W9-AAW-306

SECOND CUSTOM EDITION FOR JROTC
A CHARACTER AND LEADERSHIP DEVELOPMENT PROGRAM

FOUNDATIONS FOR SUCCESS
IN LIFE, CAREER, HEALTH AND WELLNESS

With material selected from:

Health: *Skills for Wellness*
by Kathy Teer Crumpler, Deborah Prothrow Stith, and B.E. Pruitt

Keys to Preparing for College
by Carol Carter, Joyce Bishop, Sarah Lyman Kravits, and Lesa Hadley

Career Fitness Program: Exercising Your Options, Sixth Edition
by Diane Sukiennik, William Bendat, and Lisa Raufman

PEARSON
Custom
Publishing

PEARSON
Prentice
Hall

Short text excerpts taken from the following sources unless otherwise noted:

Health Skills for Wellness, Third Edition
by B.E. (Buzz) Pruitt, Ed.D., Kathy Teer Crumpler, M.P.H., and Deborah Prothrow-Stith, M.D.
Copyright © 2001 by Prentice Hall, Inc.
A Pearson Education Company
Upper Saddle River, New Jersey 07458

Keys to Preparing for College
by Carol Carter, Joyce Bishop, Sarah Lyman Kravits, and Lesa Hadley
Copyright © 2001 by Prentice Hall, Inc.

The Career Fitness Program: Exercising Your Options, Sixth Edition
by Diane Sukiennik, William Bendat, and Lisa Raufman
Copyright © 2001, 1998, 1995, 1992, 1989, 1986 by Prentice Hall, Inc.

Copyright © 2005, 2002 by Pearson Custom Publishing
All rights reserved.

This copyright covers material written expressly for this volume by the editor/s as well as the compilation itself. It does not cover the individual selections herein that first appeared elsewhere. Permission to reprint these has been obtained by Pearson Custom Publishing for this edition only. Further reproduction by any means, electronic or mechanical, including photocopying and recording, or by any information storage or retrieval system, must be arranged with the individual copyright holders noted.

The term "Thinking Maps" and the term "Thinking Maps" with the graphic forms of the eight Maps have registered trademarks. No use of the term "Thinking Maps" with or without the graphic forms of the eight Maps may be used in any way without the permission of Thinking Maps, Inc. For use of Thinking Maps® in the classroom, inquiries regarding Thinking Maps® and training can be made to Thinking Maps, Inc., 1-800-243-9169, www.thinkingmaps.com.

Excerpts from *Content Knowledge: A Compendium of Standards and Benchmarks for K-12 Education*, reprinted by permission of McREL. Copyright © 2003 McREL: Mid-Continent Research for Education and Learning, 2550 S. Parker Road, Suite 500, Aurora, CO 80014.

Printed in the United States of America

10 9 8 7 6 5 4 3 2 1

ISBN 0-536-81440-6

2005280007

EM/JS

Please visit our web site at *www.pearsoncustom.com*

PEARSON CUSTOM PUBLISHING
75 Arlington Street, Suite 300, Boston, MA 02116
A Pearson Education Company

Brief Contents

Table of Contents

Foundations for Success

Chapter 1

Know Yourself–
Socrates

Lesson 1

Self-Awareness

Key Terms

assessment
associate
cluster
differentiate
introspection

What You Will Learn to Do

- Determine your behavioral preferences

Linked Core Abilities

- Build your capacity for lifelong learning
- Treat self and others with respect

Skills and Knowledge You Will Learn Along the Way

* Explain the four clusters of behavior in the Winning Colors® framework
* Illustrate your behavioral preferences using the four Winning Colors®
* Identify strengths for each behavior cluster
* Express appreciation for your own uniqueness
* Define the key words contained in this lesson

Introduction

You may notice that some people behave or conduct themselves like you, and others behave quite differently. For example, one person may be very quiet and contemplative while another may be the life of the party. Identifying your own preferences and the preferences of others can be an important building block in the foundation for your success. This knowledge can help you to understand situations as they unfold, improve your communication with others, and influence people and situations to get the results you desire.

Natural Tendencies

Everyone has preferences. How these are developed in each of us is a complex combination of things. Whether you are born with them or learn them—nature or nurture—can be an interesting question to explore. It is also interesting to think about how much preferences guide our behavior.

Behaviors that feel comfortable can all be considered to be natural tendencies, or your personal preferences. You might simply identify these behaviors as "the way you do things."

Being aware of personal preferences is an important step. Understanding others, being aware of what makes them tick, is another important interpersonal skill. You will learn more about that in the following lesson, "Appreciating Diversity through Winning Colors®."

Learning to Grow

Self-awareness is just the beginning of a lifetime of growth and learning. After you understand what you prefer, what is comfortable for you, it is much easier to branch out of your comfort zone to learn new behaviors. You have options regarding how you behave in any situation, rather than reacting in whatever way feels natural to you. Those natural reactions might not be the best way to handle situations.

It is in these moments when you choose to be a bit uncomfortable that you have the most potential to learn and grow. This is especially true if you select the areas for development because you have a personal reason to do so. Motivation is a powerful influence on your success.

The Process of Self-Discovery

How do you discover more about your own natural tendencies, or preferences? The following are some ways you can enhance your self-knowledge:

- **Introspection**
- **Observation**
- **Feedback (giving and receiving)**
- **Assessment tools**

Introspection

You can pay attention and take note of your own experiences, actions, and reactions. Your own observations (**introspection**) are invaluable sources of information about who you are and what makes you tick. Paying attention to how you feel inside while you participate in a variety of activities can give you some insight into your own behavioral preferences. For example,

- **Do you feel happier when working in a group, or alone?**
- **Do you feel satisfaction when you accomplish a difficult task?**
- **Is it easy or difficult for you to tell others what to do?**

Your body language can also offer helpful clues. Paying attention to what is going on when you start to feel bored and tired—or lively and interested—is an indicator. If your body is responding positively to the situation, it is likely there are elements there that agree with your personal preferences.

Observation

In addition to what you see in yourself, the observations of others can also be helpful. Sometimes others see behaviors in us that we don't see, especially when we are too involved in activities to pay attention.

There are several key concepts to keep in mind if observation is to be a truly valuable self-discovery process.

Situation—What is going on? In terms of the situation, get a sense of the environment in which a behavior occurred. What are the significant factors? Who is involved? This context information offers additional perspective about the behavior.

Specific Behavior—What happened? For an observation to offer objective information rather than subjective, or merely an opinion, it needs to be specific. Vague comments are not as helpful as a concrete example.

Because behavior arises from complex factors, this protects us from being offensive or narrow in our interpretation, and allows for the processes of communicating our thoughts and asking questions to understand even more about others and ourselves. Jumping to conclusions often leads to errors or an incomplete picture.

Impact—What is the result? The impact also needs to be described in concrete terms when making an observation. Some results that could be observed include the following:

- **Change in body language**
- **Increased energy or animation**
- **Decreased energy or animation**
- **Focus changes**

Including impacts observed in reaction to specific behavior gives people a lot of information about not only what they are doing but how that influences people and situations.

Feedback (Giving and Receiving)

Sharing observations with others is a responsibility and a privilege. This kind of information can be given in a helpful or a harmful way. Sharing an observation is an interpretation of reality. This is true whether you are observing your own behavior or that of others. So, be kind—and real—to yourself and to others when sharing your observations.

Feedback from others is simply their impression or opinion, particularly when a belief or value judgment is included. Try asking for specific examples when getting feedback from others, since observations are more reliable when they are based on fact. An opinion is more understandable when backed up with specific examples.

Assessment Tools

Putting some structure around observations, inner thoughts, feedback, and specific examples helps to make sense out of all this information. That's where **assessment** tools come in. They are valuable instruments that you can use in your quest for self-knowledge.

One set of extremely applicable tools is Winning Colors®. The Winning Colors® process supports self-discovery in a positive and affirming way. Winning Colors® is about what you can do, not what you can't.

You actually have more behavior options than you ever imagined, and the four categories make new behaviors easy to comprehend and put into practice.

Because people understand the categories and processes so quickly, you can expect to make some interesting self-discoveries using the Winning Colors® assessment tool. You can then use the information to make a positive difference in your communication and in your life.

Key Note Term

assessment – the act of evaluating or appraising a person's ability or potential to meet certain criteria or standards

Winning Colors®

Similar to other assessment tools, Winning Colors® groups human behavior into categories. Categories help us to understand complex information, by associating related data. To **associate** means to group things together when they have common characteristics. To **differentiate** means to make a distinction or state a difference between things so we can tell them apart.

Purpose and Process

Winning Colors® is a present time behavior indicator. It can be used to

- **Improve understanding of how to cooperate and communicate with others**
- **Provide clues to motivation**
- **Clarify learning styles**
- **Offer insight to conflict resolution style**
- **Uncover essential aspects of communication**

Key Note Terms

associate – to group things together when they have common characteristics

differentiate – to make a distinction or state a difference between things so we can tell them apart

Behavior Clusters

Winning Colors® focuses on present behavior, a unique and very valuable characteristic of this tool. Four categories have been identified. Each of the four categories includes behaviors that have enough characteristics in common to form a group (**cluster**).

Each category is labeled in a way that helps you remember the behaviors that go in that group.

Key Note Term

cluster – a number of similar things growing together, or of things or individuals collected

Builder Behaviors (Brown, Decide)

Do you have behaviors that tend toward taking over and being in charge? Do you like to know the "bottom line" and be in control of people or things? Do you like giving orders and being "top dog"?

If you have developed these behaviors, you are a strong BUILDER. You might use the color BROWN or compare these behaviors to the brown of the earth to describe this part of you.

Planner Behaviors (Green, Think)

Do you have behaviors that tend toward being quiet and contemplative? You like to devise and develop strategies. You act only after you have considered all the details, and you have many creative ideas.

If you have developed these behaviors, you are a strong PLANNER. You might use the color GREEN or compare these behaviors to the growing grass or leaves to describe this part of you.

Adventurer Behaviors (Red, Act)

Do you have behaviors that tend toward action? You are always on the go. You like to be on stage and take risks and chances whenever possible. You act on the spur of the moment. You know what to do in an emergency before anyone else.

If you have developed these behaviors, you are a strong ADVENTURER. You might use the color RED or compare these behaviors to fire to describe this part of you.

Relater Behaviors (Blue, Feel)

Do you have behaviors that tend toward showing feelings? You like to share your feelings with others and have them share theirs with you. You enjoy talking a lot.

If you have developed these behaviors, you are a strong RELATER. You might use the color BLUE or compare these behaviors to the wide expanse and depth of the ocean to describe this part of you.

Your Key to Success

The key to success is to be balanced. Note the gymnast in Figure 1.1.1; her success depends not only on physical balance but also on mental balance as well. Think

Figure 1.1.1: Balance is one of the keys to a successful life.

Courtesy of Eli Reed/Magnum Photos.

when it is time to think (planner—green), decide and "bottom line it" (builder—brown), feel when it is time to feel (relater—blue), and take action when it is time to take action (adventurer—red).

It is crucial that you understand that you are capable of developing all four clusters, but you may presently be emotionally attached or locked into one cluster more than another. For whatever reason, certain behaviors have worked for you or felt more natural, so naturally you developed those more than the others.

Be forewarned—a single strength can get you into trouble. For example, if you favor acting quickly (adventurer), you may act without thinking (planner) or considering the feelings of others (relater). Or, if you have strong planner (green) but no adventurer behaviors (red), you may be unable to get up in front of a group of people and speak out clearly and confidently without being embarrassed. Everyone benefits from the ability to shift between behavioral styles as needed, depending on the situation.

Conclusion

It's true that you can significantly improve your life by acquiring new behaviors to attain your goals. Making decisions, particularly effective ones, and making them quickly, is a complex set of behaviors. Because behavior is learned and can be reinforced until it becomes a habit, you have the power to choose new behaviors, even if they feel unfamiliar and alien to you today.

Taking an active approach in discovering your strengths and enhancing behaviors you find desirable is a healthy lifestyle choice. This lesson presented some information to help guide you on the path to self-discovery. As Socrates said, "Know thyself." It is the beginning of wisdom.

The following lesson delves further into the Winning Colors® process and shows you how to develop your awareness of others so you can become sensitive to the differences and similarities among all people.

Lesson Review

1. **Which behavior cluster do you see yourself in? List five reasons for this choice.**

2. **How can you use observation today to learn something new about yourself?**

3. **How can you use introspection to learn something new about a friend?**

4. **Choose one behavior cluster you feel you need to improve. Explain why.**

Appreciating Diversity through Winning Colors®

Chapter 1

Key Words

comfort zone
natural
preference

What You Will Learn to Do

- Apply an appreciation of diversity to interpersonal situations

Linked Core Abilities

- Communicate using verbal, nonverbal, visual, and written techniques
- Treat self and others with respect

Skills and Knowledge You Will Gain Along the Way

- Identify key characteristics for each Winning Colors® behavior cluster: Builders, Planners, Adventurers, and Relaters
- Determine factors that impact the behavior of others
- Determine factors that impact how others perceive your behavior
- Select behaviors that promote success in a variety of situations
- Define the key words contained in this lesson

Introduction

Understanding yourself is an important aspect of creating a successful and happy life. It is also essential to develop your awareness of others so you can become sensitive to the differences and similarities among all people. This lesson covers the key characteristics for the Winning Colors® behavior cluster that was introduced in the previous lesson and presents factors that impact the behavior of others.

We're All Different

As a young child, you became familiar with behaviors you were exposed to by your parents. These behaviors were influenced by your parents' personalities as well as your own. Because these behaviors became familiar, you got "attached" to them; you attached a positive emotion to them, sometimes solely because they were what you knew, even though they might be negative or hurtful behaviors. This principle is crucial to understanding how to communicate effectively, and this is the first clue in understanding the makeup of anyone's **comfort zone**.

When you have identified the present strengths of your own behavioral clusters as well as those of others, you have targeted this comfort zone. Generally people are more at ease if allowed to communicate within their individual comfort zones.

Asking or expecting others to behave outside their comfort zone is as hard on them as believing for yourself that you should be good at something you've never learned. Remember, though, even an old dog can learn new tricks.

Seek First to Understand

A behavior that is **natural** for you might not be so for others. Assuming that all behaviors are natural for all individuals can lead to unreasonable expectations of others and unnecessary frustration for yourself. Instead, keep in mind that others might be approaching ideas and situations a little differently than you.

> ### Key Note Terms
>
> **comfort zone** – behaviors that seem natural; behaviors you exhibit without realizing what you're doing
>
> **natural** – based on an inherent sense of right and wrong; occurring in conformity with the ordinary course of nature, not marvelous or supernatural; formulated by human reason alone rather than revelation; having a normal or usual character

Courtesy of US Army JROTC.

Awareness-Enhancing Behaviors

There are three awareness-enhancing behaviors that can help us understand and communicate better with others: introspection, observation, and feedback. Introspection is self-examination or the process of looking at ourselves to make sure that we first understand where we are, how we act, and what someone might expect of us. It is a self-analysis that determines why we behave or act the way we do and helps us understand what reaction might be expected in different situations. Introspection is an opportunity to look inward instead of always looking outward to other people and their behavior.

Observation is the act of taking in information and provides you with an opportunity to observe someone that is different from you to learn from their verbal and nonverbal behavior. It is an attempt to learn why someone acts the way they do. It is a tool that can be used to develop a better knowledge of others' behaviors.

Feedback is another opportunity to provide constructive information to someone that you have observed from the standpoint of learning more about their behavior and to effect better communication. Effective feedback is a process whereby someone can learn how well their verbal and nonverbal behavior is matching their intentions. It can provide information to a person that can be used to continue or change a behavior or the way he or she is acting. It involves the person giving the information and the person that receives the information.

The EIAG Process

The EIAG (Experience, Identify, Analyze, Generalize) model is a reflection process that can be used after each experience or action to help you understand what happened and why. It is a process to assist you in understanding other people and their behavior. After you have *experienced* an event or observed another person's behavior, you *identify* or describe what happened. You can ask yourself the following questions:

- **What did the other person do?**
- **What did you do?**
- **How did the other person react?**
- **How did you react?**

The next step is to *analyze* the experience. Again ask yourself questions about the experience. For example,

- **Why did the other person act in that way?**
- **Why did you act the way you did?**
- **How have things been going for you?**
- **What has been going on in your life?**

In the final step you *generalize* or come up with some general rules or principles that might apply not only to this situation but also to similar situations in the future. Again ask yourself some questions to help you develop your future behavior, such as the following:

Chapter 1   Know Yourself—Socrates

- What will you do in the future when you encounter another situation like this one?
- What would you do differently if you had to do it over again?
- What advice would you give another person who is about to have a similar experience?
- What can you do to make sure your behavior will go well the next time you have this type of experience?

Effective Communication

Developing awareness of others can help you become a more effective communicator. By having insight into another's **preferences**, you may be able to adapt your personal communication skills and your behavior in such a way that other people are more likely to hear, understand, and respond in a positive way. This is because you're "speaking their language," and what you say makes sense to them. When you speak out of a completely different behavioral style, you're much more likely to encounter resistance because they do not fully understand what you're trying to say.

Key Note Term

preference – the act of preferring, the state of being preferred; the power or opportunity of choosing

Winning Colors® Power Words

It has been found through years of research that certain words affect people differently. Through word association discoveries, it has been learned that the mere mention of a particular word produces tension in certain individuals. This is the basis of the lie detector test. When a question is asked, the person becomes emotionally involved and begins to perspire.

When you speak with a person with Planner behaviors, you succeed by using Planner power words. The same is true if you want to communicate successfully with those inclined to Builder, Adventurer, and Rolater behaviors.

The following is a list of words and phrases for each Winning Colors® behavior cluster. After identifying an individual's natural "cluster," use the list to help you communicate effectively with him or her.

Your Planner Power Words

- Changing and improving
- Analyzing
- Being my best
- Dreaming
- Caring
- Inner life
- Thinking
- Inventing
- Knowing more

- Exactness
- Planning
- Revolution
- Knowing the future
- Freedom of thought

Your Builder Power Words

- Always leading people
- Power
- Results
- Responsible
- Duty
- Tradition
- Money
- Be prepared
- I give directions
- Do it my way
- I like to get things done now

Your Adventurer Power Words

- Test the limits
- Do it now
- Excitement
- Fast machines
- Fun
- Doing
- Action
- Risk
- Challenge
- Act and perform
- Freedom

Your Relater Power Words

- Always liking to be with people
- Hugs are special when I choose
- Friendly
- Giving
- I see everything

- Romantic
- Let's get along with each other
- Wanting people to like me

Conclusion

Being aware of what motivates people is worth your time and attention. The information and insight you gain can help you be more effective in all your relationships.

You have been given words and behaviors that will assist you in having the best possible success as a leader or communicator with others after you have identified their comfort zones.

Think when it is time to think (planner—green), decide when it time to decide (builder—brown), feel when it is time to feel (relater—blue), and act when it is time to act (adventurer—red).

The following lesson introduces you to the personal growth planner. You need to have goals in your life, and those goals should be clearly defined so you know how to achieve them.

Lesson Review

1. How can assuming something about a friend or family member lead to disappointment or frustration?

2. What differences and similarities do you see in yourself and your best friend? How do those differences and similarities affect your friendship?

3. List five words you would use to communicate effectively with an adventurer.

4. Give an example of how you would use the EIAG model to change your behavior.

Personal Growth Plan

Key Words

adaptability
assertion
change orientation
deference
emotional intelligence
intrapersonal
persistence

What You Will Learn to Do

- Develop a plan for personal growth

Linked Core Abilities

- Build your capacity for lifelong learning

Skills and Knowledge You Will Gain Along the Way

- Match the key emotional skills to the relevant skills dimensions
- Develop strategies for growth in two emotional skill areas
- Plan self-directed development activities
- Define the key words contained in this lesson

Introduction

You need to have goals in your life, and those goals should be clearly defined so you know how to achieve them. For example, to choose a certain career or lose a specific number of pounds, you should have a well-defined strategy for getting from where you are now to where you'd like to be in the future. You've probably heard the old adage, "If you don't know where you're going, any road can lead you there." Likewise, if you don't know where you are, how do you know which road to choose? This lesson presents a personal growth plan that you can use to make certain you achieve the goals you set for yourself.

Most of the success-oriented products being marketed today, such as trendy diets and get-rich-quick programs, focus on a goal and tell you how to get there. These programs assume that if you "do as they do," you will be successful. The problem with this approach is that one method of planning doesn't work for everyone. Those who created the programs don't know where you are today, so how can they give you directions to where you want to go?

The Personal Skills Map

All of us at one time or another have taken a trip and gotten lost. Did you stop and ask for directions, look at a map, or call the person at your destination to get more information about how to get to where you're going? Regardless of the method you chose, you first had to ascertain, "Where am I now?" Only then could you determine how to get where you were going. The Personal Skills Map (a short version is on page 18) offers a way to discover where you are now and shows you how to get to where you want to go.

The Personal Skills Map helps you identify where you are now and shows you what you need to know to accomplish your goals.

The Success Profiler

The Success Profiler is a systematic, research-based assessment and skill-building system designed for the following purposes:

- **Adapt to change**
- **Develop leadership skills**
- **Enhance ability to learn**
- **Promote sensitivity/diversity**
- **Build teamwork skills**
- **Prevent violent behavior**

Rather than attempting to address knowledge and skills, this approach focuses on the **emotional intelligence** needed for success in key emotional skill areas. The assessment helps you identify those skills you need to develop, those that need strengthening, and those that can use some enhancement.

> ### Key Note Term
>
> **emotional intelligence** – a learned ability to identify, experience, understand, and express human emotions in healthy and productive ways

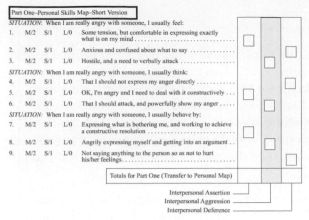

Part One–Personal Skills Map–Short Version

SITUATION: When I am really angry with someone, I usually feel:

1. M/2 S/1 L/0 Some tension, but comfortable in expressing exactly what is on my mind . . . .

2. M/2 S/1 L/0 Anxious and confused about what to say . . . .

3. M/2 S/1 L/0 Hostile, and a need to verbally attack . . . .

SITUATION: When I am really angry with someone, I usually think:

4. M/2 S/1 L/0 That I should not express my anger directly . . . .

5. M/2 S/1 L/0 OK, I'm angry and I need to deal with it constructively . . .

6. M/2 S/1 L/0 That I should attack, and powerfully show my anger . . . . .

SITUATION: When I am really angry with someone, I usually behave by:

7. M/2 S/1 L/0 Expressing what is bothering me, and working to achieve a constructive resolution . . . .

8. M/2 S/1 L/0 Angrily expressing myself and getting into an argument . .

9. M/2 S/1 L/0 Not saying anything to the person so as not to hurt his/her feelings . . . .

Totals for Part One (Transfer to Personal Map)

Interpersonal Assertion
Interpersonal Aggression
Interpersonal Deference

Courtesy of US Army JROTC.

You begin the process of identifying where you are now by completing a four-part profiler assessment. After it's completed, you will transfer your results onto your personal map.

The personal map is divided into 14 critical areas—key emotional skills. The following section covers these critical areas.

Self-Esteem

The Self-Esteem scale indicates a self-perceived level of personal worth. Research indicates that it is the most fundamental skill, and it relates to major aspects of mental health and a healthy personality.

Interpersonal Assertion

The Interpersonal **Assertion** scale indicates how effectively an individual uses direct, honest, and appropriate expression of thoughts, feelings, and behaviors in dealings with others. It indicates an ability to be direct and honest in communicating with others without violating the rights of the other person.

Interpersonal Awareness

This Interpersonal Awareness scale indicates an individual's evaluation of his or her ability for appropriate social, emotional, and physical distance in verbal and non-verbal interactions with others.

Empathy

The Empathy scale indicates an individual's ability to sense, understand, and accept another person's thoughts, feelings, and behaviors. Empathy is a primary characteristic of a skilled communicator. People with strong empathy tend to be sociable and outgoing.

Drive Strength/Motivation

The Drive Strength/Motivation scale indicates motivation and goal-setting abilities. Drive strength shows an ability to marshal energy and motivation toward the accomplishment of personal goals.

Key Note Term

assertion – the act of asserting; to state or declare positively and often forcefully or aggressively

Decision Making

The Decision Making scale indicates perceived skill in formulating and initiating effective problem-solving procedures. The ability to make decisions is a key ingredient of self-acceptance and positive self-regard.

Time Management

The Time Management scale assesses ability to organize and use time to further individual and career goals. Ability to manage time is an ingredient in self-regard, sensitivity to needs, and perseverance in completing tasks.

Sales Orientation/Leadership

The Sales Orientation/Leadership scale indicates perceived skill in positively impacting and influencing the actions of other people. The ability to influence others in a positive way is an important aspect of leadership/sales.

Commitment Ethic

The Commitment Ethic scale indicates perceived skill in completing projects and job assignments dependably and successfully. People with a strong commitment ethic are usually perceived as dependable and committed by others, are inner-directed, and persevere in completing projects regardless of difficulties encountered.

Stress Management

The Stress Management scale assesses perceived skill in managing stress and anxiety. People with skills in managing stress positively are competent managers of time and are flexible, self-assured, stable, and self-reliant.

Physical Wellness

The Physical Wellness scale reflects the extent to which healthy attitudes and living patterns that are important to physical health and well-being have been established. Physical wellness is highly correlated to positive stress management and high self esteem. People with high scores have developed high levels of self-control over potentially harmful behavior patterns.

Interpersonal Aggression (Anger Management)

The Interpersonal Aggression scale assesses the degree to which communication styles violate, overpower, dominate, or discredit another person's rights, thoughts, feelings, or behaviors. High interpersonal aggression is related to the personality characteristics of rebelliousness, resentment, and oversensitive response to real or imagined affronts.

Interpersonal Deference (Fear Management)

The Interpersonal Deference scale measures the degree to which communication style is indirect, self-inhibiting, self-denying, and ineffectual for the accurate expression of thoughts, feelings, and behaviors. High interpersonal deference is related to the personality characteristics of apprehensiveness, shyness, and oversensitivity to threat or conflict.

Key Emotional Skills By Skill Dimension		Develop¶ (0-40 pts.)	Strengthen¶ (41-60 pts.)	Enhance¶ (61-100 pts.)
Skill Dimension 1:¶ Intrapersonal Skills	Self Esteem	□	□	□
Skill Dimension 2:¶ Interpersonal Skills	Interpersonal Assertion	□	□	□
	Interpersonal Awareness	□	□	□
	Empathy	□	□	□
Skill Dimension 3:¶ Career/Life Skills	Drive Strength/Motivation	□	□	□
	Decision Making	□	□	□
	Time Management	□	□	□
	Sales Orientation/Leadership	□	□	□
	Commitment Ethic	□	□	□
Skill Dimension 4:¶ Personal Wellness Skills	Stress Management	□	□	□
	Physical Wellness	□	□	□
		Low	Normal	High
Skill Dimension 5:¶ Problematic Behavior	Interpersonal Aggression	□	□	□
	Interpersonal Deference	□	□	□
	Personal Change Orientation	□	□	□

Courtesy of US Army JROTC

Change Orientation (Comfort Level)

The **Change Orientation** scale indicates the degree of motivation and readiness for change in the skills measured by the Personal Skills Map. A high score indicates dissatisfaction with current skills and a strong conviction of the need to make personal changes.

Integrating the Personal Skills Map and Emotional Skills

On the Personal Map, the 14 key emotional skills are grouped into 5 skill dimensions. These skill dimensions help you identify your strengths and weakness in **intrapersonal** skills (those that occur by yourself), interpersonal skills (those that occur with others), any problematic behavior that needs to be addressed, and your willingness to change (**adaptability**).

The first skill dimension is Intrapersonal Skill and includes the Self-Esteem emotional skill. This skill dimension is related to how you evaluate and accept yourself as a person.

The second skill dimension is Interpersonal Skills and consists of the Assertion, Awareness, and Empathy emotional skills. This skill dimension is related to how you interact with others and how you tend to communicate in stressful situations.

The third skill dimension is Career/Life Skills and consists of the Drive Strength/ Motivation, Decision Making, Time Management, Sales Orientation/Leadership, and Commitment Ethic emotional skills. This skill dimension focuses on skills that are important in effectively managing your daily environment and school demands.

The fourth skill dimension is Personal Wellness Skills and consists of the Stress Management and Physical Wellness emotional skills. This skill dimension is extremely important in both emotional and physical well-being.

The fifth skill dimension is Problematic Behavior and consists of the Interpersonal Aggression and **Deference** emotional skills. This skill dimension provides an indication of behaviors that negatively affect personal mental health and career effectiveness.

Key Note Terms

change orientation – a scale that indicates the degree of motivation and readiness for change in the skills measured by the Personal Skills Map

intrapersonal – occurring within the individual mind or self

adaptability – capability or willingness to adapt

Key Note Term

deference – the respect and esteem due a superior or elder; also affected or ingratiating regard for another's wishes

At the bottom of the Personal Skills Map is the Personal Change Orientation category. This score indicates your motivation and willingness to change behavior.

High scores on the Personal Skills Map indicate that you are aware of a need to improve your personal skills. It is possible that this awareness has caused some increased stress and anxiety in your life. Conversely, a low score on the map indicates that you are satisfied with your current interpersonal and intrapersonal skills and behavior.

Conclusion

Whether you are satisfied with your current skill level or desire a change, knowing where you are today can help you map a plan that leads you toward your goals.

It's nice to know that our personal skills are changeable and that we are capable of learning and growing throughout our life. If you are ready to strengthen or enhance your current skills, have **persistence** in your efforts, and use the results of the assessment to help guide you toward your personal goals, you will become a better, well-rounded individual.

In the next lesson, you will see how active learners do not wait for learning to happen—they make it happen. You will see how becoming an active learner will broaden your life experiences and help make you a more well-rounded and balanced individual.

Key Note Term

persistence – the action or fact of persisting, to go on resolutely or stubbornly in spite of opposition, importunity, or warning; to remain unchanged or fixed in a specified character, condition, or position; the quality or state of being persistent

Chapter 1

Lesson Review

Lesson Review

1. **Choose one personal skill that you'd like to improve. Explain why and how you'd like to make this improvement.**

2. **Define the term** *emotional intelligence.*

3. **How can physical wellness affect your self-esteem?**

4. **What motivates you to finish a project?**

Becoming an Active Leader

Chapter 1

Key Words

active
classify
creative
critical
objectivity
passive
predict
subjective
visualize

What You Will Learn to Do

- Determine the thinking/learning skills necessary for improving active learning

Linked Core Abilities

- Build your capacity for lifelong learning
- Apply critical thinking techniques

Skills and Knowledge You Will Gain Along the Way

- Identify the thinking types and related viewpoints necessary to address typical active learner questions
- Distinguish between traits and activities of critical and creative thinkers
- Describe the difference between objective and subjective thinking
- Distinguish between active learner and passive learner traits
- Define the key words contained in this lesson

Introduction

Active learners do not wait for learning to happen; they make it happen. You learned to crawl, stand up, walk, as well as other tasks because you wanted to learn them. This desire to learn made you ask the people around you for help. Active learning is an instinct with which you were born and will possess throughout your life. This lesson shows you how to become an active learner.

Active Learners

Active learners generally display specific traits and can

- **Identify personal goals and the steps necessary to achieve the goals**
- **Use resources to identify the people and tools available to aid in goal pursuit**
- **Learn how to solve almost any problem they ever have to face**
- **Look at situations objectively**
- **Ask the right questions**
- **Use time well because they are organized and set priorities**
- **Apply good reading, studying, and questioning skills to written materials**
- **Apply good listening skills in the classroom**
- **Find patterns and take effective notes to organize materials for studying**
- **Assess progress along the way and revise their plans**

You can probably think of additional traits that active learners possess. In contrast, **passive** learners may work hard, but they do not take charge of the learning processes. Table 1.4.1 compares the differences between active and passive learners.

Active Learners Are Self-Directed

Using active learning, you can solve problems, answer questions, formulate questions of your own, discuss, explain, debate, or brainstorm during class. **Creative** and **critical** thinking as well as the ability to view situations and problems objectively are common traits among those who are active learners.

Creative and Critical Thinking

Active learners think carefully. Thinking is a complex activity involving the brain's neurons (nerve cells) linking with other neurons as waves of impulses travel from neuron to neuron. Numerous skills comprise the act of thinking. As shown in Table 1.4.2, these skills can be grouped into two categories: creative and critical.

Key Note Term

active – characterized by action rather than contemplation or speculation

Key Note Terms

passive – acted on by an external agency; receptive to outside impressions or influences

creative – marked by the ability or power to create; given to creating

critical – of, relating to, or being a turning point or especially important juncture

Table 1.4.1: Comparing Active and Passive Learners

Active Learner Versus Passive Learner	
Passive Learner	**Active Learner**
Approaches learning as "remembering."	Approaches learning as "thinking."
Reads the textbook, takes some notes, and spends hours trying to memorize those notes.	Reads the textbook, takes some notes using a method that captures the concepts and details. Reviews the notes.
Wastes or misuses a lot of study time. Feels as if there isn't enough time to "remember it all."	Uses study time efficiently. Concentrates on remembering the major concepts and details.
May be able to recall information, but often has problems using this information in contexts other than the textbook's scenario or the way he/she memorized the material.	Can recall information and transfer the information to many different contexts.
In tests, tends to get confused if the information is not presented in a manner similar to the way he/she memorized the information.	Can use the information to respond to different types of questions in tests.
Tends to see "words" on the page rather than ideas and concepts applicable to various situations. .	Looks for the basic concepts and uses those concepts as a structure on which to build secondary concepts and details. Can apply the information to various situations when appropriate

Courtesy of US Army JROTC.

Table 1.4.2: Examples of Creative and Critical Thinking

Creative Thinking	Critical Thinking
brainstorming	analyzing
generalizing	comparing/contrasting
inventing	**classifying**
predicting	evaluating
visualizing	prioritizing

Key Note Terms

classify – to assign to a category

predict – to declare or indicate in advance; especially: foretell on the basis of observation, experience, or scientific reason

Note

For more information about neurons and brain function, see Chapter 2, Lesson 1, "Brain Structure and Function."

Active learners use both critical and creative thinking; critical thinking to define a problem and creative thinking to solve it.

Critical thinkers tend to

- **Be honest with themselves**
- **Resist manipulation**
- **Figure out how to overcome a confusing situation**
- **Ask good questions**
- **Base judgments on facts and evidence**
- **Look for connections between subjects**
- **Be intellectually independent**

Aside from being honest with themselves and resisting manipulation, creative thinkers tend to

- **Use their imaginations**
- **Daydream**
- **Practice expansive thinking (think "outside of the box")**

Active learners know when to use each type of thinking.

Objective versus Subjective Viewpoint

As you grow and mature, you learn to shift from **visualizing** the world as being centered only around yourself (**subjective**) to seeing it in a way that many people can agree on what it means (objective). **Objectivity** allows you to communicate effectively and persuasively with others. Using objectivity helps you persuade other people and can gain you allies when working toward change.

To support critical thinking, you need an objective viewpoint. You can learn to distinguish between objective and subjective observations and reactions.

If you tell how an event affected you or how you reacted to an event, you are being subjective. For example, consider the following statements.

- **His criticism of me was totally unjust and it made me angry**
- **That was the funniest movie I've ever seen**

If you tell about an event or relate a fact as anyone might see it, you are being objective. For example, consider the following:

Key Note Terms

visualizing – to see or form a mental (visual) image

subjective – of, relating to, or constituting a subject; relating to or characteristic of one that is a subject, especially in lack of freedom of action or in submissiveness

objectivity – expressing or dealing with facts or conditions as perceived without distortion by personal feelings, prejudices, or interpretations

- **It rained Saturday**
- **Sick children need good medical care**

Keep these subjective and objective viewpoints in mind when you are communicating with others. Both viewpoints are necessary in life, but learn to use them appropriately. Distinguishing between these viewpoints is especially important when you are asking questions, taking tests, or giving presentations. Table 1.4.3 shows examples of how critical, creative, objective, and subjective thinking are used.

Table 1.4.3: Using Critical, Creative, Objective, and Subjective Thinking

Three Question Types	Related Thinking Type	Related Viewpoint	Notes
What? • What are the facts? • What is the evidence or proof?	Critical thinking	Objective	Facts form the basis of most of your studies.
So what? • What do the facts mean? • What conclusion can I draw? • What else do I need to know?	Creative thinking and Critical thinking	Subjective and Objective	Use the facts to form an opinion.
Now what? • What can I do with the information now that I have the facts? • How do the facts link to other information I have?	Creative thinking	Subjective	Use the information to form a pattern or structure on which to build other facts.

Courtesy of US Army JROTC.

Asking Questions

Active learners combine critical thinking and objectivity to ask good questions. They ask questions to get a complete picture and to expand their knowledge. You can't get anywhere without asking questions. To get specific facts, ask clear, concise questions requiring an objective answer. To learn opinions and feelings, ask subjective questions.

Form the habit of asking questions and learning from everyone you meet. You may be afraid to ask questions because you think people will feel you are not very smart. Don't be afraid. The only way to learn is to ask questions. And don't forget: The dumbest question is the one that's never asked.

Answering Questions

Active learners use both types of thinking—critical and creative—to give good answers to questions. You must recognize whether a question is asking you to be objective or subjective in your answer. Recognizing what type of question is being asked will help you identify whether your answer should be subjective or objective.

Answering questions is treated in more detail in the "Test-Taking Tips and Strategies" later in this textbook. For reading, study skills, and test taking, you apply the objective and subjective viewpoints, critical and creative thinking, and techniques for asking questions.

Conclusion

Active learning is a method that allows you to participate in class. It takes you beyond the role of passive listener and note taker and allows you to take some direction and initiative during the class. Active learning can encompass a variety of techniques that include small group discussion, role playing, hands-on projects, and teacher-driven questioning. The goal is to be part of the process of your own education.

This concludes Chapter 1, "Know Yourself—Socrates." In the next chapter, "Learning to Learn," you will see how the brain is structured and how it functions. Learning styles are also presented, and you will also learn about multiple intelligences.

Lesson Review

1. Compare active learners and passive learners. Which one are you?

2. Compare and contrast *creative thinking* and *critical thinking.*

3. How can a combination of creative and critical thinking help you solve problems?

4. Explain how you can change the way you think about a situation by using an objective or a subjective viewpoint.

Learning to Learn

Lesson 1

Brain Structure and Function

Key Terms

axon
brain stem
cerebral hemispheres
cortex
dendrite
limbic system
neural plasticity
neurons
neurotransmitter
sensory flooding
sensory gating
synapse

What You Will Learn to Do

- Relate the structure and function of the brain to the learning process

Linked Core Abilities

- Build your capacity for lifelong learning
- Apply critical thinking techniques

Skills and Knowledge You Will Gain Along the Way

- Identify key areas and function of the midbrain/limbic system
- Associate major regions of the brain to their functions
- Explain the function of a neuron
- Explain the three elements involved in transmitting stimulus from outside the body to the brain
- Assess the process required to enhance brain power
- Define the key words contained in this lesson

Introduction

This lesson introduces you to the most marvelous and mysterious part of your anatomy—the human brain. Most humans never totally discover or exert the full potential of their brain. In this lesson you will explore current research on what the brain is (structure) and how it works (function). You will learn practical ways to apply complex concepts that put you in control of your own mind.

Evolution of the Human Brain

One way to look at the brain's structure is based on the theory of evolution. Only 100,000 years ago, the ancestors of modern man had a brain weighing only about a pound, which is roughly one-third the weight of our current brain. Most of this increased weight is because of a much larger cerebral **cortex**. Here most of the thinking that makes human beings such unique mammals occurs. This tremendous growth is an important aspect of the evolution of the human brain.

The Human Brain

The human brain (see Figure 2.1.1) has three parts: the neocortex (mushrooming out at the top), the **limbic system** (in the middle), and the **brain stem** (at the base).

Researchers believe the neocortex, sometimes called the *cerebral cortex,* grew out of the limbic system at some time in human evolution. Though not exclusively, the neocortex is where most higher-order and abstract thoughts are processed. The two hemispheres of the neocortex also handle input from our sensory systems, making connections between various stimuli, such as associating what we see with what we hear. This makes comprehension possible, and is how we make it all meaningful.

The neocortex, the most newly developed part of our brain, also attaches feeling and value to stimuli it receives. When humans learn, the structure and chemistry of nerve cells in the neocortex are changed.

The limbic system, once thought to be associated exclusively with emotion, is now known to process not only emotional response but also a number of higher-level thinking functions, including memory.

Key Note Terms

cortex – the highly wrinkled outer layer of the cerebrum and cerebellum (forebrain); also referred to as *gray matter*

limbic system – a group of subcortical structures (such as the hypothalamus, hippocampus, and amygdala) of the brain that are concerned especially with emotion and motivation

brain stem – the oldest part of the brain composed of the mesencephalon, pons, and medulla oblongata, and connecting the spinal cord with the forebrain and cerebrum; also referred to as the *reptilian brain*

Figure 2.1.1: The human brain.
Courtesy of US Army JROTC.

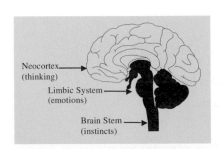

The brain stem, sometimes called the *reptilian brain* (R-complex), is considered to be the oldest part of the brain from an evolutionary standpoint. It follows then that much of the processing of basic survival needs (eating, breathing, and the fight-or-flight response) occurs here. Fight or flight is the common terminology for a complex set of reactions to a perceived threat—the organism's ability to go on red alert and respond quickly. Many of the body's systems respond automatically to increase the chance of survival when under attack.

Higher-level Thinking Skills

The brain is vital to human understanding and the ability to learn. Perhaps you've heard of higher-level thinking skills. This phrase refers to the level of information processing and response required by a particular task. Some complicated tasks can require a higher level of information processing; however, some tasks do not.

For example, when you touch a hot stove, you pull your hand away quickly. That activity does not take much thinking, and it had better not take a lot of time! In fact, your nervous system is designed to process information like that automatically, with little help from the neocortex.

Think about getting burned. What information would be helpful to store long term about that experience? Maybe the size, shape, and color of the heat source will help you to avoid the problem in the future. But the "how to" of pulling away your hand is best left to the quick reactions of nerves and muscles.

Muscles can react to nerve impulses without those impulses ever traveling up the spinal cord to the brain. The withdrawal reflex, where the finger is pulled away from the pain as muscles contract, is the simplest act that the nervous system can perform. It is automatic and unconscious; it does not involve any higher-level thinking.

Now let's look at a process we call *downshifting*. From the top to bottom view shown in Figure 2.1.1, downshifting describes what occurs when information processing moves from the higher-level thinking regions of the brain, the neocortex and even the limbic system, down into the brain stem and even into the automatic responses of reflex. Why does this happen? Why give up the ability to ponder and reflect and instead revert back to instinct and involuntary reflexes? Fear and intimidation are two main reasons downshifting occurs.

In the presence of perceived threat, survival becomes important, and the brain discerns the need for speed. Like the burn example in the previous section, your nervous system is fine-tuned enough to automatically revert to more efficient processing methods to keep the organism safe and sound. In other words, the brain will downshift from neocortex involvement to rely more heavily on the survival and emotional processing of the brain stem and limbic system whenever the organism perceives a threat.

Psychological threats can produce the same kind of fight-or-flight response needed when an animal is under attack from a predator. And to be more efficient, the brain downshifts.

Perhaps you have a lot at stake in the outcome of an upcoming geometry test. Maybe you won't pass this year if you don't complete a major writing assignment. Or maybe you know someone who believes being tough helps motivate people to perform better. Sometimes tough comes out more like put-downs and threats, instead of inspiration, high standards, and a belief in your ability to succeed.

You need your whole brain involved, especially the neocortex, to solve these problems. Fight-or-flight reactions won't help. Notice when your emotions react and your mind seems to shift into an automatic mode of response. Being self-aware of a downshift gives you the chance to incorporate your higher-level thinking skills in evaluating the situation. Then your whole brain is in operation; ideas and creativity can flow to help you determine a better way to respond to the challenge at hand. This enhanced state of being fully engaged and aware is what we call whole brain activation. Taking in and processing information in many different ways activates the whole brain.

Now that you know the basics of how the brain works, take a look at the structure of the human brain.

Major Brain Areas

The brain is composed of a number of different regions, each with specialized functions. Figure 2.1.2 shows a tripartite view of the brain's structure and function.

The brain's central core, which includes the brain stem and the midbrain, is quite different from the cerebral cortex that envelops it. The central core is relatively simple, and its activity is largely unconscious. In contrast, the cortex is highly developed and capable of the deliberation and associations necessary for complex thinking and problem solving. In humans, its size and function has increased rapidly; the older portions of the brain remain relatively static.

The Brain Stem

The brain stem seems to be inherited almost "as is" from the reptilian brain. It consists of structures such as the medulla (which controls breathing, heart rate, and digestion) and the cerebellum (which coordinates sensory input with muscle movement).

The Midbrain

The midbrain includes features that appear intimately connected to human emotion and to the formation of long-term memory via neural connections to the lobes of the neocortex. The structures contained here also link the lower brain stem to the thalamus—for information relay from the senses, to the brain, and back to muscles—and to the limbic system.

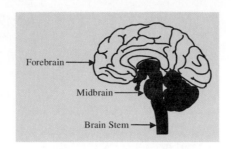

Figure 2.1.2: Another view of the brain, also showing three separate areas.
Courtesy of US Army JROTC.

The limbic system, essentially alike in all mammals, lies above the brain stem and under the cortex. It consists of a number of interrelated structures. Researchers have linked the limbic system to hormones, drives, temperature control, and emotion. One part is dedicated to memory formation, thus explaining the strong link between emotion and long-term memory.

The limbic system includes the following parts and functions:

- **The hypothalamus is instrumental in regulating drives and actions. Neurons affecting heart rate and respiration are concentrated here. These neurons direct most of the physical changes that accompany strong emotions, such as the flight-or-fight response.**
- **The amygdala appears connected to aggressive behavior.**
- **The hippocampus plays a crucial role in processing various forms of information to form long-term memories. Damage to the hippocampus will produce global retrograde amnesia.**

One important feature of the midbrain and limbic system is the reticular activating system (RAS). It is this area that keeps us awake and aware of the world. The RAS acts as a master switch that alerts the brain to incoming data—and to the urgency of the message.

The Forebrain or Neocortex

The forebrain, which appears as a mere bump in the brain of a frog, balloons out into the cerebrum of higher life forms and covers the brain stem like the head of a mushroom. This, the newest part of the human brain, is called the neocortex, or cerebral cortex, and is shown in Figure 2.1.3.

The structure of the neocortex is complicated. Most of the higher-level functions associated with human thought are enabled here.

In humans, the neocortex has evolved further than in other mammals, into two **cerebral hemispheres**. The wrinkled surface of the hemispheres is about two millimeters thick and has a total surface area the size of a desktop (about 1.5 square meters).

> **Note**
>
> For more information about the two hemispheres and how they work together, refer to the next lesson, "Left-Brain/Right-Brain."

> **Key Note Term**
>
> **neurons** – a grayish or reddish granular cell with specialized processes that is the fundamental functional unit of nervous tissue in the brain

> **Key Note Term**
>
> **cerebral hemisphere** – when looked at from the top, the brain is composed of two interconnected spheres or lobes and is the seat of higher-level thinking

Figure 2.1.3: The neocortex and all of its components.
Courtesy of US Army JROTC.

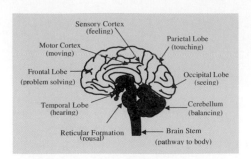

Remember that there is symmetry between hemispheres; however, not every specialized region is found on both sides. For example, highly specialized language centers exist only in the left hemisphere. The brain coordinates information between the two hemispheres and does so with startling speed and skill.

The following is a brief description of the four lobes that make up the cerebral hemispheres.

Frontal Lobes

The frontal lobes occupy the front part of the brain and are associated with making decisions, planning, and voluntary muscle movement. Speech, smell, and emotions are processed here as well. The frontal lobes control our responses and reactions to input from the rest of the system. The saying "get your brain in gear" refers to activity in the frontal lobes.

Parietal Lobes

The parietal lobes are most closely associated with our sense of touch. They contain a detailed map of the whole body's surface. More neurons are dedicated to some regions of surface area than others. For example, the fingers have many more nerve endings than the toes, and therefore they have more associated areas in the brain for processing.

The parietal lobe of the right hemisphere appears to be especially important for perceiving spatial relationships. The recognition of relationships between objects in space is important to activities such as drawing, finding your way, construction, and mechanical or civil engineering.

Temporal Lobes

The temporal lobes are associated with emotions and also contain the primary auditory cortex, which processes sound. Doesn't this provoke wonder at the profound connection between music and strong emotion?

Occipital Lobes

The occipital lobes are the primary visual cortex. This area at the back of the brain, just above the cerebellum, processes stimuli from eyes, via the optic nerve, and associates that information with other sensory input and memories.

Recall that areas crucial to long-term memory also reside at the back of the brain. These association areas interpret sensory data by relating it to existing knowledge, and are essential to memory formation. More information on memory is included in later sections of the text.

Sensory Cortex and Motor Cortex

Regions called the sensory cortex and the motor cortex are sandwiched between the frontal and parietal lobes at the top of the head. These areas specialize in the control of movement and in receiving information from the body's primary sensory systems (vision, smell, taste, touch, and sound).

Awareness of Time

According to some researchers, the lobes to the front and the back of the brain seem to be aware of the passage of time; thus the frontal lobe of the neocortex, shown in Figure 2.1.4, appears to be responsible for planning, decision making, and risk taking, while the back of the brain stores memories.

The middle section is focused on experiencing the present moment because it houses the primary sensory and motor cortex. It is busily processing information from our five senses and sending controlled signals back out to our muscles.

The Nervous System

The nervous system links the body to the external environment through sensory organs, permitting us to see, hear, taste, smell, or feel and to respond to stimuli. Through your five senses you know when the air is cold, it's early morning, and someone has a fire burning. The hot chocolate smells wonderful, and the birds are singing. But how do you know?

Sensory Systems

The five most commonly known sensory channels—our eyes, ears, skin, nose, and tongue—all rely on specialized receptor cells to take in data from the external world.

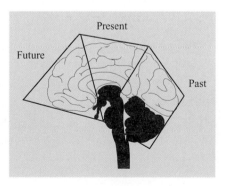

Figure 2.1.4: The lobes to the front and back of the brain are aware of the passage of time.
Courtesy of US Army JROTC.

synapse – the space between nerve cells; the point at which a nervous impulse passes from one neuron to another

sensory gating – also called the neuron spike point, regulates the transmission of stimuli to the brain

sensory overload – occurs when too much data are getting through to the brain

axon – long fibers that send electrical impulses and release neurotransmitters

dendrite – any of the usually branching protoplasmic processes that conduct impulses toward the body of a nerve cell

neurotransmitter – a chemical molecule (such as norepinephrine or acetylcholine) that transmits nerve impulses across a synapse, within and between brain cells

For example, mechanical, chemical, and electrical processes transform the glow of the sun in your eyes and its heat on your skin into electrical impulses and send them sparking along nerve fibers (called sensory neurons). Traveling at speeds up to 290 miles per hour, jumping microscopic gaps (called **synapses**) along the way, these messages make their way to nerve processing centers (called interneurons) in the spinal cord and brain. They then connect back out to your muscles and glands (called motor neurons), causing you to sweat in response to the sun's heat.

Sensory Flooding and Gating

A large amount of data comes into the brain all the time. We can't and don't pay attention to all of it. A "go or no go" signal occurs to regulate the transmission of stimuli. This is called the neuron spike point, or **sensory gating**. Without this monitoring, **sensory overload**, or flooding, would occur. This automatic physical process is a key aspect of what we actually process on a conscious level.

Sensory flooding occurs when too much data are getting through. There is some indication that disorders such as autism are, in part, caused by this type of physiological data transmission problem.

Neuron Structure

The arm and hand in Figure 2.1.5 are used to illustrate a *neuron*. The arm represents the **axon**, long fibers that send electrical impulses and release **neurotransmitters**. The hand is like the cell body and the fingers are like **dendrites**.

Messages are transmitted as electrical impulses from the senses, muscles, or other neurons. The neuron processes the impulse and then sends the message to other neurons via axons. When the impulse reaches the end of the axon, the dendrites pick up the signal as a chemical neurotransmitter synapse.

Neurotransmitters

Neurotransmitters are chemical in nature and are used to accept an electrical impulse from the axon at a synapse and relay it to the dendrites.

The neurotransmitters carry excitatory or inhibitory messages and affect behavior patterns such as pain and pleasure.

Amazing Facts About Neurons

- Fifty to 100 billion nerve cells act as information specialists in the brain and spinal cord
- Tens of billions of messages travel as electrochemical impulses every few seconds of every day of your entire lifetime
- Some single nerve cells, such as the sciatic nerve in your leg, contain dendrite branches 3 feet long
- Along these large nerve fibers, impulses travel up to 290 miles per hour

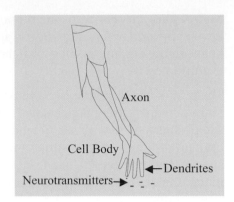

Figure 2.1.5: An arm and hand can show how a neuron works.

Courtesy of US Army JROTC.

Brain Growth

The human brain has evolved over time to a three-pound mass of tissue sparked with electrochemical interactions. Our jaws and teeth have grown smaller, infancy and childhood last longer, and we physically mature and reproduce at an older age. All these evolutionary adaptations have reserved both time and energy to devote to brain development.

Human Thought

With the advantages of a larger brain and more processing power, humans now are able to solve problems, make decisions, and generate options. Emotions are now rich and complex, giving us the ability to fall in love, nurture each other, and hope for a better future. The wonder of a more highly developed limbic system and neo-cortex is lived out each day in processes we often take for granted.

Looking closely at complex processes such as learning, you can see how these processes can bring further advantages. With understanding comes the ability to make choices to improve our lives. And these choices can literally make our physical body work better by increasing the size, number, and connections between neurons, the basic cellular building block of the human nervous system.

Growing Dendrites, Making Connections

The billions of nerve cells connect to each other in billions of combinations, forming trillions of pathways for nerve signals to follow. This results in dendritic growth. The dendrites continue to grow throughout your lifetime.

Neural Plasticity

In addition to adding and refining neural networks through the growth of dendrites, the human brain is capable of adapting specialized nerve functions for another critical use when called on to do so.

Key Note Term

neural plasticity – concerns the property of neural circuitry to potentially acquire (given appropriate training) nearly any function

Neural plasticity concerns the property of neural circuitry to potentially acquire (given appropriate training) nearly any function. For example, the connections between the eye and primary visual cortex suggest that neural circuits are wired by evolution exclusively for sight.

The brain's amazing adaptive ability has been demonstrated by the research of many scientists. Neural plasticity is an important adaptation. Similar to other tissue plasticity, neural plasticity tends to occur when called on for special skill development or fine-tuning existing capabilities. For example, when a musician makes special demands for left-hand skills in the process of learning how to play the piano, the brain adapts by increasing the number of neural circuits in the right primary motor cortex.

Similarly, the area of the brain devoted to the right index fingertip (what's known as the reading finger) is larger in Braille readers compared to that for their non-reading fingertips, or for sighted readers, according to researchers Pascual-Leone & Torres in 1993.

Interesting Facts About Brain Growth

- We produce no new nerve cells after roughly the time of birth. These cells must be nurtured because they must work for the next 80 years or so.

- Our infant brain demonstrates on-the-job training; the brain is being used at the same time it is being assembled.

- We are fairly helpless at birth. Less than 1 percent of the portion of our brain circuitry that will be dedicated to receiving sensory information needed for perception and cognition is functional at that point.

- At birth, 100 billion nerve cells in our cerebral cortex set about wiring incredibly complex circuits (some 5,000 to 10,000 connections to each nerve cell).

- Through learning mechanisms in the brain, the brain continues to rewire and change its circuitry throughout our lives.

Memory Systems

Researchers have identified different types of neural systems that store memories, each with their own focus and purpose. Perhaps you've heard of long- and short-term memory. One way to categorize memory system is in terms of how the brain intends to use the information: for short-term processing needs or as a reference that will be useful to solve problems in the future.

Have you ever heard of the term *muscle memory*? Perhaps you're aware that people can ride a bike, swim, play the piano, or demonstrate a dance step after not doing those activities for many years. Recent research indicates that nerve fibers in the muscles, and not just the brain, are actually involved in some of this long-term memory storage. It's as though, with enough repetition, the body will store signals to make body parts move in certain ways. That way, when the body is called on to do those things, the processing time is faster. You literally can do things "without even thinking about it."

Memory Storage

Recall the idea that both sides of the brain are processing sensory data about the same thing at the same time, but in different ways. This theory regarding how the brain hemispheres both specialize and synchronize was presented in the previous textbook section.

The research indicates that one system handles the detail work while the other creates a framework. The two systems are called *taxon memory* and *locale memory*.

Taxon memory handles rote memorization of data. Multiplication tables, spelling words, and the bones of the hand are examples of data that use the taxon memory system. It requires effort, such as repetition and practice, to store taxon memories (rote learning).

The locale memory system, on the other hand, stores mental maps. These are configurations of information connected to events or associated information (map learning).

Memory Retrieval

The brain has the ability to withdraw information stored in taxon memory more readily when information is stored as part of one of the locale memory system's mental maps. Anything you can do to increase the creation of a mental map, or schema, is critical to long-term memory storage.

For example, continuous, repeated practice is one way to aid memory and retrieval capacity. Another method is to create associations with things you already know, to take your understanding to a new level and enable application of the information in more complex ways.

Involving additional sensory systems is helpful to increase retrieval possibilities. Some people find using body movements will aid long-term storage and retrieval. These "kinesthetic/tactile learners" will recall a telephone number by repeating the movements needed to press the phone keys. Others might recall a rhythm or sound pattern formed when saying the numbers out loud. We'll further explore these interesting differences in Lesson 4, "Multiple Intelligences," later in this chapter.

Intelligence Defined

The ability to solve a problem is one way to define intelligence. Another way to describe intelligence is to talk about the ability to create something or to contribute in a tangible way to one's social system or culture.

These words describe a great deal of human activity. In fact, problem solving is one way experiments are designed to test the intelligence of other species. Researchers present a task to the animal and observe what resources the animal brings to bear on the problem for task completion. For example, monkeys have been known to use sticks to access food or playthings.

The ability to solve a problem—from "the food is out of reach" to "how do we get to the moon"—or the capacity to create a product is how Howard Gardner defines intelligence in his theory of multiple intelligences. These capabilities are considered distinguishing characteristics of intelligent life. For Gardner to include a specific problem-solving style as a defined intelligence, the activity must meet additional criteria. For example, to make Gardner's list, each particular intelligence must have specific regions of the brain specialized to support that function.

> **Note**
>
> Howard Gardner is the John H. and Elisabeth A. Hobbs Professor in Cognition and Education at the Harvard Graduate School of Education. He also holds positions as Adjunct Professor of Psychology at Harvard University, Adjunct Professor of Neurology at the Boston University School of Medicine, and Chair of the Steering Committee of Project Zero. To learn more about Gardner and his theory of multiple intelligences, go to *http://www.infed.org/thinkers/gardner.htm.*

Organisms that do not take in sensory information, process that information, and make decisions about what action to take based on that information are, by definition, less intelligent. The amoeba that takes in nutrients as it drifts around in the water is not solving problems. Its biological processes support food intake in that environment. Without a food source, it would die. It would not be capable of generating any options to enhance survival.

You, on the other hand, are capable of resourceful ingeniousness when it comes to solving problems in order to survive. For more information on this exciting subject, take a look at Lesson 4, "Multiple Intelligences," later in this chapter.

Conclusion

Knowing how the brain functions should give you a better understanding for how we humans are so much alike yet can behave and react to similar stimuli in completely different ways. Knowing how your brain works may make it easier for you to learn, communicate, and resolve conflict.

In the following lesson, you will learn about the left- and right-brain activity. You will learn which side of the brain controls creative activity, and which controls analytical thought.

Lesson Review

1. **Which section of the brain makes humans different than animals?**

2. **Name the three parts of the brain.**

3. **Which part of the brain senses time?**

4. **Explain how both sides of the brain process sensory data differently.**

Left Brain/Right Brain

Key Words

analysis
bilateral transfer
cognition
complementary
corpus callosum
dominant
global
hemisphere
local
specialize
synchronize
synthesis

What You Will Learn to Do

- Distinguish between the functions of left brain and right brain

Linked Core Abilities

- Apply critical thinking techniques

Skills and Knowledge You Will Gain Along the Way

- Identify the activity descriptions and functions of brain hemispheres
- Describe the differences between global and analytical thinking
- Explain how brain dominance helps determine personality and behavior
- Determine personal information processing preferences
- Define the key words contained in this lesson

Chapter 2

Introduction

There are two sides to the brain: the left side, and the right side. In this lesson, you will learn why the brain is divided into two distinct sides, and which side of the brain controls specific activity, such as creative ideas and objective, analytical thought. You will also learn about split-brain research as well as the brain hemispheres.

Visualizing the Brain

Can you imagine what your brain looks like? Close your eyes for a few seconds and visualize it positioned in the space inside your head; then, open your eyes again.

What did you see? As shown in Figure 2.2.1, your brain looks like an English walnut with the shell removed. It has a deeply wrinkled surface with a clearly marked fold that divides it into a left and a right half.

Another way to visualize what your brain looks like is by doing the following demonstration. Make a fist with both hands and put them together in front of you, about chest high and knuckles up. Look down at your fists. This will give you an idea of the physical appearance of your brain. From this view, you can clearly see the separation between the left and right halves. Figures 2.2.2 through 2.2.5 show other views of the brain.

Why is the brain divided into a left and right side? For hundreds of years, scientists believed that the two sides were mirror images of each other. Because nature equips us with two eyes, ears, legs, and kidneys that perform the same function, why not both sides of the brain?

Only within the last 40 years has science shown that the left- and right-brain **hemispheres** have unique and specific functions. Before this breakthrough, brain function was a mystery. More than 90 percent of all science known about the brain is directly or indirectly related to left-brain/right-brain research, which scientists also refer to as split-brain or hemisphere specialization research.

Key Note Term

hemispheres – half of a symmetrical shape

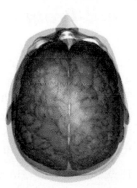

Figure 2.2.1: The wrinkly surface of the human brain.
Courtesy of US Army JROTC.

CORPUS CALLOSUM

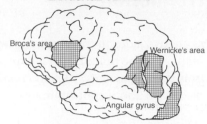

The corpus callosum is the bundle of fibers that connects the two hemispheres.

Figure 2.2.2: View of the corpus callosum.
Courtesy of US Army JROTC.

LANGUAGE CENTERS

Broca's area
Wernicke's area
Angular gyrus

The language centers (Broca's area, Wernicke's area and angular gyrus) are usually located in the left hemisphere.

Figure 2.2.3: The language centers of the brain.
Courtesy of US Army JROTC.

MEMORY STRUCTURES

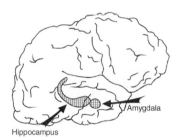

Amygdala
Hippocampus

The amygdala and hippocampus located in the midbrain are responsible for transforming short-term memory into long-term memory.

Figure 2.2.4: The memory structures of the brain.
Courtesy of US Army JROTC.

RETICULAR ACTIVATING SYSTEM

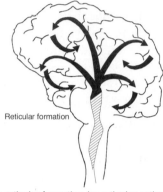

Reticular formation

The reticular formation (or reticular activating system) is the seat of consciousness that is responsible for mental alertness, and it connects the conscious and subconscious minds.

Figure 2.2.5: The reticular activating system.
Courtesy of US Army JROTC.

Split-Brain Research

Key Note Term

corpus callosum – the bundles of fibers (axons) connecting the two sides of the brain; white matter

In the 1950s and early 1960s, neurosurgeons who were treating patients with uncontrollable epileptic seizures decided to perform a radical type of brain surgery. They completely separated the two halves of the brain, creating a split brain, by cutting through the **corpus callosum**, the bundle of fibers that connects these halves. To the doctors' surprise and pleasure, these patients suffered no change in intelligence, personality, or daily function and their seizures stopped.

However, split-brain patients did report oddities and curiosities. For example, one patient had difficulty learning to associate names with faces. Many patients reported subtle memory difficulties, and most patients complained that they no longer dreamed. These reports initiated a tremendous interest in research, thus creating a rapid buildup of knowledge about the brain.

Research in sleep labs proved that split-brain patients do indeed dream, which is indicated by a special brain wave pattern and rapid eye movement below the closed eyelid. These patients could not remember their dreams because one side of the brain is responsible for dream activity and the other side records the dream into words. Because the doctors had disconnected the two sides, the brain could not share this information between the two hemispheres.

Other research suggested that the two sides of the brain have a specific set of functions. Victims of automobile accidents with injuries to the left side of the head lost the ability to speak, but they could still sing. Persons with right-brain damage lost memory of faces and an orientation to their surroundings, even their home (referred to as spatial orientation). These early findings illustrated that speech and language functions are on the left side of the brain and facial recognition, spatial orientation, and music functions are on the right side. Both hemispheres of the brain are involved in higher **cognition** functioning, with each half of the brain specialized in **complementary** fashion.

Key Note Terms

cognition – the mental process of knowing

complementary – supplying mutual needs or offsetting mutual lacks

Hemispheric Specialization

The expression *left-brain/right-brain* refers to specialized functions of the two hemispheres. Scientific research with healthy human subjects used a new brain scan technique called positron emission tomography (PET) to confirm these findings.

Individuals were connected to a machine that mapped brain activity by lighting up to show which part of the brain was active. In a typical experiment, the researcher gave each subject a series of tasks to perform and then recorded which side of the brain was most active. Results indicated that activities involving numbers, logic, word puzzles, sequential tasks, and **analysis** were more active on the left side of the brain, whereas activities involving music, imagination, colors, or creative expression were more active in the right hemisphere. Evidence suggests that the right brain has a **global** bias, while the left brain has a **local** bias. In other words, the right hemisphere sees the picture, and the left hemisphere sees the components of the picture.

Key Note Terms

analysis – the study of something complex, its elements, and their relations

global – involving the entire earth; comprehensive, total

local – a particular place

The distinctiveness of the left- and right-brain functions has led to the notion that humans have two brains. Although research shows that each hemisphere may be in charge of a specific set of functions, neither side has exclusive control of those functions. Both sides can interchange roles.

Figure 2.2.6 graphically displays a summary of those functions for both sides of the brain.

Brain Hemisphere Learning

Research identifies the left brain as the Academic Brain because educators generally emphasize its processes in the traditional classroom, resulting in certain groups using hemisphere specialization to explain limitations of traditional learning. On the other hand, research identifies the right brain as the Artistic Brain because it is in charge of creative talents.

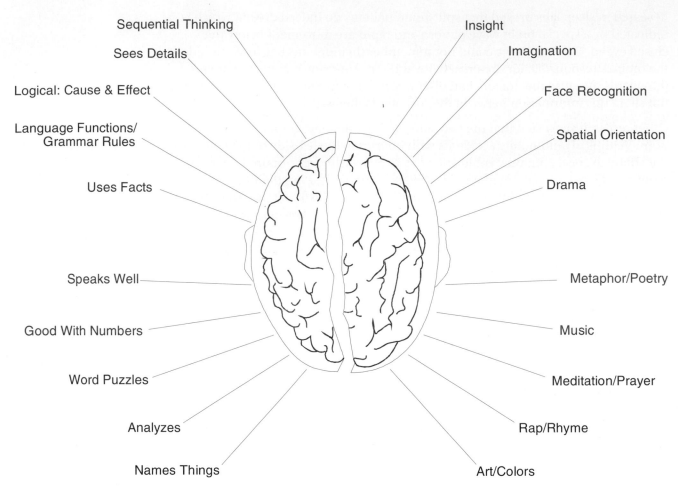

Figure 2.2.6: Left-brain/right-brain functions.
Courtesy of US Army JROTC.

Although fields such as science and medicine now pay more attention to these brain processes, education has traditionally neglected the right side, leaving half of a student's brain potential undereducated. However, more and more school systems are using whole-brain learning techniques.

Recently, educational researchers have shown that a balanced involvement of both sides of the brain in the classroom can create surprising learning gains in many types of students: children, adult learners, the so-called mentally dull, and the genius. Thus, these studies conclude that learning can proceed at astounding rates when teachers have students integrate both sides of their brain in a lesson. For example, kindergarten teachers who use music, dance, storytelling, drama, or numerous other right-brain activities as part of their routine teaching strategy not only aid the left-brain learning of their students but also aid them in learning at incredible rates. After third grade, when the use of these aids typically diminishes, learning rates drop significantly as well.

Brain Hemispheres

The brain splits up functioning and then coordinates and **synchronizes** information processing from the two hemispheres. Split-brain research in the 1960s resulted in some early views of a logical-creative functional split. This simplistic understanding has evolved to a more complex view.

Brain scanning technology has been instrumental in furthering our knowledge base in the area of brain function, specialization, and synchronization. The brain devotes areas to **specialized** tasks. For example, there are clearly areas in the cortex devoted to visual and auditory data, as well as areas that deal specifically with language, memory, and so on.

Different, specialized brain areas process related information at the same time (such as visual data, sound, and smells). These associations enhance long-term memory storage. These initial or level-one processing areas then transfer (hence the term **bilateral transfer**) processed data into another area for higher-level thinking skills and further processing. Distinct data are then integrated.

The processing appears to take place in levels. That is, initial processing seems to focus on the sensory input. Integration occurs between areas. Higher-level thinking skills get involved to make sense of the data.

This all happens very quickly, but there is both a sequential nature and a spiraling nature to the increasingly complex processing that occurs. That is, the brain has the ability to apply increasingly sophisticated analytical and evaluative thinking and it does so progressively. The brain also **synthesizes** new information and experiences with existing knowledge, memories, beliefs, values, and emotions.

The Dominant Side of the Brain

This lesson introduces you to the concept of brain preference, or brain hemisphere dominance, and explains brain preference from a personal, cultural, and career perspective. In class, you may have the opportunity to complete a brain preference test that will tell you which part of your brain you prefer.

As more knowledge about the brain became available, professionals in fields such as science, medicine, and education asked more questions. One interesting line of research explored the question of whether people rely on one side of the brain more than the other. Is one side of the brain **dominant**?

Researchers believe that brain dominance determines a person's preferences, problem-solving style, personality characteristics, and even career choices. For example, a right-brain individual will quickly get a feeling for a situation; a left-brain person will usually ask a lot of questions first. Table 2.2.1 reflects additional differences between left- and right-brain dominance.

There is nothing good or bad about either preference. Both orientations can be equally successful in accomplishing a single task; however, one may be more appropriate over the other depending on the situation.

Key Note Terms

synchronize – to happen at the same time; coincide

specialized – to become adapted to a specific function

bilateral transfer – the ability of the brain to transmit data processed in one hemisphere and coordinate and integrate it with data processed in other areas

synthesis – the combining of separate parts to form a coherent whole, as for a concentrated study of it

Key Note Term

dominant – exercising the most influence or control

Table 2.2.1: Personal Preference

Left Dominance	Right Dominance
Classical music	Popular music
Being on time	A good time
Careful planning	To visualize the outcome
To consider alternatives	To go with the first idea
Being thoughtful	Being active
Monopoly, Scrabble, or chess	Athletics, art, or music

How Brain Preference Develops

Researchers have determined that brain preference does not come from a person's conscious choice about which side of the brain to use. Researchers want to know more about if children inherit their brain preference from their parents (obtained from nature), is it socialized from early childhood experiences (obtained from nurture), or a combination of both. Different studies on how brain preference develops suggest the following:

- **Dominance is present at birth, but children may not be able to establish it well until they are five years old; other studies suggest that children continue to develop their brain preference until they reach puberty**
- **A strong relationship exists between the brain preference of infants and their parents, suggesting that genetics has a major influence on brain preference**
- **Early childhood experiences, or nurturing, can play a major part in brain preference development**

Dominance and Career Choice

As children grow, they will continue to prefer activity on one side of the brain, which eventually can reflect in their choice of a major in college or a career preference. College students who major in literature and the humanities show a greater degree of right-brain activity, compared to those majoring in science and engineering that show high left-brain activity.

Studies have also indicated that brain dominance can be inferred from a person's occupation. Typically, lawyers, chemists, mathematicians, and accountants are left-brain dominant because these occupations require logical, sequential, and analytical skills. Characteristically, musicians, actors, athletes, and artists are right-brain dominant because they rely on right-brain functions such as body sensing, rhythm, color imagery, and spatial orientation.

Distinctions in brain preference also exist within the same occupation. Corporate and contract lawyers are often more left-brain oriented than domestic and criminal lawyers. Rock musicians and recording artists are often more right-brain dominant than classical musicians. Successful managers and administrators in the same field may have different brain dominances. The manager who works well with people most likely has a right-brain tendency, while administrators who do a lot of planning tend have left-brain dominance. Careers in the military follow this same pattern; some are more left-brain oriented, while others are more right-brain oriented.

Your Own Brain Preference

By now you are probably very curious about your own brain preference and have definite feelings about which side you prefer. Knowing your brain preference is important because it determines certain likes, dislikes, skills, and weaknesses.

These preferences may develop very early in your life and may become more extreme as you develop and grow older. For instance, if you are good at basketball, but not at reading, you would most likely spend more time playing basketball than reading. Thus, your abilities and personality may become one-sided. To become a well-rounded, actualized person, you need to consciously develop the less preferred side of your brain.

Thinking Better

In today's society, a crisis exists in how people think; that is, oftentimes people do not think independently or creatively. This lesson gives you the opportunity to examine how you think, how you can improve your thinking process and problem-solving style, and how to balance brain functions to obtain better results. Successful people know how to use their whole-brain functions to solve their problems successfully.

Verbal and Visual Thinking

Each side of the brain has its own thought process, which appears in our conscious mind as voices or pictures. The left brain produces verbal thought while the right-brain creates pictures or visualizations (known as visual thought). Researchers also believe that emotional feelings, hunches, gut reactions, and so on—which people attach to these voices and pictures—represent a third brain input called kinesthetic thought. The combination of these three processes is the way people program their brains to accomplish their life goals.

Verbal Thought

People experience verbal thought through self-talk. Psychologists use self-talk extensively today to help individuals with many of their life problems by giving them thought-stopping techniques to break the habit of negative thinking. For example, star athletes go to sport psychologists to learn how to apply positive self-talk to improve their game. Statements used to condition positive self-talk are affirmations—high-quality statements that promote successful thinking and feeling. People who make the most of affirmations like them so much that they adopt them as personal slogans. Additionally, thinking about an affirmation and repeating it over and over will make it a part of an individual's self-talk; it programs the brain to bring about the desired end result.

The following affirmations are examples that one can use to promote success in learning or for life in general:

- **Learning is something I enjoy immensely**
- **My memory is sharp; my mind is powerful**
- **I am kind, patient, and compassionate with myself**
- **I have the energy and determination to tackle and solve my toughest problems**
- **I have everything it takes to achieve my goals, beginning now**

Visual Thought

The visual pictures that you form in your mind may be crystal clear and in full color or they may be fuzzy, fragmented, and unstable. Some people visualize only in black and white; others do not make pictures at all. People also experience visual thought while they are daydreaming. As a child, visual thinking is prevalent, but by fourth or fifth grade, outside influences can discourage children from daydreaming. Many adults consider it to be a waste of time. However, visual thought is very important and is the beginning point of anything new in one's life. Everything created by humans once existed as a picture in somebody's mind.

The expression *a picture is worth a thousand words* means that visual pictures impress the memory better than verbal thoughts. For example, students who routinely visualize what they read in books perform better on tests and most people remember faces longer than names. Our society may give verbal thinking more importance, but it appears that visual thinking has more brainpower. The following examples are ways you can develop your visual thought power to bring about desired outcomes.

Flashback

Flashback uses constructive daydreaming to strengthen right-brain processes. When you need more energy or motivation to get a task done, such as studying for a difficult exam, flash back to a time when you had plenty of energy and enthusiasm, for example, when you were on a hike with friends or washing cars to earn money for a trip. Get in touch with what you were experiencing in detail. Recall how you were breathing and moving. Try to match the feeling of expectancy, of being connected to a purpose, and of getting on with things to complete them. When you come out of your flashback, bring this energy with you and apply it to the task at hand—studying for that difficult exam.

Flash-Forward

When you desire to accomplish a task, such as advancing in rank in JROTC, making the honor roll, or obtaining a scholarship for college, flash forward to that event. Imagine precisely how you expect to experience it. See your name on the honor roll and feel the pride swell in your chest. Feel your breath stop and your entire body warm in response to your acceptance letter. Experience how you will accept congratulations—perhaps with humility from your superiors and with unrestrained joy from your closest friends. Visit this scene in your mind often as you continue to prepare for your goals. You will be using goal-state visualization, a very powerful mental technique, to obtain what you want in life.

For best results, use verbal and visual thinking together and amplify the effect with strong feelings and emotions (kinesthetic thought). Say your affirmations aloud and see yourself acting or feeling the way they suggest. After you start your goal-state visualizations, monitor your self-talk and make sure it supports your goals. If something happens to create discouragement, talk yourself up with an appropriate affirmation, like: "There's nothing to fear but fear itself," or "I'll turn down my fear and turn up my confidence." When your verbal thoughts, mental pictures, and feelings are in harmony with your goals, you will be activating the strongest force on earth a made-up mind.

Your Problem-Solving Style

Would you like to be able to solve your problems, including those that you consider to be very difficult, with some form of a process or style? You probably already do but have never thought about it before. In the activities for this lesson, you will have the opportunity to complete an exercise that will test your problem-solving style to see if it is left brain or right brain. Both sides have advantages and limitations; however, depending on the circumstances, one of the sides or styles will provide the lead for you to make the best solution. For best results, learn how to combine the left and the right sides of your brain to solve problems, especially those very difficult ones.

Conclusion

Knowing about the functions of the brain is good, but knowing something definite about your own brain is better. So far you know that the left- and right-brain hemispheres have specialized functions and, in many instances, educators emphasize the left brain and neglect the right brain.

During your stages of learning, growth, and personal development, the world can and will present different types of challenges that will place complex demands on your brain. Know how to use your brain efficiently. Know your individual brain preference and your problem-solving style and then use both sides of your brain to set and accomplish goals and to tackle those difficult challenges.

The following lesson covers learning style and processing preferences. Learning is a complex, interrelated system of accessing information, getting it into the brain, and processing that information to solve problems or support activities. Understanding learning styles leads to success.

Lesson Review

1. Define the term *corpus callosum.*

2. Which side of the brain is commonly known as the Academic Brain? Which is known as the Artistic Brain?

3. Are you more left- or right-brain dominant? Explain why.

4. Explain why you feel you are more of a verbal or visual thinker.

Lesson 3

Learning Style and Processing Preferences

Key Terms

auditory
kinesthetic
mode
motivation
perception
reflex
schema
sensory
tactile

What You Will Learn to Do

- Explain how learning styles and preferences can impact learning

Linked Core Abilities

- Build your capacity for lifelong learning
- Apply critical thinking techniques

Skills and Knowledge You Will Gain Along the Way

- Assess the uniqueness of individual learning styles and preferences
- Distinguish among the three sensory (perceptual) systems
- Explain the essential elements of the learning process
- Contrast an automatic and purposeful response to stimuli
- Explain the five phases of learning in the Dunn and Dunn learning model
- Explore how to expand beyond your current preferences
- Define the key words contained in this lesson

Introduction

People learn in different ways. Learning is a complex, interrelated system of accessing information, getting it into the brain, and processing that information to solve problems or support activities.

This lesson covers different learning styles and preferences. You will learn about the three sensory systems and how to tell the differences between them. You will also explore your own individual learning style and preference, and discover how to expand beyond it.

Learning Styles

Learning styles describe the various ways people gather as well as process information. Each of us has a propensity for looking, listening, or touching: some read the instructions for Monopoly, others ask to hear the rules explained, still others get the dice rolling and learn as they play. Furthermore, we each have our most productive time of day, favorite chairs to sit in, and other environmental factors that help us concentrate or feel energized.

Understanding learning styles leads to success. After you know what learning environment works best for you and what your preferred learning style is, you will see how you can use your preferred learning style to move information through the learning process and thereby:

- **Learn new information more quickly and efficiently.**
- **Remember new information for a longer period of time.**
- **Increase your ability to recall the information more quickly and completely for performance, discussion, or test taking.**

The Learning Process

When you learn something, you are acquiring a skill, knowledge or attitude. The process of learning, shown in Figure 2.3.1, involves the ability to take in data, process it, store it, and retrieve it at a later time.

Key Note Term

reflex – denoting or of an involuntary action in which the motor nerves act in response to a stimulus from an impression made on the sensory nerves

Your five senses (hearing, seeing, touching, tasting, and smelling) take in stimuli from the environment. The stimuli are subconsciously filtered, causing you to focus on some stimuli and ignore others. Those selected stimuli are sent to the brain (organism) for processing, where they are linked to prior knowledge, evaluated against your beliefs, and stored in memory. The stimuli, if encountered again, will then elicit a learned response.

If you touch a hot iron for the first time, the burning sensation is sent to your brain. The brain processes it as pain. This causes the **reflex** response of removing your hand quickly. The learned response, however, would be to not touch the iron again.

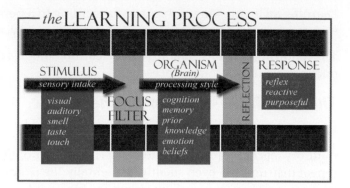

Figure 2.3.1: The learning process.
Courtesy of US Army JROTC.

Preferred Learning Environment

Can you identify personal experiences that illustrate your preferences for a good learning environment? Can you recall times when learning frustrated you? If you examined each of those times, you would probably see that you were working outside of a preferred environment. The following are aspects of the environment that have an impact on the learning process:

- **Sound.** Some people need it absolutely quiet in order to concentrate. Others work or study more effectively only if there is music or noise around them.

- **Light.** Too little or too much light can either inhibit or encourage learning. Many adolescents usually prefer soft or dim lights to study.

- **Design.** Refers to the formal or informal settings and furniture in the room where you study. For instance, do you use a desk or do you prefer the floor, bed, or just the chair?

- **Time of day.** Some people are night people and others are early morning workers.

- **Food intake.** Your need to eat, drink, or chew gum while studying or working.

- **Social aspects.** Preference to work or study alone, with a partner, or in a group.

Perceptual Modalities

Clearly our ability to learn is dependent on our ability to take in, filter, select, process, and then apply new information.

We take in new information through our five senses: hearing, seeing, touching, tasting, and smelling. For most humans, three of the senses dominate our **perceptions**. Perceive means "to become aware of through the senses," and **mode** simply means the method, route, or way. Thus, perceptual modality is another term used to describe the different **sensory** channels.

Humans tend to rely on seeing, hearing, and touching as the primary methods for taking in stimuli from our environment. Of course, a physical limitation might exist that limits one of the senses and the person might have to adapt. In other mammals, dogs, for example, smelling and tasting are highly developed.

Key Note Terms

mode – method, route, or way

perception – awareness of one's environment through physical sensation; ability to understand

sensory – of or relating to an awareness or a mental process due to a stimulation of a sense organ

auditory – of or pertaining to hearing

kinesthetic – a sensory experience derived from a sense that perceives bodily movement

tactile – of or relating to, or perceptible through, the sense of touch

Learning styles are often categorized according to a person's strongest sensory system; thus we have **auditory**, **kinesthetic/tactile,** and visual learners.

The following sections explore several learning models that consider how preferences affect the learning process.

The Big Three—Auditory, Kinesthetic, and Visual

How do you gather information? What is your strongest sensory system?

Auditory learners are the listeners. This 30 percent of the population may need to repeat instructions, even silently, to mentally "hear" information as they commit it to memory. They learn well by discussing ideas and asking questions. They like cooperative learning and group projects.

Kinesthetic/tactile learners gather meaning through touch and movement. All young children depend heavily on this strength, which is why it's so hard to walk through an art gallery with a small child who wants to "see" by touching. About 5 percent of the population holds onto this style throughout their adult lives, continuing to learn best through physical interaction.

About 65 percent of us are visual learners who gather information best by looking, reading, and watching. Visual learners may tune out spoken directions and favor illustrated explanations or charts. They "see" ideas in the mind's eye, remembering visual details from places they've visited.

Adaptive Systems

With increased use, our sensory systems—and their associated neural networks in the brain—become more sensitive and are able to process data more efficiently. In turn, people are able to come up with more skilled responses. For example, not only do concert pianists have more finely tuned abilities to hear sound than the average person, but their fine motor skills, and the sensitivity of their very fingertips, are increased through the growth of neuronal connections. Thus the adage *Practice makes perfect* actually has a physical reason for being true.

The brain can also adapt to meet specialized needs when there is a physical disability or injury. For instance, a nonhearing person handles sophisticated language tasks, like storytelling, with no auditory stimulus and limited ability to speak aloud. Most of us create language by making words come out of our mouth. However, a nonhearing person is likely to tell a story by using sign language.

Although some people think that each of us is born with given strengths, others believe that we develop strengths through our experiences and skill-building activities. The bottom line is that people have strengths. Being aware of your strengths allows you to leverage those strengths to achieve your goals and increases your ability to make an informed choice to develop in key areas.

Metacognition

You have the ability to bring your perceptions and processing into conscious consideration. We call this process thinking about thinking or metacognition. It is the simple process of becoming more aware.

In the learning process, metacognition can be a valuable tool for self-development. Paying attention—becoming more aware of your perceptions and thoughts and more deliberate in your choice of responses—is all part of developing as a person.

Attention and Motivation

An important component of our learning is the process of directing our attention. This brings us squarely into the question of **motivation**. What do we focus on and why?

Your motivation or personal interest is an important component of what you consciously choose to focus on. You may ask yourself the following questions:

Key Note Term

motivation – something that causes a person to act

- **What is the payoff or reward?**
- **Are you learning for pleasure or for the avoidance of pain?**
- **Are you grades oriented or learning oriented?**
- **Are you learning to please yourself or someone other than yourself (parent, friend, teacher, officer)?**

Data Selection and Attention

You have the ability to direct your attention and decide what to focus on. For the sake of efficiency, however, these decisions are often made subconsciously. Lots of data come in all the time, and we can't and don't pay attention to all of it. A lot of these data, depending on your goals, are potentially unimportant and therefore distracting. A "go or no go" signal occurs to regulate the transmission of stimuli. Thus, the sounds of the air conditioner or refrigerator, visual field activity, traffic noise, and so on are simply ignored in terms of conscious thought.

This physical fact reflects an important reality in the learning process. Given the billions of sensory messages taken in and processed constantly, a key activity stands out as extremely important, namely, the ability to filter and select what data to focus on.

When some stimuli are present over a period of time, we adapt to them. Continuing stimuli of constant intensity will stop activating the receptors; in other words, we "tune out." Think about what this means about how you learn.

If your teacher's voice drones on and on, with the same pitch, the same tone, and the same type of words, your brain tends to switch off and filter that sensory input. The same thing occurs if you keep trying to solve a problem in the same way. The magic of active learning happens when you use a variety of stimuli. Even small changes can make a big difference in activating different regions of the brain.

Moving from a short lecture, to building something, to reading quietly, to talking over ideas with another student—this changes the manner in which information is taken in and processed. A mixture of activities will stimulate the brain with different types of impulses, to keep those receptors firing. Learning becomes even more activated when there are spaces in the constant data flow for quiet reflection.

Mental Filters

Not only are the data being absorbed, but they are also being evaluated against prior knowledge and then interpreted. After you have gathered your selected stimuli, you group them into a cluster that you can label, so that the label makes sense to you. This helps you to know, almost without thinking about it, whether it's safe to reach out and touch the hot iron.

You have a stored set of beliefs in your memory called a **schema**. The schema is an outline of the way things are—your own representation of reality. These beliefs cause you to monitor and select the stimuli you take in and to which you pay attention. These internal models limit the data you are curious about and explore.

Key Note Term

schema – a pattern imposed on complex reality or experience to assist in explaining it, mediate perception, or guide response

Ladder of Inference

In *The Fifth Discipline Field Book*, Peter Senge describes a type of schema called the Ladder of Inference, shown in Figure 2.3.2. In this model, we begin with real data or experience (stimuli), and from that data we select the data to which we pay attention. Then we attach meaning to this selected data, make assumptions, and draw conclusions. From our conclusions, we adopt beliefs about the world, which then cause us to take actions and help determine the data we will select the next time. This mental pathway can be a slippery slope that will often lead to misguided beliefs.

> ### Note
>
> Peter Senge is founding chair of the Society for Organizational Learning (SoL). His current areas of special interest focus on decentralizing the role of leadership in organizations so as to enhance the capacity of all people to work productively toward common goals.

For example, if you believe that a particular person doesn't like you, you tend to only see and hear those actions or statements that support your belief. This is another way you filter information.

Processing Strengths

In addition to the preferred input modality, there are clear differences in processing preferences. This tends to break down in alignment with the right-brain and left-brain specializations discussed in an earlier lesson. For example, activities involving numbers, logic, word puzzles, sequential tasks, or analysis are normally more active on the left side of the brain, whereas activities involving music, imagination, colors, or creative expressions are normally more active on the right side. As you grow, you continue to develop a brain preference; that is, you will prefer activity on one side of the brain over the other.

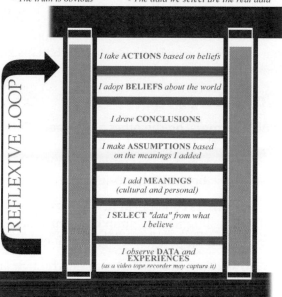

the
LADDER *of* INFERENCE
*Our ability to achieve the results we
truly desire is eroded by our feelings that:*

- *Our beliefs are the truth*   - *Our beliefs are based on real data*
- *The truth is obvious*   - *The data we select are the real data*

REFLEXIVE LOOP

I take **ACTIONS** *based on beliefs*

I adopt **BELIEFS** *about the world*

I draw **CONCLUSIONS**

I make **ASSUMPTIONS** *based
on the meanings I added*

I add **MEANINGS**
(cultural and personal)

*I SELECT "data" from what
I believe*

I observe **DATA** *and*
EXPERIENCES
(as a video tape recorder may capture it)

*Figure 2.3.2: Peter Senge's
Ladder of Inference.*
Courtesy of US Army JROTC.

Figure 2.3.3 shows that during the memory phase of the learning process, learning occurs in both hemispheres. That is, both sides have the ability to perceive information, new ideas, and so on and then organize that information so you can later recall and use it.

Thus we have global and analytic learners in accordance with the brain's ability to focus the abilities of the left hemisphere on details and of the right hemisphere on the big picture.

In other words, besides visual, auditory, or kinesthetic intake strengths, people lean toward one of two styles for processing information: analytic (those individuals who see the individual elements most clearly) and global (those individuals who focus on the big picture).

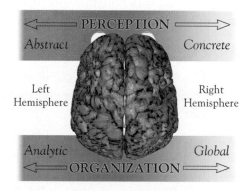

PERCEPTION

Abstract   *Concrete*

Left
Hemisphere   Right
Hemisphere

Analytic   *Global*

ORGANIZATION

*Figure 2.3.3: Learning
occurs in both brain
hemispheres during the
memory phase.*
Courtesy of US Army JROTC.

Analytic Learners

Analytic learners examine information by breaking it down bit-by-bit and arranging it logically. One person's tidy suitcase displays a bent for order and sequence, as does a penchant for lists and punctuality.

An analytic learner is happiest when his or her life marches forward predictably, when he or she can follow a plan and know the rules. Analytic learners are able to see the trees through the forest, which helps keep them (and those around them) rooted and productive.

Global Learners

Global learners, on the other hand, may miss a few trees, but they can surely see the forest. They organize by clustering information into groups. Their focus is drawn to the larger ideas underpinning the details; they concern themselves with the purpose behind the specifics.

Global learners can appear disorganized because of their impatience with minutiae and their willingness to jump between ideas in random ways. They'll bend the rules, including schedules and deadlines, to fit what they see as a greater purpose.

We are all capable of absorbing data through any of our senses and of processing new information in many different ways. This is a tribute to the brain's amazing adaptability and resourcefulness. Nonetheless, knowledge of our strengths and learning preferences helps us to understand our own processes, enabling us to make choices that will empower us as lifelong learners.

Learning Models

Think about your favorite class. Does the teacher lecture? Do you do experiments or go on field trips? Does the teacher show video clips or movies? Do you work in groups? Do you use role-play to act out different scenarios? Chances are, your teacher is using learning activities that match your learning style and processing preferences.

Everyone can learn, but not everyone learns in the same way. Where learning is concerned, there is no one approach that fits all people. If instruction is designed and implemented with consideration of different styles of learning, learners are able to increase concentration as well as process and retain more difficult material.

Models of Learning

Models help make sense of our world. They provide a framework or structure to help us understand a large or complex concept and break it down into discrete, manageable units.

Learning models provide teachers with an organized system for creating an appropriate learning environment and planning instructional activities. Learning models affect what the teacher does, what the student does, the organization of the classroom, the nature of the procedures, the types of materials, and the instructional tasks.

In this section, you will examine two distinct, but complementary, learning models: the *Dunn and Dunn learning styles model,* and *Kolb's model of experiential learning.* Each of these models is based on your individual learning styles and processing preferences. The use of the learning styles model requires teachers to reorganize the instructional environment and instructional activities in order to move from methods that were primarily dominated by lectures to classrooms that facilitate several simultaneous approaches to learning. Both of these models have years of research support behind them as well as validation through practical classroom applications.

Nine Facets of Brain-Compatible Learning

The learning process is all about how we take in, filter, store, and organize information in our brain. This research on how the brain perceives and processes information leads us to a greater understanding of how we learn and how it forms the underlying principles on which learning models were built.

The nine facets of brain-compatible learning, adapted from *Brain: Compatible Learning for the Block,* (Williams & Dunn, Corwin Press, 1999) are as follows:

- *Learning becomes relevant through personal context.* **Students need to understand how this new information relates to their "own life."**

- *Learning is dependent on motivation.* **Students need to be motivated in order to commit the new information to memory.**

- *Learning is reinforced through hands-on experience.* **This experience enables the student to put a concept or theory in context and examine the parts that make up the whole.**

- *Learning requires linking new information to prior knowledge.* **The brain has a much greater capacity to take in and store new information that it can relate to something already learned. Teachers need to help students make these connections.**

- *Learning is achieved more efficiently when information is chunked.* **By grouping together related information, the brain forms a schema, or concept, and assigns meaning.**

- *Learning is enhanced with time for reflection.* **Reflection, or thinking about what was just learned, helps put the new information in long-term memory. Activities such as group discussions, questioning, and writing in a journal all aid in this process.**

- *Learning is retained longer when associated with senses and emotions.* **The more senses that are involved in the learning experience, the more stimuli have a chance of reaching long-term memory.**

- *Learning occurs in an environment that fosters and accommodates various ways of being smart.* **We all have multiple intelligences that need to be accommodated and strengthened. We will discuss this in depth in the next section.**

- *Learning is a high-energy activity.* **If not rehearsed, new information will begin to fade after 30 seconds. It is essential that instructors cover new information several times and in a variety of ways.**

The Dunn and Dunn Learning Styles Model

Developed by Rita and Kenneth Dunn, this model, as shown in Figure 2.3.4, emphasizes the organization of the classroom and the use of a variety of instructional activities and procedures. The model is based on the premise that for a student to have the best opportunity to learn, the instructional techniques must match each student's individual learning style. This model does not address the curriculum content or instructional goals and objectives.

The Dunn and Dunn model involves two main activities:

- **Identifying the individual learning style**
- **Planning and implementing learning activities that accommodate the student's individual learning style strengths**

In this model, the learning style is defined as the preference for or aversion to variables within five identified groups of stimuli.

The five stimuli groups or dimensions encompass environmental, emotional, sociological, physiological, and psychological areas. The stimuli deal with how the learners perceive, interact, and respond within the learning environment. Within these groups are 21 variables, or elements, for which a learner may have a preference.

Environmental Preferences

- **Sound.** Do you like background music or do you prefer quiet while studying?
- **Light.** Do you prefer dim or bright light while studying or concentrating?
- **Temperature.** Do you prefer the room temperature to be cool or warm while engaged in learning activities?
- **Design.** Refers to the furniture arrangement that the student prefers. Do you normally sit at a desk (formal) or do you prefer the couch, bed, floor, or pillows (informal)?

Figure 2.3.4: The Dunn and Dunn learning styles model.
Courtesy of US Army JROTC.

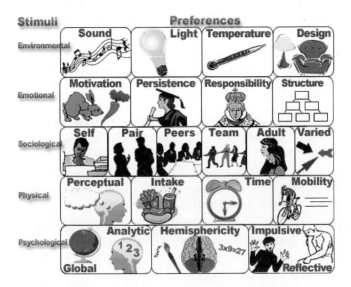

Emotional Preferences

- **Motivation.** Are you self-motivated to learn? Or are you primarily motivated by adult feedback and reinforcement?

- **Persistence.** This relates to the learner's attention span and ability to stay on task. Do you prefer to work on one task or do you like to work on a variety of tasks simultaneously?

- **Responsibility.** Do you prefer to work independently with little supervision or do you prefer to have frequent feedback and guidance?

- **Structure.** Do you like step-by-step instructions or do you prefer to be given an objective and left alone to decide how to complete the task?

Sociological Preferences

- **Self.** Do you prefer working on a task by yourself?

- **Pair.** Do you prefer working on a task with one other person?

- **Peers and Teams.** Do you like working as a member of a team?

- **Adult.** Do you like to work with an adult or teacher?

- **Varied.** Do you like routines or patterns or do you prefer a variety of procedures and activities?

Physical Preferences

- **Perceptual.** Are you a visual, auditory, or kinesthetic/tactile learner?

- **Intake.** Do you prefer to drink, eat, or chew gum while studying?

- **Time.** Refers to the time of the day when you have the most energy. Are you an early bird or a night owl or somewhere in-between?

- **Mobility.** Can you sit still or do you prefer to be moving while involved in a learning task?

Psychological Preferences

- **Global/analytic.** Are you a big picture person or are you more detailed oriented?

- **Hemisphericity.** Do you have left brain tendencies (sequential learner) or right-brain tendencies (simultaneous learner)? This overlaps with the global/analytic preferences.

- **Impulsive/reflective.** Do you tend to make decisions quickly or do you take time to consider all the options?

How Learning Styles Affect Instruction

After you have an understanding of the preferences that affect your learning, how does that understanding translate in the classroom? As you've already learned, the models influence what the teacher does, what the student does, what the classroom looks like, and the materials and learning activities you use.

Teacher's Role

The teacher's primary role in both of these models is that of facilitator and leader. Of course, the first responsibility of the teacher is to identify the student's learning styles. The most effective method is an instrument called a Learning Style Inventory (LSI), which is a self-evaluation that the students complete.

Next, the teacher must arrange the physical classroom to accommodate the different learning styles. Some students might prefer an informal setting, while others might perform better in a more traditional desk and chair.

Finally, the most difficult and time-consuming responsibility of the teacher is to plan and develop a variety of alternate learning activities that will accommodate the different learning styles of the students (role-plays, instructional games, reading, individual assignments, group discussions, writing in a journal, and so on).

Student's Role

Each student is responsible for developing an understanding of his or her learning preferences and using that understanding to enhance his or her own learning experience. Armed with the knowledge of how they learn, students should be able to select appropriate activities so that they will be able to learn more quickly and retain the new information. Studying should be much more productive.

Kolb's Experiential Learning Model

Similar to the Dunn and Dunn model, Kolb's model of experiential learning, as shown in Figure 2.3.5, recognizes the need to address individual differences in learners. Each advocated that in order to be effective, instruction must be modified to accommodate a variety of learners and learning styles.

The Kolb model is a holistic approach to learning that deals primarily with processing preferences by which information is obtained, stored, sorted, and utilized. It defines a four step learning process and then goes on to describe the four learning styles (preferences) used within the process.

The learning cycle is a series of experiences, and each stage of the cycle is associated with a distinct learning style. You can enter the cycle at any of the four processes:

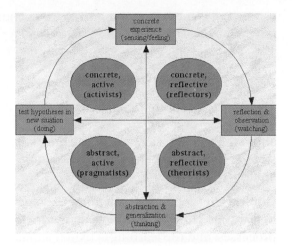

Figure 2.3.5: Kolb's model of experiential learning.
Courtesy of US Army JROTC.

- **Concrete experience** occurs when the learner is actively experiencing an activity (such as a science lab or a field class).

- **Reflective observation** occurs when the learner is consciously reflecting back on that experience.

- **Abstract conceptualization** happens when the learner is being presented with or trying to conceptualize a theory or model of what is (or is to be) observed

- **Active experimentation** happens when the learner is trying to plan how to test a model, theory, or plan for a forthcoming experience.

The four quadrants within the learning cycle represent the four personal learning styles. Because each is based on two dimensions, it is somewhat more complex than the Dunn and Dunn model. According to Kolb's model, the four learning styles include theorists, pragmatists, activists, and reflectors.

Theorists (or Assimilators)

People who adapt well to this learning style like to learn using *abstract conceptualization* and *reflective observation* (lectures, papers, analogies) and like to ask such questions as "How does this relate to that?" The instructional approach for theorists includes using case studies, readings, and thinking alone. Theorists' strengths lie in their ability to create theoretical models. They are often more global thinkers and are concerned with abstract concepts.

Pragmatists (or Convergers)

People who adapt well to this learning style like to learn using *abstract conceptualization* and *active experimentation* (laboratories, field work, observations). They ask, "How can I apply this in practice?" The instructional approach that works best with pragmatists includes peer feedback and activities that apply skills. They prefer to be self-directed, autonomous learners.

Activists (or Accommodators)

People who adapt well to this learning style like to learn using *concrete experience* and *active experimentation* (simulations, case studies, homework). They tell themselves "I'm game for anything." The instructional approach for activists includes practicing the skill, problem solving, small group discussions, and peer feedback. They tend to solve problems intuitively and rely on others for information.

Reflectors (or Divergers)

People who adapt well to this learning style like to learn using *reflective observation* and *concrete experience* (logs, journals, brainstorming). They like time to think about the subject. The best instructional approach to use with reflectors would be lectures that leave plenty of reflection time. Their strengths lie in an imaginative ability.

Our learning comes from all four quadrants, but each person has one favorite form of learning. The ideal learning environment should include each of the four processes, and the learning activities should be flexible so that the learner can spend additional time on his or her preferred learning style.

The following is an example of teaching someone how to ride a bike using the Kolb model of experiential learning:

- **Reflectors:** Thinking about riding and watching another person ride a bike
- **Theorists:** Understanding the theory and having a clear grasp of the biking concept
- **Pragmatists:** Receiving practical tips and techniques from a biking expert
- **Activists:** Leaping onto the bike and trying to ride it

Is There One Best Way to Learn?

Your mind is the most powerful tool you will ever possess. You are accomplished at many skills and can process all kinds of information. However, when you have trouble accomplishing a particular task, you may become convinced that you can't learn how to do anything new. Not only is this perception incorrect, but it can also damage your belief in yourself.

Every individual is highly developed in some abilities and underdeveloped in others. Many famously successful people were brilliant in one area but functioned poorly in other areas. Winston Churchill failed the sixth grade. Abraham Lincoln was demoted to a private in the Black Hawk War. Louis Pasteur was a poor student in chemistry. Walt Disney was fired from a job and told he had no good ideas. What some might interpret as a deficiency or disability may be simply a different method of learning. People have their own individual gifts; the key is to identify them.

There is no one best way to learn. Instead, there are many different learning styles, each suited to different situations. Each person's learning style is unique. Knowing how you learn is one of the first steps in discovering who you are. Before you explore your learning style, consider how the knowledge you will gain can help you.

What Are the Benefits of Knowing Your Learning Style?

Although it takes some work and exploration, understanding your learning style can benefit you in many ways—in your studies, the classroom, and the workplace.

Study Benefits

Most students aim to maximize learning while minimizing frustration and time spent studying. If you know your strengths and limitations, you can use techniques that take advantage of your highly developed areas while helping you through your less-developed ones. For example, let's say you perform better in smaller, discussion-based classes. When you have the opportunity, you might choose a course section that is smaller or that is taught by an instructor who prefers group discussion. You might also apply specific strategies to improve your retention in a large-group lecture situation.

Following each of this chapter's two assignments, you will see information about study techniques that tend to complement the strengths and shortcomings of each intelligence or spectrum. Remember that you have abilities in all areas, even though some are dominant. Therefore, you may encounter useful suggestions under any of the headings. What's important is that you use what works. During this course, try a large number of new study techniques, keeping those you find to be useful.

Classroom Benefits

Knowing your learning style can help you make the most of the teaching styles of your instructors. Your particular learning style may work well with the way some instructors teach and be a mismatch with other instructors. Remember that an instructor's teaching style often reflects his or her learning style. After perhaps two class meetings, you should be able to make a pretty good assessment of teaching styles (instructors may exhibit more than one). After you understand the various teaching styles you encounter, plan to make adjustments that maximize your learning. See Figure 2.3.6 for some common teaching styles.

Assess how well your own styles match up with the various teaching styles. If your styles mesh well with an instructor's teaching styles, you're in luck. If not, you have a number of options.

Bring Extra Focus to Your Weaker Areas

Although it's not easy, working on your weaker points will help you break new ground in your learning. For example, if you're a verbal person in a math- and logic-oriented class, increase your focus and concentration during class so you get as much as you can from the presentation. Then spend extra study time on the material, make a point to ask others from your class to help you, and search for additional supplemental materials and exercises to reinforce your knowledge.

Figure 2.3.6: Teaching
Styles.

Reprinted from *Keys to Success:
How to Achieve Your Goals*,
Third Edition, by Carol Carter,
Joyce Bishop, and Sarah
Lyman Kravits, 2001),
Prentice Hall, Inc.

Teaching Styles

Lecture	Instructor speaks to the class for the entire period; there is little to no class interaction.
Group discussion	Instructor presents material but encourages class discussion throughout.
Small groups	Instructor presents material and then breaks class into small groups for discussion or project work.
Visual focus	Instructor uses visual elements such as diagrams, photographs, drawings, and transparencies.
Verbal focus	Instructor relies primarily on words, either spoken or written on the board or overhead projector.
Logical presentation	Instructor organizes material in a logical sequence, such as by time or importance.
Random presentation	Instructor tackles topics in no particular order or disgresses from the intended topic.

Ask Your Instructor for Additional Help

For example, a visual person might ask an instructor to recommend visuals that would help to illustrate the points made in class. If the class breaks into smaller groups, you might ask the instructor to divide those groups roughly according to learning style, so that students with similar strengths can help each other.

Convert Class Material during Study Time

For example, an interpersonal learner takes a class with an instructor who presents the big picture information in lecture format. This student might organize study groups and, in those groups, focus on filling in the factual gaps using reading materials assigned for that class. Likewise, a visual student might rewrite notes in different colors to add a visual element—for example, assigning a different color to each main point or topic or using one color for central ideas and another for supporting examples.

Instructors are as individual as students. Taking time to focus on their teaching styles, and on how to adjust, will help you learn more effectively and avoid frustration. Don't forget to take advantage of your instructor's office hours when you have a learning style issue that is causing you difficulty.

Career Benefits

Because different careers require differing abilities, there is no one "best" learning style. Develop self-knowledge through honest analysis and then accurately match what you do best with a career that makes the most of your strengths. Specifically, how can knowing your learning style help you in your career?

You will perform more successfully. Your learning style is essentially your working style. If you know how to learn, you will be able to look for an environment that suits you best. You will perform at the top of your ability if you work at a job in which you feel competent and happy. Even when you are working at a job that isn't your ideal, knowing yourself can lead you do on-the-job choices that make your situation as agreeable as possible.

You will be able to function well in teams. Teamwork is a primary feature of the modern workplace. The better your awareness of your abilities, the better you will be able to identify what tasks you will best be able to perform in a team situation. The better your awareness of personality traits—your own as well as those of others—the more skillful you will be at communicating with and relating to your coworkers.

You will be more able to target areas that need improvement. Awareness of your learning styles will help you pinpoint the areas that are more difficult for you. That has two advantages: (1) You can begin to work on difficult areas, step by step. (2) When a task requires a skill that is tough for you, you can either take special care with it or suggest someone else whose style may be better suited to it.

Now that you know you have something to gain, look at some ways you can explore your particular learning style.

Learning Results

So, what are the tangible results of learning? If your parents ask, "What did you learn today?" can you answer the question accurately and completely?

The basic response to new information is to check it against what you already know and then to either discard it, store it, or act on it. As we've discussed, you can do some of this processing unconsciously. When threatened, people can react quickly without rational thought. Detailed memories are stored with events that happen very quickly. That's why a smell or sight can trigger a memory long forgotten; the memory is stored intact, the connections are there, and the whole thing can come back in vivid detail when triggered.

It is important to be able to recall information when you need it and to make connections between different things you've learned. These connections, linking new stimuli to prior knowledge, are called mental maps. The amazing thing is that your brain can actually improve by increasing the number of connections and clarifying your internal mental maps.

These mental maps, or reference points, are among your greatest assets for taking in new data quickly and easily. You need them to have a framework, or schema, in which to store the data. Otherwise, your brain may drop data out of short-term memory without storing it long term, or your brain may store information in a way that prevents access to it.

Conclusion

The learning process enables you to acquire knowledge, skill, and attitudes. As you become more aware of how you learn, you'll be able increase your abilities to absorb new information and apply it in new situations. You'll also remember information longer and improve your recall ability.

Knowing how you prefer to learn and understanding how you do learn are very important aspects that can help you to succeed in school, in your employment, and in your career. Learning models facilitate the process of linking instructional activities to individual learning styles, thereby increasing the learner's ability to acquire and retain knowledge.

The next lesson covers the concept of multiple intelligences. In this lesson you will learn that we use our different intelligences to solve problems, choose a profession, and excel in different aspects of our lives.

Lesson Review

1. **Give an example of your preferred learning environment. Why do you prefer this?**

2. **Are you an auditory, kinesthetic, or visual learner? Why?**

3. **Do you consider yourself an analytical or a global learner? Why?**

4. **Define the term *schema*.**

Lesson 4

Multiple Intelligences

Key Terms

bodily/kinesthetic intelligence
interpersonal intelligence
intrapersonal intelligence
logical/mathematical intelligence
musical/rhythmical intelligence
naturalist intelligence
verbal/linguistic intelligence
visual/spatial intelligence

What You Will Learn to Do

- Use your intellectual strengths to improve academic performance

Linked Core Abilities

- Build your capacity for lifelong learning
- Apply critical thinking techniques

Skills and Knowledge You Will Gain Along the Way

- Assess Gardner's impact on the understanding of intelligence
- Identify the eight types of intelligence
- Distinguish between inter- and intrapersonal intelligence
- Examine how to strengthen intelligence
- Define the key words contained in this lesson

Introduction

In his book, *Frames of Mind*, Howard Gardner introduced his theory of multiple Intelligences. Almost immediately, his theory took the educational community by storm. There are books, instructional strategies, tests, learning centers, and research studies centered on his theory that each individual is intelligent in a unique way. He asserts there is no single way of being smart and that the question should be "How are you smart?" not "How smart are you?" With that question, he revolutionized the thinking about the definition of intelligence.

> **Note**
>
> Howard Gardner holds positions as Adjunct Professor of Psychology at Harvard University, Adjunct Professor of Neurology at the Boston University School of Medicine, and Chair of the Steering Committee of Project Zero. To learn more about Dr. Gardner, go to *http://www.pz.web.harvard.edu/PIs/HG.htm*.

Everyone is different from everyone else in appearance, interest, ability, talent, and personality. The brain is no exception. We all have different kinds of minds. We use our different intelligences to solve problems, to choose a profession, and to excel in different aspects of our lives. Some of us are good with language: We talk and write easily, tell good stories, and express our thoughts clearly. Others of us are designers who can decorate a room, design a house, or landscape a yard. Some are artistic and can create songs, draw paintings, play an instrument, or choreograph dances. Others are scientists or inventors who can solve problems, study issues, or do experiments. And some are team players that are good at working with, understanding, and influencing other people.

Eight Kinds of Intelligence

Traditionally, intelligence has been associated with certain standardized tests, such as the IQ test or the SAT; however, these tests only measure verbal and mathematical abilities. Gardner, on the other hand, defines intelligence as the "ability to solve problems or create products that are valued in one or more cultures or communities." He believes that, among other criteria, intelligence is universal to all human beings, regardless of where you live or your culture.

Gardner has identified eight intelligences:

- **Bodily/kinesthetic**
- **Visual/spatial**
- **Logical/mathematical**
- **Verbal/linguistic**
- **Musical/rhythmical**

- **Naturalist**
- **Interpersonal**
- **Intrapersonal**

He believes there are more types of intelligence, but only eight have met his stringent criteria for inclusion. You can think of these as "languages" that most people speak and can be understood regardless of cultural, educational, or ability differences.

Bodily/Kinesthetic Intelligence

Bodily/kinesthetic intelligence (see Figure 2.4.1) is the gift of physical prowess, coordination, fitness, and action. It is manifested in the skills of athletic performing, dancing, doing, experiencing, fixing, forming, making, and repairing.

Learning activities that tap into this intelligence include acting, body language, choreography, constructing, energizers, experiments, field trips, games, learning centers, manipulating, pantomimes, role-plays, sports, and the use of materials and tools.

Visual/Spatial

Visual/spatial intelligence is the gift of visually representing and appreciating concepts, ideas, and information (visual thinking). People who possess this intelligence like to draw, build, design, and create things.

Learning activities that tap into this intelligence include artwork, blueprints, cartoons, designs, drawings, films, graphic organizers, illustrations, layouts, photography, manipulatives, maps, models, murals, posters and charts, props, sculptures, storyboards, and videotapes.

Logical/Mathematical

Logical/mathematical intelligence is the gift of reasoning and thinking in symbols and abstractions. It is manifested in the skills of calculating, computing, problem solving, and logic. If you have strong logical/mathematical intelligence, you are a questioner.

Key Note Terms

bodily/kinesthetic intelligence – the gift of physical prowess, coordination, fitness, and action

visual/spatial intelligence – the gift of visually representing and appreciating concepts, ideas, and information (visual thinking)

Key Note Term

logical/mathematical intelligence – the gift of reasoning and thinking in symbols and abstractions

Figure 2.4.1: Dancing is a form of bodily/kinesthetic intelligence.
Courtesy of Alon Reininger/ Contact Press Images.

Learning activities that tap into this intelligence include analogies, computer games, deductive and inductive reasoning, formulas, graphs and information organizers, learning logs, outlines, problem solving, puzzles, statistics, surveys, symbols, and time lines.

Verbal/Linguistic

Key Note Term

verbal/linguistic intelligence – strong language and literacy skills

If you are endowed with **verbal/linguistic intelligence**, you have strong language and literacy skills. You are good at listening, reading, speaking, and writing.

Learning activities that tap into this intelligence include biographies, books, crosswords, debates, dialogues, discussions, e-mail, internet searches, letters, magazines and newspapers, poems, readers' theater, reports, research, short stories, speeches, and storytelling.

Musical/Rhythmical

Key Note Terms

musical/rhythmical intelligence – the gift of melody, music, rhyme, rhythm, and sound

naturalist intelligence – environmental awareness

Musical/rhythmical intelligence (see Figure 2.4.2) is the gift of melody, music, rhyme, rhythm, and sound. It is manifested in the skills of playing an instrument, vocal performance, appreciation of sounds and music, and timing and patterns.

Learning activities that tap into this intelligence include ballads, cheers and chants, choirs, tapping, drumming, folk songs, imitations, jingles, percussions, raps, songs, and sound reproductions.

Naturalist

A **naturalist intelligence** is an environmental awareness. If you have this kind of intelligence, you understand the interrelationships of the natural world. It is manifested in the skills of classifying, observing, appreciating, and understanding nature; recognizing patterns in nature; and identifying the impact and consequences on the environment.

Figure 2.4.2: Playing a musical instrument is a form of Musical/ Rhythmical intelligence.
Courtesy of Donald Smetzer/ Tony Stone Worldwide.

Learning activities that tap into this intelligence include astronomy, bird watching, ecology, environmental issues, field studies, gardening, geology, native plants, nature walks, outdoor education, mythologies, pattern identification, recycling, and weather forecasting.

Interpersonal

People with **interpersonal intelligence** (see Figure 2.4.3) are socializers. They have the gift of working with people and understanding the complexities of human relationships. It is manifested in the skills of caring, collaborating, communicating, empathizing, leading, and peacemaking. They like to work in groups.

Learning activities that tap into this intelligence include case studies, class discussions, classroom roles and responsibilities, constructivism, cooperative learning, group projects, interviews, jigsaw, pen pals, service learning, shared homework, structured conversations, team building, and tutoring.

Intrapersonal

Intrapersonal intelligence is the gift of inner thought, self-awareness, and self-reflection. It is manifested in the skills of goal setting, self-assessing, and self-regulating. People with intrapersonal intelligence prefer to work alone.

Learning activities that tap into this intelligence include authentic assessments, autobiographies, calendaring, choice theory, diaries, goal setting, independent reading, meditations, metacognition, personal essays, personal planning time, portfolios, quiet or reflection time, reflective or response journals, and rubrics.

Key Note Term

interpersonal intelligence – the gift of working with people and understanding the complexities of human relationships

Key Note Term

intrapersonal intelligence – the gift of inner thought, self-awareness, and self-reflection

Figure 2.4.3: Socializers demonstrate Interpersonal Intelligence.
Courtesy of Richard Pasley/Stock Boston.

Conclusion

Understanding how your own body works to support the learning process helps you become a more active learner. We all have multiple intelligences; however, some are stronger than others. As you engage in learning activities that are compatible with how your brain takes in, processes, and stores information, learning will occur more naturally, and comprehension and recall will increase. The power to learn quickly and to apply what you've learned is in your hands when you know how the process works.

In the next lesson, you will learn how to read for meaning so you can get the most out of all the materials you read for school, work, and play.

Lesson Review

1. List the eight kinds of intelligence.
2. Which learning activities tap into musical/rhythmical intelligence?
3. Do you possess more interpersonal or intrapersonal intelligence? Why?
4. Define the term *naturalist intelligence.*

Study Skills

Chapter 3

Thinking Maps®

Key Words

analogies
Brace Map
Bridge Map
Bubble Map
Circle Map
Double Bubble Map
Flow Map
Multiflow Map
relating factor
Tree Map

What You Will Learn to Do

- Use Thinking Maps® to enhance learning

Linked Core Abilities

- Apply critical thinking techniques

Skills and Knowledge You Will Gain Along the Way

- Identify the types of thinking processes
- Relate thinking to learning
- Correlate thinking processes to the eight Thinking Maps®
- Use Thinking Maps® to visually depict a learning objective
- Define the key words contained in this lesson

Introduction

Describing an item or a concept can be difficult. It's probably not hard for you to describe a flower or a dog, but it might be difficult to keep your description organized in your mind. And what gets even trickier is when you're asked to describe or define main and supporting ideas of a story, or the cause and effect of a specific action. Your thoughts and ideas can easily get confused, or you might even forget some of your descriptions and conceptual thoughts.

Thinking Maps® were created to help you organize your thinking so that you can construct knowledge much like an engineer uses a certain set of tools to build a new bridge. This lesson introduces you to Thinking Maps® and covers how each of the eight maps shown in Figure 3.1.1 can be used to develop a common thinking-process language. Keep in mind as you read through this lesson how thinking and learning go hand in hand.

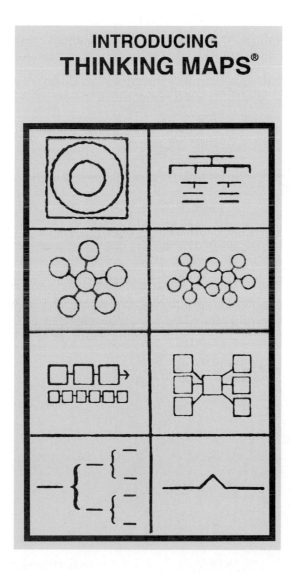

Figure 3.1.1: The eight Thinking Maps®.
©2004 by Thinking Maps, Inc.

Types of Thinking Maps®

Thinking Maps® are visual learning tools. Each map is based on a fundamental thinking process, such as describing a quality, sequencing, classifying, comparing and contrasting, and can be used together as a set of tools for showing relationships. These maps—the Circle Map, Bubble Map, Double Bubble Map, Tree Map, Brace Map, Flow Map, Multi-Flow Map, and Bridge Map—all serve a specific purpose for different types of thinking processes. The following sections describe the eight types of Thinking Maps® and how they can best aid you in your learning process.

The Circle Map

Key Note Term

Circle Map – tool used for brainstorming

The **Circle Map** (see Figure 3.1.2) is used for brainstorming ideas. It is used to define in context and answer the question, "How are you defining this thing or idea?" In the center of the circle, use a word, number, picture, or any other sign or symbol to represent an object, person, or idea you are trying to understand or define. Write or draw any information that puts this object, person, or idea into context. This type of map shows the most random type of thinking.

The square around the map is a frame of reference. It tells how you know or learned about the context. A frame of reference can be used with any type of Thinking Map®.

The Bubble Map

Key Note Term

Bubble Map – tool used for describing qualities

The **Bubble Map** (see Figure 3.1.3) is used to describe qualities of a person, place, or thing. In the middle circle, write the name of the object that you want to describe; then, in the six surrounding circles, write the adjectives or adjective phrases that describe that object and answer the question, "Which adjective would best describe this object?" By the time your Bubble Map is finished, it may look similar to a web or a cluster.

Bubble Maps are also useful for developing vocabulary, distinguishing between fact and fiction, and valuing/evaluating. Bubble Maps should not be used for brainstorming; the Circle Map is best for that.

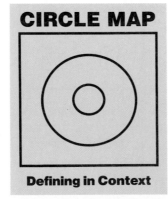

Figure 3.1.2: The Circle Map.

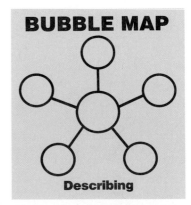

Figure 3.1.3: The Bubble Map.

©2004 by Thinking Maps, Inc.

The Double Bubble Map

The **Double Bubble Map** (see Figure 3.1.4) is used for comparing and contrasting. In the larger center circles, write the words for the two items or objects being investigated. In the middle bubbles, use adjectives, adjective phrases, and other terms that show similarity between the two objects and answer the question, "What are the similarities and differences?" In the outside bubbles, as connected respectively to the two objects, write the words that describe their different qualities.

The Tree Map

The **Tree Map** (see Figure 3.1.5) is used for classifying and categorizing objects and ideas according to common qualities and information about the category. It answers the question, "What are the main ideas and supporting details of the topics?" On the top line, write the category name. On the second level list the subcategories and then below each subcategory, write the specific members.

Tree Maps can be used for hierarchical classifications as well as for informal groupings of themes, concepts, and ideas.

The Brace Map

The **Brace Map** (see Figure 3.1.6) is used to analyze physical objects and shows part-whole relationships. It answers the question, "What are the parts of the whole physical object?" On the line to the left, write the name of the whole object. On the lines within the first brace to the right, write the major parts of the object; then follow within the next set of braces with the subparts of each major part.

Brace Maps can also be used to identify the anatomy of any object as well as developing special reasoning.

The Flow Map

If you need to sequence or order information, use the **Flow Map** (see Figure 3.1.7). It answers the question, "What happened?" In the outside rectangle, write the name for an event or sequence. In the larger rectangles, flowing from left to right, write in the major stages of the event. In the small rectangles below, write in the substage of each major stage.

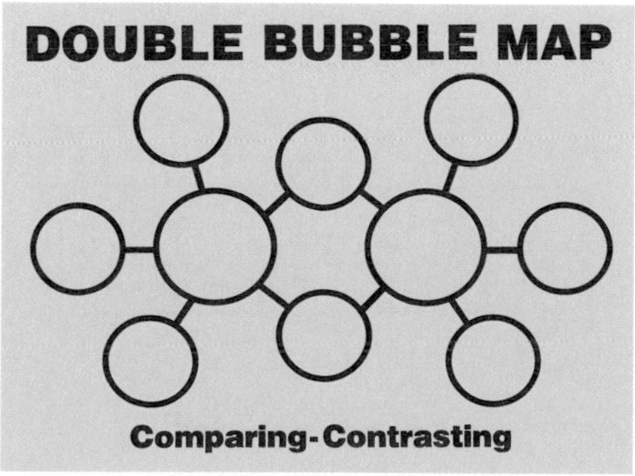

Key Note Term

Double Bubble Map – tool used to compare and contrast

Key Note Term

Tree Map – tool used for classifying and categorizing

Key Note Terms

Brace Map – tool used to analyze a physical object and its parts

Flow Map – tool used to determine sequencing

Figure 3.1.4: The Double Bubble Map.

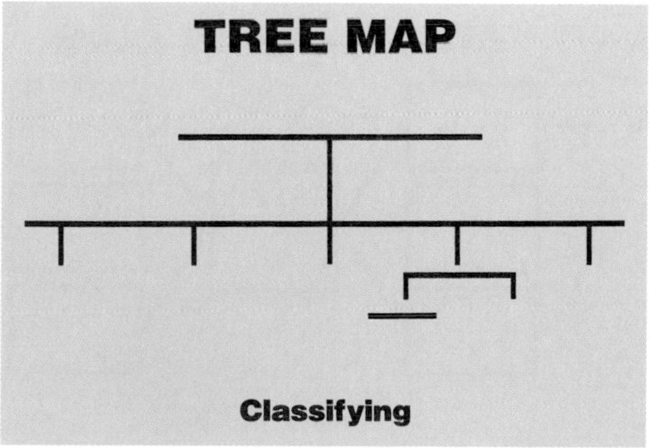

Figure 3.1.5: The Tree Map.

©2004 by Thinking Maps, Inc.

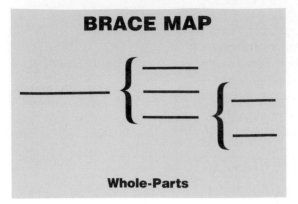

Figure 3.1.6: The Brace Map.

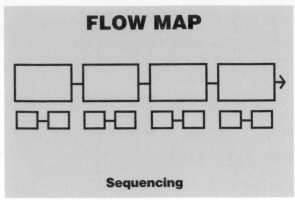

Figure 3.1.7: The Flow Map.

©2004 by Thinking Maps, Inc.

Other uses for the Flow Map include the sequence of a plot, a timeline, order of operations, and framing long-term outcomes.

The Multi-Flow Map

The **Multi-Flow Map** (see Figure 3.1.8) is used for showing and analyzing cause-and-effect relationships. It answers the question, "What are the causes and effects of the event?" In the center rectangle write an important event that has occurred. On the left side of the event, write the causes of the event; on the right side, write the effects of the event.

As you identify more causes and effects, add them to the map. If you are studying a system, you will find that there are effects in the system, which, in turn influence initial causes. This circular cause-and-effect relationship is called a feedback loop.

The Bridge Map

The **Bridge Map** (see Figure 3.1.9) gives you a tool for applying the process of seeing **analogies** and answers the question, "What is the guiding metaphor?" On the line to the far left, write the **relating factor**. On the top and bottom of the left side

Key Note Terms

Multi-Flow Map – tool used for seeing cause-and-effect

Bridge Map – tool used for seeing analogies

analogies – resemblance in some particulars between things otherwise unlike

relating factor – the similar phrase that fits both sides of an analogy

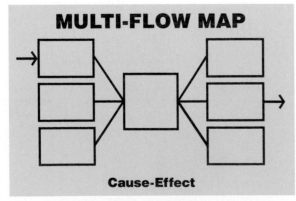

Figure 3.1.8: The Multi-Flow Map.

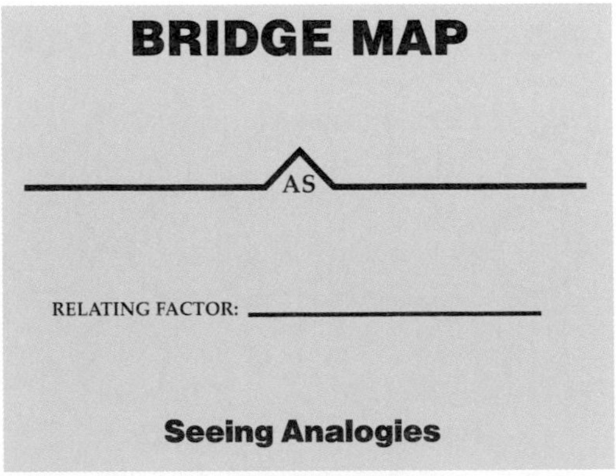

BRIDGE MAP

Seeing Analogies

Figure 3.1.9: The Bridge Map.

©2004 by Thinking Maps, Inc.

of the bridge, write the first pair of things that have this relationship. On the right side of the bridge, write the second pair of relationships that have the same relationship. This line of the bridge represents the relating factor that is "bridged over" from one side of the analogy to the other.

Conclusion

Each Thinking Map® defined in this lesson was designed to help you develop a consistent way to process your thinking so you can learn more effectively. From brainstorming to comparing/contrasting, from sequencing to seeing analogies, Thinking Maps® are tools that can aid you in keeping your ideas organized and your research easy to read. They also provide ways to stimulate your thinking.

In the following lesson, you will learn how to hone your study skills to make the most of your study time and learn all you can.

Lesson Review

1. Give an example of when you would use a Circle Map.
2. Why would you not want to use a Bubble Map for brainstorming?
3. Explain how a Brace Map can be used in the study of geography.
4. Define the term *analogy*.

Lesson 2

Reading for Meaning

Key Words

analogy
antonym
appositive
comprehension
concept
context
hypothesis
inventory
mood
prediction
properties
purpose
strategy
synonym

What You Will Learn to Do

- Select reading comprehension strategies to enhance learning

Linked Core Abilities

- Communicate using verbal, nonverbal, visual, and written techniques
- Apply critical thinking techniques

Skills and Knowledge You Will Gain Along the Way

- Identify the purposes of reading
- Distinguish among reading comprehension strategies
- Distinguish among the types of context clues readers use to determine word meaning

- Recognize how to apply vocabulary strategies to enhance vocabulary context
- Relate vocabulary in context strategies to reading comprehension
- Define the key words contained in this lesson

Introduction

Every day you are bombarded with things to read—junk mail, billboards, newspapers, magazines, and books. Sometimes it is hard to decide what to read and what to throw away. You read for many reasons: to gain information, for entertainment, to pass the time, or to study. If you want to improve your reading skills, read as much as you possibly can. You should read everything interesting; even the backs of cereal boxes and comic books will increase your reading speed and comprehension. Soon, reading will come easily and it will be more enjoyable. But do not give up looking for the types of material that you find interesting. All it takes is one good book and you will be enjoying the written word for all it is worth.

Reading is a communication skill that many people find difficult; however, similar to the other communication skills, practice will make reading easier and more enjoyable. This lesson covers a few guidelines you can follow that may make reading simple and more pleasurable.

Previewing

Preview (or scan) the material, especially a book, before you begin to read it. Previewing consists of looking over the table of contents, index, and title page. Search for familiar concepts and ideas that the material discusses. Do not spend too much time previewing but do allow enough time to become familiar with the contents.

Courtesy of Alan Marsh/First Light.

Questioning

After you preview the material, make a list of questions related to the topic about which you are reading. Your preview should help you come up with relevant questions. Make your questions detailed. Remember that you can increase your knowledge by asking questions. Also, your reading will be more directed because you will be looking for specific answers.

The following are three different kinds of questions you can ask to gain better understanding of what you are reading.

- **Empirical Questions.** These questions ask for information contained in the material that you are reading. They are questions to which the answers are factual. An example of an empirical question is "When did this event take place?"

- **Value Questions.** These questions reflect values or point of view. Answers to value questions are based on opinion. An example of a value question is "Do I agree with the principles expressed in this book?"

- **Analytical Questions.** These questions ask for a definition of what we mean by the words used in the question. Often they need to be asked before the other two types of questions are asked. For example, if you were asked, "How much of the material in this lesson did you comprehend?" you would first have to ask the question, "How do you measure comprehension?"

You will use all three types of these questions during your studies.

Reading and Note Taking

Key Note Terms

inventory – an itemized list of current assets; a catalog of the property of an individual or estate; a list of goods on hand; a survey of natural resources; a list of traits, preferences, attitudes, interests or other abilities used to evaluate personal characteristics or skills

purpose – something set up as an object or end to be obtained

After you have previewed your material and developed questions about the material, you are ready to read. Clear your mind of all personal challenges, open up the book, and begin the first page slowly. Keep a dictionary nearby so you can look up unfamiliar words as you go along. As you read, take notes in the column of the book (if it is your own book) or on a separate sheet of paper. You will be making an **inventory** of the information in the topic.

Schedule breaks during your reading. Do not try to read for a long period of time or you may become bored or sleepy. Also, do not read little sections at a time or you may easily become confused and distracted. Allow yourself at least half-hour intervals of reading time and then reward yourself with a five-minute break. During your break, walk around, stretch, or get a glass of water or a piece of fruit but have the self-discipline to return to your reading after the five-minute period is over.

As you progress in school, your instructors will require you to do research, give speeches, and prepare reports on material that may or may not be familiar to you. To complete these assignments, you may have to read as much material on your given subject as you can. Because you are reading for a **purpose** other than enjoyment, it may be helpful to first scan the material, then read it and take notes.

Courtesy of Ken Karp.

Taking notes on your reading gives you the opportunity to pick out the facts that are important to you. You will also remember what you are reading because you have to translate the material into your own words. Reading combined with note taking is an excellent way to remember important facts and to become familiar with new and challenging material.

Outlining

Outlining is an important part of reading. After you have read through the material once, create an outline. Your outline should capture the main points or ideas and answer the questions that you came up with earlier. If you have a large reading assignment, you may find it easier to outline sections of the material rather than trying to outline the entire assignment at once. You will find outlining a helpful tool for you when it is time to review the material you have read for a test.

Hints for Difficult Reading

Sometimes you must read about difficult subjects. For difficult reading materials, use the following suggestions to assist you in understanding the material better.

- **Look for key words in your material.**

- **Hold a mini-review at the end of each paragraph. When reading a paragraph, you will see that it contains a main idea or topic. Notice that the other sentences support the main idea. If you determine what the main idea is first, you will better understand the concept of the paragraph.**

- **Listen as you read the material aloud.**

- **Ask an instructor questions about the material.**

- **Find a tutor who can help you to understand the material better.**

- **Explain what you have read to another person.**

Courtesy of Ken Karp.

- Take notes while you read the material; make an outline when you finish reading.

- After reading your material, take a break from it. Work on or think about other projects.

- Find another book, reference materials, and/or textbooks that cover the same topic. Sometimes other books can describe the same topic and concepts more clearly.

- Imagine that what you are reading is real. Look at the pictures in the book and develop mental pictures in your mind about the material. Try to imagine that you are a part of them.

- Keep a dictionary nearby so you can look up unfamiliar words as you read.

Reading Comprehension Strategies

The following reading comprehension strategies will assist you in gaining a better understanding of what you read.

Key Note Terms

strategy – the art of carefully devising or employing a plan of action or method designed to achieve a goal; the art or science of planning and directing large-scale military operations and campaigns

prediction – something that is foretold on the basis of observation, experience, or scientific reason

Directed Reading-Thinking Activity (DR-TA)

The DR-TA reading comprehensive **strategy** is used to predict or define the author's purposes for writing the material you are reading. When you read, select relevant data, evaluate it, and use it to form **predictions** of the content of the material based on the information that you acquire. In this lesson, you can predict that the author wants to help you improve your reading comprehension.

GIST

Have you heard the expression, "Did you get the gist of the movie?" *Gist* means the main point of the movie. In the GIST reading comprehensive strategy, the letters actually stand for *Generating Interactions between Schemata and Text*. The strategy asks you to focus on short passages in your reading, three to five paragraphs in length, and create summaries for each passage in a structured step-by-step process. This will help you comprehend, or get the gist of, the passage.

Think-Alouds

Think-alouds help you monitor your comprehension and apply self-correction strategies to get the most out of your reading. Five strategies that can be used during think-alouds are as follows:

- Develop a **hypothesis** by making predictions. For example, by reading the introduction in this lesson, you can make a prediction that this lesson is about learning how to become a better reader.

- Develop images by describing the pictures forming in your mind from the information that you are reading. For example, when you continue with the lesson, you might picture yourself reading a schoolbook.

- Link new information with your prior knowledge by sharing analogies. For example, while reading this lesson, you remember how you became a better football player when you approached each game with a plan. You now apply that **analogy** to becoming a better reader by following the plan in this lesson.

- Monitor comprehension by verbalizing a confusing point. For example, sometimes it can help your comprehension by talking through a point in the reading that might be confusing.

- Regulate comprehension by demonstrating strategies. For example, if your predictions about the meaning of this lesson turns out not to be what you originally thought, you can talk it through until you can comprehend the correct meaning of the lesson.

Key Note Terms

hypothesis – an assumption or concession made for the sake of argument; an interpretation of a practical situation or condition taken as the ground for action

analogy – resemblance in some particulars between things otherwise unlike

Question-Answer Relationships (QARs)

As stated earlier in this lesson, one of the guidelines to help you become a better reader involves asking questions about the material that you have read. The type of question you ask must be based on the information you need to answer the question. In this reading comprehension strategy, you must draw on two different information sources to answer your questions: the information in the material that you read and the information inside your head. For example, you can find the answer to the question "What are some hints to help you understand difficult reading?" in the lesson material. However, if your question was "Does one hint work better for you than another?" you would have to rely on your knowledge of what works best for you.

Vocabulary Comprehension

Reading forms the basis of your study skills. An active learner pursues information on his or her own through reading. Class reading assignments provide a chance for you to practice all the skills you have learned from this chapter. This lesson covers vocabulary comprehension.

Studying vocabulary increases word recognition. As you read, you recognize the meaning of words and interpret the information in the text. The more you read, the more new words you acquire and understand. This builds your vocabulary, makes reading become easier and faster, and raises your reading comprehension.

Six Strategies to Improve Vocabulary Comprehension

The following sections show you strategies to help improve vocabulary comprehension: context clues, word structure, and word mapping. Each clue will help you build your vocabulary and get more out of what you read.

Context Clues

Learning the meaning of words from the **context** of your reading material can be the most useful strategy to increase your vocabulary comprehension. Using the context that surrounds an unknown word helps to reveal its meaning.

There are several different types of context clues that you can use to find the meaning of a word within the context of what you are reading.

- **Definition.** The author equates the unknown word to a word that is known or more familiar to you. For example, "Physiology is a branch of biology that deals with the functions and activities of life or of living matter (as organs, tissues, or cells)."
- **Synonyms.** The author pairs the unknown word with a **synonym** or other closely related words. For example, "The President's wife possessed the traits of a promising leader: wisdom, judgment, and sagacity."
- **Comparison Clues.** Often an unfamiliar word is used in comparison with a familiar word. Your knowledge of the familiar word may help you figure out the meaning of the new one. For example, "The thatch in the roof was as likely to burn as any other straw."

Another example of a comparison clue is the use of an **appositive**. An appositive uses two adjacent nouns that refer to the same thing. For example, using the words poet and Burns adjacent to each other in the phrase "a biography of the poet Burns" helps define both words.

- **Contrast Clue.** In a comparison clue, you learn that a new word is like a known word. In a contrast clue, you learn that a new word is different from the known word. For example, "At night the street was pacific, unlike the crowded, noisy chaos it was during the day."
- **Examples in Context.** You can predict the meaning of an unfamiliar word when it is used with an example of a familiar word. For example, "At the show we saw magicians, ventriloquists, and other performers."
- **Inferring Meaning from Context.** The author sets a **mood** (ironic, serious, funny, etc.) in which the meaning of the unknown word can be hypothesized. For example, "The tormented lion roared in pain as he tried to escape from his captors."

Word Structure

Sometimes a word can give clues to the meaning in its structure. Analyzing the word's structure and **properties** is a vocabulary strategy that you can use to figure out the word's meaning. When you approach an unknown word, you can guess at its meaning by breaking down the parts of the word.

Key Note Terms

context – that which surrounds a particular word and determines its meaning

synonym – one of two or more words or expressions of the same language that have the same or nearly same meaning in some or all senses

appositive – a grammatical construction in which two usually adjacent nouns having the same referent stand in the same syntactical relation to the rest of a sentence: as the poet and Burns in "a biography of the poet Burns"

Key Note Terms

mood – a conscious state of mind or predominant emotion

properties – a quality or trait belonging and especially peculiar to an individual or thing

Longer words can be some of the most difficult to figure out, but they can be put into categories that will help you.

- **Compound words are two known words joined together. Examples include match-maker and bookkeeper.**
- **Words that contain a familiar stem to which an affix (prefix or suffix) has been added. Examples include *micro*scope and taste*less*.**
- **Words that can be broken down into regular pronounceable parts. Examples include subterfuge and strangulate.**
- **Words that contain irregular pronounceable parts so that there is no clear pronunciation. Examples include louver and indictment.**

Word Mapping

A vocabulary word map is a graphic organizer that helps you think about new words or **concepts** in several ways.

To build a word map, start by entering the new word in the middle of the map; then fill in the rest of the map with a definition, synonyms, **antonyms**, and a picture to help illustrate the new word. This is shown in Figure 3.2.1.

Visual Imaging

When you use visual imaging, you think of a word that either looks like or sounds like the word whose meaning you are trying to learn. Thinking of the picture of the look-alike word and/or image will help you remember the word and its meaning.

For example, the word *potable* means suitable for drinking. You can break the word down to a familiar word, *pot*. You can then associate the word *pot* with something you can put in it, such as water. When you see the new word potable you will picture a pot with water for drinking and remember that the word potable means something suitable for drinking.

Look for Root Words

Searching for the root of a word can sometimes help you understand the meaning of the word. For example, related words are built on the same root and differ in their use of prefixes and suffixes. Each time a different prefix or suffix is added to

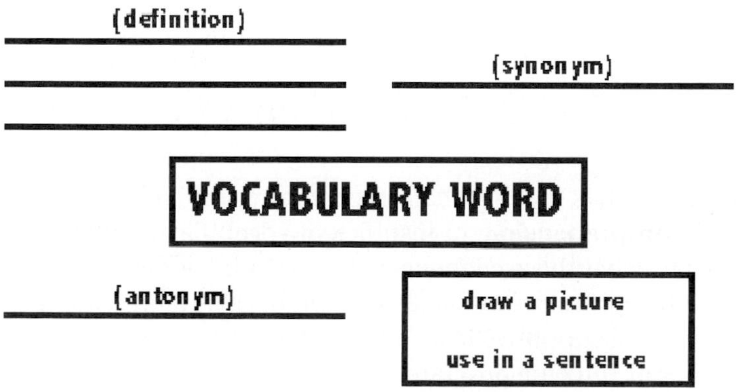

Figure 3.2.1: Building a word map.
Courtesy of US Army JROTC.

Key Note Terms

concept – an abstract or generic idea generalized from particular instances

antonym – a word of opposite meaning (the usual antonym of good is bad)

the root you have a different word with a different meaning. For example, the words *act*, *activate*, *action*, *activity*, *active*, *acting*, and *react* all contain the root word *act*. Although the parts of the speech change, the meaning of the word *act* in each word helps you understand the meaning of each word. Some root words do not change their spelling when suffixes are added, for example, detect and detective; other root words do change their spelling, for example, decide and decision.

Use the Dictionary

A dictionary is a wonderful tool for learning. It can help you spell, define, and explore the history of words. If you cannot comprehend a word by following the other strategies, it is time to turn to the dictionary. Spend some time learning how a dictionary is organized. Dictionaries arrange words alphabetically and include the following features:

- **Guide Words** are boldfaced words in the top corners of the page that indicate the first and last words listed on that page.
- **Main Entries** are boldfaced words listed at the left side of each column of words.
- **Definitions:** the meanings for each main entry. If there are many meanings, they are numbered separately.
- **Example Sentences** show a particular meaning of the word.
- **Parts of Speech** show if a word is a noun, a verb, an adjective, and so on with examples showing how the word is used in each instance, especially if it can function as more than one part of speech.
- **Syllable Structure** shows the word written with breaks between syllables.
- **Pronunciation:** An indication of the way the word sounds.

Some suggestions that may help you include the following:

- Read. The more you read, the more words with which you will come in contact.
- Use newfound vocabulary in your everyday communication (writing, speaking).
- Become familiar with the glossary of your textbooks.
- Become familiar with the dictionary. Understand the pronunciation keys as well as why there are multiple meanings for words.
- Try to learn five new words a day. Use them when communicating. This practice will help you retain the words in your long-term memory.

What Are Some Challenges of Reading?

Key Note Term

comprehension – the act or action of grasping with the intellect

Everyone has reading challenges, such as difficult texts, distractions, a lack of speed and **comprehension**, or insufficient vocabulary. Following are some ideas about how to meet these challenges. Note that if you have a reading disability, if English is not your primary language, or if you have limited reading skills, you may need additional support. Most colleges provide services for students through a reading center or tutoring program. Take the initiative to seek help if you need it. Many accomplished learners have benefited from help in specific areas.

Working Through Difficult Texts

Although many textbooks are useful learning tools, some may be poorly written and organized, perhaps written by experts who may not explain information in the friendliest manner for nonexperts. Because texts are often written to challenge the intellect, even well-written texts may be difficult to read.

Generally, the further you advance in your education, the more complex your required reading is likely to be. You may feel at times as though you are reading a foreign language as you encounter new concepts, words, and terms. Assignments can also be difficult when the required reading is from *primary sources*—original documents rather than another writer's interpretation of these documents—or from academic journal articles and scientific studies that don't define basic terms or supply a wealth of examples. Primary sources include the following:

- **Historical documents**
- **Works of literature (novels, poems, and plays)**
- **Scientific studies, including lab reports and accounts of experiments**
- **Journal articles**

The following strategies may help you make your way through difficult reading material:

- **Approach your reading assignments head-on.** Be careful not to prejudge them as impossible or boring before you even start to read.

- **Accept the fact that some texts may require some extra work and concentration.** Set a goal to make your way through the material and learn, whatever it takes.

- **When a primary source does not explain concepts, define them on your own.** Ask your instructor or other students for help. Consult reference materials in that subject area, other class materials, dictionaries, and encyclopedias. You may want to create your own mini-library at home. Collect reference materials that you use often, such as a dictionary, a thesaurus, a writer's style handbook, and maybe an atlas or computer manual (many of these are available as computer software or CD-ROMs). "If you find yourself going to the library to look up the same reference again and again, consider purchasing that book for your personal or office library," advises library expert Sherwood Harris.

- **Look for order and meaning in seemingly chaotic reading materials.** The information you will find in this chapter on the SQ3R reading technique and on critical reading will help you discover patterns and achieve a greater depth of understanding. Finding order within chaos is an important skill, not just in the mastery of reading but also in life. This skill can give you power by helping you read (think through) work dilemmas, personal problems, and educational situations.

Managing Distractions

With so much happening around you, it's often hard to focus on your reading. Some distractions are external: the telephone or a child who needs attention. Other distractions come from within, as thoughts arise about various topics, for example, a paper due in art history or a Web site that you want to visit.

Identify the Distraction and Choose a Suitable Action

Pinpoint what's distracting you before you decide what to do. If the distraction is *external* and *out of your control*, such as outside construction or a noisy group in the library, try to move away from it. If the distraction is *external* but *within your control*, such as the television or telephone, take action; for example, turn off the television or let the answering machine answer the phone.

If the distraction is *internal*, different strategies may help you clear your mind. You may want to take a study break and tend to one of the issues that worries you. Physical exercise may relax and refocus you. For some people, studying while listening to music helps to quiet a busy mind. For others, silence may do the trick. If you need silence to read or study and cannot find a truly quiet environment, consider purchasing sound-muffling headphones or even earplugs.

We all have distractions. Talk with or write one of your close friends about the proactive way in which you are dealing with your distractions. Solicit your friend's perspective on how he or she handles similar issues.

Find a Study Place and Time That Promote Success

Any reader needs focus and discipline in order to concentrate on the material. Finding a place and time to study that minimizes outside distractions will help you achieve that focus. Here are some suggestions:

Read Alone Unless You Are Working With Other Readers

Family members, friends, or others who are not in a study mode may interrupt your concentration. If you prefer to read alone, establish a relatively interruption-proof place and time, such as an out-of-the-way spot at the library or an after-class hour in an empty classroom. If you study at home and live with others, try putting a "Quiet" sign on the door.

Find a Comfortable Location

Many students study at a library desk. Others prefer an easy chair at the library or at home, or even the floor. Choose a spot comfortable enough for hours of reading but not so cushy that you fall asleep. Make sure that you have adequate lighting and aren't too hot or cold. Choose a regular reading place and time. Choose a spot or two that you like and return often. Also, choose a time when you feel alert and focused. Try reading just before or after the class for which the reading is assigned, if you can. Eventually, you will associate preferred places and times with focused reading.

Turn off the television. For most people, reading and television don't mix.

Courtesy of Superstock.

Building Comprehension and Speed

Most students lead busy lives, carrying heavy academic loads while perhaps working a job or even caring for a family. It's difficult to make time to study at all, let alone handle the reading assignments for your classes. Increasing your reading comprehension and speed will save you valuable time and effort. Because greater comprehension is the primary goal and actually promotes faster reading, make comprehension your priority over speed.

Methods for Increasing Reading Comprehension

Following are some specific strategies for increasing your understanding of what you read:

Continually Build Your Knowledge Through Reading and Studying

What you already know before you read a passage will determine your ability to understand and remember important ideas. Previous knowledge, including vocabulary, facts, and ideas, gives you a context for what you read.

Establish Your Purpose for Reading

When you establish what you want to get out of your reading, you will be able to determine what level of understanding you need to reach and, therefore, on what you need to focus. A detailed discussion of reading purposes follows later in this chapter.

Remove the Barriers of Negative Self-Talk

Instead of telling yourself that you cannot understand, think positively. Tell yourself: *I can learn this material. I am a good reader.*

Think Critically

Ask yourself questions. Do you understand the sentence, paragraph, or chapter you just read? Are ideas and supporting examples clear? Could you explain what you just read to someone else? Take in the concepts that titles, headings, subheadings, figures, and photographs communicate to you.

Methods for Increasing Reading Speed

The average American adult reads between 150 and 350 words per minute, and faster readers can be capable of speeds up to 1,000 words per minute. However, the human eye can only move so fast; reading speeds in excess of 350 words per minute involve *skimming* and *scanning*. The following suggestions will help increase your reading speed:

- **Try to read groups of words rather than single words.**

- **Avoid using your finger to point to your reading because this will slow your pace.**

- **When reading narrow columns, focus your eyes in the middle of the column. With practice, you'll be able to read the entire column width as you read down the page.**

- **Avoid *vocalization*—speaking the words or moving your lips—when reading.**

- **Avoid thinking each word to yourself as you read it, a practice known as subvocalization.**

Expanding Your Vocabulary

Vocabulary is a work in progress—part of lifelong learning is continually learning new words. A strong vocabulary increases reading speed and comprehension; when you understand the words in your reading material, you don't have to stop as often to think about what they mean. Improve your vocabulary by reading and writing words in context and by using a dictionary.

Reading and Writing Words in Context: Natural Language Development

Most people learn words best when they read and use them in written or spoken language. Although a definition tells you what a word means, it may not include a context. Using a word in context after defining it will help to anchor the information so that you can remember it and continue to build on it. Here are some strategies for using context to solidify your learning of new vocabulary words.

- **Use new words in a sentence or two right away. Do this immediately after reading their definitions while everything is still fresh in your mind.**

- **Reread the sentence where you originally saw the word. Go over it a few times to make sure that you understand how the word is used.**

- **Use the word over the next few days whenever it may apply. Try it while talking with friends, writing letters or notes, or in your own thoughts.**

- Consider where you may have seen or heard the word before. When you learn a word, going back to sentences you previously didn't "get" may solidify your understanding. For example, most children learn the Pledge of Allegiance by rote without understanding what *allegiance* means. Later, when they learn the definition of *allegiance,* the pledge provides a context that helps them better understand the word.

- Seek knowledgeable advice. If after looking up a word you still have trouble with its meaning, ask an instructor or friend to help you figure it out.

Use a Dictionary

When reading a textbook, the first "dictionary" to search is its glossary. The definitions there are usually limited to the meaning of the term as it is used in the text. Standard dictionaries provide broader information such as word origin, pronunciation, parts of speech, and multiple meanings. Using a dictionary whenever you read will increase your comprehension. Buy a standard dictionary, keep it nearby, and consult it for help in understanding passages that contain unfamiliar words.

You may not always have time to use the following suggestions, but when you can use them, they will help you make the most of your dictionary.

- Read every meaning of a word, not just the first. Think critically about which meaning suits the context of the word in question and choose the one that makes the most sense to you.

- Substitute a word or phrase from the definition for the word. Use the definition you have chosen. Imagine, for example, that you read the following sentence and do not know the word *indoctrinated:*

  - The cult indoctrinated its members to reject society's values.

- In the dictionary, you find several definitions, including *brainwashed* and *instructed.* You decide that the one closest to the correct meaning is *brainwashed.* With this term, the sentence reads as follows:

- The cult brainwashed its members to reject society's values.

Facing the challenges of reading is only the first step. The next important step is to examine why you are reading any given piece of material.

Why Define Your Purpose for Reading?

As with other aspects of your education, asking questions will help you make the most of your efforts. When you define your purpose, you ask yourself *why* you are reading a particular piece of material. One way to do this is by completing this sentence: "In reading this material, I intend to define/learn/answer/ achieve . . . ." With a clear purpose in mind, you can decide how much time and what kind of effort to expend on various reading assignments.

Achieving your reading purpose requires adapting to different types of reading materials. Being a flexible reader—adjusting your reading strategies and pace—will help you to adapt successfully.

Purpose Determines Reading Strategy

When you know why you are reading something, you can decide how best to approach it. There are four reading purposes: reading for understanding, reading to evaluate critically, reading for practical application, and reading for pleasure.

In college, studying involves reading for the purpose of comprehending the material. The two main components of comprehension are *general ideas* and *specific facts or examples*. These components depend upon each other. Facts and examples help to explain or support ideas, and ideas provide a framework that helps the reader to remember facts and examples.

- **General ideas.** Reading for a general idea is rapid reading that seeks an overview of the material. You search for general ideas by focusing on headings, subheadings, and summary statements.

- **Specific facts or examples.** At times, readers may focus on locating specific pieces of information, for example, the stages of intellectual development in children. Often, a reader may search for examples that support or explain general ideas, for example, the causes of economic recession. Because you know exactly what you are looking for, you can skim the material quickly.

Critical evaluation involves understanding. It means approaching the material with an open mind, examining causes and effects, evaluating ideas, and asking questions that test the writer's argument and search for assumptions. Critical reading brings an understanding of material that goes beyond basic information recall.

A third purpose for reading is to gather usable information that you can apply toward a specific goal. When you read a computer manual or an instruction sheet for assembling a gas grill, your goal is to learn how to do something. Reading and action usually go hand in hand. Remembering the specifics requires a certain degree of general comprehension.

Some materials are read for entertainment, such as *Sports Illustrated* magazine or the latest John Grisham courtroom thriller. Recreational reading may also go beyond materials that seem obviously designed to entertain. Whereas some people may read a Jane Austen novel for comprehension, as in a class assignment, others may read her books for pleasure.

Conclusion

Reading is an essential skill because you use it every day of your life. Do not allow weak reading skills to interfere with the life goals that you have set for yourself. You will need to be a good reader to succeed in school, obtain a job, and advance in the work force. As with your other communication skills, you must practice reading daily to improve your reading skills.

Learning vocabulary is an ongoing process. It continues throughout your entire life. Look at the following examples:

- **At the age of 4 you probably knew 5,600 words**
- **At the age of 5 you probably knew 9,600 words**
- **At the age of 6 you probably knew 14,700 words**
- **At the age of 7 you probably knew 21,200 words**
- **At the age of 8 you probably knew 26,300 words**
- **At the age of 9 you probably knew 29,300 words**
- **At the age of 10 you probably knew 34,300 words**

This demonstrates that the older you become, the more you learn, and the more vocabulary you will know. No matter what your age, you must continue to learn. Words are "symbols" for ideas. These ideas formulate knowledge which is gained largely through words.

[Some of the material used in this lesson was adapted from

- Virginia Tech—Division of Student Affairs—Cook Counseling Center at www.ucc.vt.edu
- Mrs. Dowling's Virtual Classroom at www.dowlingcentral.com/MrsD.html
- Context Area Reading: Literacy Across the Curriculum
- *Keys to Success: How to Achieve Your Goals*, Third Edition by Carol Carter, Joyce Bishop, and Sarah Lyman Kravits (2001), Prentice Hall, Inc.

Chapter 2

Lesson Review

1. How does previewing material help your comprehension?
2. Compare and contrast empirical, value, and analytical questions.
3. Explain three hints for difficult reading.
4. How does note taking help you remember important facts?

Study Habits That Work for You

Chapter 3

Key Words

allocate
aural (auditory)
compare
contrast
efficient
enumerate
inference
interpret
justify
paraphrase
prove

What You Will Learn to Do

- Develop personal study and test-taking strategies

Linked Core Abilities

- Build your capacity for lifelong learning
- Apply critical thinking techniques

Skills and Knowledge You Will Gain Along the Way

- Relate personal learning preferences to study habits
- Identify effective study skill strategies
- Identify test preparation strategies
- Distinguish among various note-taking tips and strategies
- Define the key words contained in the lesson

Introduction

The idea of studying can cause anxiety in some students. Becoming a good student does not happen automatically or overnight, and it requires time and patience. Studying is a process that is learned through trial and error. You have to discover a strategy that works for you and adapt it for different learning situations. The most important thing you can do is to make studying a priority.

This lesson guides you through various studying strategies. You will learn about time management, how to take good notes, and much more.

Study Skills

The word *studying*, as illustrated in Figure 3.3.1, includes homework assignments along with writing papers, and seeking information to prepare presentations. To write a paper you must perform research, arrive at critical judgments, and put your thoughts into coherent sentences and logical paragraphs. To prepare for a presentation, you perform the same tasks, but are then required to stand and present orally before others.

Good study skills support

- **Being efficient.** You are probably busy and you want to get as much out of your study time as possible. You need to study as much material as possible in the amount of time that you have.

Key Note Term

efficient – productive of desired effects; especially: productive without waste

Figure 3.3.1: A student studying for an upcoming test.
Courtesy of Larry Lawfer.

- **Being effective.** You want good results for the amount of time that you spend. You want to take good notes and commit them to memory so you do not have study those notes again.

- **Taking tests.** The more that you learn the first time when you study, the less you need to do before the test.

- **Demonstrating the basics.** You can produce good written assignments and presentations.

Other skills can be included, such as identifying resources, taking good notes, and researching information. These skills support your personal goals and your desire to increase your general knowledge. As an active learner, you do not just use study techniques for homework. If you identify a topic of interest or a career goal not included in your school subjects, you can pursue it. If you want to know about the early attempts of women pilots, a biography on your favorite musician, or how to make ice cream, you can find the information.

Study skills include the following:

- **Comprehending (understanding what you read)**
- **Thinking critically and objectively**
- **Thinking creatively and subjectively**
- **Identifying patterns**
- **Using reference materials**
- **Identifying resources**
- **Using time wisely**
- **Selecting strategies**

Developing an Effective Study Strategy

A strategy is a plan of action for attaining a goal. The word *strategy* implies a plan. Develop a strategy to use these study skills for homework and schoolwork. Your strategy reflects what you think works for you. If you think a study suggestion will not work for you, try to think what would. For example, is it easier for you to study alone or with a group? After you have decided to study, keep the following hints in mind:

- **Choose a quiet place where you can study**
- **Study at one particular time each day; do not change the time that you study**
- **Avoid noise and distractions**
- **Ask friends and family to support your efforts while you are studying**
- **Learn to say no to distractions: the phone, friends, chores, and TV**
- **Hang a "Do Not Disturb" sign on your door**
- **Allow sufficient time for sleep**

- Schedule 50-minute blocks of study
- Schedule as much study time as possible during daylight hours
- Clear your mind of all thoughts when you are trying to remember something
- Give yourself a break; include some leisure time

Personal Learning Preferences

You need to find the reading, writing, and study approaches that fit your schedule, your learning style, and your learning needs. The strategy factors and recommendations are probably things all students can agree on, but where, how, and when you study involves your personal preferences.

Productive studying occurs when you have everything you need when you begin. Being prepared is a signal to your mind that you are ready to study seriously and accomplish your objectives.

SQ3R—A Reading/Study System

You often read textbooks in the same way you read books for entertainment; you read without stopping from the first page to the last page of the chapter. This works when you are reading novels, but it is not likely to help you understand and retain what you read in your textbooks. Survey/Question/Read/Recite/Review (SQ3R) provides a different study system for reading textbooks that will increase your understanding and retention of what you read.

The steps for SQ3R are as follows:

- **Survey.** Before you read a chapter, do a quick reading to get an overview. Look at the headings, chapters, and setup of material.
- **Question.** Establish the purpose of your reading. Ask yourself: Why am I reading this? What am I looking for? When your mind is actively searching for answers to questions, it becomes engaged in learning.
- **Read.** A slow, thorough reading aimed at understanding the content will help find answers to the questions you first raised.
- **Recite.** Reciting material as you go, exercising your **aural** ability to learn, retrains your mind to concentrate and learn as it reads. **Paraphrase** what you have read into your own words.
- **Review.** Reviewing is an ongoing process. Check the accuracy of your recall with the text you have read.

Key Note Term

aural (auditory) – of or relating to the ear or to the sense of hearing; of, relating to, or experienced through hearing

paraphrase – a restatement of a text, passage, or work giving the meaning in another form

No study technique is guaranteed 100 percent of the time. It is important to decide when to use each study technique. Different study strategies work best in different situations.

Time Management

Some students seem to study well without trying. How is it that some students easily manage their study time while others cram hopelessly at the last minute? The answer is simple: People who manage their time wisely will plan well ahead.

Writing down your plan of study makes your responsibilities less overwhelming. Use the following as an example of your plan.

Manage Your Time

To effectively manage your time, you should

- **Monitor your time and set priorities on your assignments**
- **Reflect on how you spend your time**
- **Be aware of when you are wasting your time**
- **Use "dead time" wisely (time between classes, waiting for a bus, riding the bus, and so on)**
- **Identify your most productive time**

Keep a "To-Do" List

A to-do list can help you organize the hours in your day and enable you to accomplish everything you need to get done.

- **Write down tasks that you have to do, as shown in Figure 3.3.2**
- **Decide priorities—what to do at the moment, what to schedule later, what someone else can do**
- **Check off items you have done to give yourself a sense of completion**
- **Know that the satisfaction of "crossing off" the completed task can yield a sense of accomplishment and reward**

Use a Planner Calendar (Daily/Weekly/Long-Term Planner)

There are several excellent reasons to use a planner calendar, such as the following:

Figure 3.3.2: Example of a to-do list.

Reprinted from *Health Skills for Wellness*, Third Edition, by B. E. (Buzz) Pruitt, Kathy Teer Crumpler, and Deborah Prothrow-Stith, (2001), Prentice Hall, Inc.

Things to Do Today	
Find out driver's ed. schedule	A
Finish Math assignment	A
Take trash out	A
Help Matt rebuild bicycle	B
Watch TV	C
Clean room	B

- Use a planner so you can always plan ahead
- Enter dates for course quizzes, exams, important papers, project deadlines, holidays, breaks, and study days
- Write down assignments, appointments, classes, errands, and meetings
- Always check the next day's schedule (go to sleep knowing you are prepared for tomorrow)
- Review course work each week

Checkup

Every few days, give your study plan a checkup.

- Ensure you are taking the best advantage of your time
- Ensure you are studying when you planned to study
- Determine if there are areas where you can use your time more efficiently

Post your calendar and study plans in your study area. Chart your progress, check off finished tasks, and give yourself a periodic studying checkup.

Making the Most of Class Time

Attending classes takes a large part of your day. Here are a few hints to help you get the most out of the time that you spend in class.

- Be prompt. Always be on time for class. When you're late, it shows a lack of interest and can be disruptive to other students.
- Be prepared. Do your homework and review your notes before class to prepare to ask questions. Prepare for discussion courses before class.
- Ask your questions about the last assignment before the teacher starts the new class.
- Attend with attention. Avoid distractions, concentrate as the instructor covers the content, and listen before writing.
- Take notes.
- Be sure you understand homework assignments before leaving the class.
- Schedule time to go over the classroom material after class.

Listening

Preparation before class makes listening in class easier. Know what to expect so that you will know what to listen for. Good listening skills are an important part of your life. If you listen well, you will improve your study, speaking, and writing skills. Effective listening enables you to comprehend information and then process it to formulate new ideas and to make sound decisions—essential characteristics that are necessary for communicating properly.

Note Taking

Good reading and listening skills are the basis for effective note taking. Developing good note-taking skills takes lots of practice and experimenting until you find a style that you like.

Concentrate in class to get the most out of note taking. When you need to clarify a point, ask questions. Be specific. Leave blanks for words, phrases, or ideas that you missed and fill in the gaps later. If the teacher emphasizes or writes a special point on the blackboard, put it in your notes. Always record the teacher's examples.

Pay as much attention to note taking in the last few minutes of class as you would during the beginning and middle of the class. Reading assignments before class, being alert in class, and reviewing your notes after class will help you to perfect your personal note-taking style.

Note-Taking Hints

Learning good note-taking techniques is an invaluable skill that can help you in school as well as in business meetings later in your life. Here are a few hints that can help you find a comfortable method:

- **Do not try to write down every word that the speaker says**
- **Condense the information**
- **Listen for key phrases and transitions such as**
  - **"The four causes were"**
  - **"To sum up"**
  - **"Therefore"**
  - **"In conclusion"**
  - **"In summary"**
  - **"This is important"**
  - **"Remember"**
  - **"Memorize"**
  - **"You should know"**
- **Listen for information that the speaker repeats; it is probably important**
- **Words such as "because," "in addition," and "later" are normally keys to relationships that the speaker is presenting**
- **If you miss something, ask the speaker to repeat it**

Test-Taking Techniques

Two essentials for test taking are knowledge and attitude. You are in control of these two essential factors.

Knowledge means that you are prepared. As an active learner, you are most likely knowledgeable about the topics on which you will be tested. You are studying all the time to gain that knowledge about the changing topics as you advance in your studies.

Attitude can help you control your feelings prior to an exam. You are calm and cool. Your attitude can help you do well on a test. Work on your attitude before going into the test.

You also need knowledge about another area—test-taking techniques. After you are knowledgeable about these techniques, you don't have to study them again.

You should include the following in your test taking techniques:

- **Have a strategy for taking the entire test**
- **Recognize characteristics of specific question types and directions**

You either know the material or you don't. Being nervous won't improve your performance. Being nervous can cause you to forget the material and lower your grade. When you are tense and anxious, you drain energy away from your test performance. Tell yourself that you will do well. Repeat positive statements to yourself.

Some sample positive statements follow:

- **I can keep my cool because I studied; I'll put that information together in inspired new ways that help me shine**
- **Tests are challenges, but I can do it**
- **I can keep calm and think logically**
- **I planned my work so I didn't have to cram**
- **I'll stay calm and let my memory work**
- **I think extremely well during tests**

Preparing for Tests

The best preparation for taking tests is to keep up with assignments. Complete all study assignments when they are assigned, and take notes in class and while studying. Keep a copy of all previous study materials and all graded work.

Review your class notes each day. At the end of each week, review all reading assignments.

The expression *a picture is worth a thousand words* means that visual pictures impress the memory better than verbal thoughts. For example, students who routinely visualize what they read in books perform better on tests.

When a test is announced or anticipated, identify the material that will be covered in the test. For best test-taking results, you should create a study plan for yourself. Determine what review material you have and how much time you have to study for the test; then make a schedule for yourself. Divide the study material into small, easily completed chunks. For example, during one study period, review your class notes. In the next study session, review your homework, as shown in Figure 3.3.3.

Divide your study time to help you overcome any fears you may be experiencing. Familiarize yourself with test question styles and directions. Keep calm and cool; think positively. And **allocate** your time carefully.

On the day of the test, follow these tips to help you achieve your best results.

- **Arrive early.**
- **Take your seat and breathe deeply.**
- **Let go of negative feelings about the test.**
- **Pace the test by looking over the entire test and allotting your time, or look over as much of the test as you are allowed to see at one time.**
- **Read the test directions slowly and carefully before you answer the first question. Reread the directions if necessary.**
- **Pick the parts of the test that you know and do those first. Answer the easiest questions first. Don't spend a lot of time on the questions you need to figure out.**
- **Keep an eye on the time. Assess how much time you have to finish unanswered questions.**
- **Look for answers to the hard questions in other parts of the test.**
- **When you are unsure of the correct answer, try to eliminate the obvious wrong choices.**
- **Review your test answers before you turn them in.**

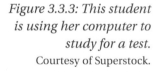

Key Note Term

allocate – to apportion fo a specific purpose or to particular persons or things

Figure 3.3.3: This student is using her computer to study for a test.
Courtesy of Superstock.

Taking the Test

Tests are composed of two main components: the directions or directives and the test questions. You just learned that you should review the test directions to help you answer questions correctly and that you should answer the easiest questions first. The following material will introduce you to several different question directives, followed by some helpful information regarding test question formats.

Directives

The following is a list of test directives and definitions. Test directives tell you how to answer questions.

- **Compare.** Examine qualities or characteristics to discover resemblances. Compare is usually stated as "compare with." You are to emphasize similarities, although differences may be mentioned.

- **Contrast.** Stress dissimilarities or differences of things, qualities, events, or problems.

- **Criticize.** Express your judgment on correctness or merit. Discuss the limitations and good points or contributions of the plan or work in question.

- **Define.** Definitions call for concise, clear meanings. You must keep in mind the class to which a thing belongs and whatever differentiates the particular object from all others in the class.

- **Describe.** In a descriptive answer, you should recount, characterize, sketch, or relate in narrative form.

- **Diagram.** If you are asked to diagram, present a drawing, chart, plan, or graphic representation in your answer. Generally, you are expected to label the diagram and in some cases add a brief explanation or description.

- **Discuss.** This word directs you to examine, analyze carefully, and present considerations both for and against the problem or topic involved. This type of question calls for a complete and detailed answer. As you discuss, you may compare, contrast, define, and describe.

- **Enumerate.** This word specifies a list or outline form of reply. In such questions, recount one by one the points required.

- **Evaluate.** This word specifies a careful appraisal of the problem, stressing both advantages and limitations. Evaluation implies authoritative and, to a lesser degree, personal appraisal of both contributions and limitations.

- **Explain.** In explanatory answers, you must clarify and interpret the material you present. In such an answer, state "how or why," reconcile any differences in opinion or experimental results, and, where possible, state causes. Make plain the conditions that laid the foundation for the topic.

- **Illustrate.** This word requires you to explain or clarify your answer to the problem by presenting a figure, picture, or concrete example.

- **Inference.** When asked to infer, you are required to make a determination of a given problem based on the proposition, statement, or judgment considered as true within another problem.

- **Interpret.** An interpretation question is similar to one requiring explanation. You are expected to translate, solve, or comment on the subject and usually to give your judgment or reaction to the problem.

Key Note Terms

compare – a test directive that requires you to examine qualities or characteristics to discover resemblances; usually stated as "compare with;" similarities are usually emphasized although differences can also be mentioned

contrast – a test directive that stresses dissimilarities, differences, or unlikeness of things, qualities, events, or problems

enumerate – a test directive that specifies a list or outline form of reply; in such questions, recount one by one the points required

inference – a test directive; when asked to infer, you are required to make a determination of a given problem based on the proposition, statement, or judgment considered as true within another problem

interpret – a test directive; you are expected to translate, solve, or comment on the subject and usually to give your judgment or reaction to the problem

justify – a test directive where you are instructed to justify your answer; you must prove or show your grounds for decisions; in such an answer, present evidence in convincing form

prove – a test directive with questions that require proof or ones that demand confirmation or verification; establish something with certainty by evaluating and citing evidence or by logical reasoning

- **Justify.** When you are instructed to justify your answer, you must prove or show your grounds for decisions. In such an answer, present evidence in a convincing form.

- **List.** To list is to enumerate. You are expected in such questions to present an itemized series or tabulation. Such answers should always be given in concise form.

- **Outline.** An outline answer is an organized description. Give the main points and essential details. Omit minor details. Present the information in a systematic arrangement.

- **Prove.** A question that requires proof is one that demands confirmation or verification. Establish something with certainty by evaluating and citing evidence or by logical reasoning.

- **Relate.** If you are asked to relate or show the relationship, emphasize the connections and associations in descriptive form.

- **Review.** A review specifies a critical examination. Analyze and comment briefly in an organized sequence on the major points of the problem.

- **State.** In questions directing you to specify, give, state, or present, you are called on to express the high points in brief, clear narrative form. Omit details and illustrations or examples.

- **Summarize.** To summarize, give in condensed form the main points or facts of the problem or topic. Omit all details, illustrations, and elaboration.

- **Trace.** To trace, give a description of progress, historical sequence, or development from the point of origin. Such narratives may call for probing or deduction.

Question Formats

Tests are used to determine how much you know about a given subject. The questions are used to elicit response and come in many forms. Typically, questions can be objective or subjective in nature. Objective questions, such as multiple choice and binary choice, test your ability to recall, compare, or contrast information and to choose the right answer among several choices. The subjective question, such as an essay question, demands the same information recall but asks that you use critical thinking strategies to answer the question and then organize, write, and revise a written response.

This section covers five question formats:

- **Multiple choice**
- **Binary choice**
- **Short answer**
- **Essay**
- **Reading comprehension**

Each question format is described with tips for answering the question format.

Multiple Choice

Multiple-choice questions are the most popular format. Typically, you are given four possible answer choices and are asked to select the best answer or most appropriate response.

Read the question carefully and determine if you are to select one correct response or select several correct responses.

An answer choice of "All of the above" is typically one of the answers. If more than one choice is correct, "All of the above" is probably correct as well.

If you don't know the answer immediately, try to eliminate obviously incorrect answer choices. Also, you can check to see if any other question has the answer to your question or a clue as to the correct response.

Binary Choice

Binary-choice questions are really multiple-choice questions with only two choices. Typical answer choices for this question format are the True/False, Yes/No, and Agree/Disagree.

Pay attention to qualifiers and negatives. Qualifiers like "never," "always," "none," and "only" usually indicate a false statement. They require the question statement be 100 percent correct to be true. Qualifiers like "sometimes," "often," "generally," and "frequently" usually indicate a true statement.

Negative words such as "can't" and "no" can be confusing. Try to evaluate the statement without the negative word.

Short Answer

Short answer or fill-in-the-blank questions require you to know (recall) the answer; binary-choice and multiple-choice questions test your ability to recognize and select the correct choice among several possible choices.

Look for grammatical clues within the question to help you determine the correct answer. If you can think of several correct answers, let your teacher know and you may be rewarded with a clue as to the answer he or she is looking for.

Essay

Remember that the essay is a subjective question that demands information recall and also asks you to use critical thinking strategies to answer the question. You must then organize, write, and revise a written response.

Start by identifying how much time you can devote to answering the question. Jot down key words or ideas so you can retrieve them later when writing your essay.

Begin with a strong sentence that clearly states your essay's main theme. Follow that with the key points that you will discuss. Expand on your key points by writing a paragraph for each point.

Reading Comprehension

In reading comprehension questions, you read a short paragraph and answer questions about it. Comprehension is especially critical during test taking. You must read and interpret correctly the test directions, the questions, and the answers. Questions can relate to the reading's main theme. Questions may also ask for general or specific information about the reading material.

You will find it helpful to read the questions before you read the text.

Conclusion

Remember to divide your study time; keep calm and cool; and think positively. Becoming a good student does not happen automatically or overnight. It requires time and patience. Studying is a process that is learned through trial and error. You have to discover a strategy that works for you and adapt it for different learning situations. Most importantly, make studying a priority.

By understanding test-taking techniques, keeping a positive attitude, overcoming your fears, and following the tips for answering different questions formats found in this lesson, you will improve your test-taking ability.

This ends Chapter 3, "Study Skills." The next chapter looks at the importance of developing good communication skills. You will learn how to communicate effectively so you can get your message across with no misunderstanding.

Lesson Review

1. Which ten hints for studying will work for you? Which won't? Why?
2. List the study skills you might want to improve for yourself.
3. What would you add to your to-do list today?
4. Define the term *paraphrase*.

Communication Skills

Chapter 4

The Communication Process

Key Words

audience analysis
channel
feedback
mixed messages
noise
nonverbal
receiver
setting
verbal

What You Will Learn to Do

- Demonstrate how the communication process affects interaction between individuals

Linked Core Abilities

- Communicate using verbal, nonverbal, visual, and written techniques
- Treat self and others with respect

Skills and Knowledge You Will Gain Along the Way

- Describe the communication model for interpersonal interactions
- Compare verbal and nonverbal means of communication
- Explain how to avoid mixed messages
- Evaluate your communication style
- Define the key words contained in this lesson

Introduction

Every day, one of your main activities is communicating with others. You communicate at home, at school, with your friends, and in the community. Some of you might also communicate in a job environment. For adults, communication at work can be the difference between success and failure. This lesson shows you the importance of good communication, and how you can communicate more effectively.

The Need for Communication

You fulfill many different needs through communication, while effective communication can give you considerable pleasure. It is pleasing when you have a stimulating conversation with a friend. You are also pleased when you participate in a group discussion that leads to a solution for a problem. You are happy if a letter you write is answered, and it's confirmed that the recipient took what you said seriously.

Sometimes, however, communication does not work, and you end up feeling frustrated.

You have a disagreement with a friend and do not know what to say to fix it. There may be certain subjects your parents do not want to discuss at all. You write a message to someone who completely misunderstands what you said. It's very easy to misinterpret e-mail and get a totally unexpected response.

Even though you have been communicating since birth, you might not always be as effective as possible. Effective communication seems to be a problem for many people.

All communication depends on understanding others and having them understand you. Much of your communication is intended to influence what people think and feel. Most of the time, you want someone to take some action as the result of your communication. You want a friend to spend vacation time with you; you want your friends to like each other; you want your parents to give you permission to go somewhere; you want your employer to more clearly answer a question you have.

Perhaps your most important need is to maintain and improve your relationships with others. You use communication to discover other people's needs and share your own needs with other people.

Our need for communication is important in all areas of our lives. To live is to communicate.

A Definition of Communication

Communication is a process in which people are able to transfer meaning between themselves. The communication process allows people to share information, ideas, and feelings. This is the transfer of meaning. When no meaning is transferred, no communication has taken place.

Courtesy of David M. Grossman/Photo Researchers.

Seven Communication Skills

There are many ways to communicate. Your ability to read, listen, think, study, write, remember, and speak are the seven communication skills that will help you to express your feelings, knowledge, and ideas. Communication is innate within everybody; from the cries of a baby, to the smile of a friend, and to the handshake of your doctor. Everybody uses communication skills differently. In JROTC, as in your other high school courses, you will have many opportunities to improve these skills.

Elements of Communication

The communication process (see Figure 4.1.1) is made up of various elements. These elements are communicators (senders), messages, receivers, **channels** (written words, sound, sight, radio, and television), **feedback**, noise, and **setting**.

- **The communicator is the originator of the message. Speakers, writers, artists, and architects can all be considered communicators.**

- **The message is made up of ideas, data, and feelings the communicator wants to share. The medium may be a speech, essay, painting, or building.**

- **The channel is the route traveled by the message as it goes between the communicator and the receivers.**

- **The receiver is the audience for whom the message is intended. The communicator must gain the receiver's attention to have effective communication.**

- **Feedback allows communicators to find out whether they are "getting through" to the receivers. You get feedback from your instructors, your parents, and your friends.**

- **Noise is interference that keeps a message from being understood. Physical noise keeps a message from being heard. For example, the physical noise of a loud television program may interfere with reading a letter. Psychological noise occurs when the communicators and the receivers are distracted by something. For example, the psychological noise caused by hunger can prevent concentration.**

- **Setting is the time, place, and circumstances in which communication takes place. It can also be considered the context and environment in which a situation is set.**

Key Note Terms

channel – in communication theory, a gesture, action, sound, written or spoken word, or visual image used in transmitting information

feedback – the return or a response to information, as in the evaluation of a communication; the return of evaluative or corrective information to the sender (point of origin)

setting – the context and environment in which a situation is set; the background; the time, place, and circumstances in which a narrative, drama, or film takes place

receiver – one or more individuals for whom a message in intended

noise – that which interferes with the successful completion of communication; a disturbance, especially a random and persistent disturbance that obscures or reduces the clarity of communication

Figure 4.1.1: By using "I" messages, you can communicate your feelings without blaming or judging others.
Courtesy of Blair Seitz/Photo Researchers.

Communicating Effectively

After you understand the process of communication, you can begin to understand why communication does or does not work.

In an ideal situation, the message is perceived in the way it was intended. For example, you write an apology to your friend for a mistake that you made. If the friend accepts the apology, the communication worked. If the friend was offended by your message and the apology was not accepted, the communication did not work.

Your communication may not have worked due to a problem with the message (not written or spoken clearly), the channel used may not have been the best choice (writing a note rather than speaking in person), or psychological noise may have interfered (the recipient couldn't hear over loud noise in the room). Asking the right questions about why communication did not work is the best way to improve communication skills.

Most of us already have considerable communication skills. We have been sending and receiving **verbal** and **nonverbal** symbols all our lives.

Key Note Terms

verbal – of, relating to, or associated with words

nonverbal – being other than verbal; not involving words: nonverbal communication

Note

Verbal symbols utilize the words in a language to stand for a particular thing or idea. Nonverbal symbols allow us to communicate without using words. Facial expressions and gestures are examples of nonverbal symbols.

Courtesy of Larry Lawfer.

Nevertheless, we have all had times when we have not communicated as effectively as we should. You may have received a lower grade on a paper than you expected. You may have unintentionally hurt someone's feelings. An instructor may not have understood a question when you asked it in class.

You can work to increase the likelihood of effective communication. There are certain basic steps to follow when preparing any oral or written communication.

The following six steps for effective communication are not always used in sequence, nor are they exclusive of each other. Tailor them to your own style and approach; you will not use all these steps each time you communicate. These steps will help you focus your attention on how to increase your effectiveness as a communicator.

- **Analyze your purpose and your audience. Make sure you know why you are communicating and to whom you are addressing your ideas. Knowing about the receivers of your communication is called an audience analysis.**

- **Conduct the research. Use a variety of resources.**

- **Support your ideas. Find facts, figures, data, statistics, and explanations that give credibility to your ideas. The more you can back up your ideas, the more your audience will understand what you are communicating.**

- **Get organized. Use an outline or notes to organize your ideas into a logical sequence. A logical sequence helps your audience follow along with you.**

- **Draft and edit. Use language to your best advantage. There may be many ways to express the same idea. Look for the best way. If you are unclear about what you are saying, you may be sending mixed messages.**

- **Get feedback. Test your work with one or more people. Testing your communication with others will ensure that you are not the only one that can make sense out of what you are saying.**

Key Note Terms

audience analysis – the examination of the characteristics that describe the receivers of communication, to include categories such as age, background, education, political opinions, and location

mixed messages – communication transmitted by words, signals, or other means from one person, station, or group to another with unclear meaning to the receiver

Conclusion

Communication is how you transfer ideas to other people. Because communication does not always work as you intend, you must ensure that your message is delivered so you get your point across without any misunderstanding.

It's important to understand your audience and your purpose. You should conduct research and support your ideas. You should decide on an organization for your information and outline your ideas.

Follow the basic steps and people will pay attention to your ideas and be impressed by your ability to express yourself.

Part of being a good communicator is learning to listen more effectively. The following lesson deals with the topic of becoming a good listener.

Lesson Review

1. Name the various elements of communication presented in this lesson.
2. Define the term *communication*.
3. Compare and contrast verbal and nonverbal communication.
4. Explain how getting organized might help you with a homework assignment.

Chapter 4

Becoming a Better Listener

Key Words

hearing
listening
thought speed
trigger words

What You Will Learn to Do

- Use active listening strategies

Linked Core Abilities

- Communicate using verbal, nonverbal, visual, and written techniques
- Treat self and others with respect

Skills and Knowledge You Will Gain Along the Way

- Explain how barriers prevent effective listening
- Compile a list of trigger words
- Identify four tips to improve effective listening skills
- Define the key words contained in this lesson

Introduction

Listening is the neglected communication skill. We spend nearly half of our communication time listening, but few of us make any real effort to be better listeners. This lesson takes a look at way that you can become a better listener. By learning to listen, you can respond more appropriately and communicate better with those around you.

Learning to Listen

Although all of us have had instruction in reading, writing, and speaking, we rarely get any training in listening. This seems like a misplaced emphasis when you consider that out of all the time we spend communicating (70 percent of our awake time), 10 percent of that time is spent writing, 15 percent is spent reading, 30 percent is spent talking, and an overwhelming 45 percent is spent listening.

Good listening is important to everyone. In the business world, listening is the communication most critical for success; but listening also is important in other places—at home, in school, in houses of worship, in civic clubs, and at social gatherings. Listening is important, not only for gaining information but also for the building of relationships.

Listening is the skill that can make or break a relationship. It is as important for you to understand the person as it is to understand what the person is saying. There is a lot more to listening than just understanding the meaning of words.

The Process of Listening

Listening is a complex process. It is an essential part of the total communication process. Unfortunately it is a part that is often ignored. There are two reasons why this happens.

Speaking and writing, which are the sending parts of the communication process, are highly visible and are much easier to evaluate. You are much more frequently tested on what you read than on what you hear.

Also, we are not as willing to improve our listening skills. Much of this unwillingness results from our incomplete understanding of the listening process. To understand the process, we must first define it.

You can define the listening process as the process of receiving, attending, and understanding messages transmitted through the medium of sound. Often the steps of responding and remembering may follow. Figure 4.2.1 shows the flow of the message from the sender to the receiver, and what the receiver does when the message is heard.

Figure 4.2.1: Process of
listening.
Courtesy of US Army JROTC.

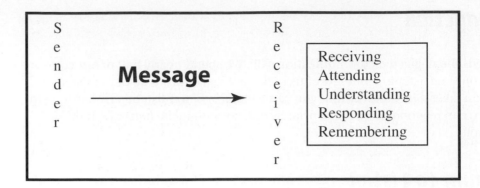

Receiving

Speaking is the call to **listening**. The speaker has not communicated until the receiver interprets and understands the message sent. Remember that **hearing** and listening are not the same. *Hearing* is the reception of sound. *Listening* is the attachment of meaning to sound. Hearing is, however, a necessary step for listening, and an important component of the listening process.

Attending

Hearing is only the first part of listening. You must then interpret, appreciate, or evaluate what you are hearing. Good listening requires energy and concentration, even though you tend to think of it as an automatic process. After you have received a message, you must attend to it. Whether or not you attend to an incoming message is a choice you actually have to make. Until you pick up the math book and study for the test, you have not attended to the message that a "math test is tomorrow."

Understanding

Effective communication depends on understanding. That is, effective communication does not take place until the receiver understands the message. Understanding must result for communication to be effective.

Responding

Sometimes a response is appropriate during communication. There are several types of responses.

- **Direct verbal responses.** These may be spoken or written.
- **Responses that seek clarification.** This involves asking for further information.
- **Responses that paraphrase.** You may say, "in other words, what you are saying is. . . ." A paraphrase gives the sender a chance to confirm that you understand the message.
- **Nonverbal responses.** Sometimes a nod of the head or a "thumbs up" may communicate that the message is understood.

Key Note Terms

listening – making an effort to hear something; paying attention

hearing – to perceive by the ear; to listen attentively

Responding is a form of feedback that completes the communication transaction. It lets the sender know that the message was received, attended to, and understood.

Remembering

Memory is often a necessary and essential part of the listening process. What is the relationship between memory and listening? Understanding the differences between short-term memory and long-term memory will help explain the relationship.

With short-term memory, information is used immediately, as with looking up phone numbers. This type of memory can only hold a limited amount of information, and is very sensitive to interruption.

Long-term memory allows you to recall information and events hours, days, weeks, and sometimes years later. For example, think of all the things you can remember that happened to you as you were growing up.

Types of Listening

Different situations require different types of listening. You may listen to obtain information, improve a relationship, gain appreciation for something, make discriminations, or engage in a critical evaluation.

Although certain skills are basic and necessary for all types of listening (receiving, attending, and understanding), each type requires some special skills. Before you can fully appreciate the skills and apply the guidelines, you must understand the different types of listening.

Informative Listening

With this type of listening, the primary concern is to understand the message. Much of your learning comes from informative listening. For example, you listen to lectures or instructions from teachers, and what you learn depends on how well you listen. If you listen poorly, you are not equipped with the information you need. There are three key factors for informative listening.

- **Vocabulary.** Increasing your vocabulary will increase your potential for better understanding.

- **Concentration.** Sometimes it is hard to concentrate because more than one thing is going on at a time. Perhaps the listeners are preoccupied with other thoughts, or with their own needs. It may also be true that they are just not interested. Others have not learned how to concentrate while listening. They have not made themselves responsible for good listening. Concentration requires discipline, motivation, and acceptance of responsibility.

- **Memory.** You cannot process information without bringing memory into play. Memory helps informative listening in three ways. It provides the knowledge bank for you to recall experiences and prior information. It also allows you to create expectations and make decisions concerning what you encounter by calling on your past experiences. Finally, it allows you to understand what others say. Without memory of words and concepts, you could not communicate with anyone else and understand the meaning of messages.

Relationship Listening

The purpose of relationship listening (see Figure 4.2.2) is to either help an individual or to improve the relationship between people. Although relationship listening requires you to listen for information, the emphasis is on understanding the other person. Three behaviors are key to effective relationship listening: attending, supporting, and empathizing.

- **Attending.** In relationship listening, attending behaviors indicate that the listener is focusing on the speaker. Little things such as nodding your head or saying "I see," will let the speaker know that you are involved.

- **Supporting.** Many responses have a negative or nonsupporting effect. For example, interrupting the speaker or changing the subject are not supportive. Sometimes the best response is silence. Three characteristics describe supportive listeners:
  - They are careful about what they say
  - They express belief in the other person
  - They demonstrate patience (they are willing to give the time)

- **Empathizing.** What is empathy? It is not sympathy, which is a feeling for or about another. Nor is it apathy, which is a lack of feeling. Empathy is feeling and thinking with another person. This characteristic enables you to see, hear, or feel as others do. It allows you to "walk in someone else's shoes." Empathetic listening is critical to effective relationship listening.

Appreciative Listening

Appreciative listening includes listening to music for enjoyment, to speakers because you like their style, to your choices in theater, television, radio, or film. It is the response of the listener, not the source of the message, which defines appreciative listening. The quality of appreciative listening depends in large part on three factors: presentation, perception, and previous experiences.

Figure 4.2.2: Relationship listening requires a great deal of attentiveness.

Courtesy of Paul Barton/The Stock Market/Corbis Images.

- **Presentation.** Presentation encompasses such factors as the medium (the form or way it is presented), the setting, or the style and personality of the presenter.

- **Perception.** Your attitudes determine how you react to and interact with the world around you. Perceptions are critical to how and whether or not you appreciate the things to which you listen.

- **Previous experiences.** Sometimes the experience you have had in the past influences how you appreciate or enjoy things. If you know too much about the topic, you may be too critical about it. If you associate pleasant experiences with the topic, you may have a more positive attitude toward the subject.

Critical Listening

Critical listening goes beyond appreciative listening because it adds the dimension of judgment. Critical listening is listening to comprehend and then evaluate the message. The ability to listen critically is especially essential in a democracy. For example, to make an informed decision in any governmental election, or to form intelligent opinions, you must be able to listen to all the information presented to you, evaluate what is relevant and what isn't, and come up with your own ideas. Not knowing, understanding, or critically listening to the information leads to misunderstanding of any issue.

Discriminative Listening

By being sensitive to changes in the speaker's rate, volume, force, pitch, and emphasis, the discriminative listener can detect both small and major differences in meaning. Small clues can strengthen relationship listening. Small differences in sound can enhance appreciative listening. Sensitivity to pauses and nonverbal cues allow critical listeners to more accurately judge not only the speaker's message, but the intentions of the message as well. There are three skills important for discriminative listening.

- **Hearing ability.** Obviously, for people who do not hear well, it is difficult to discriminate among sounds.

- **Awareness of sound structure.** Listeners that understand the structure of the language being used for the message will have an advantage in discriminative listening.

- **Ability to integrate nonverbal cues.** Words do not always communicate true feelings. The way they are said or the way the speaker acts may be the key to understanding the true or intended message.

Effective listening, whether informative, relational, appreciative, critical, or discriminative, requires skill.

Barriers to Effective Listening

To become a better listener, it is important to understand the barriers that can get in the way of effective listening. After you understand these barriers, you can work to overcome them. These barriers include the following:

- **Laziness.** Effective listening can be hard work.

- **Internal distractions.** Sometimes you have a lot on your mind, which makes it hard to concentrate on what someone else is saying to you.

- **Past relationships.** Both a poor and an excellent past relationship with the speaker can affect how you listen.

- **Lack of trust.** Believing that the speaker has betrayed your trust or that the speaker does not have your best interests in mind is a barrier that can hinder effective listening.

- **Lack of self-confidence.** If the speaker does not sound confident, you will have a harder time staying focused on what you hear.

- **Prejudice.** Prejudice can affect how you hear the speaker as well as how you receive the information.

- **The "halo" effect.** If the speaker has an association with someone or something you already like, you are much more likely to be receptive to the speaker as well as the information. You may not question what you should question.

- **The "horns" effect.** If the speaker has an association with someone or something about which you have negative feelings, you may not listen the way you should.

- **External distractions.** Sometimes there are a lot of things going on in the same location where you are trying to listen to the speaker.

- **A different level of power between you and the speaker.** Either you may have the authority, or the speaker may. Either way, it can impact how you listen.

- **Gender preferences.** You may have different expectations because of the gender of the speaker.

- **Emotionality on the part of the speaker.** If the speaker becomes passionate about the topic, it may distract you from hearing the real message.

- **Prejudging the message before the entire message has been delivered.** Sometimes a speaker will say something at the start of a speech or conversation that may distract you from effectively listening to the rest.

- **Allowing personal characteristics of the speaker to get in the way.** If the speaker is unkempt or dresses sloppily, for example, you might not pay attention to everything that is said.

- **Not caring about the speaker.** Being indifferent to the person can affect how well you pay attention to the message.

- **Interrupting.** Sometimes the listener is so excited about an idea he or she wants to share that the listener does not wait for the speaker's thoughts to be completed. This distracts both the listener and the speaker.

- **Trigger words.** Some words evoke an emotional response that prevents effective listening. These words are distracting because they make you concentrate on something else besides what is being said. If a speaker uses the word *lottery*, your mind might wander to untold riches. Words like *homework* or *test scores* may also distract you.

- **Delivery style.** Sometimes the way the speaker communicates can be distracting. The speaker might have a very monotone voice or may stutter. Some people continuously put in verbal pauses like "uh" or "you know." Any of these things may cause you to concentrate more on the delivery than the content.

Key Note Term

trigger words – words that evoke an emotional response that prevents effective listening

How to Be an Effective Listener

There are many guidelines that will help you to become a more effective listener (see Figure 4.2.3). Most involve listening "actively" while others speak.

- **Find an area of interest.** Listen with a purpose. Be interested. Try to organize what you hear.

- **Judge content, not delivery.** Do not stop listening because the sender does not meet expectations. Listen to the words. Look for the message.

- **Hold your fire.** Do not get overstimulated by the message. Do not react until the message is complete. Keep your emotions in check. Do not interrupt because you believe that what you have to say is more important or more correct. There will be time for you to react later. The speaker may surprise you and wind up saying what you want to say.

- **Listen for ideas.** Focus on the person's central ideas. Do not get bogged down in the details. Try to listen at a higher level. Listen for new knowledge or concepts.

- **Be flexible.** Vary the ways in which you attempt to remember the information. Concentrate on finding the best way to learn the information.

- **Work at listening.** Establish and maintain eye contact. Acknowledge understanding. Stay tuned in.

- **Resist distractions.** Concentrate on the speaker. Tune out other things that may be going on. Turn off the things you can control, like the TV or the radio. Try not to do several things at the same time. Focus on the sender.

- **Exercise your mind.** Challenge yourself to listen totally. Try it for short time and then make it longer and longer. See if you can listen to an entire presentation without losing concentration.

- **Keep your mind open.** Communication efficiency drops to zero when we hear certain trigger words, such as communist, Democrat, or Republican. Everyone has words that evoke an emotional response. Effective listeners are aware of keeping their convictions and emotions in check.

- **Capitalize on thought speed.** Most of us talk at 120 words a minute. Our thinking speed is about 500 words a minute. That gives us a lot of spare time while a person is speaking to us. Poor listeners let their minds wander. Good listeners think about what is being said by anticipating the point, summarizing, weighing evidence, or looking for nonverbal clues.

> **Key Note Term**
>
> **thought speed** – the amount of time it takes for people to hear a thought and process it; this is typically a good deal faster than speaking time

Conclusion

So now you know the parts of the listening process. You know there are various types of listening. You have read about barriers to effective listening and tips for overcoming those barriers. Use this information to improve your skills and become a better listener. Remember, improved listening involves work, but the results are well worth the effort.

Now that you've learned how to be a better listener, the following lesson helps you learn to communicate in groups. You will examine some of the characteristics and social influences that can affect group communications.

Lesson Review

1. Explain why listening is so important in learning.
2. Choose one type of response and discuss it.
3. How can critical listening help you with a friend or family member?
4. Define the term *thought speed*.

Lesson 3

Communication in Groups

Key Terms

ascendant
authoritarian
barriers
distortion
dysfunctional roles
filter
grapevine
groupthink
rapport
social roles
task roles

What You Will Learn to Do

- Analyze how you communicate in group situations

Linked Core Abilities

- Communicate using verbal, nonverbal and written techniques
- Treat self and others with respect

Skills and Knowledge You Will Gain Along the Way

- Define roles adopted by individuals in groups
- Describe types of productive and nonproductive behaviors
- Identify personal behavioral tendencies within group interactions
- Discuss how to communicate with people of different personalities
- Define the key words contained in this lesson

Introduction

Key Note Term

barriers – an obstruction; anything that holds apart or separates

In this lesson, you examine some of the characteristics and social influences that can affect group communications. In addition, you will have the opportunity to see how communication **barriers** and breakdowns can affect your ability to communicate effectively and how you can establish credibility through your communications.

The Art of Communication

The art of communicating is a skill that you must develop. Using words so that listeners or readers understand their meanings is a difficult task because of differences in background, education, and experience of individuals with whom you are trying to communicate.

Throughout this lesson, remember that the purpose of communication is to make known and exchange information, thoughts, opinions, or feelings by speech, writing, or gestures. It is a transmission and interchange, by any means, of information, feelings, and direction. A communicator must remember that communication is a circular process, with both parties being free to present as well as to receive ideas, feelings, and attitudes (see Figure 4.3.1).

Elements of Communication

Remember, the communication process is made up of various elements. These elements are communicators (senders), messages, receivers, channels (written words, sound, sight, radio, and television), feedback, noise, and setting.

Figure 4.3.1: These students are enjoying an opportunity for open communications in a small group.
Courtesy of Larry Lawfer.

The group communication process follows the same format. In groups, the communicator may send a message to several receivers that attach different meanings or interpretations to the message and, in turn, may offer different feedback.

Group Communication

Whenever there is a group of people together for any length of time, there will be social groups. Membership in these groups normally depends on factors such as skill, ability, job assignment, ethnic background, interests, or values. If you look around your school, you will probably be able to identify many social groups.

Roles in Group Communication

At some point in your life, you have probably heard the saying, "You can either be a leader or a follower." This statement might lead you to believe that there are just two possible roles you can assume within a group, when, in fact, there are a number of potential roles that you might play at any given time. Leadership is actually the combination of a variety of roles within a group that moves the group toward its goals.

Roles are the characteristic and expected social behavior of an individual within a group. We all have unique skills, strengths, and talents which, when contributed to the group, enable the group to operate effectively and be successful. When we communicate with one another in a group situation, we assume certain roles based on these unique skills, strengths, and talents. Some of these roles enable us to complete tasks, while others build and strengthen the group. Still others are destructive or harmful to the group communication process.

The Roles We Play

Within any group, roles will naturally evolve during the group formation process, and may change over time. Group dynamics and communication can either be accelerated or hindered based on the roles we assume.

Though many different roles exist, they fall into the following three major categories.

- **Task roles** are those roles that help the group accomplish a specific task
- **Social roles** are those roles that help the group maintain itself as a group
- **Dysfunctional roles** are those roles, which are destructive and block group communication

Task Roles

In order to accomplish a goal and achieve results, members of the group must take on task-oriented roles that will fit in with the objectives of the group as a whole. For example, if your group was responsible for putting on a fund-raiser to raise money

Key Note Terms

task roles – roles assumed during the group communication process that help the group accomplish a specific task

social roles – roles that individuals assume during the group communication process that help maintain the group

dysfunctional roles – roles assumed by individuals within a group that are destructive and block group communication

for a school trip, you might need people to suggest ideas and gather information. You would also need someone to plan the event, and someone to coordinate it. These are all task roles. The following are descriptions of some of the task roles (this is not an exhaustive list).

- **Initiator.** Suggests new ideas and proposes solutions.
- **Opinion seeker.** Looks for options; seeks ideas and suggestions from others.
- **Coordinator.** Organizes the various activities of team members and shows relationships between ideas.
- **Energizer.** Stimulates the group to a higher level of activity.
- **Recorder/secretary.** Keeps a record of group actions.
- **Information giver.** Offers facts or generalizations to the group.
- **Information seeker.** Asks for information about the task; seeks data.
- **Evaluator.** Measures decisions against group goals.
- **Spokesperson.** Speaks on behalf of the group.
- **Planner.** Prepares timelines, schedules, and organizes group logistics.

Social Roles

To maintain the group as a unit, it is also necessary that some people assume social roles to promote social interaction and a healthy group dynamic (see Figure 4.3.2). These roles are less concerned with the task at hand, and more concerned with team growth and cohesiveness. The following are some social roles.

- **Encourager.** Praises the ideas of others; warmly receptive to other points of view and contributions.
- **Volunteer.** Offers whatever is needed.
- **Group observer.** Keeps records of group activities and uses this information to offer feedback to the group.
- **Compromiser.** Moves the group to another position that is favored by all group members by coming "half way".
- **Gatekeeper.** Keeps communication channels open by encouraging or facilitating the participation of others or by proposing regulation of the flow of communication.
- **Standard setter.** Suggests standards or criteria for the group to achieve; standards may apply to the quality of the group process or limitations on acceptable individual behavior within the group.
- **Summarizer.** Raises questions about the direction which the group discussion is taking by summarizing what has been discussed and showing where it deviates from group objectives.
- **Reality tester.** Subjects group accomplishments to a set of standards for the group; this role examines the "practicality" or the "logic" behind a suggestion of group discussion.
- **Mediator.** Mediates the differences between group members. Attempts to reconcile disagreements and relieves tension in conflict situations.

Figure 4.3.2: What role is the student who is speaking playing in this group?
Courtesy of Nancy Sheehan.

Dysfunctional Roles

When an individual has competing needs or a personal agenda that is not in harmony with that of the group, the result will often be one of frustration. This frustration frequently manifests itself through behaviors that block effective group communication. The following list shows some examples of dysfunctional roles.

- **Aggressor.** Attacks other group members, deflates the status of others and shows aggressive behaviors.
- **Blocker.** Resists movement by the group.
- **Recognition seeker.** Calls attention to him- or herself.
- **Self confessor.** Seeks to disclose nongroup related feelings or opinions.
- **Dominator.** Asserts control over the group by manipulating other group members.
- **Help seeker.** Tries to gain the sympathy of the group.
- **Nonparticipator.** Chooses not to participate in group discussions.

You need to be careful when labeling dysfunctional roles, because these behaviors may be subject to interpretation. You may see a particular group member as a blocker, when they in fact see themselves as a reality tester. It is important to be aware of the lens through which you view the behavior of others.

Choosing Your Role

The role a person plays largely depends on his or her personality, preferences, and abilities. Some roles will come more naturally than others, and you may fill more than one role at the same time. For example, you could be an opinion seeker and an encourager at the same time. In other cases, you may also share roles with others members of the group.

Within group communications, the qualities that members bring to a group affect their ability to accept influence uncritically, increase cohesiveness, mediate conflicts, and solve problems. These characteristics are another important dimension that affects the roles we play within a group. Our credibility and our attitudes can influence our behaviors, and the way others perceive us.

Likewise, a personality trait is a tendency to behave in a consistent way in different situations. These traits are also important in determining our role in group communications. We can classify the numerous personality traits into six broad categories. They appear in some combination in each of us; however, your predominant trait will influence how you interact within a group.

Key Note Terms

authoritarian – characterized by or favoring absolute obedience to authority, as against individual freedom

ascendant – dominant in position or influence; superior

- **Authoritarianism.** An **authoritarian** person thinks that there should be status and power differences between people. As group members, these people use their power when in a position of leadership. They are firm, demanding, directive, and not likely to accept the ideas of others.

- **Social sensitivity.** This trait, also known as empathy, is an understanding of the feelings of others. It shows a person's ability to look at what is happening from the perspective of the other person.

- **Superior tendencies.** Group members who possess high **ascendant** tendencies tend to assert themselves and exert dominance over others. These group members influence group decisions; however, they tend to make remarks that build themselves up at the expense of others and display stern behavior that works against success in dealing with others.

- **Self-reliance and dependability.** Group members who show these traits demonstrate a sense of responsibility. They possess such characteristics as integrity, self-esteem, self-reliance, and self-control. They are successful in helping the group to accomplish its goals. People with high self-esteem tend to resist influence attempts and threats made by others; whereas, people with low self-esteem tend to be influenced by someone who has higher self-esteem.

- **Unconventionality.** Unconventional group members do not behave in expected ways. They do not seem to be interested in the group's objectives, and their behavior keeps the group from its work.

- **Emotional stability.** Anxiety and adjustment are two widely studied indicators of emotional stability. An anxious group member will worry about some uncertain or future event although there is no apparent cause for his or her worry. On the other hand, if an individual is well adjusted, relating well to his or her environment, that person appears to have emotional control and stability. Adjustment is positively related to group effectiveness, motivation, development of cohesiveness, and high morale.

Influences of a Social Group

Not only can there be one or more social groups within an organization, they can have a great deal of impact on the operation of the organization. By uniting, members of a social group (or of social groups if there are more than one in an organization) can influence a leader's action, or the actions of the leadership in the organization, in regard to making decisions on policies, rules, or procedures.

Definition of a Small Group

Most people would define a small group as having at least three and no more than twelve or fifteen members as shown in Figure 4.3.3. A group needs to have at least three members; otherwise it would be difficult to make decisions. With three members, coalitions can be formed and some kind of organization is present. Too large of a group (more than twelve or fifteen members) inhibits the group members' ability to communicate with everyone else in the group.

Within the group, roles will evolve and procedures will be developed as to how the group functions. A group must have a common purpose or goal and they must work together to achieve that goal. The goal brings the group together and holds it together through conflict and tension.

Decision Making in Groups

Many groups meet to solve problems or make decisions. Typically, a six-step approach is used when making decisions within a group.

1. **Identify the problem. What is the problem? What is wrong with the current situation?**
2. **Analyze the problem. What are the issues in play in your group's situation?**
3. **Identify the goals. What are the goals of the final decision?**
4. **Generate the solution(s). Generate as many solutions as possible. Avoid groupthink by listing many solutions. (Groups experiencing groupthink do not consider all alternatives and they desire unanimity at the expense of quality decisions. They are focused on reaching a decision, not finding the best solution.)**
5. **Evaluate and select the solutions. Measure each solution against the goals from step three.**
6. **Implement the solution(s). Enact the chosen solution(s).**

Brainstorming

Another option for decision making is brainstorming. When brainstorming, group members are encouraged to generate as many ideas about a particular topic as they can. Group members should be encouraged to say anything that comes to

Key Note Term

groupthink – the situation where a group does not consider all available alternatives due to the desire to reach consensus

Figure 4.3.3 These three people compose a small group.
Courtesy of Lawrence Migdale.

mind when brainstorming. Every idea is written down and judgments about ideas are saved until later, when the group returns to all of the ideas and selects those that are most useful.

Nominal Group Decision Making

Nominal group decision making is a group decision-making tool used when the group must place a set of options in a preferred order. To use the nominal method, group members work individually to list all alternatives to a problem or issue. Sometimes, the nominal method is used after a brainstorming session is held. The group facilitator asks each group member to individually rank all of the options from highest to lowest priority. Finally, the facilitator computes an average score for each idea. The lowest score is the highest priority for the group.

There are many ways that a group can make a final decision, decide on a solution, or come to agreement. Some of the most popular ways of making the decision include:

- **Consensus.** The group members all agree on the final decision through discussion and debate.
- **Compromise.** Through discussion and readjustment of the final plan, group members come to agreement by giving up some of their demands.
- **Majority vote.** The decision is based on the opinion of the majority of its members.
- **Decision by the leader.** The group gives the final decision to its leader.
- **Arbitration.** An external body or person makes a decision for the group.

Leadership in Groups

Leadership is concerned with control and power in a group. Leadership can be aimed at either maintaining the social relationships in the group or facilitating the group to achieve its task. Groups will sometimes have two leaders: one for the social dimension and one for the task dimension.

Some researchers believe certain people are born with traits that will make them good leaders in all situations. A second perspective is that the group's leader selects an appropriate leadership style for the given task. A third way of understanding leadership says that to some degree, leaders are born with traits that make them good leaders, but that they also learn how to become leaders and use strategies appropriate to a given situation.

There are four main styles of leadership:

- **Autocratic.** The leader uses his or her authority to make decisions.
- **Democratic.** Authority is shared and all group members help make decisions.

- **Laissez-faire.** A "hands-off" style in which the leader allows the group to make its own decisions.

- **No leader.** No one in the group exercises leadership. This style, says researchers, leads to group disintegration and is followed by autocratic leadership.

Communication Barriers

In Lesson 2, you learned that there are many barriers to effective listening. These barriers can also interfere with effective communication in groups and lead to the **distortion** of communication. After you understand how these barriers impact group communication, you can do your part to overcome them.

Key Note Term

distortion – twisted out of true meaning; reproduced improperly

- **Laziness.** Effective communication can be hard work.

- **Internal distractions.** Sometimes group members may have a lot on their minds, which makes it hard for them to concentrate on what someone else is saying.

- **Past relationships.** If members of the group have either a poor or an excellent past relationship with each other, this can affect communication.

- **Lack of trust.** Believing that other members of the group have betrayed your trust or that they do not have your best interests in mind is a barrier.

- **Lack of self-confidence.** If a group member does not sound confident, another member may have a harder time staying focused.

- **Prejudice.** Prejudice can effect both how we hear others as well as how we receive the information.

- **The "halo" effect.** If a group member has an association with someone or something the group already likes, the group is much more likely to be receptive to the member as well as the information. Members may not question what they should question.

- **The "horns" effect.** If a group member has an association with someone or something about which the group has negative feelings, the group may not listen the way they should.

- **External distractions.** Sometimes there are a lot of things going on in the same location where the group is trying to listen to each other.

- **A different level of power between members.** One member may have the authority, and one not. Either way, it can impact how members communicate.

- **Gender preferences.** One group member may have different expectations because of the gender of another member.

- **Emotionality on the part of a member.** If a member gets passionate about the topic, it may distract other members from hearing the real message.

- **Prejudging the message before the entire message has been delivered.** Sometimes a member will say something at the start of a speech or conversation that may distract another member from effectively listening to the rest.

- **Allowing personal characteristics of another member to get in the way.** If one group member was dirty or smelled unpleasantly, for example, another member might not attend to everything that is said.

- **Not caring about another group member.** Being indifferent to a person can affect how well another member pays attention to the message.

- **Interrupting.** Sometimes a group member is so excited about an idea he or she wants to share, that the member does not wait for the communicator's thoughts to be completed. This distracts both the sender and the receiver of the message.

- **Trigger words.** Some words evoke an emotional response that prevents effective communication. These words are distracting because they make group members concentrate on something else besides what is being said. Sometimes trigger words will represent different things to different members of a group. This also leaves room for misinterpretation.

- **Delivery style.** Sometimes the way information is delivered can be distracting. One group member might have a very monotone voice or may continuously put in verbal pauses like "uh" or "you know." Any of these things may cause other members to concentrate more on the delivery than the content.

Psychological Barriers

Each member of a group has psychological needs. If these needs are not met, it can create problems. Psychological barriers to communication are more difficult to identify and overcome than other barriers, and require leaders and group members to possess and apply knowledge of human nature to each situation.

Key Note Term

filters – a person who alters information or a method of altering information as it is being passed from one person to another

Since everyone has a unique combination of factors (or **filters**) such as needs, values, beliefs, experiences, education, goals, and so on (all of which combine to make up a person's character), it is through these filters that group members can see and hear the existence of possible psychological barriers. Consequently, it is through an understanding of how these filters can drive and/or influence one's character, either independently or collectively, that people can learn to avoid potential communication problems, including these barriers.

Guidelines to Avoid Barriers

Aim at your target. Group members always want the target of their communication to understand the message thoroughly; therefore, before sending a message, take a moment to aim at the target. Form the content and tone of the message so that it hits the target squarely and correctly—on the first try.

Use several channels of communication and repeat important communication. Since barriers can easily filter or block information, communicators must often use several methods to relay the information. In addition, repeat important communication to ensure the information gets out to everyone.

Communication Breakdowns

The number one cause of wasted energy and productivity within groups is communication breakdown. Communicating effectively is a vital part of a group's success. It is imperative that each member of the group communicate effectively if the group is to succeed. Factors that completely disrupt the flow of information are communication breakdowns. The following are four situations that can cause a total breakdown.

Competing for a Person's Attention

People or things that compete for a person's attention may be one cause for a breakdown in communication. Competition for attention occurs when a person receiving the information is trying to do several tasks at once. For example, when somebody interrupts you, one solution that you can implement is to stop working, clear your mind, and concentrate on the new subject until you understand it, then resume work as before the interruption occurred.

However, if you are the person doing the interrupting, you should handle the situation differently. Your first step is to recognize that the other person is busy. If your concern can wait, let it. If you must interrupt, make it as short as possible.

Situations Affecting Self-Esteem

A communication breakdown can often result from a situation that affects the self-esteem of the parties involved. In such cases, if you are aware that certain people do not get along with each other, or have not established a **rapport**, consider this when giving a message that must go to or through the other.

Misunderstandings

Misunderstanding what someone expects of you is another factor that can lead to a communication breakdown. When one group member does what they think another member wants them to do, but actually they do not do what is expected, there is a serious lack of communication.

Misunderstandings often occur when a person uses a word or phrase to describe an action or event rather than actually describing what took place. For example, saying there was a "fight" between Bonnie and Cheryl is quite different from saying Bonnie and Cheryl do not like each other and had an argument last night over what to watch on television.

Another cause of misunderstandings is the use of jargon. Jargon occurs when social or professional groups use certain words that have special meanings because of the nature of the group. Communication breaks down when people outside the group, or new people to that group, do not understand the special meanings.

Distortions, Interpretations, and Filters

As you can see, group communications do not always run smoothly. In addition to various social influences or barriers, frequently someone will distort, dilute, change, or stop the information flow before it reaches everyone for whom the sender intended it. As information travels from one group member to another, each member has the opportunity to make it more specific by adding, changing, deleting, or refining the message.

Most communication processes are not always accurate or perfect since each person in a group must interpret what was said. Two more examples of opportunities for miscommunication are **grapevine** and rumor.

Key Note Term

rapport – a relationship, especially one of mutual trust

Key Note Term

grapevine – an informal, often secret means of transmitting information, gossip, or rumor (that is usually incomplete or does not make sense) from one person to another within an organization or institution

Conclusion

Communicating is one of the most important things you do in life. *Do not think that it comes easily!* You must practice good communication skills daily; then you will gradually see results and be able to communicate effectively and confidently in a group. The spectrum of roles within the group communication process is much richer than just leaders and followers. By increasing our awareness of the diversity of those with whom we interact, and stretching our own capacities, we can develop the skills to communicate effectively and productively within a group.

This concludes the chapter, "Communication Skills." In this chapter, you learned about the communication process, how to become a better listener, and the importance of communicating in groups.

Lesson Review

1. Define the three major categories of group roles.
2. Describe three types of productive and three types of nonproductive behaviors individuals display within group interactions.
3. Identify your personal behavioral tendencies within group interactions.
4. How would you communicate with people with different personalities?

Conflict Resolution

Lesson 1

Causes of Conflict

Key Terms

active listening
conflict
effective speaking
frustration
harassment
hostility
miscommunication
relationships
solutions
territorial
understanding

What You Will Learn to Do

- Determine causes of conflict

Linked Core Abilities

- Do your share as a good citizen in your school, community, country, and the world

Skills and Knowledge You Will Gain Along the Way

- Recognize the impact of conflict on relationships
- Describe the four basic causes of conflict
- Analyze five different types of conflicts
- Use "I" statements to facilitate effective communication
- Define the key words contained in this lesson

Introduction

What does **conflict** mean to you? Is it frightening or exciting? Is it interesting or unpleasant? Do you typically avoid it, or are you more likely to confront it?

It is inevitable that you will encounter many different forms of conflict throughout your lifetime. To make appropriate decisions and gain confidence in resolving conflicts, you must be able to

- **Recognize potential conflict situations before they occur**
- **Recognize the warning signs and the sequences of events that can fuel conflicts**
- **Predict possible consequences and stay attuned to ways to stop the conflict from occurring (or escalating)**

This lesson introduces basic guidelines to managing conflicts. You will learn about the causes of conflict, what you can do to prevent them, as well as the importance of maintaining good communication in these situations.

Conflict and How It Affects Us

Conflict can be defined as any situation where incompatible activities, feelings, or intentions occur together. It is an everyday occurrence at home, at school, on the job, or anywhere there are people with different beliefs, values, and experiences.

If not carefully managed, conflict can escalate to violence and harm your personal **relationships**, creating wounds that will never heal. When conflict is avoided and important issues are left unresolved, it may lead to resentment, creating a tense environment. However, if you take the necessary steps to resolve a conflict, you may find that "clearing the air" reduces tension and brings about an **understanding** that makes the relationship more open and honest in the future.

We most often find ourselves in conflict with those with whom we spend the most time: parents, friends, coworkers, teammates, and so on. You must learn to recognize that your long-term relationship with these people is more important than the result of any short-term conflict. Calmly discussing issues may often bring about a quick resolution or a realization that a problem doesn't actually exist.

Causes of Conflict

There are many ways in which conflicts can begin: misunderstandings, embarrassment, hurt pride, prejudice, and peer pressures are just a few. Most of the factors or situations that lead to conflict can be classified as resulting from

- **Varied perspectives on the situation**
- **Differing belief systems and values resulting from personal background and accumulated life experiences**
- **Differing objectives and interests**

If you recognize a potential conflict situation early, you may be able to prevent it from escalating into a dangerous fighting situation. By applying conflict management techniques, you will be able to reduce the levels of anger and **frustration**, which will make it easier to resolve the problem.

Types of Conflict and Their Warning Signs

To make good decisions and effectively manage conflict in your life, you must be able to recognize the warning signs of a potential conflict situation. Most types of conflicts belong to one of the five categories presented in the following list:

- **Relationship.** Conflicts that occur because of strong negative emotions, stereotypes, miscommunications, or repetitive negative behaviors. Harassment is a relationship conflict.

- **Data.** Conflicts that occur because people are misinformed or lack information to make good decisions. If you are late to the drama club meeting because you thought it started at 2:00 p.m., but it actually began at 1:00 p.m., then you might find yourself in a data conflict.

- **Interest.** Conflicts that result when one party believes that in order to satisfy his or her needs, the needs of an opponent must be sacrificed. A conflict over what you perceive to be an "unfair situation" would be an interest conflict. For example, if your whole soccer team had to run an extra five miles at practice because John, a teammate of yours, was late for the second time this week, you would have an interest conflict.

- **Structural.** Conflicts that arise out of limited physical resources (including time), authority, geographic constraints, organizational changes, or other external forces. A territorial dispute is a structural kind of conflict. Similarly, if you are scheduled to begin work at your part time job at 3:00 p.m. on Wednesdays, but band practice is not over until 4:00 p.m., then you have a structural conflict.

- **Value.** When people attempt to force their own personal beliefs or values on others. For example, if a friend keeps asking you to help him cheat on his chemistry exam, you might have a value conflict on your hands. Another example of a value conflict would be the debate over capital punishment.

Although there are many types of conflict that you may inevitably encounter, we are going to examine three common types of conflict that you may find at school, at home, or in your community: sexual harassment, other personal harassments (being picked on), and "unfair" situations. The following is a description of each of these kinds of conflict and some of the warning signs that accompany them.

Sexual Harassment

Four out of every five students say that they are sexually harassed often or occasionally. Sexual **harassment** is unwelcome behavior of a sexual nature that is both demeaning and wrong. These unwelcome behaviors are sexual advances, requests for sexual favors, and other physical, verbal, or visual conduct of a sexual nature.

Specifically, sexual harassment includes explicit sexual propositions; suggestive comments; sexually oriented kidding, teasing, or practical jokes; offensive or obscene language or gestures; displays of offensive or obscene printed visual material; and physical contact of a sexual nature. The most common form of sexual harassment, although oftentimes used unintentionally or subconsciously, is to address a person as "dear," "honey," "sweetheart," or some other "term of endearment."

Other Personal Harassments (Being Picked On)

Harassers use verbal, physical, or visual means to annoy or pick on someone, possibly because of their race, ancestry, national origin, religion, age, physical or mental disability, sex, or sexual orientation. Oftentimes, harassers like to pick on people who lack self-confidence by using derogatory remarks, slurs, jokes, cartoons, pictures, or certain gestures that demean, ridicule, or torment the individual.

Unfair Situations

"That's not fair!" is a cry that can represent every aspect of your life's development. It involves following rules regardless of whether you like them or not, reaching compromises with others, and respecting the rights of others. When someone makes a decision that may be fair for some, yet unfair for you and others, it is oftentimes hard to accept the answer to the questions, "From whose perspective was that decision made?" or "What criteria was used to make that decision?" Remember, fair does not mean equal.

Risk Factors for Violence

When scientists talk about preventing a disease such as cancer, they focus on eliminating those factors that put people at risk for the disease. The same reasoning has been applied to the study of violence. Violence-prevention experts have identified some specific risk factors for violence. Poverty, exposure to media violence or to

Figure 5.1.1: The frustration and hopelessness that sometimes accompany poverty may lead to increased violence.
Courtesy of Yvonne Hemsey/Gamma-Liason, Inc./Getty Images.

family violence, the availability of weapons, drug abuse, and membership in gangs are all important risk factors for violence. Figure 5.1.1 shows a poverty-stricken area that could be ripe for violence. As you read about these risk factors, think about the ways each one might increase the likelihood of violence.

Poverty

Statistics show that violence rates are highest in poor urban communities where unemployment rates are high. The term *free-floating anger* is used to describe the frustration and **hostility** that sometimes result when people feel unable to improve their lives. A lack of jobs, money, adequate food, health care, and respect from others all contribute to feelings of hopelessness and anger. When free-floating anger is already high, a minor event may trigger a person to react more violently than normal. It is important to emphasize, however, that most people who are poor do not demonstrate violent behaviors. The anger and frustration of poverty are just two of many risk factors for violence.

Media Violence

From your first cartoon to the latest movie, music video, or video/computer game, you have learned that violence, excitement, and entertainment go together. You can probably recall lines or scenes from action movies that show violence as a reasonable response in many situations. What these scenes do not show, however, are the real results of violence—pain, tragedy, remorse, and more.

Studies suggest that people's attitudes, especially those of young children, can be shaped by media violence. Because children have had little real-life experience, they may interpret what they see on television quite literally. Children who witness a lot of media violence may grow up with an exaggerated sense of the amount of violence in the world. They also may tend to overreact with violence when confronted with threatening situations in their own lives.

Recently much attention has been focused on the media's portrayal of violence toward women, especially in some kinds of music and music videos. The audience for these forms of entertainment is mostly teenagers and young adults. Some people suspect that these media portrayals are partly responsible for the rise in dating violence, rape, and other forms of violence toward women. Do you think this could be true?

Family Violence

Children learn by imitating the behavior of parents and other important people in their lives. It is not surprising, then, that children who grow up in violent homes are more apt to use violence to solve their own problems. Violence may be the only problem-solving strategy that these children know.

How can children learn nonviolent methods for handling anger? The most effective way is to see such methods used by adults in solving their own problems and in disciplining their children. Parents need to discourage their children from fighting by suggesting alternative ways to resolve disagreements, too. Also, parents can impart antiviolence values by discouraging children from playing with certain toys or watching violent movies or television shows and by sharing their own feelings about violence with their children.

<aside>
Key Note Term

hostility – unfriendly state or action
</aside>

Availability of Weapons

Do guns kill people or do people kill people? This difficult question gets to the heart of a controversial issue—the relationship between weapons and violence.

Some people do not believe that the availability of weapons is an important risk factor for violence. They point to countries such as Switzerland, where guns are found in nearly every household. Yet, homicide rates in Switzerland are very low. Other people, however, disagree. They point to comparisons like the one shown in Figure 5.1.2. This graph compares homicide rates in two cities that are similar in many respects except one. Gun ownership is much more tightly regulated in Vancouver, British Columbia, than in Seattle, Washington. What does this graph suggest about the availability of guns?

Most people do agree that when weapons are used in fights, fights are more deadly. Yet the majority of people who purchase handguns in this country do so for protection. By having a gun, however, statistics show that these people are actually doubling their chances of being killed in a fight. What results is an unending cycle. High homicide rates lead to an increase in gun purchasing, which, in turn, leads to an increase in homicide rates. This then leads, once again, to more gun purchasing. Such a cycle may be difficult to break.

Drug Abuse

Would it surprise you to learn that 50 percent of all homicide victims have alcohol in their bloodstreams? Would you expect the statistics to be similarly high for assailants if they were known?

Although there is a correlation between violence and alcohol use, the reasons behind it are not entirely clear. Alcohol affects the brain, clouding a person's sense

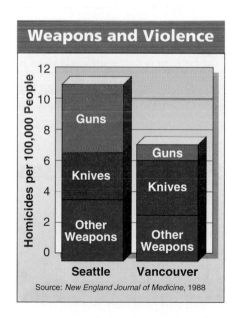

Figure 5.1.2: The homicide rates by each weapon in the two cities.

of judgment. A lack of judgment may lead a person to say or do things that he or she ordinarily would not. This behavior may lead to a fight. In other cases, however, alcohol is used more as an excuse or "to get up the nerve" to carry out preplanned acts of violence.

Drugs other than alcohol also are linked to violence. Similar to alcohol, illegal drugs such as crack cocaine can affect a person's judgment and behavior. In addition, people who are addicted to drugs may resort to robbery or other crimes to get money for drugs. Because many drugs are illegal and sold for a large profit, the people who sell drugs often carry weapons. Both of these facts add to the threat of violence.

> **Note**
>
> Drug and alcohol use will be covered in Unit 4, Chapter 3, Lesson 1.

Membership in Gangs

Key Note Term

territorial – of or relating to the geographic area under a given jurisdiction

The term *gang* describes a variety of groups, from criminal organizations to loose bands of rowdy teens. Generally the term *gangs* refers to groups that are organized to control a specific neighborhood or "turf." Such gangs are called **territorial** gangs or "fighting" gangs because they will fight those who intrude on their turf. Most gangs sell drugs, and many have moved into the lucrative suburban and rural drug markets.

Although young people join gangs, about two-thirds of gang members are adults. They recruit poor students from troubled families. Often the recruits know of no other way, except gang membership, to gain a sense of belonging or community. Holding elaborate initiation ceremonies, wearing certain colors and jewelry, and using secret hand signs are some of the ways gang members identify themselves. To join a gang, new members may undergo a beating, or gang leaders may order them to commit a crime, such as robbery, kidnapping, rape, or murder. Quitting a gang can be much more difficult than joining one.

Small, nonterritorial gangs can form in any town. These groups may identify with a style of music or dress that sets them apart from their peers. Similar to all gangs, these groups isolate their members from the community.

Strategies for Resolving Conflicts

You have control over how you choose to deal with conflict. In some cases, the best course of action is to walk away or do nothing at all. You may find it best to ignore the conflict if

- **The issue or situation is unimportant or trivial to you**
- **You will probably not see the other person again**
- **The other person is just trying to provoke a fight**
- **The timing is wrong and a cooling-off period is needed**

Although choosing to walk away from a conflict may be difficult, doing so in these situations will demonstrate a great deal of maturity and self-control.

In other cases, however, it is best to confront the conflict. Avoiding the issue will not resolve it, and unresolved, lingering conflict can lead to resentment, hostility, and may even escalate to violence. In these situations, using a process to manage the conflict and establishing certain ground rules will help you to resolve the issues peacefully. The basic steps in managing conflict are as follows:

- **Prepare yourself to deal with the conflict**
- **Find a mutually agreeable time and place**
- **Define the conflict**
- **Communicate an understanding**
- **Brainstorm to find alternate solutions**
- **Agree on the most workable solution**

Prepare to Deal with Conflict

We all experience emotions in reaction to conflict. These emotions can include nervousness, fear, embarrassment, anger, frustration, and anxiety. These are strong feelings that can propel you into inappropriate or destructive behavior. Take time to identify your feelings. If not acknowledged, these emotions will become a barrier to resolving the conflict.

We need to maintain emotional control to communicate in a calm, even tone. Screaming and name-calling will only serve to worsen the situation. Some techniques that people use to remain calm and release tension in stressful situations include: deep breathing, vigorous exercise, counting to 10, pounding or yelling into a pillow, and talking to a friend.

Find a Mutually Agreeable Time and Place

Choose a place to discuss the conflict that is comfortable and nonthreatening for both of you and where you can be alone. Some people may feel compelled to act in an aggressive way if they have an audience.

You should also make sure that you have chosen a time when you are both calm and ready to discuss the issues at hand.

Define the Conflict

Two of the most important skills that you need to develop in order to effectively manage conflict are: **effective speaking** (expressing your needs, feelings, and reasons) and **active listening**. In other words, your ability to send and receive clear messages. Each person involved in the conflict must communicate "their perspective or feelings on the situation," "what they want," and "why." Be sure to describe the conflict in clear, concrete terms, focusing on behaviors, feelings, consequences, and desired changes. Be specific and start your sentences with "I," not "You."

"I" messages are statements that tell how you feel. They are the most appropriate way to express your feelings in a calm and respectful manner. By using "I" messages, your communications do not take on a blaming or accusatory tone. "I" messages

Key Note Terms

effective speaking – expressing your needs, feelings, and reasons

active listening – to go beyond comprehending literally to an empathetic understanding of the speaker

have three parts: to state a feeling, to describe a specific behavior, and to state how it affects you. An example of the parts of an "I" message include "I feel" (state feeling) when you (describe specific behavior) because (state how it affects you). For example, "I feel hurt when you tell someone something I told you in secret because I didn't want anyone else to know."

> **Note**
>
> More guidelines for conflict resolution using Winning Colors® communication tools are described later in this chapter.

Communicate an Understanding

In addition to defining the conflict, each party must also feel that they have been heard and understood. This is where active listening comes into play. Request that the other person describe how the situation looks and feels from their perspective. Listen to really understand the other person's feelings and needs. Try to step back and imagine how you would feel if you were in the other person's shoes. Make sure that the other person knows that you are trying to understand his or her point of view. You may want to repeat back your understanding of what you have heard, or you could say something similar to, "I know this issue is important to you because . . . ". Sometimes, however, you will find that it is necessary to *agree to disagree*.

Brainstorm to Find Alternate Solutions

Key Note Term

solution – an action or process in solving a problem

To resolve a conflict, both of you must identify possible **solutions**. When identifying potential solutions to the conflict, it is important to remain positive and be open to compromise. Remember that the conflict is a problem for both of you to solve together, not a battle to be won. You should take turns offering alternative solutions, examining the consequences of each solution. Be creative and focus on solutions rather than pass blame. Do not be judgmental of the other person's ideas.

Agree on the Most Workable Solution

To reach an agreement on a solution, you both need to be committed to resolving the conflict. The conflict ends when both parties reach an agreement that meets everyone's needs and is fair to both of you.

Putting It All Together

Use Table 5.1.1 as an aid to help you remember the steps for effectively managing conflict in your life.

If you cannot reach an agreement, the conflict may need to be resolved through mediation or arbitration (these topics will be discussed in Lesson 2).

Table 5.1.1: Phrases to help manage conflict

I want . . .	You both have the conflict. You must work together to solve it constructively and respectfully.
I feel . . .	You both have feelings. You must express them to resolve the conflict. Keeping anger, frustration, hurt, fear, or sadness inside only makes the conflict more difficult to resolve.
My reasons are . . .	You both have reasons for wanting what you want and feeling as you do. Ask for each other's reasons and ensure you understand them. Recall that at times you must agree to disagree.
My understanding of you is . . .	You both have viewpoints. To resolve the conflict constructively, you must see the conflict from both sides.
Maybe we should try . . .	You both need to come up with wise agreements that make both people happy.
Let's choose and shake!	You both must select the agreement that seems fair. You should not agree on a solution that leaves one party happy and the other unhappy.

Communication Skills

Although **miscommunication** can lead to conflict, good communication is the key to settling problems peacefully.

Language is extremely powerful. If you have ever heard the phrase *those are fighting words*, you know that there are some words that can escalate a conflict and others that can be used to diffuse one. An example of some fighting words includes never, always, unless, can't, won't, don't, should, and shouldn't. Likewise, good communication is blocked when either party blames, insults, puts the other down, interrupts, or makes threats or excuses. On the other hand, words that can be used to de-escalate a conflict include maybe, perhaps, sometimes, what if, seems like, I feel, I think, and I wonder. Try to use these words when facing a conflict situation.

Nonverbal communication, or body language, also has a tremendous impact on those who observe and interpret it. It can encourage or discourage a fight. When trying to resolve a conflict, be sure to maintain eye contact, and use a tone of voice that is sincere and not intimidating or sarcastic. You should also keep your legs and arms uncrossed, and your fists unclenched.

Successful conflict resolution and negotiation depends on the use of positive communication skills.

Key Note Term

miscommunication – failure to communicate clearly

Conclusion

Conflict is a natural part of life. It can be positive or negative depending on how you choose to manage it. By recognizing potential conflicts and their warning signs, and using conflict management strategies to help you make appropriate decisions, you will have confidence and be better prepared to deal with conflict in the future.

In the following lesson, you will learn a variety of conflict resolution techniques. You will learn that conflict resolution depends on the attitudes and behaviors of the people involved in the conflict, including your own attitude toward the people and the situation.

Lesson Review

1. **Do you feel that media violence has affected you? Why or why not?**

2. **List the six basic steps to resolving conflict.**

3. **Explain how good communications skills might help you in a conflict situation.**

4. **Define the terms *conflict* and *territorial*.**

Conflict Resolution Techniques

Key Terms

apologize
compromise
mediation
negotiation
resolution

What You Will Learn to Do

- Apply conflict resolution techniques

Linked Core Abilities

- Do your share as a good citizen in your school, community, country, and the world

Skills and Knowledge You Will Gain Along the Way

- Apply awareness of differences in behavior preferences (Winning Colors®) to conflict situations and resolution

- Evaluate the steps to managing conflict

- Assess personal conflict management skills

- Recognize different hot buttons and the behavior style they indicate

- Evaluate the pros and cons of alternatives to determine potential solutions to conflict

- Define the key words contained in this lesson

Introduction

Key Note Term

resolution – the process or capability of making distinguishable the individual parts of an object, closely adjacent optical images, or sources of light such as the sharpness and clarity of a picture

The success or failure of any conflict **resolution** depends on the attitudes and behaviors of the people involved in the conflict. This lesson offers some strategies for seeking peaceful solutions to conflicts. The skills covered in this lesson promote positive and nonviolent conflict resolution, and include the following:

- **Awareness of others**
- **Awareness of the distinctions between self and others**
- **Listening skills**
- **Compromise**
- **Ability to express one's own thoughts and feelings**
- **Ability to respond to the feelings of others**

These are skills that you need to develop throughout your life. Although conflict is inevitable, you have control over your own response to the situation, and your actions can either diffuse or escalate the conflict. Remember that reacting defensively or judgmentally can trigger the same response in others.

Winning Colors® and Conflict Resolution

Effective communication skills are a key factor in the conflict resolution process. Sometimes to resolve a conflict, you need to go beyond your own comfort zone of preferred behaviors to facilitate good communications with the other party.

As discussed in Chapter 1, Winning Colors® is an assessment tool that is used to classify behaviors into four dominant categories:

- **Planners.** Planners are quiet and introspective. They like to be correct and are very detail oriented. They have excellent listening skills. They are calm, cool, and collected on the outside. They are likely to hide their feelings.

- **Builders.** Builders are natural leaders. They are up-front with people, expressing themselves openly and directly. They like rules, law, order, and direction and do not hesitate to tell others what they should do. Builders are typically punctual, dependable, and loyal.

- **Relaters.** Relaters are very social. They want to be liked and they love to talk. Relaters share their ideas and feelings readily. They work well in teams and need to be shown appreciation.

- **Adventurers.** Adventurers are action oriented. They are bored unless there is fun, excitement, and things are moving. They live in the present. They are flexible and thrive on spontaneity, and do not like structure.

Using an assessment tool such as Winning Colors® will not only help you evaluate your own behavioral strengths and weaknesses, but it will also give you valuable insights into the behavioral characteristics of the people you interact with on a daily basis. Surely no one is going to walk up to you and say "My name is Bob and I'm an Adventurer," so you will have to listen carefully and observe clues in the other person's body language and speech patterns.

With insight and awareness, you will be able to adapt your communication skills and behavior to be able to negotiate a peaceful solution to a conflict.

Hot Buttons

By observing and identifying the behavioral characteristics and tendencies in others, you can determine how to best communicate with them to resolve a conflict. For example, some people respond better to facts and figures; others are more concerned with feelings and emotions. Hot buttons are strategies that you can use to communicate in a way in which the other person is more likely to hear you, understand you, and respond positively. In other words, it is important that both persons involved in a conflict speak the same language. To illustrate this metaphor, imagine trying to negotiate a settlement if you were speaking English and the other party was speaking Chinese. You would not get very far.

When you are speaking to someone who exhibits planner behaviors, you succeed by using planner hot buttons. The same is true if you want to communicate successfully with those who most clearly exhibit builder, relater, and adventurer behaviors.

Hot buttons for planners include the following:

- **Take a serious approach**
- **Show interest; be patient, calm, and collected**
- **Give ample warning before confronting them with a conflict**
- **Supply details and allow more time for decisions**
- **Try not to impose time constraints**
- **Respond in terms of causes rather than exterior effects**
- **Be prepared for interior understanding rather than exterior caring**
- **Show that you are competent and striving to understand the subject**
- **Be a good listener and sounding board**
- **Avoid silly talk and babbling**
- **Respond with new and innovative ideas**

Hot buttons for builders include the following:

- **Take a bottom-line approach**
- **Explain directions step-by-step**
- **Let them know what is expected of them**
- **Do not repeat unless requested to do so**

- Be concise and clear in your speech
- Know the hierarchy of command and give it proper deference
- Look for law, order, and routine
- Make sure your actions deliver results
- Be prepared

Hot buttons for relaters include the following:

- Take a friendly approach
- Talk in a personal way and volunteer to help out
- Show genuine concern, smile, and be kind
- Respect their feelings by not imposing your feelings on them
- Show personal appreciation
- Give them opportunity to express themselves
- Validate their emotions and feelings

Hot buttons for adventurers include the following:

- Take a light-hearted/fun/action approach
- Move it; be an action-centered person
- Keep the discussion in the here and now
- Be willing to change and be flexible
- Show you are competitive and a winner
- The more spontaneous you are, the more you will be appreciated
- Have an easy-come-easy-go manner with good humor to win you points
- Give immediate results or feedback whenever possible
- Avoid theoretic explanations
- Create result-oriented action plans consistent with common goals

Evaluating Consequences

Your response to a conflict should not be a knee-jerk reaction, but rather a carefully considered response. It is important to think through the consequences of your behaviors before you act on them. If you act hastily or in anger, your behavior may add fuel to the fire and conflict could escalate to violence.

> ### As You Go Through This Lesson
> Focus on these questions as you read this lesson.
> - What should always be a person's first concern in any conflict?
> - That strategies are important for resolving conflicts peacefully?

One method of analyzing a response to a conflict is to list three or more alternative solutions at the top of a sheet of paper; then record all of the positive and negative consequences of each option. This forces you to take the time to brainstorm and predict all the possible outcomes you could expect. The result will be a more reasonable and well-thought-out response.

Your goal should be to agree on a nonviolent solution in which both party's needs are met. Remember, if the conflict is over something trivial, or if you will not have contact with the person again, you could choose to ignore the conflict or to **apologize** to settle it peacefully.

Key Note Term

apologize – to make an apology or express regret for a wrong

Preventing Fights

If, after reading this chapter, you have concluded that fighting does not solve problems you may now be wondering what peaceful alternatives exist. You also may doubt whether it is really possible to pursue peaceful solutions if the other person wants to fight.

Although it is certainly not always easy to avoid fighting, it can be done. As you read these strategies, you may come up with ways to adapt them to particular situations or personalities. You may also come up with strategies of your own that you can share with friends, siblings, and others that you care about.

Recognizing a Conflict Early

When people who know each other fight, there is usually a history of events that led to the fight. Events such as name-calling or rumor-spreading may go on for a day, a week, or more before a fight breaks out. By recognizing that a potential fight situation is building, you may be able to prevent it. The earlier you deal with problems, the lower the levels of anger, and the easier it can be to resolve the problem.

Learning to Ignore Some Conflicts

Not all conflicts require that you respond. In some situations it may be smartest to walk away and do nothing at all. You may decide it is best to ignore a situation if

- **It is unlikely you will ever see the person again**
- **The person or situation is not very important to you**
- **The conflict is based on rumors that may not be true**
- **The conflict is over something trivial or silly**
- **The person is just trying to make you angry so you will fight and get into trouble**

Some people think that ignoring a conflict is a sign of cowardice. Actually, it is a sign of maturity and self-control to walk away from some situations. Fighting out of pride or to "save face" may instead be an act of cowardice. As shown in Figure 5.2.1, walking away is one option.

Figure 5.2.1: When a conflict is over something unimportant, it may be best to simply walk away.
Courtesy of Ken Karp.

In deciding how to deal with any conflict, your safety should always be your first concern. If you think that a person might be more angered if you ignore the situation, you need to proceed carefully. It is important to trust your judgment and be prepared to try a new tactic if your first choice does not diffuse the situation.

Confronting a Person Wisely

In some cases it may not be advisable or even possible to ignore a conflict. The person may be someone with whom you are in frequent contact, or the issue may be too important to ignore. In these cases you may decide to confront the person, as shown in Figure 5.2.2. The way in which you handle the confrontation, however, is critical to its success. The steps described here can help you resolve things peacefully.

Choose the Time and Place Carefully

It is always best to confront a person when the two of you are alone. If friends are present, the person may think you are intentionally trying to embarrass him or her in front of them. The person may feel pressured to start a fight to avoid embarrassment. Choosing a time when the person is alone and when both of you are calm can help avoid a fight.

It is also important to avoid a confrontation when a person has been using alcohol or drugs. Alcohol and drugs impair judgment and may increase the likelihood of fighting. Never use alcohol or drugs yourself. If you suspect the other person is under the influence of drugs, postpone your discussion until another time.

Figure 5.2.2: When confronting a person about a problem, find the steps you can take to negotiate a peaceful solution.

Courtesy of Bob Daemmrich/Stock Boston.

Stay Calm

Although it can be difficult to remain calm when you are upset, it is important for keeping peace. Try to keep your voice low and calm. By avoiding screaming or name-calling, you can remain in control of the situation.

Analyzing Risks and Benefits

You just took a seat on a crowded subway when the person seated next to you lights up a cigarette. When you point out the **No Smoking** sign, the person replies, "Too bad. If you don't like it, move!" Make a list of the potential risks and benefits of confronting the person again. What would you do?

Everybody has his or her own technique for keeping calm under pressure. Some people find it helpful to rehearse the confrontation beforehand with an uninvolved person. Other people use deep breathing or count to 20 when they feel their tempers beginning to rise. Despite all your efforts, however, you may find yourself unable to keep calm and control your temper. If that happens, it may be best to try to postpone your discussion until a later time.

Negotiate a Solution

There are skills for effective communication and **negotiation**. Skills such as using "I" messages, assertiveness, and seeing the other person's point of view are important for resolving conflicts peacefully. Making statements such as, "I get upset when . . ." or "I know this issue is important to both of us . . ." can open the lines of communication without putting the other person on the defensive. Showing an understanding of the other person's feelings can also help keep emotions under control. Some other strategies that may be useful in negotiating a peaceful solution include the following:

Key Note Term

negotiation – discussion or conference that is aimed at bringing about a settlement

Key Note Term

compromise – a settlement of differences reached by mutual concessions

- **Do the unexpected.** If, instead of being hostile, you are friendly, confident, and caring, the other person may relax his or her guard. Try to make the situation seem as if it is not serious enough to fight about. The person may agree and decide to work with you to resolve things.

- **Provide the person with a way out.** Sometimes fighting breaks out simply because people see no other way to resolve things without losing pride. To avoid fighting, present the person with **compromise** solutions that you both can live with. By saying something like, "Let's try this for a week and see how it goes," you give the person an easy way out.

- **Be willing to apologize.** In some situations, be willing to say "I'm sorry" or "I didn't mean to embarrass you." Apologizing does not mean that you were wrong or that you are a coward. Instead, a sincere apology can be the quickest way to diffuse a fight.

Helping Others Avoid Fights

When you are not personally involved in a conflict, you can still play an important role in preventing fights. You have learned how friends and acquaintances can put pressure on people to fight. These same people, however, could instead play a key role in preventing fights.

Mediation

Key Note Term

mediation – working with opposing sides in order to resolve a dispute or bring about a settlement.

A growing number of schools today are training students in the skill of **mediation**. Mediation is a process for resolving conflicts that involves a neutral third party. As is true for all people involved in a conflict, mediators need to think about their own safety first. Mediators should never get involved in heated conflicts that have the potential for turning violent at any moment.

Your Role as an Onlooker

How can friends and acquaintances help reduce the pressure that others feel to fight? Friends can use their influence in many positive ways. A person can show disapproval of fighting by

- **Ignoring people when they talk badly about others**
- **Refusing to spread rumors or to relay threats or insults to others**
- **Staying away from potential fight scenes**
- **Showing respect for people who can apologize to others, ignore insults, and otherwise avoid fights**

People who advise friends to ignore someone's insults or not to hold grudges do their friends a very important service. They help keep their friends safe from the potential of deadly violence.

Getting Help When You Need It

Controlling anger and avoiding potentially violent situations are not skills that can be learned overnight. They are, however, skills that can be mastered.

If you are not satisfied with the way you now deal with anger, many people can help you. Parents, teachers, coaches, school counselors, and members of the clergy are just some of the people you can turn to for help. If these people cannot help you themselves, they may be able to refer you to trained counselors who can. By asking for help, you take an important first step toward gaining control over your behavior and your future.

Another time when it is important to ask for help is when a friend reveals plans of violence to you. Such plans should always be taken seriously, especially if your friend talks about using a weapon. Although it is never easy to break a friend's confidence, it is critical for you to share your friend's plans with a trusted adult. Doing so is a true act of caring. It shows that you care too much to let your friend be lost to violence.

Focus on Issues: How Can Schools Be Kept Safe?

Jonesboro, Paducah . . .

Littleton, Conyers . . .

The list of schools that have experienced terror in their hallways seems to grow each year.

Surprisingly, however, school violence is actually declining. There are fewer homicides, fewer assaults, and fewer students carrying weapons into class. What has increased is a kind of random violence that seems more intent on the act of killing rather than a desire to injure a specific person. It may be the ultimate mark of isolation that these murderers cannot even identify an actual enemy.

The struggle against random violence has led to a variety of ideas:

- Metal detectors, see-through backpacks, and security guards to reduce the number of weapons

- Checklists and social workers to identify and help at-risk teens

- School uniforms to help end cliques and isolation

- More school activities to involve students

- A reduction in the violence of music, movies, and video and computer games

What do you think should be done to keep schools safe from violence? Explain.

Conclusion

Effective communications are essential to successful conflict resolution and negotiation. Sometimes we misinterpret what others say, or vice versa; however, if we practice self-awareness and seek to understand others, we will be much more successful in maintaining healthy relationships. Understanding your own communications style, being able to appreciate others, and adjusting accordingly will enable you to resolve conflicts successfully.

This concludes Chapter 5, "Conflict Resolution." Next, you will learn about the NEFE High School Financial Planning Program. This program can help guide you to a more secure financial future.

Lesson Review

1. Using your Winning Color®, explain how you would find a solution to conflict.

2. Explain how evaluating consequences should be important before responding to a situation.

3. Why is it important to choose the time and place to confront a friend or family member about a problem?

4. Who would you go to if you could not manage anger on your own? Why would you choose that person?

Chapter 5

Lesson Review

Presenting Skills

Lesson 1

Becoming a Better Writer

Key Terms

active voice
autobiography
bibliography
biography
body
conclusion
conjunction
entice
fragment
information cards
introduction
passive voice
plagiarism
predicate
source cards
subject
thesis statement

What You Will Learn to Do

- Organize writing for a specific purpose

Linked Core Abilities

- Communicate using verbal, nonverbal, visual, and written techniques

Skills and Knowledge You Will Gain Along the Way

- Identify situations where writing is an appropriate form of communication
- Describe various writing techniques
- Explain how to use writing to express your needs
- Describe how to effectively organize writing assignments
- Define the key words contained in this lesson

Introduction

Writing is one of the acts or processes used to exchange ideas. When all is working well, when sentences are grammatically correct, when words are carefully chosen, when paragraphs are soundly structured, communication is usually successful. People will read your sentences, understand your meaning, and respond accordingly.

Writing is one of the most important means of communication, so your writing must be simple, readable, and understandable. With a little practice and desire, writing is an art that anyone can master. Your writing will take many forms. In school, you will often have to write papers for your classes. These may include term papers, a **biography**, or an **autobiography**.

To write well, you must first define the purpose of your writing, organize your thoughts, and make an outline—only then are you ready to write. This process is not always easy, but all it takes is the desire to write clearly, hard work, and following a few guidelines.

The Basics of Writing

Writing a paper is similar to writing a speech. You must first decide on a topic, research the topic, and organize your material. After you have organized your material, you are in a position to begin writing your paper. The elements of a paper are also similar to those of a speech. You should have an **introduction**, **body**, and a **conclusion**. As you continue to read, you will see how similar these elements really are to a speech.

> **Note**
>
> Although writing for reading, such as writing a paper, is similar to writing for speaking, such as writing a speech, there is a difference. Keep in mind that the reader will be reading silently, so the way you create your sentences should be different than the way you'd write if someone was reading out loud.

Research

Research is probably the most important part of your paper. When you begin your research, be determined to find all the information you can; however, be sure that the information you select is accurate and relevant to your topic.

You may want to start your research at the school library. Carry index cards with you so that you can make or use them as **source cards** or **information cards**. For each book or reference that you find on your topic, use the source cards to correctly record the title, author or authors, publisher, copyright date (usually just the year), and place of publication (city and state). Not only do these source cards help you to keep track of where your information came from, but they are the basis for

Key Note Terms

biography – the history of a particular person, as told by someone else

autobiography – the biography of a person, written by that person

Key Note Terms

introduction – the beginning of a paper, speech, or lesson plan

body – the main part of a paper, lesson plan, or speech

conclusion – the final part of a paper, speech, or lesson plan; also referred to as a summary; a final opinion reached through research and reasoning

source cards – a card that is used to record the title, author, publisher, copyright date, and place of publication (city and state) of resources being used during research for a project (paper, speech, and so on)

information cards – cards used to collect data for a report or paper

bibliography – a list of sources of information on a specific subject; the description and identification of the editions, dates of issue, authorship, and typography of books or other written materials

your **bibliography** when you finish your paper. Later you can organize your bibliography by alphabetizing your source cards. Give each source card a code such as a number or letter. Place the code in the upper left corner.

After you have your books, magazines, articles, and other resource materials recorded on source cards, begin taking notes from these books on index cards. These will become your information cards. Write your code numbers from your source cards on the upper left corner of your information cards so you can identify which notes came from which publication. Also, write the page number you found the notes on your information cards.

After researching your topic at the school library, you may want to venture out to other libraries, such as the city or county library, looking for supplemental materials. When you have finished this library work, do not stop your research. Contact experts on your subject and set up interviews with them. This can be exciting because you are gathering more information for your paper and you are also meeting new people and establishing contacts. Perhaps you can also look for reliable sources on the Internet. Internet research can save you some time, as seen in Figure 6.1.1.

> **Note**
>
> Not everything you read on the Internet is true or correct. Be sure you visit reputable Web sites when gathering information from the Internet.

Although research is sometimes a frustrating process, it is important to stick with it. Be curious and always open to new ideas. Through your research, you will discover the main theme of your paper and experience one of the joys of learning.

Figure 6.1.1: Research on the Internet can provide additional sources of supplemental materials.
Courtesy of Ken Karp.

Organization

After you have completed your research, you should be able to develop the main point of your paper. This main point is similar to the specific purpose of a speech. The main point of a paper is called a **thesis statement**.

Now you are ready to develop your outline. Take your information cards and place them in related groups. Arrange the related groups in the order in which you think they should logically appear in your paper. Experiment with different types of order or arrangements. Rearrange and regroup them as often as necessary. If you have time, put your cards away for a night and rework them the next day. Remember, this outline does not have to be exact. You can still be flexible at this point. After all, you are looking for the best way to present the material you collected.

Finally, when you finish arranging your information cards based on your initial thoughts about the topic, begin writing the outline. The outline allows you to organize your thoughts and record them on paper. The most traditional outline is the Roman numeral/capital letter style outline; however, you do not have to use this type. If you are more comfortable with another type of outline, by all means, use it. Your outline is far too important to confuse matters by using an unfamiliar or cumbersome format.

Writing Your Paper

After completing your research and organization, you are ready to begin writing the paper. As mentioned earlier in this lesson, your paper needs an introduction, body, and a conclusion. Some students compose their papers on a computer, as seen in Figure 6.1.2.

Introduction

Your introduction grabs the reader's attention and introduces the topic. It is important to **entice** your readers into your paper, so make sure you have a catchy, exciting, and well-organized introduction.

Key Note Term

thesis statement – the main point of a paper that you try to support through research

Key Note Term

entice – to attract or lure; to encourage someone to participate

Figure 6.1.2: Some students key their paper drafts on a computer to save time.
Courtesy of Bob Daemmrich.

Body

The body of your paper is where you explain and document what you know about the subject based on your research. Tell the readers your main points, which should support your thesis statement; then support these main points with examples and facts.

Use one idea per paragraph. Your information cards should help you do this and your outline should help you to stay organized and on track with your topic. The first time you write the paper should be nothing more than a rough draft; therefore, do not worry too much about grammar and spelling. You will be revising this draft, probably several times, so worry about those details later. In your first draft, you are still looking at presenting the information in the most logical order. In later drafts, you can rearrange the order as necessary, add or delete information, and correct the grammar and spelling.

Conclusion

Your conclusion is the last opportunity for you to tell the readers what you want them to remember. Use this space to pull your paper together and to leave the reader with a sense of accomplishment.

Rewrites

After you have completed your first draft, rewrite and revise your paper then rewrite your paper again, if time permits. Rewriting is a major part of the development of your paper. Do not ignore this step! Try to leave at least one day between revisions. When you leave time between rewrites, you are able to review your work with a fresh state of mind. Use rewrites to reword your material and to polish your grammar and spelling.

Have others review your work. They can help find errors and clarify statements.

Plagiarism

Plagiarism is illegal. It is the stealing of someone else's work or ideas without giving them the proper credit or, in some cases, obtaining permission to use the material. You can commit plagiarism by simply, and in many instances unintentionally, copying someone else's ideas, words, or pictures/graphic illustrations.

To avoid plagiarism, always give the appropriate credit to every resource you used when writing the paper. The most common ways to give credit are to use footnotes, endnotes, quotation marks (mentioning the source), or a bibliography. Refer to your English textbook or to a writing style handbook for suggestions on formats. Whichever system you use, you will find the information on your source cards very helpful.

Courtesy of US Army JROTC.

Key Note Term

plagiarism – the act of copying the ideas or words of another and claiming them as one's own

Note

There are a variety of writing style handbooks available. One that is widely used is *The Chicago Manual of Style*. You can take a look at this and other style handbooks in any library.

Principles of Writing

As a writer, there are six principles that you should use as a guide when writing. By adhering to these six principles, you will be able to keep your writing focused on the topic, written to the correct target audience, concise, complete, logically arranged, and grammatically correct. These principles are audience level, accuracy, brevity and completeness, clarity, coherence, and unity.

Audience Level

When you write, you should do so for a particular audience, just like you would for a speech. Although most of your writing in high school will be assignment related, you may have the opportunity to write articles for the school paper or yearbook, reports for an after-school club, or flyers for your after-school job. Because of the different audiences these items would reach, you should not write them in the same manner. Instead, you would tailor them to each audience.

Be careful not to write at too high or too low of a level for your audience. This may seem hard to do, but it is extremely important. The purpose of your writing is to explain your topic or to present information, not to prove how much you know or how little you may think your reader knows about the subject. It is not your job to alienate the audience.

Accuracy

Your work must be free of factual and mechanical errors. It should represent only essential and accurate facts. Correct use of grammar, punctuation, and spelling will also contribute to clarity and understanding.

Brevity and Completeness

Include in your paper only the information that is essential or pertinent to cover the topic. In other words, keep your writing brief and to the point. Do not stray from your main point as that only distracts the reader and could take attention away from your desired outcome or conclusion. To cover a subject completely while keeping the length of the paper to the absolute minimum requires careful analysis and many rewrites; however, never sacrifice clarity or completeness just to gain brevity.

Clarity

You must make a special effort to keep your writing clear, crisp, and fully under-standable. Ensure that your readers understand your intention. Do not try to impress them with your vocabulary. The best way to obtain clarity in your writing is by practicing the following guidelines:

- Use short sentences.
- Avoid explaining something that the reader already knows.
- Use simple, familiar words to describe objects. Also, avoid vague words that do not relate precisely to your topic.
- Use verbs in the active tense. For example, instead of "The ball was thrown by John," write "John threw the ball."
- Avoid long phrases when one or several words will do and avoid wordiness (or the use of unnecessary words). For example, use "now" instead of "at the moment."
- Select words and phrases that express your exact meaning and can have only one interpretation.
- Use words that bring an image to mind. If a reader can picture something, he or she will have a better chance of understanding what you are trying to write.

Because of the importance of writing grammatically correct work, common errors in grammar are described in detail later in this lesson.

Grammatical Errors

When a piece of writing is flawed, the process of communication breaks down; the transfer of information stops as the reader tries to translate your meaning.

There are many flaws that can damage your writing; among the most serious are ungrammatical sentences. Grammatical errors include fragments; run-on sentences; subject/verb agreement; shifts in person, number, tense, voice, and tone; and faulty pronoun reference.

Fragments

A sentence is an independent clause that can stand alone. It has a **subject** (tells what or whom the sentence is about) and a **predicate** (tells what the subject does). A **fragment** is a dependent clause (a word group that lacks a subject or a predicate).

The following is an example of a fragment:

In the basement and the attic

Here is an example of a complete sentence:

We searched for the missing book in the basement and the attic.

Run-on Sentences

A run-on sentence occurs if two or more independent clauses are joined without a **conjunction** (joining word such as "and" or "but") or appropriate punctuation.

Here is an example of the correct way to write this:

Organize a résumé according to your education, work experience, career objectives, and recreational interests review your needs carefully before stating a career objective.

Courtesy of US Army JROTC.

Key Note Terms

subject – tells what or whom the sentence is about

predicate – tells what the subject does

fragment – a word group that lacks a subject or a predicate

Key Note Term

conjunction – joining words such as "and" or "but"

In the second example, the run-on sentence is written in two complete sentences.

Sometimes a conjunction is used to connect two related clauses, such as shown in the following example.

A good résumé will include carefully chosen detail, and it will create an impression of depth without overwhelming the reader with your life history.

Subject/Verb Agreement

Subjects and verbs agree with one another in number (singular or plural) and person. Agreement as to number means that the verb may have a different spelling, depending on whether the subject is singular (one) or plural (more than one).

The following is a singular example:

The musician is a professional.

Here is a plural example:

The musicians are professional.

The verb in these examples changed when the subject went from singular to plural.

Person is a term that indicates whether the subject is the one speaking (first person); the one spoken to (second person); or the one spoken about (third person).

First person	I walk to the store.
Second person	You drive to the store.
Third person	Joey runs to the store.

Shifts

Shift, as defined in grammar, is an abrupt change of perspective within a sentence or between sentences.

An example of a shift in person is as follows:

People are tempted to go off their diets when we go on vacation.

This is a shift from third person ("people") to first person ("we") within the same sentence.

A shift in number is as follows:

If the books belong to the boy, return it.

The previous sentence is a shift from plural ("books") to singular ("it") within the same sentence.

A shift in tense changes when the time of an action changes (past, present, future). An example of a shift in tense is as follows:

Mrs. Hopkins arrives at her desk and went directly to work.

The sentence above is a shift from present tense (arrives) to past tense (went).

Voice is a term that indicates whether the writer has emphasized the doer of the action (**active voice**) or the receiver of the action (**passive voice**). Avoid shifting voices within a sentence, as shown in the following example.

We went to the post office (active) and the letters were mailed (passive).

Here is one way to write this using only the active voice:

We went to the post office and mailed the letters.

"We" took the action of going to the post office and mailing the letters.

A shift in the tone of your writing can also confuse your readers. Tone refers to the quality of language (word choice, sentence structure) that creates for your reader an impression about your work and you, the writer. Your tone may be formal or informal. After you adopt a certain tone, use it consistently. The following paragraph shows a shift from formal to informal:

> **In your letter of May 16, 2001, you requested that we pay the balance of our bill, in the amount of $25.31. You know, if you people would get your act together and correct the problems we told you about, maybe you would get your money.**

Faulty Pronoun Reference

A noun is a word that names a person, place, or thing. A pronoun is a word used in place of a noun. Pronouns help avoid unnecessary repetition in our writing. For example, the following is repetitive use of a noun:

Although Seattle is damp, Seattle is my favorite city.

Rather than using Seattle twice in the same sentence, a pronoun can be used, as shown in the following example:

Although Seattle is damp, it is my favorite city.

Pronoun reference is a term that describes the relationship between a pronoun and its noun.

Noun ← Pronoun

The *gentleman* bowed to *his* partner.

For a pronoun to function correctly, it must refer clearly to a well-defined noun, as in the previous example. *His* can refer to only one noun in the sentence, *gentleman*. When a pronoun does not refer clearly to its noun, readers will be confused, as shown in the following example.

Mr. Jones extended an invitation to Mr. Smith after he returned from his trip.

In this example, it is not clear who took the trip—Mr. Jones or Mr. Smith. The following clarifies the sentence, showing that Mr. Jones was clearly the traveler.

After Mr. Jones returned from his trip, he extended an invitation to Mr. Smith.

Writing More Clearly

Writing a grammatically correct sentence is no guarantee that you will communicate effectively. Grammatically correct writing can still be unclear. After you are confident that your sentences are grammatically correct, examine your choice of words.

Have you expressed yourself clearly? Have you avoided using jargon that may make your meaning unclear? Have you refrained from overusing to be or to have as main verbs? Have you chosen the better voice for your verb? Learning about these choices and thinking about them when you write will improve the clarity of your writing.

Wordiness

Delete words, phrases, and clauses that do not add directly to the meaning of a sentence. Try to be less wordy and more to the point. Say your sentences to yourself with fewer words and see if the meaning stays the same. If so, use the version with fewer words. The following is a wordy sentence:

Under all circumstances and in every case, always check the oil level in your car when you stop at a service station.

This can be written so that it's more to the point, as shown in the following example:

Always check the oil level of your car when you stop at a service station.

Jargon

Jargon consists of "shorthand" words, phrases, or abbreviations that are known only to a relatively small group of people. You should avoid jargon for two reasons:

- **Your audience may not understand what you are saying or writing**
- **Your message will be unclear when you rely on overused phrases as a substitute for original thinking**

Always choose your words carefully and know what they mean. Do not depend upon phrases that add syllables but not substance. For example, a jargon-filled sentence might read like the following:

Semipermanent dyadic relationships provide the adolescent with the opportunities for trialing that make for a more secure union in the third and fourth decades.

This can be reworked for clarity by cutting out the jargon, as shown in the following example:

Going steady when you are a teenager helps prepare you for marriage later on.

Overuse of "to Be" and "to Have"

Relying too heavily on forms of "to be" and "to have" as main verbs will diminish the effectiveness of your sentences. These words lack force as main verbs and do not establish the clearest possible relationship between the subject of a sentence and its predicate. When possible, substitute a verb that more clearly expresses action than "to be" or "to have." For example, the following sentence shows little imagination:

Ms. Smith was at the office door.

By changing the verb so that it's clearer, the reader gets a better idea of what Ms. Smith was doing.

Ms. Smith stood at the office door.

Active and Passive Voice Sentences

Sometimes the same sentence can be written in more than one way. Consider the following:

The lawyer had won the case.

The case had been won by the lawyer.

The first example emphasizes the lawyer. It tells you something about the lawyer. The lawyer is the subject of the sentence. Because the lawyer is the one that did something (won the case), and you are writing about the lawyer, this is called active voice.

The second example emphasizes the case. It tells you something about the case. The case is the subject of the sentence. Because the case is the object that had something done to it (it was won by the lawyer), and you are writing about the case, this is called passive voice. The following are examples of active and passive voice:

Active: Babe Ruth hit the ball.

Passive: The ball was hit by Babe Ruth.

The passive voice is less direct and less forceful than the active voice. Use the active voice whenever possible, unless it does not convey the meaning you intended.

Organizing a Paragraph

A paragraph is a collection of sentences logically arranged and focused on a narrowly defined topic. Similar to sentences, paragraphs rarely occur alone. They are parts of larger units: the business letter, the memorandum, or the essay for school.

Learning about the composition of paragraphs is important in that the success of any larger form is entirely dependent on the success of its component parts. A letter will fail to communicate if any of its paragraphs are poorly structured or poorly developed.

The Topic Sentence

The topic sentence tells the reader the main idea of the entire paragraph. The topic sentence should be just broad enough and narrow enough to allow approximately five to seven sentences about the topic. Depending on the topic, there could be more sentences. If some of your sentences are about a different subject, perhaps you should be starting a new paragraph with a new topic sentence.

Use topic sentences as an aid in organizing your writing. When you properly focus a topic sentence, you have a solid basis on which to include or exclude information as you write a paragraph.

A good topic sentence also enables the reader to anticipate the contents of a paragraph and thus to follow your ideas as they are expressed.

Unity

Your writing must adhere to a single main idea or theme. Apply this principle not only to each sentence and paragraph but to the entire paper. This is where your initial outline comes in very handy. Give unity to each paragraph by making each sentence contribute to the main idea of the paragraph. At the same time give unity to the paper by making each paragraph support the main idea of the paper. A paragraph is said to have unity when each sentence contributes to the main idea of the paragraph. Any sentence that does not relate to the main idea of a paragraph needs to be deleted or rewritten. To achieve unity in each paragraph, you may want to develop a plan or outline for each paragraph that would include the topic and each point supporting the topic. If the paragraphs in your paper tend to lack unity, you may use the following questions to assist you in revising them. Is the main idea of the paragraph clearly stated or implied? Does the subject or idea of the paragraph change one or more times? Are all sentences in the paragraph relevant to the main idea? If you answered yes to any of these questions, go back and revise your paragraph so that each sentence supports the main idea.

Coherence

Coherence is the logical development and arrangement of a subject. You can achieve coherence by thinking the subject through and seeing it as a whole before you arrange the parts logically and begin writing. A paragraph has coherence when the relationship between sentences is clear and when there is an easy and natural transition or flow from one sentence to the next. To achieve coherence, you need to arrange sentences in a clear and logical order. There are several ways to arrange sentences in a logical order. The simplest and most common way is the time order. Each sentence is arranged in a chronological or time sequenced order. Often the idea in a paragraph has time elements and can easily be arranged in a time sequence of events. Another example of a logical order is the order of climax. In this type of paragraph, the least important sentence or idea in the paragraph comes first followed by sentences of increasing importance that leads to the final or climax sentence of the paragraph. Other paragraphs may begin with a general statement type sentence followed by sentences that support the general statement with particular details. Sometimes sentences can be linked by the use of pronouns. The following sentences provide an example of using pronouns to link or transition from one sentence to the next.

The squad leader is the organizer and leader of the patrol. He is the boss. He runs the show. etc.

Using your outline and rewrites will help you to achieve coherence.

Paragraph Transitions

Providing a smooth flow or transition from one paragraph to another is even more important than the transition between sentences. Transitional words such as *first, then, next, additional,* and *finally* and phrases like *just as significant, more important, for example* (or giving examples) and *most important of all* are very useful particularly when the paragraphs are arranged according to time order or the order of climax. Look at the paragraph on *Active and Passive Voice Sentences,* the first transition paragraph used the phrase *The first example,* and the next one used the phrase *The second example* to make the transition from one paragraph to the next. Another approach is to repeat a word or phase that is used in the first sentence of a paragraph in the first sentence of the transition paragraph. For example, look at the paragraph on *The Topic Sentence.* All three paragraphs in this subject begin with either *The topic sentence, Use topic sentences,* or *A good topic sentence.* The key phrase used to make the transitions from one paragraph to the next is "topic sentence." Using your outline and a good paragraph plan will help you achieve a smooth transition between each paragraph.

Conclusion

Written communication is another way we transfer ideas among ourselves; however, your message has to be perceived the way you intended it to be perceived.

You must understand your audience and your purpose for writing. You should conduct research and write to support your ideas. You should decide on an organization for your information and outline your ideas.

After you start writing, you need to understand some fundamentals of the English language. For people to respect and respond to your message, they must not be distracted by poor writing or inappropriate language. Follow the basic rules and people will pay attention to your ideas and be impressed by your ability to express yourself.

In the following lesson, you will learn that there is a difference between writing for reading and writing for speaking. You will learn how to write effective speeches that get your message across to your audience.

Lesson Review

1. Name the three elements of a paper.
2. What is a thesis statement? Why is it important?
3. Give an example of writing to a specific audience. Create two sentences—one for a beginning-level audience and one for an advanced-level audience.
4. What jargon do you use in everyday speech? Who understands this jargon, and who doesn't?

Lesson 2

Creating Better Speeches

Key Words

articulate
commemorative
demographics
dramatic statement
descriptive
eye contact
impromptu
logical
modulation
operational
persuasive
statement
tone
vocal qualities
volume

What You Will Learn to Do

- Write a speech for a specific purpose

Linked Core Abilities

- Communicate using verbal, nonverbal, visual, and written techniques

Skills and Knowledge You Will Gain Along the Way

- Identify ways to create interesting speech introductions
- Compare different types of speeches and different occasions for which speeches are used
- Describe how to organize effective speeches
- Define the key words contained in this lesson

Introduction

Throughout your life you will be asked to give speeches. These speeches may be formal presentations or just a few words at an informal occasion. Whatever the situation, you will probably feel nervous. Don't worry; this is natural. Most people become anxious when someone asks them to talk in front of a group. Relax, establish **eye contact** with your audience, and tell them what you want them to know in your own words. After the first minute, you should begin to feel more comfortable. You will then be well on your way to delivering a successful speech. This lesson shows you how to create effective speeches of all types.

One of the best ways to be a successful speaker is to be completely prepared. Although this may not be possible with an **impromptu** speech, preparing for other types of speeches, such as a **commemorative** speech, will require an organized and designed speech.

The six basic steps of preparing for public speaking are as follows:

- **Analyze the purpose and audience**
- **Conduct your research**
- **Support your points**
- **Organize your information**
- **Draft and edit your speech**
- **Practice, practice, practice**

Key Note Term

eye contact – looking someone directly in the eyes

Key Note Terms

impromptu – without planning or rehearsal

commemorative – honoring the memory of; speaking in honor of

Analyze Purpose and Audience

It's important to understand the purpose of your speech as well as to whom the speech is directed. Is your speech to sway opinion? Is it to report on a specific topic? Does your audience know anything about the topic, or are you presenting a new idea? This section discusses these issues when creating and presenting your speech.

Purpose

It is important to identify the purpose of your speech because it will keep you focused as you analyze your audience and begin to organize your speech.

The purpose of a speech depends on the type of speech you are giving (or required to give), your topic, and the audience level. In some cases, there may be a general purpose and/or a specific purpose. You may make decisions along the way based on the purpose of your speech. The general purpose for an informative speech might simply be to inform the audience about your topic. A specific purpose, however, states the main idea (or ideas) of the speech. The specific purpose should be written in one sentence to ensure that its intent is clear and concise. For example, if you are giving a speech to an eighth grade graduating class on the advantages of taking Army JROTC, the following statements could represent your topic, general purpose, and specific purpose:

- **Topic.** Army JROTC
- **General Purpose.** To inform eighth graders about JROTC
- **Specific Purpose.** To inform the graduating class at Center Middle School about the advantages of taking Army JROTC in their ninth grade year at Lakeview High School

Audience

The goal of every speech and speechmaker is to win a response from the listeners. To accomplish this, you need to have some basic knowledge about your audience, which might include the following:

- **What knowledge does the audience already have about this topic?**
- **What additional information will the listeners most want to know about the topic?**
- **What particular aspects of the topic will be most relevant to the audience?**
- **What is the audience's attitude about this topic?**
- **How can you best gain and hold their interest and attention?**
- **What do you need to think about as far as language level of the audience?**
- **What interests do you share with your listeners?**
- **What is the occasion of the speech?**
- **How much time should you allow for your speech?**

Additionally, you should try to learn some **demographics** about the audience. Demographics are statistical information about groups of people. These data tell you about group characteristics, not individuals. You can learn about the audience's:

- **Age**
- **Occupation**
- **Religion**
- **Ethnic or cultural background**
- **Gender**
- **Physical characteristics**
- **Economic status**
- **Educational background**
- **Political affiliations**

You can learn about your audience by personal observation, information from others, interviews, and questionnaires.

The more you know about your audience, the more you can gear your talk toward their needs and interests, and the less likely you will be to offend anyone.

The best speakers focus on the audience. Good speakers know that the best collection of information will not substitute for a good audience analysis.

Key Note Term

demographics – dealing with the vital and social conditions of people

---

Select a Topic

Sometimes a topic is assigned to you; other times you are given the opportunity to select your own topic. There are several methods that can be used to make a selection:

- **Analyze your own interests.**
- **List broad categories of topics or subtopics under one broad category.**
- **Engage in personal brainstorming to list as many topics as you can think of in a short amount of time.**
- **Identify current topics of interest in the news.**
- **Cluster topics to think of a concept or an idea about which you know something. Write and circle that topic in the middle of the page and then spend about ten minutes letting your mind freely associate other topics related to the concept. This is different from just listing various topics because with clustering, all the topics are related in some way. After you have finished, you can pick the pieces that can be developed into a speech. Ask yourself the following questions:**
  - **Are you interested in the topic?**
  - **Will you enjoy talking about this topic?**
  - **Do you want to entertain, inform, or persuade?**
  - **What can you do to make the topic more interesting?**
  - **Will the topic offend some members of your audience?**
  - **Does the occasion of the speech have a special purpose?**
  - **Do you know anything about this topic?**
  - **Do you have any interest in learning about this topic?**

After you have selected your topic, confirm whether it is appropriate for your audience and for yourself. Is it appropriate ethically, and is it appropriate for the occasion? Narrow the topic appropriately for your time constraints. You are now ready to conduct your research.

Getting Started

The general purpose and the specific purpose of the speech are developed early in the speech preparation process, usually before you conduct any research. You do, however, need to have a certain amount of information to write a thesis **statement**, such as:

- **Topic.** Army JROTC
- **General purpose.** To inform eighth graders about service learning
- **Specific purpose.** To inform the graduating class at Center Middle School about the advantages of participating in service learning and how they can get started
- **Thesis statement.** Participating in service learning will allow you to learn outside the traditional classroom environment and help fill a need in the community.

> **Key Note Term**
>
> **statement** – the act of stating, declaring, or narrating

The thesis statement is a one-sentence summary of the speech. It acts like the topic sentence in a written composition. It is a complete sentence that tells exactly what your speech is about. After you have your general and specific purposes and your thesis statement, you are ready to conduct your research.

Conduct Your Research

There are many ways to conduct research on your topic, such as the following:

- **Personal experience**
- **Newspapers**
- **Online newspapers**
- **Public libraries**
- **Library catalog**
- **Reference works**
- **Periodicals**
- **Nonprint materials**
- **Online libraries**
- **School libraries**
- **State/local agencies online**
- **Personal interviews**

Personal Interviews

Personal interviews can be helpful if they are easily obtainable. The information-gathering interview is an especially valuable form of research. The interview allows you to view your topic from an expert's perspective, to take advantage of that expert's years of experience, research, and thought. You can use an interview to collect facts and to stimulate your own thinking. Often the interview will save you hours of library research and allow you to present ideas that you could not have uncovered any other way. And because the interview is a face-to-face interaction with an expert, many ideas that otherwise would be unclear can become more understandable.

Courtesy of US Army JROTC.

Why Research?

Research is used to increase speech effectiveness as well as to enhance your credibility. You will want to know the most recent information. Knowing about any new controversies and the latest information will help you understand the audience's attitudes and will assist you in developing strategies for the best approach.

Remember to write down where you are finding all your information. You may need to go back and find more data, and you also need to give credit to your sources during your speech.

Support Your Points

Knowing the details that support the ideas within your speech will allow the audience to look at you as an expert. They will be more likely to give you their undivided attention. There is an art to giving a credible and well-supported speech. Support for your points can come in several forms.

Facts and Figures

Facts and figures are statements and verifiable units of information. You can impress an audience if you include a lot of facts and figures. You must make sure they are accurate.

Descriptive Statistics

Descriptive statistics explain things in terms of size or distribution. These statistics are powerful because they give the impression that they are the result of a thorough scientific study. When evaluating statistics one should consider the source, seek multiple sources, cite the statistic completely, and try to use current and relevant statistics. For example, if you were naming someone as the greatest tennis player of all time, just making the statement is not as impressive as giving the statistics that support the statement.

Statements of Authority

Statements of authority let you "borrow" the credibility of the expert. In the previous example of naming the world's greatest tennis player of all time, if you can also quote a well-known tennis player who agrees with your estimation, your writing would carry a lot more credibility.

Narratives

Narratives are examples in the form of stories. Audiences will often listen to narratives when they will not listen to anything else. Be sure that the audience sees the relationship between the story and the point you are making. Narratives should always have a beginning, middle, and end, and should be interesting, while avoiding unnecessary details and excessive length.

Definitions

There are three types of definitions: logical, descriptive, and operational. A **logical** definition is the dictionary definition. A **descriptive** definition describes how a word derives from the root word of its culture. **Operational** definitions tell how the object relates to how it works or operates.

Humor

If you are trying to build credibility, humor can be effective because people like to hear a good joke, and they are likely to remember it and associate it with serious ideas. Political candidates use humor in their speeches.

> **Key Note Terms**
>
> **logical** – the dictionary definition
>
> **descriptive** – describes how a word derives from the root of its culture
>
> **operational** – tells how the object relates to how it works or operates

Remember, use humor only at appropriate times during the speech, illustrated in Figure 6.2.1. There are clearly some speeches where the use of humor would not be appropriate at all. When explaining to a group of youngsters why their behavior was inappropriate, humor may be out of place.

Logic, Testimony, Statistics, and Facts

Logic, testimony, statistics, and facts are the support types that can prove your points. Without this support, the points you make in a speech will be less **persuasive**. Supporting information will also clarify, add interest to, and make memorable your points.

Outline Your Information

After you have gathered information and found the supporting logic, facts, testimonies, or statistics, the next step is to create an outline of your information.

Outlining your points will help you see the main themes in your speech, let you add to your notes, and ensure your speech will flow naturally. You can write an outline in words and phrases or in complete sentences, but it is best to use as few complete sentences as possible. By avoiding complete sentences, you will limit the temptation to just read your speech from your notes.

When outlining your main points and supporting ideas, make sure that all of them support the goal and purpose of the speech.

Key Note Term

persuasive – to have the power to persuade

Figure 6.2.1: Humor can be used as part of the introduction of a speech as well as a way to relax the speaker and the audience.
Courtesy of Larry Lawfer.

There are several ways to organize the information. Before you start, think about the various alternatives available to you.

- **Topical organization allows you to present several ideas related to one topic. These ideas follow a logical order. This is one of the most common ways to organize ideas.**

- **Chronological organization uses time sequence for the framework. Chronological organization is important for speeches that require background information.**

- **Spatial organization arranges material according to physical space. You may use spatial order in speeches involving geographical locations.**

- **Classification puts topics into categories. This pattern fits many speeches.**

- **Problem/solution puts the problem in the first part of the outline, and the solution into the second part.**

- **Cause/effect organization describes the cause of a problem in the first part of the outline, and describes the effect in the second part.**

Regardless of how you format your outline, it should contain the following elements:

- **Title**
- **Specific purpose**
- **Thesis statement**
- **Introduction, which may be outlined or written in full**
- **Body of the speech in outline format**
- **Conclusion of the speech, which may be outlined or written in full**
- **Bibliography of sources or references consulted**

Write an Introduction

After you have an outline of the information that is the body of your speech, you need to think about how you will introduce the information. The introduction accomplishes the following:

- **Grabs the audience's attention**
- **Introduces the topic**
- **Shows the importance of the topic**
- **Presents the thesis of the topic**
- **Forecasts the major ideas**

There are many ways to get the attention of your audience. Some of the following may suit your needs:

- **Wait for silence**
- **Tell a joke**
- **Tell a story related to the topic or about your research**
- **Ask a question**
- **Quote a famous person**
- **Make a dramatic statement**
- **Use a gimmick**
- **Compliment the audience**
- **Point to a historical event**
- **Refer to the occasion**

Key Note Term

dramatic statement –
a phrase or sentence
meant to capture the
attention of the
audience

Different types of speeches require different types of introductions. You need to decide what will work for your topic and your audience.

Within the introduction, give a preview of your presentation. The preview is usually only a sentence or two long. Be brief and be clear. After the introduction, your audience should know exactly what you are talking about and, in some cases, why.

The Body of Your Speech

The body of your speech should take about 75 percent of the allotted time. In this main section of the speech you want to reinforce your general and specific purposes. Support your main idea with examples. These ideas should be carried throughout the speech in a logical order and be supported by data.

The main body of the speech is typically divided into main points, usually two to five. These main points should be similarly worded and approximately equal in importance.

Make sure you use words that your audience will understand. Eliminate complex sentences and try to speak as naturally as possible. Make the body of the speech similar to the body of a report: organized, concise, and to the point.

Write a Conclusion

The conclusion of a speech is also similar to the conclusion of a report. The conclusion should be short and review the main ideas. Wrap up your ideas and remember to leave time for your audience to ask questions. Do not rush through the conclusion. This is your final opportunity to tell the audience that you are an informed and confident speaker.

The conclusion can be very effective when it ends with a surprising statement. Such a statement can make your presentation unforgettable.

Transitions

Transitions are statements that connect different parts of your speech. Transitions look back at what you have stated and connect it with the next item you are discussing. It is especially important to have a transition between your introduction and the body of your speech, and the body of your speech and your conclusion. Adding transitions make your speech sound polished and prepared.

Use Visual Aids

Visual aids can be a stimulating part of your speech. They allow the speaker the freedom to use overheads, slides, charts, pictures, film, or anything else that helps your audience relate to the topic. Visual aids can be handwritten or drawn, or they can be computer generated. Usually, visual aids are prepared ahead of time. Occasionally, they can be drawn, on chart paper or a board, during the presentation. This is usually when input from the audience is required.

Visual aids are successful when they help keep the audience interested in the topic. You can use them to support any part of your speech. For example, visual aids can capture the audience's attention in the introduction, support your main idea(s) in the body, and leave the audience with a favorable impression during the conclusion.

If you decide to use visual aids, do not let them distract you. Prepare your visual aids ahead of time and practice with them. Do not display them until you are ready to use them. When you are finished with a visual aid, remove it or cover it so it does not distract your audience. Try to use only a few visual aids. Visual aids should add to your speech, not be the main substance of your speech.

When you give your speech, make sure you focus your attention on the audience. Do not talk to your visual aids, or turn your back to the audience. Make sure the point of the visual aid is clear to the audience. If you are giving out materials such as handouts, do not give them out during your speech. Distribute them before or after the speech.

Practice

You have probably heard the expression *Practice makes perfect*. This is definitely true in speech preparation. The more you practice, the more polished you will sound, and the less you will have to rely on your notes.

Practice in front of the mirror, your family, or one or more friends. If you can, do a dry run in the room in which you will deliver the actual speech. Use your visual aids to make sure they work. Perhaps you can even record yourself practicing and see how it sounds. You may hear some places where you are not communicating effectively. Each time you practice you will find ways to improve your speech.

> **Note**
>
> When you practice your speech, be sure to time how long it takes you. You might need to add more material, or cut some, depending on the length of time you have to present. And be sure to have your practice "audience" ask questions.

During the Presentation

If you have analyzed your audience, done your research, organized the information, written your outline or notes, and practiced your delivery, you are almost done. Of course, you still need to deliver the actual speech!

There are certain steps you must remember:

- **Capture the audience's attention.**
- **Establish eye contact.**
- **Articulate your words. Do not mumble.**
- **Stand up straight, do not shift your body and shuffle your feet. Do not put your hands in your pockets.**
- **Do not use phrases such as "okay," "you know," "um," "I mean," and "well."**
- **Establish an acceptable volume. Do not screech or use a monotone voice.**
- **Do not talk to your visual aids. Face the audience at all times.**

Key Note Term

articulate – to speak clearly and effectively

Presentation Guidelines

Here are some guidelines for ethical speech and delivery in communication:

- **Understand the power of the lectern. Being in front of people gives you a certain amount of credibility.**
- **Speak truthfully and be sure of your facts.**
- **Be willing to rock the boat. Stand for what you believe, but do not alarm your audience.**
- **Do not lie.**
- **Avoid excess and inappropriate emotional appeals.**
- **Use credible and current sources.**
- **Avoid ambiguity. Be concrete in your statements.**

Verbal Communication

Key Note Term

vocal qualities – the characteristics of someone's speaking voice

In verbal communication, it is up to you to use your voice and **vocal qualities** to drive home your ideas and information. You have control over rate, volume, pitch, pause, articulation, and pronunciation. Your voice can help you in the following ways:

Rate

The rate at which you speak is very important. It should not be too fast or too slow. Vary the rate at which you speak to add emphasis to your presentation.

Volume

Volume is another verbal technique that can add emphasis to your speech. Make sure you can be heard in the back of the room.

Pitch

Pitch is the use of notes (higher or lower) in a voice range. Speak in a range and **tone** that is comfortable for you and move up or down your scale for emphasis. **Modulation** in your voice will keep the audience listening.

Pause

Pause gives you time to take a breath and collect your thoughts. It also gives the audience time to absorb your points and ideas.

Articulation/Pronunciation

Articulation is the art of speaking intelligibly and making proper sounds. Listen to yourself and make your words distinct and understandable. The more clearly you articulate, the more confident you will sound.

Even if you articulate clearly, you can still mispronounce a word. Mispronunciation distracts listeners from focusing on the content of the speech.

Key Note Terms

volume – the amplitude or loudness of a sound

tone – a sound of distinct pitch, loudness, vibration, quality, or duration: the particular or relative pitch of a word or phrase

modulation – to change or vary the pitch, intensity, or tone

Conclusion

Speech is the most widely used medium of communication. The main purpose of any speech or presentation is to deliver clear and specific ideas to the listeners. Preparing and practicing your speech is the best way to have a positive speaking experience.

You will have many opportunities to give speeches during your life. The better prepared you are, the more comfortable you will feel, and the more successful you will be. Giving speeches is a science with definitions, terms, and processes. Study these and practice them, and you will soon be a competent speaker.

The following lesson looks at how you can become a better speaker. You will learn how to use your voice and your body language to your advantage when you're in front of an audience.

Lesson Review

1. Why is it important to analyze the purpose of your speech?

2. Define the term *demographics*.

3. Choose three ways to get your audience's attention and explain how these work.

4. During a dry-run practice, what can you do if your speech is too long or too short?

Lesson 3

Becoming a Better Speaker

Key Terms

constructive criticism
coping strategy

Chapter 6

What You Will Learn to Do

● Present a speech for a specific purpose

Linked Core Abilities

● Communicate using verbal, nonverbal, visual, and written techniques

Skills and Knowledge You Will Gain Along the Way

● Identify ways to improve speaking skills
● Develop a plan to improve speaking ability by avoiding common mistakes
● Develop coping strategies for stressful speaking situations
● Define the key words contained in this lesson

Introduction

Most individuals spend seven out of every ten waking hours communicating; three-fourths of this communication is through speech. The average person speaks some 34,020 words a day. That is equal to several books a week, more than 12 million words a year. With all that speaking, the likelihood of an individual being asked to give a public speech is high.

When you were younger, being the center of attention was probably fun. Now that you are older, you are probably much more concerned with your appearance and what people think of you. You may be much more nervous about public speaking. With the right knowledge and practice, you can minimize this nervousness.

Speeches are not made alone in a room. When you give a speech, there is always an audience. You and the audience have a two-way relationship. You give the speech to the audience. In turn, the audience gives you their attention and reaction, which is called feedback. The advantage of oral communication is that it is a face-to-face process of mutual give and take.

At some point, you will be asked to speak in front of your class, at a family gathering, at a club group, or some other public environment. Perhaps you have already experienced these situations. If so, you know that being nervous can be the hardest hurdle to overcome.

> ## Note
> "The human brain is a wonderful thing. It operates from the moment you are born until the first time you get up to make a speech." – Howard Goshorn

Coping with Nervousness

Recent studies show that speaking in front of a group is by far the greatest fear of most people. It ranks ahead of the fear of dying, riding in an airplane, or failure in other areas of one's personal life.

You have probably already had to talk in front of a group of people. You may have felt one or more of the following common symptoms of nervousness:

- **Shaking knees**
- **Dry mouth**
- **Quivering voice**
- **Stomach pains**
- **Loss of memory**

Coping Strategies

One of the most important concepts on which you should focus when you are nervous about speaking in public is that you are not alone. Whatever group you are facing, look around and realize that you have something in common with everyone there. Every person you see has been, or will be, in your situation at some time. In many cases, such as classroom speaking, you are all members of the same group.

> **Note**
>
> "There are two types of speakers: those that are nervous and those that are liars."
> – Mark Twain

Another **coping strategy** to deal with nervousness is to realize that you look more confident than you actually feel. Think about all the newscasters you have seen on television. Many of them have said that they feel stage fright, yet it is rarely noticeable. Look how many instructors must stand before a classroom and keep the attention of their students. For many individuals, being in the spotlight is their profession or career. For other individuals, presenting a speech is an occasional event, such as in speech classes. For everyone, feeling the symptoms of nervousness is ordinary, but it rarely shows.

Keep in mind that your listeners are there to hear what you have to say. Assume they are a friendly crowd. They are not "out to get you." They are waiting to learn some interesting information.

Another important point to remember is to concentrate on your speech content. Do not concentrate on how you are saying it. If you are discussing a subject in which you are interested, the audience will perceive this. If you are more focused on your gestures and your emphasis on certain words, both you and the audience will be distracted.

Be aware of your nervousness before you begin and deal with it. Take some deep breaths and perhaps even do some stretches. Give yourself some time to collect your thoughts.

The best way of all to overcome nervousness is to know that you are prepared. Proper preparation and rehearsal can help to reduce fear by 75 percent. Practice your speech in front of a mirror. Try to practice enough so that your use of notes will be minimal. If you know your subject very well, and are solidly prepared, you will balance your nervousness with a strong feeling of confidence. The audience will see your level of confidence. Whether speaking to a small group or several hundred people, most people feel nervous. Accomplished speakers like the late Dr. Martin Luther King Jr., as seen in Figure 6.3.1, overcome their nervousness by proper preparation and practice.

To review, the following are some strategies for coping with and overcoming nervousness:

Key Note Term

coping strategy – technique used for dealing with a difficult situation

Figure 6.3.1: Martin Luther King Jr. giving a speech to a large audience.

Courtesy of Miller Francis/Life Magazine © 1963, Time, Inc./Getty Images.

- **Look at the audience and know that they all feel nervous when giving a speech**
- **Remember that the audience is there to hear what you have to say**
- **Concentrate on the subject**
- **Keep in mind that your nervousness does not show**
- **Prepare, prepare, prepare**
- **Practice, practice, practice**
- **Breathe deeply**

Tips for Presentation

After you have gathered the necessary information for your speech, you are ready to present it. When you stand before your audience, remember the strategies for dealing with nervousness. Take a few seconds, breathe deeply, and begin your presentation. Proper breathing techniques can reduce fear by 15 percent.

Remember to be yourself. Think positively while you are in front of the audience. Know that the audience is there to learn and listen.

Establish eye contact with members of the audience. Some members of the audience may not return the eye contact. The solution is to establish eye contact with the individuals who are returning your interested look. Remember, this is the way to begin talking with your audience and not just to them. You are communicating with both your words and your eyes.

When you are giving a speech, you should not read from your notes. Only glance at your notes occasionally to be sure that you are following the outline and format of your speech.

Try to avoid a lot of body shifting. The movements and gestures you make can be very distracting to the audience. Shuffling your feet or scratching your ear will cause the audience to lose concentration.

Also avoid those interrupting pauses such as, "Uh," "You know," "I mean," "Well," and "So." Adding these phrases is a very common habit for speakers. It can also be a hard habit to break, and one that will take some effort and concentration.

Everyone makes mistakes when they are speaking. If you accidentally say a wrong word or you suddenly lose track of where you are, do not panic, but attempt to smile. Smiling through your fumbles tells the audience that although you made a slight mistake, you are still in control of the situation. Correct it if it is an important point. If it is not, disregard your blunder and continue with your presentation. Go a little more slowly and take your time, maintaining your concentration.

What is equally important in giving a speech is concluding it. When you are finished, do not rush back to your seat. Be professional and ask if anyone has any questions. Look around with composure and if there are no questions, politely say, "Thank you" and go sit down. If there are questions, answer them as well as you can. If the information has already been covered in the speech, do not give an extensive explanation. Be brief. Remember, you are the expert on the subject.

Basic Speech Structure

All types of speeches basically have a beginning, middle, and an end. They use a standard format for organization. You tell the audience what you are going to say, you say the main part of your speech, and then you tell the audience what you told them.

While preparing your speech, follow the six basic steps to effective speech writing.

1. **Analyze the purpose of the speech and the audience.**
2. **Conduct research and gather information.**
3. **Support your ideas.**
4. **Organize all the material.**
5. **Draft and edit the speech.**
6. **Practice and get feedback.**

Types of Speeches

There are several major categories of speeches:

- **Informative**
- **Persuasive**
- **Actuating**

- **Argumentative**
- **Entertaining**
- **Impromptu**

The purpose of each speech varies, depending on what you are attempting to accomplish as a speaker.

The Informative Speech

The speech to inform does exactly what it says; it informs or tells the audience about something. It delivers information so that the audience can grasp and remember important data about the subject. The goal is for the audience to accomplish understanding of the subject. An example is a presentation on how to gain rank in JROTC.

The Persuasive Speech

The speech to persuade attempts to change the audience's minds and/or behavior toward something. An example is persuading other students to become cadets.

The Actuating Speech

The speech to actuate is a motivating speech similar to the persuasive speech, but the difference is that the speech to actuate calls for immediate action. For example, suppose your school principal announces that the school team needs to be encouraged about a big upcoming game. The resulting action may be in the form of a school pep rally.

The Argumentative Speech

The argumentative speech must be structured as most other speeches. It must rely on logical appeals. This type of speech is also known as a kind of reasoned persuasion. Many debates in social and political fields are based on this kind of speech. Another common example is the closing argument an attorney makes during a courtroom trial.

The Entertaining Speech

The speech to entertain is used to relay a message in an entertaining manner. Humor plays an important part in this speech. For this reason, the entertaining speech can be difficult to present because humor is of a personal nature. If an entertaining speech is presented well, however, it can be very effective. When someone is being honored, very often another person will make a humorous speech about the honoree, perhaps telling a funny story about the person.

The Impromptu Speech

The impromptu speech is something a little different because most impromptu speeches are presented without elaborate preparation. The word *impromptu* means "to do something without preparation or advance thought—off-hand." Here are some tips, benefits, and techniques related to impromptu speaking.

Note

"It usually takes me more than three weeks to prepare a good impromptu speech."
– Mark Twain

Practicing

For beginners, impromptu speeches are necessary in helping the individual to gain self-confidence and the ability to "think on your feet." Impromptu speaking is an effective training device. The more practice you have in giving impromptu speeches, the better qualified you will be to deliver prepared talks. Suppose your instructor asks you to stand up and give an impromptu presentation on why you decided to join the Army JROTC. Pause for a few seconds before you begin and collect your thoughts.

Benefits

If you sound smooth and polished when giving an impromptu speech, both you and your audience will be impressed. By practicing, you will be capable of putting your thoughts into logical order. You will talk clearly and convincingly to your audience without any notes. Remember that your audience will not be expecting an elaborate speech, but they are there to hear you tell them something of interest

Techniques

The best way to be prepared for the "unprepared" is to stay up-to-date in your field of interest. Clipping and saving articles and reading newspapers or news magazines are ideal ways to do this. Communicating with people who share your area of interest also helps you broaden your understanding.

Imagine a storehouse in your mind where you will file these different bits of information. When you stand to speak impromptu, you will be prepared to pull out the needed data from your mental file. For example, reading up on Army JROTC and discussing your future in it with your instructor will add to your ability to discuss this subject with your audience.

One way to organize your thoughts for an impromptu speech is to use a "past, present, future" format. Speak first about the past of the subject, such as the history of the Army JROTC and what has been done to increase the number of cadets; then, speak about the organization and the role it plays today by considering what is happening now and what kind of learning takes place. Finally, contemplate the future. Consider what things may change, what improvements may be made, and where Army JROTC may be ten years from now.

Another procedure to use in your presentation is to support your ideas with examples or statistics. In addition, try to find experiences from your past that will add to your speech and make your points believable. For example, suppose your instructor asked you to make a speech about seatbelts and whether or not you favor a mandatory law for wearing them. You could talk about how you feel wearing seatbelts is a wonderful idea. But, most people already know that. You would not be telling them anything they did not already know. Instead, state why a mandatory law is a good idea by attaching it to something you have seen, heard, or read in the news. You could say something like the following: "I read in the newspaper the other day that a family of four survived a car accident because they were wearing seatbelts. The report said that if it were not for that, they would have been thrown violently from their car. More than likely, they all would have died."

Also, always be sure to take your time. Of course, some situations require a minimum or maximum time. Remember that you will need to collect your thoughts and to wait for the audience to quiet down. Most important, do not rush head-on into your presentation. Concentrate on what you are saying and what you want to say.

Finally, try to stay on the subject. Keep focusing on the topic in your mind so that your examples or stories are extended from that basis. Practicing at home will help you be prepared in the classroom or anywhere the impromptu situation arises. Pick any object in your room or any story in the newspaper. Contemplate what you could say about it. Speak about the item while timing yourself.

Tips for Impromptu Speaking

Remember the following techniques to improve impromptu speaking:

- **Stay knowledgeable on a variety of topics**
- **Try a format such as "past, present, future"**
- **Support your ideas with examples or statistics**
- **Add personal experiences**
- **Do not rush; collect your thoughts**
- **Concentrate on what you are saying**
- **Stay on subject**
- **Practice giving impromptu speeches**

Constructive Feedback

Key Note Term

constructive criticism – feedback that is helpful and productive

Sometimes you will be called on to provide feedback on another person's speech. It is important to realize that feedback need not always be negative or destructive. It should be **constructive criticism**.

The purpose of giving feedback is to improve someone's performance in some way. In its most effective form, it provides constructive advice, direction, and guidance in an effort to raise performance levels.

Effective feedback stresses both strengths and suggestions for improvement. In giving constructive feedback, you must be straightforward and honest; you must also respect the speaker's personal feelings. Feedback is pointless unless the speaker profits from it; however, praise just for the sake of praise has no value unless the only goal is to motivate or improve self-concept.

Effective feedback reflects your consideration of the speaker's need for self-esteem, recognition, confidence, and the approval of others. Ridicule, anger, or fun at the expense of the speaker have no place in constructive feedback.

To give constructive feedback, listen carefully to the speaker. Focus on the following:

- **The actual content of a speaker's effort**
- **What actually happened during the speech**
- **The observed factors that affected performance of the speech**

Conclusion

Speech is the most widely used medium of communication. The main purpose of any speech or presentation is to deliver clear and specific ideas to the listeners. Practicing the impromptu speech is an ideal way for many individuals to gain self-confidence and the ability to communicate "on their feet."

Although fear of speaking is common, studies show that one of the most admired qualities in others is their ability to speak in front of a group.

Similar to writing, speaking is a skill. After you grasp the basics, the rest is practice, polish, and style. You may be embarrassed by initial mistakes, but you will survive. Few of us will become great speakers, but all of us can become more effective speakers if we take the time to practice the basics.

This concludes Chapter 6, "Presenting Skills." In the next chapter, you will learn to manage conflict.

Lesson Review

1. Explain one of your coping strategies that work for you when you're nervous.
2. What is the basic speech structure?
3. List the six different types of speeches covered in this lesson.
4. Compare and contrast constructive and destructive criticism.

Managing Conflict

Lesson 1

Managing Anger (Emotional Intelligence Program)

Key Terms

anger management
aggression
assertion
change orientation
deference
empathy

What You Will Learn to Do

- Apply anger management strategies

Linked Core Abilities

- Take responsibility for your actions and choices
- Treat self and others with respect

Skills and Knowledge You Will Gain Along the Way

- Determine the common causes and effects of anger in interpersonal relationships
- Select strategies for controlling anger
- Explain the role of empathy in reducing anger
- Define the key words contained in this lesson

Introduction

Key Note Term

aggression –
a tendency to be hostile
or quarrelsome

At some point in life, every human being feels angry. Anger is usually a healthy and normal emotion, but for some it can get out of control and become destructive. Uncontrolled anger can lead to failed relationships, loss of employment, and physical illness. It can also cause hurt feelings, frustration, annoyance, harassment, **aggression**, disappointment, and threats. This lesson is designed to help you understand the nature of anger, and how to manage it.

Understanding What Causes Anger

According to Dr. Charles Spielberger, anger can be explained and defined as "an emotional state that varies in intensity from mild irritation to intense fury and rage." Similar to other emotions, anger is usually accompanied by physiological and biological changes; when you get angry, your heart rate and blood pressure go up, as do the levels of your energy hormones, adrenaline, and noradrenaline. Other physical symptoms of anger can include the following:

- **Headaches**
- **Gastrointestinal disorders**
- **Respiratory disorders**
- **Skin disorders**
- **Disabilities of the nervous system**
- **Circulatory disorders**
- **Aggravation of existing physical symptoms**
- **Emotional disturbances**
- **Suicide**

Note

Dr. Charles Spielberger is a leading researcher in the link between anger and heart failure. He is a recipient of the APA Award for Distinguished Professional Contributions to Applied Psychology as a Professional Practice. Dr. Spielberger is currently on staff at the University of South Florida.

Anger can be triggered by external or internal events. For example, you could get angry at a fellow student or supervisor, or at being in the slow line at the grocery store. Memories of traumatic or enraging events can also trigger angry feelings.

Expressing Anger

For many, the natural way to express anger is to respond in an aggressive manner. Anger is an adaptive response to threats that can inspire powerful, often aggressive, feelings and behaviors. These feelings allow humans to fight and to defend themselves when attacked. When faced with survival, a certain amount of anger is healthy and necessary; however, lashing out at nearly every person or event that causes you to feel angry isn't appropriate or productive.

The three main approaches to managing anger are expressing, suppressing, and calming. Expressing your angry feelings in an assertive—not aggressive—manner is the healthiest way. To do this, you have to learn how to make clear what your needs are and how to get them met without emotionally or physically hurting others. Being assertive doesn't mean being pushy or demanding; it means being respectful of yourself and others.

Unexpressed anger can create other serious problems. It can lead to pathological expressions of anger, such as passive-aggressive behavior (getting back at people indirectly without telling them why, rather than confronting them) or a personality that seems cynical and hostile. People who are constantly putting others down, criticizing everything, and making cynical comments haven't learned how to constructively express their anger.

Anger can be suppressed and then converted or redirected. This happens when you hold in your anger, stop thinking about it, and focus on something positive. The aim is to inhibit or suppress your anger and convert it into more constructive behavior. The danger in this type of response is that if it isn't allowed outward expression, your anger can turn inward—on yourself. Anger turned inward may cause hypertension, high blood pressure, ulcers, or depression.

Another method for controlling anger is to calm yourself down inside. This means not just controlling your outward behavior but also controlling your internal responses, such as taking steps to lower your heart rate, calming yourself down, and letting your feelings subside.

Anger Management

Anger management reduces your emotional feelings and the physiological changes that anger causes. You can't get rid of, or avoid, the events, objects, or people that make you angry, nor can you change them; however, you can learn to control your reactions to them.

Anger is normal, and a universal emotion that everyone experiences from time to time. When you are angry, you experience strong feelings that can propel you into inappropriate or destructive behavior. Anger, if left unchecked, can easily spiral out of control and lead to violence. The people in Figure 7.1.1 can easily become destructive if their emotions are not managed.

Key Note Term

anger management – learning to control and manage the emotion of anger; managing your anger so it comes out in a healthy and constructive way

Your response to anger, however, is completely within your control. Mastering the techniques of anger management will help you keep calm in a tense situation and avoid violence.

Anger management skills must be practiced throughout your lifetime. After you have gained control over your anger, you can work toward resolving conflict in a nonviolent way.

What Makes People Angry

You probably have met someone who is more "hotheaded" than others. This person gets angry more easily than others, and is more intense than the average person. There are also those who don't show their anger by raising their voice but are irritable and grumpy. Easily angered people don't always yell and throw things; sometimes they withdraw socially, sulk, or get physically ill. People who are easily angered can't take things in stride, and they're particularly infuriated if the situation seems somehow unjust, such as being corrected for a minor mistake.

So why do some people get angrier than others? Genetics might have something to do with it. There is evidence that some children are born irritable, touchy, and easily angered, and that these signs are present from a very early age. Another reason may be sociocultural, where anger is looked at as a negative emotion. Those who aren't taught that it's perfectly normal to express anger in a healthy way don't learn how to handle it or channel it constructively.

To deal with and manage anger, it's best to find out what triggers angry feelings and then to develop strategies to keep those triggers from tipping you over the edge.

Strategies for Managing Anger

There are several ways that you can manage your anger and express it in a positive and constructive manner and end up with the results you want. These strategies include learning to relax, changing the way you think, solving problems, and learning to communicate better. The following sections cover these strategies.

Figure 7.1.1: Anger can be either a constructive or destructive emotion.

Courtesy of Donna Binder/Impact Visuals.

Chapter 7   Managing Conflict

Using Relaxation to Manage Anger

Relaxation techniques can include deep breathing and relaxation imagery. It can help to breathe deeply from your diaphragm while slowly repeating to yourself a calming word or phrase such as "easy does it" or "relax." You can also use relaxation imagery, such as using a soothing experience from your memory to calm yourself down. Try to imagine a calming picture in your head—maybe a day at a beach or listening to your favorite music—to help get your emotions under control. Learn to use these techniques whenever you're in a stressful or tense situation.

Changing Your Thinking

As a general rule, angry people swear or speak in highly colorful terms that reflect their inner thoughts. When you're angry, your thinking can become exaggerated and dramatic, and you may tend to see situations as absolutes. Try to avoid using words such as *never* or *always* when talking about yourself, someone else, or a specific situation. Instead of thinking that the situation is terrible and your life is ruined, try telling yourself that the situation is annoying, but it's not the end of the world. Keep in the front of your mind that getting angry is not going to fix anything, that it won't make you feel better, and that it may actually make you feel worse.

Change Orientation

Change orientation is a reflection of your level of satisfaction with your current behavior. Your view of how satisfied you are with yourself and the world around you is an important starting point for planning personal change. To engage in personal change and get your anger under control, you need to understand personal change, feel good about making person changes, and choose healthy ways to make those changes. Some areas of self-reflection include the following:

- **How you feel about yourself as a person**
- **How you relate to your family**
- **If you are satisfied with the way you manage your time**
- **If you are satisfied with your leadership ability**
- **If you are satisfied with the way you handle personal relationships**
- **If you are satisfied with the way you relate to people**

Change orientation can be a tremendous tool in converting powerful emotions into positive change.

> **Key Note Term**
>
> **change orientation** – a reflection of satisfaction or dissatisfaction with current emotional skills and abilities

Solving Problems

Sometimes anger and frustration are caused by real problems; not all anger is misplaced, and is often a healthy, natural response to difficulties. Many people believe that every problem has a solution, and it can add to your frustration to find out that this isn't always true. In situations that seem unsolvable, the best attitude to bring is not to focus on finding the solution but rather on how you handle and face the problem.

Make a plan and check your progress along the way. Resolve to give it your best but do not punish yourself if an answer doesn't come right away. If you can approach a problem with your best intentions and efforts and make a serious attempt to face it head-on, you will be less likely to lose patience and fall into all-or-nothing thinking, even if the problem does not get solved right away.

Learning to Communicate and Listen Better

Key Note Term

deference – the degree to which a person uses a communication style or pattern that is indirect and effectual for accurate expression of thought and feeling

Deference is the degree to which an individual employs a communication style or pattern that is indirect, self-inhibiting, self-denying, and ineffectual for the accurate expression of thoughts, feelings, or behaviors. It is reflected by communications that are indirect or that convey unclear or mixed messages. Deference can result in effective communications that negatively affect relationships.

Deferential behavior may actually make people angry at times because deference frequently masks suppressed anger or rage. People who are aware of their emotional states recognize anger and use positive self-assertion to negotiate the outcomes they seek. Sometimes deference is just good common sense, such as when you defer to an angry cop. But oftentimes deference takes the place of healthy self-assertion and ends up triggering more inner anger.

Key Note Term

assertion – the ability to clearly communicate personal thoughts and feelings

When communicating anger, **assertion** is key. Assertive communication is a positive way of talking with people and clearly expressing thoughts and feelings in a way that promotes understanding, caring, and respect. A person who communicates assertively respects the right of others. It enables a person to communicate effectively, even during difficult situations that involve strong and intense emotions. Do you feel that assertive communications might resolve the conflict exhibited in Figure 7.1.2?

When you're confronted with an angry person in a heated discussion, slow down and think through your responses. Don't say the first thing that comes into your

Figure 7.1.2: Fighting is not a constructive way to deal with anger. What other methods of handing anger work for you?

Courtesy of Barbara Burnes/Photo Researchers.

head; rather, think carefully about what you want to say. At the same time, listen carefully to what the other person is saying and take your time before answering.

Phrase your responses in as much of a calm and nonthreatening manner as possible. Try to keep from becoming defensive and saying something that will cause the situation to escalate. Many times, if you show **empathy** toward an angry person's concern, that is listening carefully and sharing in that person's feelings, you can help to calm that person and get a volatile situation under control. By remaining calm and staying focused on what you're hearing as well as how you want to respond, you can manage an angry situation much better than just flying off the handle. The following is a quick reference for anger management techniques.

Key Note Term

empathy – the ability to accurately understand and constructively respond to the expressed feelings, thought, behaviors, and needs of others

- **Take time to calm down. You need to maintain emotional control to communicate in a calm, even tone. Yelling and insulting will only serve to worsen the situation.**

- **Identify the source of your anger and know what triggers it.**

- **Use words to describe your needs and explain your feelings.**

- **Turn your anger into energy. You could exercise vigorously, write down what is making you angry, daydream about things that make you happy, do something useful for yourself or for someone else, pound or yell into a pillow, or blow up a balloon. Keep a list of the activities that you can do at different times so you do not have to think about what to do when you become angry.**

- **Share your angry feelings with a friend, teacher, parent, coach, counselor, or clergy. This always proves to be an excellent antidote.**

Getting Help

Did you get a payoff the last time you got angry? Did other people give you what you wanted because you were louder, tougher, stronger, and could intimidate them? This question reflects your character and self esteem: "I feel good about making others give in to me by becoming angry."

If you feel that your anger is out of control or you can't figure out where your anger comes from, you might consider counseling to learn how to handle it better. A psychologist or other licensed mental health professional can work with you to develop a range of techniques for changing your thinking and your behavior. Tell a counselor, social worker, or therapist that you have problems with anger; you want to work on getting this emotion under control, and ask about an approach to anger management.

Conclusion

Anger is a normal and healthy emotion, and it needs to be expressed. Learning how to constructively express anger and how to manage it is a skill that will benefit you throughout your entire life. You can use a variety of techniques covered in this lesson, from relaxation to better communications; but if these methods don't work for you, counseling is a good and healthy option.

In the following lesson, you will learn how to incorporate the skills you learned here when dealing with diversity and resolving conflict.

Lesson Review

1. **What physical and biological changes occur in the body when you get angry?**

2. **Choose a relaxation technique and explain it.**

3. **How can thinking about what you want to say in a heated discussion help to keep the situation under control?**

4. **Have you ever been in a situation that has gotten out of hand due to anger? What did you do? How did you handle this?**

Lesson 2

Conflict Resolution and Diversity (Hate Comes Home)

Key Terms

anti-Semitism
bigotry
hate-related words
prejudice
racism
scapegoating
stereotype

What You Will Learn to Do

- Develop strategies for resolving conflict in a diverse, multicultural setting

Linked Core Abilities

- Do your share as a good citizen in your school, community, country, and the world
- Treat self and others with respect

Skills and Knowledge You Will Gain Along the Way

- Assess how age, race, ethnicity, gender, and other aspects of diversity impact perceptions of self and others
- Compare two or more points of view and the reasons behind them
- Clarify particular points of disagreement and agreement
- Identify appropriate intervention guidelines
- Identify techniques for reducing conflict within a diverse population
- Define the key words contained in this lesson

Chapter 7

Introduction

Although acts of bias such as stereotyping, jokes, labeling, and racist comments may seem harmless, they form the foundation for feelings of hate that ultimately can lead to prejudice, discrimination, violence, and genocide. History provides examples of the ways in which **stereotyping**, **scapegoating**, **bigotry**, **anti-Semitism**, dehumanization, and discrimination can escalate to murders. This section explores how acts of bias can lead to conflict, and how confronting bias can help to avoid violence.

> ## Note
>
> To learn more about scapegoating and anti-Semitism, check out the Anti-Defamation League's Web site at www.adl.org. The ADL monitors hate groups around the world and is a good resource for Holocaust information.

Hate-Motivated Behavior

Hate-motivated behavior is an act or attempted act intended to cause emotional suffering, physical injury, or property damage through intimidation, harassment, bigoted slurs or epithets, force or threat of force, or vandalism motivated in part or in whole by hostility toward the victim's real or perceived ethnicity, national origin, immigrant status, religious belief, gender, sexual orientation, age, disability, political affiliation, or race. Or, simply defined, it is an expression of hostility against a person or property because of the victim's race, religion, disability, gender, ethnicity or sexual orientation that does not meet the necessary elements required to prove a crime. This definition provides a common definition that enables schools and law enforcement agencies to develop a reporting system to document these behaviors. These acts may not be considered crimes or hate crimes but should be reported and considered as serious as a hate crime because they can be as emotionally damaging as any hate crime and can have long-lasting effects on students and teachers.

Students must take responsibility for their own behavior and meet the standards of conduct established by their schools and society in general. Bullying is perhaps the most underrated problem in our schools and can be motivated by prejudice, intolerance, or hate. Bullying can include name-calling, teasing, harassment, extortion of lunch money, harsh pranks, or jostling in a hallway. Victims often are left with emotional scars long after the incident. Reducing hate-motivated behavior requires selfless acts by teachers a well as students.

The *Hate Comes Home* program is a virtual-experience interactive CD-ROM that allows students to become the lead character in a plot immersed in everyday occurrences of bias and hate-motivated behavior. It includes a discussion of the distinction between hate crimes and hate bias incidents as well as a Culture Tree graphic exercise. By participating in the Culture Tree exercise, students will spend time identifying how one's own personal behavior reinforces or combats prejudice. Students will also discuss the many roles that people can find themselves faced

Key Note Terms

stereotype – a formulized conception, notion, or attitude

scapegoating – the action of blaming an individual or group for something when, in reality, there is no one person or group responsible for the problem; it targets another person or group as responsible for problems in society because of that person's group identity

bigotry – bitter, intolerant, and prejudice

anti-Semitism – feeling or showing hostility towards Jews; persecuting Jews

with when a bias act occurs, for example, sometimes they perpetuate prejudice, sometimes they observe others acting in a prejudiced manner, and sometimes they are the victims of prejudice. Only then can students begin to develop skills to confront prejudice and discrimination in their schools and communities.

Hate Crimes Statistics

Hate crimes are crimes committed against individuals or groups or property based on the real or perceived characteristics of the victims. These crimes have been plaguing our country for centuries, tearing at the very foundation of our country and destroying our neighborhoods and communities. Hate crime statutes vary from state to state and may cover bias-motivated crimes based on religion, gender, sexual orientation, ability, national origin, or ethnicity of the victims. In 2002, 7,462 hate crimes, involving 9,222 victims, were reported to the FBI. Schools increasingly have a legal, as well as moral, responsibility for combating hate crimes because so many of the perpetrators and victims are of school age. According to a 2001 Bureau of Justice Statistics Special Report,

- **33 percent of all known hate crime offenders were under 18; another 29 percent of all hate crime offenders were 18 to 24**
- **30 percent of all victims of bias-motivated aggravated assaults and 34 percent of the victims of simple assault were under 18.**

Hate behavior generates humiliation, shock, outrage, fear, and anxiety in the victim and in the victim's community. When such an incident occurs at school, the entire school community experiences a loss of safety. Feelings of vulnerability, insecurity, and alienation become common. Ultimately, these feelings produce a negative school climate where not only is school safety questioned, but also learning is disrupted and instruction is preoccupied with classroom management. According to the National Center for Education Statistics,

- **In 2001, 12 percent of students ages 12 through 18 reported that someone at school had used hate-related words against them in the previous six months**
- **In both 1999 and 2001, 36 percent of students saw hate-related graffiti at school**

Why Diversity Matters

Diversity matters to every living human being. When a group or segment of the population is excluded or oppressed, everyone is denied. For communities to not only survive, but also to thrive, each person needs to be aware and sensitive to *all* the members of the community. When all segments of a community are respected and utilized, it benefits everyone involved. How many different cultures are represented in Figure 7.2.1?

America is the most diverse nation in the world. Our ethnicity, religion, life experiences, and so on make each of us unique. It is beneficial to everyone to learn to accept what is different and respect it.

Key Note Term

hate-related words – derogatory words having to do with race, religion, ethnicity, ability, gender, or sexual orientation

Figure 7.2.1: Diversity is an important part of our society.
Courtesy of C. J. Allen/Stock Boston.

Hate, Stereotypes, and Racism

Key Note Terms

prejudice – a judgment or opinion formed without knowing the facts; hatred or fear of other races, nations, creeds, and so on

racism – the practice of racial discrimination, persecution, or segregation based on race

You might have seen the bumper sticker, "Hate Isn't a Family Value." No one is born with hatred or **prejudice** toward another person; hate, stereotypes, and **racism** are learned behaviors and feelings. Sometimes human beings have negative feelings toward another simply because they are different. Sometimes cultural dress, actions, and attitudes are misunderstood and misinterpreted. Other times, a news story about a single individual might sway your opinion about an entire group of people. Was the young man in Figure 7.2.2 born with hatred toward other races?

Knowledge and information are the most powerful tools you have at your disposal to combat hate, stereotypes, and racism. How can you learn about other cultures and combat racism and stereotyping?

● **Know your roots and share your pride in your heritage with others.**

● **Celebrate holidays with extended family and friends. Use such opportunities to encourage storytelling and share personal experiences across generations.**

Figure 7.2.2: Prejudice is a learned behavior.
Courtesy of Paul Brou/Picture Group, Inc.

- Invite friends from backgrounds different from your own to experience the joy of your traditions and customs.

- Be mindful of your language; avoid stereotypical remarks and challenge those made by others.

- Speak out against jokes and slurs that target people or groups. Silence sends a message that you are in agreement. It is not enough to refuse to laugh.

- Be knowledgeable; provide as much accurate information as possible to reject harmful myths and stereotypes. Discuss the impact of prejudicial attitudes and behavior.

- Read books that promote understanding of different cultures as well as those that are written by authors of diverse backgrounds.

Why Conflict Occurs

Conflict can arise for the smallest and most insignificant of reasons. One person makes an off-handed racial slur or a disparaging comment about someone's cultural background. Heated words are exchanged, tempers flare, conflicts escalate, and, all too often, violence results. And when conflict arises, many teens feel they have no choice but to fight. Although conflicts and disagreements are an inevitable part of life, they do not have to lead to violence.

When you try to resolve conflicts and disagreements, you find that conflicts don't have to be avoided, nor do they necessarily lead to violence. Conflict can actually be a positive force in your life; it can provide you with an opportunity to take a close look at yourself, your attitudes, and your beliefs. If resolved positively, conflicts can actually help strengthen relationships and build greater understanding of yourself and those around you.

Conflict Management and Resolution

Conflicts can be managed and resolved through several different options. Sometimes it's best to combine methods to get the problem solved and avoid the conflict from escalating to a violent end. The following sections discuss some conflict management and resolution solutions available to you.

Win-Win Approach

The win-win approach is about changing the conflict from adversarial attack and defense, to cooperation. It is a powerful shift of attitude that alters the whole course of communication (see Figure 7.2.3).

While people battle over opposing solutions (such as "Do it my way!" "No, that's no good! Do it my way!"), the conflict is a power struggle. What you need to do is change the agenda in the conversation. The win-win approach says "I want to win and I want you to win, too." A win-win approach rests on the following strategies:

Figure 7.2.3: By working together and learning about different groups, tolerance can replace prejudice.
Courtesy of David Young-Wolff/PhotoEdit.

- **Going back to underlying needs: Why did the conflict start and what will the outcome resolve?**
- **Recognition of individual differences**
- **Openness to adapting one's position in the light of shared information and attitudes**
- **Attacking the problem, not the people**

Compromise is usually the key to the win-win approach. Even if the conflicting parties simply agree to disagree, everyone wins.

Creative Response Approach

The creative response to conflict is about turning problems into possibilities. It is about consciously choosing to see what can be done rather than staying with a bad situation. It is affirming that you will choose to extract the best from the situation.

You can take a conflict and turn it into an opportunity for discussion and healthy debate.

Appropriate Assertiveness Approach

The essence of appropriate assertiveness is being able to state your case without arousing the defenses of the other person. The secret of success lies in saying how it is for you rather than what the other person should or shouldn't do. Attaching the statement "The way I see it . . . ," can help tremendously. A skilled "I" statement goes even further. When you want to state your point of view helpfully, the "I" statement formula can be useful. An "I" statement says how it is on my side, how I see it.

Use an "I" statement when you need to let the other person know you are feeling strongly about an issue. Others often underestimate how hurt, angry, or put out you are, so it's useful to say exactly what's going on for you. What you can realistically expect is that an appropriate "I" statement made with good intent

- **Is highly unlikely to do any harm**
- **Is a step in the right direction**
- **Is sure to change the current situation in some way**
- **Can/will open up to possibilities you may not yet see**

Empathy

Empathy is about rapport and openness between people. When it is absent, people are less likely to consider your needs and feelings. The best way to build empathy is to help the other person feel that they are understood. That means being an active listener.

There are specific listening activities relevant to different situations: information, affirmation, or inflammation. Use active listening when offering advice won't help. To use active listening:

- **Don't ignore or deny the other party's feelings.**
- **Read the nonverbal as well as the verbal communication to assess feelings.**
- **Check back with the other party about their feelings as well as the content even though they may only be telling you about the content. If you're not sure how they feel, ask them "How do you feel about that?" or "How did that affect you?"**
- **Reflect back what you hear them saying so they can hear it themselves.**
- **Reflect back to them what you hear them saying so they know you understand.**
- **If you get it wrong, ask an open question and try again, such as "How do you see the situation?"**

When you empathize, you let the other person know that you're trying to relate and understand how they feel and what brought them to the point of conflict.

Manage Emotions

People's behavior occurs for a purpose. They might be looking for ways to belong, feel significant, or self-protect. When people perceive a threat to their self-esteem, a downward spiral can begin. People can be led into obstructive behaviors in the faulty belief that this will gain them a place of belonging and significance. How you respond to their difficult behaviors can determine how entrenched these become.

The secret is to break out of the spiral by supporting their real needs without supporting their destructive faulty beliefs and alienating patterns of reaction. Convince them that you respect their needs. Build trusting relationships and support their need for justice and fairness.

Conclusion

The world is made up of many different kinds of people from different cultures, races, ethnic backgrounds, creeds, and religions. As the world gets smaller and smaller, the ability to resolve conflict in a multicultural society becomes more and more important. The first step to conflict resolution is to understand different cultures and backgrounds and get rid of racial bias and prejudice. From there, conflict resolution can happen through several different methods.

In the following lesson, you will learn about mediation and the skills it takes to mediate a situation.

Lesson Review

1. **Explain why diversity matters to every human being.**

2. **Define the term *anti-Semitism*.**

3. **Choose a conflict management and resolution method and discuss it. Have you ever used this method to resolve a conflict?**

4. **What is a hate crime? Why do hate crimes occur?**

Lesson 3

Conflict Mediation

Key Terms

anger management
arbitration
empathy
mediation
violence prevention

What You Will Learn to Do

- Apply mediation techniques to resolve conflict

Linked Core Abilities

- Do your share as a good citizen in your school, community, country, and the world
- Treat self and others with respect

Skills and Knowledge You Will Gain Along the Way

- Differentiate between arbitration and mediation
- Compare mediation techniques
- Identify techniques for reducing conflict
- Define the key words contained in this lesson

Introduction

The National Center for Education Statistics reports that approximately 37 percent of high school students have been in a physical fight within the last year and 18 percent of high school students have carried a weapon at least once within the past 30 days. These alarming statistics illustrate the fact that the instances of violence have become all too common in our schools. Safety has become a primary concern in what is supposed to be a nonthreatening learning environment.

One of the best ways to handle violence in schools and prevent its spread throughout the community is to defuse disputes and resolve any conflict before it turns violent.

In this lesson, you learn how you can take personal responsibility for **violence prevention** by acting as a peer mediator to help others resolve conflicts in a nonviolent manner.

Mediation

What would happen if you tried to resolve a conflict yet could not brainstorm any solutions that were acceptable to both parties? Or if the emotions became overheated to the point where you could no longer continue negotiations? If you fail to resolve a conflict through negotiation, the conflict may need to be resolved through **mediation** or **arbitration**. Mediation, from the Latin word meaning *middle*, literally means putting another person in the middle of the dispute. The mediator is an independent third party that acts as a facilitator, and can be another student. In fact, studies show that peer mediation programs, where students are trained to resolve disputes of other students, have proven to be relatively successful. The goal of mediation is to help the disputing parties find and agree on a win-win solution in which each party's needs are met.

Mediation is usually contrasted with arbitration, which should be used as a last resort. Arbitration is the submission of a conflict to a disinterested third party, an adult such as a teacher or principal, who makes a final and binding judgment to decide who is right. Typically, arbitration leaves at least one person with anger about the decision and resentment toward the arbitrator. However, both people involved in the conflict should abide by the decision made by the arbitrator, and agree to let go of the conflict with no hard feelings toward either person.

Role of a Mediator

A mediator facilitates a discussion between the parties with the dispute by asking open-ended questions that encourage a discussion of solutions as seen in Figure 7.3.1. Unlike an arbitrator, mediators will not issue orders, find fault, investigate, impose a solution, or make decisions for the parties. Mediators try to help the people with a dispute reach their own agreement and achieve practical, sustainable resolutions. A mediator, however, cannot enforce agreements after they have been reached. It is up to all parties to enforce and implement their own agreements.

Key Note Terms

violence prevention – discouraging or hindering acts of physical force that cause injury or abuse

mediation – working with opposing sides to resolve a dispute or bring about a settlement; the process in which conflicts are resolved with the help of a neutral third party

arbitration – to submit for decision to a third party who is chosen to settle differences in a controversy

As a rule, mediators should

- **Be honest**
- **Remain objective**
- **Act in good faith**
- **Show empathy but avoid becoming emotional**
- **Use good communication skills**
- **Listen effectively**
- **Summarize accurately**
- **Think critically**

As with any conflict situation, mediators should not get involved in a heated argument that has the potential for turning violent at any moment.

Steps to Mediating a Conflict

Have you ever helped two friends reach an agreement or helped to settle an argument between siblings? If so, you have mediated a conflict. Mediation may take place with two students or a larger group as depicted in Figure 7.3.2. Mediation is a simple, straightforward process. The procedure for a successful mediation includes the following steps:

1. **Introductions.**
   - **Explain the mediator's role**
   - **Mediator emphasizes neutrality**
   - **Establish the ground rules such as confidentiality, respect, no name-calling or vulgar language, and no interruptions**
   - **Explain the steps of a mediation**
   - **Ask questions**

> **Key Note Term**
>
> **empathy** – the capacity to experience the feelings of another as one's own

Figure 7.3.2: Peer mediation has proven to be successful in many schools around the country.
Courtesy of Bob Daemmrich.

2. **Tell the story.**

   - **Both parties tell their side of the story to the mediator**

   - **Mediator summarizes each party's point of view including facts and feelings**

   - **Mediator makes sure that each party understands the conflict**

3. **Explore possible solutions.**

   - **Ask both parties how they can solve the problem**

   - **Write down all solutions**

   - **Check off only those solutions to which both parties can agree**

4. **Don't give up.**

   - **Keep trying until you can reach an agreement; you may have to trade something that one side wants for something that the other side has**

   - **Ask the parties to write down the agreement in their own words**

   - **Ask all parties to sign the agreement**

Peer Mediation in Schools

Peer mediation has proven to be an effective tool for conflict resolution in schools. The Troy Police Department of Troy, Michigan, working with the local schools and the local Boys and Girls Club created a peer mediation program for schools. This new program provides peer mediation at any time of the year within the city limits. Mediation referrals are passed along by teachers or other individuals to the community services officer who contacts the disputants' parents and with their approval brings the two sides together with two peer mediators and an adult monitor. The program uses volunteer student mediators. Schools nationwide are adopting peer mediation programs; 8,500 schools currently use youth-led mediation to resolve conflict, according to the National Institute for Dispute Resolution. One seventeen-year-old volunteer sees his role as getting the disputants to understand their feelings and figure out their own solution. The job of the mediator is to get the parties to understand how each feels; it is not to suggest a solution but to ask questions that lead them to their own solution. A typical mediation is an hour-long session at the Boys and Girls Club and includes the disputants, two volunteer teen mediators, and an adult monitor. The mediation process builds confidence for everyone present. Another example of a success story is the problem-solving approach taken at West Mecklenburg High School in Charlotte, North Carolina. In this program students are asked to identify and help solve problems such as discipline, parking in the school's lot, and smoking in the bathrooms. Student suspensions due to fighting and disruptive behavior decreased by 59 percent.

Steps in the Arbitration Process

Arbitration is usually the last effort to resolve a conflict before going to court. It is an alternative to the court system. It is used in various businesses and between buyers and sellers of various products. For example, the state of California has a binding arbitration process for car buyers who are dissatisfied with the car they purchased. New York State has a Lemon Law Arbitration in which arbitration services are provided for vehicle owners having disputes with the manufacturer or dealers of a new, used, or leased vehicle. The parties involved in the conflict must accept the appointment of an arbitrator and must accept the arbitrator's decision in order for arbitration to work. A preliminary meeting is held to set the rules for the process; each party submits statements, claims, and information to the arbitrator; the arbitrator reviews all the information provided; a hearing is held where all pertinent information, statements, witnesses, and claims are presented from both sides; and finally the arbitrator makes a binding decision. The disadvantage of arbitration is that one or both parties in the process may disagree with the decision and may come away from the process with anger and resentment.

Role of a Bystander

Even if you are not personally involved in a conflict as one of the disputing parties or the mediator, you have a responsibility to do your part to prevent violence by

- **Refusing to spread rumors**
- **Refusing to relay threats or insults to others**
- **Staying away from potential fight scenes**
- **Showing respect for people who use good judgment in ignoring insults or other trivial forms of conflict**

Appeal to your peers to help control a situation and reduce the potential for violence.

Adapted from "Juvenile Peer Mediation Expands Beyond Schools" and "School Violence Reduced When Students Participate in Problem Solving," articles at the International Academy of Mediators Web site www.mediate.com, December, 2004.

Conclusion

Key Note Term

anger management – employing steps to control feelings of anger or rage

We all have a responsibility to try to resolve conflicts in a productive and non-violent way. When a conflict occurs, try first to negotiate a resolution. If that fails, involve a classmate or teacher to mediate the conflict. By negotiating and/or mediating conflicts, you are developing valuable **anger management**, problem-solving, and conflict-resolution skills that you will use throughout your life.

The next lesson covers violence prevention. You will learn what to look for in a potentially violent situation and what steps you can take to stop violence before it happens.

Chapter 7

Lesson Review

Lesson Review

1. What is the role of a mediator?
2. What are the steps to mediating a conflict?
3. Explain why it's important to hear both sides of a story.
4. Define the term *arbitration*.

Violence Prevention (Violence Prevention Profiler)

Key Terms

decision-point
prevention
violence

What You Will Learn to Do

- Apply strategies to prevent violence

Linked Core Abilities

- Do your share as a good citizen in your school, community, country, and the world
- Treat self and others with respect

Skills and Knowledge You Will Gain Along the Way

- Differentiate between violent and non-violent responses to anger
- Compare violence prevention techniques
- Select strategies for preventing violence
- Define the key words contained in this lesson

Introduction

The National Center for Education Statistics reports that approximately 37 percent of high school students have been in a physical fight within the year, and 18 percent of high school students have carried a weapon at least once within the past 30 days. These alarming statistics illustrate the fact that the instances of violence have become all too common in our schools. Safety has become a primary concern in what is supposed to be a nonthreatening learning environment.

In earlier lessons you learned processes for effectively managing conflict and negotiating a fair solution; however, what if the negotiation is unsuccessful, and you cannot reach an agreement to settle the conflict? What other steps can you take to prevent a conflict from escalating to violence? In this lesson you will learn how you can take personal responsibility for violence **prevention**.

Key Note Term

prevention – to stop or prevent an event or act from occurring

Statistics Don't Lie

Youth violence is a widespread problem in the United States. Consider the following statistics:

- About 9 percent of murders in the United States were committed by youth under 18 in 2000. An estimated 1,561 youth under the age of 18 were arrested for homicide in 2000

- Youth under 18 accounted for about 15 percent of violent crime arrests in 2001

- One national survey found that for every teen arrested, at least 10 were engaged in violence that could have seriously injured or killed another person

- About one in three high school students say they have been in a physical fight in the past year, and about one in eight of those students required medical attention for their injuries

- More than 1 in 6 students in grades 6 to 10 say they are bullied sometimes, and more than 1 in 12 say they are bullied once a week or more

- Suicide is the third leading cause of death among teenagers. In 2000, 1,921 young people ages 10 to 19 died by suicide in the United States

- About 1 in 11 high school students say they have made a suicide attempt in the past year

Do all you can to help prevent violence!

What You Can Do to Prevent Violence

Somewhere everyday, someone is dealing with violent behavior. Whether it's a child being bullied by a classmate or a shop owner being robbed at gunpoint, violent acts occur everywhere. Although **violence** has become more common in recent years, it is still an unacceptable way to resolve issues and problems.

Teenagers (see Figure 7.4.1) and young adults can play an important role in reducing and preventing violence. Consider some of the following ideas.

Key Note Term

violence – physical force used to do injury; any infringement of rights

Figure 7.4.1: When confronting a person about a problem, what steps can you take to negotiate a peaceful solution?
Courtesy of Bob Daemmrich/Stock Boston.

Start with Yourself

Try to broaden your social circle to include others who are different from you. Be mindful of your language and avoid stereotypical remarks and challenge those made by others. Speak out against jokes and slurs that target people or groups. Silence sends a message that you are in agreement. It is not enough to refuse to laugh.

Make a commitment not to contribute to violence in any way. Do not bully, tease, or spread negative gossip about others. Respect others and value differences. Try to broaden your social circle to include others who are different from you.

Understand Diverse Cultures, Traditions, and Lifestyles

Learning about others' cultures and traditions can help you be more compassionate and understanding. It can also help you better understand points of view that are different from your own. Talk with your friends, parents, and teachers about how you and your classmates can respond to hateful attitudes and behaviors. Newspapers, magazines, movies, and television shows that you've seen on these subjects can be great ways to start a discussion about hate crimes and intolerance.

Get Involved

Get involved in your school and community. Identify any hate group active in your community; then share the information by publishing an article in a school or local newspaper or talking to community groups or groups of students. Volunteer with a community group, play sports, write a play or poem, play a musical instrument, or join a club or after-school program.

Join a Group That Promotes Tolerance

Join with other students to create anti-hate policies and programs in your school. Coordinate an event that brings diverse people and groups together. Find ways to show support and solidarity for groups when one of their members is a victim of hate violence.

Learn about effective programs and what other teens are doing around the nation. Find out how to plan and start a program, run a meeting, develop publications, and work with the news media.

Avoid Alcohol and Drugs

Stay away from alcohol and drugs as well as people who use them. There is a strong link between the use of alcohol and drugs and violence. For more information about drugs and alcohol abuse as well as their prevention and treatment, see the earlier lessons, "Use and Effects of Drugs, Alcohol, and Substances" and "Critical Decisions about Substances."

Learn About Conflict Resolution

Many schools, churches, and after-school programs offer training in conflict-resolution skills. This training might include the following:

- **Learning about a win-win approach to resolution**
- **Turning problems into possibilities**
- **Becoming a more empathetic listener**
- **Practicing assertiveness, not aggressiveness**
- **Learning the art of negotiation**

Do Not Carry a Gun or Other Weapons and Avoid Those Who Do

Carrying a gun is unlikely to make you safer. Guns often escalate conflicts and increase the chances that you will be seriously harmed. If someone is threatening you and you feel that you are in serious danger, do not take matters into your own hands. Find an adult you can trust and discuss your fears or contact school administrators or the police. Take precautions for your safety, such as avoiding being alone and staying with a group of friends if possible (see figure 7.4.2).

Take the Pledge

You can take the Student Pledge Against Gun Violence and adhere to it to make your school and community safer.

I will never bring a gun to school;

I will never use a gun to settle a personal problem or dispute;

I will use my influence with my friends to keep them from using guns to settle disputes.

My individual choices and actions, when multiplied by those of young people throughout the country, will make a difference. Together, by honoring this pledge, we can reverse the violence and grow up in safety.

Figure 7.4.2: When walking through a deserted area, always walk with someone and be aware of your surroundings.
Courtesy of Ken Karp.

Most of us have learned from an early age that it is wrong to "tattle," but in some instances it is the most courageous thing you can do. Tell a trusted adult, such as a teacher, guidance counselor, principal or parent. If you are afraid and believe that telling will put you in danger or lead to retaliation, find a way to anonymously contact the authorities. Before someone reaches a **decision-point** and performs a violent act that can change their life and the lives of those around them, tell someone who can help.

Take the Initiative to Make Your School and Community Safer

Join an existing group that is promoting nonviolence in your school or community or launch your own effort. The Justice Department's youth Web site (http://www.usdoj. gov/kidspage/) can connect you with national organizations and provide you with information and resources to take action in your community. Learn about effective programs and what other teens are doing around the nation. Find out how to plan and start a program, run a meeting, develop publications, and work with the news media.

Conclusion

Although violence has always been a problem in the United States, the number of deaths and serious injuries increased dramatically during the late 1980s and the early 1990s as more and more youth began to carry guns and other weapons.

Key Note Term

decision-point – the point where a decision to act is made

Since then, however, the tide has begun to turn. Between 1992 and 2001, juvenile arrests on weapons charges dropped 35 percent; the juvenile arrest rate for murder fell 62 percent, dropping to its lowest level in more than two decades; and the juvenile arrest rate for violent crimes dropped by 21 percent. Clearly, considerable progress has been made, but youth violence does still remain a serious problem in the United States. With your help, however, these statistics can drop even lower.

This concludes Chapter 7, "Managing Conflict." In Chapter 9, "Career Planning," you will learn how to explore career possibilities and opportunities and create a career development portfolio. The following chapter, "Making a Difference with Service Learning," offers some ideas about working in your community.

Lesson Review

1. **What ways can you get involved in your school or community to help prevent violence?**

2. **Why is it important to learn about other cultures and ethnicities in an effort to prevent violence?**

3. **How can the use of drugs and alcohol lead to violent acts?**

4. **Explain how bullying is considered violence.**

Making a Difference with Service Learning

Lesson 1

Orientation to Service Learning

Key Terms

community service
debriefer
facilitator
orientation
recorder
reflection
reporter
service learning
timekeeper

What You Will Learn to Do

- Identify the components of service learning

Linked Core Abilities

- Apply critical thinking techniques

Skills and Knowledge You Will Gain Along the Way

- Compare the types of service opportunities within your community
- Identify the benefits of serving others within a community
- Associate the roles and responsibilities of service learning teams
- Define the key words contained in this lesson

Introduction

You have probably noticed that people who seem to find the most satisfaction in life are those actively engaged in doing something to make the world a better place for everyone. They seem happy because they are making a difference. Have you ever helped a friend through a difficult time, stopped to help change a flat tire, or take food to a sick neighbor? Then you know why people who help others appear to be more genuinely content with their lives.

Unfortunately, although you know you will feel good, it is probably not easy for you to get started. You are not alone. Many people find it awkward to reach out. However, after you take those initial steps and begin making a difference, the difficulties disappear. Feelings of accomplishment and generosity of spirit make the effort and time you spent worthwhile.

So how do you get started in service? First, look around you. There are problems and people in need everywhere. You do not have to look very far to find hunger, illiteracy, pollution, illness, poverty, neglect, and loneliness. Decide on an urgent need or one that you find most compelling. What matters most is that you make a commitment to address the need in a positive way.

After you have chosen a need, select a project that will help you accomplish your goal of making a difference. President John F. Kennedy reminded everyone to "Ask not what your country can do for you; ask what you can do for your country." Planning and carrying out the **service learning** project will help you selflessly "do" for your neighbor, your community, your state, your country, and the world.

The author Aldous Huxley said, "Experience is not what happens to you; it's what you do with what happens to you." Service learning takes that belief to heart. It is not enough to take positive actions; you must learn from your actions. For example, starting a paper recycling program is a worthy project; it can become more meaningful when you learn more about why it is important, reflect on your experiences, identify what you learned, analyze how you've changed, and decide other ways you can recycle and help others commit to recycling.

Service learning experiences can become the starting point for self-awareness, self-improvement, and self-fulfillment. In the process of making a difference for others, you make a difference in yourself.

What Is Service Learning?

Service learning is an active and experiential learning strategy where students have a direct impact on an identified need that interest and motivates them. It requires sequential lessons that are organized so **orientation** and training come before the meaningful service activity and structured reflection follows the activity.

> **Key Note Term**
>
> **service learning** – an environment where one can learn and develop by actively participating in organized service experiences within one's own community

> **Key Note Term**
>
> **orientation** – the act or process of orienting or being oriented, for example, being oriented on the first day of college

facilitator – one who facilitates; one who leads team discussion

recorder – one who take notes for the team and organizes information

reporter – one who represents the team voice and reports team findings

timekeeper – one who keeps track of time and plans the schedule

debriefer – one who encourages team members and leads discussions after presentation and team discussion

Structured Teamwork

Service learning requires active participation in structured teamwork much like sports (see Figure 8.1.1). Working within small teams and solving problems together will help you become active participants. Each member is assigned a team role:

- **Facilitator.** The facilitator leads team discussions to identify needs and prepare service learning activities.
- **Recorder.** The recorder takes notes for the team and organizes information.
- **Reporter.** The reporter represents the team voice and reports team findings.
- **Timekeeper.** The timekeeper keeps track of time and plans the schedule.
- **Debriefer.** The debriefer encourages team members and leads discussion after presentation.

Cadet teams should determine, plan, and execute service learning activities with the aid of their instructor.

Orientation and Training

Orientation and training activities are necessary to prepare you and other participants for the service experience. Integrating what you are learning in class with the service activity is a key goal of service learning. This step requires in-class lessons, followed by selecting a service project that relates to the curriculum and meets academic standards.

You should be familiar enough with the material to conduct the service project you have selected. Part of the planning process will require you to determine what you need to know before the activity and to train yourself accordingly.

If possible, speak with representatives or others involved with the service you have selected to see what to expect. Orient yourself with the service goals, those you will be helping, other organizations or people that you may need to contact, and so on. In other words, learn what you need to know before starting the service experience and plan for all potential circumstances.

Meaningful Service

It is your responsibility to initiate and plan service activities to correspond to the lesson material. Although there should be at least 15 cadets per service experience,

Figure 8.1.1: Sports promote good health as well as teamwork.
Courtesy of Craig Hammell/The Stock Market.

you can either work in committees on one project or small teams on separate projects. For example, you may want to divide the project components among three teams of five cadets each. Learning should be an active and social experience that is meaningful to you and those involved. Within your teams, choose a service activity that

- **Addresses a real and important need another group is not addressing**
- **Is interesting and challenging**
- **Connects you to others within the community or world**
- **Challenges you to develop new skills**
- **Requires little or no money**
- **Is achievable within the time available**
- **Has a positive effect on others**

Structured Reflection

Reflection, or taking time to observe, analyze, and integrate actions with learning, is an important part of the learning process. A strong reflection helps you develop skills and extend learning from the service experience. You may use many types of reflection: learning logs and essays; team and class discussions; performances; graphic organizers; and public presentations. Using learning logs throughout the experience to record thoughts, feelings, knowledge and processes will help you organize what you have learned.

Within your teams, share what you have learned by discussing your answers to open-ended questions before, during, and after each service experience. Reflection questions should encourage observation, analysis, and integration.

Community Service versus Service Learning

Community service in many states is dispensed by a judge or court system as mandatory work for infractions of the law. Some students and members of the community view this type of service as punishment. What students learn is that they don't ever want to be forced to do "service" again. Today, many high schools include community service hours as a graduation requirement; though intentions are good, sometimes the emphasis is on quantity of hours, not the quality of the project.

Service learning, on the other hand, is a step up from community service; it brings academics to life and is driven by student involvement (see Figure 8.1.2). You should identify essential needs in your school or community and then decide on your own projects. In addition, you should plan and carry out your own projects and take responsibility for your own learning. Reflecting on the experience will reveal the importance of your service work and the impact you are making on yourself and others.

Key Note Term

reflection – a thought, idea, or opinion formed or a remark made as a result of mediation; consideration of some subject matter, idea, or purpose

Key Note Term

community service – any form of service provided for the community or common good

Chapter 8

Plan and Train for Your Exploratory Project

Key Words

experiential learning
exploratory project
field education
problem-based learning
training

What You Will Learn to Do

- Prepare for a service learning project

Linked Core Abilities

- Build your capacity for lifelong learning
- Communicate using verbal, nonverbal, visual, and written techniques
- Do your share as a good citizen in your school, community, country, and the world

Skills and Knowledge You Will Gain Along the Way

- Select an exploratory project
- Identify the steps needed in conduct a service learning experience
- Identify the essential components of a chosen service learning project
- Develop a plan addressing various circumstances and outcomes of the project
- Define the key words contained in this lesson

Introduction

There are several points to consider before undergoing service learning. Planning ahead will prepare you both mentally and physically to undertake the challenge. Before you select a service learning project in class, your instructor should familiarize you with service learning by guiding you in an **exploratory project** within the community. This will help you select a service project and demonstrate the steps to conducting a proper service learning experience.

Exploratory Project Purpose

The exploratory project is an introduction to a service learning activity that utilizes **experiential learning** and **problem-based learning** principles. The purpose of a teacher-planned exploratory project is to provide students with a meaningful experience, expose them to how it feels to serve, and stimulate their thinking about possible service learning activities.

One of the primary benefits of engaging in an exploratory project is to understand what service learning entails. Service learning is not community service, although many confuse the two. Until you participate in service learning, you will not have a real-life experience to justify the difference.

Exploratory projects help you capture a vision of how to make a difference in the world. After you get involved, you may begin to see the world through different glasses. In addition, as you work to address one need in the community, several other unmet needs will begin to surface. Your vision of the world may change when you begin to see critical needs where you never saw them before.

Suggested introductory projects could include going to a hospital or nursing home to visit residents, distributing food at a food bank, or volunteering at a local Red Cross or hospital program, such as that depicted in Figure 8.2.1.

Before participating in service, familiarize yourself with the following steps to conduct a proper service learning experience:

1. **Complete a preassessment of skill level using the Personal Skills Map from the JROTC Success Profiler.**

2. **Determine a school, community, or national need you can fill relating to class curriculum.**

3. **Brainstorm and select a meaningful service project that meets proposed guidelines.**

4. **Start a learning log to record new knowledge, thoughts, and feelings throughout all phases.**

5. **Plan and organize details of the service activity and discuss expectations.**

6. **Participate in a meaningful service activity that meets the service learning guidelines (Form 219-R).**

7. **Discuss and reflect on what you experienced (observation).**

Key Note Terms

exploratory project – a teacher-planned introductory project to service learning, intended to provide students with a meaningful experience, expose them to how it feels to serve, and to stimulate their thinking abut possible service learning activities

experiential learning – gaining practical knowledge, skills, or practice from direct observation of or participation in events or in a particular activity

problem-based learning – an instructional Strategy that promotes active learning where problems form the focus and learning stimulus and problem-solving skills are utilized

Figure 8.2.1: Volunteering your time in a hospital is just one way to help members of your community.
Courtesy of Michal Heron.

8. Discuss and reflect on what you gained from the experience (analysis).

9. Discuss and reflect on what you can do with the new information (integration).

10. Complete a project summary report and a final group evaluation form to judge teamwork and other activities.

11. Brief the experience to community members, administration, classmates, and so on.

12. Complete a post-assessment using the personal skills map and related analysis to determine plan of action.

Choosing a Service Activity

After participating in an exploratory project, you should be able to select your own service activity that meets an important need and integrates the curriculum.

It is very important that you participate in selecting a service activity that is meaningful to you and others. Brainstorm service ideas relative to the lesson curriculum and program at hand. Then as a class or team, select the service activity.

Service learning opportunities can use **field education** principles to incorporate scholastic programs with the curriculum. You can integrate programs such as the following:

- **Lions-Quest Skills for Action®**
- **Groundhog Job Shadow Day®**
- **NEFE High School Financial Planning Program®**
- **You the People®**
- **Chief Justice®**
- **Cadet Ride®**

Key Note Term

field education – performing service and training to enhance understanding with a field of study

In field education, you perform the service as a part of a **training** program designed primarily to enhance understanding of a field of study while providing substantial emphasis on the service.

Besides integrating curriculum and service, you will learn more about the different types, models, and terms of service in the next lesson, "Project Reflection and Integration." Service learning projects can vary from addressing a littering problem to raising funds for a specific cause (see Figure 8.2.2).

Key Note Term

training - to form by or undergo instruction, discipline, or drill; to teach so as to make fit, qualified, or proficient

Planning the Service

After you have chosen an activity, you must plan the essential facets for project completion and prepare or train yourself for what is to come.

This is where service learning begins. Service learning efforts should start with clearly stated goals and the development of a plan of action that encourages cadet responsibility. You can achieve those goals through structured preparation and brainstorming such as discussion, writing, reading, observation, and the service itself. Keep the goals consistent with the level of the activity planned and ensure that the goals and plan of action draw on the skills and knowledge of your team. When corresponding goals to the curriculum, try to determine academic content standards you will address through the service.

Besides determining goals and standards, plans should be comprehensive to ensure adequate preparation for each step or task. Determine a description of the task(s) and answer the following questions:

- **Who will be involved?**
- **What is involved and needs to be done?**
- **When will each step take place?**
- **Where will it all take place?**
- **Why will we do it?**
- **How will it work?**

For example, you might decide to visit a local veterans' hospital. You could discover the needs of the elderly patients that reside there by discussions with the hospital's administrative personnel or possibly by meeting with the residents themselves. You

Figure 8.2.2: Collecting trash to address a littering problem or raising funds for a special cause are both meaningful and effective service learning projects.
Courtesy of Bob Daemmrich.

should also determine where the project fits into the curriculum. Together, you might decide that the patients need to have younger people help them write letters to family members, assist with their wellness and fitness, or plan and lead activities.

> ### Service Learning Success Story
>
> During lessons on planning and social responsibility, cadets in Gastonia, North Carolina, decided to plant a garden at a nursing home. Their preplanning resulted in a specially designed, waist-high "no stoop garden" so seniors could help maintain the plants and flowers. This is a good example of how the needs of the elderly were taken into consideration when the garden plan was developed.

If you are aware of children who have a hard time learning to read, you could plan a service activity to a local elementary school. Because teachers rarely have extra time on their hands to spend one-on-one with these children, certain schools may welcome JROTC cadets who could come and spend time reading or listening to the children read. You do not have to limit this service to reading; consider helping in mathematics or other subjects. Remember to maximize the use of your participating cadets' skills and knowledge. Contact your local Junior Achievement office at http://www.ja.org, for more service learning suggestions to help teach elementary students. You can also find service learning projects ideas by searching the Internet.

Do not forget to accomplish the administrative details during the preparation phase. Teams often overlook these requirements or assume that someone else will do them. You must obtain permission from school administrators to conduct the service learning activity as a field trip and arrange for transportation, lunch, parental release/permission slips for participating cadets, and the necessary supplies and equipment to perform the activity. Invite administrators, counselors, community members, and so on to be on your advisory board so that they will become more involved with your project.

Training for the Service

Before participating in the service activity, prepare yourself for different circumstances or outcomes. This may involve learning about the subject matter you will be expected to know to complete the tasks you have laid out or discussing different outcomes and expectations within your teams. Try your best to be prepared for different situations you may encounter. Within teams, or as a class, brainstorm and discuss potential hazards you may encounter, and precautions you should take to make the task run smoothly.

Pretend you are taking a bus to a children's hospital with a group of cadets to tutor sick children who cannot be in school. You may need to train yourselves on particular academic subjects, research what grade levels will be represented, and locate the hospital. Also, make sure to pair up and plan a meeting time and place.

Executing the Service

In this phase there are a few rules to remember. Arrive on time and always be courteous. You are representing your school and you should act accordingly at all times. Also, ensure that you understand the task or goal at hand. If you are not sure, ask a person in authority, who should be able to point you in the right direction. If you are a team leader, make sure your team members feel completely comfortable with the tasks. Finally, if a situation or problem arises that needs an authority's attention (for example, an accident occurs and someone is hurt), take what actions you can and have someone contact the person in charge.

Being well organized and completely prepared are fundamental for a successful execution phase. For example, if you are going to build a garden such as the one mentioned earlier in this lesson,

- **Ensure you have the correct tools and supplies to complete the service**
- **Know the name or names of the contacts for the particular service you are performing**
- **Identify alternate group leaders in case there are absences**
- **Assign cadets to work on projects according to their experience and abilities**
- **Be thoroughly prepared to complete the task but be flexible to make changes because things may not go as you planned them**

Remember, you are there to render a service for your community.

Conclusion

The exploratory project will introduce you to service learning through active participation. From there, you will be ready to choose your own service activity. At that time, remember that good planning is the key to a successful service learning venture. Training may be necessary to complete the task, and learning should be the focus as well as making a difference through service.

You should now be prepared to use the proposed steps and planning procedures to conduct a proper service learning experience.

Lesson Review

1. Define the term *problem-based learning*.
2. Why is it important to participate in a service activity that means something to you?
3. What materials might you need if you were visiting children in a hospital?
4. Name three projects in your community you might want to join.

Lesson 3

Project Reflection and Integration

Key Terms

advocacy service
after action review
analysis
direct service
indirect service
integration
observation
placement
project

What You Will Learn to Do

- Evaluate the effectiveness of a service learning project

Linked Core Abilities

- Communicate using verbal, nonverbal, visual, and written techniques
- Apply critical thinking techniques

Skills and Knowledge You Will Gain Along the Way

- Relate the projected goals of a service learning project to the final outcomes
- Identify ways to integrate service learning into the JROTC curriculum
- Outline service learning objectives for the future
- Define the key words contained in this lesson

Introduction

Now that you have an idea of what service learning is all about, what comes next? After the exploratory project you will be able to determine and conduct appropriate service learning activities. Before choosing activities, you should know about the models, terms, and types of service available, and how to integrate service with what you are learning in class.

After you have completed a service activity, you should follow it up with a structured reflection, demonstration of learning, and evaluation of the service learning.

Short-Term versus Long-Term Service

You need to understand how to meet others' needs through either short-term or long-term service activities. Short-term service projects include the following:

- **Restoring a historical monument during history lessons**
- **Raising money at an event for charity during the financial planning lessons**
- **Visiting a nursing home while discussing wellness and fitness issues**

Long-term service projects include the following:

- **Adopting a local waterway while studying environmental issues**
- **Setting up an advocacy campaign to raise financial resources for shelters during the financial planning lessons**
- **Organizing an after-school tutoring program during lessons on teaching skills**

Models of Service

Key Note Terms

project – a task or problem engaged in usually by a group of students to supplement and apply classroom studies; service learning projects are initiated and planned by cadets with instructor guidance

placement – service learning activities carried out beyond the classroom in a pre-existing, structured situation

Service can be done anywhere to reinforce what you are learning in class; you do not even have to leave the school grounds. The two models of service include **projects** and **placements**.

Project Model

Service learning projects are initiated and planned by cadets with instructor guidance. Tutoring elementary children in subjects you are currently studying or starting a recycling program based on information from your geography lessons are examples of service projects.

Placement Model

Service learning placements are activities carried out beyond the classroom in a preexisting, structured situation. The placement organization typically assigns responsibilities to students individually. Examples include teaching lessons for Junior Achievement or volunteering for Special Olympics during fitness lessons.

Three Types of Service

The three types of service are **direct**, **indirect**, and **advocacy**. These service types are described in the following sections.

Direct Service

Direct service involves face-to-face contact with those being served in either project or placement models of service learning. Examples of direct service include working in a soup kitchen or working with disadvantaged children while you are studying about group communication. Figure 8.3.1 demonstrates both a short-term and a direct service type project.

Indirect Service

Indirect service requires hands-on involvement in a service activity without any face-to-face contact with those served. An example would be raising money for a veterans' hospital or e-mailing deployed soldiers during your military lessons. Figure 8.3.2 illustrates an indirect service type project.

Advocacy Service

Advocacy services do not require face-to-face contact with those served. Advocacy involves speaking out on behalf of an issue or cause. For example, starting a schoolwide poster campaign to teach others about an issue would be an advocacy service.

Integrating Service Learning

Because the learning should equal the service in service learning, it is important to integrate classroom content with the chosen service. Service learning should reinforce curriculum content and standards for you to benefit academically, personally,

Key Note Terms

direct service – involves face-to-face contact with those being served in either project or placement models of service learning

indirect service – hands-on involvement in a service activity without any face-to-face contact with those served

advocacy service – the act or process of supporting or providing a service toward a cause or proposal that does not require face-to-face contact

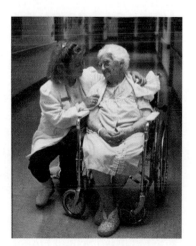

Figure 8.3.1: Visiting patients of a nursing home is both a short-term and a direct service type project.
Courtesy of J. Lotter/Tom Stack & Associates.

Figure 8.3.2: Raising funds
for the March of Dimes is
an example of an indirect
service project.
Courtesy of Larry Lawfer.

and socially. Applying content standard material to real-life experiences will give
you a better understanding of the curriculum.

When conducting a service learning project, take time to pinpoint the standards
you should address and ways to assess your learning. As a team or class, consider:

- **What standards are we addressing?**

- **What should we know or be able to do?**

- **What assessments can illustrate our learning?**

Not only will you fulfill an important need with your service project, but you will
also be learning the national standards in a more relevant and engaging manner.

Service Learning Examples

Field education integrates curriculum programs with service learning. This section
presents examples of how you can integrate service learning with curriculum
related programs, including the following:

- **Lions-Quest Skills for Action®**

- **You the People®/Chief Justice®**

- **Groundhog Job Shadow Day®**

- **Cadet Ride®**

- **Winning Colors®**

- **NEFE High School Financial Planning Program®**

Lions-Quest Skills for Action®

Lions-Quest Skills for Action® (SFA) is a student-centered program based on combining learning with service. The program is divided into four parts and a Skills Bank. The program curriculum is an elective that advocates service, character, citizenship, and responsibility.

The Skills for Action curriculum helps guide you through the crucial steps of conducting service learning activities. Those steps include identifying needs, choosing and planning a project to address the need, carrying out the project, and reflecting on experiences and exploring what was learned throughout the project.

You the People and Chief Justice®

There are a variety of ways to incorporate service learning with You the People (YTP) and Chief Justice®. After you are grounded in YTP citizenship skills and have formed groups, you can identify a service learning activity to integrate into the skill-building curriculum.

For example, you could create, circulate, and publicize a petition that addresses a community issue and create a videotape to document the issue for community officials.

Groundhog Job Shadow Day®

Groundhog Job Shadow Day® (GJSD) is a nationwide effort to introduce students to the skills and education needed to make it in today's job market by letting them explore various career options.

For example, you may decide to start a Job Shadow effort to link the schools to the community; then organize a career day or GJSD to make it possible for high school students in the community to explore different career opportunities.

For details about the program, go to http://www.jobshadow.org.

Cadet Ride®

The Cadet Ride® is an extension of American history that allows you to choose different historical characters to research. You can reenact them on site or in the classroom and then complete a related service learning activity.

You first need to identify issues that still relate to the community today, such as homeless veterans or victims of terrorist attacks; then take time to discuss how you can use what you have learned to improve the community/world issue. Finally, complete a related service learning activity, taking time to reflect on each phase of the experience.

Project examples used with the Cadet Ride® include supporting war memorials or assisting in veterans' hospitals or shelters. Specifically, you could decide to educate others on the service of Lieutenant General Maude, who died in the line of duty at the Pentagon on September 11, 2001. In addition, you could plan a memorial for him and/or other victims to commemorate the acts of war that occurred at the World Trade Center, the Pentagon, and in Pennsylvania.

Winning Colors®

Winning Colors® states that everyone is capable of developing decision making, thinking, feeling, and action behaviors. One example of a service learning project would be to teach senior citizens or elementary students about Winning Colors® and its precepts of discovering their personal needs and developing a plan to help them achieve a successful balance.

> **Note**
>
> You can earn two hours of college credit with Winning Colors® and a service learning project. Ask your JROTC instructor for more details.

For more information about Winning Colors® go to http://www.winningcolors.com.

NEFE High School Financial Planning Program®

The National Endowment for Financial Education (NEFE) High School Financial Planning Program® (HSFPP) is designed to teach practical money management skills to introduce financial planning through course work. Numerous service learning activities can be integrated into the NEFE HSFPP® curriculum. Chapter 11, "NEFE High School Financial Planning Program," includes six lessons regarding money management.

> **Note**
>
> You can earn two hours of college credit when you do the NEFE curriculum and a service learning project. Ask your JROTC instructor for more details.

Suggested service learning activities related to the NEFE HSFPP® include the following:

- **Teach elementary students Junior Achievement material in relation to HSFPP**
- **Provide a budget assistance program**
- **Host a Credit Awareness or Financial Fitness Fair**
- **Develop budgets and spreadsheets for local services**
- **Start an Investment Club in school**
- **Design, produce, and distribute informative posters**
- **Shop for homebound seniors' groceries**

For more information, call NEFE at (303) 224-3510 or visit *http://www.nefe.org*.

Integration with Additional Unit Content

Besides using applicable curriculum programs in service learning, you may decide to integrate additional content and services. The key is to connect the service activity with the course curriculum.

For example, after studying harmful effects of tobacco and drugs, you could teach elementary school kids by putting together an antidrug advocacy program. You could create banners, skits, and instructional materials and then plan and coordinate the elementary program teaching.

After the Service

After the service, you will participate in an **after action review** so you can reflect, demonstrate, and evaluate. This will be done in three phases, as described in the following sections.

Structured Reflection Phase

Remember, a strong reflection helps develop skills and extend your learning from the service experience. Besides keeping a running learning log of entries, you should hold team discussions to answer open-ended questions before, during, and after each service experience. Sharing what you learned with your teammates and listening to others will add to your learning experience.

Types of reflection questions to ask about the service learning experience include the following:

- **Observation**/*What.* What did I do?
- **Analysis**/*So What.* What did it mean to me?
- **Integration**/*Now What.* What will I do because of what I accomplished or learned?

This phase provides you with a structured opportunity to think about what you just did for your community and to describe the feelings that stimulated your actions throughout this activity. Experience indicates that reflection is the key to successful service learning programs.

After you actually perform the service, you should come together as a group to contemplate your service experiences in a project summary report, learning logs, essays, and class discussions. You should thoroughly describe what happened during the activity; record any differences your activity actually made; and try to place this experience in a larger context. Specifically, do you believe you successfully accomplished your service learning goals? If not, why? What can you do better the next time? Share your feelings and thoughts. Discuss experiences that made you happy, sad, or angry; events that surprised or frightened you; and other topics related to the activity.

Demonstration Phase

In the demonstration phase you share with others your mastery of skills, creative ideas, and the outcomes from this project; you then identify the next steps to take to benefit the community. The actual demonstration can take many different forms. For example, you might

- **Give a presentation to peers, faculty, or community members about the activity**
- **Write articles or letters to local newspapers regarding issues of public concern**
- **Extend the experience to develop future projects that could benefit the community**

Key Note Term

after action review – reflecting on what was learned after an act

Key Note Terms

observation – an act or instance of examining a custom, rule, or law; an act of recognizing and noting a fact or occurrence often involving measurement with intruments; a record or description so obtained

analysis – the separation of a whole into its component parts for individual study; a study of something complex, its elements, and their relations

integration – the act or process or an instance of forming, coordinating, or blending into a functioning or unified whole

Evaluation Phase

A goal in JROTC is to couple high service with high integration of course content to maximize learning and skill development as well as meet identified needs. When evaluating your service learning activities, reflect on accomplishments and determine ways to improve.

High service meets a clear and important need and is organized and implemented by students. High integration with curriculum addresses classroom goals, incorporates classroom content, and improves course-related knowledge and skills. Use the following quadrants to rate your service learning experience.

Quadrant 1

Example: After studying financial planning lessons from the National Endowment of Financial Education, cadets teach Junior Achievement lessons to elementary students and assist them in making posters to advocate financial responsibility.

Quadrant 2

Example: Cadets organize a drive for stuffed animals and blankets after learning about work skills and participating in Groundhog Job Shadow Day®.

Quadrant 3

Example: Teacher directs cadets to send e-mail to deployed service members after studying a historic event through a Cadet Ride®.

Quadrant 4

Example: Teacher assigns cadets to perform a color guard in the community after studying lessons in "You the People".

Service Learning Authentic Assessments

Authentic assessments that evaluate the service activity and student learning are imperative to a successful service learning initiative. Choose assessment tools that measure and affirm learning, program goals, and impact on the need identified to determine potential improvements.

Service learning lends itself to performance-based assessment, enabling you to exhibit what you have learned in a hands-on and meaningful context. Be sure to take advantage of college credits available through service learning and your curriculum.

Conclusion

In addition to teaching you the value of volunteering, service learning fosters your development of citizenship skills as well as personal, social and thinking skills. It teaches service responsibilities and prepares future service commitments. Most important, service learning builds a spirit of cooperation among you, your peers, the school, and the community.

This concludes Chapter 8, "Making a Difference with Service Learning." In the following chapter, "Career Planning," you will learn how to start forming career decisions.

Lesson Review

1. List the three types of services and give an example of each.

2. Choose one service learning curriculum-related program and discuss it.

3. Define the term *placement*.

4. State what you learn through the evaluation phase.

Chapter 9

Career Planning

Lesson 1

Career Exploration Strategy

Key Terms

advancement
attitude
aptitude
career
employee
entrepreneur
internship
job
job posting
mentor
occupation
profession
promotion
telecommuting
virtual worker
vocational

Chapter 9

What You Will Learn to Do

- Investigate a career

Linked Core Abilities

- Take responsibility for your actions and choices
- Apply critical thinking techniques

Skills and Knowledge You Will Gain Along the Way

- Identify personal strengths and interests and link them to possible career paths
- Identify jobs/careers of interest
- Explain the difference between a job and a career
- Determine qualifications and education/training necessary for desired career

- Discuss the effects of education and training on a career
- Identify the steps in developing a career exploration strategy
- Analyze future job trends
- Define the key words contained in this lesson

Introduction

As a high school student, you are faced with many decisions. Selecting a career may be one of the most important decisions that you make. Although some students in your class may know exactly what they want to do after graduating from high school, others may not. If you are one of those who have not yet decided, don't panic as the student is Figure 9.1.1 is doing! This is the time in your life to try different things, to discover your interests, and to understand how your interests relate to career decision making.

Because much of your adult life will be spent working, it is important to start as early as possible selecting a career. When determining your interests and personal preferences about a career, you may want to consider how much education you want to pursue. Is it important for you to find a career that has high prestige, allows you to work independently, is especially creative, or relates to other common work values? This lesson helps you start planning for your future.

Planning a Career Strategy

Developing a satisfying career requires careful planning and informed decision making. This is an exciting time for you, but it can also be overwhelming. You must spend time gathering information, understanding what alternatives you have, and thinking about your personal preferences in regard to your career. The career decisions that you make in the next few months or years will not be the only career decisions that you will make. Most people have many careers over the course of a lifetime, but the decisions you make soon will be key ones. Therefore, to use your career exploration strategy as a tool to help you make those important career decisions; it should focus on three tasks:

Figure 9.1.1: Do not panic over career decisions; rather, do some career planning and research.
Courtesy of James Whitmer.

- Discovering your aptitude, interests, abilities, and personal preferences
- Matching your aptitude, interests, abilities, and preferences with occupations
- Learning where and how to get information on different careers

If you have not yet decided what type of a career you would like, now is the time to start planning a strategy that will help you to decide. In addition to teaching you career exploration skills, developing a career exploration strategy can motivate you to learn more about yourself and the occupations that you might find rewarding. Such a strategy can help you to see how your aptitude, interests, abilities, and personal preferences match career opportunities.

An effective career exploration strategy can also help you to decide whether you want to attend college, a **vocational**-technical school, join one of the military services, or go directly into the world of work after high school.

Identifying What You Want to Become

Do you know at this time in your life what career or job you would like to pursue after graduating from high school? Your answer can be anything: doctor, plumber, hot dog salesman, **entrepreneur**, instructional designer, baseball star, electrician, and so on. In the *Dictionary of Occupational Titles* the Department of Labor lists over 2,000 different jobs performed in the United States.

Although you may believe that discovering your aptitudes for certain jobs or careers may seem like a difficult task, it can actually be easier than identifying a career that interests you. Your guidance counselor (career counselor, occupational specialist) has career tests that can match your skills, abilities, and interests with specific job titles. The results of these tests allow you to eliminate jobs that may not be suited for you (because you scored low on them) so that you can concentrate your time and research on those jobs that better match your skills, abilities, and interests.

The Armed Services Vocational Aptitude Battery (ASVAB) test is a good indicator of how well you have developed your academic and occupational abilities. It measures aptitudes that are related to success in different types of civilian or military jobs. The U.S. Department of Defense (DoD) has provided the nationally normed, multiaptitude test battery to high schools and post-secondary schools since 1968. The ASVAB Career Exploration Program has been designed to encourage students to increase their level of self-knowledge and to understand how that information could be linked to civilian and military occupational characteristics.

The ASVAB program was recently redesigned to be helpful to virtually all students, whether they are planning on immediate employment after high school in civilian or military occupations, or further education at a university, community college, or vocational institution. Visit www.asvabprogram.com/ for more information.

There are several Web sites that are dedicated to helping you assess your potential in the job market. Some offer a free assessment and some offer the assessment for a fee. The following Web sites are just a few examples:

Key Note Terms

vocational – of, relating to, or being in training for a skill or trade to be pursued as a career

entrepreneur – one who organizes, manages, and assumes the risks of a business enterprise

- **www.assessment.com:** Provides a free online career assessment test and appraisal through MAPP, also known as Motivational Appraisal of Personal Potential
- **www.careerexplorer.net:** Offers aptitude and assessment testing to help you find a satisfying career

> **Note**
>
> To find other career assessment sites, simply use your favorite search engine and search for "career assessment."

When thinking about your future, you should first consider all the jobs that interest you the most and why. Try to understand what draws you to those professions. Then, identify the qualities and traits that you have for those jobs as compared to the requirements for them.

Maybe you do not have any idea what you would like to do. If that is the case, you might be eliminating some career choices because of negative thinking:

- **You assume certain jobs are not realistic**
- **You do not have the resources to pursue certain jobs or careers**
- **You may not have direct experience**
- **You feel that you cannot even guess at jobs or careers that may interest you**

What Am I Going to Do After Completing High School?

This is a question that you may be asking yourself right now. Because you have been in school most of your life, you might be wondering, "What will I do after graduation? Should I go to college or look for a job? Do I have any other alternatives? What about technical or vocational training? Is college something I can handle now, or should I wait until later? Do I have the resources to obtain further education? If I do try to find a job, what kind should it be? Should I join the military? How do I find out which occupations are best for me? Where will I likely succeed and be most satisfied?"

To answer those questions, you should find out as much as possible about the many career opportunities that exist, and which ones match your aptitude, interests, abilities, and personal preferences. To do all of that, you will need the following:

- **Information about your aptitude, interests, abilities, and personal preferences**
- **Information about the world of work, including educational requirements, work environment, and career opportunities for specific occupations**
- **Information on how to match your personal characteristics to the characteristics of the world of work**

You must first decide how you will conduct your career exploration, how many hours you plan to take in your search process, and a date when you will make a tentative decision. The time limitations you set are important. It is easy to postpone big decisions. If you commit yourself to a plan, you are less likely to become overwhelmed by such a big decision.

The deadline that you set is there to help you make timely decisions about your future. It does not mean you must make a career decision that is not changeable.

You may even find it helpful to set a time in the near future to review your research. That review will give you the opportunity to see if you are still satisfied with your choices. When looking for a career, it is important to be creative. Explore all possible avenues. Use techniques such as brainstorming, researching, networking, canvassing, testing, counseling, and volunteering to assist you in making your career decisions.

What's Hot in the Career Market

Not sure what kind of career to pursue? You might want to consider the computer or health fields. The number of jobs in these areas is projected to grow very quickly within the next few years. According to the U.S. Bureau of Labor Statistics, the ten occupations with the fastest projected employment growth for 1996 through 2006 are the following:

1. Database administrators, computer support specialists and all other computer scientists (118% more jobs by 2006)

2. Computer engineers (109%)

3. Systems analysts (103%)

4. Personal and home care aides (85%)

5. Physical and corrective therapy assistants and aides (79%)

6. Home health aides (76%)

7. Medical assistants (74%)

8. Desktop publishing specialists (74%)

9. Physical therapists (71%)

10. Occupational therapy assistants and aides (69%)

As you can see, the top three careers with projected growth are related to the Information Technology (IT) field. One of the reasons for the interest in the IT field, which involves working with computers, is that it provides the opportunity to work at home by the use of an electronic linkup with a central office, called **telecommuting**. There are thousands of organizations throughout the country that offer the benefit of telecommuting to their employees. Improved work performance and employee morale, reduced operating costs for items such as office space, and a more efficient work environment all contribute to the benefits of telecommuting. Employees who telecommute are sometimes called **virtual workers** because they are performing work tasks virtually, via the Internet, phone, and fax machine. Another in demand career field will be almost any career in the health sciences area, such as a dental hygienist.

Key Note Terms

telecommuting – working at home by the use of an electronic linkup with a central office

virtual worker – employee who telecommutes and performs work tasks virtually, via the Internet, phone, and fax

Brainstorming

Spend 10 minutes listing careers that you know you are not interested in. Next, spend another ten minutes listing all the careers that you think may interest you. Finally, evaluate both lists. Commit yourself to exploring the possibilities you like the most. Set a date to review the list to see if you still feel the same way about the choices you have made. Remember, you can always change your mind at any time during the career exploration process and add or delete choices from your lists as you learn more about those choices.

Researching

Two good resources that should be available in your school career center or library are the *Occupational Outlook Handbook* and the *Dictionary of Occupational Titles*.

- The *Occupational Outlook Handbook* is a career information resource produced by the U.S. Department of Labor that provides detailed information on approximately 250 civilian and military occupations.

- The *Dictionary of Occupational Titles* (DOT) defines civilian careers and assigns them a DOT code. As a result of an extensive task analysis performed by the authors of that book, you can link comparable occupations. This capability is particularly important when linking civilian to military occupations, and vice versa, to determine occupational counterparts.

Other resources that you may want to consider for obtaining information about career fields are *Dunn and Bradstreet's Million-Dollar Directory, Thomas Registry of Corporate Profiles*, and *Standard and Poor's Corporation Registry*. These books should also be available in your school career center or library.

Your research should also include the following:

- Visit a local Job Services office. This office has more **job postings** in more occupations than any other single source.

- Use the yellow pages in the telephone book. The yellow pages group companies together according to what they do or make. Try to match your interests or abilities with a company most likely to meet them.

- Read the newspaper ads. These ads list job categories alphabetically. Remember, the type of work you can do may be listed under several different categories.

- Listen to the radio or television and read the business section of the newspaper to find out what new businesses may be opening.

- Visit local Chambers of Commerce, professional societies, or community organizations, attend trade shows, or go to industrial or craft unions.

- Contact city, county, state, and federal personnel offices.

Networking

Networking means meeting people and making contacts. It is one of the most successful ways that people learn about job or career openings. Ask your friends, relatives, or neighbors about possible careers. People who are working often hear about job openings before businesses make them public, and those people may be able to give you "the tip of a lifetime."

Canvassing

Talk with professionals and the people who visit your school during career day. Attend the career days sponsored at most technical or vocational schools, junior or community colleges, and the major colleges and universities that are in your area. Use these events to learn about the requirements for entering into various occupations.

> **Key Note Term**
>
> **job posting** – A published notice of a job vacancy

Additionally, make appointments with managers or other key people in the fields in which you are most interested. Generally, people will gladly take a few minutes of their time to discuss their career field with you.

Testing

There are a variety of tests that can help you determine your **aptitude**, interests, and abilities. This may refer to your capability to learn a particular type of work or your potential for general training; both are measurements that are essential for success in determining a career.

You may have already taken a career test. Career tests match possible careers to your interests and they also give you an idea about the type of job for which you are best suited. You can obtain additional information about career tests from your instructors, the media center, or any of the school counselors.

Counseling

Guidance and career counselors and occupational specialists are available in most schools and communities to help you make decisions about your career. If you think you will have trouble making up your mind about a career, speak to a counselor for assistance. Counselors and occupational specialists can match your aptitude, interests, and abilities with potential jobs or career fields. Remember, it is important to start your career plan early and these counselors and occupational specialists will be able to help you.

Volunteering/Working a Summer Job

After you make a decision about your career, consider volunteering for a job that relates to your career decision or working a summer job in that field. For example, if you want to be a teacher, find a job at a camp or day care center. If you want to be a doctor, volunteer at a hospital. Volunteering and working part-time can help you decide if the career choice you made is right for you.

Although making money may seem important, an **internship**, volunteer work in an area that interests you or while in college a student assistant position, as depicted in Figure 9.1.2, can be more beneficial in the long run. Besides, a job in itself is a good learning experience.

> ### How Will a Summer Job Help My Future?
>
> A summer job can
>
> - Give you work experience
> - Boost your self-esteem and make you more responsible
> - Give you references for future jobs/careers
> - Give you the chance to meet a role model or **mentor** who can help you plan your future
> - Help you grow and learn your true interests and talentsw

Key Note Term

aptitude – the capabilities that you have developed so far that indicate your readiness to become proficient in a certain type of activity

Key Note Terms

internship – an advanced student or graduate, usually in a professional field (such as medicine or teaching) gaining supervised, practical experience (such as a hospital or classroom)

mentor – a trusted counselor or guide

Figure 9.1.2: A student assistant position with a college professor will provide a mentor and valuable information about careers in the professor's discipline.
Courtesy of Brian Smith.

When Should I Choose a Career?

Nearing high school graduation, you may be feeling pressured into making a decision about what career to pursue. At this point in your life, however, you may not be prepared to make that kind of a decision. You may not even be aware of all the career possibilities that exist, especially since so many new careers are created yearly! Unfortunately, in the United States, our society does pressure young adults to make career decisions that can have a lasting effect. What happens if you choose the wrong career? What if you want to change your mind after a few years of study?

It may help ease the pressure to know that the U.S. Department of Labor has estimated that "young people of high school age should expect to have an average of fourteen jobs throughout their lifetimes, in possibly six to eight different career fields." What a change from a generation ago when individuals often began working right out of high school and worked for the same company until they retired!

What does this prediction about the job market mean for you? On the positive side, it probably means you will never be locked into one particular job. You will have the opportunity to try new skills, learn new information, and experience new adventures throughout your life. On the other hand, it will mean you will have to have or develop the skill of being flexible with your career. You will need to learn how to transition from one job to another with minimum time, training, and possibly even education.

If you are unsure about what career you want to pursue, relax. Career counselors will tell you that it is okay not to be locked into a career decision at your high school graduation. In fact, they will most likely urge you to take some time to self-reflect, explore your options, take exploratory classes, and make an informed decision when you feel comfortable doing so.

But taking the pressure off doesn't mean you should stop thinking about your options now. This is the perfect time to begin exploring what the future holds in terms of employment and to begin reflecting on your personal values, interests, and skills.

What Should I Know about the Future Job Market?

Although no one can predict the future perfectly, you can look at trends and get a general picture of what the job market will be like a few years down the road. The Bureau of Labor Statistics offers the following information for the years 1996–2006:

- Industry employment growth is projected to be highly concentrated in service-producing industries, with business, health, and education services accounting for 70 percent of the growth:
- Health care services will increase 30 percent and account for 3.1 million new jobs.
- Educational services are projected to increase by 1.3 million teaching jobs.
- Computer and data processing services will add more than 1.3 million jobs.
- The labor force will become increasingly diverse:
  - The labor force growth of Hispanics, Asians, and other races will be faster than that for blacks and white non-Hispanics, stemming primarily from immigration.
  - Women's share of the labor force is expected to increase from 46 percent to 47 percent.
- Jobs will be available for job seekers from every educational and training background.
- Almost two-thirds of the projected growth will be in **occupations** that require less than a college degree. However, these positions generally offer the lowest pay and benefits.
- Jobs requiring the least education and training—those that can be learned on the job—will provide two of every three openings due to growth and replacement needs.

Job growth varies widely by educational and training requirements:

- Occupations that require a bachelor's degree are projected to grow the fastest. All of the twenty occupations with the highest earnings require at least a bachelor's degree. Engineering and health occupations dominate the list.

> **Key Note Term**
>
> **occupation** – the principal business of one's life

- **Education is essential for getting a high-paying job; however, many occupations, such as registered nurses, supervisors of blue-collar workers, electrical and electronic technicians, automotive mechanics, and carpenters do not require a four-year college degree, yet they offer higher-than-average earnings.**

These projected trends give only a brief profile of what the future job market will be like. One thing does seem certain: The more technological skills you learn, the better your chances of landing a high-paying job. Figure 9.1.3 illustrates predictions about occupations that will have fast growth, high pay, and largest numerical growth.

Figure 9.1.4 illustrates job growth rates based on education and training.

Don't despair if you are passionate about a career that isn't listed in the top 25 future jobs. If you are passionate about a specific career, you should pursue that goal! Although you might find that you have to work harder at finding a job, that you have to work more than one job until you can pursue your dream full-time, or that you don't earn as much money as others, you will be happy in your **profession**. Greater job satisfaction will reflect positively in other areas of your life.

Additionally, if you diversify your skills, have a well-rounded background, and continue to be a lifelong learner, you will find that you have more opportunities, and that it is easier to move into a wide variety of jobs.

Exploring Careers

As a high school student, this may be the first time you've seriously explored your career options; however, career exploring and planning may occur many times over the course of your life. As society advances, new opportunities are created. If you continue to explore careers and keep up-to-date with your skills and education, you will be ready when something new and challenging comes along.

One of the most important points to remember right now is that you do have time. In fact, the first two years of college are generally spent fulfilling general education requirements such as math, writing, communications, arts, science, and social sciences. These freshman- and sophomore-level classes give students an opportunity to strengthen critical-thinking skills and develop a solid background in the basics that will help them succeed in upper-level classes and give them the opportunity to explore various fields of study.

As you begin college, you will have several opportunities to meet with an academic adviser to discuss career goals and academic planning. If, at an advising session, you are given a degree plan that you are uncertain about, don't worry. You are not locked into pursuing that degree. Advisers often give you this one or degree plans to get you to think about your college and career goals. These degree plans list all of the courses a student in that field of study is required to complete to earn a certificate or degree. After you have declared a major, these degree plans act as a contract between you and the college. If you are following an established degree plan and the school revises and changes the degree plan, you will probably not be required to take additional classes, only the classes listed on your original degree plan. Often, the first two years of any degree plan are similar because every student is completing the general education requirements.

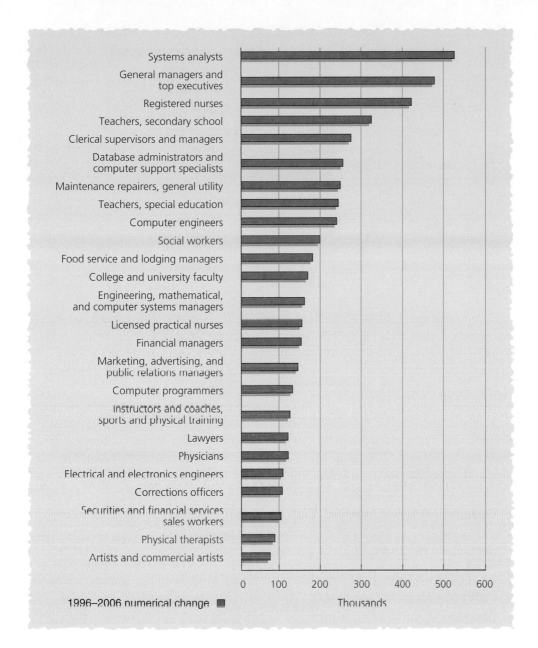

Figure 9.1.3: Occupations with largest numerical growth.

Reprinted from *1998–1999 Occupational Outlook Handbook*, Washington, DC: U.S. Department of Labor.

Although you are free to change degree plans whenever you want, you should be advised that the best time to change majors is before you take a significant number of upper-level courses. Often, the credits for one degree don't match those for another, so you end up taking extra semesters to complete your degree. If you are using financial aid to pay your college expenses, the money may run out, and you will have to pay for the extra classes on your own.

Choosing a degree plan, or career, can be a difficult task; however, you can begin the exploration process right now so that the decision becomes less complicated. Two steps you should consider are self-assessments and occupational research.

Figure 9.1.4: Growth rates by education.
Reprinted from *1998–1999 Occupational Outlook Handbook,* Washington, DC: U.S. Department of Labor.

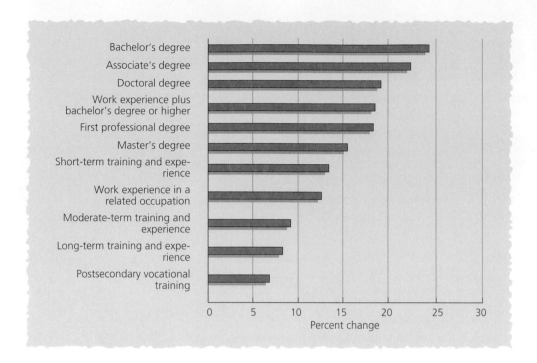

Self-Assessments

Self-assessment tools are created to help individuals gather information about themselves. Some assessments focus on your personality, values, interests, and work styles; other assessments focus on skills and competencies. Examples of available self-assessments include the following:

- **Campbell Interest and Skill Survey.** Matches interests and skills to occupations
- **Career Skills.** A computerized program that determines the type of skills a student would like to use in his or her work
- **Choices.** A computerized interest and skills inventory
- **Compass.** Measures basic skills
- **Discover.** A computerized guidance tool that assesses interests, abilities, values, and skills and matches those with the world of work
- **FOCUS II.** Identifies interests, skills, and values and relates them to occupations
- **Myers-Briggs Type Indicator.** Determines personality and matches it to work styles
- **Self-Directed Search.** Matches interests and abilities to career fields
- **SIGI Plus.** A computerized guidance tool that looks at interests, personality, values, and occupational options
- **Strong Interest Inventory.** Matches interests to occupations

Another valuable self-assessment tool is the *Prentice Hall Self-Assessment Library* on CD-ROM.

These assessments will ask you questions about yourself, your interests, your values, and your skills. Your high school counseling office, the U.S. Department of Labor, or the career counseling office at any college can provide you with a number of self-assessments.

You can also choose to create your own self-assessments. For example, you could

- **Look at your personal mission statement to reflect on your personal values.**

- **Create a table that lists all your accomplishments. For each accomplishment, list the skills you used in that activity.**

- **Write in your journal about the things that interest you, your aspirations, and people you admire.**

- **Compare jobs you have had or would like to have. Create a list of pros and cons associated with each job.**

- **Create a list of your personal traits and characteristics and think about what jobs might match them.**

- **Join activity clubs and organizations to see what interests you. Evaluate what you like or dislike about your experience.**

- **Take a class that focuses on career exploration. Your high school, local adult basic education, community education center, or local college may offer these courses.**

- **Complete a personality-style inventory and compare the results to various job requirements.**

The process of self-assessment is ongoing because you grow and change with each new experience. What you value now may not be as important in a few years, and you need to take these changes into account when you are considering careers.

After completing one or more self-assessments, you should have a self-profile that you can match to various jobs. If you work through specific programs in career centers, your self-assessment tool may give you a computer-generated list of suggested careers that would suit your profile. Think of this as a starting place for more specific types of research about careers and occupations.

Occupational Research

In addition to self-assessments, you should also plan to spend time researching occupations. Your research may include looking through books and occupational guides, but you may also want to interview someone in the job you are considering, shadow someone in the job, take on part-time work in that field, volunteer, or try a cooperative education experience.

There are specific points of information you should gather during your research. For example, you will want to find out answers to the following questions:

- **How much knowledge or training would I need to be hired for this job?**

- **What kind of other skills would I need to learn (communication skills or team-building skills, for example)?**

- **What kind of responsibilities would I have in this job?**

- **What are the working conditions of this job?**

- **What opportunities for advancement would I have in this job?**
- **What is the salary range for this job?**
- **What is the future outlook for this job?**
- **What are similar jobs that I might consider?**

The place to begin researching jobs is your high school counseling office or library. Most likely, it will have specific occupational guides that you can browse through, as well as numerous books, videos, and computer programs that offer comparable information. As you complete your research, take notes and compare the various jobs you research but don't feel pressured into making a decision immediately. Leave your options open as you work through the exploration stage of **career** planning.

Interviewing people performing the job you are interested in is a great way to obtain more information and makes the information from the books real for you. You can ask questions that might not have been answered in your previous research as well as questions that pertain to specific geographic jobs. For example, the research might show you that there are a large number of available jobs nationwide, but in an interview you might discover that there are a very limited number of job openings in your city or state. Interviews can also open the door for you to shadow someone performing the job.

Job shadowing is an opportunity for you to work side by side with someone who is hired in that profession. Depending on the type of job, you might find yourself observing others, or you may even get the chance to help. Benefits of job shadowing include discovering both the good and bad aspects of a particular job, learning about the job environment, and making contacts with others in the profession. Job shadowing may also open the door for you to be hired in part-time employment.

One of the best ways to find out if a particular type of work is suited to you is to do it. There are several ways: part-time or full-time paid work and volunteer work. At this point in your education, you may find that you are too busy with academic and extracurricular activities to take on a job, which is okay because you are learning valuable skills in school, organizations, and sports. But when you evaluate your time, you may discover that you could work one or two days after school or one day of the weekend. You don't want to overload yourself; however, even a minimal amount of work experience will certainly help you decide whether you like certain jobs and teach you work-related skills such as communication, leadership, team building, and problem solving. You may even get referrals for future jobs.

Cooperative education provides you with the opportunity to have paid employment in positions that complement your academic program. Although most co-op positions are obtained at the college level, more and more high schools are taking the initiative and offering high school students co-op positions. In these cases, students generally take classes for half a day and work for half a day.

If you have the opportunity to complete a co-op program, make the most of it by developing learning objectives in consultation with your supervisor, monitoring your progress, and making changes to your goals and strategies, if necessary.

However you choose to research occupations and careers, take time to reflect on your experiences. What do you like or dislike about the job? Do you like the work environment and the pace of the job? Do you have the skills, or can you easily learn the skills, to make you successful in the job? Does the job challenge or bore you? Would you be happy in the job for more than a few years? Does the career offer multiple yet similar job opportunities that you could take advantage of?

As you analyze these questions, consider whether you want to pursue this type of job. If not, consider yourself lucky that you discovered that answer now, not five or ten years down the road. If you do think this is a career worth pursuing, it may be time to think about what to major in at college.

How Are Careers and Majors Related?

After you have decided on the type of career you want to pursue, you should research the type of skills and education you will need. The required education will indicate what type of degree you will need and what you will need to major in. A major is a group of classes that are required to earn a degree in a specific area. Some careers, such as heating and air-conditioning technology or business and office technology may only require a one-year certificate or a two-year degree. These types of careers take very specialized training and education, so you will need to declare your major early in your academic career so that you can get into the classes you will need.

Some careers don't require specific majors in entry-level positions. For example, a person entering a career in marketing might major in marketing, accounting, communications, or public relations. As you research your career options, find out what type of major or degree is required so you can plan accordingly.

Understanding the Differences Between a Job and a Career

Throughout this book, you will see the words *job* and *career*, each being defined differently. Basically, a **job** is a series of tasks or activities that are performed within the scope of what is called work. These tasks relate to a career in that a career is a series of jobs. However, a career is more than just jobs; it is a sequence of **attitudes** and behaviors that are associated with work and that relate to your total life experience. A career is really an integration of your personality with your job activities. Therefore, your career becomes a primary part of your identity or your self-concept. This is illustrated in Table 9.1.1.

Although they are often used interchangeably, the words *career* and *job* have different meanings. Jobs can be both the individual pieces of a career or random, isolated events in a person's work history. Careers are formed over time; they consist of related jobs that build on one another. One job does not make a career; several jobs do.

Key Note Terms

job – a position of work or employment that is performed regularly in exchange for payment; a task or undertaking; a specific activity or piece of work

attitude – a feeling, emotion, or mental position regarding a fact or state

Table 9.1.1: Job versus Career	
What is a Job?	**Example**
A piece of work, task or undertaking	Babysitting, mowing lawns; duty done by agreement to pay
What is a Career?	**Example**
A principal business or profession	Teacher, engineer, writer; occupation or lifework

Working behind the counter at a fast-food restaurant until you can do something else is a job. If, however, your goal is to become a manager and invest in franchises someday, it is the first step in a career. The knowledge and skills gained from working behind the counter are a foundation on which you can continue to build as you move up in the fast-food industry.

In the past, people chose a career early in life, and they tended to stay in it most of their lives. Farmers worked on their farms, secretaries stayed in the office, and teachers taught until retirement. More recently the trend in America has shifted toward multiple careers. You can now expect to have four or more careers in your life. Furthermore, with the rapid changes in society as well as in economic conditions, jobs, and technologies, many traditional jobs are becoming obsolete.

This is markedly different from the world in which your parents worked. Thus, the expectation that after you find a job, you are home free, secure, or set for life is no longer realistic. The traditional **employee** contract, although unwritten, implied an honest day's work for an honest day's wage, employee loyalty in exchange for job security, and raises and **promotions** in return for seniority. Today's new employee contract simply implies continued employment for individuals who possess skills that continuously meet a business need.

More than ever it is important to give considerable thought to what you want to do and structure your training and education to be relevant both to your interests and to trends in the job market. You will find it beneficial to assess your skills and identify those that are transferable from a previous career to a newly emerging field with a minimum amount of retraining. Knowing yourself and developing a plan of action based on both your needs and the needs of the job market will help you embark on the career most satisfying for you rather than just following the latest trends in one field or another.

Demands in the job market rapidly come and go. Some time ago, teachers were in great demand; then, for about a decade, there was a glut of teachers on the market. Now there seems to be a renewed need for teachers in the workforce. The same is true of engineers. If you base your career decision primarily on current trends, by the time you obtain the training necessary to get into the hot field, it may well have cooled down. This strategy leaves you with slim prospects for a job that can lead to a career, and quite possibly with skills and training in a field that you weren't terribly excited about in the first place (except as a quick opportunity).

Key Note Terms

employee – one employed by another, usually for wages or salary

promotion – the act or fact of being raised in position or rank

You have the potential to be satisfied in any number of occupations. Getting to know yourself better through self-assessment will help you identify careers that are best suited to your personality. People who are not prepared for change allow that change to make decisions for them. They are often frustrated and unhappy because they are forced to work at jobs they don't enjoy. They may never have realized that they have choices, or perhaps they never took the time or energy to become aware of their preferences. They settle for less than what might be best for them. Dad says "get a job in business" even though his child has a special talent in art. The high school adviser recommends engineering because scholarships are available. The employment department directs a job applicant into an electronics training program because there's an opening. By knowing your own preferences, you will be ready to manage your career path instead of merely following others' suggestions.

Striving for Career Satisfaction

Survey after survey on job satisfaction among American workers indicates that well over 50 percent are dissatisfied with their jobs. In a study for *U.S. News & World Report*, people were asked to name the three things that contribute most to their quality of life. The top categories for men and women were "job/career satisfaction," "relationship with family," and "money." Because people may be changing jobs and careers several times in their lives, it is more important than ever before to have accurate knowledge about yourself and the world of work

In its annual Labor Day survey for 1999, the Gallup poll indicated that only 39 percent of workers are completely satisfied with their jobs. In another Gallup survey, two-thirds of a group of adults said if they were starting all over, they would try to get more information about their career options. You will face the need to continually reevaluate yourself and your career path. It is useful to know about the changing world of work and which occupations allow you to best express yourself and best use your strengths and talents. When analyzing your personal assets, it is to your advantage to ultimately think about the total job market. Search for jobs that will lead you into a career. You will benefit greatly from identifying a variety of alternatives that allow you to express your personality. Once you have looked within yourself and identified what you want and need in a job, changes will be easier to make because you'll know when you have outgrown one job and need a new one.

For most people, career planning is not a simple, straightforward, linear process in which they follow certain prescribed steps, end up at a specific destination, and live happily after. It is instead a feedback loop that continues to self-correct as you add information about your changing self and the world around you. You are constantly revising your career plan as you grow and change. This means that there isn't any one "right" career. Instead, there are many careers in which you could be equally happy, equally successful, equally satisfied.

You are looking, then, not for the one right career but for the series of alternatives and career options that seem to make sense for you, given your background, your personality, your career and life stages, and the changing world.

Choosing and Changing Careers

Each one of us, regardless of our stage in life, is in some phase of career development. You may be starting your first job or looking for a job. You may be planning for your first career, reentering the job market after some time at home, considering your next career, planning for part-time employment, or looking for meaningful volunteer experience.

Because there is no crystal ball that will predict the one right career for you, you will want to consider several options as you explore career development. It is possible to survey your needs, values, interests, skills, aptitudes, and sources of information about the world of work to create a broader career objective. Some careers do have established or common career paths. Teachers, for example, often start out as tutors, work up to student teacher, and then become an assistant teacher before taking on the task of a full-time teacher. In the marketing profession, people often start in sales; therefore, you need to think about career goals in the sense of their being both short term and long term. A short-term career goal is one that can be rather quickly attained. For example, in the process of career planning, you may discover you want to be a lawyer. Law is considered a long-term career option because it generally takes many years of study and preparation; however, a short-term career goal related to law might be obtaining a job as a legal secretary or a paralegal. Either of these would give you the opportunity to work in an environment that excites and energizes you long before you actually achieve your final and ultimate career goal. In addition, relevant experience enhances your appeal to future employers.

Real-Life Stories

Sandra was 17 when she started her first secretarial job in a legal office. For 10 years she was happy being a secretary involved with the legal profession. This left her time to raise her family. But her employers encouraged her to continue her education. Not only did she attend evening courses, but she also became involved with the Professional Secretaries' Association. By the time her children were grown, she had completed a two-year college degree program, served as president of her association, started a training course to become a paralegal, been promoted to legal assistant, and is now teaching legal terminology at a local community college.

There is a final, important reason that this effort at personal assessment is crucial as the first step in your career-planning process. After you know who you are and what your preferences and talents are, you can better make sense of the information that continually bombards you regarding the world of work. It's almost impossible to read a newspaper, listen to a news broadcast, visit a Web site, or watch a television show that does not have some implication for you and your career. In fact, you may feel you suffer from information overload. Looking at the want ads and reading about employment projections and trends can cause confusion, frustration, and often discouragement about what place you might have in this elusive job market.

One of the best ways to achieve a sense of control and perspective on this constant stream of information is to know who you are, so that when you are listening, reading, watching, and experiencing, you will have a means of processing information through your consciousness, through your personality and preferences, and through your values and skills. Eventually, you will be able to recognize and reject information that does not apply to you, and to internalize and add to your career plan information that does. If a group setting such as a career class is available to you, all the better! The opportunity to discover yourself and expand your horizons is multiplied by the added benefit of group interaction.

Conclusion

This lesson explained the importance of career exploration skills and career planning. Specifically, it introduced a career exploration strategy, discussed how to link information about yourself to specific occupations, and showed you how to use that strategy in making career decisions. You should be able to organize information about yourself and the world of work and be able to see which occupations best fit your aptitude, interests, abilities, and preference.

Many people never work at jobs or careers that use their full talents and abilities or that interest them. You do not have to work at a boring job. You can do something that interests you and still make good money.

By answering the following two questions that career seekers must answer, you are on your way to a satisfying and personally meaningful career:

- **What do you want to do?**
- **What are you suited to do?**

In the following lesson, you will learn how to create a career development portfolio and use it as you expand your ideas about the perfect career for you.

Lesson Review

1. **Explain the difference between a job and a career.**
2. **What are some of the experiences you've had that might lead you to your career?**
3. **What kind of job or career would you like to have? What do you need to do to get it?**

Lesson 2

Career Development Portfolio

Key Words

employment application
interview
networking
portfolio
resume
success

What You Will Learn to Do

- Assemble a personalized career portfolio

Linked Core Abilities

- Communicate using verbal, nonverbal, visual, and written techniques
- Take responsibility for your actions and choices

Skills and Knowledge You Will Gain Along the Way

- Explain the importance of developing and maintaining a career portfolio
- Identify components to include in a career portfolio
- Identify what best represents personal achievements and goals
- Describe documents to include in a career portfolio
- Define the key words contained in this lesson

Introduction

What do you want to become? What are you suited to do? What do you need to do to prepare? These questions and many more like them are what you must try to answer to prepare for your future. This lesson focuses on the career development portfolio, its importance, and its development and maintenance.

The better you prepare, the better your chances of achieving **success** and doing something that you enjoy. A career portfolio is a tool that helps you document evidence of your successes. The portfolio provides information about you and your achievements over time. It is a type of scrapbook that contains evidence of your accomplishments, your educational development, and your career growth.

By maintaining an up-to-date portfolio, you will be able to quickly reference needed information when applying for jobs, colleges, or scholarships.

Key Note Term

success – the gaining of fame or prosperity

What Is a Career Portfolio?

A portfolio is a file that contains an organized collection of your work based on your personality, goals, and aspirations. It provides insight and information on you and your achievements and growth over time. It presents an in-depth picture of your skills and competencies. It also provides a means to reflect on important areas of your life development and the impact of education on future lifestyle and career choices. It contains information that promotes what you want others, specifically future employers and schools, to know about you.

Why Create a Career Portfolio?

There are many good reasons to create and maintain a career development portfolio. A portfolio is tailored to meet your needs and requirements. It serves as your record of achievement. A portfolio will

- **Serve as an ongoing record of your completed work. Your portfolio will contain copies of good work from all of your classes, including information on projects in which you are involved that will be ongoing from year to year. It will provide you with a historical record that you can apply to other projects.**

- **Allow you to evaluate and see your improvement and growth, including how much you have done over the course of a nine-week period, semester or quarter, this year, or all the years of your high school experience.**

- **Serve as evidence of your accomplishments, even if you transfer from one school to another.**

- **Update your parents on your progress.**

- **Furnish you with a record of areas in your growth and development that may require additional work.**

- Help you with the application process for future jobs and/or enrollment in colleges or universities.
- Prepare information for school and job interviews.

Your Personal Career Portfolio

The following sections show you how to create a career development portfolio that suits your own personality, goals, and aspirations. As you begin to use this information, you will be able to see how important pieces of your life fit together so that you can feel confident and optimistic about your future. During the development and use of your career portfolio, you are encouraged to talk with your parents, instructors, counselor, and other supportive people in your life. They can best advise you on the type of information that you should save in your portfolio; information that promotes what you want others to know about you.

Creating Your Career Portfolio

By now, you may be able to pause and reflect on certain things you have learned, your likes and dislikes about them, your personality, your dreams for yourself, the things you wonder about, the things that frustrate you, and especially the things that you like most about yourself. When creating your career development portfolio, apply these thoughts and reflections to the areas of

- Self-knowledge/self-analysis
- Your life roles
- Past, present, and future educational development
- Career exploration and planning

Although portfolios will vary based on the needs of the individual and the audience, there are some basic requirements to all portfolios. They are as follows:

- A personal cover page
- A table of contents
- A personal statement
- A **résumé**
- Letters of reference—as many as possible
- Transcripts (optional)
- Samples of your school work from different subject areas to include why they are significant
- References and contact information

Your career development portfolio is still missing one essential element: an address book. The names, addresses, and phone numbers found in an address book represent the contacts that a person makes and develops over many years of **networking**. Fellow JROTC cadets, other classmates, teammates, your parents'

Key Note Terms

résumé – a short account of one's career and qualifications prepared typically by an applicant for an employment position

networking – meeting people and making contacts; the exchange of information or services among individuals, groups, or institutions

friends, your friends' parents, people met at camp, church, or acquaintances made while traveling are contacts that may become an important part of your future. They may be future clients, customers, colleagues, or employers.

Evaluating Your Career Portfolio

A **portfolio** is not complete unless you evaluate it thoroughly. Remember that the portfolio represents you. The following are some questions you should ask yourself to ensure that you have developed a quality product.

Key Note Term

portfolio – a document that contains a student's achievement over time and provides an in-depth picture of the student's skills and competencies

- **Are the required documents included?**
- **Have you edited it to make sure that there are no errors?**
- **Is the portfolio neat and organized?**
- **Is the portfolio labeled properly?**
- **Is it pleasing to the eye?**
- **Does it represent you as a person?**

Maintaining Your Career Portfolio

You should review the information in your portfolio at least three times per year and remove anything that is outdated. Your objective is to keep your career development portfolio as responsive to your future needs and interests as possible. This portfolio should be the best record of your school and work accomplishments.

When Should I Begin to Build a Portfolio?

You may be saying to yourself, "Why do I need to worry about creating a portfolio now? I'm not going to apply for jobs until after graduation." That may be true, but because there are so many uses for portfolios, the time to start building one is now. Remember, a portfolio is a collection of your work and accomplishments, so you need to collect those documents as you complete them.

The wrong time to start building a portfolio is the night before a deadline. Building a professional-looking portfolio takes time. As you are applying for admission and scholarships, you will need to collect specific documents, such as transcripts and test scores. Because you are collecting these documents from various sources, the process may take weeks.

Start today by requesting any documents you may need and by reflecting on what you have done that will demonstrate the kind of person you are. Find the evidence that will prove your abilities.

What Information Can Be Found in a Portfolio?

There isn't just one set of guidelines for assembling and using portfolios. As you go through life, you will need to customize your portfolio depending on its purpose. Not only might the contents change but also the form of the portfolio.

All portfolios are different depending on their purpose. For example, a person who is using a portfolio for promotion purposes has much different information in the portfolio than a person who is applying to serve in the Peace Corps.

Furthermore, your portfolio may take on different forms. Someone who is applying for a job as a Webmaster for a large corporation would probably choose to create a digital or electronic portfolio; a person applying for an accounting position in the same corporation may have a more traditional portfolio.

Additionally, you may choose to customize your portfolio based on the way you use it. As you are searching for scholarships to apply for, you will want to note not only their required documents but also the values they desire. When you are aware of your audience and their expectations, it is easy to tailor your work to their desires. This is not to say that you will lie in your portfolio, but rather that you will empha-size some skills or accomplishments over others, and you may even choose not to include some material.

For example, if you are applying for a scholarship based on academic merit, you would naturally want to showcase achievements in that area. However, if you are applying for a scholarship based on service to the community, you would want to discuss how you've volunteered at the local Boys and Girls Club, led a campaign to introduce a recycling program in your neighborhood, and participated in a fund-raiser for juvenile diabetes. See Table 9.2.1 for questions you should consider when customizing your portfolio.

Table 9.2.1: Customize Your Portfolio

Purpose	Why are you creating this portfolio?	Application to a particular school or academic program? Is it for a job? A scholarship? An award?
Audience	Who will be reading this portfolio?	Will they be supervisors? A scholar-ship committee made up of faculty, staff, and students? Peers? Faculty? Community members?
Format	How should I present this information?	Should it be presented in a notebook? A folder? Electronically?
Required	Have I included all the required documents that have been requested?	Can I, or should I, include other relevant documents? Will I be penalized for including additional documents? Have the documents been revised or updated?
Other Information	What information should be contained in a cover letter that explains the portfolio?	Do I need multiple copies of the portfolio? Who are the individuals I can contact if I have questions?

You may feel like you have little to put in your portfolio at this time. After all, perhaps you've never had a paying job or won any state competitions. Don't let that stop you. If you've been actively participating in academics and in your school activities, you probably have plenty to include. The following are suggestions of what to include in your personal portfolio, which is dependent on its purpose and audience.

- **A copy of your personal mission statement and long- and short-term goals.** An admissions counselor, scholarship committee, or prospective employer would already know a great deal about you and what you value by reading your personal mission statement. Having stated goals and a plan of action for reaching those goals impresses others. It shows you have reflected on what is important to you (your values) and made decisions about how to live your life according to those values.

- **A copy of your résumé.** Even though you may not have had many paying jobs, you should include those you have held, as well as any volunteering you have done and projects you have worked on for organizations you belong to. For example, if you were the recording secretary for an organization for two years, you should list that. It demonstrates your commitment to the organization, as well as your leadership potential, organizational skills, and communication skills. Your résumé doesn't need to be elaborate, but it does need to be clearly written so that others can glean information about you from it.

- **Copies of transcripts, your diploma, and any certifications you have earned.** This information would be appropriate when applying for admission and scholarships; however, it might not always be appropriate. Use your best judgment when including this information.

- **Copies of any awards you have received.** If needed, include an explanation about the award. Often the award itself is explanation enough and is telling evidence of your personal character and abilities.

- **Copies of recommendation letters.** If you have excelled in particular classes or have done exceptional work for an individual, consider asking for a letter of recommendation. These letters could be rather general letters that describe the relationship you have with the individual (this person's student for two years, for instance), a description of the work you have accomplished, your skills, and general information about your character. If you need specific information for a specific purpose, don't hesitate to tell the person so the letter can be most effective.

- **Copies of names of references and their contact information.** References are people who will vouch for you and your skills. They may be contacted and asked specific questions about your abilities. Make sure the contact information—phone numbers, mailing address, e-mail address—is kept current. Also make sure you get permission to use them as references. It is an uncomfortable situation for someone to be called and asked to give a reference when that person is not expecting it. The opposite is also true: If the person named as reference is expecting to be called, he or she can be prepared to discuss your achievements and give a strong, positive profile of you.

- **Copies of your work samples.** Admissions counselors, scholarship committees, and prospective employers often want specific examples of work you have completed. Outstanding writing samples are very helpful, so you might consider including a copy of an essay or article you wrote. Group projects are also appropriate if you include a description of your participation and leadership in the project. Also consider including a piece of work that demonstrates your level of critical and creative thinking. Perhaps you designed an advertising campaign for your yearbook. Include copies of some of the work you created.

- **Any other requested information or materials that will showcase your skills.** For example, if you are planning on majoring in early childhood education, you would want to find a way to demonstrate your skills in working with children. You might write a summary of your experiences that describes how you've learned to effectively manage caring for children of various ages, how you've learned to solve problems, and how you completed a study on children's nutrition and snacks.

Your portfolio might look a little different every time you use it. Keep in mind the purpose of the portfolio when you are selecting items to include in it.

The following are some other suggestions to keep in mind:

- **Use cover letters.** If you are sending your portfolio to someone, include a cover letter that explains why you are sending the portfolio and a brief description that highlights the contents.

- **Put your materials in a logical order.** If you are responding to a specific scholarship application that asks for specific materials, put the materials in the order in which they are listed on the application.

- **Include the appropriate information and the appropriate amount of information.** You want the person reviewing your portfolio to get a clear and complete profile of you, but you don't want to overwhelm that person. If you make him or her wade through excessive information, that person may not bother to look at any of it. Be complete, but don't go over the limit.

- **Organize your materials.** If you include a great deal of information, find a way to make it accessible. For example, you might include tabs or staple sections separately.

- **Keep your materials current.** As you grow as a student, the work you produce will reflect that growth. Your thinking, writing, and leadership skills will strengthen, and you want the work in your portfolio to reflect that growth. Exchange your old examples for new ones.

- **Keep your references current.** For example, as you eventually move through college and get ready to enter the job market, you will replace the letter from your high school forensics coach with a letter from a college instructor. Likewise, when you work for different employers, always ask them for letters of recommendation or for permission to use them as references.

- **Make sure your portfolio looks neat and professional.** With today's easy access to computers, there really isn't a reason to include handwritten cover letters, resumes, or other information. This will be especially true when you approach graduation from college and will use your portfolio in the job market.

- **Get feedback.** Have your portfolio critiqued by an individual who can give you good advice. The process of assembling a portfolio is much the same as writing an essay. You should go through the process of having the portfolio critiqued and revised in order to present a high-quality profile of yourself.

Building a Portfolio

Do you remember the old adage, "Rome wasn't built in a day"? The same is true for effective portfolios. You may have tried to write a paper the night before it was due or study for a test an hour before taking it. What was the result? Was the paper the best it could be? Did you get every question on the test correct? Probably not. Building a strong portfolio also takes time, and like a paper you write for your English class, it probably will need to be revised—possibly more than once.

As you begin to create your portfolio, think of its purpose in general terms. This should be a collection that you can pick and choose from when you are assembling portfolios for specific reasons.

You should probably consider investing in a small file in which you can keep your materials. Most of the time, you will want to send copies of documents, instead of originals, so you should have separate folders for each document. Make sure you mark the original in some way so that you won't accidentally send it away. Keep a few copies of the original ready in case you need to assemble multiple copies of the portfolio at one time. This is especially helpful if you are going to apply for admission to several different colleges or for multiple scholarships.

You should spend some time brainstorming your accomplishments and activities. At this point in the process, don't edit yourself or leave anything out. It's best to gather as much information as possible before you decide what is important and what isn't. When law enforcement agencies are investigating a crime, they are required to collect every type of information possible before they actually present the case. Think of your portfolio as evidence that proves your abilities; you also should collect as much information as possible before presenting your case.

The following are suggestions for collecting information:

- **Fine-tune your personal mission statement, and keep a copy in your files. Even if you don't use it in all the portfolios you send out, having it and using it will keep you focused on your goals.**

- **Get copies of transcripts and test scores from your school.**

- **Begin drafting your résumé. If you don't know how to write a résumé, check with your counselor or English teacher, who should have a packet of information for you. Or you can purchase one of the many how-to books at your local bookstore.**

- **Consider carefully whom you might ask to write a letter of recommendation for you. Choose three or four individuals and talk to them personally about what your goals are and why you would like them to write a letter for you. You might consider asking teachers, employers, club or activity sponsors, or adults who know you well. When they have written their letters, be sure to thank them.**

- **List all the awards you have earned and make copies of the certificates that accompany the awards. Don't forget to include community service recognition as well as school activities.**

- **Sort through completed school assignments that demonstrate your academic abilities. Choose ones that emphasize your thinking and writing abilities.**

After you have a collection of materials ready, create a sample portfolio that you can have critiqued. Teachers or counselors who know you well would be good people to ask because they may remember something you've done but haven't included. After they have looked at it and given you suggestions for improvement, begin to revise. If your reviewers are willing to look at it again, let them. When you are happy with the materials, file them away until you need to assemble a portfolio for a specific purpose.

After completing your portfolio, you should be able to reflect on your accomplishments with a sense of pride and confidence. You will discover how valuable your work as a student, volunteer, participant, and leader has been. By creating a portfolio, you showcase not only your accomplishments as an individual but also your qualities and character. This should give you the motivation and self-confidence to move ahead with your life.

Keeping Your Portfolio Strong

Even when you get accepted into college or get the scholarship or job you want, your work with your portfolio won't be over. You should consider your portfolio a living document that needs to steadily grow as you do. As you improve your skills and your thinking and as you participate in new experiences, you should document these accomplishments and add this evidence to your growing portfolio file. And as your older material becomes out-of-date and irrelevant, remove it from your files.

One way to keep your portfolio growing is to create and then take advantage of opportunities that you excel in. For example, you could find a campus organization to participate in and volunteer to be an officer, or you could join a community service organization. And, of course, you could take a co-op, internship, or job that will prepare you for the career you want after college graduation.

Creating a portfolio now will keep you organized and ready for any opportunity that may come your way.

Preparing a Winning Résumé

The purpose of the résumé is to get an interview. Similar to an advertisement, the résumé should attract attention, create interest, describe accomplishments, and provoke action. Brevity is essential; one page is best, and two pages are the limit. The résumé tells the prospective employer what you can do and have done, who you are, and what you know. It also indicates the kind of job you seek. The résumé must provide enough information for the employer to evaluate your qualifications, and it must interest the employer enough so that you will be invited for an interview.

Writing a well-constructed résumé requires that your research be completed before compiling the résumé. You need to keep in mind the type of employer and position as well as the general job requirements in order to tailor your résumé to the specific requirements and personality of the employer. To be most effective, your résumé should be designed to emphasize your background as it relates to the job being sought. It should also look neat, clean, and organized. This means word-processed with no errors and then laser-printed or photocopied on high-quality paper (see Figure 9.2.1).

Portfolios

The portfolio is an expanded résumé. It is usually a folder containing the basic résumé and samples of your work related to the job objective. It is a good idea to be storing work samples now. For instance, a marketing specialist will send a potential

Figure 9.2.1: This student is using the computer and the Internet to develop and proof his résumé.
Courtesy of Bob Daemmrich/The Image Works.

employer a résumé along with fliers, brochures, and ads created in past jobs. For a marketing student with limited experience, the folder could include copies of term papers, proposals completed for classes, and homework assignments related to the job objective. Portfolios are useful to have during information interviews, when you are at association meetings and networking, or upon request in an interview.

Preparation for Composing Your Résumé

Although stating an objective is considered optional by some experts (because it can be stated in your cover letter), it is to your advantage to include it on the résumé. In actuality, one résumé should be designed for each job objective. Remember, there are no jobs titled "anything."

The job objective is a concise and precise statement about the position you are seeking. This may include the type of firm in which you hope to work, such as a small, growing company. A clear objective gives focus to your job search and indicates to an employer that you've given serious thought to your career goals. When time does not allow you to develop a résumé for each of several different jobs that interest you, the job objective may be emphasized in the cover letter, which will be discussed at the end of this chapter, and omitted from the résumé.

A job objective is sometimes referred to as a goal, professional objective, position desired, or simply objective. It can be as specific as "community worker," "personnel assistant," or "junior programmer"; it can be as general as "management position using administrative, communications, and research skills" or "to work as an administrative assistant in a creative atmosphere and have the opportunity to use my abilities." The more specific the objective statement the better; a clear objective enables you to focus your résumé more directly on that objective. The effect is pointed, dramatic, and convincing.

A résumé summarizes your particular background as it relates to a specific job. It summarizes your career objectives, education, work experience, special skills, and interests. Visualize a pyramid or triangle with the job objective at the top and everything beneath it supporting that objective.

In writing the rough draft of your résumé, prepare 5" x 3" index cards for each job you've held (see Figure 9.2.2).

The front of your index card should contain the following information:

- **Name, address, phone number of employer, and immediate supervisor at work site**
- **Dates employed (month/year to month/year)**
- **Job title**
- **Skills utilized**

Figure 9.2.2: Front and back of the résumé index card. The format can be easily adapted for use in creating a computer file. Reprinted from *The Career Fitness Program Exercising Your Options*, Sixth Edition, by Diane Sukiennik, William Bendat, and Lisa Raufman, (2001), Prentice Hall, Inc.

Elaine's Espresso House
555 Stevens Circle   April 2000–December 2000
Roanoke, VA 23640
(540) 555-1211

Supervisor: Position:
Joe Smith   Bookkeeper & Shift Supervisor

Skills Utilized:

Related well with continuous flow of people. Attentive to detail; organized; energetic.

Bilingual—Spanish/English

Functions:

Management	—Coordinated service with customer needs, payroll, scheduled employees.
Communications	—Welcomed guests. Directed staff in performing courteous and rapid service. Responded to and resolved complaints.
Bookkeeping	—Maintained records of financial transactions. Balanced books. Compiled statistical reports.

The back of the card should show the duties divided into functional areas.

When choosing information to include in your résumé, avoid anything that may not be considered in a positive light or that has no relationship to your ability to do the job, such as marital status, number of children, political or religious affiliation, age, photos. When in doubt, leave it out.

Using Action Words

Remember that your writing style communicates the work activity in which you have been involved. Use phrases and document experiences that both involve the reader and make your résumé outstanding and active. The following are basic guidelines for selecting your "power" words:

- **Choose short, clear phrases**
- **If you use sentences throughout, keep them concise and direct**
- **Use the acceptable jargon of the work for which you are applying. Remember, you want your prospective employer to *read* your résumé**
- **Avoid general comments such as "My duties were . . ." or "I worked for . . ." Begin with action words that concisely describe what your tasks were. For example:**
  - **Developed more effective interviewing procedure**
  - **Evaluated training program for new employees**
- **List the results of your activities. For example:**
  - **Reduced office filing by 25 percent**
  - **Developed interview evaluation summary form**
  - **Increased efficiency in delivering services**
- **Don't dilute your action words with too many extraneous activities; be *selective* and sell your *best* experiences**
- **Target your words to the employer's needs**

The following are examples of action words that could be used in your résumé:

accomplished	evaluated	negotiated
achieved	expanded	organized
analyzed	facilitated	oriented
arranged	guided	planned
built	implemented	processed
controlled	improved	produced
created	increased	proved
demonstrated	initiated	raised profits
designed	inspired	reduced costs
developed	interpreted	researched
directed	invented	sold
effected	led	supervised
encouraged	managed	supported
established	motivated	wrote

Using the Correct Key Phrases

In many large companies, human resources personnel now scan résumés into computer files and databases for storage and later retrieval. According to a poll by a management consulting firm, 31 percent of 435 human resource professionals indicated their firms used résumé banks for recruiting. Many experts say the percentage of large and midsize companies using such programs is far higher, with employers such as The Walt Disney Company and MCI Inc., leading the way in their use of résumé banks. A growing biotechnology firm, Amgen, Inc., receives more than 225 résumés a day, about 60 percent in conventional paper format and 40 percent by e-mail or fax. All end up in an automated tracking system. The manager of employment systems at Amgen, Inc., says automated tracking allows the company to consider all applicants for all available jobs, which is especially important in a growing company. When an opening occurs, employers search their banks and databases for résumés using certain key phrases relevant to the position. For example, a company looking for "B.S., Information Systems, dBase, Lotus 1-2-3" would first retrieve résumés containing these key words.

Depending on the field in which you hope to work and the type of companies to which you will apply, this information may be vital to your writing a résumé that gets retrieved during a key word search. In such cases, the appearance and style of your résumé will be less significant than the manner in which you describe your specific skills; be certain to use concrete nouns to summarize past experience.

References

The expression *References available on request* is usually sufficient on a résumé and is typically placed at the end. Although you don't have to list specific names on the résumé, you should have at least three people in mind who can talk about your work habits, your skills, and your accomplishments. When you are job hunting, ask these people in advance if you may use them as references, informing them of your job objective so they will be prepared if a prospective employer calls. Many college placement centers act as a clearinghouse for the collection of résumés and references. You establish a file, and the center sends out your résumé and references when you make a request. The placement center often makes this service available for alumni, and it may have reciprocal agreements with other colleges across the country.

The Appearance of Your Résumé

The appearance of this document is important. Your résumé must be typed clearly, spaced well, and visually attractive. Remember that many employers skim only the first page of a résumé. Thus, it is crucial that your material be strategically placed so that what is most likely to be read is most relevant to the job desired. Employers have been known to receive hundreds of résumés each day, giving them only minutes to review each one. Therefore, even if you must use two pages, the first is more crucial. Experts advise against using a résumé preparation service. An employer can usually spot a canned résumé and might assume that the applicant lacks initiative or self-confidence. The time you spend writing your résumé will be time well spent. It will give you the opportunity to summarize what you have to offer to an employer.

Personal computers and résumé writing or word processing software can help turn an average-looking résumé into a class act. If possible, store your résumé and cover letter on a floppy disk or in hard-drive memory for easy retrieval and updating. Many duplicating shops have personal computers available for an hourly fee.

Although offset printing was once the preferred method of producing résumés, quick copies made at professional copy centers are now acceptable if they are reproduced on high-quality equipment and are clean and free of smudges. Use an attractive bond paper for these copies of your résumé; usually a neutral color such as ivory or white is best. Copy centers typically have a wide selection of stationery available. It is often useful to have a career counselor, potential employer, family member, or friend review a draft of your résumé before duplicating your final copy. Ask for a careful check of content, format, grammar, spelling, and appearance. Even if you plan to send your résumé electronically via computer, make sure it is completely error-free.

Electronic Résumés

Whether you prepare your résumé yourself or have it prepared professionally, after you have a document you can be proud to send to potential employers, you will need to make slight modifications to create the scannable version. Electronic résumés are entered into a résumé bank, which means they are subject to electronic, as well as human, scanning. You may need to create two or more versions of your résumé, emphasizing various skills and key words. You may also seek assistance from students who have prepared effective résumés (see Figure 9.2.3).

Guidelines for preparing and submitting electronic résumés

When preparing a résumé, keep the following in mind:

- Your résumé will be viewed with 80-character lines and 24 lines to a screen page
- Use an 8½" x 11" page format (If you plan to fax it, print it on white paper)
- Use an easy-to-read typeface (font), such as Times, Helvetica, or Palatino, at a point size of 10 or 12
- Avoid tabs (use the space key), underlines, boxes, columns, italics, and shading
- Use boldface type and bullets to emphasize words
- Use key skill words from a job description or advertisement
- Some résumé banks offer fill-in-the-blank templates, complete with instructions
- E-mail a copy of your résumé to yourself to see what it looks like (You can do this from an Internet site that allows you to create your own résumé using its format)

You will find this process easier if your résumé is on computer disk. You are then free to copy it and make changes to the copy. This allows you to keep your hard work safe and protected in the original file. If your résumé is prepared professionally, you may also want to have the service prepare an electronic version. It will provide you with a disk containing the file, so you may create the electronic version yourself if you feel competent to do so. The key is to work from a copy, not the original.

Figure 9.2.3: Other students that have been through the process of developing an electronic résumé can be of great assistance.
Courtesy of Loren Santow/Tony Stone Images.

Another reason to have your résumé on disk is that employers and online résumé distribution services often have different requirements for file formats and design specifications. The Web site for an online résumé distribution service or potential employer will provide you with company-specific details; it may also offer assistance in preparing this very important promotional piece about you. The human resources department of a potential employer may also be able to provide you with electronic résumé information.

Although it is highly recommended that your traditional résumé be no more than one page, your electronic résumé may be longer. The computer will easily scan more than one page. It uses all the information on your résumé to determine if your skills match available positions. The computer searches for key words. Those key words can often be found in a general job description matching the position title for which you are applying. They also appear in classified ads and job postings. Or you may be able to glean some during information interviews. Be sure to write your résumé to reflect the skill needs of the position, which is another reason why you may want to prepare multiple versions of your résumé.

Refer to the Guidelines for Preparing and Submitting Electronic Résumés on page 285 for detailed how-to information. You may want to learn more about electronic résumés. Your career center will have many books on the subject, and résumé Internet sites are excellent sources for additional information.

Types of Résumés

There are three general types of résumé: functional, chronological, and combination. Comparing the following two sample work experience entries will give you some idea of the basic difference between functional and chronological résumés, which are referred to in Figure 9.2.4.

The next part of this lesson discusses all three types in detail. The combination résumé, as the name implies, is a combination of functional and chronological.

The Functional Résumé

A functional résumé presents your experience, skills, and job history in terms of the functions you have actually performed rather than as a simple chronological listing of the titles of jobs you have held. Similar to any résumé, it should be tailored to fit the main tasks and competencies required by the job you are seeking. Essentially, you redefine your past experiences according to the functions in the job for which you are applying. You should select and emphasize those activities from previous employment that relate to the specific job sought and deemphasize or omit irrelevant background.

	NAME Address Phone Number
Job Objective	State and describe as specifically as possible. Refer to the *Dictionary of Occupational Titles* for appropriate descriptive vocabulary.
Education	Depending on your job objective and the amount of education you have had, you may want to place this category directly after Job Objective. (However, if your job experience is more relevant to the position being applied for or if your education is not recent, you will want to list job experience prior to education.) Most recent education should be listed first. Include relevant credentials and licenses.
	Example: As employers, educational institutions are usually more concerned with appropriate degrees than other employers. Include special workshops, noncredit courses, and self-taught skills when they are appropriate to your job objective.
Experience	Describe *functionally* (by activities performed) your experience relevant to the particular job for which you are applying; start with the most relevant and go to the less relevant. Include without distinction actual job experience, volunteer experience, your work on class projects, and school and class offices held. Alternatively, show your experience *chronologically*, listing your most recent professional experience first.
	There is no need to stress dates unless they indicate that you have been continuously advancing toward this job objective.
	Use action verbs; do not use full sentences, unless you decide to write your resume as a narrative.
	Use the *Dictionary of Occupational Titles* to help you describe accurately what you have done, always keeping in mind how your experience relates to your job objective. Remember to use words and skills related to your job objective to describe yourself in the cover letter and during the interview.
Special Skills	Put this optional category directly after Job Objective if you feel that your professional experience does not adequately reflect the talents you have that best support this job objective.
	Examples: Facility with numbers, manual dexterity, patience, workshops you have led, writing ability, self-taught skills, language fluency.
References	Available on request.
	(Use references only if you have space and if the names are well known to potential employers.)

Figure 9.2.4: Résumé guidelines.
Reprinted from *The Career Fitness Program Exercising Your Options,* Sixth Edition, by Diane Sukiennik, William Bendat, and Lisa Raufman, (2001), Prentice Hall, Inc.

For example, an administrative assistant might perform some administration, communications, and clerical functions. A secretary for an elementary school rewrote his résumé to highlight these categories. To better define the skills used in his secretarial job, he researched the job description of executive secretary and office manager in his school personnel manual and located the description of administrative assistant in the *Dictionary of Occupational Titles*. He then compiled his résumé to show how his executive secretarial responsibilities related to the administrative assistant position desired. Assess how your past work or life experience can be described in such categories as marketing, human resources, finance, community services, or research and development.

Suggestions for Job Descriptions

Descriptions in the *Dictionary of Occupational Titles* and in some personnel manuals provide a source of helpful phrases and statements to use in describing your own job history and experience. The following two descriptions, for example, would be useful to you in composing a functional résumé for a job in business. However, you would use only relevant sentences, adapting them to your personal background.

Office Manager

- Coordinates activities of clerical personnel in the organization
- Analyzes and organizes office operations and procedures such as word processing, bookkeeping, preparation of payrolls, flow of correspondence, filing, requisitioning of supplies, and other clerical services
- Evaluates office production, revises procedures, or devises new forms to improve efficiency of work flow
- Establishes uniform correspondence procedures and style practices
- Formulates procedures for systematic retention, protection, retrieval, transfer, and disposal of records
- Plans office layouts and initiates cost reduction programs
- Reviews clerical and personnel records to ensure completeness, accuracy, and timeliness
- Prepares activity reports for guidance of management
- Prepares employee ratings and conducts employee benefits and insurance programs
- Coordinates activities of various clerical departments or workers within department

Administrative Assistant

- Aids executive in staff capacity by coordinating office services such as personnel, budget preparation and control, housekeeping, records control, and special management studies
- Studies management methods in order to improve work flow, simplify reporting procedures, and implement cost reductions
- Analyzes unit operating practices, such as recordkeeping systems, forms control, office layout, suggestion systems, personnel and budgetary requirements, and performance standards, to create new systems or revise established procedures
- Analyzes jobs to delineate position responsibilities for use in wage and salary adjustments, promotions, and evaluation of work flow

- **Studies methods of improving work measurements or performance standards**

If you are applying for a specific job, ask the human resources department for a copy of the job description; then tailor your résumé to the skills listed in that description.

Creating a Functional Résumé

Beginning or returning workers who have had no paid experience often find it particularly hard to make their activities sound transferable to the world of work. They dismiss their experience as academic work or homemaking, which they mistakenly think differs markedly from work in business; however, they usually have been performing business functions without realizing it. People without paid work experience and people returning to the job market after taking time out to be homemakers can persuade employers to recognize their ability and practical experience if they describe their life in categories like the following:

Management

- **Coordinated the multiple activities of five people of different ages and varying interests, keeping within tight schedules and continuous deadlines**
- **Established priorities for the allocation of available time, resources, and funds**

Office Procedures

- **Maintained lists of daily appointments, reminders, items to be purchased, people to be called, tasks to be accomplished**
- **Handled all business and personal correspondence; answered and issued invitations, wrote stores about defective merchandise, made hotel reservations**

Personnel

- **Recruited, hired, trained, and supervised household staff; negotiated wages**
- **Motivated children to assume responsibilities and helped them develop self-confidence**
- **Resolved problems caused by low morale and lack of cooperation**

Finances

- **Established annual household budget, and monitored costs to stay within expenses**
- **Balanced the checkbook and reconciled monthly bank statements**
- **Calculated take-home pay of household staff, made quarterly reports to the government on Social Security taxes withheld**

Purchasing

- **Undertook comparison shopping for food, clothing, furniture, and equipment, and purchased at various stores at different times, depending on best value**
- **Planned meals according to savings available at different food stores**
- **Shopped for insurance and found lower premiums than current coverage, resulting in substantial savings**

Pros and Cons of the Functional Résumé

The functional résumé is especially useful if you have limited work experience or breaks in your employment record. If you are changing fields, you need not include dates or distinguish paid activities from nonpaid volunteer activities. By omitting or deemphasizing previous employers' names, you downplay any stereotyped assumptions that a prospective employer may make about previous employers (McDonald's, the PTA, a school district). Similarly, highlighting skills and deemphasizing job titles help direct the future employer to the fact that you are someone with specific abilities that may be useful in the present job opening. This format also can emphasize your growth and development.

To use this format effectively, you must be able to identify and write about your achievements. This sometimes requires the assistance of an expert résumé writer. Additionally, some employers may prefer résumés that include exact dates and job titles.

The Chronological Résumé

The chronological résumé is the traditional, most often used résumé style. It lists your work history in reverse chronological order, meaning the most recent position or occupation is listed first. The work history should include dates employed, job title, job duties, and employer's name, address, and telephone number.

Pros and Cons of the Chronological Résumé

The chronological résumé is most useful for people with no breaks in their employment record and for whom each new position indicates continuous advancement or growth. Recent high school and college graduates also find this approach simpler than creating a functional résumé.

As dates tend to dominate the presentation, any breaks or undocumented years of work may stand out. If your present position is not related to the job you desire, you may be eliminated from the competition by employers who feel that current experience is the most important consideration in reviewing résumés. However, if you emphasize skills in your present job that will be important to the new position, this will be less of a problem.

The Combination Résumé

If you have major skills important for success in your desired job in addition to an impressive record of continuous job experience with reputable employers, you can best highlight this double advantage with a combination of the functional and chronological styles of résumé. This combination style usually lists functions followed by years employed with a list of employers. The combination style also satisfies the employer who wants to see the dates that you were actually employed.

Cover Letter Guidelines

One sure way to turn off a prospective employer is to send a résumé with no cover letter. Other turnoffs are sending a form letter addressed to the Personnel Manager or addressing your letter Dear Sir, only to have it received by a female manager.

A cover letter is used to announce your availability and introduce the résumé. It is probably one of the most important self-advertisements you will write.

The cover letter should indicate you have researched the organization and are clearly interested in a position there. Let the person to whom you are writing know what sources you used and what you know about the firm in the first paragraph—to get his or her attention and show your interest.

You may have heard people say, "It's not what you know, but who you know that counts." This is only partly true, but nonetheless important. You can often get to know someone with only a little effort. Call or, better yet, visit the organization and talk to people who already hold the job you want. Be tactful and discreet, of course. You're not trying to take their position from them. Ask about training, environment, salary, and other relevant issues; then in your cover letter, mention you talked with some of the firm's employees, and these discussions increased your interest. You thereby show the reader you took the initiative to personally visit the company and that you know someone, if only casually.

Basic principles of letter and résumé writing include being self-confident when listing your positive qualities and attributes, writing as one professional to another, and having your materials properly prepared. Figure 9.2.5 shows résumé cover letter guidelines.

Address
City, State Zip
Date

Name of Person
Company Name
Street Address or P.O. Box
City, State Zip

Salutation: (Dear M ______________: or Greetings:)

The first paragraph should indicate what job you are interested in and how you heard about it. Use the names of contact persons here, if you have any.

Sample Entry: Your employment advertisement in Tuesday's *News-Chronicle* indicating an opening for an administrative assistant is of special interest to me. Mary Smith, who is employed with your firm, suggested I write to you. I have heard that Rohn Electronics is a growing company and needs dynamic employees who want to learn and contribute to the firm.

The second paragraph should relate your experience, skills, and background to the particular position. Refer to your enclosed resume for details, and highlight the specific skills and competencies that could be useful to the company.

Sample Entry: During the last five years, I worked as office manager. In this position, I improved office efficiency by investigating and selecting word processing equipment. I understand that your opening includes responsibilities for supervising and coordinating word processing procedures with your home office. I was able to reduce my firm's operating costs over 30 percent by selecting the best equipment for our purposes.

The third paragraph should indicate your plans for follow-up contact and that your resume is enclosed.

Sample Entry: I would appreciate the opportunity to apply my skills on behalf of your company. For your examination, I have enclosed a resume indicating my education and work experience. I will call your office early next week to determine a convenient time for an appointment to further discuss possible employment opportunities.

Sincerely,

NOTE: Don't forget to sign the letter.

Your first and last name
Enclosure (or Attachment)

Figure 9.2.5: Résumé cover letter guidelines.
Reprinted from *The Career Fitness Program Exercising Your Options*, Sixth Edition, by Diane Sukiennik, William Bendat, and Lisa Raufman, (2001), Prentice Hall, Inc.

If at all possible, address your letter to a specific person, with the name spelled correctly and with the proper title. These details count. Your opening paragraph should contain the "hook." Arouse some work-related interest. Explain (very briefly) why you are writing. How did you become interested in that company? Summarize what you have to offer. Details of your background can show why you should be considered as a job candidate. The self-appraisal that went into preparation of your résumé tells what you can and like to do and where your strengths and interests lie. Your research on the prospective employer should have uncovered the qualifications needed. If your letter promises a good match—meaning your abilities matched with the company's needs—you've attracted attention.

Keep your letter short and to the point. Refer to your résumé, highlighting relevant experiences and accomplishments that match the firm's stated needs. Ask for an interview. Indicate when you will be calling to confirm a convenient time for the interview. Let your letter express your individuality but within the context of the employment situation.

The cover letter should be individually typed for each job desired. Always review both cover letter and résumé for good margins, clarity, correct spelling, and accurate typing. Appearance does count.

Application Forms

Key Note Terms

employment application – a form used in making a request to be considered for a job position

interview – a formal face-to-face meeting, especially one conducted for the assessment of an applicant

A final type of form, accepted sometimes as a substitute for a résumé, is an application form. The **employment application** is a form used by most companies to gain necessary information and to register applicants for work (see Figure 9.2.6). This information becomes a guide to determine a person's suitability for both the company and the job that needs filling. You should observe carefully the following guidelines.

You will probably be asked to fill out an employment application form, usually before the **interview** takes place. With this in mind, it is good practice to arrive at the employment office a little ahead of the time of your interview. Bring along a pen and your résumé or personal data sheet. You will be asked to provide your name, address, training or education, experience, special abilities, and possibly even your hobbies and interests. Practically all application forms request that you state the job you are seeking and the salary you have received in the past. Most firms require an applicant to complete an application form.

Many times the employer wants to make certain rapid comparisons and needs only to review the completed company employment application forms on file. For example, Ms. Ford needed a stenographer who could type fast. She examined many application forms of people who had word processing skills. By referring to the same section each time, she quickly thumbed through dozens of applications, eliminating all candidates who had only average speed. Thus, there was no need for her to examine résumés or read dozens of letters to find out exactly how fast each candidate could type.

Date _____

PERSONAL INFORMATION:

Name _____
      Last   First   Middle

Address _____
      Street   City   State   Zip

Telephone Number (_____) _____   Are you over 17 years of age? ❑ Yes ❑ No

POSITION WANTED:

Job Title _____ Date Available _____ Salary Desired _____

Check any that apply: ❑ Full Time ❑ Part Time ❑ Day Shift ❑ Night Shift

EDUCATION:

Begin with high school; include any military school you may have attended:

NAME OF SCHOOL   LOCATION OF SCHOOL   DEGREE OR COURSE OF STUDY

List any Academic Honors or Professional Associations:

WORK EXPERIENCE:

List last three employers. Start with the current or most recent.

Name and Address of Employer _____

Dates Worked _____ Pay _____ Reason for Leaving _____

Job Title _____ Job Description _____

Name and Address of Employer _____

Dates Worked _____ Pay _____ Reason for Leaving _____

Job Title _____ Job Description _____

Name and Address of Employer _____

Dates Worked _____ Pay _____ Reason for Leaving _____

Job Title _____ Job Description _____

Computer Skills (describe) _____   Typing Speed _____ wpm
(if applicable)   (if applicable)

Do you have any physical condition or handicap that may limit your ability to perform the job applied for? ❑ Yes ❑ No
If yes, what can be done to accommodate your limitation?

Have you ever been convicted of a felony? ❑ Yes ❑ No If yes, give kind and date.
A conviction will not necessarily disqualify you from employment.

Are you legally entitled to work in the U.S.? ❑ Yes ❑ No Can you provide proof of citizenship after employment? ❑ Yes ❑ No

Are you a veteran? ❑ Yes ❑ No If yes, give dates:

List the names of three references whom we may contact who have knowledge of your skills, talents, or technical knowledge:

    (1)   (2)   (3)

Name and Relationship
(Supervisor, Teacher, etc.)

Address

Telephone & Area No.

I certify, by my signature below, that any false or omitted important facts in my answers on this application may be cause for dismissal.

Applicant's Signature _____   Date _____

Figure 9.2.6: Sample employment application. Reprinted from *The Career Fitness Program: Exercising Your Options*, Sixth Edition, by Diane Sukiennik, William Bendat, and Lisa Raufman, (2001), Prentice Hall, Inc.

Neatness Counts

The way in which an application form has been filled out indicates the applicant's level of neatness, thoroughness, and accuracy. If two applicants seem to have equal qualifications but one form is carelessly filled out, the application itself might tilt the balance in favor of the other applicant. Unless your handwriting is especially clear, print or type all answers. Look for "please print" instructions on the form.

Sometimes you may apply for a job by mail, and a form will be sent to you. The application form should be carefully, completely, neatly, and accurately filled out. You should then return it to the company, and you may also attach a copy of your résumé. When you have completed the application, go over it again. Have you given the information asked? When an item asked for is not applicable, have you written in N/A (not applicable or not available)?

Filling out application forms

1. Fill out the application form in ink or use a typewriter.

2. Answer every question that applies to you. If a question does not apply or is illegal you may write N/A, meaning not applicable, or draw a line through the space to show that you did not overlook the question.

3. Give your complete address, including zip code.

4. Spell correctly. If you aren't sure how to spell a word, use the dictionary or try to use another word with the same meaning.

5. A question on job preference or "job for which you are applying" should be answered with a specific job title or type of work. Do not write "anything." Employers expect you to state clearly what kind of work you can do.

6. Have a prepared list of schools attended and previous employers. Include addresses and dates of employment.

7. Be prepared to list several good references. It is advisable to ask permission of those you plan to list. Good references include

   a. A recognized community leader

   b. A former employer or teacher who knows you well

   c. Friends who are established in business

8. When you write or sign your name on the application, use your formal name, not a nickname. Your first name, middle initial, and last name are usually preferred.

9. Be as neat as possible. Employers expect that your application will be an example of your best work.

Conclusion

This lesson provided various examples of résumés, cover letters, letters of introduction, and application form reminders. If you have not already started on a career development portfolio before this school year, start now! Create a portfolio that is responsive to your future needs and interests. To be complete, it should contain documentation on your goals; educational development; career exploration; planning; and self-analysis. Start today by planning what you want to accomplish along with the how and when you can complete it. Use a portfolio to organize your school accomplishments and career planning and to help you achieve success. Putting the résumé together is now your job. With a little work and some advice from family and friends, you can put together a professional-looking résumé and cover letter that will "wow" a potential employer.

Next, you will be introduced to the many opportunities you have in military careers.

Lesson Review

1. What are the different types of résumés covered in this lesson?
2. Why do you need different résumés for different job applications?
3. What information should you include in a cover letter?
4. What is the point of an employer having you fill out an application, even though you have a résumé?

Military Career Opportunities

Chapter 9

Key Words

Active Duty
commissary
counterpart
enlistment
exchange
prerequisite
recruiter
Reserves

What You Will Learn to Do

- Relate the military to your career goals

Linked Core Abilities

- Build your capacity for lifelong learning
- Take responsibility for your actions and choices

Skills and Knowledge You Will Gain Along the Way

- Explain the difference between the three career paths available in the U.S. Armed Forces
- Identify four ways to become a commissioned officer
- Identify basic enlistment qualifications and processes to enter the military
- Describe benefits provided to enlisted members of the military
- Describe the purpose of the Selective Service
- Define the key words contained in this lesson

Introduction

The military is one of the largest employers of high school graduates in full-time positions. The U.S. Armed Forces hire over 365,000 enlisted and officer personnel each year. The military is one more career option to consider in your career planning. Serving in the armed forces allows you to contribute to your own advancement and to your country at the same time. In this lesson, you will explore military careers and benefits. You will also match military opportunities to your career interests.

> **Note**
>
> For more information on military **enlistment** and education programs, go to http://www.todaysmilitary.com.

Key Note Term

enlistment – to engage a person for duty in the armed forces

Types of Military Career Paths

The military offers three career paths for its members: the noncommissioned officer path, the warrant officer path, and the commissioned officer path. The following sections introduce you to these career paths.

Noncommissioned Officers

Noncommissioned officers (NCOs), as seen in the uniform of the day in Figure 9.3.1, are enlisted personnel who have advanced above the first three entry-level positions and hold supervisory positions over other lower-ranking enlisted members. Within the Army, NCOs are known as "the backbone of the Army" because they actually supervise the details involved in accomplishing the unit's mission.

Figure 9.3.1: An Army NCO in the uniform of the day.
Courtesy of US Army JROTC.

Noncommissioned officers' ranks start at pay grade E-4. They are better known as corporals in the Army and Marine Corps; petty officers third class in the Navy and Coast Guard; and sergeants in the Air Force. However, there are E-4s who are not noncommissioned officers. Those are specialists in the Army and senior airmen in the Air Force. Specialists and senior airmen are technicians in their field and, as such, do not normally supervise lower-ranking personnel.

Warrant Officers

A warrant officer ranks between an enlisted person and a second lieutenant in the Army, Air Force, and Marine Corps or between an enlisted person and an ensign in the Navy and Coast Guard. As technical specialists, each branch of service primarily assigns them to duties in their area of expertise.

Commissioned Officers

Commissioned officers are the professional leaders of the military. The president of the United States appoints them, and the Senate confirms them to hold positions of authority in the Armed Forces. Officers range from Second Lieutenant in the Army, Air Force, and Marine Corps (or ensign in the Navy and Coast Guard) to General of the Army or Air Force and Fleet Admiral of the Navy or Coast Guard. An officer's role is similar to that of a manager or executive in the civilian world. Officers are typically responsible for setting and meeting objectives by managing lower-ranking officers and enlisted personnel.

Military Career Groups

Within the three types of military career paths mentioned in the previous section, you can find a variety of career groups. The following introduces you to these groups.

Noncommissioned Officers

Noncommissioned officers specialize in 1 of 12 military career groups, as follows:

- **Human services occupations**
- **Media and public affairs occupations**
- **Health care occupations (note the medical lab assistant specialist doing lab work in Figure 9.3.2)**
- **Engineering, science and technical occupations**
- **Administrative occupations**
- **Service occupations**
- **Vehicle and machinery mechanic occupations**
- **Electronic and electrical equipment repair occupations**
- **Construction occupations**

Figure 9.3.2: A medical lab assistant conducting lab work is the same in civilian life as in an Army career.
Courtesy of Stacy Pick/Stock Boston.

- **Machine operator and precision work occupations**
- **Transportation and material handling occupations**
- **Combat specialty occupations**

Of these 12 categories, all have civilian **counterparts** except combat specialty occupations. A specialty is a particular branch of a profession or field of study to which its members devote or restrict themselves. The military offers over 2,000 job specialties within these 12 broad areas from which enlisted personnel can choose.

Warrant Officers

Warrant officers also specialize in a single area of expertise. This area is generally in 1 of the 12 military career groups.

Commissioned Officers

Officers have two areas of concentration or specialties. The primary area of concentration is further divided into fields such as combat arms, combat support, and combat service support. The secondary or functional area of concentration is a career field unrelated to the primary area of concentration. Each branch of the service normally assigns a secondary specialty to their officers after they have become qualified in their primary specialty.

Military Career Paths: Prerequisites

To follow your chosen military career path, you must meet certain **prerequisites**. This means that you must meet specific qualifications before reaching your military goal. This might include working your way up through the ranks, taking a training course, or completing a degree program.

> ### Key Note Term
>
> counterpart – something that is similar or comparable to another, as in function or relation

> ### Key Note Term
>
> prerequisite – a requirement or condition you must meet or achieve before being able to move on to your goal

Noncommissioned Officers

You become a noncommissioned officer by advancing through the enlisted ranks. Competition among your peers is the basis for promotions within the NCO corps. Ability, job performance, skill, experience, and potential are the major considerations for advancement; however, at each grade level, there are certain minimum requirements for promotion such as time in service, time in grade (present level of work), and successful completion of skill-level examinations. Also, in some cases, there are military educational requirements which an NCO must meet.

Warrant Officers

In some branches of the service, personnel must first work their way up through the enlisted ranks; then, after meeting the required prerequisites, they may apply to become a warrant officer. However, some of the services also require you to be a certain rank before you are eligible to apply and they prefer their warrant officers and warrant officer applicants to have an associate's degree or the equivalent. In the Army, one way you can become a warrant officer is by enlisting for the Warrant Officer Candidate School in its Aviation Program.

Commissioned Officers

There are four main pathways to become a commissioned officer:

- **Completion of ROTC**
- **Graduation from a service academy**
- **Completion of Officer Candidate School (OCS) or Officer Training School (OTS)**
- **Direct appointment**

Reserve Officers' Training Corps (ROTC)

The Reserve Officers' Training Corps is a course that you can take while in college. The Army refers to its course as the Senior ROTC program (or SROTC). SROTC is a two- to four-year program that has extensive military training both on campus and at summer camps.

Many colleges and universities across the country offer one or more ROTC programs for the Army, Navy/Marine Corps (the Marines do not have their own program), and Air Force. In some cases, you may be eligible for a military scholarship (where the military pays most of the educational costs plus a monthly stipend of $150 for up to 10 months per year) or financial aid while participating in ROTC. After graduating from college and successfully completing the ROTC training, you become a commissioned officer. This commission will incur an eight-year service obligation. Participants must be younger than 27 years of age for the Army—25 for the other services—when commissioned. Cadets wear the proper ROTC uniform on certain days during the school year.

Service Academies

There are four service academies for which you can apply and receive a commission in the U.S. Armed Forces. Applicants for the U.S. Military Academy at West

Point, New York (for Army applicants), the Naval Academy at Annapolis, Maryland (for Navy and Marine applicants), and the Air Force Academy at Colorado Springs, Colorado, must be nominated, usually by a member of Congress, to be considered. Nominations for the Coast Guard Academy at New London, Connecticut, are made competitively on a nationwide basis, that is, congressional nominations are not required.

Each academy is a four-year program in which you can graduate as a military officer with a bachelor of science degree. At these academies, the government pays your tuition and expenses. In return, you are obligated to serve six years on **Active Duty** and two years in an inactive reserve status. Applicants must be at least 17 years of age but not older than 22; a U.S. citizen; of good moral character; able to meet the academic, physical, and medical requirements; not be married or pregnant; and not have any legal obligations to support family members. Acceptance to an academy is highly competitive. Each year, they receive between 10,000 and 12,000 applications. Of those who qualify, only about 1,200 receive appointments.

Key Note Term

Active Duty – a condition of military service where members are on full duty, or subject to call, at all times to respond quickly to the nation's emergencies

Officer Candidate/Officer Training Schools

If you are a college graduate with a four-year degree and do not have any prior military experience, you may join the service of your choice with a guaranteed option to attend Officer Candidate School (OCS) or Officer Training School (OTS). Course lengths vary by service, but they are normally less than six months. Then, after successfully completing the training, you are eligible to become an officer.

If you earn a degree while serving on active duty, you may apply for OCS or OTS. You must first meet all of the prerequisites and your unit commander must approve your request. Additionally, each state National Guard has its own Officer Candidate School that takes applicants directly from its own units. If they successfully complete the training, they are commissioned and are usually sent back to the unit from which they came to serve as officers.

Direct Appointment

A person in a professional field, such as medicine or law, may receive a direct appointment and become a commissioned officer even without prior military training. The grade that a professional receives on entering into the military depends on two factors: years of schooling and prior experience in that profession. For example, a professional could start out at the grade of captain. The appointment of professionals accounts for the majority of the direct appointments made by the services.

Within the US Army, over 70 percent of its new officers come from ROTC each year. Within the other branches of the armed forces, about 15 percent of the military's new officers come from the service academies, 25 percent from officer candidate/training schools, 45 percent from ROTC, and 15 percent from direct appointment.

Enlisted Commissions

Selected enlisted personnel from each service may qualify for appointment to one of the four service academies or may be eligible to attend an SROTC program. Other enlisted commissioning programs are as follows:

- The Army's Green to Gold program
- The Navy's BOOST (Broadened Opportunity for Officer Selection and Training) program
- The Army Medical Department's Enlisted Commissioning Program
- The Navy Enlisted Commissioning Program
- The Marine Corps Enlisted Commissioning Education Program
- The Airman Education and Commissioning Program
- The Coast Guard's Precommissioning Program for Enlisted Personnel

In the last five programs, qualified enlisted personnel may collect full pay and allowances while attending college full-time. Those who graduate and finish an officer candidate program receive their commissions.

An enlisted person may also receive a direct appointment as an officer if that person demonstrates performance far above the standards called for in his or her occupational field and does not have a disciplinary record.

> **Note**
>
> Appointments of this nature are extremely rare.

Remember, to join the military as an officer, you must have a bachelor's degree. Certain scientific and technical fields, such as medicine or law, require advanced degrees.

If you are interested in any of the options discussed in this lesson, your JROTC instructors, the school guidance or career counselors, and/or service **recruiters** will be able to give you the information you need.

Key Note Term

recruiter – a member of the armed services who enlists new members into the armed forces

Benefits of Military Service

The military can offer an exciting and rewarding career. It is important to research the career options that are available to you. When you enter the military, you must sign a contract that commits you to serving a specific amount of time. In return, the military offers you a variety of benefits, such as participation in sports (see Figure 9.3.3). Table 9.3.1 summarizes the benefits available.

Selective Service

It is the legal obligation of young men to register with Selective Service when they turn 18 years of age. Failure to register can result in jail time, a fine, and other serious consequences. Not knowing about Selective Service registration is not a justifiable excuse under the law.

Figure 9.3.3: Participating in sports and other recreational activities is just one benefit of military service.
Courtesy of US Army JROTC.

Table 9.3.1: Summary of Employment Benefits for Enlisted Members

Benefit	Description
Vacation	Leave time of thirty days per year
Medical, Dental, and Eye Care	Full health, medical, hospitalization, dental, and eye care services for enlistees and most heath care costs for family members; in remote sites, this care is available from civilian sources (dental care, especially for family members, is with civilian care under a dental plan)
Continuing Education	Voluntary educational programs for undergraduate and graduate degrees, or for single courses, including tuition assistance for programs at colleges and universities
Recreational Programs	Programs include athletics, entertainment, and hobbies, such as softball, basketball, football, swimming, tennis, golf, weight training, and other sports
	Parties, dances, and entertainment
	Club facilities, snack bars, game rooms, movie theaters, and lounges
	Active hobby and craft clubs, and book and music libraries
Exchange and **Commissary** Privileges	Food, goods, and services at military stores are available, generally at lower costs and tax-free, although the commissary does charge a small surcharge
Legal Assistance	Many free legal services for help with personal matters

Key Note Terms

exchange – a store at a military installation that sells merchandise and services to military personnel and authorized civilians

commissary – a supermarket for use by military personnel and their dependents located on a military installation

Who Must Register

The Military Selective Service Act states that male U.S. citizens and male immigrant aliens residing in the U.S. who are between the ages of 18 and 26 must register in a manner prescribed by proclamation of the president. The proclamation under which registration is presently required was signed on July 2, 1980. It provides that young men must register with Selective Service within 30 days of their 18th birthday.

A man is exempt from registering while he is on full-time active duty in the U.S. Armed Forces. Cadets and midshipmen at service academies are included in the exemption. Members of the National Guard and **Reserves** not on full-time active duty must register unless they have reached age 26 or are already registered.

Lawfully admitted nonimmigrant aliens (for example, those on visitor or student visas and members of diplomatic or trade missions and their families) are not required to register. Parolees and refugees who are aliens residing in this country must register.

Those who are unable to register on schedule due to circumstances beyond their control—for example, those that are hospitalized, institutionalized, or incarcerated—do not have to register until they are released. After release, they have 30 days in which to register. Handicapped men who live at home must register if they are reasonably able to leave the home and go into a public place. A friend or relative may help a handicapped man to fill out the form if he is unable to do so by himself.

The fact that a man is required to register does not mean that he is certain to be drafted. If Congress should authorize a draft, a registrant within the group subject to induction would have his eligibility for service determined based on his individual situation at that time.

> ### Key Note Term
>
> **Reserves** – a military force withheld from action for later decisive use; forces not in the field but available; the military forces of a country not part of the regular service

---

Frequently Asked Questions About Selective Service Registration

Q. What is Selective Service?

A. The Selective Service system is a government agency. Its job is to provide men for service in the Armed Forces if there is a national emergency.

Q. What is Selective Service registration?

A. When you register, you add your name to a list of all men in the nation, ages 18 to 25. The Selective Service would use this list to identify men for possible military service in a national emergency.

Q. Do females have to register?

A. No, by law they do not.

Q. What happens if there's a draft?

A. There has not been a draft since 1973, but if there was an emergency, and Congress ordered another draft, Selective Service would conduct a birth date lottery to decide the order in which to call men. The Selective Service would first call men who turn 20 in the calendar year in a sequence determined by the lottery. If the military needed more, the Selective Service might then call those men who are 21 to 25, youngest first.

Q. Do I have to register?

A. Yes, it is the law. If you do not register and the government prosecutes you, it could send you to jail for up to five years and/or fine you up to $250,000. Not registering hurts you in other ways, too. You would not qualify for federal student grants or loans, job training benefits, or most federal employment.

Q. Is registration hard?

A. No, it is simple. Just go to any post office and ask for a Selective Service registration card. Fill in your name, address, telephone number, date of birth, and Social Security number. Then, give the card to the postal clerk. The clerk will ask to see some identification so bring your driver's license or some other piece of identification. It takes only about five minutes.

Q. Do I have to register at a post office?

A. Maybe not. You may receive a registration card in the mail, or you can obtain a card from your local recreation or social service center. If so, just fill it out and mail it to Selective Service. Check with your JROTC instructors; they may be able to register you over the Internet. Finally, check with your school's guidance office; you may be able to register there.

Q. Can I register online?

A. Check the Selective Service Web Site at www.sss.gov for online registration.

Q. When should I register?

A. Register within 30 days of your 18th birthday. If you are applying for federal student aid or job training, you can register up to 120 days before you turn 18 to avoid delays. If you cannot register on time because you are in a hospital or prison, you do not have to register until you are released. You then have 30 days in which to register.

Q. What if it's more than 30 days after I've turned 18 and I haven't registered?

A. Register at a post office immediately. Selective Service will accept a late registration, but the longer you wait, the longer you are breaking the law.

Q. Do all men have to register?

A. To make the system fair, the law requires all 18-year-old men to register. The only young men exempt from registration are foreigners who are in the U.S. temporarily as tourists, diplomats, or students; personnel on active duty in the Armed Forces; and students at U.S. service academies. Immigrant noncitizen males, 18 to 25 must register.

Q. How do I prove I registered?

A. After you register, Selective Service will mail you a card. Keep it as proof that you have registered. You may need it if you apply for federal employment, federal student aid, or job training. If you do not get your card within 90 days of registering, write to: Registration Information Office, P.O. Box 94638, Palatine, IL 60094-4638. Or call 1-847-688-6888.

Q. What if I change my address?

A. Notify Selective Service of your new address on a Change of Information form. You can get one at any post office. Or you can use the Change of Address form that comes with your acknowledgment card.

Conclusion

Serving in the armed forces allows you to contribute to your own advancement and to your country at the same time. The Army, Navy, Marine Corps, Air Force, and Coast Guard combined offer numerous opportunities each year for high school graduates in positions similar to those found in the civilian sector. Remember, the military is one more career option to consider in your career planning.

With fast facts and frequently asked questions, this lesson provided pertinent information for young male adults about the Military Selective Service Act and Selective Service registration. This lesson pointed out that it is not hard to register and that there are numerous ways that men can register. The main thing for males to remember is that when you are within 30 days of your 18th birthday, register.

In the following lesson, you will learn about what it takes to prepare yourself for college. You will explore what it takes to apply to a school, and what it takes to get in.

Lesson Review

1. **Compare and contrast the different career paths offered in the military.**

2. **Which noncommissioned career group interests you the most? Why?**

3. **What are the prerequisites for becoming a warrant officer?**

4. **Who must register for the draft? When must they register?**

Lesson 4

College Preparation

Key Terms

academic
admissions
aptitude test
college
distance education
financial aid
grants
registration
scholarships
tuition
university

What You Will Learn to Do

- Create a College Preparation Action Plan

Linked Core Abilities

- Take responsibility for your actions and choices

Skills and Knowledge You Will Gain Along the Way

- Discuss different types of colleges
- Describe the admissions process
- Explore ways to finance college
- Identify educational institutions and majors that fit personal needs
- Define the key words contained in this lesson

Key Note Terms

college – an independent institution of higher learning offering a course of general studies leading to a bachelor's degree; a part of a university offering a specialized group of courses; an institution offering instruction, usually in a professional, vocational, or technical field

university – an institution of higher learning providing facilities for teaching and research, and authorized to grant academic degrees; specifically, one made up of an undergraduate division that confers bachelor's degrees, and a graduate division that comprises a graduate school and professional schools, each of which may confer master's degrees and doctorates

distance education – learning that takes place via electronic media linking instructors and students who are not together in a classroom

tuition – the price of or payment for instruction

Introduction

This lesson helps you prepare for college. It tells you what you need to know about the different types of colleges, the admission process and requirements, and ways to finance college.

Deciding Whether College Is Right for You

Before you can begin preparing for college, you have to ask yourself a few questions. "What are my reasons for attending college?" "What are my reasons for not attending college?"

Attending college is not the only way to attain your career goals. It is possible that certain careers can be pursued without a traditional four-year college program. Take nursing for example. You must earn either a two-year associate degree or a four-year baccalaureate degree to qualify for a job as a registered nurse. However, in a two-year program at a community college, you would not take the courses in management and public health found in the four-year counterpart, but you would get more clinical experience.

If a traditional **college** or **university**, as shown in Figure 9.4.1, does not cover your career choice, you might explore the opportunities that a business, trade, or technical school has to offer. The length of study at these schools varies from a few weeks to a few years. You can learn a particular skill or trade and earn a diploma, certificate of completion, or a license following program completion. Some examples of occupations for which these schools can provide instruction are court reporting, hairstyling, computer repair, and cooking.

Another alternative to a four-year college program is e-learning, or **distance education**. Distance education has its advantages. The reduced need for buildings, housing, and personnel costs may make **tuition** more affordable.

Online classes through distance education institutions or universities are often more convenient and can be taken at different times and places. Other distance education programs may make use of other technologies, including video, audio, audio graphics, text-based correspondence, radio, broadcast TV, and so on. Additionally, many employers offer distance education classes on the job.

If your career choice does not require going to college, you need to first identify the workplace skills and experiences needed to pursue your career goals and then find the resources that help you reach them.

The Admissions Process

The process of applying to college should begin in the fall of your high school senior year. If you are applying to more than one college, the process can become overwhelming. It is important that you are organized and have your career development portfolio up to date.

Figure 9.4.1: Arriving on a traditional college campus at the beginning of a new school year.
Courtesy of Brian Smith.

The following steps outline the major tasks involved in the **admissions** process.

1. **Gather applications from the colleges you are considering.**
2. **Know the application deadlines for each college.**
3. **Complete and mail each admission application.**
4. **Apply for financial aid (keep in mind application deadlines).**
5. **Apply for scholarships (keep in mind application deadlines).**
6. **Apply for campus housing if you are not living at home while you attend college.**
7. **Make your college choice, enroll, and register for classes.**

General Admission or Entrance Requirements

Admission or entrance requirements can differ from one college to another; however, there are basic criteria that are required for the majority of colleges.

One of the basic admission requirements is that you must have graduated from an accredited high school or have earned a GED (General Equivalency Diploma). Many colleges require specific coursework or curricula from high school. For example, a college could require that you have four years of English, three years of math, two years of history and science, as well as a required number of course electives. Some colleges look at your grade point average, your rank in class (this is usually found on your school transcripts), and/or standardized test scores such as ACT (American College Test) or SAT (Scholastic **Aptitude Test**.)

Ways to Finance College

You have your list of colleges that you would like to attend. Everything is perfect, from the exact major you want, to the size of the campus, to a picture perfect location. Your next step is to look at the costs and figure out which ones you can afford. For most students, the tuition and other higher education expenses require seeking funding from someplace other than parents. There are two forms of **financial aid**

Key Note Term

admissions – the act or process of admitting

Key Note Terms

aptitude test – a standardized test designed to predict an individual's ability to learn certain skills

financial aid – a grant or subsidy to a school or individual for an educational or artistic project

Key Note Terms

grants – monetary awards based on financial need that do not need to be paid back to the grantor

scholarships – grants-in-aid to a student, as by a college or university

academic – belonging or pertaining to higher education

funding for college: gift aid and self-help aid. Ask your instructor about the JROTC Financing College CD that provides an outlined plan to help you learn about all available college financial options.

Gift Aid

Gift aid does not have to be paid back. It can come from a variety of sources: businesses and foundations, community groups, and the colleges and universities to which you apply. There are two forms of gift aid:

- **Grants that are awarded based on your financial need**
- **Scholarships that are awarded based on your academic merit**

Self-Help Aid

You or your parents may need to borrow money for your college education. Loans are normally repaid with interest. Some loans do not need to be repaid until you have graduated or left college for some other reason.

Student employment is another form of self-help aid. There are three common forms of student employment:

- **Federal and state work-study programs**
- **Teaching assistantships and research assistantships**
- **Regular part-time employment during the academic year or the summer months**

Finding college funding can be a complicated and confusing process. Following a few ground rules will give you an advantage in navigating the process.

- **Make contact with your college's financial aid office early**
- **Have all of the verification information you need by submittal deadlines**
- **Organize your information and keep your portfolio files updated**

Choosing an Educational Institution That Fits Your Needs

Choosing a college is probably one of the first major decisions you will make in your life. This is where the work that you put into your career development strategy begins to pay off. You have a plan and it will help you make the best possible decision as to which college to attend.

The following tips will help you choose the right college:

- **You will most likely receive brochures from colleges through the mail; read them and if you are interested, request more information**
- **Request information from other colleges in which you are interested**
- **Talk to your parents, friends, and other family members about college, the colleges they attended, and their personal experience with college**

- Write down what you are looking for in a college
- Make a "wish list" of colleges you would like to attend
- Complete the process by narrowing down the list to three to six schools
- Apply to each of these colleges

Degree Programs

Clearly, a student should select a college that is going to serve his or her needs in the best way possible. One of the first options you should research is whether a college you are considering offers majors in your area of interest. Not all colleges offer all types of majors; that would be redundant and impossible. Often, state institutions offer programs that emphasize majors that are different from those of other institutions in the state. For example, one state college may emphasize medicine, another may emphasize engineering, while yet another college may emphasize education. If you are not yet sure what you want to major in, you should select a college that most closely emphasizes your interests. Remember that two- and four-year degree programs have general education requirements, and students take those classes in their first two years. During this time period, you will have the opportunity to more thoroughly explore majors, and if it is necessary, you can transfer to a different college that offers the degree you desire.

Transfer Options

Students sometimes choose to attend a two-year community college the first two years. This is a viable option to consider when selecting a college. If you do plan to attend a two-year college and then transfer to a four-year college, you need to be very careful in selecting classes. Two-year colleges generally have articulation agreements, which mean that the four-year colleges will automatically accept credit for specific classes taken at two-year schools. It is your responsibility to get in writing a list of classes that can be easily transferred. After you have this list, don't stray from it; otherwise, you will find yourself repeating classes, incurring additional costs, and delaying your graduation. Graduating from a four-year college or university in four years needs to be one of your college career goals. Note the student in Figure 9.4.2 that graduated in four years, all smiles.

Faculty Reputation and Research

Depending on your major area of study and the type of degree you are pursuing, faculty reputation and research may be a concern for you. If you are interested in knowing about the faculty, the best way to get some answers is to visit them! Make appointments to see them and talk to them about their work; this will let them know that you are a prospective student who is serious about your future!

If, however, you are not able to visit faculty in person, you should visit through the college home pages on the Web. Many instructors post not only office information but also course syllabi, schedules, and specific assignments. These sites will at least give you a general idea of what to expect if you should enroll in one of those classes.

Figure 9.4.2: Graduating from a four-year college in four years is a desirable goal.
Courtesy of Frozen Images/The Image Works.

Accreditation

All legitimate colleges go through an accreditation process. They are evaluated by independent accrediting agencies that periodically review the school's curriculum, standards, and results.

Additionally, programs within the college should be accredited in their specific discipline. Specific professional programs should be accredited by the appropriate accrediting agency in their field. For example, a nursing program should be accredited by the National League for Nursing, or an Emergency Medical Technician (EMT)/paramedic program should be accredited by the Joint Review Committee on Educational Programs for the EMT/paramedic. If you can't find information about the accreditation, you should ask. Making sure you are in a top-notch program is ultimately your responsibility.

If the college you are considering is not accredited by a regional accrediting association or the programs within the college are not accredited, you should probably consider a different college.

Scholarship, Work-Study, Internship, Co-op, and Job Placement Opportunities

Because college is a costly venture, you should find out what types of financial aid and employment opportunities each college provides and how to apply.

Scholarships can help a great deal when you are faced with college expenses because they provide financial assistance that does not need to be repaid. Some scholarships are based on financial need; other scholarships may be based on special talents or academic performance. Generally, you must submit financial aid applications to apply for any type of financial aid. After you've received the required paperwork, apply for as many scholarships as possible. Even small scholarships can help pay for books and supplies that you will need.

Work-study jobs are another way to help with college expenses; in addition, you may get lucky enough to land a job that will look good on your résumé when you graduate. These jobs are located on the college campus, and the supervisors often attempt to work around students' class schedules. Work-study jobs may range from 5 to 20 hours a week. When you visit a campus, check out the campus job board and see if you might qualify for any. These jobs go quickly, so the sooner you apply, the better chance you will have.

Academic Considerations

Does each college provide the following academic considerations?

- The academic degree that I want
- Faculty who focus on students and who are current in their professional field
- Appropriate accreditations
- Scholarships, work-study opportunities, internships, co-ops, and job placement programs

Intern and co-op positions give students an opportunity to work in the career field in which they are studying. Although internships and co-ops are all different, the point of these programs is to give students an opportunity to apply the knowledge they have gained in the classroom while gaining on-the-job experience. Intern and co-op programs place students in jobs in the community and in work with professionals in their field. Many positions pay very well, and students are sometimes offered full-time positions when they graduate. A college with a healthy intern or co-op program is worth serious consideration; it demonstrates that the college has a realistic view of employer expectations and employment opportunities.

Finally, in terms of academics, you should research the school's job placement rate. Find out how many graduates are employed after graduation. If there is a high job placement rate, it indicates that the school is well-respected from an employer's point of view.

Student Services and Activities

The quality and quantity of student services and activities can tell a prospective student a great deal about the college. Student services that cater to special needs and populations should be obvious, and a variety of activities that build a sense of community should appear on a campus calendar.

Student Services

Some student services are basic to every college campus—advising centers, financial aid offices, tutorial services, career development and placement services, counseling centers, and libraries. These are key offices to visit when making your college selection. Personnel in these services who are clearly student-friendly, professional, knowledgeable, and up-to-date reflect a campus with the same qualities.

A thorough investigation also includes researching auxiliary student services and organizations. Auxiliary services might include a student health center, eating facilities, technological laboratories, and cultural programs. Certainly if you are interested in pursuing a degree in computer science, you want to attend a college that is committed to technology and provides up-to-date computer labs and software. Likewise, if you want to major in Latin American studies, you should attend a campus that clearly reflects a commitment to cultural studies and programs.

Student Organizations

Student organizations can be a key factor in your college experience. Becoming involved in student organizations is one way to connect with your campus and make you feel a part of that community. Because there is such a wide variety of student organizations you should be able to find one that interests you. For example, you may want to join a fashion merchandising club, a technology club, a drama club, or an intramural sports team. Your involvement in student organizations demonstrates your commitment to an idea and allows you the opportunity to work with other individuals with similar beliefs and values. Furthermore, student organizations provide key opportunities to strengthen your leadership skills, and future employers may be very interested to hear about your involvement.

Student Athletics

For some students, athletic programs have no weight in making a decision about which college to attend; for others, however, athletics are a major factor. If you are basing your decision on athletics, you should consider the following.

Graduation Rates for Athletes

How many athletes in the college have graduated during the last five years? If there is a low graduation rate, that school probably isn't the best choice. After all, what good is going to college if you don't get a college degree? A few athletes have the ability to turn professional, but most don't; in the long run, you would be better off to be on a team that has a sound reputation and record for stressing academics and graduation. There is a more physical and metal stress on student athletes (see Figure 9.4.3).

Figure 9.4.3: Student athletes have more physical and metal stress than other students.
Courtesy of Mike Valeri/ FPG International.

Program Completion Time

How long does it take most athletes to complete a program of study? Although it is common for athletes to take longer than regular full-time students to complete a program of study, that time shouldn't be excessive. If student athletes are taking longer than five or six years, it's a good bet that academics aren't stressed until after eligibility has expired.

Scholarships

What kinds of scholarships are available for student athletes? If you truly have a talent to offer the university and are capable of successfully completing your academic commitment, you should expect that university to offer some scholarship or financial assistance. An athletic recruiter should be able to answer your questions about financial assistance clearly. Be sure to get any offers of assistance in writing before you sign any letters of intent.

NCAA Probationary Status

What is the National Collegiate Athletic Association probationary status of the team you are considering? If you find yourself being recruited by a team that is serving probation because of violations, find out the cause of the probation. If this team has broken rules under the current coaching staff, you should probably not spend a great deal of time considering this team. If, however, the violations occurred under a different staff, you may be okay. Perhaps they are in the process of rebuilding a program, and you could be instrumental to the team.

Athletic Status

What will your athletic status be as a first-year student? Will you be red shirted? Or will you be an active team member? These are questions that may affect financial aid and scholarships, so you should have a clear idea about your status before you commit to a team.

Special Student Athletic Services

What types of special services are given to student athletes? Because of demanding practice and traveling schedules, student athletes can have difficulties keeping up with academic demands. It is important to find out if your team offers services such as tutorial programs designed especially for athletes.

Practice and Traveling Schedules

How long will you be expected to practice each day, and how extensive are the travel schedules? If you discover that your schedule will be difficult, you may need to make a tough decision about whether you want to participate in collegiate athletics. After all, your goal is to get a solid education and degree, so decide where you are willing to concentrate your efforts.

Student Activities

In addition to student organizations, a college should sponsor student activities that provide a sense of campus community. Perhaps there are homecoming celebrations, holiday events, special concerts, or movie nights. Although these activities might not be the deciding factor in your college decision, they do play an important role in campus living and provide not only entertainment but a sense of campus pride.

Tuition

Cost is a fundamental concern when selecting a college or university. One of the two major expenses is tuition, the price your courses will cost you per credit hour. A few things to keep in mind when looking at tuition costs include full- or part-time tuition and in-state or out-of-state tuition.

Tuition expenses can range from very low to tens of thousands of dollars and are usually presented in two different ways: the total cost of tuition for full-time students and the cost of tuition per credit hour for other students.

Full-Time Status

College classes are presented by credit hours, depending on the amount of time spent in class, and a full-time student takes at least twelve credit hours per semester, which is usually four classes. If a full-time student chooses to enroll in more than twelve credit hours, there is usually no extra charge for the extra credit hours unless a student takes eighteen or more credit hours—not something a first-year student should even consider. Additionally, health and activity fees are also included in the cost of full-time tuition. Depending on the college, these fees may cover the cost of such privileges as using the campus health center; attending sports, music, and theater events; and using special campus facilities such as computer labs. Meal plans may be available, but the price of the meal plan is not included in the tuition fee, nor is the price of textbooks.

Part-Time Status

If you will not be able to attend classes on a full-time basis, you will pay your tuition fees by a credit-hour rate. For example, if you take two classes that are each three credit hours, you will pay for six hours of tuition. If the tuition costs $150 per credit hour, you will pay $900 to take those two classes. Health and activity fees are not included in the credit-hour rate but may be available at an additional fee.

In-State Tuition

In-state tuition simply means that you will be attending a college located in the state in which you reside. These fees are substantially lower than out-of-state tuition. For example, one college lists its in-state tuition as $1,200, but out-of-state tuition at the same college is $4,100.

Out-of-State Tuition

Out-of-state tuition is sometimes referred to as nonresident tuition. Residential requirements vary from state to state. For example, colleges located on state borders may have special agreements to accept students from neighboring cities in the adjoining state, so if you are considering attending a college in a different state, be sure to find out these requirements. Out-of-state tuition may be four or five times more expensive than in-state tuition, so it may be financially beneficial to attend an out-of-state college on a part-time basis until residency has been established. Additionally, some colleges offer special scholarships to be used specifically to cover this added expense.

Does Tuition Reflect the Quality of Education I Will Receive?

Although a $30,000-a-year school is likely to be viewed as more prestigious than a $10,000-a-year school, does a degree from a prestigious school really give a graduate a substantial competitive edge in the job market? Opinions differ, but you should remember that employers are looking for well-educated applicants, not applicants with expensive degrees. What you choose to do with your educational opportunities is more important than the price tag of your tuition. Many successful individuals have started their college careers at less expensive community colleges and then transferred to a four-year college.

Housing Options and Expenses

Tuition may seem as though it should be the largest expense you pay, but the biggest expense is often housing if you choose a campus in a different city or state than where you live. As an in-coming first-year college student, your housing options may be limited. Some campuses require that first-year students live on campus and in specific dorms; however, other campuses may not have these types of requirements. Before deciding where you want to live, you should consider the pros and cons of all options.

Residential Halls

Although some students groan at the thought of living in the residential halls, or dorms, the reality is that residential life offers many advantages for first-year students. Living in the residential halls allows you to meet and make new friends (see Figure 9.4.4), participate in residential team-building activities, and live in a protected and safe environment that is close to all your collegiate activities.

Figure 9.4.4: Living in the dorm provides an excellent opportunity to make friends and network.
Courtesy of Jacques Chenet/Woodfin Camp & Associates.

Residential regulations vary from campus to campus, but generally there are several options from which students can choose. For example, you may be able to live in a room that you share with only one roommate, or you may choose to live in a suite with several other students. Additionally, residential halls are sometimes reserved solely for certain groups of students, such as athletes, women, or honor students.

If you are a person who needs a great deal of privacy and solitude, the residential halls may not be the best choice for you. But for many students the residential halls give them the opportunity to make lasting friendships, to connect with student tutors and mentors, and to sharpen people skills.

Fraternity and Sorority Houses

Although images from the movie *Animal House* may come to mind when you think of living in a fraternity or sorority house, fraternities and sororities do offer a viable housing option that rarely reflects the movie. This option, however, may not be available until your sophomore year or even later, depending on the fraternity or sorority. And there are varying eligibility requirements for joining fraternities and sororities that should be taken into consideration before considering this an option.

The living arrangements in fraternity and sorority houses are often similar to residential halls in which you have two or more roommates. In some instances, the members reside in "sleeping porches," very large rooms that house all members.

The cost of living in a fraternity or sorority is sometimes comparable to living in residential halls but can sometimes be much more expensive, depending on the organization. Be sure to thoroughly research this expense if you do decide to pledge.

Apartments

Most students are excited at the prospect of living in an apartment for the first time, and with careful shopping and planning, apartment living may be the least expensive housing option. Apartments can offer privacy and independence that residential halls and fraternity or sorority houses can't, but that privacy and independence can come with a higher price tag than is expected. For example, you may have to pay utilities, security deposits, and transportation costs to get to and from school. You may also have to pay extra for a furnished apartment.

Apartments can cost you in other ways, as well. For example, if you are a first-year student in a new city, you may not know any other students. Living alone in an apartment does not offer you the opportunity that you would have in a residential hall to easily meet other students. And, by living in an apartment, you may have to sacrifice some of the safety that comes with living on campus. If you share the apartment with one or more roommates, however, these financial and social expenses may seem reasonable, and apartment living might be your best choice.

Parents' or Relatives' Homes

The very least expensive housing option is to continue to live at home with your parents or to live with a relative. Often, you can live free and have the added bonus of having meals with your family and access to conveniences such as laundry facilities. Even if you are required to pay rent, it is usually much less than you would have to pay elsewhere.

One disadvantage of living at home or with relatives may be the lack of the degree of independence that other students have. For example, if your friends are living in the residential halls and have freedom to stay out as long as they want, you may be tempted to do the same. Sometimes parents aren't willing to give college students that much independence.

If you choose to live at home or with a relative, it is imperative that you sit down and discuss expectations before problems arise. Parents may be more willing to compromise and bend their rules if you discuss this with them prior to following through with your plans.

Because housing is one of the greatest expenses you'll encounter as a college student, it is important to research the options carefully for each college you consider. Your choice needs to be livable, both financially and socially. For example, if you are a person who is extremely shy and it is difficult for you to meet others, living in an apartment could further isolate you and make your college experience unbearable. Weigh your options carefully and be fair to yourself.

Table 9.4.1 shows some important questions you should ask yourself before making a decision about housing.

Resources for Making an Informed Decision

Collecting the information you need to make an informed decision may seem like an overwhelming task; however, most of the information can be found in a few key places.

Much of the initial information can be found in college catalogs, which list detailed information about degree programs, classes, tuition and housing expenses, and some student services. This type of information can also usually be found online by clicking on the colleges' home pages.

Table 9.4.1: University Housing Choices	
Options	**Questions to consider**
Residential Hall	Will I live with someone I know or someone I haven't met before? How will I manage distractions from other residents?
Fraternity or Sorority House	Will I be able to manage my schoolwork, time, money, and fraternity activities effectively? Will I be able to say no to fun activities when I have tests to study for and papers to write?
Apartment	Will I share the apartment with a roommate? How will I meet friends and get involved in campus life?
Home	Will I have the same freedoms that I would have if I were living elsewhere? Will I be expected to pay rent or have other household responsibilities?

Many online services exist for the sole purpose of helping you compare institutions. These services are free and provide a wealth of information. If you use an online service, carefully check its sources of information, data collection methods, and sponsors. The following sites can help you make informed decisions:

- **Petersons: www.petersons.college.com**

- **CollegeNET: www.collegenet.com**

- **U.S. News & World Report's College Ranking: www.usnews. com/usnews/edu/ college/rankings/rankindex_brief.php**

- **The Princeton Review Online: www.review.com/college/default.asp**

- **www.fastweb.com**

- **University of Illinois Library Collection: www.library.uiuc.edu/edx/rankings.htm**

After you have narrowed your choices, it is imperative that you visit the college campuses and meet with individuals who can answer specific questions for you. Before arriving, you should make appointments to see representatives in the offices such as financial aid, student advising, housing, and your major area of study. These individuals can help answer your questions and provide you with key information that will help you make the most informed choice.

After you've selected the college of your choice, you will have to complete a series of steps before you can actually attend. This process may seem like a giant maze with one hurdle after another, but getting organized and understanding the steps will help you accomplish your goal.

In this section, you explore answers to the following questions:

- **What are the common admission requirements?**
- **How do I complete the admission process in an organized manner?**
- **What does early admission mean, and what are its advantages?**
- **What do I need to know about financial aid?**
- **How will I register for classes?**

Common Admission Requirements

One of the first steps you need to take is to apply for admission. Most colleges require similar information before admitting you, but it is important to find out exactly what your college requires so that your admission process is smooth and expedient.

Admission Definitions

Colleges offer one of two types of admission: open and competitive. Open admission means that the college will accept any incoming freshman who has earned a high school diploma or GED and who has placed within the required range of scores for tests such as the American College Testing Program (ACT) or the Scholastic Assessment Test (SAT). Students with low test scores or GPAs may be admitted on a provisional status until they successfully complete developmental courses that will increase their skill level, or they may be directed to attend a community college to take developmental courses there. Competitive admission means that the college demands specific requirements before admitting a student. Those requirements might mean a higher-than-average GPA, a high class ranking, or recommendations from professionals in the field.

Commonly, colleges have open admission but competitive admission within specific programs. For example, a college may have open admission for freshmen, but when a student completes the sophomore year, that student may have to apply to enter a particular program such as social work or education.

Minimum Required Information for Admission

Even colleges with open admission policies require a record of your past academic performance. You should begin a permanent file that contains the following documents:

- **High school transcripts and documentation of grade point average**
- **College transcripts if you've taken courses while still in high school**
- **Documentation of class ranking (usually found on transcript)**
- **Documentation of ACT or SAT scores**

Keep this file current and in a convenient place so that your documents are easily accessible if you want to apply to more than one college.

Transcripts

Transcripts are a permanent list of classes and the grades you've earned in those classes. High school transcripts may also contain information about overall grade point average, attendance, and class ranking. College transcripts will list all classes you enroll in and the grades you earn. It will list classes you withdraw from and audit, as well. Grade point averages, earned degrees, and graduation honors will also be listed on college transcripts.

High School Grade Point Averages

Even colleges with open admission policies demand that students have completed a precollege curriculum and have earned a GPA that meets their minimum standards. This baseline varies from college to college, so research your college's admission standards to see if you qualify.

A somewhat common GPA minimum standard is 2.5; however, if students don't have a 2.5 GPA or if they've earned a GED, a college may accept that if the student has earned a higher-than-minimum score on ACT or SAT composite scores.

Precollege Curriculum

Preparatory curriculum varies from state to state, but, in general, colleges with open admission policies insist that incoming college students have completed specific requirements in the core academic areas. Commonly, those requirements include completing four units of English, three units of math, three units of social science, three units of natural science, and two units of foreign language. If you are nearing graduation and haven't completed a precollege core of classes, you might want to consider summer school.

Tests

As part of their admission process, colleges generally require the scores of a standardized test. The two tests that are most common are the American College Testing (ACT) Program and the Scholastic Assessment Test (SAT). The scores of these tests are used differently by colleges that have competitive admission than by colleges with open admission.

Colleges with competitive admission use these scores as one means of selecting students. Students with high ACT or SAT scores may be accepted to a number of colleges while students with average to low ACT or SAT scores may have difficulty getting accepted to schools with competitive admission.

Colleges with open admission use ACT and SAT scores to determine if students meet basic academic competency. If a student scores low in specific areas, that student may be admitted on a provisional basis until the deficiency can be corrected by taking basic developmental courses.

Occasionally community colleges will not require that you submit ACT or SAT scores; however, these colleges will require that you take a placement test at the college. These scores are used to place students in courses that are best suited for their academic abilities. If the college you are considering requires that you complete a placement test, make sure you know when and where you take the test because these tests are required before you can enroll in classes.

Students who have completed precollege curriculum, earned high GPAs, and scored in the above-average to high range on the ACT or SAT may want to consider taking the College Level Examination Program (CLEP) test. CLEP tests will determine whether a student has college-level knowledge about a particular subject. When a student "CLEPs" out of a class, this means the student will get credit and will pay for the class but will not have to actually take the course.

Although tests are an important part of the admission process, admissions counselors understand that test scores are only one indicator of how well a student may do. If you have lower-than-expected test scores, you should emphasize other strengths you have as a student.

Completing the Admission Process in an Organized Manner

Even though colleges require the same general information for admission applications, there is a great deal of information to keep organized. Starting a filing system early will help you through the process. We suggest you keep separate files for copies of all the general information we've discussed.

In each file, keep three or four copies of each document and label the original so you don't accidentally mail it. Most colleges only require photocopies of documents until admission has been approved. At that time, colleges can request that you send official transcripts. Sending copies will save you a great deal of money if you are applying to several colleges.

Also, keep a file that contains a copy of your admission application for each college you apply to. Attach to each application a list of all documents you have submitted. When you have received notice of your admission status, place that notice in your file until you have made your decision.

When you apply for admission to a college, do so in an organized manner, as shown in "Applying for Admission," to make a good first impression:

- **Write a cover letter that discusses required information for competitive admission colleges**
- **Complete every question on the application**
- **Attach all required documents in order**

Some colleges provide online admission applications on their Web pages. If you choose to apply electronically, don't forget to follow up with the appropriate documents.

Applying for Admission

- Obtain an admission application through your counselor, directly from the college, or from its online resource
- Obtain copies of high school transcripts
- Obtain copies of test scores, such as ACT or SAT
- Complete and mail application and required documents

Advantages to Early Admission

Early admission has two different meanings. In some cases, high school students can apply for early admission to a college and take classes while still in high school. There are often specific requirements for this type of early admission that may include a specific grade point average, an interview process, and referrals from high school officials. Clearly this type of early admission is advantageous because it allows students to get a feel for college to see if they would like to attend there after high school. It is also a way to complete general education requirements and take time to explore personal interests.

The other definition of early admission is simply completing the admission process early in the year prior to attending. For example, students planning to attend college in the fall may complete an early admission process in the spring or early summer. This type of early admission also has its advantages. Besides having a larger selection of classes from which to choose, a student who applies early may also be able to take advantage of special orientations or introductory sessions. These orientations may give students one-to-one mentoring, a stay in campus housing, special advising sessions, and social time to meet other new students.

Financial Aid

While you are in the process of applying for admission to the colleges that you are considering, you should also apply for financial aid. Seeking help from various sources of financial aid has become a way of life for much of the student population. Education is an important but often expensive investment. Per the website www.collegeboard.com, a four-year private school in 2004-2005 will average $20,082 for one year's tuition. A four-year public university will average $5,132 per year.

Not many people can pay for tuition in full without aid. In fact, almost half of students enrolled receive some kind of aid.

Most sources of financial aid don't seek out recipients. Take the initiative to learn how you (or you and your parents, if they currently help to support you) can finance your education. Find the people on campus who can help you with your finances. Do some research to find out what's available, weigh the pros and cons of each option, and decide what would work best for you. Try to apply as early as you can. The types of financial aid available to you are loans, grants, and scholarships.

Loans

A loan is given to you by a person, bank, or other lending agency, usually to put toward a specific purchase. You, as the recipient of the loan, must pay back the amount of the loan, plus interest, in regular payments that stretch over a particular period of time. Interest is the fee that you pay for the privilege of using money that belongs to someone else.

Loan Applications

What happens when you apply for a loan?

1. **The loaning agency must approve you. You (and your parents) may be asked about what you (and any other family members) earn, how much savings you have, your credit history, anything you own that is of substantial value (such as a car), and your history of payment on any previous loans.**

2. **An interest charge will be set. Interest can range from 5 percent to over 20 percent, depending on the loan and the economy. Variable-interest loans shift charges as the economy strengthens or weakens. Fixed-rate loans have one interest rate that remains constant.**

3. **The loaning agency will establish a payment plan. Most loan payments are made monthly or quarterly (four times per year). The payment amount depends on the total amount of the loan, how much you can comfortably pay per month, and the length of the repayment period.**

Types of Student Loans

The federal government administers or oversees most student loans. To receive aid from any federal program, you must be a citizen or eligible noncitizen and be enrolled in a program of study that the government has determined is eligible. Individual states may differ in their aid programs. Check with the financial aid office of the colleges you apply to find out details about your state and those colleges in particular.

Following are the main student loan programs to which you can apply if you are eligible. Amounts vary according to individual circumstances. Contact your school or federal student aid office for further information. In most cases, the amount is limited to the cost of your education minus any other financial aid you are receiving.

Perkins Loans

Carrying a low, fixed-rate of interest, Perkins loans are available to those with exceptional financial need (need is determined by a government formula that indicates how large a contribution toward your education your family should be able to make). Schools issue these loans from their own allotment of federal education funds. After you graduate, you have a grace period (up to nine months, depending on whether you were a part-time or full-time student) before you have to begin repaying your loan in monthly installments.

Stafford Loans

Students enrolled in school at least half-time may apply for a Stafford loan. Exceptional need is not required. However, students who can prove exceptional need may qualify for a subsidized Stafford loan, for which the government pays your interest until you begin repayment. There are two types of Stafford loans. A direct Stafford loan comes from government funds, and an FFEL (Federal Family Education Loan) Stafford loan comes from a bank or credit union participating in the FFEL program. The type available to you depends on your school's financial aid program. You begin to repay a Stafford loan six months after you graduate, leave school, or drop below half-time enrollment.

Plus Loans

Your parents can apply for a Plus loan if they currently claim you as a dependent and if you are enrolled at least half-time. They must also undergo a credit check to be eligible, although the loans are not based on income. If they do not pass the credit check, they may be able to sponsor the loan through a relative or friend who does pass. Interest is variable; the loans are available from either the government or banks and credit unions. Your parents will have to begin repayment sixty days after they receive the last loan payment; there is no grace period.

For a few students, a loan from a relative is possible. If you have a close relationship with a relative who has some money put away, you might be able to talk to that person about helping you with your education. Discuss the terms of the loan as you would with any financial institution, detailing how and when you will receive the loan as well as how and when you will repay it. It may help to put the loan in writing. You may want to show your gratitude by offering to pay interest.

Grants and Scholarships

Both grants and scholarships require no repayment and therefore give your finances a terrific boost. Grants, funded by the government, are awarded to students who show financial need. Scholarships are awarded to students who show talent or ability in the area specified by the scholarship. They may be financed by government or private organizations, schools, or individuals.

Federal Grant Programs

There are a number of federal grant programs available to part- and full-time students, depending on their needs. These grants include the Pell grant and Federal Supplemental Educational Opportunity Grant.

Pell Grants

These grants are need based. The Department of Education uses a standard formula to evaluate the financial information you report on your application and determines your eligibility from that score (called an EFC, or expected family contribution, number). You must also be an undergraduate student who has earned no other degrees to be eligible. The Pell grant serves as a foundation of aid to which you may add other aid sources, and the amount of the grant varies according to the cost of your education and your EFC. Pell grants require no repayment.

Federal Supplemental Educational Opportunity Grants (FSEOG)

Administered by the financial aid administrator at participating schools, FSEOG eligibility depends on need. Whereas the government guarantees that every student eligible for a Pell grant will receive one, each school receives a limited amount of federal funds for FSEOGs, and after it's gone, it's gone. Schools set their own application deadlines. Apply early. No repayment is required.

Work-Study

Although you work in exchange for the aid, work-study is considered a grant because a limited number of positions are available. This program is need-based and encourages community service work or work related in some way to your course of study. You will earn at least the federal minimum wage and will be paid hourly. Jobs can be on campus (usually for your school) or off campus (often with a nonprofit organization or a local, state, or federal public agency). Find out who is in charge of the work-study program at the colleges where you apply. Many students today have to find part-time work (see Figure 9.4.5) to help finance their college education.

Make Financial Arrangements

- Obtain financial aid forms from your high school counselor or directly from the college you are applying

- Completely fill out forms, sign the forms, and mail to the appropriate address

- Determine how to apply for scholarships, and follow through on the instructions

- Apply for part-time on-campus jobs, if necessary

- Apply for bank loans, if necessary

- Apply for and put down appropriate deposit or down payment for residential halls or apartments

- Check on fees for other expenses such as meal plans, parking, activities, and insurance

There is much more to say about these financial aid opportunities than can be discussed here. Many other important details about federal grants and loans are available in the *2005–2006 Student Guide to Financial Aid*. You can check out this guide at http://studentaid.ed.gov/students/publications/student_guide/2005_ 2006/ english/site-map.htm. You might also find this information at a college financial aid office, or you can request it by mail, phone, or online service:

Figure 9.4.5: Many college students work part-time to finance their education. Courtesy of Ken Karp.

Address:	Federal Student Aid Information Center P.O. Box 84 Washington, D.C. 20044
Phone:	1-800-4-FED-AID (1-800-433-3243) TDD for the hearing-impaired: 1-800-730-8913
Web site:	www.studentaid.ed.gov/students/publications/student_guide/index.html

Scholarships

Scholarships are given for different kinds of abilities and talents. Some reward academic achievement, some reward exceptional abilities in sports or the arts, and some reward citizenship or leadership. Certain scholarships are sponsored by federal agencies. If you display exceptional ability and are disabled, are female, have an ethnic background classified as a minority (such as African American or Native American), or are a child of someone who draws benefits from a state agency (such as a POW or MIA), you might find scholarship opportunities geared toward you.

All kinds of organizations offer scholarships. You may receive scholarships from individual departments at your school or your school's independent scholarship funds, local organizations such as the Rotary Club, or privately operated aid foundations. Labor unions and companies may offer scholarship opportunities for children of their employees. Membership groups such as scouting organizations or the YMCA might offer scholarships, and religious organizations such as the Knights of Columbus or the Council of Jewish Federations might be another source.

Sources for Grants and Scholarships

It can take work to locate grants, scholarships, and work-study programs because many of them aren't widely advertised. Ask at your school's guidance office or a college's financial aid office. Visit your library or bookstore and look in the section on college or financial aid. Guides to funding sources, such as Richard Black's *The Complete Family Guide to College Financial Aid* and others, catalog thousands of organizations and help you find what fits you. Check out online scholarship search services. Use common sense and time management when applying for aid. Fill out the application as neatly as possible, and send it in on time or even early. In addition, be wary of scholarship scam artists who ask you to pay a fee up front for them to find aid for you.

After you have completed the financial aid process and have decided which college to attend, you will register for classes.

Registering for Classes

Key Note Terms

registration – the act of registering

After you have been accepted to the college you will attend, you will need to go through the **registration** process for classes. Even though many colleges allow students to register for classes online, you should set up an appointment with an adviser the first time so that you have a clear understanding of the classes you will need to complete in order to earn a degree. In fact, the safest move is to meet with your adviser every semester so that your progress will be monitored.

When you meet with your adviser, you will receive a degree plan. This is a list of courses you will be required to successfully complete in order to graduate with a specific degree. Keep this list. A degree plan acts as a legal document between you and the college. Should the college decide to change the degree plan before you graduate, you probably will not be required to take additional classes if you are clearly progressing on an approved degree plan.

Register for Classes

- Meet with an adviser (this may be a faculty member or a staff member who works in student services) to determine which classes you will enroll in.

- Create a class schedule that will be based on your academic needs, as well as your personal needs. Take into consideration extracurricular activities or jobs you might be involved with.

- Take registration documents to the appropriate office.

- Pay registration fees or a down payment to hold your classes.

After you have registered for classes, you will be on your way. There may be other decisions you will need to make, including housing, meals, and transportation. These, too, are important decisions and will have an impact on your college experience, so work through these decisions carefully.

When you begin your college experience, continue to evaluate and refine your personal mission statement and your long- and short-term goals, as well as your personal skills and study skills. These are skills you can take with you on your journey of lifelong learning.

Keep Track of Information

In your search for the right school, you will be visiting several campuses and checking out many options. With all the information you have to gather, it would be easy to get confused or forget what one college offers as compared with another. Use Table 9.4.2 to help compare and contrast different schools, what they offer, what they cost, what they require for admission, and what activities interest you.

Table 9.4.2: College Comparison Worksheet			
	College 1	**College 2**	**College 3**
Location • Distance from home			
Size • Enrollment • Physical size of campus			
Environment • Type of school (2 yr, 4 yr) • School setting (urban, rural) • Location and size of nearest city • Co-ed, male, female • Religious affiliation			
Admission Requirements • Deadline • Tests required • Average test scores, GPA, rank • Notification			
Academics • Your major offered • Special requirements • Accreditation • Student-faculty ratio • Typical class size			

(continued)

Table 9.4.2: College Comparison Worksheet (continued)

	College 1	College 2	College 3
College Expenses • Tuition, room and board • Estimated total budget • Application fee, deposits			
Financial Aid • Deadline • Required forms • Percent receiving aid • Scholarships			
Housing • Residence hall requirement • Meal plan			
Facilities • Academic • Recreational • Other			
Activities • Clubs, organizations • Fraternity/sorority • Athletics, intramurals • Other			
Campus Visits • When • Social opportunities			

Conclusion

After you have gone through the process of picking a major, applying for financial aid, choosing and applying to a college, you now wait to get accepted. After you are accepted, you will need to contact your chosen school to find out its registration procedures. There are no guarantees in this process, but you can be assured that if you followed the suggestions in this and the other lessons in this chapter and are committed to the process, and motivated to succeed, you will reach your career goals.

This concludes the career planning chapter. In Chapter 10, "Planning Skills and Social Responsibility," you will learn how to set goals, how to manage your time, how to make good choices, and about cadet etiquette.

Lesson Review

1. How will you determine if college is right for you? What are your options?

2. What options are available to you to pay for your education?

3. What are the differences between a loan, a grant, and a scholarship?

4. Define the term *distance education.*

Planning Skills and Social Responsibility

Lesson 1

Making the Right Choices

Key Terms

criteria filter
idleness
intuition
routinization

What You Will Learn to Do

• Apply effective decision-making processes to personal situations

Linked Core Abilities

• Build your capacity for lifelong learning
• Take responsibility for your actions and choices

Skills and Knowledge You Will Gain Along the Way

• Relate how decision making impacts life
• Distinguish between decision making and problem solving
• Distinguish among effective and ineffective decision-making strategies
• Identify the features and benefits of the decision-making processes
• Define the key words contained in this lesson

Introduction

Making the right or wrong decisions can shape your life. Whether you make these decisions consciously or unconsciously, they represent how you respond to the opportunities, challenges, and uncertainties of life. You will have many decisions to make as you go through your life, such as the following:

- **Will I go to college?**
- **What college will I select?**
- **What will I study?**
- **Where will I live?**
- **When will I get married?**
- **Who will I marry?**
- **When will I change jobs?**
- **How will I invest my money?**
- **When should I retire?**

Asking and answering these questions establishes your future. You will fulfill many roles in your life, from student to career person, from homeowner to parent. The decisions you make in those roles define your successes and failures.

Use a Decision-Making Process

Even more important than what you decide is *how* you decide. The way to increase your odds of making a good decision is to learn to use a good decision-making process—one that helps you get to a solution with a minimum loss of time, money, energy, or comfort.

An effective decision-making process will

- **Help you focus on what is important**
- **Be logical and make sense for you**
- **Allow you to think of both the factual and the emotional consequences of your actions**
- **Not require an unreasonable amount of research**
- **Allow you to have an informed opinion**
- **Be easy to use and flexible**

An effective decision-making process will be valuable to you both for major decisions as well as the minor, more common decisions. The more you use a process to make decisions, the more it will become a natural part of your problem solving, and the more efficient you will become. As you grow more skilled in decision making, it will become second nature to you. Others may even start asking you for help with their decisions, as seen in Figure 10.1.1.

Figure 10.1.1: Sometimes two heads are better than one in making decisions.
Courtesy of Gary A. Conner/PhotoEdit.

The F-I-N-D-S Decision Process

Faced with a decision you have to make, you may do a lot of worrying. Worrying about making a decision generally does not accomplish anything.

You need to separate the issues, examine the facts, and work toward reaching a decision. The important thing is to follow a process. One such decision-making process is a simple five-step plan called the F-I-N-D-S plan.

The F-I-N-D-S decision-making model consists of

- **Figuring out the problem**
- **Identifying possible solutions**
- **Naming the pros and cons of each choice**
- **Deciding which is the best choice and then act on it**
- **Scrutinizing the decision**

Identifying the Problem

You cannot solve a problem until you have clearly defined the problem. Try to identify the problem in clear and precise terms.

For example, suppose you decide that you are unable to go to a concert. Simply stating the problem in vague terms, "I am not able to go to the concert Saturday night," won't get you there. Did you make another commitment for the same night? Are you unable to borrow the car for the evening? Are you grounded for the week of the concert? Or maybe you just don't have the funds for the ticket.

If the money for the ticket is what is keeping you from the concert, state the problem as, "I need to come up with $45.00 for the cost of the ticket." This is a much clearer statement of the problem.

Developing Possible Solutions

You can brainstorm by yourself, or involve others to create a list of possible solutions as seen in Figure 10.1.2. The more people you can question about your problem, the more likely it is that you will hit on the best solution.

Every idea that comes up should be considered. Sometimes the best answers are developed from an idea that does not seem feasible when you first hear it. Make an initial list of possible solutions. Look at your list. See if any other ideas come to you, evolving from something on the initial list.

When you are satisfied that you have a good number of possible solutions, you are ready to narrow down the possibilities.

Listing the Pros and Cons of Each Solution

After you have come up with a list, take each possible solution and think about what it would take to accomplish that solution. Think of the consequences of each idea.

In the concert ticket example, you may be able to earn the money, borrow the money, steal the money, or use your savings. Obviously, stealing the money is eliminated when you think of the consequences and the morality issue. You may decide to borrow the money from your parents or a friend and then pay it back over the next month from the money you earn at your part-time job. Perhaps the concert is important enough for you to use money from your savings. Maybe your job will pay enough between now and the concert for you to purchase the ticket.

While you are considering your choices, ask yourself some questions:

- **Will I feel good about this choice?**
- **How will my family feel about this choice?**
- **Will certain risks be involved?**

Figure 10.1.2. This student is reviewing her initial list of possible solutions.
Courtesy of Nick Gunderson/Tony Stone Images.

- **Am I willing to take such risks?**
- **Will this choice be satisfying to me?**
- **How will I feel about this choice when I look back at it in the future?**

After you have considered the possibilities and the consequences, you are ready to make a decision.

Choosing the Best Option and Implementing It

The list of possibilities and consequences should clearly indicate one or more "best choices." Don't worry if there are several good answers. There will be situations in which more than one decision will get you to your goal. Taking out a loan or using your savings may both be equally good decisions to pay for that concert ticket. Don't be afraid to make a decision and stick with it.

There are techniques you can use to simplify the choices. Depending on the type of choice you are making, one of the following techniques may help you narrow down your choices:

Key Note Terms

criteria filter – a standard, rule, or test on which a judgment or decision can be based

idleness – passing time without working or while avoiding work

intuition – instinctive knowledge or perception without conscious reasoning or reference to a rational process; keen insight

routinization – a process or decision that you have routinely used in the past that helps you in current situations because you have established a decision-making pattern

- **Criteria filter.** There may be some fixed set of criteria that the alternatives must meet. For example, if you were choosing a car, there may be a maximum amount that you can spend.
- **Idleness.** You may decide to do nothing, let others decide for you, or just wait and see what happens. You will have identified the consequences of this choice and will have to deal with those consequences. Sometimes, however, not making a decision is actually making a decision. For example, if you decide not to go on a trip to France, you are actually deciding to stay home.
- **Intuition.** Sometimes you follow your heart and make a decision based on your feelings and emotions. You go with what your gut tells you. For example, when you are offered two part-time jobs with equal pay and benefits, you may decide to go with one because "it just feels right."
- **Routinization.** There may be a decision that you have routinely made in the past that may help you now. For example, if you always study for your Friday math quiz on Thursday afternoon, you will have an easy time figuring out when you will need to study each week.

After you have made a decision, it is important to monitor the results. Both right and wrong decisions can teach you something for the future decisions you make.

Scrutinizing the Decision

This is where the learning takes place. If the result was successful, you will know that this was a good solution if the problem should come up again. If the decision did not lead to success, you will know that it would be best not to make that decision again.

Conclusion

The ability to make good decisions takes a lot of practice. Using a process (such as F-I-N-D-S) may seem like a large amount of work just to make a decision. Like many other things, after you start using the process—whether for major or minor decisions—you will find that solving problems and making decisions will become easier and easier. You will learn from the wrong decisions as well as the right decisions. With a good process, you increase the odds that your decisions will be well thought out and the results will be positive.

Next, you will take a look at goals and what it takes to set goals. You will also learn the importance of setting reasonable goals for yourself and others.

Lesson Review

1. What roles do you think you will play in your life? How can a decision you make about one role affect how you respond to another role?

2. What are the decision-making components of the F-I-N-D-S model?

3. Why is it important to include others in your decision-making process?

4. After you make a decision, what would be the consequences if you change your mind?

Lesson 2

Goals and Goal Setting

Key Words

goal
goal setting
long-term goal
mid-term goal
short-term goal

What You Will Learn to Do

- Develop a personal goals action plan

Linked Core Abilities

- Build your capacity for lifelong learning
- Take responsibility for your actions and choices

Skills and Knowledge You Will Gain Along the Way

- Define goals
- Differentiate between short-, mid-, and long-term goals
- Analyze goals to determine what makes them meaningful
- Identify criteria for well-defined goals
- Define the key words contained in this lesson

Introduction

Have you ever gotten into the car and started driving with no destination in mind? How would you know which route to take if you didn't know where you wanted to go? How would you know when you had arrived?

Think of a **goal** as your destination. The most efficient way to get from one place to another is to identify the final destination and follow a map that will guide you in your journey. Goals give you direction and keep you focused on a purpose. If you go through life without goals, you will probably waste a lot of time and energy. Time wasted can never be recaptured. Sometimes it is important to discuss your goals with friends in order to determine what is most important to you (see Figure 10.2.1).

Setting and achieving goals is one way to achieve a more fulfilling life. This lesson not only introduces you to types of goals and to the concept of **goal setting**, it also explains why goals are important and how to set them.

What Is a Goal?

A goal is an end to which an effort is directed. In other words, you establish a target and then take careful aim and shoot for it. A goal should also be something that is important to you and consistent with your values. Some goals are more difficult and time-consuming than others, and sometimes you may initially fail to achieve your goal. When this happens, you can modify the goal somewhat and try to hit it again. You cannot succeed if you do not keep trying.

Key Note Term

goal – an aim or purpose; an end to which effort is directed

Key Note Term

goal setting – planning done to reach a desired goal

Figure 10.2.1: Discussing your goals with friends can help you determine what is most important to you.
Courtesy of Larry Lawfer.

Writing Goals

It is important to write your goals down. A written goal can be read over and over again until it becomes imprinted on your brain. If a goal exists only in your head, it is just a dream and may be forgotten; but a written goal statement is a declaration of the outcome one plans to achieve. For a goal to be effective, however, it must be **Specific**, **Positive**, **Achievable**, and **Measurable**. You can use the acronym S-P-A-M to evaluate the goals you set against the following criteria.

- **Specific.** It must be explicit, clearly defined and have a specific plan of action. For example, "I will be a better student" is too vague to be a useful goal; however, "I will get an A on my next history exam" is more specific and therefore a much better goal.

- **Positive.** You are telling yourself that you will do something, not that you *might*, or you *think* you can. For example, "I want to do 60 sit-ups in a minute" is only a desire; however, "I will do 60 sit-ups in a minute" is a positive goal. A positive goal statement is very powerful.

- **Achievable.** The goal has to be within your power to make it happen through your own actions. It must be something you have a reasonable chance of achieving.

- **Measurable.** The goal must be defined in terms of results that are measurable or actions that can be observed. If your goal is not measurable, you will not know if you have attained it.

Why Goals Are Important

If you allow only outside forces to rule your life and set goals for you, you might feel bored, overwhelmed, or unsure of the decisions you face. By setting and achieving your own goals, however, you have the means to establish a framework that will build confidence, reduce stress, and ease decision making.

Some goals may seem overwhelming; however, by setting interim goals you can break down a goal into tasks that are more manageable, reducing your level of stress and anxiety. This process also enables you to explore and plan out all the steps necessary to reach the goal. When you have a map, the journey does not seem as daunting.

Accomplishing the goals you set for yourself gives you a good feeling and builds self-confidence. You can feel proud of a job well done. This is another benefit of setting goals. By setting goals, you can avoid wasting your time, energy, and effort. Goal setting makes the difference between mediocrity and excellence.

Types of Goals

Goals are divided into three categories: **short-**, **mid-**, and **long-term**. You can accomplish short-term goals in an hour, a day, or a week. They may often be the beginning steps to mid-term or long-term goals. Short-term goals do not require

Key Note Terms

short-term goal – a goal that can be accomplished in a short period of time, often without much planning or effort

mid-term goal – an intermediate goal; sometimes a step to a long-term goal

long-term goal – a life goal; a goal that requires a lot of time and planning to accomplish

much planning because you can usually accomplish them in very little time. An example of a short-term goal would be, "I will complete my homework assignment for algebra class and turn it in on time."

Mid-term goals are of intermediate length that often require more time and planning than short-term goals, especially if they lead to another goal. A mid-term goal may also be a step that leads to achieving a long-term goal. An example of a mid-term goal would be, "I will get an A in algebra this semester."

Long-term goals require a lot of time and planning to accomplish. They are usually your life goals. Setting a goal to become a doctor is a long-term goal. The planning for these goals may begin early in your life, even if you do not realize it. These goals may even begin as things you wish for instead of things to do. An example of a long-term goal would be, "I will get accepted to a top-rated engineering school." As you can see, this goal would take years of planning and work to fulfill.

Learning to Set Goals

Think about what your life would be like if you had everything you wanted. If that was ever the case, you would not have any goals to accomplish, and without goals, life would not have any direction or commitment. By setting goals, you are able to direct your life and commit to that direction. The kind of life that you have in the future is closely related to the goals you set today. Therefore, you must constantly strive to set meaningful and realistic goals for yourself and to do your best to achieve them.

Developing a goal plan begins with deciding which goals are important to you. After you have clearly defined a goal (consistent with S-P-A-M criteria), you need to begin planning how to achieve it. If a goal is too big, plan various smaller, interim steps that will enable you to reach the long-term goal. Never put yourself in a position where your goals are overwhelming; you may fail simply because the steps involve too much effort at one time. Keep your goals challenging, but realistic. The feeling of accomplishment that comes with completing each small step can inspire you to reach your larger, long-term (or life) goals. Figure 10.2.2 shows one way to write out a plan for achieving your goals.

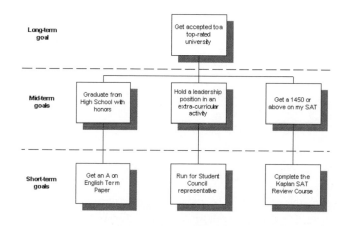

Figure 10.2.2: Writing out and mapping your goals can help you succeed.
Courtesy of US Army JROTC.

Goal setting is an ongoing process. Goals are also a source of motivation as seen in Figure 10.2.3. Because goals get you through every day of your life, you must continually reevaluate your goals. Some mid- or long-term goals require sacrifices now so that you can achieve your objectives later. You must discipline yourself to reach long-term goals, resulting in greater happiness and self-fulfillment.

Figure 10.2.3: This student has set his goals and is now motivated to move forward.
Courtesy of Prentice Hall.

Conclusion

Goals are very important to your life's development; without them, you would have no direction or commitment. Goals fill the need for disciplined work, play, study, and growth. They provide a framework that will help you organize and prioritize the events in your life. When you set and achieve a goal, you feel a sense of personal satisfaction and pride.

Time management will be covered in the following lesson. You will learn how to schedule your time to better be able to meet your goals.

Lesson Review

1. Why is it important to write down and list your goals?
2. Compare and contrast short-, mid-, and long-term goals.
3. List three personal goals—one short-, one mid-, and one long-term goal.
4. Why are the three goals you just listed important to you?

Chapter 10

Time Management

Key Words

agenda
procrastination
time management
time wasters

What You Will Learn to Do

- Develop a personal time management plan

Linked Core Abilities

- Take responsibility for your actions and choices
- Apply critical thinking techniques

Skills and Knowledge You Will Gain Along the Way

- Distinguish between time efficiencies and time wasters
- Relate time management to your personal goals
- Develop daily, weekly, monthly, and quarterly/semester time management plans
- Define the key words contained in this lesson

Introduction

Think back to this morning. How was it for you? Did you get up on time? Did you have breakfast? Did you have time to do what you expected to do or what your parents expected you to do? Now, think back to last evening. Did you finish your homework? Did you take care of your share of the household chores? Did you watch your favorite television program?

Frustration creeps in when you do not manage time well. On a scale of 1 to 10 (1 being poor use of time and 10 being good use of time), how well did you manage your time yesterday? If you can honestly answer 9 or 10, give yourself an A. If you answered 7 or below, you need to organize your day better in order to gain control of your time and your life. Setting priorities and planning your time effectively can eliminate stressful situations in your life (see Figure 10.3.1).

Every day you are given a precious gift—the gift of time. You get 24 hours, but how you choose to use this time makes all the difference. When you take responsibility for your time—by planning your day and building a schedule to achieve your goals—you are practicing **time management**.

This section teaches you how to plan your day and how to execute your plan. Planning your day will help you target academic and personal goals, manage the increasing demands on your time, reduce stress, increase successes, and achieve greater satisfaction and enjoyment of life.

The Perfect Day

You can divide the day into five blocks of time: before school, during school, after school, before bed, and bedtime.

Key Note Term

time management – the process of effectively using time to gain control of events, conditions, and actions

Figure 10.3.1: Learning to set priorities and plan your time effectively can eliminate stressful situations such as running to class late.
Courtesy of Deborah Davis/ Tony Stone Images.

Before School

Consider the morning as that part of the day from the time you wake up until the time you leave for school. What is a perfect morning?

- What time would you get up?

- How long would you need to take care of your personal hygiene, grooming, and dressing?

- How much time would you need to take care of your other responsibilities, such as helping to get your younger sister or brother ready, feeding the pets, or taking out the trash?

- What other activities must you complete before school and how long do they take?

During School

The time you spend in school can be a productive time to organize the rest of your day.

- What assignments take top priority?

- Which assignments will take the most time to complete?

- Will you need to spend time in the library?

After School

- Consider what goes on after school.

- This period can amount to between two to four hours, and it should include meaningful activities as well as leisure time and time to rest.

- Do you participate in a club, in a sport, or in the band?

- Do you work after school?

- Is there time before, during, or after practice or work to accomplish something meaningful?

- If you do not practice or work everyday, what would be the best use of your time after school and before dinner?

Before Bed

To have a perfect morning, you must definitely get some things accomplished in the evening, after dinner, and before you go to bed on the preceding day.

- How much time should you spend doing homework and chores?

- How much time is left for talking on the phone or watching television?

- What is your nighttime ritual before going to bed? Do you choose your clothes for the next day, pack your book bag, or prepare your lunch? How long does all that take?

- What time do you need to go to bed to get your "forty winks" of sleep? For most of us, eight hours of sleep is almost essential.

- What else do you need to do after dinner and before bed? Planning a perfect evening sets the stage for a perfect tomorrow.

Bedtime

Just before going to bed, you can take a few moments to plan the following day, and review what you've already accomplished.

- **Did you complete everything you wanted to do?**
- **Do you need to get up earlier than usual to finish a task?**
- **What does the next day bring?**

Creating a Daily Activity Matrix

Before you can begin to manage your time effectively, you need to know how you currently spend your time. Completing a daily activity matrix, shown in Figure 10.3.2, can help you in this endeavor.

Examine the matrix. If you take the total time spent on these activities and subtract that from 1,440 (the number of minutes in a day), you end up with the number of minutes you spend in unscheduled activities. Is some of this time wasted? Remember that time wasted can never be regained. There are many ways that people waste time each day. Some of the most common **time wasters** are:

- **Procrastination.** This is putting something off that needs to be done. For example, you procrastinate writing the essays for your college application because it is burdensome.
- **Poor organization.** If you spend every morning looking for your backpack before you catch the bus to school, you are poorly organized, and you are wasting time.

Key Note Terms

time wasters – activities that do not promote the effective use of time

procrastination – the act of putting off something that needs to be done

Activity	Minutes a Day	Days a Week
School		
School related extracurricular activities		
Playing sports (not school related)		
Homework and studying		
Watching TV		
Playing videogames		
Reading for pleasure		
Shopping		
Work		
Chores and family responsibilities		
Spending time with friends		
Spending time with family		
Church and all related activities		
Eating		
Sleeping		
Other:		

Figure 10.3.2: Daily activity matrix.
Courtesy of US Army JROTC.

- **Crisis management.** Do you spend a lot of time solving large and immediate problems? For example, you forgot you had a math quiz today, so now you have to drop everything else and cram for your quiz. This is a time waster because if you had planned better, you would not have had a crisis in the first place.

Could your time be better spent elsewhere?

Now that you have thought about it, you are ready to organize your day on paper. You should always write down your plans, keeping in mind that if you fail to plan, you plan to fail.

Tools for Time Management

There are three simple tools that students can use to ensure their time management effectiveness. These tools, a monthly calendar, a daily schedule/plan, and a "to-do" list, when used together on a daily basis, will ensure a more efficient and more effective time manager.

A Monthly Calendar

The monthly calendar is an important planning document. All appointments, class schedules, work schedules, meetings, sporting events, and other activities or events need to be entered or recorded on the monthly calendar first. Using a monthly calendar properly will provide you with a week at-a-glance and a month at-a-glance planning document. You can see all activities or events for any week or a particular month. Why do you need such a tool? Used properly, you will be better able to schedule activities and events without double scheduling or scheduling events on top of each other, which can be very embarrassing and time consuming.

The monthly calendar should never be used as a "to-do" list. Having class schedules, meetings, and so on on the same document is very confusing and can cause a lack of control as well as add unnecessary stress to your day. Most monthly calendars have a place for additional notes. This section is a good place to list events or activities that will take place in a certain month but not necessarily on any particular day. This note section is a good place to record reminders. For example, a friend or relative in another state may ask you to call them in March. To avoid losing that information, where would you record it? You can record it under the note section on the month of March. Figure 10.3.3 is an example of a monthly calendar. Monthly calendars are available in any office supply store or discount store as well as many businesses that give them out during December and January each year.

Daily Planning and Goals

Think about what you want to accomplish in school this year, and what part of it is achievable within the next six weeks. Do you want to

- **Make the honor roll?**
- **Work toward earning an academic, military, or athletic scholarship?**
- **Write an article for the school newspaper?**

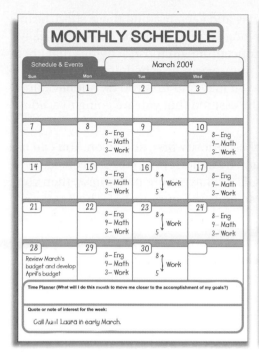

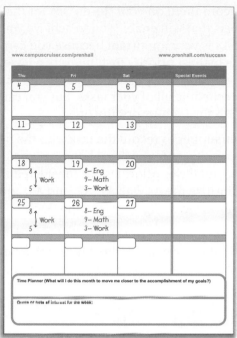

Figure 10.3.3: Monthly calendar or schedule which is used for weekly and monthly planning. Courtesy of Prentice Hall.

A daily plan should be aligned with your short-term and mid-term goals, which will, in turn, enable you to achieve your long-term goals. When you know that your daily activities are helping you achieve your goals, you will see that there is an increased meaning in the tasks you do every day and you will feel a sense of accomplishment at the end of the day, knowing that you are working toward the achievement of your goals. When you take responsibility for planning your daily activities, you are in control of your own destiny.

The first step toward creating a daily plan, as seen in Figure 10.3.4, is to prioritize your daily tasks, assigning a higher priority to those that are most important to you.

Figure 10.3.4: A daily planner with one page for a "to-do" list and one page for the daily schedule. Courtesy of US Army JROTC.

Record them on your "to-do" list for that day and keep in mind those short-term goals that will enable you to achieve your long-term goals. Prioritizing your daily tasks is very important because you can concentrate on those activities that are of the highest priority first. Items of a lesser priority can be scheduled around the high priority tasks as they fit into the day. You may find that you do not have time to schedule all of your tasks, but you can be assured that you are going to accomplish the highest priority ones.

Remember to record the task with the highest priority first, and so on. You can use a priority system using a letter assignment. The highest priorities are considered As, and lower priorities are considered Bs. It you have more than one A, then you prioritize the As with A1, A2, and A3, and so on (see Figure 10.3.5). The B tasks are prioritized using the same approach.

After you have prioritized all of your daily tasks, you are ready to create a daily schedule or plan for the day. Use this type of written daily schedule to serve as a reminder of specific events, due dates, responsibilities, and deadlines.

The Big Picture

Planning one day at a time is like admiring a beautiful forest, one tree at a time. If the forest is your life, you may need to get an overview to see where the paths through the forest are leading. In the same way, you should plan in larger time

Figure 10.3.5: A one page daily schedule that includes a daily schedule of events on the left side of the page and a to-do list on the right side of the page.
Courtesy of Prentice Hall.

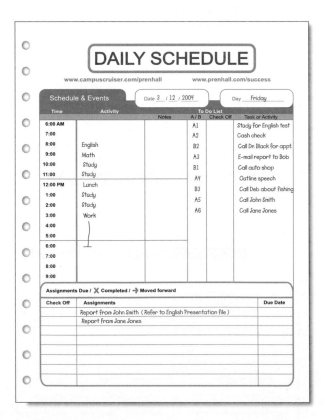

Chapter 10 Planning Skills and Social Responsibility

frames to ensure your days are leading you toward your goals. The daily plan takes you through 24 hours of life and keeps you active in the here and now. The weekly plan shows you how to balance your life. You will discover that 168 hours is enough time to work, practice, study, attend meetings, spend time with your family, and have fun with your friends, too.

The quarter or semester plans show you the big picture far in advance. You can plan your days and weeks better if you have developed a quarter or semester schedule. The monthly calendar is an excellent tool to use to plan each semester. A school semester lasts approximately five months; the monthly calendar (see Figure 10.3.3) will help you visualize your plan. Monthly calendars display week by week when all of your tests, projects, mentoring activities, papers, science or math fairs, key social events, athletic or JROTC events, field trips, national test dates, family vacations, and so on are due or will occur. You will be able to determine which weeks are heavily scheduled. You can use the light weeks to start studying and preparing for the heavier weeks.

Plan Your Work, Work Your Plan

The following tips will help you to more effectively know how to plan your work for a day, week, or longer (quarter or semester) and enable you to do better at working your planning process.

- Make time every evening to review your day and plan your tomorrow.

- Reevaluate your goals every week and write short-term goals on your planning sheets. Stay committed to your goals.

- Prioritize your "to do" list.

- Make a list of things you can accomplish in 15- and 30-minute blocks of time. For example, dusting or emptying the trash, reviewing class notes, learning new Spanish vocabulary (already written on index cards), reviewing mentoring activities, or learning how to work one new math problem. Be ready to fill the in-between times with something useful.

- Use a timer to move you along during tight periods, such as mornings before school.

- Schedule something fun every day. Do your work first and reward yourself with something fun.

- Record your favorite television programs and watch them during planned leisure times.

- Be flexible; shift things around when necessary. Do not get discouraged if you are thrown off schedule by unavoidable circumstances.

- As you finish a task, cross it off your "to-do" list. Add anything you did that was not on the list and then cross it off. Adding and crossing tasks off your list is not only a way of keeping track of what you have accomplished but also a way of acknowledging your accomplishment.

- Enjoy the sense of satisfaction that comes from accomplishing something, no matter how small, and taking definite steps toward your goals.

Conclusion

Few people ever plan to fail, but many people fail to plan. Time is the great equalizer; everyone gets the same amount every day. Whether it is used or abused often determines who rises to greatness and who falls to failure. Daily, weekly, monthly, and long-term (quarter or semester) planning puts you in charge of your life. Setting specific goals will give you a track to run on and a course to follow. You will know what it is you want, and you will go for it!

The cadet who routinely plans, reviews the plan, and adjusts it to the ups and downs of life will find this planning process very rewarding. Planning can help you to manage life's increasing demands while targeting academic and personal goals. Daily triumphs, no matter how small, will translate into goal achievements, generating greater satisfaction and enjoyment of life.

Now that you're familiar with how to plan your time more efficiently, you will most likely have more time to attend social functions. The following lesson covers the cadet etiquette guide. You will learn the best ways of interacting at social events and will gain the self-confidence to always present yourself in the best light possible.

Lesson Review

1. **What is your favorite time of the day? Why?**

2. **How can planning your day give you more free time?**

3. **List three items you'd put in your daily schedule.**

4. **Define the term *procrastination*.**

Lesson 4

Cadet Etiquette Guide

Key Terms

comradeship
curtly
dining-in
dining-out
etiquette
martial
monopolize
palate
place cards
protocol
receiving line
repast
sorbet
stag
stilted
tines

What You Will Learn to Do

- Learn proper etiquette for various events

Linked Core Abilities

- Treat self and others with respect
- Apply critical thinking techniques

Skills and Knowledge You Will Gain Along the Way

- Prepare invitations and thank-you notes
- Exhibit appropriate etiquette when making introductions
- Demonstrate proper dining etiquette
- Define the key words contained in this lesson

Introduction

During your high school years, JROTC experience, and life after graduation, there will be occasions when you will be encouraged to interact with people on a social level. By knowing the rules of proper etiquette, you will not only make a good impression, but you will also be more relaxed and confident in these situations.

This lesson is designed to provide information on proper social conduct and behavior, an important element in your character development. Although the lesson concentrates on the etiquette and manners required at your Cadet Ball, this information carries over into other aspects of your life.

Etiquette is a code of behavior or courtesy based on rules of a polite society. Manners are socially correct ways of acting as shown in prevalent customs. Manners are based on kindness, respect, thoughtfulness, and consideration. Good manners are timeless, whereas the rules of etiquette may vary with the changing times.

As you read about the rules of proper etiquette and the practice of good manners, remember that social etiquette and good manners are nothing more than common courtesy, sincerity, and consideration for others. It is important to treat others in the same way that we want others to treat us. This is the very foundation on which a polite society is built.

Key Note Term

etiquette – a code of behavior based on rules of a polite society

Making Introductions

Introductions should be simple, direct, and dignified, and the act of making them should be an occasion of formality. They should be made whenever people gather socially, even for a short period of time. Introductions should be made automatically and immediately when discovering that two people do not know each other. You may make these introductions or have someone else do it (as in a **receiving line**), but you cannot neglect an introduction without running the risk of being rude or negligent. There is nothing mysterious about making introductions, unless you do not know what to do.

Key Note Term

receiving line – a group of people, including the host and honored guests, who stand in line and individually welcome guests attending a function, as at a formal reception

The Receiving Line

Introductions at a formal reception, such as the annual Cadet Ball, may often include a **receiving line**. It is customary, and often mandatory, that all cadets and their guests go through the receiving line after arrival. The people who might be in the receiving line are as follows:

- **The host (senior Army instructor or commander of the unit holding the reception)**
- **The spouse or guest of the senior Army instructor or unit commander**
- **The ranking honored guest and his or her spouse/guest**
- **Other dignitaries with their guests**

At a reception, such as the Cadet Ball, the lady precedes the gentleman through the receiving line. The gentleman, whether or not he is the ROTC cadet, introduces the lady first and then himself to the Cadet Adjutant, who often announces the names of all attendees to the host. A lady or gentleman attending **stag** should introduce him or herself to the adjutant. Even though the adjutant may be a friend of yours, do not shake his or her hand. The adjutant will announce your name to the host as you step in front of him or her. A simple, pleasant greeting and a cordial handshake are all that is necessary when moving through a receiving line. Save lengthy conversation for later. Should your name get lost in the line, repeat it for the benefit of the person doing the greeting.

In the absence of an adjutant, the lady still precedes the man through the receiving line. He introduces her first and then introduces himself directly to the host. After you have finished this line, you may proceed to the serving of refreshments or conversation with other guests and await the signal for the next event. If the receiving and dining rooms are separate, do not enter the dining room until that signal is given.

For the remainder of the event, you will be responsible for making introductions as you move around the room and during dinner. The following guidelines explain what you need to do.

Key Note Term

stag – unaccompanied by someone of the opposite sex; traditionally, a man who attends a social affair without escort of a woman

Formality of Introductions

When making an introduction, avoid the use of elaborate phrases. Recall that introductions should be simple and direct. The most generally accepted introductions are as follows: "Captain Smith, may I introduce . . ." or "Mrs. Foster, I would like you to meet. . . ." You should not say "Meet Joe."

It is a general rule that you introduce juniors to seniors (this applies to age and military rank), gentlemen to ladies, and so on. However, the degree of formality used when making the introduction depends on the position of the persons involved and/or the solemnity of the occasion.

Examples of Formal Introductions

When introducing someone to a dignitary, mention the dignitary first to show respect for the office he or she holds. Ensure that you use the correct formal title or appellative for the dignitary when making the introduction.

- **Introduce a doctor, judge, or bishop by their titles.**
- **Introduce members of Congress by Senator or the Honorable.**
- **Introduce a Catholic priest by Father, and an archbishop by Your Grace. Some Protestant clergy use titles such as Reverend, Pastor, or Doctor, whereas others prefer to be addressed as Mr., Mrs., Miss, or Ms. It is best to ask the individual how he or she prefers to be introduced before the introduction is made.**
- **Introduce military personnel by their rank; for example, when introducing your guest to one of your JROTC instructors, you might say "First Sergeant Allen, I would like you to meet Miss Jones."**

If the situation arose where you had to introduce a teacher to a parent, you would use the teacher's name first. For example, "Major Cooper, I would like you to meet my mother, Mrs. Eastern." If both of your parents were there, you would introduce the woman first and then the man, such as, "Major Cooper, I would like you to meet my parents, Mrs. Eastern and Mr. Eastern."

Examples of Less-Formal Introductions

When introducing two people who you know very well and who have heard you talk of the other, you may be more casual. For example, to introduce a squad buddy to your sister, you might simply say, "Susie, this is Pete." In this example, it is perfectly acceptable to make the introduction using the first names of both people; however, do not make an introduction to an adult, senior, and so on, using that person's first name.

In some cadet battalions or military academies, cadets have only one formal title as far as introductions are concerned—that of cadet. In those situations, the rank structure is not used when addressing cadets socially. For instance, you would say, "Doctor Jones, this is Cadet Draper," not "Doctor Jones, this is Cadet Lieutenant Draper." Furthermore, at some schools cadets may be addressed as "Mr. Draper" or "Ms. Draper" during conversations. For example, "Mr. Draper, I am pleased to meet you."

Methods of Making Introductions

When making an introduction, speak each name slowly and clearly so there can be no possibility of misunderstanding on the part of either person. When you are on the receiving end of an introduction, make a special point of listening to the other person's name. If you forget the name, or did not hear it, ask—with an apology—for the name to be restated; then, use the name several times in conversation. This will help you remember it.

When being introduced, it is proper to return a courtesy such as, "Nice to meet you," "Hello," "I am really glad to meet you," or "How do you do?" If you were the one making the introduction, it is not appropriate to walk off and leave the two people staring at each other. As the person who made the introduction, you should either say something about each person to get a conversation started or excuse yourself so that you and your guest can continue to move about the room or participate in some other event.

When starting a conversation, mention something of common interest to both parties. For example, "Captain Davis, I would like you to meet Michael Knight. Captain Davis is my senior Army instructor, Michael. Sir, Michael hopes to enroll in JROTC next year."

Before taking leave of the person whom you just introduced, your guest should respond with "Good-bye, I am very glad to have met you" or something to that effect.

Note

In taking leave of a group, it makes no difference if you were introduced or merely included in their conversation; you politely and quietly respond good-bye to anyone who happens to be looking at you, without attracting the attention of those who are unaware that you are leaving.

When and How to Shake Hands

When gentlemen are introduced to each other, they typically shake hands. Additionally, ladies who are JROTC cadets shake hands during introductions. However, as a more general rule, whenever a lady or gentleman extends their hand as a form of greeting, the receiving party should reciprocate the gesture. Nothing could be more ill-bred than to treat **curtly** any gesture made in spontaneous friendliness. At the end of the introduction and/or conversation, those who were drawn into it do not usually shake hands when parting.

A proper handshake is made briefly; but there should be a feeling of strength and warmth in the clasp. At the same time, maintain eye contact with the person whose hand one takes, as shown in Figure 10.4.1. Do not shake a hand violently, grasp the hand like a vise, keep the handshake going for a long period of time, or offer only your fingertips.

Other Forms of Introductions

If seated, one rises to acknowledge an introduction and remains standing while other members of the party are being introduced to one another. When being introduced to ladies or gentlemen who are seated, you need not rise if rising may inconvenience others at the table.

Key Note Term

curtly – rudely brief or abrupt, as in speech or manner

Figure 10.4.1: An Army JROTC cadet shaking hands.
Courtesy of StockDisc/Fotosearch.

When being introduced to a lady out-of-doors, a gentleman in civilian clothes may remove his hat. In addition, a gentleman will ordinarily remove his glove to shake hands unless he is a member of a color or honor guard. If he is confronted with a sudden introduction when he has gloves on and it is awkward to remove a glove while the other person has their hand outstretched, it is better to shake hands with the glove on with no apology.

> **Note**
>
> You would also use these rules as part of general public behavior, even in casual situations.

If you desire to introduce two people who are not near each other, you would typically take the junior to the senior, the young lady to the older person, the gentleman to the lady, and so on.

When in doubt whether two people have met, it is perfectly permissible to ask. Be sure to address the senior first, using a courtesy such as "Colonel Smith, have you met Miss Jones?" If they have not met, make the introduction. Usually, most people will consider your question as tantamount to an introduction, and will proceed with the how-do-you-dos. The important thing is not to assume that people know each other. There is no harm in introducing people who have already met; it is, however, quite inconsiderate to have strangers together without an introduction.

It may sometimes be an erroneous assumption that every cadet knows every other cadet. Do not hesitate to introduce cadets if you are not sure they know each other.

Some people have a difficult time remembering names. Not remembering a name is a common failing and can be easily forgiven. However, forgetting a name is not an excuse for not making an introduction. If necessary, ask for the person's name—with appropriate apologies—before starting the introduction. For example, "I beg your pardon, sir (or ma'am), but I have forgotten your name. Thank-you, sir (ma'am). Colonel Smith, I would like you to meet Miss Jones."

In certain situations, you may find it necessary to introduce yourself to another person. If you are next to someone you do not know and no one is around to make an introduction, it is perfectly acceptable to make your own introduction. Use a greeting such as "Hello, I am Tom Frazier," while shaking that person's hand. Do not say, "What's your name?" A good reply to you would be "Ted Wentworth, nice to meet you." It is then up to both people to start their own conversation.

Dining Tips

Table manners are an important part of social conduct. Proper manners around the table are not just reserved for special occasions; you should use them whenever you dine. Relaxed politeness is the key to any dining situation. When you know what to do, you can relax and enjoy yourself. This section will help you learn the rules of the table.

Manners and Courtesies Before Eating

A gentleman does not sit down until all the ladies at his table are seated. He can help with the seating by holding the chair, first for his guest, then for other ladies near him if the ladies outnumber the men. He does this by pulling out the lady's chair from the table far enough for her to move easily in front of it. Then, as the lady sits down, he gently pushes the chair under her until she is seated. When all ladies at the table are seated, he may then take his seat by going around the left side of his chair. Posture at the table should be straight but not stiff.

If a lady leaves the table at any time, the gentleman who seated her rises. When the lady returns to the table, her escort or the gentleman who seated her rises and the courtesies mentioned in the preceding paragraph are repeated.

The polite dinner guest will not touch anything on the table, not even the napkin, until after the blessing (or invocation) has been said or until it is obvious that there will be no blessing. Then you may pick up your napkin and partially unfold it on your lap. Do this inconspicuously; do not unfold a dinner napkin completely or above the table.

At a large dinner, there may be a vast array of silverware at the place setting, consisting of one or two knives, two or three forks, and two or three spoons. This is shown in Figure 10.4.2. If there is any doubt about the correct piece of silverware to use for a particular course, one generally starts with the outside piece of silverware and works inward. If you end up without a spoon or a fork, it is appropriate to ask for a replacement.

Specialized pieces of silverware, for which their function is self-explanatory, include the butter knife, soup spoon, dessert fork and spoon, iced tea spoon, oyster fork, and fish knife and fork. The number of pieces of silverware indicates the number of courses to expect. A six-course meal, for example, might include soup, fish, **sorbet** (a **palate** cleanser), salad, an entree, and dessert. The placement of the silverware indicates the order of these courses.

Key Note Terms

sorbet – a fruit-flavored ice served for dessert or in between courses as a palate refresher

palate – the sense of taste

Methods, Manners, and Courtesies of Eating

Different methods, manners, and courtesies of eating exist, depending on various situations. You should be familiar with the proper use of silverware, how to eat with your fingers as well as with a soup spoon, the differences between American and European styles of dining, and more.

American versus European Styles of Eating

In the American style of eating, cutting food should be done, as shown in Figure 10.4.3, by holding the fork in your left hand, **tines** down with your index finger on the back of the fork, secure the food being cut with the knife, which is held in your right hand. Cut in front of the fork, not behind it. After cutting not more than two or three bites of food, place the knife on the plate and transfer the fork to your right hand. This is called the zigzag method.

Key Note Term

tines – slender pointed parts of a fork; prongs

Figure 10.4.2: A place setting can be confusing if you're not familiar with it. Courtesy of US Army JROTC.

Figure 10.4.3: American style of eating. Courtesy of US Army JROTC.

When not using your knife and fork, place them together across the top of your plate, as shown in Figure 10.4.4. This is the resting position. When you have finished the main course, place the knife and fork beside each other on the dinner plate diagonally from the upper left to lower right, or from the 10:00 to the 4:00 position. This is the finished position and indicates that your plate may be removed.

In the Continental or European style, hold the fork in your left hand and the knife in your right hand. Cut and eat with your fork, tines down, while still holding it in your left hand. The knife can remain in your right hand throughout the meal to cut food or to help push bits of food onto the fork. Only one bite of food is cut and eaten at a time.

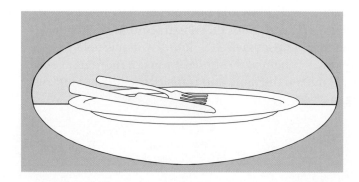

Figure 10.4.4: Resting position, American style. Courtesy of US Army JROTC.

Chapter 10 Planning Skills and Social Responsibility

When not using your fork, rest it diagonally on the left side of the plate with the tines down and close to the center of the plate. Rest the knife diagonally on the right side of the plate with its point toward the center of the plate. When finished, place them as described in the American style with the fork tines down.

Proper Use of Silverware

Various rules govern how to properly use silverware.

- **After you have used a piece of silverware, do not place it back on the table.**

- **Do not leave a used spoon in a cup; place it on the saucer.**

- **Do not leave a soup spoon in a soup bowl, although you may leave it on a soup plate if one is provided; otherwise, place it on the dinner plate when not in use.**

- **Do not lay a knife with the handle on the table and the tip of the blade on the edge of the plate. This also applies to the fork.**

- **Leave unused silverware on the table in its proper position.**

Proper Way to Eat Soup and Finger Foods

When eating soup, the motion of the spoon should be away from you while filling it. Sip from the side of the spoon; do not slurp. If it is necessary to tip your soup bowl, tip it away from you. If your soup is too hot to eat, let it sit until it cools; do not blow on it.

Bread, rolls, biscuits, nuts, fresh fruit, olives, celery, radishes, raw carrots, cookies, and small cakes may be eaten with your fingers. Place finger foods such as these on the bread plate, or in the absence of that plate, on the salad or dinner plates.

As seen in Figure 10.4.5, break your individual servings of bread, rolls, and large biscuits into small pieces before buttering and eating them, one piece at a time. Do not cut these items. Buttering and eating a whole roll or whole slice of bread is also not appropriate.

Proper Use of a Napkin

You should not tuck the napkin under your belt or wear it like a bib. Napkins are for dabbing lips, catching spills, and covering sneezes. Do not use a napkin to blow your nose. Never lick your fingers; always use your napkin.

Before taking a drink of water or any other beverage, wipe your lips with your napkin to avoid leaving smears on the glassware. One quick, light pass with the napkin should suffice.

Figure 10.4.5: Break bread, rolls, and biscuits with your fingers before you butter them.
Courtesy of US Army JROTC.

If you must leave the table during dinner, say, "Excuse me, please," with no explanation, and place your napkin on your chair. When leaving the table after dinner, place the napkin on the table in loose folds to the right of your plate. Do not refold, crumple, or twist it. Also, push your chair to the table on every occasion.

Basic Table Manners

The following are hints regarding table manners. Follow each one in any situation where you might be dining.

Key Note Term

place cards – a name card for a formal dinner

- If **place cards** are used, do not move or remove them. In addition to indicating the specific seating arrangement, place cards are used to make guests feel welcome and to help people get to know one another in large social settings.

- Take small bites. Large mouthfuls of food are unsightly. Do not chew with your mouth open or make loud noises when you eat. It is not polite to talk with food in your mouth.

- If you burp, say "Excuse me," to no one in particular and continue eating. Do not make a big deal out of it.

- Hats, gloves, cameras, purses, sunglasses, and so on do not belong on the table. If it is not a part of the meal, do not put it on the table. Hats and gloves belong in the cloakroom. You may place cameras and purses under your chair.

- Your hands should go no farther over the table than is necessary to eat and to pass things. Between courses, place your hands in your lap or at your side. Do not place your elbows on the table.

- If you cannot easily reach something on the table, ask for it to be passed to you with a please and a thank-you. If you are the one passing something, place the items on the table for the person to pick them up. When passing salt and pepper, pass them together.

- If food spills off your plate, you may pick it up with a piece of your silverware and place it on the edge of your plate.

- If you drop something, leave it on the floor until the meal is over; then pick it up. If a piece of your silverware falls onto the floor, pick it up if you can reach it and let the server know you need a clean one. If you cannot reach it, tell the server you dropped a piece of your silverware and ask for a clean one.

- Do not season your food before you have tasted it.

- Hold a long-stemmed glass with the thumb and first two fingers of your right hand at the base of the bowl or on the stem.

- It is not appropriate to ask for a "doggy bag" during a formal occasion.

- Do not reprimand a server. Make any complaints to the person (cadet) in charge of the ballroom arrangements.

- If food gets caught between your teeth and you cannot remove it with your tongue without being too noticeable, leave the table and go to the restroom where you can remove the food in private.

- At the end of dinner, and after the host and honored guests have departed, make sure that you say good-bye to everyone at your table before departing.

Table Talk

Conversation is an important part of social interaction around the table. It is perfect for the enjoyment of good companionship and a pleasant meal. A few important tips are as follows:

- Try not to talk too quickly or too slowly.

- Keep the conversation light. Small talk includes casual, unofficial, interesting things in everyday life such as the weather, music, upcoming events, movies, or sports. Keep topics of conversation safe and noncontroversial. Avoid discussions about religion, race, politics, or any controversial issue. Avoid health issues, off-color jokes, and gossip.

- Answer respectfully when addressed.

- Be mindful of engaging in conversation with a person who has just taken a bite of food. Remember, do not talk with food in your mouth.

- Loud voices/laughter can be disturbing to others. Do not yell; use a pleasant tone of voice that can be heard only at your table. Do not use profane, abusive or vulgar language.

- Be a good listener. Give others a chance to talk. Do not **monopolize** a conversation. Pay attention to the person speaking by giving eye contact; do not look at other people when someone is talking to you.

- Do not interrupt. Allow the other person to finish what he or she is saying before speaking. If you and another person start talking at the same time, give way quickly in a friendly manner with a simple, "Go ahead, please."

- Do not ridicule or laugh at an unfortunate remark or someone's mistake. Although a good conversationalist does not contradict someone in a social setting, it is okay to disagree. In those instances, start by saying, "I disagree with you because . . ."

Key Note Term

monopolize – to take exclusive ownership or control

The Cadet as a Guest

When you are invited to attend a social event, which could be a short afternoon visit, a dinner party, or the annual Cadet Ball, you have certain obligations that you must observe as a guest.

Invitations

You must understand the invitation: what you are invited for, where it will be held, when you should be there, and what you should wear. A written invitation will usually spell out most of these things quite clearly. Certain things are implicit in an invitation, as you shall see.

The R.S.V.P.

R.S.V.P. comes from the French expression "Repondez s'il vous plait," which means "please reply." On many invitations, you will see the R.S.V.P. followed by a telephone number. In this case, the courtesy of a prompt reply by telephone is required to permit the host, hostess, or planning committee to properly plan the event. Call within two or three days to accept or decline the invitation and make your call between 9 a.m. and 6 p.m.

> **Note**
>
> R.S.V.P. means that you must reply to the host to let them know if you can or cannot attend the function to which you've been invited.

> **Note**
>
> More on telephone courtesies is covered in the section on "Other Courtesies."

If your plans for that day are unsettled or indefinite, do not pass this problem on to the prospective host or hostess. It would be much better to outright decline the invitation than to give a complicated account of your indefinite social activities. Even if the other arrangement or engagement is tentative; it is best to decline the invitation. After you have declined, however, do not call back if your plans change.

When declining, it is sufficient to say to the host or hostess that a conflicting duty or social engagement prevents you from accepting. You are at liberty to turn down an invitation because you do not wish to go; however, you should exercise good judgment on the invitations you refuse.

If, after you accepted an invitation, an illness or an absolute emergency prevents you from attending, call the host or hostess immediately with regrets and apologies.

You are not at liberty to invite someone else along unless the invitation clearly indicates the number and names of those invited.

There are several variations of the R.S.V.P. that are coming into widespread use, especially on informal invitations.

- **"R.S.V.P. Regrets Only." This invitation means that the prospective host or hostess is expecting you unless you notify otherwise that you cannot come. If you can accept, you need not reply, just be there on time.**

- **Invitations by phone. When accepting an invitation by phone, it is a good idea to repeat back all of the essential information so that there is no misunderstanding. If you must first check your calendar before answering, get all the details and explain that you will call back as soon as you have done so. Thank the caller for the invitation, make sure you have the phone number, and promise to call right back; then make sure you do.**

Where

Most written invitations will indicate exactly where the function is being held. Some invitations may include a small map for your convenience.

When

Invitations to dinners, receptions, and weddings will usually give a time. For dinners and receptions, this is the time at which you should arrive, no earlier and no later. You will need to plan your timing so that you can be punctual. The time on a wedding invitation is the time the ceremony begins; therefore, you should allow sufficient time to be punctual.

If you are invited to an open house from 3 p.m. to 6 p.m., you may arrive any time after 3:00 and depart before 6:00. You are not expected to stay the entire three hours. After a dinner party, you should stay at least an hour; otherwise, it hints of "eat-and-run" rudeness.

What to Wear

The invitation may specify what you should wear. For example, cadets would most likely wear their Class A uniform to the annual Cadet Ball. In this situation, male guests should wear a suit while female guests should wear either short or long evening attire.

Some invitations may simply indicate that the dress is formal, informal, or casual. Ensure that you understand what these terms mean. If you are in doubt, ask the host or hostess what to wear when you call to R.S.V.P. As a general rule, use the following guidelines:

- **Formal: For gentlemen, a suit may be acceptable, although a tuxedo or uniform equivalent is preferred; for ladies, a short or long evening gown may be appropriate.**

- **Informal: For gentlemen, a sport coat and tie is appropriate; for ladies, a dress appropriate for daytime wear or a nice pantsuit is acceptable.**

- **Casual: For gentleman, nice slacks and a sport shirt is appropriate; for ladies, a sundress or nice pants and blouse is appropriate. In some situations, jeans or shorts and a nice shirt or blouse may be acceptable.**

Courtesies When a Guest at Smaller Functions

When attending an open house or a small dinner party, seek out your host and/or hostess immediately upon arrival and greet them. A crowded room should not keep you from properly greeting your host and hostess. You should also delay getting any refreshments until after you have properly greeted them.

Because the host and hostess are in charge, let them run things. As a polite, unassuming guest, you should help by making conversation and joining wholeheartedly in whatever activities they have planned.

You should not sit when other guests are standing in your presence.

Prior to leaving, you must thank your host and hostess for a wonderful time. Even if there are still dozens of people present, you must seek them out to say thank you and good-bye.

Thank-You Notes

Thank-you notes should be written within two or three days, but no more than a week, after you have been a guest at someone's home. A thank-you note should be handwritten in ink on quality writing paper. Stationary sets that provide matching paper and envelopes are recommended. Be conservative in the choice of color and design. Plain white is always acceptable. Some of the requirements for a thank-you note are as follows:

- **Spell out the month, the notation 3/9/05 is not used socially. This should be written as March 9, 2005. Place the date in the upper-right corner just below the fold line on the informal notepaper.**

- Ensure there are adequate margins on both sides of the paper; leave about one and one-fourth inch on the left side and about three-fourths inch on the right, depending on the size of the paper.

- Place the salutation, such as "Dear Mrs. Elliott," at the left margin.

- Indent the first line of each paragraph; bring each subsequent line out to the left margin.

- Place the complimentary close approximately as far to the right as the date at the top of the page. "Sincerely," or "Sincerely yours," with your first and last names are acceptable complimentary closes. Do not use "Yours truly" and reserve the use of "Love," for a family member or close friend followed by your first name only.

- Do not use "Cadet" or your cadet rank in your signature.

- Your return address belongs on the envelope, not under your signature.

There should be a minimum of three paragraphs in the thank-you note. The first expresses your thanks specifically and in detail for the occasion. The last briefly summarizes your thanks. There must be one or more paragraphs in the middle on any topic you choose about the occasion you attended. Do not invite yourself back in your thank-you note.

Key Note Terms

stilted – stiffly or artificially dignified or formal; pompous; lofty

repast – a supply of food and drink served as a meal

When expressing yourself, be yourself! If you do not normally speak a **stilted** or flowery language, do not sound that way in your note. Sincerity is far more important than eloquence. "I was overwhelmed by the sumptuousness of the **repast** in your exquisite domicile" is pretty silly from most people. "I enjoyed the dinner in your attractive home" sounds much more natural. If you particularly enjoyed the soup, or if the chocolate cream pie was out of this world, by all means say so in your note.

Sincerity is the first rule in social correspondence. Simplicity is the second rule. You can hardly go wrong with a few simple and direct statements of the things that pleased or amused you. Write just as you would say it to someone you know very well. Also, use correct grammar and spelling and keep it neat.

The thank-you note is an individual responsibility. If more than one of you enjoyed a dinner party at someone's home, it is not proper to send one thank-you note. Each of you should write your own note.

To address an envelope, ensure that you use a block style; include the proper title with the name (such as Mr., Mrs., Miss, Dr., Colonel, SGM and so on); place the city, two-letter state abbreviation, and zip code on the same line.

Place your return address on the front top left-hand corner of the envelope. You may use an address label for this purpose. You may also include "Cadet" in your title but not your cadet rank: Cadet John C. Scott is acceptable, but Cadet Captain John C. Scott is not correct.

If you are on the planning committee for the Cadet Ball, you should also send thank-you notes to the special guests, the organizations that sponsored the event, and the organizations that provided services and entertainment.

Other Courtesies

Life is full of ways to show courteous behavior toward others. This section shows just a few ways you can act in a thoughtful and civilized manner.

Telephone Courtesies

The telephone is a valuable time-saver and an effective means of communication. Here are some tips for proper telephone usage.

When calling a private residence to respond to an R.S.V.P., it is most proper to call between 9:00 in the morning and 6:00 at night. Avoid calling during meal hours. If you are in doubt, ask the person you are calling if this is a convenient time and offer to call back later if necessary. Let the phone ring at least six times to allow the person to reach the phone.

Identify yourself when placing a call. Unlike talking to someone face-to-face, the person on the other end of the phone may not recognize your voice until you identify yourself. While talking on the phone,

- **Be polite. This applies to any conversation.**
- **Speak slowly and clearly. Do not eat, drink, or chew gum.**
- **Do not sneeze or cough into the receiver. Turn your head or excuse yourself.**
- **Do not carry on a conversation with someone in the room.**
- **Call back immediately if you get disconnected and you placed the call.**
- **When answering a call for someone else, say, "May I ask who is calling?" This sounds better than "Who is this?"**

There is also proper etiquette to follow if you dial a wrong number. No matter how careful you are you may still dial a wrong number. When that happens, apologize to the person who answers. That person is not interested in hearing a story about how you misdialed, just tell him or her "I'm very sorry to have disturbed you," hang up, ensure you have the correct number, and then try again. It is inexcusably rude to hang up without an apology.

When leaving a message on an answering machine, clearly state your name, the date and time of your call, and a brief message. Leave a phone number only if you need to be called back.

Cellular Phone Courtesies

Because cell phones can be used virtually anywhere, their users need to remember commonsense courtesy. Results from a nationwide survey indicate that wireless users need to improve their phone etiquette and put people ahead of phone calls. A few tips are as follows:

- **Use of wireless phones is prohibited in most schools and at school functions.**
- **Use of wireless phones during social gatherings or appointments is not appropriate.**

- Do not place a cell phone on the table during a meal. It is also considered impolite to make or receive cell phone calls during a meal.

- Do not drive and use a cell phone. If you need to have a conversation while driving, be sure to pull off the road while talking.

- Do not use a wireless phone when it will inconvenience or disturb others.

- Use should be limited in public places or gatherings to safety or emergency reasons.

Helping Others

If an older woman or an invalid gentleman wants some support, it is appropriate for you to offer your arm. The cadet does not offer his or her hand. Hand holding in public is not appropriate and is considered a public display of affection. Public displays of affection are improper when in uniform. A cadet may offer his or her hand only when it is not practical to offer the arm, for example, to help an elderly lady or gentleman out of a car. Offer your hand palm up but do not force it on the person to whom you are offering it. Withdraw your hand as soon as it is no longer needed.

When walking with a lady, a gentleman should walk on the curbside or on her left if there is no curb.

If a gentleman arrives at a door first, he should open it and allow others to pass through. If a lady arrives at the door first and opens it, the gentleman may hold the door for her to continue.

If you are driving or riding to the social in a privately owned vehicle, open the car door for your passenger first on the right side of the car, then go around it and take your seat, either behind the wheel or in the back seat beside your guest. When you reach your destination, walk around the car and open the door for your guest if he or she has not already exited the vehicle.

Being Responsible for Your Guest

Depending on the nature of the social occasion, cadets should inform their guests about the traditions and courtesies of it before arriving. Using the Cadet Ball as an example, cadets should inform their guests about appropriate dress, conduct, the receiving line, traditions of the mess, and so on. Remember, if you invite a guest, you are responsible for your guest's behavior. If you have duties to perform after you arrive at the social, arrange for someone else to act as an escort for your guest until you are free. Introduce your friends and ensure that your guest's time is fulfilling.

Respect to Seniors

By this time in JROTC, you should not have any difficulty in showing respect to military seniors; in fact, it should be automatic.

You should also show respect for elders, as well as parents, teachers, and others in a position of authority. In short, you should treat all persons with whom you have contact with the utmost respect.

Because it is unacceptable to use slang or poor grammar such as "yeah," "nope," or "un-huh" to a JROTC instructor, it is also socially rude to say these things to others.

You may also encounter situations when seniors address you by your first name. Although this may be flattering, under no circumstances should you address a senior by his or her first name unless that person specifically asks you to do so.

Grooming

Nothing less than scrupulous attention to all aspects of personal hygiene will make you socially acceptable. Be certain that you are well groomed every time you make an appearance socially. One dirty or untrimmed fingernail may seem like a small thing to you, but it may be the basis for a negative impression. You will not have a second chance to make a first impression. The following are just a few of the basics you should already be doing to ensure your appearance is up to standards.

- **Ensure your hair is clean, neatly trimmed or styled, and combed at all times.**
- **Shower daily and use a deodorant as part of your daily routine.**
- **Brush your teeth and floss daily. Try to brush after meals.**
- **For young men who already have to shave, if it is necessary for you to do so once or twice a day to be presentable, then do so.**

Good grooming is an individual responsibility. It should not be necessary for an instructor or a senior cadet to tell you to maintain proper personal hygiene. Additionally, for cadets, ensure that your uniform is clean, pressed, and presentable.

Other Everyday Courtesies

Use "please," "thank you," "you're welcome," "excuse me," and "I'm sorry" naturally and sincerely in conversations. Say, "excuse me" if you accidentally brush against someone. You can also say "I beg your pardon" but do not use the phrase "pardon me."

You may chew gum in public as long as you do it in a nonoffensive way—quietly and inconspicuously. Do not chew gum in formal situations, at work, if you are a host or hostess, or if you are around food.

In public places, do not make a lot of noise with friends that might upset other people.

Do not push ahead of anyone. Wait your turn in line to go though a door, into an elevator, or onto an escalator.

Planning a Cadet Ball

A major prerequisite for ensuring that the Cadet Ball (and for that matter, any social occasion) is successful is careful planning. The first important act is the appointment of a Cadet Ball chairperson by the senior Army instructor. This chairperson should have authority to make many of the required planning decisions, although some of these decisions may be subject to the approval of the senior Army instructor.

One of the first duties of the cadet chairperson should be to review the reports on file for previous Cadet Balls. These reports will acquaint the chairperson with his or her responsibilities, which include the following (this list is not all inclusive):

- Establishing committees, appointing committee leaders, and providing them with the necessary people and other resources. He or she is also responsible for supervising these committees. At a minimum, the chairperson should establish committees for

  - Advertising
  - Decorating
  - Entertainment
  - Food
  - Fund-raising
  - Invitations, including the special guests
  - Program and seating arrangements

- Establishing short-and long-term goals, identifying the tasks necessary for the achievement of these goals, and delegating the tasks to committees for execution.
- Identifying problem areas and lessons learned from previous Cadet Balls and preventing them from reoccurring.

The chairperson and all committee leaders should think through all of the details thoroughly and develop a plan to get everything done. You should be sure to establish alternative (or backup) plans where necessary. This way you can be sure of avoiding last minute embarrassment.

Send out invitations as early as possible. If some guests do not accept, you still have time to invite others without offending them with a last minute invitation. Ensure that the invitation clearly states the location, time, and dress requirements. Let your guests know exactly what is being planned and what is expected of them.

Helpful planning tips include the following:

- Ensure that all arrangements are carefully made for the special guests
- Select a band that plays an arrangement of music as well as music that does not offend anyone
- Arrange to have a photographer
- Arrange to have several nice door prizes if you can find sponsors to donate them
- Give credit in the program to all sponsors as well as to individuals and organizations that assisted in putting the Cadet Ball together
- Rehearse the Color Guard, the sequence of events, and any special activities at the designated location at least one day prior to the actual event
- Coordinate with the designated location to ensure they prepare the correct number of meals, have the correct number of chairs and tables, and that seating is in accordance with the seating chart

History of Military Dining-Ins

You should be familiar with the terms **dining-in** and **dining-out**. These terms refer to formal dinners, which are intended for military members only (dining-in) or to which guests are invited (dining-out). The **protocol** for these affairs often reflects long-standing traditions within a regiment or corps of the armed forces.

Key Note Terms

dining-in – a formal military dinner for military members only

dining-out – a formal military dinner to which non-military guests are invited

protocol – a code of precedence in rank and status and of correct procedure in ceremonies; a form of etiquette observed in ceremonies; a combination of good manners and common sense that allows for effective communication

Dining-in has its roots in Europe and may extend all the way back to the Roman practice of holding great banquets to celebrate victory and parade the spoils of war. The customs and traditions of our contemporary dining-in come from those of the British Army regimental mess. The British mess provided a time for satire, solemn formality, and horseplay. It was an excuse for living beyond one's means and an occasion to observe long-standing customs and traditions of the regiment. The first recorded American dining-in occurred in September 1716 when Governor Spotswood of Virginia, along with a company of Rangers, celebrated after crossing the mountains and descending into the Shenandoah Valley.

Even today, there is still ample reason to observe the dining-in tradition. The intent of the dining-in is to promote cordiality, **comradeship**, and esprit de corps. In addition, it is hoped that participation in this worthy tradition will stimulate enthusiasm to prevent it from dying out.

The primary elements are a formal setting, posting of the Colors, invocation, traditional toasts (may be at the conclusion of dinner), a fine dinner, comradeship of cadets, benediction, retirement of the Colors, and **martial** music.

Toasting

The custom of toasting is universal. It is a simple courtesy to the person being honored. It is not proper to drain the glass at the completion of each toast; therefore, know how many toasts are being given so that you will know how much to drink with each toast. It is also not proper to raise an empty glass to make a toast. Toasts are made standing up. One person will present the toast by saying, "Ladies and Gentlemen, the president of the United States" or "Ladies and Gentlemen, I propose a toast to the president of the United States." All will then raise their glasses and say "the president" or "to the president," respectively.

On the presentation and retirement of the Colors, face toward the Colors at attention until the ceremony is completed; then, remain standing for the toasts and the invocation at the beginning of the program. You are expected to rise again for the benediction at the end of the program.

Key Note Terms

comradeship – companionship

martial – of or relating to army or military life

Conclusion

Learning proper social conduct is an important part of your growth and character development. Although there are many forms of etiquette that pertain to almost every social occasion that you will encounter in life, the intent of this lesson was to familiarize you with proper manners and etiquette for the single most important social event in JROTC—the Cadet Ball.

Lesson Review

1. What is the difference between etiquette and manners?

2. Explain why it is important to present a good appearance at all times.

3. Compare American-style dining with European-style dining.

4. Give three examples of proper dinner conversation topics; give three examples of improper dinner table topics.

Lesson 1

Setting Financial Goals

Key Terms

delayed gratification
goal
needs
SMART goals
values
wants

What You Will Learn to Do

- Determine personal financial goals

Linked Core Abilities

- Take responsibility for your actions and choices

Skills and Knowledge You Will Gain Along the Way

- Identify the components of the five-step financial planning process
- Differentiate between needs and wants
- Describe how values can influence decisions
- Define the key words contained in this lesson

Chapter 11

Introduction

You'll come into contact with money almost every day for the rest of your life. When you're at work, you're earning money; when you're at the mall, you're spending money. Used poorly, money can be a source of anxiety and lead to financial problems. Used wisely, money can be a tool to help you achieve your goals and dreams. That's the goal of the National Endowment for Financial Education (NEFE) High School Financial Planning Program—to teach you how to responsibly and effectively manage your money for the rest of your life. The NEFE High School Financial Planning Program has three main objectives:

- **Learning the financial planning process—what it is and what it can do for you**

- **Applying the process through assignments you will complete that relate to your experiences with money**

- **Taking control of your finances, starting today**

> **Note**
>
> You will find this lesson in your NEFE High School Financial Planning Program Student Guide.

For more information go to www.nefe.org/hsfppportal/index.html, call (303) 224-3511, or write:

National Endowment for Financial Education
5299 DTC Blvd., Suite 1300
Greenwood Village, CO 80111

Financial Planning: Your Road Map

Key Words

cash flow
decision making
opportunity cost
restraint
SMART goals

What You Will Learn to Do

- Determine personal financial goals

Linked Core Abilities

- Take responsibility for your actions and choices

Skills and Knowledge You Will Gain Along the Way

- Differentiate between needs and wants
- Describe how values can influence decisions
- Compare SMART goals
- Discuss how goals impact actions
- Define the key words contained in this lesson

Introduction

Do you ever find that you don't have enough money to buy something or participate in an activity? You may have already found that you need to make choices
because your cash supply is limited. In this learning plan you will compare your
wants and needs. You will also set personal financial goals as the first step in creating your own financial plan.

> **Note**
>
> You will find this lesson in your NEFE High School Financial Planning Program Student
> Guide.

For more information go to www.nefe.org or write:

NEFE The High School Financial Planning Program
5299 DTC Blvd., Suite 1300
Greenwood Village, CO 80111

Lesson 3

Budgeting: Don't Go Broke

Key Words

budget
cash management
expenses
federal income tax
fixed expenses
gross income
income
Medicare tax
net income
payroll deductions
P.Y.F.
Social Security tax
state income tax
taxes
variable expense

What You Will Learn to Do

- Outline a personal budget

Linked Core Abilities

- Take responsibility for your actions and choices

Skills and Knowledge You Will Gain Along the Way

- Identify the purpose of a budget
- Determine resources available for financial objectives
- Explain how to construct a simple budget
- Define the key words contained in this lesson

Introduction

What do you spend your money on? Do you take in more money than you spend, or do you find yourself needing to borrow money to make purchases? A budget is a useful way to help you identify where your money goes and figure out how to make the most of it. When you are in control of your spending, you are able to make your money work for you. In this learning plan you will create a personal budget that will match your financial goals.

> **Note**
>
> You will find this lesson in your NEFE High School Financial Planning Program Student Guide.

For more information go to www.nefe.org or write:

NEFE The High School Financial Planning Program
5299 DTC Blvd., Suite 1300
Greenwood Village, CO 80111

Savings and Investments: Your Money at Work

Chapter 11

Key Words

bond
capital gain
compounding
diversification
earned interest
inflation
interest
invest
mutual fund
rate of return
Rule of 72
savings
stocks
time value of money

What You Will Learn to Do

- Forecast personal savings and investments

Linked Core Abilities

- Take responsibility for your actions and choices

Skills and Knowledge You Will Gain Along the Way

- Describe reasons for saving and investing
- Describe how time, money, and rate of interest relate to meeting specific financial goals
- Describe basic investment principles
- Describe various savings and investment alternatives
- Define the key words contained in this lesson

Introduction

You can earn money by working or receive money as gifts. Another way to earn money is to make your money work for you. You can earn interest on savings or receive earnings from smart investments. In this learning plan you will examine different ways to put your money to work by saving and investing. You will also consider saving and investing habits that will help you meet your financial goals.

> **Note**
>
> You will find this lesson in your NEFE High School Financial Planning Program Student Guide.

For more information go to www.nefe.org or write:

NEFE The High School Financial Planning Program
5299 DTC Blvd., Suite 1300
Greenwood Village, CO 80111

Chapter 11

Credit: Buy Now, Pay Later

Key Words

annual fee
annual percentage rate(APR)
bankruptcy
credit
credit history
credit report
debt
finance charge
grace period
interest
loan term

What You Will Learn to Do

- Appraise personal credit worthiness

Linked Core Abilities

- Take responsibility for your actions and choices

Skills and Knowledge You Will Gain Along the Way

- Identify the advantages of using credit
- Identify the various costs related to credit
- Compare common sources for building credit
- Discuss the factors to consider when establishing credit
- Define the key words contained in this lesson

Introduction

Think of a time you borrowed money from a friend or family member. Were you able to build a good borrowing reputation by promptly repaying the money? Were the terms to repay the money fair? When you are in a situation when you need to make a large purchase such as a car, you might need to borrow money from a bank or another financial business. To use this type of credit wisely and avoid problems, you need to know what is involved. In this learning plan you will explore ways to use credit. You will also consider your rights and responsibilities of using credit.

> **Note**
>
> You will find this lesson in your NEFE High School Financial Planning Program Student Guide.

For more information go to www.nefe.org or write:

NEFE The High School Financial Planning Program
5299 DTC Blvd., Suite 1300
Greenwood Village, CO 80111

Lesson 6

Insurance: Your Protection

Key Words

deductible
insurance
insurance premium
risk management

What You Will Learn to Do

- Relate insurance to current and future personal needs

Linked Core Abilities

- Take responsibility for your actions and choices

Skills and Knowledge You Will Gain Along the Way

- Describe how insurance works
- Identify general types of insurance, including health, property, life, disability, and liability
- Discuss the costs associated with insurance coverage
- Define the key words contained in this lesson

Introduction

Have you ever been injured, in an accident, or had property damaged? Chances are, someone had to pay for those unexpected medical bills or costs for repairs. People use insurance as a way to protect themselves from unexpected losses. In this learning plan you will explore how different types of insurance protect you from losses. You will also uncover strategies to handle financial risk and ways to lower insurance costs.

> **Note**
>
> You will find this lesson in your NEFE High School Financial Planning Program Student Guide.

For more information go to www.nefe.org or write:

NEFE The High School Financial Planning Program
5299 DTC Blvd., Suite 1300
Greenwood Village, CO 80111

Teaching Skills

Preparing to Teach

Key Terms

competency
learning objectives
learning outcomes
lesson plan
measurable
prerequisite
training aids

What You Will Learn to Do

- Prepare to teach

Linked Core Abilities

- Communicate using verbal, nonverbal, visual, and written techniques

Skills and Knowledge You Will Gain Along the Way

- Describe five critical elements you need to consider in preparing to teach
- Write effective learning outcomes
- Describe at least six tips for planning a lesson
- Define the key words contained in this lesson

Introduction

Being an instructor, or an assistant instructor, will be a challenging experience for you. It is for anyone—even experienced teachers. Teaching is also a rewarding experience because you will have the opportunity to help younger cadets learn the skills they need to succeed. As an added bonus, you will find that when you teach, you learn more about the competency and content.

In this lesson, you will consider five critical elements that are important to your success when you teach:

- **Motivation**
- **Learning Outcomes**
- **Training Aids**
- **Lesson Plans**
- **Knowing the Content**

Motivation

To effectively teach a class, you must be motivated. Motivation is a drive that comes from within you. When you get excited about doing something, you will discover that you have the necessary motivation to do that task well; however, the opposite is also true. If you do not get excited about the task, you will lack the necessary motivation and drive to perform the task successfully. In teaching, just doing an okay or a satisfactory job is not enough. When your instructors give you the opportunity to become a student instructor, consider it a challenging and exciting opportunity to give students in your class the solid education they deserve.

Learning Outcomes

Key Note Term

learning outcomes – describe what students should know and be able to do as the result of a learning experience

As a student instructor, your primary responsibility is to help students achieve the **learning outcomes** for the lesson your instructor has assigned you to teach. The learning outcomes for a lesson describe what students should know and be able to do when they successfully complete the lesson.

Each JROTC lesson also includes performance standards that describe how students and the instructor will know when they are succeeding, learning activities that explain how students will achieve the learning outcomes, and assessment activities that tell how students will demonstrate their learning.

Competencies and Learning Objectives

As you prepare to teach a lesson, you will need to focus on two types of learning outcomes: *competencies* and *learning objectives*.

- A <u>competency</u> describes the major skill or task addressed in the lesson. Each lesson targets one competency.

- <u>Learning objectives</u> describe the supporting knowledge and skills needed to perform a specific competency. Learning objectives break the competency into smaller pieces that make learning easier and provide benchmarks by which students and instructors can measure progress toward achieving the lesson competency. Each lesson targets several learning objectives.

Key Note Terms

competency – a major skill or task that describes what a learner will be able to do as a result of a specific lesson

learning objective – a supporting skill, knowledge, or attitude leading to mastery of a competency

Example:

Competency	Apply mediation techniques to resolve conflict
Learning Objectives	a. Differentiate between arbitration and mediation
	b. Describe the role of a mediator and the qualities required to fulfill that role
	c. Establish ground-rules for the mediation process
	d. Facilitate the steps in the mediation process
	e. Adapt active listening skills to the mediation process
	f. Define key words: arbitration, empathy, mediation, facilitate

Writing Competency and Learning Objective Statements

Both competencies and learning objectives begin with one measurable action verb. Action verbs require students to <u>do</u> something: create a product, make a decision, solve a problem, or perform a task. Verbs such as "understand," "learn," and "know" are <u>not</u> action verbs and therefore <u>should not be used</u> in a competency or learning objective.

Table 12.1.1 shows examples of measurable action verbs. Refer to this list as you learn to write competencies and learning objectives in this lesson

Competencies and learning objectives are written in the same manner:

1. **Write a simple, one-sentence statement that describes the skill that students will learn to do in the lesson.**
2. **Begin the statement with an action verb.**
3. **Add the content, object, or performance.**
4. **Add descriptive words.**
5. **Check to be sure that the competency and learning objectives are observable (you can see the product or watch the performance) and measurable (you can evaluate the quality).**

Action Verb	Object	Descriptive Phrase
Apply	mediation techniques	to resolve conflict

Key Note Term

measurable – able to be observed and evaluated for quality

All learning objectives must be realistic, attainable, observable, and **measurable**. At the end of each period of instruction, you should be able to administer a test based on the criteria of the objective and on the material you presented. Likewise, students should be able to pass a test or at least demonstrate to the best of their ability, that they have a basic understanding of the material you presented.

Note

The process of develop learning objectives is by far more complex and detailed than presented here; however, this material should give you an appreciation for what learning objectives are and the basic developmental procedures.

Table 12.1.1: Sample Action Verb List		
act	discuss	predict
answer	distinguish	prepare
apply	estimate	produce
arrange	explain	rate
build	give examples of	record
calculate	identify	reply
change	illustrate	report
choose	join	restate
classify	judge	revise
compare	justify	schedule
compete	list	select
compose	match	show
compute	measure	solve
contrast	modify	state
create	name	summarize
define	organize	use
demonstrate	outline	verify
describe	perform	write/rewrite

Training Aids

Key Note Term

training aids – materials such as computers, handouts, chalkboards, and so on that enhance and support teaching

Training aids are materials and tools that help students learn and help you teach. Training aids include delivery tools such as computers, overhead projectors, television sets with videocassette recorders, and chalkboards, as shown in Figure 12.1.1. They also include items that present content such as PowerPoint presentations, posters, handouts, worksheets, and so on.

To make a training aid effective, you must use it properly. Use training aids as part of your lesson; however, your entire lesson cannot rely on the use of training aids.

When you find a training aid that you like, rehearse your lesson with it. The following pointers will enable you to use training aids effectively:

- **A training aid should adequately support the material in your lesson. Clearly explain how the training aid relates to the lesson learning outcomes and content.**

- **Do not talk to your training aids. Keep your eye contact with your class as much as possible.**

- **Make sure your training aids are large enough for everyone to see, and if the training aids use sound, loud enough for everyone to hear.**

Figure 12.1.1: The chalkboard can be an effective training aid if use properly.
Courtesy of US Army JROTC.

Lesson Plans

A well-designed lesson plan is your guide for teaching an effective lesson that is accomplished within the allotted timeframe. Without a lesson plan, it would be very difficult to ensure that the students achieve the competency and learning objectives and that you teach in an organized manner. Prior to teaching, be sure to carefully review the lesson plan and the information included in the related student learning plan such as the competencies, learning objectives, performance standards, learning activities, and assessment activities. In the next lesson, you will learn how to develop and use lesson plans.

Key Note Term

lesson plan – an organized, well-written plan for how an instructor will facilitate student learning

Knowing the Content

As you review the learning plan prior to teaching, make sure that you know the content. (See Figure 12.1.2.) You must be prepared to explain concepts, answer questions, provide demonstrations of required skills, and facilitate the designated learning activities. Be sure to practice presenting information, giving instructions, and providing demonstrations prior to class. Finally, use the eight tips for preparing to teach to make sure that you are ready to teach each lesson effectively.

Eight Tips for Teaching

When teaching a class, use these eight tips to prepare to teach effectively. These tips will help you to capture the attention of your class, keep their attention throughout the class period, build their respect in your ability as a teacher, and ensure that they meet the intended learning outcomes of the lesson:

Figure 12.1.2: You must prepare for the lessons you will teach.
Courtesy of Phyllis Picardi/Stock Boston.

Figure 12.1.3: Friends can provide valuable insight into your lesson during rehearsals.
Courtesy of Mark Richards/ PhotoEdit.

Key Note Term

prerequisite – required before moving to the next step, level, class, and so on

- Use an opening that will grab the attention of the class.

- Practice the material that you plan to present to the class. Pay close attention to your pace. Know how long each section of your lesson will take. (See Figure 12.1.3.)

- Inform the students of the learning outcomes (competencies and learning objectives) for the lesson and your expectations.

- Briefly review any material from previous lessons (prerequisites) that relates to the material you are teaching.

- Inform or advise the students of any precautions, safety requirements, or special instructions regarding the lesson.

- Present the material according to your lesson plan. Use your training aids effectively. Describe any assignments or practical exercises you plan to give and ensure the class knows how to accomplish them.

- Use demonstration and practice activities, when appropriate, to reinforce your instruction. Give your class examples that will help them understand and complete their assignments.

- Conclude by reviewing the main points of the lesson by referring back to the learning outcomes for the lesson. Allow time for questions. That is one way to determine how well the class understood the material. If possible, review any information that the class did not fully understand. You may wish to make a list of supplemental material students can review OR set aside time to work individually with students.

Conclusion

When conducting a class or assisting someone else to teach, proper preparation is essential to do your best. Create strong learning outcomes, develop a lesson plan, learn the content, identify the training aids you will use, and motivate yourself.

Classes have a set time period and your job is to effectively complete the lesson within that time. Remember your job is to *help* the students learn; not to learn for them. Encourage your students to share the responsibility for learning by actively engaging them in the process. If you are well-organized, well-prepared, and interested in the content, you will put yourself and your class at ease and make learning enjoyable for all of you.

Lesson Review

1. What are the five critical elements you need to consider while preparing to teach?

2. What are the two types of lesson learning outcomes?

3. What might be the outcome if you didn't develop a well-written and organized lesson plan?

4. What training aid do you find to be the most effective and easiest to use as an instructor and student?

Lesson 2

Using and Developing Lesson Plans

Key Words

facilitator
focus
energizer
inquire
gather
apply
process
reflection

What You Will Learn to Do

- Develop a lesson plan

Linked Core Abilities

- Build your capacity for lifelong learning
- Communicate using verbal, nonverbal, visual, and written technique

Skills and Knowledge You Will Gain Along the Way

- Explain the purpose of a lesson plan
- Describe the four-phases of a lesson plan
- Relate teaching and learning to the four phase lesson plan model
- Relate learning activities to learning objectives
- Associate active learning principles to effective lesson plan development
- Define the key words contained in this lesson

Chapter 12

Introduction

During your life, both in school and out, you may be called upon to teach others about a content area in which you have some expertise. As a JROTC cadet, you may be asked to teach some aspects of the JROTC curriculum to other cadets. In order to be prepared for these situations, it is helpful to know how to plan and execute a lesson.

Lesson plans are essential tools for teaching. Instructors use a lesson plan to organize the information and activities they plan to use in class. In some cases, lesson plans help to standardize how competencies and learning objectives are taught by a large number of teachers to ensure that all students meet the same standards for performance. In these cases, the lesson plan would show teachers:

- **What students need to learn**
- **What material they should teach**
- **To what extent they should teach the material**
- **In what sequence they should teach the material**
- **What strategies and learning materials they may use to teach**

Lesson Plans

JROTC lesson plans identify the target competency and learning objectives for each lesson. They provide detailed guidelines for facilitating cadet learning activities. The lesson plans should be used in conjunction with student learning plans as tools for planning, guiding, and assessing learning. The lessons incorporate sound learning principles such as multiple intelligences, the Four-Phase Lesson Plan, brain-based learning techniques, reflection, and authentic assessment.

Learning Plans

JROTC learning plans are designed to support cadet learning. Learning plans are written for cadets. They answer the questions cadets need to know about what they will learn including the target learning outcomes (competencies and learning objectives), the criteria for performance, and the activities and assignments they will need to complete in order to learn, practice, and perform the competency. Learning plans guide cadets through the learning activities and assessment activities included in the lesson plan and help cadets take responsibility for their own learning.

To be used most effectively, cadets should have the learning plan for each lesson at the beginning of class. Engaging in a review of the learning plan at the start of each lesson, instructors or cadet leaders should:

- **Highlight the target competency, performance standards, and learning objectives**
- **Explain why that information is important; for example, criteria tells learners how they will be evaluated on their performance**

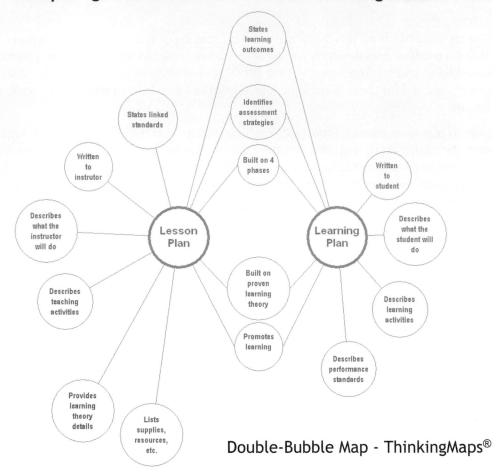

States learning outcomes

States linked standards

Identifies assessment strategies

Written to instrutor

Built on 4 phases

Written to student

Describes what the instructor will do

Lesson Plan

Learning Plan

Describes what the student will do

Describes teaching activities

Built on proven learning theory

Describes learning activities

Promotes learning

Provides learning theory details

Describes performance standards

Lists supplies, resources, etc.

Double-Bubble Map - ThinkingMaps®

- Show cadets how learning plans can help them keep track of the activities they need to complete
- Guide cadets to refer to and use the learning plan throughout the learning process

The Four-Phase Lesson Plan

JROTC lesson plans consist of four phases: Inquire, Gather, Process, and Apply. The following sections examine these phases in more detail:

Inquire Phase

The purpose of the **inquire** phase is to motivate and engage the students, helping them connect new learning to past experience. During the inquire phase you will also refine the lesson starting point by examining what your students already know and can do. Activities in the inquire phase can help to answer these questions:

- **What do students know?**
- **What don't students know?**
- **What misunderstandings do students have?**

Key Note Term

inquire – the phase in a lesson plan designed to connect new learning to past experience

- **What past experiences do they bring to the lesson?**
- **What do students want to know?**
- **What is the purpose of the lesson?**
- **How motivated are the students to learn the content?**
- **What are some practical reasons for students to participate in the lesson?**

During this phase you may want to use an icebreaker or **energizer** in your lesson. These are physically active games or other activities that motivate and engage learners and introduce the lesson topic.

Gather Phase

After you determine the lesson's starting point, you are ready to help your students **gather** information about what they need to know about the subject matter. You want students to acquire important facts and concepts so they may develop a better understanding and build their skills.

The purpose of the gather phase is to research and collect information from a variety of sources, to synthesize information, to evaluate existing information, to collect data, to evaluate ideas, or to observe new skills. Some important questions you can ask during this phase are:

- **How can you help students think through the concepts they need to understand?**
- **How can students actively engage in collecting the information they need to learn?**
- **How do the new concepts and ideas connect with what they already know and can do?**
- **What can students do to make sense of the new information?**
- **What new understandings can students construct?**

Process Phase

The third phase is called the **process** phase. The purpose of this phase is to use new information, process new ideas, and practice new skills. The following questions can help your students during the process phase:

- **How can students explore concepts through a variety of learning activities that support multiple intelligences?**
- **What ways can students show relationships among the data or concepts?**
- **What can students do to reinforce their understanding of the new concept?**
- **How can students practice and improve their ability to apply the new knowledge and skills?**
- **What feedback will help students improve their competence?**

Apply Phase

The purpose of the **apply** phase is to help students make real-life applications of the new information or ideas. Students can consider ways to integrate the lesson concepts or skills with other curriculum areas. They can also plan ways to transfer their learning into personal use outside the classroom. Questions that can help both the instructor and students during this phase are:

Key Note Terms

energizer – a learning activity designed to motivate and engage learners

gather – the phase in a lesson plan designed to assist learners in gathering new ideas and information

Key Note Term

process – the phase in a lesson plan designed to provide opportunities for practicing new skills and processing information

apply – the phase in a lesson plan designed to provide opportunities for students to demonstrate their competence and expand their ability to use it in their lives

- What else can be done with the information?

- What else is needed to make the information usable?

- How can students demonstrate their ability to apply their new knowledge and skills in ways that are different from those experienced in the lesson?

- How can students demonstrate their ability to apply their new competence in their lives?

The Three Components of Each Phase

There are three components that are common to each of the four phases in the lesson plan. They are Direct Student Focus, Learning Activity, and Reflection.

Direct Student Focus

As a teacher, you have a responsibility to help your students **focus** on specific elements of the learning activity. You will guide their thought processes and help them focus on key processes or content during the learning activity. You will eliminate or filter extraneous information so students can direct their attention to what is critical for their learning.

For example, if the students watch a video, you will identify specific elements of the video on which to focus; if you have the students read a chapter in a book, you could list the details you expect them to extract from their reading; if the students do research on the Web, you can help clarify the research topics or important information needed from the research; and so on.

The competency and learning objectives presented in the student learning plans serve as excellent tools for directing student focus. By teaching students to refer to them and referencing them for your students as you teach, you will go a long way toward directing student focus.

Learning Activities

A learning activity is an activity designed to help students learn to perform the competency. As a teacher, you should plan activities that best present the information and allow students the opportunity to participate in the learning process. (See Figure 12.2.1.) Learning activities should relate to the learning objectives for each competency and engage students in active learning experiences for each phase of the lesson plan.

Learning activities in the **inquire** phase should set the stage for learning by capturing the students' interest and helping them connect with what they will learn. As the instructor, your primary role in the **inquire** phase is consultant. As the consultant in this phase, your job is to inspire the students to learn and to assess what the students know and what they need to learn to achieve the competency.

Typical learning activities that are effective in the inquire phase include:

- Agree/disagree worksheets

- Graphic Organizers and Thinking Maps

- Analogies or metaphors

Figure 12.2.1: Teaching is more than just writing on a board in front of a class. Courtesy of Len Rubenstein/ Index Stock Imagery.

- **Pre-quizzes or pre-tests**
- **"Group" graph or "4 corners"**
- **Panel discussions**
- **Debates**
- **Homework reviews**
- **Other**

In the **gather** phase, learning activities are designed to help students obtain information from you, fellow classmates, and the learning materials. The instructor's primary role in the **gather** phase is that of presenter and resource person. As the presenter, you present information; you also serve as a resource—directing students to information, coordinating student activities, observing their progress, and answering student questions.

Typical learning activities that are effective in the gather phase include:

- **Graphic organizers and Thinking Maps**
- **Computer searches**
- **Jigsaw**
- **Interviewing experts**
- **Demonstrations**

- **Generating examples**
- **Socratic questioning**
- **Constructivist questions**
- **Field Trips**
- **Other**

In the **process** phase, learning activities should provide opportunities for students to practice new skills and help students evaluate the importance and usefulness of what they are learning. (See Figure 12.2.2.) Students also have an opportunity to check their grasp of the lesson material. Your primary role in the **process** phase is **facilitator**. As the **facilitator**, you serve as a guide or coach, coordinating student activities, observing performance, providing feedback, and answering student questions.

Typical learning activities that are effective in the process phase include:

- **Games**
- **Laboratory experiments**
- **Role Play**
- **Peer teaching**
- **Rehearsal**
- **Simulations**
- **Reciprocal teaching**
- **Graphic organizer and Thinking Maps**
- **Interviews**
- **Student designed homework activities**
- **Other**

Key Note Term

facilitator – one who leads a discussion or guides an activity

Figure 12.2.2: Practical application and field trips are very effective in the learning process.
Courtesy of Paul Mozell/ Stock Boston.

Learning activities designed for the **Apply** phase, engage students in active learning experiences that help them transfer the new information or skills outside the classroom and demonstrate their mastery of the competency. In this phase your primary role is that of mediator. As the mediator, you serve as a mentor, helping students to consider ways that the new knowledge and skills can be applied to their everyday lives and how it connects to what they are learning in other classes. You also provide feedback as students complete assessments that require them to demonstrate their competence. As the mentor, this is your opportunity to encourage students to make improvements in their performance when needed, and most importantly, to celebrate their successes!

Typical learning activities that are effective in the apply phase include:

- **Action research**
- **Portfolios**
- **Personal goals and objectives**
- **Creative connections**
- **Problem-based projects**
- **Demonstration of competence**
- **Peer and instructor review of products and performance**
- **Self evaluation of learning and developed or expanded competence**
- **Other**

Reflection

The **reflection** process is important because it causes students think about the importance and purpose of what they are learning and to see how the learning activity has helped them learn. Reflecting also helps the brain store information into long-term memory.

As the teacher, ask questions that help students think about, reflect on, or make sense of their learning experiences. Having students discuss or write down what they understand helps them clarify their thinking and improve their understanding, as well as strengthen their memory connections.

The Four-Phase Lesson Plan is based on a learning model in which lecture and reading is minimized, and in which group discussion, learning by doing, and teaching others is emphasized. In each of the four phases, students reflect on what they have learned, how they have learned it, and what they are going to do with it.

Key Note Term

reflection – an activity that requires learners to think about and communicate their learning experiences

Conclusion

For teachers, lesson plans provide the map or blueprint for teaching and facilitating a well-designed lesson. The Four-Phase Lesson Plan facilitates the planning and teaching processes. As you develop each phase of your lesson plan, remember to include activities that address the following components: Direct Student Focus, Learning Activities, and Reflection.

Be sure to provide learning plans for your students. Learning plans help your students take responsibility for their own learning by guiding them through the learning process and answering the following questions:

- **Why is this important?**
- **What will I learn?**
- **How will I demonstrate what I have learned?**
- **What strategies will help me learn?**

If you are called upon to teach a lesson, your students will benefit from this well-organized approach.

Lesson Review

1. List the four lesson plan phases. Choose one and explain it.
2. What are the three components of each lesson plan phase?
3. Define the term *facilitator* and explain what a facilitator does.
4. Explain how a student learning plan should be used to effectively support student learning.

Delivering Instruction

Key Terms

brainstorming
case study
coach-pupil exercises
conference
demonstration
discussion
gaming
group performance
independent exercises
lecture
practical exercise
role-playing
team practical exercises

What You Will Learn to Do

- Use effective teaching methods to deliver instruction

Linked Core Abilities

- Communicate using verbal, nonverbal, visual, and written techniques

Skills and Knowledge You Will Gain Along the Way

- Compare lesson objectives to learning objectives
- Distinguish among the seven teaching methods
- Identify the five types of practice exercises
- Define the key words contained in this lesson

Introduction

From time-to-time, you may be required to present a portion of the course content. When this occurs, you will need to know some of the finer points necessary to teach that instruction.

Recall that in the "Preparing to Teach" lesson, you learned how to prepare yourself to teach, develop learning objectives (consisting of tasks, conditions, and standards), and use training aids. In the "Developing Lesson Plans" lesson, you learned how to develop four-phase lesson plans (inquire, gather, process, apply). You may want to review all or a portion of that material before proceeding with this lesson.

In this lesson you learn different teaching methods and when to use each method, such as demonstration and lecture, five practical exercise formats, and the rehearsal process.

Types of Teaching Methods

The method of instruction is how you choose to conduct your class. Sometimes, the subject you are teaching dictates which method to use. There are many different types of instruction from which to choose. The following sections give you some ideas about different methods of instruction.

Lecture

Key Note Term

lecture – teaching method designed to provide instruction on a task or topic

The **lecture** is an informative talk given to a class (see Figure 12.3.1). During a lecture, the teacher does most of the talking; questions and answers usually occur at the end of the lecture. Because the teacher limits the interaction during the presentation, this method provides the fastest dissemination of information.

Figure 12.3.1: Lectures can be an effective method of teaching.
Courtesy of Barbara Stitzer/ PhotoEdit

Use lectures when the subject you are teaching is unfamiliar to your class and it is the best method for preparing students to practice the task. Generally, this method involves learning knowledge-based information. Knowledge-based information is that which you need to know or understand. Examples of JROTC subjects for which you might use a lecture are history, citizenship, or technology awareness.

When preparing for a lecture, be sure to research your topic, organize your thoughts using the outline of the lesson plan, and rehearse. Remember to use your training aids while practicing. Ensure that you are comfortable with your topic because you will be doing most of the talking.

The question and answer session at the end of the lecture gives your class the opportunity to ask for clarification or additional information, and it gives you the opportunity to reemphasize the lesson learning objectives.

Discussion/Conference

There are two names for this method of teaching. During a **conference**, the instructor involves the entire class in a **discussion** of the subject being taught by asking leading questions to get the class to think about and discuss the main points.

This method of instruction is more interesting than a lecture and is ideal for subjects such as current events, topics that require practical exercises (such as first aid and map reading), and topics where a majority of the class is having difficulty learning.

Experienced teachers recommend using a conference when conducting reviews because it enables them to ensure that the class is comfortable with the text material.

Demonstration

Demonstration is a method of instruction that requires class participation. Use this method to show the class how to do a task and to have them practice performing the task. This method holds the students' interest because they are actively involved in the learning process.

Advance planning and preparation are especially important for demonstrations to ensure that everything goes smoothly and to avoid interruptions or problems that would make the demonstration less realistic.

Practical Exercises

The **practical exercise** is a type of instruction where a learner performs, under controlled conditions, the operation, skill, or procedure being taught (see Figure 12.3.2). In a practical exercise, class members learn by doing. It is one of the most effective methods for teaching skills. Practical exercises are often used in conjunction with other methods, such as after a lecture or demonstration.

Demonstrations and practical exercises lend themselves to classes such as *Leadership Lab*, *First Aid*, *Map Reading*, and *Cadet Challenge*.

You will learn more about practical exercises later in this lesson.

Key Note Terms

conference – a teaching method where the instructor involves the entire class in a discussion of the subject being taught by asking leading questions to get the students to think about and discuss the main points

discussion – a teaching method where the instructor involves the entire class in a discussion of the subject by asking leading questions to get the students to think about and discuss the main points

demonstration – a teaching method that requires hands-on class participation

practical exercise – a maneuver, operation, or drill carried out for training a discipline

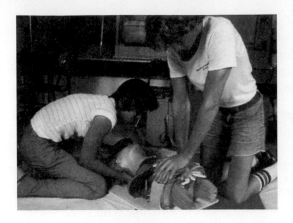

Figure 12.3.2: In this practical exercise, students are demonstrating their new learned CPR skills.
Courtesy of Frank Siteman/ The Picture Cube.

Brainstorming

Key Note Term

brainstorming – a teaching method that consists of group problem-solving techniques involving the spontaneous contribution of ideas from all members of the group

Brainstorming is a problem-solving technique in which instructors give participants a problem and have them bring into the discussion any ideas that come to mind. All ideas are gathered and recorded, without evaluation, before any are discussed. Preferably, the ideas are recorded someplace where all the participants can see them—for example, on a flipchart, whiteboard, or chalkboard.

In some situations, you may limit idea gathering to 5–15 minutes. After gathering the ideas, have the participants discuss them and decide on the best solution or course of action. It is your job, as the instructor, to facilitate this process.

To conduct a successful brainstorming session, you should

- **State the objectives and ground rules of the session up front so that the group members know of the session and what is expected of them**
- **Encourage input from all group members**
- **Recognize nonverbal cues that group members want to have input, and respond accordingly**
- **Keep the session moving and on track**
- **Avoid judging any ideas offered by the group during the idea-gathering phase**
- **Facilitate the group by constructively evaluating the various ideas and in reaching consensus on a solution, idea, or course of action**

Case Study

Key Note Term

case study – a teaching method that consists of an oral or written account of a real or realistic situation

A **case study** is an oral or written account of a real or realistic situation, with sufficient detail to make it possible for the learners to analyze the problems involved and determine possible solutions. There may be many right answers.

Many case study exercises involve group discussions. In this case, you should follow the same rules as described for the discussion/conference. Be prepared to provide relevant and constructive feedback.

Gaming

Gaming consists of activities where participants compete to try to achieve or exceed a certain standard in performing a skill relevant to the learning objectives of the lesson.

Learner-Focused Delivery

Learner-focused delivery, or learner-centered approach to instruction, is a process that begins with determining the needs of the student. It is when the learning objectives put the focus on the student and learning rather that the teacher and teaching methods. It is based upon the methodology known as instructional design using the ADDIE Cycle.

ADDIE is an acronym that stands for:

- **Analysis.** Establish the learner's current state of knowledge and skills in the subject area.
- **Design.** Detailed planning of the lesson with objectives based on learning outcomes.
- **Development.** Develop learning materials according to the design and learning styles.
- **Implementation.** Lesson is delivered as specified, monitored, and evaluated.
- **Evaluation.** Feedback the evaluation data to provide revision as needed.

Each student has different needs when it comes to learning. Each has different life experiences and a different knowledge base. Each student has a different way of learning or learning style. Some learn visually by observing or viewing information; others are auditory learners or learn by hearing or listening; and some learners are kinesthetic learners or learn by doing or are hands on learners. For learning to be most effective it should be tailored specifically to the individual student.

When developing a lesson plan, an instructor needs to consider a learner-focused delivery in choosing the type of teaching method that will be employed. For example, if most of the learners are auditory learners, the lecture method will be more effective. However, if some of the learners are kinesthetic learners, demonstrations with practical exercises will have to be added to the delivery plan. A learner focused delivery approach is more time consuming and requires more work but the results are more effective learning. Sometimes the instructor does not have the time or the resources to follow the ADDIE process. Nevertheless, to ensure effective learning, always use a combination of different teaching methods. For example, a lecture can be followed by a demonstration and a practical exercise. By combining several teaching methods to your delivery, you will be reaching more of your students and meeting their individual learning needs.

<aside>
Key Note Term

gaming – a teaching method that consists of activities where participants compete to try and achieve or exceed a certain standard in performing a skill relevant to the learning objectives of the lesson
</aside>

Practical Exercise Formats

In the best practical exercises, the tasks that learners perform should be as close as possible to those they will be expected to perform on their assessment or evaluation. The most common types of practical exercises are discussed in the following sections.

Group Performance/Controlled Exercises

In **group performance**/controlled exercises, learners work together at a fixed rate. Everyone does the same thing at the same time. One caution with this practical exercise type is that learners may imitate the performance without actually understanding it.

Independent Exercises

Learners work alone at their own pace in **independent exercises**. As the instructor, you will circulate around the classroom and supervise, providing assistance and feedback as necessary.

Role-Playing

In **role-playing** exercises, learners are given different roles to play in a situation, and they apply the concepts being taught while acting out realistic behavior. This type of exercise is especially useful for training interpersonal skills, such as leadership or counseling, or interactive skills in a realistic, but controlled situation.

> **Note**
>
> Role-playing can also be classified as a method of instruction.

Coach-Pupil Exercises

In **coach-pupil exercises**, learners work in pairs or small groups, alternately performing as instructor and student. Coach-pupil exercises are extremely useful when time is short or when there are too few instructors.

Team Practical Exercises

In **team practical exercises**, learners work together as a team to perform the desired tasks. This method integrates basic skills into team skills.

Reviews and Rehearsals

As part of your preparation for delivering instruction, you should rehearse prior to attempting to deliver the instruction. Even if you have delivered the instruction many times, rehearsing will help you get into the proper mindset and iron out any problems that you may have had in the past.

Key Note Terms

group performance – a controlled practical exercise where learners work together at a fixed rate

independent exercises – a practical exercise format where learners work alone at their own pace

role-playing – a practical exercise format where learners are given different roles to play in a situation, and apply the concepts being taught while acting out realistic behavior

Key Note Terms

coach-pupil exercises – a practical exercise format where learners work in pairs or small group, alternately performing as instructor and student

team practical exercises – a practical exercise format where learners work together as a team to perform the desired tasks

Reviews

If you have revised or adapted your materials, review them one last time to ensure you are comfortable with their content, format, and flow. It is also a good idea to look over your references and training aids again.

Rehearse

To help you rehearse, enlist family or friends to serve as an audience and to play the role of students. If possible, practice with all the equipment and training aids you will use in the classroom.

At the conclusion of your instruction, ask your audience to help you evaluate your performance to make sure that you iron out all trouble spots and are conducting the instruction at the proper pace (see Figure 12.3.3).

Figure 12.3.3: Having friends provide feedback after you rehearse your lesson is an effective way to fine-tune your presentation skills.
Courtesy of I. Marshall/The Image Works.

Conclusion

Teaching is more than just getting up in front of an audience and talking. You need to develop learning objectives and create a lesson plan identifying the best method for the presentation. Then you need to review the material and rehearse so you become comfortable delivering the instruction.

If you are asked to instruct others, creating a lesson plan, selecting the most appropriate lesson method, and rehearsing your presentation will increase your confidence level and allow you to conduct a well-received lesson.

Next you will learn the importance of adding variety in your lesson plan. You will also learn about cooperative learning strategies.

Lesson Review

1. **Choose one type of teaching method and explain it.**

2. **Why would one type of teaching method work better than others for different topics and settings?**

3. **List the most common types of practical exercises.**

4. **What methods would you choose to review and rehearse before delivering instructions?**

Key Terms

cooperative learning
strategy
team-building exercises

What You Will Learn to Do

- Incorporate a variety of strategies into a lesson plan

Linked Core Abilities

- Communicate using verbal, nonverbal, visual, and written techniques
- Apply critical thinking techniques

Skills and Knowledge You Will Gain Along the Way

- Assess the benefits of using cooperative learning strategies in the classroom
- Select cooperative learning strategies that encourage team building
- Select cooperative learning strategies that require students to respond to questions posed in the lesson
- Select cooperative learning strategies that help learners gather, share, and learn a great deal of material in a short amount of time
- Explain how incorporating a variety of learning styles and multiple intelligences benefits learners in a classroom
- Define the key words contained in this lesson

Introduction

In the lesson, "Delivering Instruction," you learned a variety of teaching methods, some involving individual effort, and others encompassing group work.

In this lesson you learn how to structure group exercises into a cooperative learning experience for the class.

Cooperative Learning Strategy

A **cooperative learning** strategy is one in which a team of students work with and depend upon each other to accomplish a common goal. Each team member is responsible for

- **Achieving an individual goal**
- **Instructing the other team members**
- **Receiving information from the other members**
- **Helping their teammates achieve their individual goals**
- **Reaching the group goal**

The team members work both independently and as a group to gather, disseminate, discuss, and incorporate information into a single cohesive element.

A cooperative learning strategy is best used when the learning goals are important, both mastery and retention are important, and the task is complex or conceptual.

As you progress through this lesson, you learn some strategies that can help build good teamwork, strategies that can help students respond to and discuss questions raised in the lesson, strategies that can help students learn the material quickly, and some benefits of cooperative learning.

Team Building Strategies

Teams are composed of a group of individuals associated together in work or activity. Because you are going to form teams when using a cooperative learning strategy just as we do in sports (see Figure 12.4.1), it only makes sense to try and have the best teams possible. Table 12.4.1 shows **team-building exercises** that you can employ to help you foster good team spirit. What team-building strategies were employed by the team shown in Figure 12.4.2?

Question Strategies

In a standard classroom, the teacher asks questions from time to time and calls on one or more students to answer the question. When a student wants to ask a question, he or she will raise a hand and wait for teacher recognition before speaking.

Key Note Term

cooperative learning – a teaching strategy in which teams of students work with and depend upon each other to accomplish a common goal

Key Note Term

team-building exercises – strategies that can be employed to help foster team dynamics; examples include team color, name, and logo

Figure 12.4.1: Team building is an essential part of cooperative learning just as it is in sports programs.
Courtesy of Craig Hammell/
The Stock Market.

Table 12.4.1: Team-Building Exercises

Team Cheer	The team creates a cheer to be used when the group has accomplished a task and is celebrating.
Team Color	The team chooses a color that represents the personality of the group members.
Team Excellence Symbol	The team decides on a physical symbol formed by the group that indicates they have finished an assigned task and that they fulfilled the requirements of the task.
Team Food	The team selects a food (candy, fruit, gum, and so on) that the whole group enjoys and can be used as part of their celebrations.
Team Logo	The team designs a logo that visually represents the group.
Team Name	The group decides on an appropriate name for the team.
Team Song	The team creates a song or selects a song that reflects the group's personality.

Figure 12.4.2: What team-building strategies were used by this team?
Courtesy of Catherine Karnow/Woodfin Camp & Associates.

Key Note Term

strategy – the art of carefully devising or employing a plan of action or method designed to achieve a goal

Group dynamics make the standard question and answer format difficult to use. Table 12.4.2 shows a series of **strategies** that you may employ in a cooperative learning situation to facilitate question response and discussion in a group setting.

Gather, Share, and Learn Strategies

Despite the good intentions of teachers, events can occur that prohibit them from adhering to their lesson plans (special school assemblies, sickness, inclement weather, etc.). Table 12.4.3 shows several strategies that you may use when you are called upon to teach that will enable the groups to gather, share, and learn their lesson material in a relatively short period of time.

Benefits of Cooperative Learning

There are benefits for using a cooperative learning strategy in the classroom. One of the most important goals in education is to promote constructive relationships and positive attitudes among the student body. The group dynamics of cooperative learning require a large amount of social interaction. Students share ideas and feelings. Team members get to know one another and develop a better understanding of other individuals. The students learn to trust, depend on, and respect one another as they strive to achieve a common goal. Teammates are appreciated for what they can do and are not simply rejected for what they cannot do.

Cooperative learning groups tend to be more creative than individual students or noncooperative learning groups because the group dynamics encourage and require all team members to actively participate. More ideas are generated, the quality of ideas is increased, and there is more originality in creative problem-solving activities.

Table 12.4.2: Cooperative Learning Strategies	
Heads Together	Pairs of students get together to answer a question, solve a problem, review an assignment, react to a video, generate a discussion, and so on.
Numbered Heads Together	The team members count off (such as one, two, three, four), discuss a problem together, reach some conclusion, then randomly team members answer a question when the teacher calls their number.
Partner Interviews (PI)	Partners take turns interviewing each other to determine their level of understanding of a concept.
Round-Robin	Each team member takes a turn adding information or sharing an idea; each class member shares an insight or new learning; each team member contributes to the creation of a writing project; and so on.
Round-Robin Brainstorm	Team members take turns adding to a group brainstorm.
Squared-Shared-Partner-interviews	Pairs join with another pair to form a square and share what they gathered from their previous interviews.
Think-Pair-Share (TPS)	Individually, students think about a question, pair with another student to discuss their thoughts, and then share their thoughts with a larger group or with the class.
Team Brainstorm	Team members randomly and rapidly contribute many ideas.

Table 12.4.3: Group Strategies

Carousel	Teams work together to respond to different problems by moving from station to station or by sending their problem around the groups so other groups can contribute to the solution by responding on the chart or paper they receive.
Conversation Circles	Two circles are formed with one circle inside the other. One student from each circle faces another student. In these pairs, students discuss questions posed by the teacher. Circles rotate two to four times in opposite directions so students discuss questions with new partners.
Jigsaw	Material such as a chapter in a book, different Web sites, several articles, and so on is segmented and each team member is assigned a segment to study and/or review. Team members return to share their segment with the rest of the group.
Jigsaw and Expert Groups	Each team member is assigned a segment of information. Each member studies the assigned section independently. Members then find others from different groups who studied the same material. Together they review what they learned and reinforce the learning, clarify any misunderstandings, and fill in gaps. They become experts. They return to their original group and share their expertise.
Team Graphic Organizer	A team prepares a single graphic organizer of information.
Team Product or Project	Teams produce a product or engage in a project as a culminating activity.
Team Performance	Teams prepare a performance or presentation based on a synthesis of what they learned.

Conclusion

Cooperative learning is based on the belief that all people are good at something, have the ability to help others, and can benefit from others' help. This cooperation among all students promotes an exciting and far-reaching way of including differently-enabled students.

By creating a classroom that is cooperative and inclusive, students' acceptance and success in the general education environment will be greatly enhanced. All students and all teachers have much to gain by structuring the classroom and school environment so that it provides generous support for learning, connecting, and caring.

The following lesson introduces you to thinking maps and graphic organizers. You will learn that these visuals provide a powerful picture of information and allow the mind to "see" patterns and relationships.

Lesson Review

1. Describe how cooperative learning is beneficial to the student.

2. List the seven team-building strategies covered in this lesson.

3. Choose one question strategy and explain how you'd use this in a classroom,

4. Choose one gather, share, and learn strategy and explain how you would use this in a classroom.

Lesson 5

Thinking Maps® and Graphic Organizers

Key Words

analogies
cause and effect
classifying
comparing and contrasting
defining in context
describing
part-whole relationship
sequencing
thinking process

What You Will Learn to Do

● Use Thinking Maps® and graphic organizers as tools for teaching others

Linked Core Abilities

● Communicate using verbal, nonverbal, visual, and written techniques

Skills and Knowledge You Will Gain Along the Way

● Identify the factors associated with brain-based learning

● Describe the benefits of graphic organizers to the learner

● Compare types of visual tools

● Match thinking processes in learning to Thinking Maps®

● Define the key words contained in this lesson

Chapter 12

Introduction

Graphic organizers and Thinking Maps® are both based on the brain and educational research that supports the use of visuals in a classroom. According to Eric Jensen in *Teaching with the Brain in Mind,* 90 percent of all information that comes to the brain is visual. Robert Marzano's *Classroom Instruction That Works* cites research that proves that using visuals in a classroom improves student achievement.

Each kind of visual tool can encourage student-centered and cooperative learning. The JROTC curriculum uses both graphic organizers and Thinking Maps® within its lesson plans. In this lesson you examine the various types of visual tools and use them as you continue to improve your teaching skills.

Types of Visual Tools

Visual tools are excellent tools for learning the structure of thinking skills. Teachers have been using visuals for years to help students make abstract concepts more concrete. These visuals provide a powerful picture of information and allow the mind to "see" patterns and relationships. Some tools are perfect for simple brainstorming; others are task-specific, organizing content. Tools such as Thinking Maps® relate directly to a thinking skill or process.

What type of visual tool is being used in Figure 12.5.1?

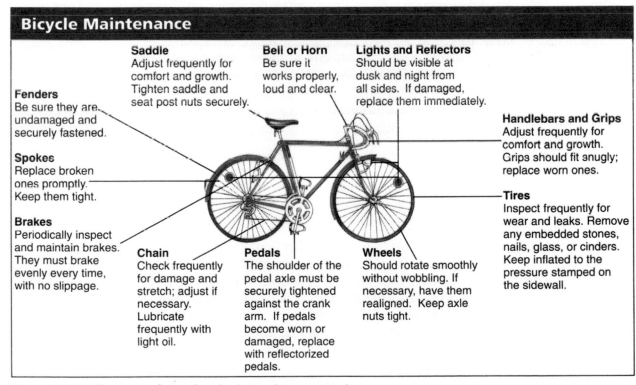

Figure 12.5.1: What type of visual tool is being demonstrated?
Courtesy of Boston Graphics.

There are three basic types of visual tools for learning and enhancing the **thinking process**. These can be defined as brainstorm webs, task-specific graphic organizers, and Thinking Maps®.

Brainstorm Webs

Brainstorm webs are visual tools used for personal knowledge and include mind mapping and webbing.

A mind map is a form of brainstorming using a free-flowing documentation process where lines connect concepts to each other. The core subject is in the center; the main spokes are like sub parts of chapters. Related ideas can be color coded, circled, or attached by lines. Pictures and words can both be used. For example, as seen in Table 12.5.1, you could use this tool to discuss what it will take for a cadet to successfully earn a high school diploma.

The concept web uses text to link main concepts and subconcepts or even sub-sub-concepts. The center circle is the main concept or idea. The smaller circles connecting to the main concept represent the sub-concepts; connected to these sub-concepts are sub-sub-concepts. For example, the center circle could be citizenship. The smaller connected circles are subconcepts related to citizenship.

These smaller circles can also be explored for additional supporting concepts. An illustration might be the subconcept of voting as a critical part of citizenship. Most cadets can't vote yet, but they could continue to explore how they might encourage voting or how they might get involved with the voting process, as seen in Table 12.5.2.

When using these tools in a teaching environment, you can ask the students to use any of these types of webs to brainstorm a topic of their choice. They are very effectively used during the inquire phase of lesson plans. Students can complete this activity alone, in pairs, or as a group. An example of how they can be used is to have students complete a web individually. Then pair up and exchange their notes. Each student should read his or her partner's web ideas and try to summarize the concept being brainstormed without any help from the cadet who created the visual. Paired students should then discuss their summaries.

Task-Specific Graphic Organizers

Task-specific graphic organizers are used for isolated tasks and are found in different textbooks. They are used to represent life cycles, timelines, and other content-specific data. One example is the Fishbone Diagram.

This structure helps cadets think of important components of a problem to solve, an issue to explore, or a project to plan. The head of the fish represents a problem, issue, or project. "Ribs" of the fish represent component parts of the problem and the related elements of each part. For example, cadets could explore how to prepare for an upcoming orienteering competition. Each rib represents the critical elements of preparation. Attached to each rib are the processes or activities that will assist in accomplishing each key element.

An example of how to use task-specific graphic organizers in a teaching environment is to have students work in pairs to survey their textbooks or other resources to look for content that could be represented by graphic organizers and visuals, such as the steps to determine direction of travel, or the timeline for how the framers created the constitution. Then have students choose and draw graphic organizers to represent their thinking about the subject or topic.

Table 12.5.1: Brainstorming

Step	Action	Graphic
1	Set up chart paper on an easel and get the markers. If possible place the paper in a horizontal position.	
2	Draw the central concept on the paper. Ask the cadets to define what the concept is—for example, graduate from high school.	
3	The cadets will brainstorm what it takes to graduate and draw pictures or images to show these items—for example, money, books, studying, and ideas are some of the information they could provide.	
4	Link the thoughts to show relationships of ideas—for example, books are needed before you can study and get your degree. Ideas as well as money are independent ideas that support receiving a degree.	

Table 12.5.2: Steps to Change the Voting Process

Step	Action	Graphic
1	Set up chart paper on an easel and get the markers. If possible place the paper in a horizontal position.	
2	Draw a circle in the center of the paper with a diameter sufficient to hold the main idea and write the main idea in the circle.	
3	Draw a connected subconcept containing a concept related to the main concept.	
4	Draw a ray out from the subconcept and place an element of voting on the ray. Add additional rays as needed.	
5	Add additional subconcepts with rays as needed to cover all the elements.	

Thinking Maps®

Thinking Maps® give students and teachers a common visual language for learning that can be used with all subject matter and across all LET levels in classrooms and whole schools. The purpose for using them is to transfer thinking processes, integrate learning, and assess progress. Thinking Maps® consist of eight graphics or maps. These maps include the Circle Map or **defining in context**, the Tree Map or **classifying**, the Flow Map or **sequencing**, the Bridge Map or **analogies**, the Multiflow Map or **cause and effect reasoning**, the Double Bubble Map or **comparing and contrasting**, the Bubble Map or **describing** qualities, and the Brace Map or **part-whole relationship**. Each one is tied directly to a specific thinking process. Look at the key word definitions for each map and notice how they are used to organize your thinking.

> ### Note
>
> The introductory "Thinking Maps®" lesson (Chapter 3, Lesson 1) contains pictures of each type of map discussed here. Each map is also defined and described in that lesson.

Thinking Maps® are most effective when they are used together to develop a learning objective, concept, or performance task, as seen in Table 12.5.3. An example of how multiple maps can be used to develop an understanding of heat injuries is illustrated in Figure 12.5.2.

Putting Them All Together

As closure for the three preceding activities, ask cadets to draw some conclusions about the effectiveness of these three different types of visual tools.

Comparing Thinking Maps® to Other Graphic Organizers

Graphic organizers and webs are commonly used strategies that help organize and process a great deal of information. They can help make relationships and connections visible or concrete. Thinking Maps® combine the flexibility of brainstorm webs and the structure of task-specific graphic organizers with a clearly defined, common thinking process language. Graphic organizers and webs help people graphically organize information. Thinking Maps® help people think about their information and construct knowledge.

The most important difference between Thinking Maps® and graphic organizers is that each Thinking Map® is based on a fundamental thinking skill.

Key Note Terms

defining in context – a process where a specific concept is defined and explored

classifying – a process of sorting things into categories or groups

sequencing – a process of ordering or examining stages of an event

analogies – a process of seeing the relating factor or the same relationship to something

cause and effect – a process of identifying the interrelationship of what results from an action

comparing and contrasting – a process of identifying similarities and differences of things

describing – a process of seeing qualities, characteristics, traits and/or properties of things

part-whole relationships – a process of identifying the relationship between a whole physical object and its parts

Table 12.5.3: Using a Thinking Map®

Step	Action	Graphic
1	Set up chart paper on an easel and get the markers. If possible place the paper in a horizontal position.	
2	Draw a square about the size of a CD-ROM case. This will be the head.	
3	Draw a horizontal line from the left side of the head to the left side of the paper. This is the backbone.	
4	Draw ribs out from the backbone above and below the backbone. Make sure they correspond and touch each other at the intersection. Add rays as needed.	
5	Instruct the cadets to write their responses for one point of view on the bottom set of bones and the other point of view on the top. EXAMPLE: On the bottom write: Problems On the top write: Materials and Transportation	

Figure 12.5.2: Using multiple maps.
©2004 by Thinking Maps, Inc.

Sweating a lot

Signs and symptoms of heat injuries

Dizzy

Heat Injuries

Heat Cramps
- Muscular pain
- Spasms
- Loss of salt

Heat Exhaustion
- Heavy sweating
- Form of shock
- Loss of fluids

Heatstroke
- Sunstroke
- Malfunction of cooling system
- Rising temperature

Move victim to a cool, shady area → Loosen the victim's clothing → Pour water on victim/fan victim

→ Have victim slowly drink water → Seek medical aid

Relating Factor Is a resut of...

Extreme thirst ⁄\ Chills ⁄\ Inability to sweat ⁄\
Heat cramps   Heat exhaustion   Heatstroke

*Extreme thirst is a result of heat cramps, just as chills is a result of heat exhaustion, just as the inability to sweat is a result of heatstroke.

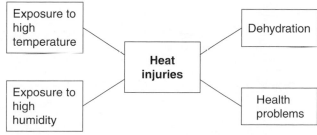

This thinking skills foundation supports three intellectual outcomes:

- **Students learn clearly stated definitions for eight fundamental thinking skills**
- **Students are applying multiple thinking skills (as maps) to complex, multistep problems**
- **Students are empowered to use these visual tools for transferring thinking skills across disciplines**

The Double Bubble Map in Figure 12.5.3 compares the similarities and differences between graphic organizers and webs and Thinking Maps®.

Which Visual Tool Do I Choose?

As you are reading content or listening to someone speak, your brain is processing the information by figuring out what to do with it. When that happens, the next step is to visualize a graphic organizer, web, or Thinking Map® that can help you understand and remember the information. If, for example, the information you receive is asking you to define something, you may choose to use a mind map, a concept map, or a Circle Map as illustrated earlier in this lesson. If you are being asked to compare and contrast something, you may choose to use a Venn diagram or a Double Bubble Map. Graphic organizers, webs, and Thinking Maps® have proven to be highly successful for the learner. When considering which visual tool to use, remember that Thinking Maps® are consistently used for a specific thinking process while the other tools are less defined and therefore are not always used in the same way for the same purpose.

Look at the example in Figure 12.5.4. Discuss with a partner or group which visual tool you feel is most beneficial and effective for learning. What are the advantages and disadvantages of each?

Figure 12.5.3: Similarities and differences.
©2004 by Thinking Maps, Inc.

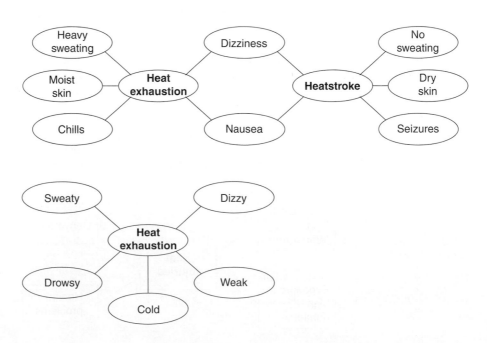

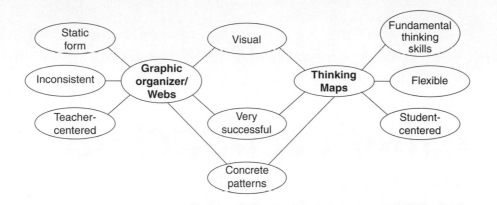

Figure 12.5.4: Contrasting and comparing visual tools.
©2004 by Thinking Maps, Inc.

Now practice picking a visual tool for learning. Think about a specific task you might do in JROTC. Choose a graphic organizer and a Thinking Map® to represent the same tasks. Share why the visual tools were chosen and which will help you retain the information the most.

Use the Double Bubble Map to help you remember the similarities and differences between Thinking Maps® and other graphic organizers.

Conclusion

Overall, Thinking Maps® and graphic organizers allow you to visually organize concepts, ideas, data, thoughts, and feelings. Choosing the appropriate map or graphic organizer depends on the type of elements that need organizing and analyzing. After the organization process is complete, understanding complex concepts, decision-making, and problem-solving becomes easier.

In the next lesson, you will learn how to use feedback in the classroom. Giving constructive feedback is one of the most important tasks you have as an instructor because you provide information that learners use to improve themselves during the course. Such feedback guides learners while they can still take corrective action.

Lesson Review

1. **Name and describe the three types of visual tools.**

2. **What are the similarities and differences between Thinking Maps® and other graphic organizers?**

3. **What are the advantages and/or disadvantages of using Thinking Maps®?**

4. **What are the advantages and/or disadvantages of using graphic organizers and webs?**

Using Feedback in the Classroom

Key Words

acceptable
clarifying
comprehensive
constructive
conviction
criteria
flexible
jargon
modify
objectivity
preconceived
rapport
reinforce

What You Will Learn to Do

- Use feedback to enhance learning in the classroom

Linked Core Abilities

- Communicate using verbal, nonverbal, visual, and written techniques

Skills and Knowledge You Will Gain Along the Way

- Describe the purpose of feedback in the classroom
- Explain four ways that feedback can be effective
- Identify the five characteristics or conditions of effective feedback
- Identify the basic ground rules and tips for giving effective feedback
- Define the key words contained in this lesson

Chapter 12

Introduction

In traditional courses individualized comments from instructors to their students are often limited to grades on papers, quizzes, exams, and the final grade; however, comments of this sort come well after instructors have evaluated learners on their course work. Such after-the-fact feedback often contributes little to learning because it is too late for learners to take corrective action. On the other hand, the most important task you have as an instructor may be to provide information that learners can use to improve themselves during the course. Such feedback guides learners while they can still take corrective action.

This lesson examines how you can give objective, **acceptable**, **constructive**, **flexible**, and **comprehensive** feedback.

Definitions and Applications

In general, feedback is any information about the results of a process. When you use a computer, for instance, you feed in the information and get back feedback. In the social sciences, feedback is the information that returns to the source of the process so as to **reinforce** or **modify** it. For example, if a coach finds that the football team is weak in defense tactics, the coach schedules the team for more tackling practice. In psychological **jargon**, feedback is called the *knowledge of results*.

In the classroom, feedback can be defined as information that learners receive from their instructor about their performance, information that may cause them to take self-corrective action and guide them in attaining the goals of the course more effectively.

Learners can receive feedback from at least five sources: themselves, the learning task, fellow cadets/students, the instructor, and from the school/cadet battalion.

Feedback is generally given for informational and/or motivational purposes. Informational feedback is generally responsible for correcting the errors that the learner commits and should always be motivating. Motivational feedback motivates the learner to try harder but does not always provide information. A pat on the back or a word of encouragement may motivate a learner but will not necessarily point out the errors in the learner's performance.

Giving Feedback to Learners

The purpose of giving feedback in the classroom is to improve learner performance. In its most effective form, it provides constructive advice, direction, and guidance to learners in their effort to raise their performance levels. Learners must understand the purpose and role of feedback in the learning process; otherwise, they may reject it and make little or no effort to improve. Feedback can also be used as a device to reinforce learning. Although all feedback cannot be used in this manner, the instructor should take every opportunity to use feedback as a means of **clarifying**, emphasizing, or reinforcing instruction.

Key Note Terms

acceptable – capable or worthy of being accepted, adequate, satisfactory

constructive – promoting improvement or development

flexible – ready to adapt to new, different, or changing requirements

comprehensive – covering completely or broadly

reinforce – to strengthen by additional assistance, material, or support

modify – to make basic or fundamental changes to give a new orientation to or to serve a new end

jargon – technical terminology or language created for a particular profession, such as computer science, that may seem strange or outlandish to outsiders who do not understand it

Key Note Term

clarifying – to make understandable

Characteristics (or Conditions) of Effective Feedback

Effective feedback stresses both learner strengths as well as suggestions for improvement. The most significant characteristics, or conditions, of effective feedback are **objectivity**, acceptability, constructiveness, flexibility, and comprehensiveness. Each of these characteristics is briefly explained in the following sections.

Objectivity

Effective feedback focuses on the learner and the learner's performance; it should not reflect the instructor's personal opinions, likes, and biases. For example, if the learner makes a speech and expresses views that conflict with your beliefs, you should give feedback on the merits of the speech, not on the basis of the agreement or disagreement with the learner's views. To be objective, feedback must be honest; it must be based on factual performance; not performance as it could have been or as you and the learner wish it had been.

Acceptability

Learners usually accept feedback when you give it with **conviction** and sincerity. Usually, you have the opportunity to establish **rapport** and mutual respect with learners before the need for giving feedback arises. If there is no such opportunity, your manner, attitude, and knowledge of the subject must serve instead.

Constructiveness

You must be straightforward and honest; you must also respect the learner's personal feelings. Feedback, then, is pointless unless the learner profits from it. Praise just for the sake of praise has no value; however, unless the only goal is to motivate or improve self-concept.

Effective feedback reflects your consideration of the learner's need for self-esteem, recognition, confidence, and the approval of others. Ridicule, anger, or fun at the expense of the learner, have no place in constructive feedback.

Flexibility

You should always remain flexible in giving feedback by avoiding mechanical, predetermined techniques and **preconceived** opinions regarding content, subject matter, and learner capability. Instead, you should consider

- **The actual content of the learner's effort**
- **What actually happens during an activity**
- **The observed factors that affect performance**

Comprehensiveness

Comprehensive feedback need not be extremely long nor must it treat every detail of the learner's performance. As an instructor, you must decide whether you can achieve the best results by discussing a few major points or a number of minor

Key Note Term

objectivity – dealing with facts or conditions as perceived without distortion by personal feelings, prejudices, or interpretations

Key Note Terms

conviction – a strong persuasion or belief

rapport – a relationship, especially one of mutual trust

Key Note Term

preconceived – to form (as an opinion) prior to actual knowledge or experience

points. You should base your feedback either on what areas need improvement or on what areas you can reasonably expect the learner to improve.

Feedback includes both strengths and weaknesses. Only you can determine a proper balance between the two. It is a disservice to learners to dwell on the excellence of their performance and neglect areas that need improving (or vise versa).

Ground Rules and Tips for Giving Feedback

There are some basic ground rules for giving feedback so it is constructive and helpful to the learner. These rules are as follows:

- **Establish and maintain rapport with learners as shown in Figure 12.6.1.**

- **Cover the major strengths and weaknesses. Try to be specific; give examples if possible.**

- **Avoid trying to discuss everything. A few well-made points may be more beneficial than numerous but inadequately developed points.**

- **Try to avoid comments with "never" or "always"; most rules have exceptions. Your feedback may be incorrect or inappropriate for certain situations.**

- **Do not criticize something that cannot be corrected.**

- **Do not criticize when you cannot suggest an improvement.**

- **Avoid being maneuvered into the unpleasant position of defending feedback. If the feedback is honest, objective, constructive, and supported, no defense should be necessary.**

- **If part of the feedback is written, it should be consistent with the oral feedback.**

To ensure the learner takes your feedback in the most constructive manner possible and use it in a positive way, the following tips can be helpful.

- **Reinforce correct performance by letting learners know what they are doing well. Your encouragement and support will mean a great deal to your learners.**

- **Make sure to base your feedback on the evaluation criteria.**

- **When you see someone doing something differently than you would ordinarily do it, consider whether it matters. Ask yourself questions such as:**

Key Note Term

criteria – a standard on which a judgment or decision is based

Figure 12.6.1: Do you think this instructor has rapport with the learners?
Courtesy of Ken Karp.

- Will it work the way they are doing it?
- Is this a better way?
- Will it cause problems for them later?
- Is it safe?

- Allow for individual variations. Consider the learner's openness to suggestions before recommending changes that are not based on the criteria.

- Identify incorrect performance as early as possible. Give feedback as soon as you see the incorrect performance.

- Try to provide feedback in the most constructive way possible. Help learners understand how to do a task correctly; do not just tell them what they are doing wrong.

- Be aware of the learners' sensitivity to correction, especially in front of other people (generally avoided whenever possible). Keep your voice down when providing individual feedback. Avoid the temptation to point out one person's mistake to the whole group as an example.

- Give feedback less often as learners' progress.

Conclusion

It is important to realize that feedback need not always be negative or destructive. In fact, positive feedback is almost always seen as warmer and more sincere than negative feedback given in identical ways.

As a potential instructor, coach, and counselor in JROTC, you must be able to give effective, positive feedback. By improving the way that you give feedback, you are improving the future performances of your teammates and classmates.

This lesson concludes the chapter, "Teaching Skills." Through this chapter, you have learned how to develop and use lesson plans, how to deliver instruction, where Thinking Maps® and graphic organizers can be useful in your classroom, and how important feedback is to keeping your students on track.

Lesson Review

1. Why feedback is generally given?
2. What are the characteristics of feedback covered in this lesson?
3. Choose one tip for giving feedback and discuss it.
4. Define the term *criteria*.

Wellness, Fitness, and First Aid

Chapter 1

Achieving a Healthy Lifestyle

Choosing the Right Exercise Program for You

Key Terms

aerobic
anaerobic
calisthenics
cardiorespiratory
isokinetic
isometric
isotonic
obesity
tone

What You Will Learn to Do

- Develop a personal exercise program

Linked Core Abilities

- Take responsibility for your actions and choices

Skills and Knowledge You Will Gain Along the Way

- Classify exercises as aerobic, anaerobic, isometric, and isotonic
- Compare the benefits of aerobic, anaerobic, isometric, and isotonic exercise
- Identify the benefits of regular exercise
- Determine the essential components of a good exercise program
- Define the key words contained in this lesson

Introduction

Key Note Term

tone – a degree of tension or firmness, as of muscle

What you eat and how much you exercise can directly affect how you look and feel. When it comes to your appearance, diet and exercise help you maintain proper weight, **tone** muscles, and healthy hair and skin. When it comes to your health, diet and exercise can lower your risk of heart disease, high blood pressure, and other health problems, including depression. Staying healthy and looking good means following a balanced diet and exercising regularly. This chapter discusses guidelines for a healthier lifestyle that will help keep you fit and feeling great, now and throughout your life. This first lesson specifically covers exercise, including types of exercises and how to stick with an exercise program.

Some people consider exercise a chore; others think it's fun. There are even those who avoid it altogether. With the right outlook, however, everyone can find an exercise program that they enjoy. More and more people find ways to keep fit, from walking to joining fitness clubs, because more and more people recognize the importance of exercise for physical and mental health.

Although the fitness craze has hit many older Americans, it has not yet reached most of America's youth. This is unfortunate because not only is exercise good for you, it can also be fun. You can form friendships with people you meet while exercising on the track or basketball court or at the gym or pool. You will feel better about yourself, improve your resistance to disease, and relieve stress found at school and work. Basically, being fit improves your overall health—both physically and mentally.

Do you think you are physically fit? Physical fitness is the ability of the heart, blood vessels, lungs, and muscles to work together to meet the body's needs. When you are physically fit, your body's systems work as a team allowing you to breathe easily and contract muscles in coordinated movement.

Your body is made for activity. Stimulating your muscles, bones, heart, lungs, and blood vessels with regular exercise helps you gain or maintain physical fitness. A program of vigorous exercise, however, is not the only important factor in fitness and a healthy lifestyle. Rest, sleep, and good nutrition are just as important. What muscles are required to move the furniture in Figure 1.1.1?

Components of Fitness

Each individual has his or her own potential of fitness. For example, you may not have the capability of becoming an Olympic weightlifter or a professional gymnast; yet you can reach your own personal best. Physical fitness can be broken down into four health-related areas: cardiorespiratory endurance, muscular strength and endurance, flexibility, and body composition. Each component is a necessary part of fitness.

Figure 1.1.1: Physical fitness is necessary for performing many tasks, such as moving furniture.
Courtesy of Ken Karp.

Cardiorespiratory Endurance

The first component, cardiorespiratory endurance, is the ability of your heart, blood vessels, and lungs to distribute nutrients and oxygen and to remove wastes. When you exercise, your heart and lungs must supply more oxygen to your muscles than they need when you are resting. When you are at rest, for example, your heart pumps about 5 to 6 quarts (5.5 to 6.6 liters) of blood per minute, but it pumps about 20 to 25 quarts (22 to 27 liters) when you are exercising.

If your heart and lungs function easily during hard exercise and recover quickly afterward, you probably have good cardiorespiratory endurance. People with poor cardiorespiratory endurance might be left short of breath and have a very high heart rate after light exercise. Their lungs and heart are unable to keep up with the muscles' demand for oxygen.

Muscular Strength and Endurance

The capacity of a muscle or a group of muscles to exert or resist a force is called muscular strength. In contrast, muscular endurance is the ability of muscles to keep working for an extended time. For example, the amount of weight you can lift is one measure of your muscular strength, as depicted in Figure 1.1.2. How long you can hold that weight—or how many times you can lift it—is a measure of your muscular endurance. You need muscular strength for all sports and most everyday activities. Acts of muscular endurance include repeated actions, such as raking leaves, shoveling snow, or doing sit-ups.

Figure 1.1.2: Which components of physical fitness are especially important in lifting weights?
Courtesy of David Madison.

Flexibility

The ability to use a muscle throughout its entire range of motion is called flexibility. This means that you can bend, stretch, and twist your joints easily. The sit-and-reach test measures the flexibility of specific groups of muscles in the back and legs, but it is also used to indicate overall flexibility. However, flexibility can vary in different joints. Some people may show poor flexibility in the sit-and-reach test, for example, yet have excellent flexibility in the shoulders and arms. Stretching exercises, if done correctly, can increase flexibility and may reduce the risk of injury during exercise.

Body Composition

The fourth component of physical fitness, body composition, is the amount of body fat compared to lean tissue, such as muscle and bone. Skinfold measurement is one method for assessing body fat. Excessive body fat has been linked with heart disease, diabetes, arthritis, cancer, and other harmful health conditions.

History Connection

Great emphasis was placed on physical fitness in the schools of ancient Greece. Students received instruction in exercise and sports such as wrestling, running, and jumping. In fact, the word *gymnasium* comes from the ancient Greek word *gymnasion,* meaning "school."

The Benefits of Exercise

What happens inside you when you run, swim, dance, play hockey, or enjoy some other form of exercise? As the muscles in your arms, shoulders, or legs alternately contract and relax, they use energy that comes from chemical reactions in which oxygen combines with nutrients. Because of the increased needs of your muscles, your heart beats faster, and you breathe more rapidly and deeply. The flow of blood to your heart, lungs, and skeletal muscles increases as your blood vessels dilate, or widen. Your blood pressure and body temperature rise, and you begin to sweat. How do these responses benefit your body? Refer to Figure 1.1.3 to help you answer this question.

Physical Benefits

Because blood circulates more rapidly through vessels during exercise, the rate at which it brings oxygen and nutrients to, and removes wastes from, your tissues is increased. This increased circulation rate is one reason why you feel refreshed and energetic after a hard workout. In addition, over time, regular exercise may increase the number of capillaries in your body. These additional capillaries provide muscles with a greater supply of blood, not just when you are exercising but at all times.

Cardiorespiratory endurance is significantly improved by an exercise program. Your heart becomes stronger and pumps blood more efficiently. Regular exercise can also lower your blood pressure and can improve the function of your lungs. An exercise program can help prevent atherosclerosis and coronary heart disease.

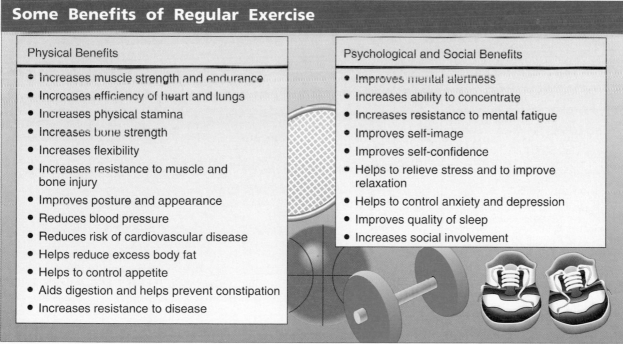

Some Benefits of Regular Exercise

Physical Benefits	Psychological and Social Benefits
• Increases muscle strength and endurance	• Improves mental alertness
• Increases efficiency of heart and lungs	• Increases ability to concentrate
• Increases physical stamina	• Increases resistance to mental fatigue
• Increases bone strength	• Improves self-image
• Increases flexibility	• Improves self-confidence
• Increases resistance to muscle and bone injury	• Helps to relieve stress and to improve relaxation
• Improves posture and appearance	• Helps to control anxiety and depression
• Reduces blood pressure	• Improves quality of sleep
• Reduces risk of cardiovascular disease	• Increases social involvement
• Helps reduce excess body fat	
• Helps to control appetite	
• Aids digestion and helps prevent constipation	
• Increases resistance to disease	

Figure 1.1.3: Regular exercise helps both physical and mental health.
Courtesy of Function thru Form.

As you stretch your muscles when you exercise, you can improve your flexibility by loosening stiff muscles and joints. When you run, swim, or do other endurance exercises on a regular basis, your muscles become stronger and are able to work longer. Regular exercise also strengthens your bones, making them thicker and denser. Strong bones and muscles are less likely to be injured than are weak ones. Table 1.1.1 show ratings of various exercises.

Table 1.1.1:

Fitness Ratings of Physical Activities				
Activity	Cardiorespiratory Endurance	Muscular Strength	Muscular Endurance	Flexibility
Aerobic dancing	3-4	2	2	3
Ballet	3	2	2	4
Baseball/Softball	1	1	1	2
Basketball	3-4	1	2	2
Bicycling (at least 10 mph)	3-4	2	3-4	1
Bowling	1	1	1	2
Calisthenics	3	3-4	3-4	3-4
Canoeing	2-3	3	3	2
Football	2-3	2	2	2
Golf	1	1	1	2
Gymnastics	1	4	3	4
Handball/Squash	3	2	3	2
Hiking (uphill)	3	1	2	2
Hockey	2-3	2	2	2
Jogging/Running (at least 6 mph)	3-4	1	3	2
Judo/Karate	1	2	1	3
Jumping Rope	3-4	1	3	2
Racquetball	3-4	1	3	2
Rowing	3-4	3	3	2
Skating (ice, roller)	2-3	1	2-3	2
Skiing (cross-country)	4	2	3-4	2
Skiing (downhill)	3	2	2-3	2
Soccer	3	2	2	2
Swimming	4	2	3	2
Tennis/Badminton (singles)	2-3	1	2-3	2
Volleyball	2	1	2	2
Walking (brisk)	3	1	3	2
Weight training	1-2	4	3	2
Wrestling	3-4	2	3	3
Rating Scale: 1 = Low, 2 = Moderate, 3 = High, 4 = Very high				

Reprinted from *Health Skills for Wellness*, Third Edition, by B. E. (Buzz) Pruitt, Kathy Teer Crumpler, and Deborah Prothrow-Stith, (2001), Prentice Hall, Inc.

Exercise can also improve or maintain body composition. A regular workout is important in keeping body fat within recommended levels. A program of regular exercise is an important factor in successful weight loss or weight maintenance.

Psychological Benefits

People who exercise regularly are likely to sleep better, feel more self-confident, and focus more productively on their work. Exercise may also increase creativity by releasing body chemicals that stimulate the brain's centers of creativity.

One of the most important psychological benefits of exercise is the reduction of emotional stress. Simple stretching exercises, for example, can help you relax tense muscles and allow you to sleep better. If you are feeling depressed, exercise can generally help make you feel better. In fact, many health professionals consider exercise an important part of a complete treatment for depression, whether the depression is mild or serious.

Have you ever experienced a sense of physical and emotional exhilaration after a hard workout? This feeling is at least partly the result of certain substances called endorphins. Endorphins, which are chemicals produced in your brain, help to give you a sense of satisfaction and pleasure. During vigorous exercise, cells within your brain produce greater amounts of endorphins.

Types of Exercise

No single exercise can improve or maintain all four components of physical fitness. Table 1.1.1 compares the fitness benefits you can receive from many activities. Notice, for example, that recreational activities such as basketball and rowing provide many health benefits. Swimming, as shown in Figure 1.1.4, is also an excellent exercise.

Exercises can be classified into different types, depending on what their performance involves. Included among these are **aerobic**, **anaerobic**, **isotonic**, **isometric**, and **isokinetic** exercise.

Figure 1.1.4: Swimming is an excellent all-around exercise that is especially good for developing cardiorespiratory and muscular endurance.
Courtesy of David Madison.

Key Note Terms

aerobic – allowing sufficient amounts of oxygen to be delivered to the muscles

anaerobic – working in the absence of adequate amounts of oxygen being delivered to the muscles

isokinetic – exercise in which muscles contract, but very little body movement takes place

isometric – building muscle strength using resistance without joint movement

isotonic – building muscle strength using resistance with joint movement

Aerobic Exercise

Nonstop, repetitive, strenuous physical activity that raises the breathing and heart rates is called aerobic exercise. Aerobic exercises increase the amount of oxygen that is taken in and used by the body. Aerobic exercise works the heart, lungs, and blood vessels. As you exercise aerobically, your heart beats faster and you breathe in more air, so your blood can supply more oxygen to your hardworking muscles. This type of physical exercise improves blood and oxygen flow to vital organs, as well as lung capacity (the ability to take in and use more air). Swimming, riding a bike, running, brisk walking, and cross-country skiing are all forms of aerobic exercise. If aerobic exercises last for at least 20 minutes at a time and are done frequently, on a regular, ongoing basis, they will improve cardiovascular endurance. Aerobic exercises are therefore especially important in maintaining the health of your circulatory and respiratory systems. As the information in Table 1.1.1 indicates, activities that provide good aerobic exercise do not always improve muscular strength. They do, however, generally improve your muscular endurance.

Anaerobic Exercise

Anaerobic exercise, on the other hand, works the muscles intensely in fast bursts of movement and does not require as much oxygen as aerobic exercise. Instead of endurance, anaerobic exercise requires bursts of power and energy and the ability to maneuver quickly. For example, a sprinter working his or her leg muscles hard in a burst of energy to cross the finish line in a few seconds is performing an anaerobic exercise. Many sports, from tennis to football, require anaerobic work to move from one point to another as quickly as possible. Imagine that for 20 minutes you exercise like the weight lifter in Figure 1.1.2. Although your overall exercise time is 20 minutes, the periods of intense physical activity come only when you actually lift the weight. Anaerobic exercise is intense physical activity that lasts only from a few seconds to a few minutes, during which time muscles use up more oxygen than the blood can supply. Anaerobic exercises usually improve the flexibility, strength, and sometimes speed at which muscles work. However, it does not specifically condition the cardiovascular and respiratory systems. Most anaerobic exercises are designed to develop specific skills, agility, flexibility, or strength. Lifting weights, sprinting, push-ups, and some forms of gymnastics, for example, are usually considered anaerobic activities.

Note

Aerobic dance programs, in which people perform a set of exercises in time to music, are offered by many community centers, YMCAs, YWCAs, and health clubs. Recreational dance can be substituted for aerobic dance as long as you dance vigorously enough to reach your target heart rate for at least 20 minutes.

Isotonic, Isometric, and Isokinetic Exercise

Other forms of exercise concentrate specifically on firming and toning muscles and building muscle strength. Working against resistance builds muscle strength. You work against resistance when you try to open a tight lid on a jar or push a heavy piece of furniture across a room. Three types of exercise—isotonic, isometric, and isokinetic—can increase the strength and endurance of specific groups of muscles. Isometric exercise builds muscle strength by using resistance without joint movement, while isotonic exercise uses resistance with joint movement. For example, when you try to pull your locked hands apart, you perform an isometric exercise. You contract your muscles but do not move any joints. Most weight training, on the other hand, is isotonic. When you do bicep curls, you contract your muscles and bend your elbows to raise the weights to shoulder level. Isotonic exercise involves the contraction and relaxation of muscles through the full range of their motion. You can perform isotonic exercises with or without weights. Through repetition of isotonic exercises, you can develop muscle strength.

Place your palms together and push them against each other. You are performing an isometric exercise in which muscles contract but very little body movement takes place. Pushing against a wall is another example of isometric exercise. Even though this activity involves little movement, your muscles are contracting and thus working. If you continue isometric exercises over a long period, the muscles you use will become stronger.

Perhaps you have seen an accident victim or injured athlete use a special machine in order to recover the use of specific muscle groups. They are performing isokinetic exercises. Isokinetic exercises are exercises that involve moving a muscle through a range of motion against a resistance, or weight that changes. Unlike isotonic exercises, isokinetic exercises, as shown in Figure 1.1.5, always use special machinery to provide the resistance. Many exercise machines in gymnasiums and fitness centers provide isokinetic exercise.

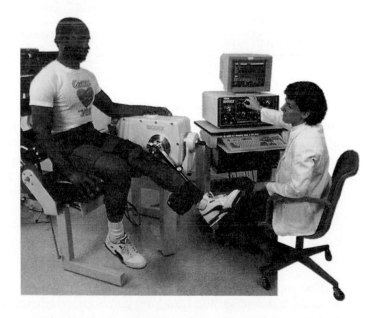

Figure 1.1.5: Physical therapists help people perform isokinetic exercises using special machinery to recover the use of muscles.
Courtesy of Larry Mulvehill/The Image Works.

Defining Your Goals

Do you want to obtain total fitness, increase your stamina, have a trimmer body, achieve better coordination, or just feel more alert? Your goals help to determine the best exercise program for you. Reexamine Figure 1.1.4, which lists different types of exercises and their benefits. If your goal is to strengthen muscles, for example, your program might include anaerobic exercises such as lifting weights. If you want to improve your cardiorespiratory endurance, you may develop a program of aerobic exercise. Basketball, jumping rope, or brisk walking will fit into this type of program. Most likely, you have a combination of goals in mind. For example, you may want to increase both your cardiorespiratory endurance and your flexibility.

Youth Fitness Fact Sheet

- Youth fitness in the United States has not improved in the last 10 years and, in some cases, has declined

- Approximately 50 percent of girls ages 6 to 17 and 30 percent of boys ages 6 to 12 cannot run a mile in less than 10 minutes

- Fifty-five percent of girls ages 6 to 17 and 25 percent of boys ages 6 to 12 cannot do a pull-up

- Boys generally perform better than girls on fitness tests, except in the area of flexibility

- Girls' scores increase until age 14, where they plateau and then decrease (except for flexibility, which continues to improve to age 17)

- American children have become fatter since 1950 (U.S. Public Health Service)

- Forty percent of children between the ages of 5 and 8 show at least one heart disease risk factor, e.g., **obesity** (overweight), elevated cholesterol, or high blood pressure

- Only 36 percent of America's schoolchildren in grades 5 through 12 are enrolled in daily physical education, with the average number of gym classes per week in grades 5 through 12 being 3.6

Adapted from the President's Council on Physical Fitness.

Key Note Term

obesity – overweight to the point of injuring health

As you create your exercise program, remember that your fitness program should be fun! Choose activities or a sport that you enjoy and will look forward to. Combine exercise with social activities; for example, take a hike with a group of your friends. You can often develop an enjoyable fitness program by expanding on the activities that are already a part of your life, as shown by the weekly exercise record in Figure 1.1.6.

The FIT Principle

The effectiveness of your exercise depends on three factors: how often you exercise, how hard you exercise, and how long you exercise at each workout session. These ingredients make up the FIT principle, which stands for frequency, intensity, and

A Weekly Exercise Program	
Sunday • Slow, 20-minute run around the pond • Two flights of stairs taken three times	**Wednesday** • Bike to school • Gym class • 40-minute basketball practice
Monday • 20-minute brisk walk to school • Gym class at school • 20-minute walk home	**Thursday** • 20-minute walk to school • Basketball game
	Friday • Gym class • 30-minute aerobics class • 20-minute walk home
Tuesday • Walk to school • 30-minute swim after school • Walk home	**Saturday** • Leaf raking for 40 minutes • Slow 20-minute run

Figure 1.1.6: What changes would you make in this weekly exercise program to suit your own needs and interest?
Courtesy of Boston Graphics.

time. To achieve fitness, you need to meet minimum standards for each FIT factor. Do you think the students in Figure 1.1.7 are FIT?

Frequency of Exercise

To stay physically fit, you should exercise frequently, preferably three or more times a week. As you become more fit, some studies suggest that if the intensity of your exercise is moderate, four times a week is most effective in increasing cardiorespiratory endurance and weight loss. If you exercise vigorously, however, do not do so more than five times a week; otherwise, injuries can result.

Figure 1.1.7. Basketball is one of many fitness-building activities that you can do with friends.
Courtesy of Mark Burnett/ Stock Boston.

No matter what your goal is, you should spread your exercise out over the week. Being inactive during the week does not prepare your body for an intense weekend workout. Weekend athletes are more likely to injure themselves than those who exercise regularly throughout the week.

Intensity of Exercise

If your goal is increased cardiorespiratory endurance, you must work your cardiovascular and respiratory systems with greater-than-normal effort through aerobic exercise. The intensity of a workout is indicated by the number of times your heart beats per minute. The more intense the exercise, the faster your heart rate.

Your maximum heart rate is your heart's top speed or your heart rate when you have exercised to the point of exhaustion. For teenagers, this rate is about 200 beats per minute. You should not try to work out at your maximum heart rate, since exercise at that intensity puts a strain on your heart. Your target heart rate, which is lower than your maximum heart rate, is the approximate heart rate you need to maintain during aerobic exercise in order to benefit from the workout. Your target heart rate depends on your age, your current level of fitness, your resting heart rate, and your maximum heart rate. It is often expressed as a range, such as 145 to 170 beats per minute. Do you think that cross-country skiing is intensive exercise (see Figure 1.1.8)?

During exercise, you need to check your heart rate regularly to determine whether it is within your target heart range. To check your heart rate, you need to stop exercising briefly and count your pulse. Your heart rate slows down quickly, so take your pulse for only six seconds and multiply by ten to get an accurate count of the number of heartbeats per minute.

The "talk test" is an easy way to check your exercise intensity. If you are so out of breath while exercising that you cannot talk, your exercise level is too

Figure 1.1.8: Cross-country skiing is good aerobic exercise. The faster you ski, the more intense the exercise becomes.
Courtesy of David Stoecklein/The Stock Market.

intense. If you can sing while you exercise, however, you probably are not working hard enough. You are working at the proper intensity if you can talk comfortably.

Exercise Time

Finally, the amount of time spent exercising affects your level of fitness. If you are just beginning an exercise program, start out with only a short period of exercise—about 10 or 15 minutes. Then increase the exercise time gradually, by no more than 10 percent a week. Once your workout program is well established, most research suggests that 20 to 30 minutes of vigorous exercise four times a week will lead to greater fitness. If your goal is cardiorespiratory improvement, you must exercise within your target heart range for 20 to 30 minutes each session. If your goal is to reduce body fat, your exercise period should be a minimum of 30 minutes, which is longer than the 20-minute minimum required for a cardiorespiratory workout. You should, however, exercise only at a moderate level of intensity—about 60 percent of your maximum heart rate. This is because, at a moderate level of intensity, your muscles tend to use body fat as an energy source, rather than the glucose that is used to provide energy for high-intensity exercise. In order to burn a significant amount of fat, you need to exercise for at least 30 minutes.

Phases of Exercise

A complete fitness workout should be preceded by warming up and followed by cooling down. Although skipping these preliminary and follow-up procedures does not always result in injury, the safest and most healthy exercises include these two phases. Increasing your exercise program needs to take place over several weeks, as illustrated in Figure 1.1.9.

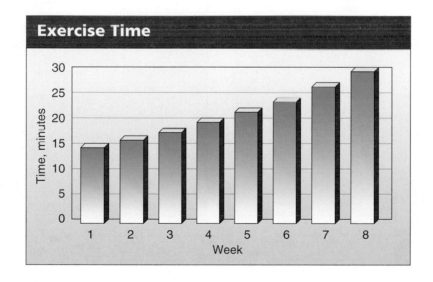

Figure 1.1.9: If you want to increase the time of your workout, do it gradually, at a rate of about 10 percent a week.

Reprinted from *Health Skills for Wellness*, Third Edition, by B. E. (Buzz) Pruitt, Kathy Teer Crumpler, and Deborah Prothrow-Stith, (2001), Prentice Hall, Inc.

Warming Up and Stretching

Before doing any type of exercise you must warm up. A warm-up is a 5- to 10-minute period of mild exercise that prepares your body for vigorous exercise. During a warm-up, your body temperature begins to rise, your heart rate picks up, blood flow to your muscles increases, and your muscles become more elastic and less likely to become injured.

Some people suggest that you go through the motions of your planned activity when you warm up. Rather than doing these movements at full intensity, do them at a slower pace. If you are planning to run, for example, start out by walking. Then gradually increase your speed until reaching your usual pace, as illustrated in Figure 1.1.10.

Your warm-up should include 5 to 10 minutes of stretching. As you know, stretching increases your flexibility, and proper stretching may decrease your chance of injury. However, it is very important to know your limits and stretch according to safe guidelines, such as those given in Building Health Skills in Lesson 2 (page 466). Don't overstretch, as that can damage ligaments and weaken joints. Stretching should be a constant, even pull on the muscles on both sides of your body. Because muscles work in pairs, you need to stretch both muscles in a pair. As you stretch each muscle group, you should feel tension but not pain. Do not bounce when you stretch, since bouncing can tear muscle fibers.

The Workout

The goal of this phase of exercise is to improve one or more of the components of physical fitness. Figure 1.1.11 summarizes the parts of a total fitness workout,

Figure 1.1.10: Walking is a good way to warm up for running.
Courtesy of Ken Karp.

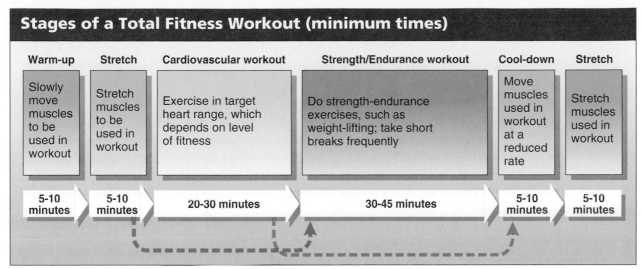

Stages of a Total Fitness Workout (minimum times)

Warm-up	Stretch	Cardiovascular workout	Strength/Endurance workout	Cool-down	Stretch
Slowly move muscles to be used in workout	Stretch muscles to be used in workout	Exercise in target heart range, which depends on level of fitness	Do strength-endurance exercises, such as weight-lifting; take short breaks frequently	Move muscles used in workout at a reduced rate	Stretch muscles used in workout
5-10 minutes	5-10 minutes	20-30 minutes	30-45 minutes	5-10 minutes	5-10 minutes

Figure 1.1.11: An exercise session may have up to six parts. Why do you need to warm up and cool down?
Courtesy of Function thru Form.

which includes strength/endurance exercises as well as those designed to improve cardiovascular fitness. Depending on your goals, you may not plan on doing both cardiovascular and strength/endurance exercises. Alternatively, you might switch between cardiorespiratory and strength/endurance workouts in successive exercise sessions. If you do both in the same session, however, the cardiorespiratory workout should be done first.

It is important to do strengthening exercises on alternating days because a full day is needed for your muscles to recover from such a workout. Also, when doing muscle-strengthening exercises, you should plan on short periods or sets of physical activity followed by rest periods during which the muscles can recover.

Cooling Down and Stretching

A slow warm-up period brings you safely from minimal to maximal activity. The cool-down is a period of milder exercise that allows your body and your heart rate to return slowly and safely to their resting states. Your cool-down should be at least as long as your warm-up. If you stop exercising abruptly, blood can collect in the muscles you were using. When this happens, blood may not return fast enough to your heart and brain. As a result, you may become dizzy and faint. Walking is a common method of cooling down.

Stretching after your cool-down loosens muscles that have tightened from exercise and prevents muscle and joint soreness. Spend at least five minutes repeating the stretches you did before your workout.

Checking Your Progress

One of the most exciting and gratifying aspects of sticking with a fitness program is seeing your progress. Your fitness will improve only gradually, so wait three or four weeks before retesting your fitness. In most exercise programs, you will begin to notice significant changes within 12 weeks. You may find that you look better, sleep better, or feel more alive. Perhaps you will notice that you have gained muscle strength, lost weight, or lowered your resting heart rate.

Your Resting Heart Rate

Someone with average cardiovascular fitness has a resting heart rate between 72 and 84 beats per minute. In general, girls and women have higher resting heart rates than boys and men. In either sex a resting heart rate below 72 beats per minute usually indicates a good fitness level. A young athlete in top competitive condition may have a resting heart rate as low as 40 beats per minute. The athlete's heart is so strong and efficient that it doesn't need to beat more rapidly to meet the body's needs. Your resting heart rate will probably not drop that low, but you may notice a drop of five to ten beats per minute after three to four weeks of exercise.

Your Changing Shape

If one of your goals is to lose body fat, you need to combine your exercise program with changes in your eating habits. As you track your progress, keep in mind that to be healthy, your body must store some fat; you cannot expect to lose all your body fat. In addition, remember that it is possible to lose fat tissue without losing weight. If you lose fat and gain muscle, you may even find that you weigh more than when you began your program. This is because muscle tissue is heavier than fat.

You will, however, have a trimmer body. To get an idea of whether you are losing body fat, you might measure and record the circumference of your upper arm at the start of your exercise program. Then measure your arm again every three to four weeks to track any changes.

To keep track of your overall progress in your workout program, you might keep a record in a table such as that shown in Figure 1.1.12. About every three or four weeks, write your fitness data in the table. Then, as the weeks go by, you can compare early data with later test results.

Progress Record					
Week	**Weight**	**Upper Arm Measurement**	**Resting Heart Rate**	**Appetite**	**Sleep Pattern**
0					
3					
6					
9					

Figure 1.1.12: A record of your progress might take the form of the table shown.

Reprinted from *Health Skills for Wellness*, Third Edition, by B. E. (Buzz) Pruitt, Kathy Teer Crumpler, and Deborah Prothrow-Stith, (2001), Prentice Hall, Inc.

Courtesy of Bob Daemmrich.

Courtesy of Melchior DiGiacomo/The Image Bank.

Figure 1.1.13: Proper safety equipment can help prevent injuries.

A Safe Workout

Anyone who exercises faces the risk of injury. Although some injuries may be unavoidable, most can be prevented by following some common-sense practices.

Equipping for Safety

You do not need expensive equipment in order to be safe. Depending on the activity you choose, you may need nothing more than sneakers. The key point is to choose the right equipment for your particular kind of exercise. Proper clothing, footwear, and protective gear help you to avoid discomfort and injury, as shown in Figure 1.1.13.

Clothing should be comfortable and allow unrestricted movement. Avoid clothing that inhibits your body's ability to cool itself through the evaporation of sweat. Also avoid any clothing that can trip you or get caught. For example, do not wear loose-fitting long pants or skirts when bicycling. Long pants and long sleeves are appropriate in sports such as skating, where falls and skin scrapes are a risk.

To protect your feet from injury, footwear must fit properly, be in good condition, and provide support and protection. Although athletic footwear is highly specialized, you probably do not need to buy expensive shoes. For example, do not waste your money on shoes meant for professional runners if your main activities are walking and bicycling.

Shoulder pads, helmets, mouth guards, and other protective gear are designed to prevent injuries in contact sports such as football and hockey. Hard-shell helmets worn by football players, hockey players, and baseball players at bat are designed to protect the head from a direct blow. Of course, you would not play a contact sport without a helmet, but did you know that you should regard a helmet as standard operating equipment anytime you get on wheeled sports equipment? A helmet should be worn each time you bike, skateboard, or roller skate. Knee and elbow pads are important equipment for skateboarders and roller skaters.

Fluids and Food

Your body can require water even when you are not thirsty. If you exercise for more than 45 minutes, you should take fluids during your exercise period. This is especially important in hot weather. To help prevent dehydration on warm days, you should have a cup of fluid a few minutes before you exercise and every 15 minutes during your exercise.

You need energy for exercising, and you get that energy from the food you eat.

Avoiding Overexertion

You may feel unusually tired during the session or even a few hours after if you exercise too intensely, too long, or too often. This tiredness is a signal that you have overworked your body. Other signs of overexertion include nausea or vomiting during or after a workout, and muscle or joint aches and pains that do not go away quickly. If you experience any of these symptoms, you need to cut back the intensity and length of your exercise. Avoid overexertion by sticking to a consistent exercise schedule, rather than occasional bursts of activity followed by periods of inactivity. In addition, always keep your exercise within your comfort level. Do not make the mistake of pushing yourself too hard in order to reach your fitness goal quickly.

Weather Considerations

Make sure your clothing is appropriate for the weather. Regardless of the air temperature, you should feel slightly cool at the beginning of your workout. When you exercise outdoors on warm, sunny days, wear light-colored clothing to reflect the sun's rays, and dress lightly to prevent overheating. The lighter or more sun-sensitive your skin is, the more you will need to protect yourself from sunburn with a sunscreen lotion.

When it is cold, your clothing should protect you from frostbite. Cover your hands and head, since you lose a lot of heat from these parts of your body. You may need a sweat suit for warmth but do not overdo it. Clothing that is too thick or heavy can inhibit the evaporation of sweat and possibly cause overheating. If you wear layers of clothing, you can regulate your temperature by taking off or adding layers as necessary.

Exercise Myths and Facts

1. MYTH: "No pain, no gain"; exercise to the point of feeling pain is the only way to improve your abilities.
   - FACT: Pain is a danger signal, a signal that you are causing harm. Sharp or sudden pain should be a signal to stop immediately.
2. MYTH: Sit-ups and other abdominal exercises will decrease fat in the stomach area.
   - FACT: You cannot "spot reduce" or lose fat just in one area.
3. MYTH: Drinking fluids before exercising can cause stomach cramps.
   - FACT: Plain water will not cause cramps. Without adequate water, you can become dehydrated, which can lead to muscle cramps and other more serious problems.
4. MYTH: Being thin is a sign of fitness.
   - FACT: Thin people who do not exercise are likely to have poor heart, lung, and muscular fitness. Cardiovascular fitness is a better indication of overall fitness than your appearance.
5. MYTH: If women lift weights, they will develop large muscles.
   - FACT: Women actually have less muscle tissue and more fat tissue than men. They also have a balance of hormones that is different from men and that prevents the development of large muscle mass.
6. MYTH: Exercise is unsafe for older people.
   - FACT: The health of elderly people can benefit greatly from moderate exercise.

Choosing the Right Exercise Program

Your exercise program should be based on your current fitness ratings and your own interests, needs, and abilities. Even if you think you are perfectly healthy, it makes good sense to check with a physician or other health-care professional to be sure your new activities will not put you at risk. After you have a physician-approved exercise plan, an exercise specialist, such as your physical education teacher, can help you select the best exercises. Moreover, he or she can give you specific pointers on the techniques that will make the activities safe and effective.

The type of exercise program you choose should have three parts: warm-up, conditioning, and cool-down.

The warm-up period allows for a slow increase in the heart rate and sends extra blood through muscles to warm them up. Your warm-up could include slow walking, mild stretching, or **calisthenics**. Remember, warm-up for five to seven minutes.

The conditioning period brings you into **cardiorespiratory** endurance and/or muscle strengthening activities. This is where most of your exercising occurs. These exercises should push your body to its normal limit, and when you are feeling strong, a little beyond. As exercising becomes easier, your normal limit should change. Walk or jog a little farther; do a few more sit-ups or push-ups. When weight training to gain bulk, increase to heavier weights; to build strength without bulk, keep lighter weights and increase repetitions. With muscle strengthening exercises, give your

Key Note Terms

calisthenics – light gymnastic exercise designed to promote good health by developing strength and grace

cardiorespiratory – of or relating to the heart and the respiratory system

WEEKLY PHYSICAL FITNESS TRAINING SCHEDULE

MONDAY	TUESDAY	WEDNESDAY	THURSDAY	FRIDAY
Warm-up/Stretching	Warm-up/Stretching	Warm-up/Stretching	Warm-up/Stretching	Warm-up/Stretching
Conditioning exercises, to include strength training	Aerobic conditioning activities	Conditioning exercises, to include strength training		Physical fitness assessment of goal measurement session
Running		Running	Unit fun run	
Cool-down/Stretching	Cool-down/Stretching	Cool-down/Stretching	Cool-down/Stretching	Cool-down/Stretching

Tuesdays and Thursdays are the "recovery" days. They allow the body to recover. Appropriate activities for these days include aerobic dance, kickball, volleyball, touch football, speed work, and/or fun runs.

(Sample)

muscles a day off between workouts to rest. Or work your upper body one day and your lower body the next. The conditioning period generally lasts twenty minutes.

Figure 1.1.14 is a sample of a weekly physical fitness training schedule. Notice how it includes the warm-up and conditioning periods as well as a cool-down period.

The cool-down period allows your heart rate to slow down, relaxes muscles, and cools the body. Slow walking, simple calisthenics, and mild stretching are good ways to cool down. Stretching during cool-down can prevent muscle cramps and soreness. Cool-down should last four to six minutes.

Sticking with an Exercise Program

Even though many people know how important exercise is to a healthy lifestyle, they have trouble sticking with an exercise program. Follow these tips and you will find it easier to keep your resolution to become or remain physically fit.

- **Think of fitness as part of your daily routine, just like brushing your teeth, going to class, or eating dinner.**
- **Set realistic and specific goals for yourself. If you have never jogged before, do not expect to jog three miles your first time out. You may become discouraged. Plan to jog one mile and stick with it, even if you have to walk part of the way. You will find that you progress quickly, building your self-confidence.**

- Exercise at least three times a week. If you exercise less than this, you probably will not see much progress, giving you an easy excuse to give up.

- Keep track of your progress in a journal. It is motivating to look back at where you started and see how far you have come.

- If you are a routine person who likes for things to remain the same, keep the same exercise routine from week to week. If you get bored easily and like change, develop several exercise routines that you can alternate from week to week.

- Exercise with a friend or group. You will get support from others and feel more committed to stick with it.

- Choose a place to exercise that is convenient for you. If the place you plan to exercise is far from home or school, you may not get there as often as you should.

- Wear comfortable clothing and shoes to make your exercise experience as pleasant as possible.

- Stay positive and have fun. Remember that you are doing something good for yourself. Be serious and consistent with your exercise routine, but enjoy it as well. If you choose an exercise program that you just cannot learn to enjoy, try something else. There is an exercise program for everyone!

CAUTION: BEFORE BEGINNING ANY EXERCISE OR DIET PROGRAM, IT IS IMPORTANT THAT YOU HAVE THE APPROVAL OF YOUR PHYSICIAN.

Assessing Cardiovascular Fitness and Determining Target Heart Rate

When you exercise, your heart and lungs must supply your muscles with more oxygen than they need when you are resting. Your heart, for example, pumps about 5 quarts (about 5.5 liters) of blood per minute when you are at rest and 20 to 25 quarts (about 22 to 27 liters) when you are exercising vigorously. Running track, as shown in Figure 1.1.15, is a great way to get a cardiovascular workout.

Your target heart rate is the heart rate you need to maintain during exercise in order to improve your cardiovascular fitness. The following is a simple test for

Figure 1.1.15: Running is one way to exercise your heart and muscles.
Courtesy of Bob Daemmrich/ Stock Boston.

Table 1.1.2

Mile Walk/Run Times in Minutes and Seconds		
Age	Girls	Boys
14	10:30	7:45
15-18	10:30	7:30

assessing your cardiovascular fitness and the procedure for determining the range in which your target heart rate should fall. These are followed by some guidelines for improving cardiovascular fitness.

Test Your Cardiovascular Fitness

Before you do this test or start an exercise program, have a physical examination to make sure that you do not have any health problems that rule out vigorous exercise. The examination should include a check of your blood pressure and resting heart rate. Do not attempt this test if you are ill or if you have a history of health problems.

> **Note**
>
> To prepare for the test, do the warm-up and stretching exercises described in this lesson.

To test your cardiovascular fitness, you must walk and/or run one mile as fast as you can. You can alternate running with walking, but your goal is to cover one mile in as little time as possible. You will need to work with a partner. Your partner should use a watch with a second hand to measure the time, in minutes and seconds, it takes you to complete the distance of one mile.

Compare Your Results to Recommended Results

Compare your score to the scores listed in Table 1.1.2. To be at a good fitness level, your time should be no greater than the minimum times listed in the table.

Take Your Resting Pulse and Determine Your Target Heart Range

To determine your resting heart rate, you will need a watch or clock with a second hand. Use your index finger or middle finger to find your pulse, either in your wrist or in your neck, as shown in Figure 1.1.16. Then count the number of pulse beats during one minute.

Subtract your resting heart rate from 200, which is approximately your maximum heart rate. Then multiply the resulting number first by 0.6 and then by 0.8.

Add your resting heart rate to each of the two numbers you obtained in the previous step. The two sums give you the range in which your target heart rate should be.

Choose an Appropriate Cardiovascular Exercise Program

Ask your physical education teacher to help you select appropriate activities for building cardiovascular fitness, such as those in the table. Select moderate intensity activities first; then switch to activities of higher intensity as your fitness improves.

Do these activities three to four times a week. Take your pulse rate immediately after you stop exercising to see if you are exercising in your target heart range. (Because your heart rate begins to decrease as soon as you stop exercising, count the beats in 6 seconds and multiply this number by 10 to get the total number of beats for 60 seconds.)

Figure 1.1.16: Taking your pulse is easy and tells you your heart rate before and after exercise.
Courtesy of Boston Graphics.

After you have been exercising regularly for a while, repeat the cardiovascular walk/run fitness test to monitor your progress.

Apply the Skill

1. Complete the timed one mile walk/run to determine your cardiovascular fitness level. Record your results. Be sure to do warm-up stretches before you begin.

2. Determine the range in which your target heart rate falls.

3. After a physical checkup by a qualified health-care professional, design a cardiovascular fitness program that will improve your fitness level.

Fitness Throughout Life

One of the most important and challenging things you can do for yourself is to start exercising now and continue your program for your entire life. If you begin and continue an exercise program when you are young, it will help you stay healthy and fit as you age. Some people are discouraged from achieving this goal because they think that exercise is too difficult or time-consuming. They do not realize that many activities that they already perform may actually be forms of exercise. In addition, fitness activities can actually be a lot of fun. Both aerobic dance classes and recreational dancing can help you become physically fit.

Fitness and Recreation

Do you have fun riding your bike to visit a friend? Is a brisk walk on a cool morning something that you enjoy? At school dances, do you love to jump and turn enthusiastically in time to fast music? Do you and your friends ever get together for a hike, a quick game of basketball, or a swim at a local lake or pool? If you answered yes to any of those questions, you already perform activities that contribute to your physical fitness. Recreational activities that involve exercise, such as walking, biking, dancing, and swimming, are an important part of a fitness program.

Fitness and Aging

As people age, they undergo physical changes. Their bodies become less flexible, and their bones tend to fracture more easily. Those changes do not, however, have to prevent older people from being physically fit. Studies have shown that moderate exercise can help reduce the effects of, and sometimes eliminate, many physical problems associated with old age, such as cardiovascular disease and arthritis. This is true even if exercise begins late in life.

Some older people mistakenly think that they need to avoid exercise to protect themselves from injury. In fact, bones and muscles are more likely to stay strong and function well if they are exercised regularly. Exercise can significantly reduce the risk of osteoporosis, a condition in which the bones of elderly people—particularly elderly women—become fragile. Older people who get little exercise are generally less healthy than those who remain active.

Moderation is especially important in a fitness program for older adults. Older people may not be able to exercise at as high intensity as they once did. Older people are more likely than younger people to develop circulatory-system problems, and the target heart rate for exercise decreases as a person ages. Elderly people also need to be especially careful not to put too much stress on bones and muscles. If older people exercise carefully and moderately, however, they can continue to benefit from regular exercise.

Finding Ways to Get Fit

Do you still think you just cannot bring yourself to plan and carry out a fitness program? Then at least try to increase your daily level of activity. Make a game out of trying to add just a little more exercise each day. If you travel mostly by car or bus, bicycle or walk instead. Use stairs instead of an elevator. If you already walk quite a bit, pick up your pace or jog for a short distance. A small amount of exercise is better than none at all. People who get even a little bit of exercise have less risk of cardiovascular disease than those who are totally inactive.

Conclusion

Regular exercise is important to maintaining your health. It can make you feel and look better and help your body fight disease. Different exercise programs have different benefits, like aerobic dancing for a strong heart and weight lifting for strong muscles. No matter what exercise program you close, remember that that most important thing is to stay active. So much in life today makes things easy for us—elevators, escalators, cars, electric appliances—that it is easy to get out of shape. In addition to an exercise program, take the stairs, walk or bike to the store; go bowling with friends instead of watching television. It can be fun, and it is all to your benefit!

In the next lesson, you will do the Cadet Challenge and participate in exercises designed for the Presidential Physical Fitness Award (PPFA) program.

Lesson Review

1. **How does aerobic exercise differ from anaerobic exercise? Give an example of each.**

2. **List three physical benefits of regular exercise.**

3. **Explain how your target heart rate affects the level of intensity of the exercise you perform to improve your cardiorespiratory endurance.**

4. **List two ways to reduce your risk of injury when you exercise.**

Lesson 2

Cadet Challenge

Key Terms

Cadet Challenge
curl-ups
flexed-arm hang
Presidential Physical Fitness Award (PPFA)
pull-ups
v-sit reach
shuttle run

What You Will Learn to Do

- Meet the physical fitness standards for the Cadet Challenge

Linked Core Abilities

- Take responsibility for your actions and choices

Skills and Knowledge You Will Gain Along the Way

- Compare the Cadet Challenge to the Presidential Physical Fitness Award
- Distinguish between the Presidential Physical Fitness Award and the National Physical Fitness Award
- Identify the five Cadet Challenge exercises
- Describe the proper techniques for the Cadet Challenge exercises
- Define the key words contained in this section

Chapter 1

Introduction

This is it! Time to put on your sneakers and start warming up for what may be the toughest part of this unit—participating in exercises designed for the Presidential Physical Fitness Award (PPFA) program. Get ready to tackle these exercises developed to test your physical ability. They require endurance, speed, strength, and flexibility. What can Cadet Challenge do for you? First, it allows you to develop an understanding and appreciation for physical fitness. Second, it shows how an exercise program can improve health and appearance, thereby improving self-confidence. Finally, there is the personal satisfaction involved in striving to achieve a goal and in recognizing and recording your own progress.

The Challenge

Ready to go? It's time for the challenge! **Cadet Challenge** consists of five exercises taken from the **Presidential Physical Fitness Award** program. The Cadet Challenge is the JROTC Physical Fitness Test. Each cadet is required to participate in the physical fitness test conducted twice each school year. Cadets who score at the 85 percent or better on each event on the test may receive the Physical Fitness Ribbon. Read the descriptions of how to execute each exercise carefully. Along with each exercise description is a box showing standards to shoot for based on your age and gender. The Presidential Physical Fitness Test is part of the President's Challenge program that encourages all Americans to make being active part of their everyday lives. To qualify for the PPFA, you must achieve a standard of 85 percent or higher on all five items of the test. In each box showing standards, the 85th percentile standards are listed in the two columns under the heading "PPFA (85%)." If you achieve a standard of 84 percent or below, but above 50 percent, you qualify for the National Physical Fitness Award (NPFA). Fifty percentile standards are listed in each box in the two columns under the heading "NPFA (50%)."

Cadets who score in the 85th percentile or above on Cadet Challenge are eligible to receive the PPFA, which consists of a round blue emblem embroidered with an eagle. Cadets who score in the 50th to 84th percentile are eligible to receive the NPFA, which consists of a round red emblem embroidered with an eagle. Those cadets who achieve Cadet Command's standards in Cadet Challenge are eligible to receive the JROTC Athletic Ribbon. Cadets who attempt all five exercises but score below the 50th percentile on one or more of them are eligible to receive a white round emblem embroidered with an eagle.

If you are a cadet with special needs or have one or more disabilities, which would directly affect your performance on these exercises, see your instructor for criteria for modified or alternative exercises.

Key Note Terms

Cadet Challenge – a physical fitness test that consists of five exercises taken from the Presidential Physical Fitness Award program

Presidential Physical Fitness Award – an award earned by achieving a standard of 85 percent or higher on the Presidential Physical Fitness Test

Improving Your Scores

The exercises in Cadet Challenge test your endurance and physical strength. Initially, it does not matter what you score on these events except to establish a base score from which to build. From there, however, it is important that you establish a routine exercise program, so that your score will improve, and along with it, your health. Work toward achieving the 85th percentile standard. If you have participated in the PPFA program in another physical education program and met the 85th percentile for your age and gender, try to achieve it again this time. If you did not meet that standard, here's a chance to improve.

Basic Rules of Exercise

As you prepare for the Cadet Challenge, remember to follow these basic rules:

- **To produce positive results, exercise at least three times a week**
- **Begin your exercise program by warming up for 5 to 7 minutes**
- **Spend at least 20 minutes on conditioning then cool down for four to six minutes**
- **With the exception of the v-sit reach, complete the exercises in the challenge during the conditioning period**
- **Make the v-sit reach part of your warm-up or cool-down**

Remember to follow an exercise program that includes aerobic exercise for the one-mile run/walk, anaerobic exercise for the shuttle run, muscle strengthening for the pull-ups and curl-ups, and stretching for the v-sit reach. If you give it your all and perform to the best of your abilities, you will

- **Have a stronger body**
- **Feel good about yourself**
- **Appreciate health and fitness**

Taking the Challenge

The Cadet Challenge consists of the following five events. A more detail explanation of each event can be found on the President's Challenge Web site at www.presidentschallenge.org/misc/downloads.aspx. From this site, you can download, *Get Fit: A Handbook for Youth.* You will also find composite records and other forms of the physical fitness program that may be used to score each cadet who participates.

Curl-ups

Conduct **curl-ups** on a flat, clean surface, preferably with a mat. Start in a lying position on your backs with your knees up so your feet are flat on the floor and about 12 inches from your buttocks. You should have your arms crossed with your

Key Note Term

curl-ups – one of the five events on the Cadet Challenge and Presidential Physical Fitness Test that consist of a sit up movement from a lying position up to the point where your elbows touch your thighs hands placed on opposite shoulders, and your elbows held close to the chest throuogut the exercise. Have a partner hold your feet at the instep. At the command, "ready, go," raise the trunks of your body, curling up to touch the elbows to the thighs; then lower your back so that your shoulder blades touch the floor/mat. This constitutes one repetition of a curl-up. During each repetition, bouncing off the floor/mat is not allowed and the fingers must touch the shoulders at all times. Complete as many curl-ups as possible in 60 seconds.

Partial curl-ups can be used as an alternative to curl-ups. Lie on a cushioned, clean surface with knees flexed and feet about 12 inches from buttocks. Do not hold or anchor the feet. Arms are extended forward with fingers resting on the legs and pointing toward the knees. Your partner should be behind your head with hands cupped under your head. Curl up slowly, sliding the fingers up the legs until the fingertips touch the knees, then back down until the head touches your partner's hands. The curl-ups are done to a metronome (or audio tape, clapping, drums) with one complete curl-up every three seconds. Continue until you can do no more in rhythm (has not done the last three in rythym) or have reached the target number for the test.

Pull-Ups

Key Note Term

pull-ups – one of the five events on the Cadet Challenge and Presidential Physical Fitness Test that consist of pulling the body up from a dead weight hanging position on a bar to having the chin clear the bar

Key Note Term

flexed-arm hang – an alternative event for the pull-up in the Cadet Challenge and Presidential Physical Fitness Test

Pull-ups are conducted using a horizontal bar approximately one and one-half inches in diameter. A doorway bar or a piece of pipe can serve the purpose. The bar should be high enough so you can hang with your arms fully extended and your feet free of the floor/ground. Assume the hanging position on the bar using either an overhand grasp (palms facing away from body) or underhand grip (palms facing toward body). Begin the exercise by first raising your body until your chin is over the bar without touching it. To complete one repetition, the body must be lowered to the full-hang starting position. During each repetition, the body must not swing, legs must not kick or bend, and the pull must not be jerky. Scoring is done on the number of pull-ups you can correctly execute. There is no time limit on this event.

The **flexed-arm hang** should be used when a cadet cannot execute one pull-up. (This event is only for the National Physical Fitness Award). Using a horizontal bar as in the pull-ups, climb a ladder until your chin is above the bar. Begin the exercise by grasping the bar with your hands, shoulder width apart, using either an overhand grasp (palms facing away from body) or underhand grip (palms facing toward body). At the command "ready, go," step off the ladder. Simultaneously, an assistant instructor will remove the ladder and prevent any forward swinging of the legs. The cadet's chin should be level above the bar. Kicking and other body movements are not permitted while you are on the bar. The stopwatch starts on the command "go" and stops when your chin rests on the bar, the chin tilts backward to keep it above the bar, or the chin falls below the level of the bar. Scores are recorded to the nearest second.

Right Angle Push-ups

Lie face down on the mat in push-up position wiwth hands under shoulders, fingers straight, and legs straight, parallel, and slightly apart, with the toes supporting the feet. Straighten the arms, keeping the back and knees straight, then lower the body until there is a 90-degree angle at the elbows, with th upper arms parallel to the floor. A partner holds your hand at the point of the 90-degree angle so that you go down only until your shoulder touches the partner's hand, then back up. The push-ups are done to a metronome (or audio tape, clapping, drums) with one complete push-up every three seconds, and are continued until you can do no more in rhythm (has not done the last three in rhythm) or has reached the target number for the PPFA.

V-sit Reach

Key Note Term

v-sit reach – one of the five events on the Cadet Challenge and Presidential Physical Fitness Test that consist of stretching a number of inches past an established baseline

The **V-sit reach** is conducted on a flat, clean floor. Use a yardstick and adhesive tape to make a baseline that is two feet long. Make a measuring line perpendicular to the midpoint of the baseline extending two feet out from either side of the baseline. Place one-inch and half-inch marks along the measuring line with "0" where the baseline and measuring line intersect. Remove your shoes and sit on the floor with the soles of your feet placed immediately behind the baseline. The measuring line should be between your heels, which should be 8 to 12 inches apart. Clasp your thumbs so that your hands are together, palms down, and place them on the floor between your legs. While your legs are held flat on the floor by a partner (or partners), perform the exercise while keeping the soles of your feet perpendicular to the floor (feet flexed). Slowly reach forward along the measuring line as far as possible keeping the fingers in contact with the floor. You receive three practice tries for the v-sit reach. On the fourth extension, hold your farthest reach for three seconds. Scores are recorded where fingertips touch the floor to the nearest half-inch. Scores beyond the baseline are recorded as plus scores, whereas those behind the baseline are recorded as minus scores.

Sit and Reach

The sit and reach exercise is done in a specially constructed box with a measuring scale marked in centimeters, with 23 centimeters at the level of the feet. Remove your shoes and sit on floor with knees fully extended, feet shoulder-width apart, and soles of the feet held flat against the end of the box. With hands on top of each other, palms down, and legs held flat, reach along the measuring line as far as possible. After three practice reaches, the fourth reach is held while the distance is recorded. Participants are most flexible after a warm-up run. Best results may occur immediately after performing the endurance run. Legs must remain straight, soles of feet against box and fingertips of both hands should reach evenly along measuring line. Scores are recorded to the nearest centimeter.

One-Mile Run/Walk

This event is conducted on a flat area that has a known measured distance of one mile with a designated start and finish line. You will be given a lightweight numbered device to carry or wear in any manner that will not slow you down while running.

Note

Use of the numbered device makes it possible to have many cadets run at one time by having them pair off before the start of the event, then having one cadet from each pair run while the other cadets keep track of the number of laps your partners complete as well as listening for your times as they cross the finish line.

Start from the standing position. At the command "ready, do," start running the one-mile distance. Although walking is permitted, try to cover the distance in the shortest time possible. Scores are recorded to the nearest second.

Shuttle Run

The shuttle run is conducted on an area that has two parallel lines 30 feet apart. The width of a regulation volleyball court can serve as a suitable area. Start from the standing position. At the command "ready, go," run to the opposite line, pick up one block, run back to the starting line, and place the block behind the line. Run back, and pick up the second block, and carry it across the line. Two runs are allowed for this event with the better of the runs recorded. Scores are recorded to the nearest tenth of a second.

More Than Healthy Rewards

The President's Challenge not only helps you get fit and stay healthy, but also rewards participants who meet or exceed program requirements. Cadets that successfully complete all events are eligible for the President's Physical Fitness Award as well as the National Physical Fitness Award.

The President's Physical Fitness Award recognizes students who achieve an outstanding level of physical fitness. Students who score at or above the 85th percentile on all events are eligible for this award. Awards can be requested by accessing the President's Challenge web site at http://www.presidentschallenge.org.

Other awards include the National Physical Fitness Award. This award recognizes students who demonstrate a basic, yet challenging level of physical fitness. Students who score above 50th percentile on all five Cadet Challenge events are eligible for this award.

The JROTC Physical Fitness Ribbon (N-2-2) is presented to cadets who receive the 85th percentile rating or better in each of the five events of the Cadet Challenge program.

The JROTC Athletics Ribbon (N-2-3) is presented to cadets who receive the 50th percentile rating or better in each of the five events of the Cadet Challenge program.

The top five male and five female cadets in each unit receive individual medals.

Building Health Skills

As you go through this or any exercise program, it's important to protect your body and build some health skills. These skills include knowing how to warm up, cool down, and stretch.

Warming Up, Cooling Down, and Stretching

Imagine that you are about to go on a five-mile bicycle ride or play your favorite sport. You know that these are strenuous activities that put stress on your bones, muscles, and tendons. How should you prepare your body for these activities? After the activity, what should you do to minimize the effects of the stress your body has just undergone?

Key Note Term

shuttle run – one of the five events on the Cadet Challenge and Presidential Physical Fitness test that consists of a 30-foot shuttle run

Figure 1.2.1: Stretching helps to pro-tect your muscles during exercise.
Courtesy of Susan Spellman.

Figure 1.2.2: The hand grasp stretches your arms and shoulders.
Courtesy of Susan Spellman.

Before a workout, use slow movements to warm up the muscles that you will use. When the muscles are warmed up, stretch them. Stretching cold muscles is not effective and can cause injury. After your workout, cool down by slowly moving the muscles you used. Then stretch these muscles as you did before the workout.

Although no single stretching routine is appropriate for every activity, the stretching exercises that follow provide a base for you to build on. It is important not to rush when you perform these movements. A pulled muscle can hold you up much longer than the few minutes of warming up/stretching and cooling down/stretching needed with each workout.

When you perform stretching exercises, do not bounce. Bouncing can tear muscle fibers, and scar tissue can form as a result.

Warming Up/Cooling Down

Before your workout, walk, jog slowly, or do the activity that you are about to participate in at a reduced pace. This warms up your muscles, preparing them for the more intense activity of the workout itself. Similarly, right after the workout, you need to continue moving your muscles at a reduced pace for five to ten minutes, as you did in the warm-up. This cool-down period helps ease the body back to normal levels of muscular activity.

> **Note**
>
> To warm up for bike riding, begin by pedaling slowly and gradually increase your speed.

Side Stretch

Stand with feet apart, knees bent, and one hand on your hip. Extend the opposite arm overhead and stretch to the side, as shown in Figure 1.2.1. Hold 15 seconds. Repeat in the other direction. Do five times in each direction.

Hand Grasp

Grasp your hands behind your back and hold. Stand with your feet apart and knees slightly bent, and lean over at the waist. Pull up your arms behind you, as shown in Figure 1.2.2, and hold 15 seconds.

Lower Back Curl

Lie on your back with legs extended. Bring one knee up to your chest. Grasp the leg behind the knee and pull the knee closer to your chest. Next, curl your shoulders toward your knee. Figure 1.2.3 shows how this is done. Hold this position for 15 seconds. Switch to the opposite leg and repeat.

Calf Stretch

Stand in a stride position with your right leg forward and hands on your hips. Lean your upper body forward. Simultaneously bend your right leg and extend your left leg back in a continuous line with your upper body. Push your left heel to the ground. Figure 1.2.4 shows this position. Hold for 15 seconds. Repeat with the other leg. Do this five times on each side.

Hamstring Stretch

Sit on the floor and extend one leg, toes facing up. Tuck your other foot against your extended thigh. Reach forward over your extended leg and slide your hands down your leg until you feel a stretch. Hold for 15 seconds. Switch to the other leg. Repeat with each leg twice.

Take five minutes to practice these stretching exercises.

Each day for a week, do the stretching routine and record how you felt before and after the routine, including any soreness or stiffness. At the end of the week, evaluate the stretching routine and your reactions to it. What are its benefits?

Note

Select a favorite sport or other physical activity and then ask your physical education teacher or coach to suggest an appropriate warm-up routine for that activity, including stretching exercises.

Figure 1.2.3: Stretch the muscles in your lower back to prevent injury while working out.
Courtesy of Susan Spellman.

Figure 1.2.4: Stretching your calves will help prevent cramping and shin splints.
Courtesy of Susan Spellman.

Conclusion

The Cadet Challenge is an introduction to exercising for a specific goal. You will see your scores improve as you continue to practice. Making healthy changes in your lifestyle and working hard to reach this goal will make you a stronger, healthier individual, both mentally and physically, and will bring you the great satisfaction of a job well done. For more information on The President's Challenge and the Presidential Physical Fitness Test and exercises, go to the President's Challenge Web site at www.presidentschallenge.org/*Get Fit: A Handbook for Youth*.

The following lesson introduces you to the importance of good nutrition. You will learn that "you are what you eat," and how a balanced diet is essential when planning a fitness program.

Lesson Review

1. Explain the Cadet Challenge.
2. Contrast the difference between the PPFA and the NPFA.
3. Describe the five Cadet Challenge exercises.
4. Explain the proper techniques for the Cadet Challenge exercises.

Lesson 3

You Are What You Eat

Key Words

calories
carbohydrates
deficient
diabetes
fats
fiber
metabolism
minerals
nutrients
osteoporosis
protein
stimulant
vitamins

What You Will Learn to Do

- Evaluate how diet impacts life

Linked Core Abilities

- Take responsibility for your actions and choices

Skills and Knowledge You Will Gain Along the Way

- Explain how calories consumed verses calories used affects body weight
- Identify the daily-required food and portions
- Identify sources and benefits of fiber in diet
- Describe the importance of water
- Describe the possible effects of a diet high in fat and cholesterol
- Explain why salt, sugar, and caffeine should be used in moderation
- Define the key words contained in this lesson

Introduction

A healthy lifestyle includes good nutrition as well as exercise. You need to eat well to maintain an exercise program. Just as a car will not run without fuel, your body will not work properly without the right **nutrients**. Eating a balanced diet also helps you maintain proper weight and lowers your risk of disease. This lesson explains the importance of a proper diet to your health.

Americans live in a fast-paced environment and frequently eat on the run. Eating on the run too often, however, may affect your nutrition and weight. You can end up consuming too many **fats** and too few vegetables and fruit, leaving you overweight and/or **deficient** in certain nutrients. Learning to eat balanced meals, even on the run, contributes to your overall well-being by helping to maintain proper weight, providing energy for physical activity, and supplying nutrients for good health.

> ## Note
>
> Although too many fats can be bad for you, your body needs a certain amount of fat from the foods you eat. Many necessary vitamins are fat-soluble only; without fat, these vitamins cannot be absorbed.

Key Note Terms

nutrients – substances found in food that allow the body to function properly

fats – nutrients made up of fatty acids that are insoluble in water and provide energy to the body

deficient – having too little of something, such as a nutrient in the body

Balancing Calories

You must eat to fuel your body. The more active you are, the more fuel your body requires. Even if you remain very still, your body uses a certain amount of energy, or **calories**, on basic functions that work automatically all the time to keep you alive, such as your heart beating, your lungs inhaling, and your nerves delivering information. You do not have much control over the amount of calories used for these basic functions. Some people's bodies naturally use more calories to sustain their basic functions; some people use less. It's often said that those who use more have a high **metabolism**, meaning they can eat more and not gain weight.

Your body also uses calories to do everything else throughout the day, from brushing your teeth, to studying, to stretching. Unlike your basic functions, however, you can control how many calories you voluntarily use throughout the day by how active you are. For example, you will use more calories if you choose to walk for an hour instead of watching television for an hour. Also, the more effort you put into an activity, the more calories you burn. For example, walking at a brisk pace uses more calories than walking at a leisurely pace.

When your body uses the same amount of calories daily than you eat daily, your weight stays the same. If you eat more calories than your body uses, your body stores the unused calories as fat and you gain weight. If you eat fewer calories than your body needs, your body uses the stored fat for energy and you lose weight. It's a balancing act between numbers of calories eaten and calories used.

Key Note Terms

calories – the amount of energy it takes to raise the temperature of one kilogram of water one degree Celsius; a measurement of energy

metabolism – the chemical process by which the body produces energy and maintains vital functions

Karen and Andrea

Here's an example of making sensible choices when choosing the foods you eat.

Karen wonders why she keeps gaining weight—10 pounds over the last year. One Saturday, she and her friend, Andrea, meet at the local fast-food restaurant for lunch. While they wait in line, Andrea says she played tennis that morning. Karen admits she slept late and watched television. Andrea orders a small soda and a salad with grilled chicken and light Italian dressing; Karen orders a double hamburger with mayonnaise only, large French fries, and a large chocolate milkshake.

Andrea shakes her head and asks Karen if she ever eats fruit or vegetables. Karen shrugs and says "sometimes." Andrea explains that she eats hamburgers and French fries every once in a while; in fact, she had that for lunch a few days ago, which is why she ordered a salad today. Andrea tells Karen that eating fruit and vegetables more often than fried foods and sweets helps her maintain her desired weight, and she feels better, too. Karen thinks about this for a moment as they sit down to eat.

Perhaps if Karen had access to the following calorie counts, she would reconsider what she ordered. Keep in mind that most people need only between 2,000 and 3,000 total calories a day. Table 1.3.1 shows the difference between the two food orders.

Table 1.3.1: Karen and Andrea's Lunch Orders

Karen's Order	Calories	Andrea's Order	Calories
Plain double hamburger with bun (1/4 pound beef)	540	Salad with grilled chicken	200
Mayonnaise (1 tablespoon)	100	Light Italian salad dressing (2 tablespoons)	50
French fries (large order)	360		
Chocolate milkshake (large)	540	Soda (small)	150
TOTAL	1540	TOTAL	400

The calories listed here are approximate; actual calories in these food items may vary at different restaurants.

Chapter 1 Achieving a Healthy Lifestyle

Even if Karen did not want a salad, she could cut her calories considerably by ordering a single hamburger with mustard and ketchup, a small milkshake, and a regular order of fries. She could also have lettuce and tomato on the burger to eat some vegetables. Her new calorie intake would look simliar to Table 1.3.2.

Table 1.3.2: An Alternative to Andrea's Lunch Order

Andrea's order	Calories
Plain single hamburger with bun (2 ounce patty)	275
Lettuce (1/2 cup)	5
Tomato (1 slice)	5
Mustard (1 tablespoon)	8
Ketchup (1 tablespoon)	15
French fries (regular order)	220
Chocolate milkshake (small)	330
TOTAL	858

If Karen really wants to lose those extra 10 pounds, however, she should skip the milkshake and replace the fries with a small salad and light dressing. This would reduce her calorie intake to about 400 for lunch. She should then get some exercise like her friend Andrea. Playing tennis for an hour uses three times as many calories as watching television for an hour. If Karen sticks to eating sensibly and exercises daily, she will start using more calories than she eats, losing those extra pounds. How many calories are contained in the food you eat? Figure 1.3.1 gives you an idea of the calories contained in everyday foods.

The Importance of a Proper Diet to Your Health

Just as important as eating the correct amount of calories to supply your body with energy and maintain proper weight is what you eat to get those calories. If you eat like Karen every day, you are giving your body too much fat, cholesterol, salt, and sugar, and denying your body many necessary nutrients. Many health problems are related to poor diets, and these problems can start when you are young. At your next physical examination, ask your doctor about your cholesterol, blood pressure, and blood sugar levels. You may be surprised to find you need to change your diet to improve your health.

The Calorie Content of Some Common Foods

Tomato
1 medium — 25

Whole milk
1 cup — 150

Cheese pizza
1 slice — 290

Egg
1 large — 80

Apple
1 medium — 80

Green pepper
1 medium — 20

Wheat bread
1 slice — 65

Potato
1 medium — 145

Ice cream
1 cup — 270

Orange
1 medium — 60

Figure 1.3.1: Of the foods shown, which two have the most calories? Which have the fewest?
Courtesy of Function thru Form.

Key Note Terms

vitamins – nutrients that occur naturally in plant and animal tissue and are required for proper function of the body

minerals – natural chemical elements of the earth used by the body to supply necessary nutrition

carbohydrates – one of the various neutral organic compounds composed of carbon, hydrogen, and oxygen (including starches and sugars) produced by plants and used to provide energy necessary for growth and other functions

protein – nutrients that are made of amino acids and that maintain body tissues and supply energy to the body

osteoporosis – a condition characterized by a calcium deficiency in the bone mass. The body pulls calcium from the bones, causing them to lose their density and possibly leading to fractures

What Should You Eat?

The United States Department of Agriculture (USDA) developed the Food Guide Pyramid to indicate how many servings of six different food groups you should eat daily to get the nutrients your body needs. If you follow these guidelines, you will get enough **vitamins** and **minerals** to keep your body's processes functioning properly, and you will have enough **carbohydrates**, **protein**, and fat to supply your body with energy. When you do not get enough of certain nutrients, you increase your risk of disease. For example, if you do not get enough calcium, a mineral found in milk products, almonds, sardines, leafy vegetables, and beans, you can develop **osteoporosis**.

To see the current Food Guide Pyramid, as offered by the USDA, check out http://www.nal.usda.gov/fnic/Fpyr/pyramid.html or Figure 1.3.2.

Figure 1.3.2: The Food Guide Pyramid divides foods into groups and indicates how many servings you should eat from each group every day?

Your body also needs **fiber**, the only form of carbohydrate that is not an energy source. Fiber aids in digestion. It prevents cholesterol, fats, and other toxic materials from entering the bloodstream and for this reason may lessen your chances of cancer and heart disease; it also helps balance your blood sugar levels, which is important if you suffer from **diabetes**. To obtain fiber, eat raw or lightly cooked vegetables, fresh fruit, beans, nuts, and whole wheat or bran breads, cereals, and crackers.

One final nutrient which contains no calories is water. Water can be obtained from drinking plain or sparkling water, fruits and vegetables and their juices, milk and yogurt, cooked cereal, rice and soups. More than 65 percent of the body is water, and, as the body loses water through normal activity and exercise, it must be replaced. Water aids in digestion, regulates temperature, carries vitamins and minerals to all parts of the body, and is important for the removal of waste products from the kidneys. Drink a minimum of five to six glasses of water a day. On the days you exercise, you may need to drink more.

Eating in Moderation

Your body needs fat for energy, but too much fat in your diet can make you gain weight and can lead to high cholesterol. Cholesterol, a type of fat, is a natural, waxy substance produced by your body and found in animal products. Your body needs some cholesterol to remain healthy, but too much is harmful. As shown in Figure 1.3.3, cholesterol forms plaque on artery walls, restricting the flow of blood within blood vessels. This leads to high blood pressure and an increased risk of heart disease. To lower cholesterol levels, lower your intake of fat by eating less meat, using oil-free dressings, avoiding fried foods, eating low-fat dairy products, and consuming lots of fiber.

Many foods, especially prepackaged foods and restaurant foods, already have added salt, so do not shake on more. Too much salt in your diet forces your body to retain unnecessary water and may contribute to high blood pressure.

Sugary foods like candy, soda, syrup, and table sugar supply you with calories and few (if any) nutrients. These foods contain "empty calories"; they give your body calories and nothing else. Avoid them while dieting, and do not eat them as a replacement for other foods that provide nutrition. Many fruits and vegetables naturally contain sugar, but they also provide many other important nutrients.

Limit your intake of coffee, tea, and sodas that contain caffeine, a **stimulant**. Although caffeine temporarily reduces drowsiness and makes you more alert, in large quantities it can upset your stomach, make you nervous and irritable, keep you awake when you want to sleep, and give you diarrhea.

Clot

Key Note Terms

fiber – coarse food made mostly of carbohydrates, such as bran or broccoli, that serves to stimulate and aid the movement of food through the digestive tract

diabetes – a disease in which the body is unable to use sugars properly

Key Note Term

stimulant – an ingredient found in beverages, food or drugs that speeds up the activity of the mind or body; a drug that speeds up the activities of the central nervous system, the heart, and other organs; for example, caffeine in tea or chocolate

Figure 1.3.3: Cholesterol shown in artery walls.
Courtesy of US Army JROTC.

Conclusion

Your body needs food for energy, just like a car needs fuel to run. How much food your body needs depends on how active you are and how many calories your body uses to keep its basic functions operating. You know you are getting the right amount of calories from food when you maintain your ideal weight. Not only does food supply you with energy, but the right foods also provide the nutrients your body needs to operate properly and lower your risk of disease. Eating a healthy, balanced diet and exercising regularly increase your chances of a long, strong, and disease-free life.

In the next lesson, you will learn more about nutrition and what it takes to properly nourish your body.

Lesson Review

1. Think about what you had for breakfast. How could you have balanced your calories better?

2. Do you feel you have a slow or fast metabolism? How can you plan your meals with this in mind?

3. Looking at the food pyramid, what food group do you need to eat more or less of?

4. Define the term *metabolism*.

Nutrition: Nourishing Your Body

Key Terms

amino acids
complex carbohydrates
fat soluble vitamins
monounsaturated fats
polyunsaturated fats
Referenced Daily Intake (RDI)
saturated fats
simple carbohydrates
water soluble vitamins

Chapter 1

What You Will Learn to Do

- Analyze how well you meet nutrient guidelines

Linked Core Abilities

- Take responsibility for your actions and choices

Skills and Knowledge You Will Gain Along the Way

- Explain the six nutrients your body requires
- Explain the difference between simple and complex carbohydrates
- Describe the role fat and cholesterol play in body functioning
- Compare saturated and unsaturated fats
- Describe ways to reduce cholesterol levels
- Compare the functions of vitamins, carbohydrates, fats, and proteins
- Identify food sources of vitamins and minerals
- Define the key words contained in this lesson

Introduction

Nutrition is the science of nourishing the body properly to reach the higher levels of dynamic living. This lesson introduces you to the six nutrients and shows you how to best provide them in a diet that is well rounded yet diversified. You will learn the newest methods available in how to choose your foods and how to read labels. Finally, you will better understand how to maintain a lean body, free from the damaging effects of carrying too much personal fat.

Our diets have radically changed during the past 35 years. With the advent of fast-food outlets, an increase in dual-career parents, and sky-rocketing numbers of single-parent households, most Americans now have a hurry-up lifestyle where proper eating habits take a back seat to convenience and lack of time.

Knowing that our lifestyles are busy and sometimes hurried, it is very important that young adults have at least a basic understanding of nutrients, how to obtain them, and how to control fat. This knowledge will lead to a more dynamic life and a higher quality lifestyle. The six types of nutrients are carbohydrates, fats, proteins, vitamins, minerals, and water.

We also refer to the first three nutrients, carbohydrates, fats, and proteins, as food-stuffs. They give us the energy for all of the bodily processes. When our body uses the foodstuffs, it releases energy. We measure this energy in calories.

> **Note**
>
> To learn more about calories, see Unit 4, Chapter 1, Lesson 3, "You Are What You Eat."

Carbohydrates

Carbohydrates are the starches and sugars found in fruits, grains, and vegetables. They have a caloric value of four calories per gram and supply us with short- and long-term energy to accomplish everything from thinking and breathing to running a race.

The short-term carbohydrates are the sugars, or **simple carbohydrates**, which are quickly digested and absorbed into the blood. The most important simple sugar is glucose, or blood sugar. Before the body's cells can use other simple sugars (such as fructose, sucrose, and lactose) for energy, a change must occur converting them into glucose. Many sugary foods are sources of simple carbohydrates; however, those such as soda and candy have few other nutrients, while fruit is an excellent source of simple carbohydrates and contains many other vitamins and minerals as well.

The long-term carbohydrates are starches, or **complex carbohydrates**, which are made up of combinations of simple sugars. They take longer to digest because the body must break them into simple sugars (glucose) before they can enter the bloodstream. When your body has extra glucose that it does not need immediately for energy, it converts it into the complex carbohydrate glycogen and stores it in

Key Note Terms

simple carbohydrate – a sugar that is found in food and the body in its simple state which supplies the body with short-term energy

complex carbohydrates – a carbohydrate that is formed by the body or by plants after the conversion of simple carbohydrates, which supplies the body with long-term energy

the muscles and liver to be released later when energy is needed, usually for short periods of strenuous activity. After your muscles and liver store as much glycogen as they can hold, your body changes the rest to body fat for long-term energy. Long distance runners use carbohydrate loading (eating large quantities of carbohydrates) to have the long-term energy they need to complete the race.

Good sources of complex carbohydrates are grains (such as bread, cereal, pasta, and rice) and starchy vegetables (such as peas, corn, beans, and potatoes), as shown in Figure 1.4.1. These starchy foods are also important sources of vitamins, minerals, and fiber. Fiber provides no calories but is roughage that aids in the movement of food through the digestive system.

Nourishing Your Body's Fuel with Fats

Fats, or lipids, perform the vital roles of maintaining body temperature, insulating body organs, providing the body with stored energy, and carrying the **fat soluble vitamins** A, D, E, and K to the cells. One gram of fat is the equivalent of nine calories of energy, more than twice the amount of carbohydrates; therefore, a minimum consumption of fats is the most sensible approach to maintaining a lean body fat content.

Triglycerides are the primary fats in the foods we eat, as well as the fats stored in body tissue. They include saturated fat, which mainly comes from animal sources and does not melt at room temperature, and **monounsaturated** and **polyunsaturated fats**, which are usually liquid oils of vegetable origin. When you eat too many calories, your liver changes them into triglycerides and stores them as fat. When you eat too many **saturated fats**, your liver makes more cholesterol than your body needs, which is unhealthy. Which of the foods in Figure 1.4.2 is low in saturated fats?

Key Note Terms

fat soluble vitamin – a vitamin that is absorbed through the intestinal tract with the help of fats and is stored in the body

monounsaturated fats – oil or fat that is liquid at room temperature, is low in hydrogen, which can lower the level of blood cholesterol

polyunsaturated fats – an oil of fatty acid containing more than one double or triple bond and is, therefore, cholesterol defensive

saturated fats – a fat that does not melt at room temperature and can raise the blood cholesterol level

Cardiovascular Disease Is the Main Killer of Americans

Your liver already produces about 1,000 milligrams (mg) of cholesterol daily and diet adds another 400 to 500 mg. Cholesterol, a waxy, sticky substance found in animal and human tissue, insulates nerves and forms hormones, cell membranes, vitamin D, and bile to aid in food digestion.

Your blood carries cholesterol by way of lipoproteins, with low density lipoproteins (LDL) carrying cholesterol from the liver to the cells to accomplish the functions mentioned. Unfortunately, the LDLs deposit any cholesterol that is not needed by the cells in the arteries, giving them the nickname of the "bad guys." Cholesterol accumulated on the inside walls of the arteries is a factor in the development of atherosclerosis. Eventually, cardiovascular disease, in the form of a heart attack or stroke, may result.

The high density lipoproteins (HDL) carry the extra cholesterol in your blood to the liver to dispose of it, thus preventing cholesterol from building up in the arteries. For this reason, HDLs are known as the "good guys." To keep cholesterol at a normal level in the body, you must lower LDL levels and raise HDL levels. Steps you can take to accomplish this are to eat less fat, especially saturated fat, maintain appropriate body weight, and participate in a regular exercise program. Eating more fiber will also help because it binds with cholesterol and carries it out of the body; and consuming monounsaturated fats, such as olive, canola, and peanut oils, raises HDLs.

Figure 1.4.1: Your body needs energy from the carbohydrates found in these foods.
Courtesy of Steven Mays.

Nourishing Your Body with Proteins

The body contains substances called proteins in every cell. They aid in the development and maintenance of muscle, bone, skin, and blood. Proteins are also the key behind keeping the immune system strong. They control the chemical activities in the body that transport oxygen, iron, and nutrients to the body cells. The body can also use protein for energy if it is low on carbohydrates and fats; but in most cases, its role as an energy source is minor. Proteins, like carbohydrates, contain four calories per gram.

The building blocks of protein are the **amino acids**. These chains of carbon, hydrogen, oxygen, and nitrogen linked together in different ways control all of the body's

Key Note Term

amino acids – the basic units of proteins, produced by living cells or obtained as an essential component of a diet

Figure 1.4.2: Of the fatty foods shown, only the olive oil is low in saturated fats.
Courtesy of Steven Mays.

chemical activities. There are 22 amino acids found in the human tissue, but the body cannot manufacture all of them. Eight (nine for children) amino acids, known as the essential amino acids, must come from the food we eat because the body cannot produce them. We refer to the food products that contain all eight essential amino acids as having complete proteins. The best sources of complete proteins are meat, fish, poultry, and dairy products. Plant foods generally contain incomplete proteins since they are either low on or lack an essential amino acid. However, plant foods can be combined easily, such as rice and beans or peanut butter and bread, to include all essential amino acids in high enough amounts to form a complete protein.

The remaining 14 amino acids are known as the nonessential amino acids. They are still necessary for bodily functioning, but are called *nonessential* because they do not have to be supplied in the diet. Instead, the body manufactures nonessential amino acids itself.

Keep in mind that although animal and dairy products are sources of complete proteins, many are often high in fat as well. As you will read later in this text, Americans get most of their protein from animal sources instead of from combinations of complex carbohydrates. You will have a healthier diet and still meet your protein needs if you consume less fatty foods and more carbohydrates in the forms of grains and vegetables.

Regulating Your Body with Vitamins, Minerals, and Water

Three important components that your body needs to be healthy are vitamins, minerals, and water. Vitamins and minerals are found in the foods you eat, and water is essential for proper hydration.

Vitamins

Vitamins are promoters of health and wellness. Unlike the carbohydrates, fats, and proteins, the body does not digest vitamins; instead, food products release them and your body tissues absorb them. Vitamins are classified as either fat soluble or water soluble. With the help of fats, the intestinal tract absorbs fat soluble vitamins (A, D, E, and K) and stores them in the body. The water in the tissues dissolves the **water soluble vitamins** (B complex and C).

Many countries have standards for vitamin and mineral requirements to recommend daily amounts needed for good health. For example, the standards for the United States are the **Referenced Daily Intakes** (**RDI**). From time to time, the federal government reviews these standards and proposes new ones as research continues and more complete information about vitamins and minerals is discovered. Table 1.4.1 shows the current U.S. RDI for vitamins.

Key Note Terms

water soluble vitamin – a vitamin that is dissolved in the water of tissues

Referenced Daily Intake (RDI) – standards developed by the U.S. government for the regulation of vitamin and mineral requirements

Table 1.4.1: Vitamins

Vitamin	U.S. RDI	Functions	Sources
A	5000 International Units (IU)	Helps maintain eyes, skin, and linings of the nose, mouth, digestive, and urinary tracts	Liver, dairy products, fortified margarine, orange fruits and vegetables, and dark-green vegetables
B-1 (Thiamin)	1.5 mg	Helps convert carbohydrates into energy	Yeast, rice, whole-grain and enriched breads/ cereals, liver, pork, meat, poultry, eggs, fish, fruits, and vegetables
B-2 (Riboflavin)	1.7 mg	Helps convert nutrients into energy; helps maintain skin, mucous membranes, and nervous structures	Dairy products, liver, yeast, fruits, whole-grain and enriched breads/cereals, vegetables, meat, and poultry
B-3 (Niacin)	20 mg	Helps convert nutrients into energy; essential for growth; aids in synthesis of hormones	Liver, poultry, fish, milk, eggs, whole-grain and enriched breads/cereals; fruit, and vegetables
B-5 (Pantothenic Acid)	10 mg	Helps convert nutrients into energy	Liver, yeast, whole grains, eggs, beans, and milk
B-6 (Pyridoxine)	2.0 mg	Aids in more than 60 enzyme reactions	Milk, liver, meat, green, leafy vegetables, and whole-grain and enriched breads/cereals
B-7 (Biotin)	0.3 mg	Helps convert nutrients to energy	Liver, yeast, milk, oatmeal, beans, nuts, and egg yolks
B-9 (Folic Acid)	0.4 mg	Aids in blood cell production; helps maintain nervous system	Liver, green, leafy vegetables, and beans
B-12 (Cobalmin)	6 micrograms (mcg)	Helps form new cells	Meat, seafood, poultry, dairy products, and eggs

(continued)

Table 1.4.1: Vitamins (continued)

Vitamin	U.S. RDI	Functions	Sources
C	60 mg	Helps maintain and repair connective tissue, bones, teeth, and cartilage; promotes wound-healing	Broccoli, brussel sprouts, citrus fruit, tomatoes, potatoes, peppers, cabbage, and other fruits and vegetables
D	400 IU	Helps regulate calcium and phosphorus metabolism; promotes calcium absorption; essential for development/maintenance of bones and teeth	Fortified milk, eggs, fish-liver oils, and sunlight on skin
E	30 IU	An antioxidant (prevents oxygen from interacting destructively with other substances) that helps protect cell membranes, maintain fats and vitamin A, and increase blood flow	Green, leafy vegetables, whole grains, seeds, nuts, vegetable oil/shortening, liver, and egg yolks
K	60–80 mcg*	Helps in blood clotting	Green, leafy vegetables, liver, tomatoes, egg yolks, and milk

*No U.S. RDI established. Amount is an estimated recommendation for dietary intake.

Points of Interest: Vitamins

According to a 10-year study of 11,348 U.S. adults, vitamin C was effective at cutting death rates from heart disease and stroke. Souces of vitamin C arc illustrated in Figure 1.4.3. The study tested three groups getting

- **50 mg or morc a day in food, plus an average supplement of 500 mg**
- **50 or more mg and no supplement**
- **Less than 50 mg with no supplement**

Men in Group 1 had a 35 percent lower mortality rate and 42 percent lower death rate from heart disease and stroke. Women in Group 1 were 25 percent less likely to die of heart disease or stroke and had a 10 percent lower mortality rate.

Taking supplements of 2,000 mg of vitamin C daily might be helpful to allergy sufferers.

Figure 1.4.3: Citrus fruits, melons, papayas, tomatoes, and peppers are all high in vitamin C.
Courtesy of Steven Mays.

Minerals

Minerals are elements found in the environment that help regulate the bodily processes. Without minerals, the body cannot absorb vitamins. Macrominerals, shown in Table 1.4.2, are minerals that the body needs in large amounts. These minerals are calcium, phosphorus, magnesium, potassium, sulfur, sodium, and chloride.

Although sodium is a macromineral, many Americans consume too much of it, which can contribute to high blood pressure. High blood pressure, in turn, can contribute to cardiovascular disease. On the other hand, many Americans do not consume enough calcium, and a calcium deficiency can lead to osteoporosis later in life.

Although the body only needs trace minerals (such as selenium, manganese, molybdenum, iron, copper, zinc, iodine, and chromium, shown in Table 1.4.3) in very small amounts, they are also essential for proper functioning of the body. For example, an iron deficiency can reduce the number and size of red blood cells, causing weakness, sleepiness, and headaches. Iron is contained in many foods as shown in Figure 1.4.4.

Point of Interest: Minerals

A study has found that heart-disease patients who received 150 mcg of chromium per day had a dramatic jump in the HDL cholesterol, the good stuff that helps keep arteries clear.

Water

About 60 to 70 percent of your body is water, with most of your blood, brain, and muscles being water and even 20 percent of your bones. Water carries the other nutrients, when dissolved, to all parts of the body where and when needed. It also aids in digestion, regulation of temperature, removal of wastes, joint lubrication, and bio-

Table 1.4.2: Macrominerals

Mineral	U.S. RDI	Functions	Sources
Calcium	1000 mg	Structure of bones and teeth; muscle contraction; maintenance of cell membranes; blood clotting; nerve impulse transmission; heart activity; Helps convert carbohydrates into energy	Dairy products, small fish (such as sardines) with bones, dark-green vegetables, dried beans and peas
Phosphorus	1000 mg	Structure of bones and teeth; muscle contraction; maintenance of cell membranes; blood clotting; nerve impulse transmission; heart activity; Helps convert carbohydrates into energy	Dairy products, small fish (such as sardines) with bones, dark-green vegetables, and dried beans and peas
Magnesium	400 mg	Structure of bones and teeth; release of energy from nutrients; formation of enzymes	Meat, poultry, fish, eggs, dried beans and peas, and dairy products
Potassium	3500 mg*	Building bones; release of energy from muscle glycogen; conduction of nerve impulse to muscle	Green, leafy vegetables, nuts, soybeans, seeds, and whole grains
Sulfur	140 mg*	Muscle contraction; maintenance of fluid and electrolyte balance; transmission of nerve impulse; release of energy from nutrients	Orange juice, bananas, dried fruit, meat, bran, peanut butter, potatoes, coffee, tea, and cocoa
Chloride and Sodium	No more than 2400 mg*	Part of sulfur-containing amino acids; firm proteins of hair, nails, and skin	Meat, wheat germ, dried beans and peas, peanuts
Table salt (sodium chloride)		Regulate blood and fluids; nerve impulse transmission; heart activity; metabolic controls	many canned soups and pro-cessed foods, pickles, soy sauce, sauerkraut, and celery

*No U.S. RDI established. Amount is an estimated recommendation for dietary intake.

Table 1.4.3: Trace Minerals

Mineral	U.S. RDI	Functions	Sources
Selenium	50–75 mcg*	Prevents breakdown of fats	Seafood, whole-grain cereals, meat, egg yolks, milk, and garlic
Manganese	5 mg*	Central nervous system; normal bone structure; reproduction	Nuts, whole grains, vegetables, fruits, tea, and cocoa powder
Fluoride	1.5–4 mg*	Tooth and bone formation	Drinking water in some places, seafood, and tea
Molybdenum	75–250 mcg*	Part of enzymes	Legumes, cereals, liver, kidneys, and dark-green vegetables
Iron	18 mg	Formation of hemoglobin; part of enzymes and proteins	Liver, kidneys, meat, egg yolks, green, leafy vegetables, dried druit, dried beans and peas, and whole-grain and enriched cereals
Copper	2 mg	Formation of red blood cells; part of respiratory enzymes	Oysters, nuts, cocoa powder, liver, kidneys, beans, corn oil, and margarine
Iodine	150 mcg	Functioning of the thyroid gland and production of thyroid hormones	Iodized salt and seafood
Chromium	50–200 mcg*	Helps the body use carbohydrates and fats; aids in digestion of protein	Liver, nuts, whole grains, Brewer's yeast, meat, mushrooms, potatoes, apples with skin, and oysters
Zinc	15 mg	Part of many enzymes; essential to synthesis of DNA and RNA; metabolizes carbohydrates, fats, and proteins; dispose of carbon dioxide; strengthen immune system; helps wounds heal; helps body use vitamin A	Meat, liver, eggs, poultry, and seafood

* No U.S. RDI established. Amount is an estimated recommendation for dietary intake.

Figure 1.4.4 These foods are rich in iron. Why is iron such an important mineral?
Courtesy of Steven Mays.

chemical processes taking place in the body all the time. Without water you would die in a few days. To maintain all the bodily functions water helps carry out, you need to consume the equivalent of six to eight glasses of water a day. If you exercise regularly, you may need as many as ten glasses, especially on the days you exercise.

Hunger and Malnutrition

As long as people can easily obtain an abundant and varied diet, it is not difficult for them to meet their nutritional needs. When such fortunate people become hungry, they can usually satisfy their need for food. However, many people in the world cannot obtain enough of the right foods, and in some cases cannot get much food at all. For them, hunger is a way of life—an ongoing, painful condition over which they have little control, as depicted in Figure 1.4.5. Poor nutrition is a serious, worldwide problem.

Malnutrition

Technically, malnutrition is any condition in which a person's nutrient consumption is inadequate or unbalanced. Most cases, however, are the result of consuming too little of one or more nutrients. Malnutrition harms every system of the body and also damages emotional well-being.

When people are malnourished, they do not have the energy to perform well in school or at work. Malnourished people are also more susceptible to disease than those who eat a healthy diet. Malnourished children usually grow much more slowly than children whose diet is adequate. If malnutrition occurs during pregnancy, the baby may weigh less than normal and have serious health problems.

Figure 1.4.5: Famine victims, such as this Somalian woman, search in vain to try to find food.
Courtesy of Jean-Claude Coutausse/Contact Press Images.

There are various types of malnutrition, including the vitamin and mineral deficiencies discussed earlier in this lesson. In one especially serious condition known as protein-energy malnutrition, the diet does not contain adequate protein, nor does it supply enough calories to meet the body's energy needs. The effects of this condition are especially severe on children because their bodies need protein and calories for growth. Severe cases can cause death, either directly through starvation or indirectly through the diseases to which its victims become susceptible. Protein-energy malnutrition is the most serious nutrition problem affecting people in developing countries today.

Malnutrition has various causes. In some cases, people may be undernourished because they are unaware of the foods that they need for good health. Also, diseases and other conditions may prevent the digestive system from absorbing nutrients. But, indirectly, poverty is by far the most common cause of malnutrition. Victims of severe poverty cannot afford to buy or grow the food they need.

A World Problem

Hunger and malnutrition are an especially severe problem in many of the world's poorer nations. Severe famines, for example, have devastated countries such as Somalia and Bangladesh. However, hunger is also a problem in more prosperous countries, including the United States. Although few people starve in the United States, many are not receiving adequate nutrition. Hungry people in the United States are those who have little or no income, such as homeless people, teenage runaways, families dealing with unemployment, and some elderly people.

Various programs and organizations are trying to solve the problem of malnutrition and provide food for those who need it. For example, the Food and Agriculture Organization of the United Nations combats hunger by helping people improve methods of agriculture and food distribution. The U.S. government sponsors the Food Stamp Program that enables low-income people to purchase the food that they need. Volunteers also work hard to help those who are hungry. For example, soup kitchens, which are often staffed by volunteers, provide meals for those in need.

Conclusion

Understanding what nutrition your body needs is essential to maintaining both physical and emotional health. Without the proper balance of carbohydrates, fats, proteins, vitamins, and minerals, you open the door to all kinds of health problems—some possibly fatal. Even with a fast-paced lifestyle, it's still possible to eat correctly and give your body the fuel it needs.

Next, you will learn about dietary guidelines. You will examine the National Academy of Sciences' 2001 report on how we should eat, as well as some alternative choices that many nutritionists advocate.

Lesson Review

1. How do carbohydrates help the body?
2. Compare and contrast monounsaturated fats and polyunsaturated fats.
3. What roles do proteins play in nutrition?
4. What are the effects of malnutrition?

Lesson 5

Dietary Guidelines

Key Words

amenorrhea
anorexia nervosa
bulimia
diuretics
electrolyte
episodic
esophageal

What You Will Learn to Do

- Relate the NAS dietary guidelines to your personal diet

Linked Core Abilities

- Communicate using verbal, nonverbal, visual, and written techniques
- Take responsibility for your actions and choices

Skills and Knowledge You Will Gain Along the Way

- Identify the nine National Academy of Sciences dietary goals
- Identify factors that affect the nutritional requirements of individuals at various life stages
- Identify signs and symptoms of anorexia nervosa and bulimia
- Examine varying viewpoints on vitamin and mineral supplement usage
- Calculate your personal blueprint
- Define the key words contained in this lesson

Introduction

Today's hurry-up lifestyles, diverse family structures, fast-food restaurants, and personal finances have all impacted on the way we eat. Thus, by our actions, America has become a country that is overweight and suffering greatly from cardiovascular disease, cancer, diabetes, and other ailments that hinder our efforts to live a dynamic lifestyle.

This lesson explains the National Academy of Sciences' report on how we should eat, as well as some alternative choices that many nutritionists advocate.

The Lifetime Eating Plan

Nutritional needs vary at different ages. There are different needs for children (age two to adolescence), adolescents, adults, and the elderly. There are also special conditions and needs for pregnant women.

For example, the special concerns for teens are that they often have erratic eating habits, their calcium requirements are high, and after the onset of menstruation, females need more iron. General dietary recommendations are to ensure you eat sufficient calories to support your growth and activity levels with high-carbohydrate foods. Also, consume iron-rich foods and keep healthy snacks available.

Pregnant women need to increase their caloric intake and to eat adequate protein, iron, calcium, folic acid, and vitamin C. Proper nutrition is essential to avoid complications, including nausea, heartburn, constipation, and gestational diabetes. General dietary recommendations are to eat two dairy servings daily and two cups of calcium-rich vegetables; also eat green leafy vegetables, legumes, broccoli, asparagus, and whole grains. Avoid overcooking. An obstetrician may recommend supplements. Drink at least eight glasses of liquid daily. Avoid alcohol and caffeine.

The New American Diet—Step by Step

Another popular eating plan is the New American Diet. This plan yields similar dietary recommendations as those explained elsewhere in these nine guidelines. However, the basis for this plan is the development of a healthier lifestyle by following a three step approach: Phase I stresses the use of substitutions to your present diet; Phase II introduces new recipes; Phase III prescribes a new way of eating.

Eating Disorders

Eating disorders such as **anorexia nervosa** and **bulimia** are common in today's society. People with anorexia nervosa experience extreme weight loss, **amenorrhea**, and a variety of psychological disorders culminating in an obsessive preoccupation with the attainment of thinness. However, for 10 to 15 percent of its victims, the disease becomes **episodic** and relentless, resulting in death from the consequences of starvation.

A person with anorexia nervosa normally exhibits the following characteristics:

> ## Key Note Terms
>
> **anorexia nervosa** – an aversion to food syndrome; an eating disorder characterized by an extreme (prolonged) loss of appetite and very decreased food intake
>
> **bulimia** – a disease (or eating disorder) with symptoms of binging and purging or overeating and vomiting
>
> **amenorrhea** – an abnormal absence or suppression of the menstrual period
>
> **episodic** – occurring, appearing, or changing at irregular intervals; incidental

- An unwillingness to maintain minimal normal body weight for the individual's age and height; weight loss that leads to the maintenance of a body weight 15 percent below normal; or a failure to gain the amount of weight expected during a period of growth, resulting in a body weight that is 15 percent below normal.

- An inordinate fear of gaining weight and/or becoming fat despite being significantly underweight.

- An unrealistic perception of body weight, size, or shape. The person "feels fat" or perceives that one specific part of the body is "too fat."

- An absence of at least three, otherwise normal, menstrual cycles.

On the other hand, people with bulimia experience alternate cycles of binge eating and restrictive eating. Purging usually follows binges, primarily by self-induced vomiting supplemented with the use of laxatives and **diuretics**. The physical and psychological results of such a struggle with bulimia include **esophageal** inflammation, erosion of tooth enamel caused by repeated vomiting, the possibility of **electrolyte** imbalances, and altered mood states, particularly anxiety and depression.

A person with bulimia normally exhibits the following characteristics:

- An episodic eating binge, characterized by rapid consumption of large amounts of food in a short time.

- At least two eating binges per week for at least three months, even possibly experiencing a loss of control over eating behavior while in the process of binges.

- Frequent purges after eating; then engages in fasting, strict dieting, or vigorous exercise.

- A constant concern over body shape, size, and weight.

If you think someone has an eating disorder,

- Express your concern about the person's health. Although the person may deny there is a problem, show that you care.

- Try to focus on feelings that the person may be experiencing, such as excessive worrying, anxiety, poor self-esteem, anger, or hurt. Encourage the person to talk about issues not related to food. Be a good listener.

- Encourage the person to talk to parents, relatives, or a health care or mental health professional.

- Talk to someone else (possibly a professional) about your concerns for that person.

- Do not label the person. That may make the person feel accused and strengthen feelings of denial.

Key Note Terms

diuretics – food, medication, etc., that promotes or tends to increase the excretion of urine

esophageal – of or relating to the esophagus (a muscular tube through which food passes from the mouth to the stomach)

electrolyte – substance that, when dissociated into ions in solution or fused, becomes electrically conducting; obtained from minerals in the diet

Getting Help for Eating Disorders

For more information about anorexia, bulimia, and other eating disorders, contact:

National Eating Disorders Association

603 Stewart St., Suite 803

Seattle, WA 98101

(206) 382-3587

www.nationaleatingdisorders.org

The National Academy of Sciences believes there is a close association between total fat intake, saturated fat, high cholesterol, and heart disease. They developed nine guidelines for reducing the risk of chronic diseases and helping to provide protection against the possibility of early disease.

> **Note**
>
> The American diet should consist of a total fat intake between 35 to 40 percent of the total calories consumed each day; however, the typical American diet consists of nearly 50% fat calories.

Guideline #1

The goals of this guideline are to reduce your total fat intake to 30 percent or less of your total calories, your estimated fatty acids (building blocks of fat) intake to less than 10 percent of your total calories, and your cholesterol intake to less than 300 milligrams. Take a look at Figure 1.5.1 and determine which of these foods has the lowest percent are of saturated fat.

Tips for achieving these goals include the following:

- **Limit your egg intake. Use two or three egg whites for every yolk. Cholesterol is in the yolk, and egg white is a great source of protein.**

- **Use skim milk non-fat or one percent milk. Purchase low-fat or non-fat cheeses, yogurt, and other dairy products.**

- **Use margarine sparingly. The soft tub or liquid margarine is best.**

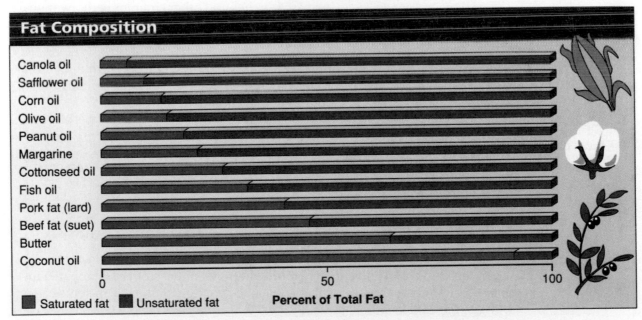

Figure 1.5.1: Which of the fat sources in the graph is lowest in saturated fat?
Courtesy of Function thru Form.

- **Read labels. Avoid foods that contain trans-fat.** Trans-fat causes the same type of damage in your arteries as saturated fats and cholesterol. Trans-fat is found in foods that contain solid plant fat, such as stick margarine, cream filling in cookies, and baking shortening.

- **When ordering in a restaurant, tell the waiter to ask the chef to use only half the oils or fat products he would normally use.**

- **Try to eat three servings of fish per week.** Cold water and deep sea running fish are best because of the high omega three oils (fat that may aid in the maintenance of the heart and blood vessels).

- **Eat lean meat and then sparingly.**

- **Bake and broil meat products, if possible.**

- **Use the lowest saturated fat cooking oils.**

- **When eating snacks, choose low-fat, low sugar content sweets.**

- **Learn how to read a label and calculate the fat content in food products.**

Figure 1.5.2 shows a sample food label that might appear on a package.

Alternative Guideline #1

An alternative goal for Guidelines #1 is to reduce fat intake to 20 percent or less of your total calories, saturated fat to 5 percent of your total, cholesterol intake to 100 milligrams, and use only 4 to 7 teaspoons of mono- or polyunsaturated fat a day.

Your eating habits can affect your health. Try to develop an eating plan that will keep you at your healthiest level and avoid eating disorders. A discussion of two acceptable eating plans and two common, potentially dangerous eating disorders was given at the beginning of this lesson.

Guideline #2

The goal of Guideline #2 is to increase starches and other complex carbohydrates, as shown in Figure 1.5.3. The typical American diet consists of 22 percent complex carbohydrates and 24 percent sugar.

General dietary recommendations are to receive 60 to 65 percent of your diet from the carbohydrate group, 50 to 55 percent of that from the complex carbohydrates, and 20 percent from sugar, with most of that coming from fruits.

> **Note**
>
> Almost all nutritionists agree with the National Academy's number two guidelines. By choosing those percentages, you will receive more than adequate amounts of fiber.

Guideline #3

The goal of this guideline is to maintain protein intakes at moderate levels. Americans receive 68 percent of their protein from animal sources (compared to 4 to 5 percent for the Chinese). There is evidence pointing to the rise in some cancers with the increase in animal protein.

The body needs no more than 0.45 of a gram of protein per pound of lean body weight per day. Since the minimum requirement is 0.16 grams per pound, 10 to

Nutrition Facts		
Serving Size: 1/2 cup (114 g)		
Servings Per Container: 4		

Amount Per Serving

Calories 260	Calories from fat 120

	% Daily Value*
Total Fat 13 g	20%
Saturated Fat 5 g	25%
Cholesterol 30 mg	10%
Sodium 660 mg	28%
Potassium 400 mg	11%
Total Carbohydrate 31 g	11%
Sugars 5 g	
Dietary Fiber 0 g	0%
Protein 5 g	10%

Vitamin A 4%   Vitamin C 2%
Iron 4%   Calcium 15%   Vitamin D 25%

* Percent (%) of a Daily Value is based on a 2000 calorie diet. Your Daily Values may vary higher or lower depending on your caloric needs:

Nutrient		2000 Calories	2500 Calories
Total Fat	Less than	65 g	80 g
Sat Fat	Less than	20 g	25 g
Cholesterol	Less than	300 mg	300 mg
Sodium	Less than	2400 mg	2400 mg
Potassium		3500 mg	3500 mg
Total Carbohydrate		300 g	375 g
Dietary Fiber		25 g	30 g
Protein		50 g	65 g

Calories per gram
Fat 9   Carbohydrate 4   Protein 4

Figure 1.5.2: A typical food label gives you information about the contents of the product.

* Note: Trans-fat will be added to food labels by January, 2006.

15 percent of your food should come from proteins and the majority of that from plant sources.

Alternative Guideline #3

The American Heart Association recommends no more than two protein servings daily. However, the U.S. Department of Agriculture recommends two to three servings of the milk, cheese, and yogurt group daily and two to three servings of the meat, poultry, fish, beans, eggs, and nuts group.

Guideline #4

The goal of this guideline is to balance food intake and physical activity to maintain appropriate body weight. Approximately 1/3 of the American population is

Figure 1.5.3: Breads are excellent sources of starch.
Courtesy of Steven Mays.

overweight. Overweight teenage boys are more likely to die at a higher than usual rate by the age 45. Teenage girls who are overweight are eight times more likely to have trouble in later years with daily routines such as climbing stairs, lifting, and walking.

To balance food intake and physical activity requires planning each day's food intake based upon these guidelines as well as each week's physical activities to include at least three 30-minute workouts. While in school, participating in sports programs and daily physical activities is the best way to accomplish this goal.

Alternative Guideline #4

Body weight is not the best indicator of measuring food intake versus physical activity. Measurement of body fat is a healthier indicator and a much more concise measuring tool in determining the best balance of food intake and physical activity. Also, the more fat that accumulates around the stomach represents more of a danger to the person.

Fewer than 10 percent of Americans over age 18 exercise vigorously and regularly. Exercise can decrease a person's chance of dying of heart disease, cancer, and a host of other illnesses.

Guideline #5

The main goal of Guidelines #5 is to avoid alcoholic beverages. Alcohol can produce the following problems with nutritional balance and wellness:

- **Upsets metabolism**
- **Produces fullness, thus the person does not eat a balanced diet**
- **Increases nutritional needs**
- **Causes inadequate assimilation (digestion and absorption) of the nutrients**

It is not easy to avoid the temptation of alcoholic beverages particular with the pressure that our peers put upon us. The best way to avoid alcoholic beverages is to make the decision not to drink an alcoholic beverage before it is offered to you.

Alternative Guideline #5

Try to avoid putting yourself into a situation that will force you to make the choice to drink or not to drink alcohol. First make the decision not to drink alcoholic beverages and let your friends know that alcohol is not for you. Whenever possible, avoid parties and other events where alcohol is served. If you have to attend these events, always plan ahead and have your decision made.

Guideline #6

The goal here is to limit the daily intake of salt to no more than 3 grams. Salt is 60 percent chloride and 40 percent sodium. Too much sodium can lead to high blood pressure in some people (those who are salt sensitive). Furthermore, salt absorbs water in the body, causing the blood pressure to increase because of the larger volume of water the heart must pass through the system. Try to avoid adding salt to your meals. It is best not to add table salt to any of your meals. All processed or manufactured food has salt added. Just read the label on any canned food and you will be surprised how much salt has already been added.

Alternative Guideline #6

There are several ways that you can cut down on your salt intake, including the following:

- **The National Academy of Sciences recommends no more than 2400 milligrams (1/2 teaspoon; 2.4 grams) of salt a day. One teaspoon of salt is equivalent to 5 grams.**
- **Switch to "lite" salt, thus reducing the sodium content by one half. You can also increase potassium (too little increases blood pressure) by using "lite" salt.**
- **Eat less processed or manufactured food.**
- **Avoid snack food or use unsalted varieties.**
- **Limit smoked foods.**
- **Limit brine prepared foods such as pickles, olives, and sauerkraut.**

Guideline #7

The goal for Guideline #7 is to maintain adequate calcium intake. Most Americans do not receive enough calcium from their normal diets. Ninety-nine percent of our body's calcium is present in the bones and teeth. One percent aids in the functioning of the blood, muscles, and nerves.

To meet its need for calcium, the body will pull calcium from the bones, causing them to lose their density. This condition, known as osteoporosis, can lead to hip, leg, and arm fractures. Diets that are low in calcium may also cause hypertension (high blood pressure) and some forms of cancer.

The referenced daily intake for ages 11 to 24 is 1200 milligrams a day. Adult men and women need 1000 milligrams. Pregnant and nursing women also need 1200 milligrams. To prevent osteoporosis:

- **Participate in lifelong weight-bearing exercises to ensure the density of the bones**
- **Avoid excessive protein**
- **Eat a diet rich in calcium (skim milk, certain fruits, and vegetables)**
- **Take calcium supplements, if needed**
- **Avoid starvation diets**
- **Avoid alcohol and smoking**

Alternative Guideline #7

A well-balanced diet following the Food Guide Pyramid guidelines, as shown in Figure 1.5.4, ensures adequate calcium intake. Make sure that there is a variety of colors on your plate each meal. For example, dark leafy green vegetable just like dairy products contain calcium.

Figure 1.5.4: The Food Guide Pyramid provides guidance for a well balanced diet.

Note

For more information on the Food Guide Pyramid, see Chapter 1, Lesson 3, "You Are What You Eat."

Guideline #8

The goal for Guideline #8 is to avoid taking dietary supplements in excess of the referenced daily intake in any one day.

There are two schools of thought on this guideline. One says that we can get all of our vitamins and minerals from our normal diet without supplementation. The other opinion is that by taking supplemental dosages of specific vitamins and minerals, we can protect ourselves from birth defects, cataracts, cardiovascular disease, and cancer, as well as strengthen the immune system.

Alternative Guideline #8

As an alternative to Guideline #8, you can

- Take a general vitamin/mineral supplement daily, not to exceed the RDI
- Take a calcium supplement
- Take antioxidant vitamins in supplemental form: vitamin C, vitamin E, and beta-carotene (See the following nutrition prescription for an additional alternative)

Note

Always consult a healthcare professional before taking any supplements.

Your Nutrition Prescription

Vitamin and mineral supplements are indispensable anti-aging weapons, but too many people use them shotgun style—a handful of this, a bunch of that—instead of coordinating them for the most life-lengthening strategy. To ensure that you are not over- or underdoing any element, you need a prescription customized for your age, gender, health, and lifestyle. Look at the Supplement Blueprint in Table 1.5.1 and see how much of each supplement you take. Then answer the following six questions. For each yes answer, follow the directions for revising the Supplement Blueprint. If you end up with more than one recommendation for a particular nutrient, follow the highest single dosage.

- Are you male? Delete iron.
- Do you smoke or live/work with a smoker, or do you live in an air-polluted area? Increase C to 1000 mg, selenium to 400 mcg, beta-carotene to 25,000 IU, E to 400 IU, copper to 3 mg, and zinc to 50 mg.
- Do you exercise at least three times a week for 20 or more minutes? Increase E to 400 IU, magnesium to 400 mg, B-1 to 100 mg, and zinc to 50 mg.
- Are you on the Pill (birth-control pills)? Increase B-6 to 50 mg.

Table 1.5.1: Personal Supplement Blueprint

Personal Supplement Blueprint		
Supplement	**Longevity Standard**	**My Dose**
Beta-carotene	15,000 IU	_____
Vitamin A	10,000 IU	_____
Vitamin B-1	25 mg	_____
Vitamin B-2	25 mg	_____
Niacinamide	100 mg	_____
Pantothenic acid	50 mg	_____
Vitamin B-6	25 mg	_____
Vitamin B-12	100 mcg	_____
Biotin	100 mcg	_____
Folic acid	400 mcg	_____
Vitamin C	500 mg	_____
Vitamin D	400 IU	_____
Vitamin E	200 IU	_____
Calcium	1,200 mg	_____
Chromium	100 mcg	_____
Copper	2 mg	_____
Iodine	150 mcg	_____
Iron*	18 mg	_____
Magnesium	200 mg	_____
Manganese	5 mg	_____
Molybdenum	50 mcg	_____
Selenium	200 mg	_____
Zinc	30 mg	_____

* Double-check with your doctor before adding iron to your regimen. Some people are prone to iron overload.

Courtesy of US Army JROTC.

- **Are you pregnant or nursing? Increase folic acid to 800 mcg, iron to 60 mg, calcium to 1300 mg, and magnesium to 400 mg. Delete A.**

- **Do you have high cholesterol levels and/or a family history of heart disease? Increase E to 400 IU, C to 1000 mg, beta-carotene to 25,000 IU, chromium to 200 mcg, and magnesium to 400 mg.**

According to Ronald Hoffman, Director of the Center for Holistic Medicine in New York City, supplements are especially important for people who do not eat (1) fresh fruits and vegetables daily; (2) dairy products more than once a week; or (3) at least two full meals a day. Some of the above recommendations are higher than the U.S. RDI's because longevity research has leapfrogged over the old standards. However, all recommendations are well within safety guidelines. Avoid taking more than the amounts suggested; mega dosing can be dangerous. Remember, check with your doctor before starting any supplement regimen.

Guideline #9

The goal for this guideline is to maintain an optimal intake of fluoride, particularly during tooth formation, which normally continues until the beginning of the teenage years. The requirement for sufficient intake of fluoride begins during pregnancy to ensure proper tooth and bone development.

Fluoride is important to tooth and bone formation. It makes the teeth harder, and they can resist decay and breakdown. Only two-thirds of the U.S. population receives fluoridated water. The National Research Council of the National Academy of Sciences recommends 1 milligram of fluoride for each liter of water consumed.

Alternative Guideline #9

Most cities and towns in the United States add fluoride to the communities' drinking water, which provides the fluoride needed to help fight tooth decay; however, it is also recommended that you brush your teeth with a fluoride toothpaste to ensure that you are providing adequate protection for your teeth.

Conclusion

The nine guidelines presented in this lesson are the results of one of the most comprehensive scientific analysis of potential health risks and benefits stemming from diet. Implementing these guidelines means that we will need to devote more time and attention to our daily diets and the risk factors associated with improper diets.

In the following lesson, you learn tips and hints to help control your intake of fats in your diet. You will also learn that some fat is essential to good health.

Lesson Review

1. **What is the goal for total daily fat intake?**
2. **What are the differences between anorexia nervosa and bulimia?**
3. **What are the signs of anorexia nervosa and bulimia?**
4. **What is the general dietary recommendation for daily carbohydrate intake?**

Controlling Fat

Key Words

basal metabolic rate (BMR)
essential fat
storage fat

What You Will Learn to Do

- Estimate your body fat content

Linked Core Abilities

- Take responsibility for your actions and choices

Skills and Knowledge You Will Gain Along the Way

- Identify the risks of obesity
- Explore tendencies that encourage fat accumulation
- Define current and desired state for healthy lifestyle
- Identify steps that can lead to a lean body fat content
- Relate food intake and physical activity to weight control
- Define the key words contained in this lesson

Introduction

In today's society, obese and overweight people, young and old, seek corrective advice from all types of organizations and individuals. These "experts," for many reasons, attempt to encourage and control what we eat, how we eat, when we eat, how much of what we eat, etc.

In this lesson, you learn how it is possible, without difficulty, to carry an amount of fat that is helpful and encourages the dynamic living principle. You will see in the simplest terms a method designed to keep you healthy and promote enjoyment of living while participating in life to your fullest potential.

Fat Control

When you are obese or overweight, you increase your risk of cardiovascular disease, high blood pressure, gall bladder disease, diabetes, and certain types of cancer. It also prevents you from performing actively at your highest potential and raising your self-esteem and self-assurance.

Determining whether you are obese or overweight is not dependent on how much you weigh on a scale. All of us have our own unique and special body types, which include our inherited strengths and weaknesses and tendencies that encourage accumulation of fat in our formative years, such as the following:

- **Family eating habits**
- **A tendency to develop more fat cells**
- **A large skeletal structure**
- **Any number of unproved theories passed down through the years**

To ensure that you follow a proper and proven method for obtaining a healthier lifestyle, we will present you with a few guidelines on learning how to control your fat intake.

The steps to controlling body fat are a combination of restricting your fat intake, adequate exercise, making the right food choices, and understanding how to measure your body fat and how to use that information in your overall wellness program.

Step 1: Restricting Your Fat Intake

Most of us are continually trying to lower our body fat. When you diet, the body says you need to store more fat instead of less fat. This causes, especially in females, the body to slow down, which reduces the fat burning enzymes. Therefore, with each diet you undertake, the body reduces more fat burning enzymes, making it harder for you to lose fat. But remember, fat levels that drop too low are also unhealthy and unsafe. A certain amount of **essential fat** is necessary to maintain the bodily functions discussed earlier.

> ### Key Note Term
>
> **essential fat** – fat which the body needs in certain amounts to maintain bodily functions

For example, most women should not go below eight percent, as this would upset the menstrual cycle, the ability to conceive children, and eventually hormonal balance. In men, the lower limit is approximately three to four percent.

Storage fat, on the other hand, is our fat reserve that can become a problem for many of us. Women in general seem to have a greater propensity to store fat. The reason for this is probably estrogen, which increases the fat-storing capability. Evidence points to the hips, thighs, and buttocks as the body's most desirable storage areas.

The following are ratings of body fat percentages by age and gender:

Key Note Term

storage fat – fat that the body keeps in reserve that can lead to over fat problems or obesity

Males ages 18 to 30:		Females ages 18 to 30:	
Athletes	6–10%	Athletes	10–15%
Good	11–14%	Good	16–19%
Acceptable	15–17%	Acceptable	20–24%
Possibly needs help	18% and over	Possibly needs help	25% and over
	(Obese/Overweight)		(Obese/Overweight)

The average-weight adult has approximately 25 to 30 billion fat cells, whereas the average overweight adult has between 60 to 100 billion. Some overweight people can have as many as 200 billion. Many factors are responsible for the development of these fat cells. Despite all the reasons, a person's growth and/or activities may or may not use all of the foods, or calories, consumed. The body will store the non-used calories as fat. For maximum benefit, keep saturated fat to a minimum. Count your total fat intake over a seven-day period. If you foul up, just cut back the next day.

When your fat content is where you desire, the next step is to develop a lifetime guideline for healthy eating. Calculate your daily intake of carbohydrates, fats, and proteins (as you did in the Journal Exercises in the previous lessons). Then choose one of the following plans and stick to it. The two plans that best enhance the dynamic living profile are #2 and #3. Whichever plan you select will require an effort on your part to make it succeed; but it will work and you can enjoy the benefits of that change.

Plan #1 (Average American Diet)		Plan #2 (The New American Diet)	
Fat	37–42%	Fat	20%
Saturated Fat	12–15%	Saturated Fat	6%
Protein	10–15%	Protein	10–15%
Carbohydrates	40–45%	Carbohydrates	60–65%

Plan #3 (The Lifetime Eating Plan)		Plan #4 (U.S. Dietary Goals)	
Fat	10%	Fat	30%
Saturated Fat	Low	Saturated Fat	10%
Protein	10–15%	Protein	10%
Carbohydrates	75–80%	Carbohydrates	60%

Step 2: Exercise–How the Body Burns Food (Calories/Energy)

In addition to eating a healthy diet, you must follow an exercise program to maintain a lean body fat content. Balancing how many calories you consume with how many calories your body burns daily is the key to maintaining body fat content and weight. People gain body fat when they consume more calories daily than their bodies use for energy. Keep in mind that one pound of body fat contains approximately 3,500 calories. Therefore, if a person wants to lose a pound of body fat in one week, he or she must burn 3,500 calories more than he or she consumes over the course of the week.

Your body burns calories even when it is at complete rest. **Basal metabolic rate** (**BMR**) is the number of calories burned at complete rest, and it varies based on age, health, and body size, shape, and weight. For example, after age 25, most people's BMR decreases approximately 1 percent because their requirements for energy slow down. In addition to your BMR, your body burns calories through muscle activity; and while you do not have much control over your BMR, you do have control over the amount of physical activity in which you participate. Obviously, the more active you are, the more calories you use.

Choose an exercise program that accomplishes the two goals of improving your heart and lungs, as well as working your muscles. You can increase the efficiency of the heart and respiratory system through exercises such as jogging, swimming, and biking that increase the heart rate and maintain it for a set period of time. The time will vary based on your age, abilities, and the exercise being performed.

The second goal of working your muscles includes toning your muscles and/or increasing your muscle size and improving your muscle strength. Because muscle burns more energy than fat, the more muscle tissue you have, the more calories you burn. This is also true of your BMR, meaning that even at rest, the more muscle mass you have, the more energy your body will burn. You can work your muscles through weight training and exercises such as push-ups and sit-ups.

Step 3: Food Control and Choice

People eat for many different reasons: they feel hungry, the time of day, they missed a meal, or they are following their families' eating routine. Whatever the reason to eat at any given time, it is the choice of food that will truly make the difference in whether you will develop an overweight problem or maintain the dynamic living profile.

As you learned in previous lessons, the most recent USDA-approved Food Guide Pyramid can be accessed at www.mypyramid.gov. This is an interactive Website where you can enter your age, gender, and level of activity to design an eating program geared towards your body type and lifestyle. For example, if you are a 16-year-old female who gets 30 to 60 minutes of exercise per day, you should be getting 2,000 calories per day, consisting of:

- **Six ounces of whole grains (breads, pastas, cereals, and so on)**
- **Two and a half cups of vegetables (it is recommended that you eat more dark green vegetables such as spinach and other leafy greens; orange vegetables such as sweet potatoes and squashes; dried beans and peas)**

> ### Key Note Term
>
> **basal metabolic rate –** the number of calories burned at complete rest; measurement of it indicates an individual's general metabolism or state of health

- **Two cups of fruit (fresh, frozen, dried, or canned, but try to go easy on the fruit juices)**
- **Three cups of milk (low- or no-fat is preferable)**
- **Five and a half ounces of lean protein foods (broiled, grilled or baked) with a variety of chicken, fish, beans, peas, nuts, and seeds**

Limit your oil (butter and other fats) intake to six teaspoons per day, and try to avoid an excess of sugar. You should strive to limit your extra oils and sugars to 265 calories per day.

Step 4: Measuring Your Body Fat

This section presents two fairly accurate methods of measuring your body fat. Follow the directions and do not be discouraged. Body types differ, and you are your own special person.

Pinch an Inch Test

Remember, your body does not need large amounts of fat. When your storage, or reserve, fat begins to melt away, you can determine the right level by using the "pinch an inch" test as a simple method of measuring and maintaining your body's fat.

You can perform the "pinch an inch" test by pinching the skin fold of your triceps (women only), waist, or thighs between your fingers. If the fat is over an inch between your thumb and forefinger, you might consider continuing your fat control program.

Estimating Body Fat

Jack H. Wilmore, an exercise physiologist at the University of Texas in Austin, created the following ways to measure body fat.

Women: Measure the circumference of your hips at the widest point and plot that measurement and your height on the chart in Figure 1.6.1. Then, using a straight

Figure 1.6.1: Estimating body fat for women.
Courtesy of US Army JROTC.

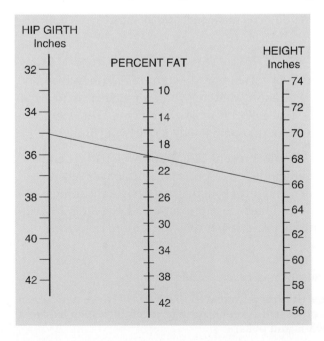

Chapter 1   Achieving a Healthy Lifestyle

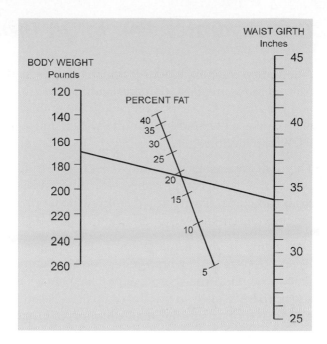

Figure 1.6.2: Estimating body fat for men.
Courtesy of US Army JROTC.

edge, draw a line connecting the two plots. Your body fat percentage is where the line crosses the percent fat column. Refer to the appropriate chart in Step 1 to see if your fat content is acceptable, good, athletic, or needs help.

Men: Refer to Figure 1.6.2 and measure the circumference of your waist at the exact level of the belly button, making sure to keep the tape perfectly horizontal. Plot that measurement and your weight on the chart at the top of the next column. Then, using a straight edge, draw a line connecting the two plots. Your body fat percentage is where the line crosses the percent fat column. Refer to the appropriate chart on in Step 1 to see if your fat content is acceptable, good, athletic, or needs help.

The Road to Fat Control

A 1992 Consumer Reports survey with 68 nutrition experts indicated a deepening concern over America's dietary habits and implicated the leading causes of death as being associated with eating and drinking. The causes of death are coronary artery disease (heart attack), cancer, cerebral vascular disease (stroke), diabetes, liver disease, bowel disorders, and osteoporosis.

The 68 experts agreed on a reasonable diet for the American people as one that closely resembles the dietary guidelines set forth by the U.S. RDI and the Department of Health and Human Services. Additionally, the experts were much more deliberate in defining an "ideal" diet as one that maximizes the immune system, reduces the risk of disease, and minimizes the process of aging.

By understanding the experts' opinions and responses, you can develop a formula that promotes a healthier lifestyle. If used properly, this formula can improve your immune system and risks against the leading causes of death, keep your body fat at a healthy level, and enhance your potential to maintain an ideal body fat content for life.

Carbohydrates: How to Eat Them

A definition of natural foods is one that fits the carbohydrate category perfectly. Natural foods are foods that are as unrefined as possible and free from additives and preservatives. Fruits, vegetables, and grains in their natural state are the key elements to a maximized immune system and a body fat content that will maintain itself for a lifetime.

There is growing evidence that a diet rich in fruits, vegetables, and grains will reduce the risk of certain cancers. Such a diet will also protect the heart and bones from early breakdown and infirmity, which limit millions of Americans from enjoying their potential.

Depending on your gender, body type, and level of activity, experts recommend at least three ounces of whole grains, a variety of fruits and vegetables, low- or no-fat dairy products, broiled, grilled, or baked meats, and a limited amount of fat and sugar. To be realistic in our hurry-up lifestyles, this may not be possible. However, evidence supports eating small amounts of these natural products several times a day for maximum benefit.

When you design your own eating program at www.mypyramid.gov, you can ensure you will be receiving all the carbohydrates you need (20 to 35 grams a day) without worrying about supplemental fiber. Plus, there is also room to enjoy a sweet treat. But remember, look at the label and keep the fat content at a reasonable level, and your sugar intake to nearly zero.

Protein: Don't Worry

If you are eating the recommended amounts of carbohydrates in a diversified manner, tests indicate you will receive your complete protein needs without concern. Most of your protein (about 85 to 90 percent) should come from plant sources or the complex carbohydrates. Studies indicate that populations eating a high degree of protein coming from animal products (as are the Americans with 70 to 75 percent) will have a higher incidence of problems.

Vitamins, Minerals, and Water: The Regulators

In general, the experts believe that you can receive your vitamins and minerals in sufficient amounts from a well-balanced diet. They also suggest that you drink water at a rate of six to eight glasses per day—more if you work out rigorously.

Planning a Balanced Diet

Up and down Elm Street, families begin the day with healthy breakfasts. The Gilmores eat bran muffins, orange juice, and shredded-wheat cereal with milk. Across the street, the Lins sit down to a traditional Korean breakfast of soybean soup with chunks of bean curd (tofu) and rice.

People's food choices are influenced by many factors, one of which is their culture. The term *culture* refers to the way of life of a group of people, including their customs and beliefs. Food is one important aspect of culture. As the two breakfasts demonstrate, different groups consume different foods. Look at Figure 1.6.3 and imagine which breakfast you would choose.

Both culture and personal preferences affect the types of food that are served in your household. Some families may dislike fish, for example, while others may choose not to eat red meat. In addition, most people respond to peer pressure when selecting food; when you eat a meal with friends, you may choose different foods than when you are by yourself or with your family. Your economic situation also plays a role in what you decide to eat. People with low incomes cannot afford to buy certain foods.

Breakfast Menu	Vegetable Group	Fruit Group	Dairy Group	Meat-Poultry-Fish-Dry Beans-Eggs-Nuts Group	Grain Group
Yogurt and fruit; whole-wheat toast		✔	✔		✔
Peanut butter on bread; orange juice; milk		✔	✔	✔	✔
Tortilla with beans and cheese; vegetable juice	✔		✔	✔	✔
Cream of tomato soup; crackers and cheese	✔		✔		✔

Figure 1.6.3: Breakfasts can be as varied as you want them to be. Which of these breakfasts would you choose?
Reprinted from *Health Skills for Wellness*, Third Edition, by B. E. (Buzz) Pruitt, Kathy Teer Crumpler, and Deborah Prothrow-Stith, (2001), Prentice Hall, Inc.

When you are making decisions about what to eat, consider the nutrition content of foods, as illustrated in Figure 1.6.4. There are many ways of meeting your nutritional needs, no matter what your preferences are. With a little imagination, you can have a variety of well-balanced meals and snacks.

Meals

What is your favorite meal of the day? Whether it is breakfast, lunch, or supper, it and your other meals should provide you with a balance of healthy nutrients.

Breakfast

Even if you are rushed in the morning, do not neglect breakfast, because many nutritionists believe that breakfast is the most important meal. After a night without food, your stomach is empty, and your body needs fuel for the day's activities. A good, balanced breakfast should provide as much as one-third of your daily food needs. If your breakfast is inadequate, you may be tempted later to eat snacks that are low in nutrient density.

Lunch

School cafeterias provide nutritionally balanced meals planned by dietitians. Some school cafeterias even offer nutritious snacks, salad bars, and special diet foods. Because lunch makes up another third of your food needs for the day, make sure that you choose nutrient-dense foods. You might, for example, eat a turkey sandwich on whole-wheat bread, a salad, a carton of milk, and an orange.

Supper

In many cultures around the world, lunch is the major meal of the day. In the United States, the biggest meal is generally the evening meal. Because you may be less physically active after this meal, supper should not account for more than the final third of your daily calorie needs. The evening meal can be an opportunity to

Figure 1.6.4: You are in control of the foods you select in the school cafeteria. Be sure to consider the nutrient value of your lunch selections.
Courtesy of Ken Karp.

Chapter 1   Achieving a Healthy Lifestyle

fill in gaps in the day's Food Guide Pyramid selections. Suppose, for example, you have not eaten foods from the vegetable group at breakfast and lunch. You might volunteer to prepare a fresh green salad for dinner that includes several vegetables, such as spinach, carrots, and celery.

Snacks

Snacks can contribute significantly to your nutritional needs if you choose them wisely. However, many snack foods, such as those frequently sold in movie theaters, vending machines, and the snack-food sections of supermarkets, are high in fats and sugar and low in nutrient density. If you fill up on chips, soft drinks, and candy bars, you may have no appetite for the nutrient-dense foods that you need. Moreover, because snack foods are often high in calories, frequent snacking may result in unwanted weight gain. Finally, many snack foods, such as soft drinks and chocolate, contain caffeine, which can cause nervousness and sleeplessness.

For snacks, choose foods with a high nutrient density. Instead of an evening snack of cookies, try satisfying your craving for sweets with some fruit. Make a bagel, not a doughnut, your after-school treat. When you go to the movies, choose unbuttered popcorn instead of chips or candy.

Fast Foods

Picture this: You and a friend drop by you favorite fast-food restaurant several times a week for a meal of double cheeseburgers, fries, and shakes. Table 1.6.1 shows a nutritional breakdown of your favorite fast-food meal.

Similar to this one, many fast-food meals are high in fat and calories. When you eat in fast-food restaurants, follow these guidelines:

- **Substitute low-fat or nonfat milk or orange juice for shakes and soft drinks**
- **Select the salad bar in place of fries and onion rings**
- **Choose a grilled chicken sandwich instead of a hamburger or cheeseburger**
- **Sauces and dressings can add a lot of fat. Use them sparingly**
- **Taste food before adding extra salt to it**

Improving Your Diet

The Food Guide Pyramid's recommendations can help you select specific kinds and amounts of food. In addition, nutrition experts have identified some general ways in which the American diet can be improved. Their recommendations, called the Dietary Guidelines for Americans, can help you plan a healthy diet.

Table 1.6.1: Calories and Fat in a Typical Fast-Food Meal

Food	Total Calories	Calories from Fat	Percent Calories from Fat
Double cheeseburger	490	245	50%
French fries	330	160	49%
Chocolate shake	290	14	5%
Total for whole meal	1,110	419	38%

- **Eat a variety of foods.** To obtain all the different nutrients you need, choose a wide selection of foods.

- **Balance the food you eat with physical activity to maintain or improve your weight.** Health problems can develop if you are too fat or too thin.

- **Choose a diet with plenty of grain products, vegetables, and fruits.** These foods are especially rich in starch and fiber.

- **Choose a diet low in fat, saturated fat, and cholesterol.** Choose lean meats, fish, poultry, and legumes instead of fatty meat. Cut away all visible fat on meats, and remove the skin from poultry. Limit fried foods, including potato chips, french fries, and doughnuts.

- **Choose a diet moderate in sugars.** Foods high in sugar are high in calories but often low in more useful nutrients. Limit your intake of sweet snacks and soft drinks.

- **Choose a diet moderate in salt and sodium.** Sodium, which is found in table salt and salty foods, has been linked to high blood pressure. Avoid eating too many salty snacks, pickled foods, luncheon meats, and canned soups. Do not add salt to foods at the table.

- **Adults who use alcohol should do so in moderation.** Alcoholic beverages are very low in nutrient density. In addition, as you will learn later, alcohol can damage every system in your body. Many adults choose not to drink at all, but those who do drink alcohol should strictly limit their intake.

Changing Nutritional Needs

Just as your body changes throughout life, so do your nutritional needs. During infancy, childhood, and adolescence, the body needs great amounts of all the nutrients necessary for physical growth. Teenagers need ample protein in their diets to support their physical growth. Adolescents also need significant amounts of iron; girls lose iron during menstruation, and boys need additional iron to support the development of muscle mass. The need for calcium also reaches its peak during the teenage years. Adolescent girls, in particular, are advised to eat calcium-rich foods as a means of preventing the weakening of bone that can occur later in life.

After adolescents become adults, their activity levels generally decrease, and continue to go down as they grow older. As activity decreases, so do energy needs. For this reason, adults need to watch their caloric intake carefully. Older adults, moreover, may need to increase the fiber in their diet as an aid to digestion. With proper attention to their nutritional needs, older people can live healthy and vigorous lives.

Managing Your Weight

Are you content with your weight, or would you like to change it in some way? If you are comparing yourself to athletes, film stars, and friends whose appearance you admire, you may be trying to achieve a weight that is unrealistic for you—and even unhealthy. When people have unrealistic expectations about their weight, they sometimes develop eating disorders such as anorexia nervosa and bulimia. However, some people do have good reasons for wanting to lose or gain weight. Those reasons relate to health, and not to some idealized concept of beauty or handsomeness.

Assessing Your Weight

Cassie and her best friend Thuy are the same height. Cassie weighs 10 pounds more than Thuy, but both girls have a weight that is appropriate for them. Thuy is small-boned, while Cassie has a larger bone structure. In addition, Cassie is very athletic, and some of her extra weight is in the form of muscle mass, not body fat. A person's appropriate weight depends on various factors, including body structure and level of activity. Your appropriate weight is one that you feel comfortable with, one that does not present any health risks. A physician or nutrition expert can help you determine your appropriate weight.

The amount of body fat, rather than weight, should be your concern. Various tests measure body fat. In one test, for example, an instrument called a skin-fold caliper is used to measure the fat deposits that accumulate under the skin.

Even though you do not have skin-fold calipers, you can get a rough idea of whether or not you have too much body fat. Pinch a fold of skin on your upper arm and estimate its thickness. If the fold of skin is more than one inch (2.5 centimeters) thick, you may have excess fat. However, remember that your estimate is not as accurate as a test done by a professional who is trained in evaluating weight problems.

Appetite, Hunger, and Metabolism

If an appropriate test has determined that you should change your weight, you will probably need to modify your eating habits. Once you have achieved a healthy weight, you will want to maintain it. To maintain a healthy weight, the number of calories that you eat each day should match the daily calorie needs of your body.

Calories are units of energy. If you eat more calories than your body can use, it will store the excess energy as fat, causing you to gain weight. A diet that contains fewer calories than you need, can make you lose weight.

Your calorie needs are partly determined by your activity level; the more active you are, the more calories you need. In addition, your basal metabolic rate—the rate at which you use energy when your body is completely at rest—affects your calorie needs. The higher your basal metabolic rate, the more calories you will burn. Various factors affect basal metabolic rate. For example, older people tend to have a lower basal metabolic rate than do younger ones. Children and pregnant women tend to have higher basal metabolic rates than the rest of the population. Regular exercise may help increase a person's basal metabolic rate.

If you are trying to change your eating habits, your task will be easier if you understand the physical and emotional factors that make you crave food. Hunger is a feeling of physical discomfort that is caused by your body's need for nutrients. Appetite, in contrast, is a desire for food that is based on emotional factors rather than nutritional need. Unlike hunger, which is an inborn response, appetite is learned. For example, suppose you smell chicken roasting. Your appetite may make you want to eat the chicken because you have learned to associate that particular aroma with a delicious taste. Your appetite may sometimes make you eat even when you are not hungry.

Appetite and hunger are not the only factors that affect people's eating behavior. Emotional stress, for example, can influence eating. Some people crave more food when they experience stress, while others lose their appetite. People may eat because they are bored or because they are with others who are eating.

Dangers of Obesity

If you frequently eat more calories than you need, you risk becoming overweight. People are overweight if they weigh more than 10 percent above their appropriate weight. The condition known as obesity (oh BEE sih tee) occurs when a person's weight is 20 percent or more above an appropriate weight. Obesity can create many serious health problems and risks, as illustrated in Figure 1.6.5. Obese people may suffer from high blood pressure and experience difficulty breathing. Being obese also increases a person's risk of heart attack, stroke, diabetes, arthritis, and certain forms of cancer. People who are significantly overweight should make every effort to reduce to a healthier weight.

Reducing Weight and Fat Safely

A sensible program of weight loss involves choosing nutritionally balanced meals and snacks. Even though you want to reduce the number of calories that you consume, you still need to make sure that you are obtaining the nutrients necessary for good health. Choose low-calorie foods that are high in nutrient density.

Recognizing Eating Patterns

Before you plan your diet, keep a diary of what you presently eat. Record the foods that you consume, when you eat them, and how you feel at these times. Use calorie guides to count the approximate number of calories you consume each day.

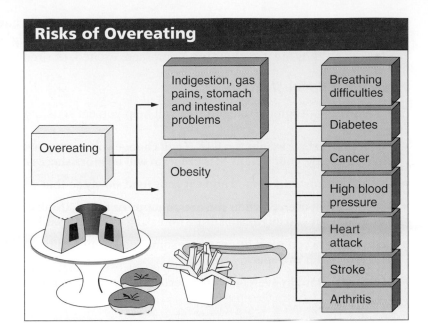

Figure 1.6.5: Overeating can lead to obesity. People who are obese have an increased risk of developing many health problems.
Courtesy of Function thru Form.

Dieting Myths and Facts

There are many myths and facts surrounding diets and dieting.

MYTH: Eating starchy foods, such as bread and pasta, will make you gain weight.

FACT: Starchy foods, or complex-carbohydrate foods, have fewer calories per ounce than fats.

MYTH: You can lose a lot of weight just by exercising.

FACT: To lose a pound by exercising alone, you would need to run for 4 1/2 hours or do aerobics for more than 6 hours.

MYTH: You can lose weight if you don't eat breakfast.

FACT: Omitting any meal is likely to make you overeat at the next meal. If you skip breakfast, you will probably eat an extra-large lunch.

MYTH: You can lose weight by eating only one food, such as grapefruit, bananas, rice, or celery.

FACT: Because one-food diets are monotonous and nutritionally inadequate, dieters return to previous eating patterns and regain weight.

MYTH: Drinking caffeine always makes your appetite decrease.

FACT: Caffeine can make the level of sugar in your blood drop. This can make you hungry.

MYTH: After you lose weight, you can then resume your former eating habits.

FACT: Maintaining weight loss means changing eating and exercise patterns for the rest of your life.

As you review your diary, you may discover eating patterns or behaviors you were not aware of. You may even find out what triggers your overeating. Some people overeat when they are disappointed, depressed, excited, or tired.

Planning Helpful Strategies

The following are some strategies that will help you eat sensibly:

- **Do not try to lose weight too fast. If you change your eating habits gradually rather than suddenly, your weight-loss program will be more successful in the long run.**

- **Take small portions of food and eat your food slowly so that you can enjoy its taste.**

- **If you tend to overeat when you are unhappy or bored, think of an enjoyable behavior that you might substitute for eating—taking a walk, for example.**

- **To avoid between-meal hunger, save some food from regular meals, such as bread, and later eat it as a snack.**

- **If you occasionally overeat, do not become upset. Just go back to your sensible eating habits.**

Exercising

Your weight reduction program should involve regular exercise, such as walking, dancing, or swimming. Changing your eating habits alone is far less effective than eating changes combined with exercise. When you decrease your calorie intake but do not exercise, your basal metabolic rate goes down. Thus your body does not burn calories as rapidly as it did before you began reducing your calorie consumption, and your weight loss slows or stops.

Fad Diets, Diet Aids, and Fasting

Many people want to lose weight very quickly, so they rely on strategies such as fad diets, pills, or fasting. These approaches are unrealistic and unsafe.

Fad Diets

A fad diet is a popular diet that may help a person lose weight but without proper regard for nutrition and other matters of health. Fad diets range from high protein, low carbohydrate diets to diets with special ingredients that are supposed to help you burn fat. These diets often exclude some important nutrients.

The weight loss achieved with a fad diet is usually only temporary. Frequently, fad diets restrict food choices too much. People become so bored with the diet's limitations that they stop dieting and begin to overeat again.

Diet Pills

Diet aids, such as pills and candies, are supposed to suppress the appetite. However, they are usually ineffective and can be habit-forming. The major ingredient in most diet pills is caffeine, which may cause nervousness, sleeplessness, and high blood pressure. Diet aids do not provide long-term weight control. If you want to lose weight and keep it off, you need to change your eating behavior rather than rely on medication.

Fasting

When people refrain from eating all foods, they are fasting. Fasting is not a healthy way to lose weight, because muscle tissue as well as fat is lost. Long-term fasting may stunt your growth. It may also put a strain on your kidneys and cause hair loss. It has even been linked with irregular menstrual periods in girls and women.

Gaining Body Weight Wisely

Being too thin can be as emotionally painful as being too heavy. You are under-weight if you weigh at least 10 percent less than appropriate. If you are under-weight, remember that teenagers as a rule need a large number of calories for growing. Eventually, your growth rate will become slower and then stop. You may put on weight when you are in your early twenties. In addition, some people are naturally thinner than others, and thinness is not a health problem unless it is excessive. However, since underweight can be an indication of health problems, underweight people should be checked by a physician.

The goal of gaining weight can best be achieved by changing any habits that keep you too thin. Eliminate snacks right before mealtimes because they may spoil your appetite. When you do snack, choose nutrient-dense foods, as shown in Figure 1.6.6, that are high in calories. Never skip a meal. At mealtimes, take bigger help-ings of food than usual. While you are increasing your caloric intake, do not neglect exercise. Exercising will help you gain healthy muscle tissue as well as fat.

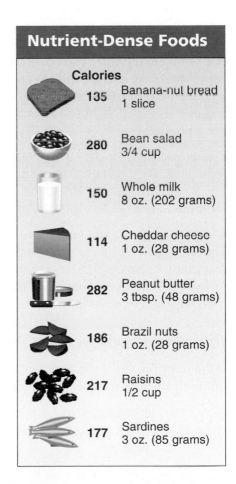

Nutrient-Dense Foods

Calories

135	Banana-nut bread 1 slice
280	Bean salad 3/4 cup
150	Whole milk 8 oz. (202 grams)
114	Cheddar cheese 1 oz. (28 grams)
282	Peanut butter 3 tbsp. (48 grams)
186	Brazil nuts 1 oz. (28 grams)
217	Raisins 1/2 cup
177	Sardines 3 oz. (85 grams)

Figure 1.6.6: If you are try-ing to gain weight, snack on nutrient-dense foods such as these.
Courtesy of Function thru Form.

Special Diets

People's circumstances may call for special diets. Certain physical conditions, such as diabetes and hypoglycemia, have special nutritional requirements. Lifestyle choices, such as the decision not to eat meat, may also affect how people meet their dietary requirements.

Diet and High Blood Pressure

As blood flows through your body, it exerts a force called blood pressure that pushes against the walls of your blood vessels. High blood pressure, or hypertension, is a condition in which this force becomes too strong. Sodium, found in table salt and many other foods, is thought to be a factor in high blood pressure. People with high blood pressure need to limit their sodium intake. They can do this by using herbs and spices instead of table salt to add flavor to foods. They also need to avoid salty snack foods, such as potato chips. Many processed foods, such as soup mixes and canned vegetables, contain large amounts of sodium. Therefore, people with high blood pressure need to read food labels carefully to avoid high-sodium foods.

Diets for Diabetics

Glucose is the principal carbohydrate that circulates in your blood and is used by your cells for energy. A substance called insulin enables glucose to pass from the blood into the body's cells. Diabetes mellitus is a disorder in which the body does not produce or properly use insulin, resulting in high levels of glucose in the blood. Symptoms may include sudden excessive thirst, an increase in appetite combined with a loss in weight, and frequent urination. Some people also feel fatigued, irritable, and confused. If you have a combination of any of these symptoms, you should see a physician.

Diabetes usually can be controlled. Some diabetics may need to take daily insulin injections. They also need to eat balanced meals and exercise on a regular schedule. Frequently people with diabetes carry a snack that they can eat to regulate their blood glucose levels if they are unable to eat a regular meal.

Diabetics' diets should help to control blood glucose levels by leaving out foods high in sugar and focusing on complex carbohydrates. The American Diabetes Association also emphasizes the importance of foods high in fiber and low in fat. Obesity is a factor in one type of diabetes, and those diabetics need to control their weight. For more information, go to www.ada.com (American Diab. Assoc.)

Diet and Hypoglycemia

If the body produces too much insulin, the level of glucose in the blood may fall dramatically. The result is a condition known as hypoglycemia, or low blood sugar.

People with hypoglycemia may experience hunger, weakness, severe headaches, and shakiness as their blood glucose levels fall. Hypoglycemics need to eat several small meals per day instead of three big ones, with foods rich in complex carbohydrates and low in fat. Concentrated sweets, such as candy, should be avoided altogether.

Vegetarianism

A person who does not eat meat is called a vegetarian. Some vegetarians eat no foods that come from animal sources. Others, however, include eggs and dairy products. Complete proteins contain all the essential amino acids, but incomplete proteins do not. Vegetarians who eat no food from animal sources must make sure that their diets contain all the essential amino acids. Complete proteins can be obtained from a combination of plant foods. For example, beans and rice are a complete protein and are illustrated in Figure 1.6.7.

Vegetarians are less likely than others to suffer from heart disease, a problem that can result from eating too much animal fat. In addition to protein, however, vegetarians must make sure that they are obtaining adequate supplies of the vitamins and minerals they need. Variety is therefore especially important in a vegetarian diet. Protein sources from the Meat and Beans group for vegetarians include eggs (for ovo-vegetarians), beans, nuts, nut butters, peas, and soy products (tofu, tempeh, veggie burgers). Check out http://www.mypyramid.gov/tips_resources/vegetarian_diets.html for more information on how you can eat a healthy vegetarian diet.

Figure 1.6.7: Because rice and beans contain complementary proteins, when you eat both together, you obtain all the essential amino acids.
Courtesy of Steven Mays.

Nutrition and Pregnancy

A woman's diet during pregnancy, see Figure 1.6.8, must provide for her needs as well as the needs of the developing baby. When a mother's diet is inadequate, she may give birth to a premature baby or a baby who weighs less than normal. A baby with a low birth weight may be susceptible to disease and slow to develop mentally and physically.

Most pregnant women should gain between 25 and 35 pounds (about 11 to 16 kilograms) during the pregnancy. To do this, they need to consume more calories than they did before pregnancy (about 300 extra calories per day). A pregnant woman also needs extra amounts of protein and the vitamin folate, since both of these nutrients are essential for the formation of the baby's cells. The minerals calcium, phosphorus, and magnesium are needed for building the baby's teeth and bones. Iron is especially important. Without it, the baby might not get enough oxygen from its mother's blood. For this reason, extra iron is often prescribed during pregnancy.

Pregnant teenagers have higher nutrient needs than any other group in the population. Since pregnant adolescents themselves are still growing, their diets need to supply both them and their babies with nutrients needed for growth. Young pregnant teenagers—those between the ages of 13 and 16—are encouraged to gain about 35 pounds (16 kilograms).

Diets for Athletes

Athletes should eat a basic well-balanced diet but with added calories to accommodate a higher level of physical activity. Most of these calories should come from an increase in complex carbohydrates. High-fat and sugar-rich foods should be avoided. During competition, athletes should drink plenty of fluids to replace water lost in perspiration.

You have probably heard of runners practicing carbohydrate loading before a long race. Carbohydrate loading consists of greatly increased carbohydrate intake,

Figure 1.6.8: During pregnancy, a woman needs to provide nutrients for herself and her developing baby.
Courtesy of David Dempster/ Offshoot Stock.

accompanied by decreased levels of exercise, in the days immediately before a competition. This practice is an attempt to make extra carbohydrates available to supply energy for the muscles. Carbohydrate loading may benefit highly conditioned athletes who participate in long-lasting sports such as marathon running. However, for most athletes, the best policy is just to eat their normal diet.

Buying Food Wisely

To choose nutrient-dense foods, you need knowledge and practice. When you buy food, do not be swayed by attractive packaging. Instead, use food labels and other information to evaluate foods as shown in Figure 1.6.9.

Food Labels

The U.S. Food and Drug Administration (FDA) requires manufacturers of foods list certain information on a food's label. Labels must provide the name and address of the manufacturer, the weight of the food, and a list of ingredients in descending order of weight. It must also indicate the number of servings per container, based on a standard serving size for that type of food.

Nutrition Information

Food labels must also provide facts about the nutrient content of the product. The nutrition information on food labels is especially important for consumers to read and evaluate. The label indicates the following for each serving:

- **The total number of calories per serving**
- **The number of those calories that come from fat**
- **The weight, in grams or milligrams, of nutrients such as saturated fat, total fat, cholesterol, sugar, dietary fiber, total carbohydrates, protein, and certain minerals**
- **The percentage of the Daily Values for different nutrients that are supplied by the food**

Manufacturers are free to volunteer additional information. Any claims relating to nutrition or health, however, must meet FDA standards.

Figure 1.6.9: When you examine a food label, you should check the fat and calorie content of the product.
Courtesy of Ken Karp/A&P Supermarket, Scarsdale, NY.

Food Additives

When you have read a food label, have you ever noticed a series of long chemical names in the ingredients list? These are food additives. Additives are chemicals that are added to a food to prevent spoiling, to control and improve color and texture, to replace or add nutrients, or to improve flavor. While some people may be allergic to specific additives, such as artificial colors, food additives are safe for most people.

Additives that are used to prevent spoilage or to keep foods from losing their natural color or texture are called preservatives. For example, the preservative *calcium propionate* prevents mold from growing on baked goods. Other preservatives keep peeled and cut fruits from becoming brown. Many preservatives prevent food poisoning and increase the length of time that a food is safe to eat.

Often when a food is canned or processed in some other way, some of its vitamins and minerals may be lost. When nutrients are added to replace those that have been lost, the food has been enriched. Some breads and cereals are enriched with the vitamins *thiamin, riboflavin, niacin,* and the mineral *iron.* If vitamins, minerals, and even proteins are added to a food that does not normally contain them, the food is fortified. Milk, for example, is fortified with vitamin D. The types of foods shown in Figure 1.6.10 are frequently enriched or fortified.

Figure 1.6.10: During processing, nutrients are added to fortified and enriched foods such as those shown here.
Courtesy of Steven Mays.

Sometimes manufacturers use additives to improve the texture or taste of foods. A leavening agent makes baked goods rise. An emulsifier (ih MUHL suh fy ur) is used to keep fats from separating from the other ingredients in a food. Emulsifiers in salad dressing, for example, keep the fat from floating to the top.

Evaluating Foods

Wise shoppers check the nutrient content of foods. Price and freshness are other characteristics to consider.

Nutrients

Carefully read the label on a packaged food. Check the number of calories and whether the food contains large amounts of fat or sugar. Compare similar foods to determine which are more nutritious. If you are choosing breakfast cereals, for example, look at the amount of dietary fiber, vitamins, minerals, and protein in different products.

Freshness

Many foods, such as meat and baked goods, have a date on their packages. This product date is an estimate of how long the product is usable. Reduced-price foods may not be a bargain if the product date has already passed.

Price

To find out which of two competing products is the better buy, compare the unit price, or cost per unit of measurement. The unit price is usually expressed in ounces or pounds. Suppose, for example, a 20-ounce loaf of bread and a 16-ounce loaf of bread both cost $1.50. The 20-ounce loaf has a unit price of about 8 cents per ounce, while the 16-ounce loaf costs about 9 cents per ounce. If both these loaves have approximately the same nutrients, which is the better buy?

Advertising and Food Choices

Advertising can have a strong influence on food choices. Often advertisers use special techniques, such as humor and lively music, to make products appealing. A television commercial for frozen waffles, for instance, may show a smiling, healthy-looking family. Yet the label on the waffles may reveal that the product is not particularly nutritious. As a smart food consumer, be aware that advertisements can mislead you.

Reading a Food Label

Every time you go into a supermarket, you see thousands of different food products: cereals in brightly colored boxes, snack foods in shiny foil bags, and frozen dinners in packages that can be used in a microwave oven. Attractive and convenient packaging is designed to make you want to purchase the product. In addition, before you even enter a store, advertisements in magazines, newspapers, and television try to convince you to buy certain foods.

To judge the nutritional value of a food, do not rely on advertisements or nice looking packages. Instead, read the food label carefully. The U.S. Food and Drug Administration (FDA) requires packaged foods to be labeled with a list of ingredients and nutrition information.

To use food labels to make healthy food choices, use the following steps:

1. Read the ingredients. Be aware of the ingredients that a food contains.

   - Become familiar with terms for different kinds of ingredients. For example, even if the word *sugar* does not appear on the label, the product may contain sugar; words ending in -*ose* are generally the names of different sugars.

   - Notice that ingredients are listed in order by weight from most to least.

   - If you have specific dietary restrictions, it is especially important to check the ingredients list first. For example, people who have an allergy for a particular food need to make sure that the product does not contain that ingredient.

2. Notice the number of servings per container. Serving sizes are standardized for over 100 different food categories, so you can compare similar food products for the number of servings they provide. For example, if you need enough lasagna to feed four people, a brand that provides four servings in one container may be a better purchase than one that provides only three servings per container.

3. Note the calories in one serving. Keep in mind that recommended daily caloric intake levels vary depending on a person's age, sex, weight, basal metabolism, and activity level. Active teenagers usually need more calories than do older people.

   - If the number of calories is high and you are trying to lose weight, you might want to choose a different food.

   - If you are trying to gain weight, a high-calorie food may be a good choice, as long as it provides useful nutrients.

4. Look at the percentages of the Daily Values. The food label indicates what percentages of the Daily Values for different nutrients are supplied by that product. For example, if the label says "Vitamin C—20%," that food supplies 20 percent of the vitamin C that the average person should obtain each day. Notice that the Daily Values are based on a diet of 2,000 calories per day.

   - Check the percentages of valuable nutrients, such as dietary fiber, iron, calcium, and vitamins. Is this food a good source of many nutrients that you need?

   - Also note the percentage of nutrients that you should limit, such as saturated fat and cholesterol. If a food is high in those nutrients, you may want to avoid it.

5. Read any health-related descriptions or claims. The FDA sets standards for the use of descriptions such as "high fiber" and "low fat." You can use those descriptions for guidance. Also notice any health claims on the package. For example, a label can indicate that high-calcium foods may help prevent osteoporosis.

Conclusion

The science of nourishing the body properly is a continually revolving door of facts, information, and misleading information. Much of the data is very conflicting and difficult to sort out, although there is some material that has remained consistent throughout the years. A basic understanding of this information will enable you to stay properly nourished.

To begin building a healthy diet, the Dietary Guidelines of Americans provides the following advice:

- **Eat a variety of foods to obtain the energy, proteins, vitamins, minerals, and fiber you need for good health.**

- **Maintain a healthy weight to reduce your chances of having high blood pressure, heart disease, a stroke, certain cancers, and the most common kind of diabetes.**

- **Choose a diet low in total fat, saturated fat, and cholesterol. Because fat contains over twice the calories of an equal amount of carbohydrates or protein, a diet low in fat can help you to maintain a healthy weight.**

- **Choose a diet with plenty of vegetables, fruit, and grain products that provide the needed vitamins, minerals, fiber, and complex carbohydrates, which can also help you to lower your intake of fat.**

- **Use sugars only in moderation. A diet with lots of sugars has too many calories and too few nutrients for most people.**

- **Use salt and sodium only in moderation.**

- **Avoid drinking alcoholic beverages. Although alcoholic beverages supply calories, they have little or no nutrients. Furthermore, drinking alcohol is the cause of many health problems and accidents.**

This lesson presented up-to-date information and numerous guidelines from which you can make proper dietary choices. However, there are still many unanswered questions, such as "What is the role of supplementation?" and "How much fat is too much?" In the future, there will be more discoveries, which will lead to unlocking more doors and to expanding our understanding and potential for a dynamic, healthier way of life.

In the next lesson, you get even more information about living a healthy lifestyle and how you can take better care of yourself.

Lesson Review

1. **What are the risks of obesity?**
2. **What tendencies encourage fat accumulation?**
3. **Describe a desired state for a healthy lifestyle.**
4. **List the steps that you can take to achieve a lean body fat content.**

Lesson 7

Taking Care of Yourself

Key Terms

ampule
bivouac
chlorine
disinfect
dysentery
galvanized
hygiene
iodine
lice
personal hygiene
purified
sanitation

What You Will Learn to Do

- Analyze the impact sanitation and hygiene has on health

Linked Core Abilities

- Apply critical thinking techniques

Skills and Knowledge You Will Gain Along the Way

- Recognize the benefits of maintaining good hygiene habits

- Explain how to keep clean in field conditions

- Explain the correlation between physical fitness and hygiene

- Identify possible results of poor sanitation

- Detail procedures of disinfecting water

- Explain how to guard against food poisoning and the spread of germs though waste

- Define the key terms contained in this lesson

Introduction

Key Note Terms

hygiene – practices or conditions that aid in good health; the science that deals with maintenance of good health and the prevention of infection and disease

sanitation – the promotion of hygiene and prevention of disease by working to keep a clean and healthy environment

Exercise, rest, and good **hygiene** and nutrition can help you stay healthy and avoid many illnesses and infections. In other words, you can prevent disease and injury by taking good care of yourself. You learned about the importance of nutrition and exercise to your health in the previous lesson. This lesson covers the importance of good hygiene habits. In particular, it discusses hygiene and **sanitation** when attending JROTC summer camp or camping on your own, with friends, or family. In these cases, you may not have the modern conveniences of clean, running water or indoor plumbing, but you must still know how to take care of yourself to help prevent illness and maintain good health.

Personal Hygiene

Key Note Term

personal hygiene – an individual's practice of taking care of him or herself in order to maintain good health

Most likely, there are certain habits that you perform routinely at the start of each day. You are probably so accustomed to doing them that you do not give them a second thought. First, you wake up after resting your body during the night. Then you shower if you did not shower the night before, wash your face, and comb your hair. It is now time for breakfast—some toast and cereal perhaps. And, last but not least, you brush your teeth and leave for school.

Now, stop for a minute and think about the activities that we have just described. They involve rest, nutrition, and cleanliness, three elements that are important to maintaining good health and are a part of **personal hygiene**.

It is easy for most of us to practice personal hygiene in our homes where there are sinks, showers, toilets, and clean water, all of which help with sanitation. In some situations, however, practicing personal hygiene and maintaining sanitary conditions take more effort and require greater care. For example, if you are camping, you may have to work harder at hygiene and sanitation depending on conditions at your campsite. Also, when you are staying in close quarters with several other people, like at JROTC summer camp, hygiene and sanitation become extremely important. The poor sanitation or hygiene habits of one person can lead to a disease or illness that affects an entire group.

Personal hygiene is important to maintain your personal health and establish your health image to other people. A neat, clean, physically fit person illustrates a healthy image and a positive leadership posture.

Principles of Hygiene

It is not always simple to apply the basic principles of personal hygiene. It takes a conscience effort to follow these principles and to stay healthy.

Field Sanitation

The following story illustrates the importance of maintaining all aspects of health and sanitation when out in the field.

On Togatabu Island in 1942, the 14th Artillery and the 404th Engineer Battalions were part of a task force preparing to attack Guadalcanal. Fifty-five percent of the engineers and 65 percent of the artillerymen contracted a disease called "Filariasis," transmitted by mosquitoes. Both units had to be medically evacuated without seeing any enemy action because they were not combat ready. The use of insect repellent and insecticides and the elimination of standing water would have prevented the spread of this disease.

Often in military history, the health of the troops influenced the course of battle more than strategy or tactics. "Historically, in every conflict in which the United States has been involved, only 20 percent of all hospital admissions have been from combat injuries. The other 80 percent have been from diseases and nonbattle injuries." (*Field Hygiene and Sanitation*, FM 21–10)

Hand Hygiene

Hand washing needs to be second nature. It is important to wash your hands after contact with an animal, after using the toilet, before eating or touching a person at risk from infection. A good routine needs to include removing of any jewelry, wetting hands with warm water, using an anti-bacterial soap If available, washing vigorously for at least 30 seconds, rinsing hands, and drying hands on a clean towel or using a hand drying machine. Figure 1.7.1 demonstrates that hand hygiene is also important in the field.

Oral Hygiene

After each meal or at least twice a day, you need to eliminate food particles and dental plaque as well as clean your gums. Visiting the dentist twice a year is also recommended. Use fluoride toothpaste and brush up and down in a light circular

Figure 1.7.1: Washing your hands is essential particularly in the field.
Courtesy of Corbis Images.

motion, in front, behind and across the top of the teeth for at least three minutes. Avoid putting objects and fingers in your mouth as well as sugar and sweets that encourage germ proliferation.

Personal Hygiene

A dirty body is a hotbed for developing germs. Dust, sweat, and other secretions, and warmth are all factors which encourage germs to multiply. A shower with effective soap and shampoo should follow any physical activity. Showering daily is necessary to maintain good personal health. Clean clothes should be worn and underwear changed daily; the fabric in clothes is a breeding ground for many germs. Imagine how you would feel if you did not bathe for a week. Now imagine how others would feel about having to be around you during that time. Uncleanliness or disagreeable odors affect the morale of others, so the solution is for everyone to take personal responsibility for their own hygiene.

Nasal Hygiene

Nasal secretions are highly contagious. Runny noses and sneezing are sources of germ dissemination. Frequent nose blowing using a disposable paper tissue clears the nostrils and limits the spread of germs. Repeated blowing of the nose can cause irritation, so use a soft tissue and blow softly.

Food Hygiene

Food poisoning is on the rise. Some of these cases can be linked to the food processing industry and centralized distribution of food. You can reduce your risk of food poisoning by following simple yet effective hygiene practices. High-risk foods include eggs and egg products, poultry, (particularly chicken), and food eaten raw. It is estimated that 50 percent of domestic food poisoning cases are due to poor hygiene in the home. Refrigeration is a means of reducing the spread of germs and not the elimination of germs. Refrigerators need to be cleaned on a regular basis. Food that needs refrigeration needs to be kept at the recommended temperature; food that does not need to be kept refrigerated should be stored as indicated on the packaging, and the date indications on food packaging should be followed.

Cooking food is an excellent way of keeping germs from spreading. Cooking food at sufficiently high temperature will eliminate many germs. Rigorous hygiene is also required in the kitchen. Always wash hands before handing food. Wash frequently any cloths and towels used in the kitchen. Avoid using wooden chopping blocks, salad bowls and spoons because nicks or cracks can create an ideal place for germs. Kitchen utensils should not be used to prepare different dishes unless they have been cleaned in between. Table and worktops should be cleaned with an anti-bacterial product between preparing different types of food. You should also watch for the country of origin of the food you eat; note the best before dates on food labels; and use the most effective practices in food preparation.

Pet Hygiene

Most people today spend a great deal of time with a pet or pets. Our pets carry a number of germs as well as affect allergy sufferers. However, it is easy to apply simple rules of hygiene without affecting the bond between people and pets. Animals need to be cleaned regularly. Also it is essential to disinfect a pet's scratch or bite with an antiseptic. Clean everything that your pet touches on a regular basis. Floor areas used by an animal should also be cleaned, paying particular attention to allergen traps such as carpets and bedding. Hands should always be washed after touching an animal.

Adapted from the Institut Pasteur's Web site, January 4, 2005.

Stay Physically Fit

People who are physically fit are less likely to get sick or injured, so participate regularly in a fitness program. Physical fitness training will also help you become adjusted to a field environment. Remember to use caution when exercising in extremely hot or cold weather particularly if you are going to run long distances (Figure 1.7.2).

Get Enough Sleep

The average person needs eight hours of sleep a night. Make sure you get enough sleep so you have the energy to effectively complete the required tasks of your day. You may have a harder time sleeping when you are away from home, bunking with others, or camping. Follow these suggestions to get as much rest as possible.

Figure 1.7.2: Staying physically fit will help you succeed in the field.
Courtesy of David Madison.

- Sleep as much as you can before going someplace where you may not be able to sleep comfortably or as much as you should

- Take catnaps whenever you can but expect to need a few minutes to wake up fully

- When in the field, follow your leader's instructions and share tasks with other cadets so everyone gets time to sleep

- After going without sleep, catch up as soon as possible

- Learn and practice techniques to relax yourself quickly

If you have not gotten enough sleep in the field and are required to remain awake and alert, try these suggestions:

- Play mental games or talk with other cadets to stay alert during dull watches or critical jobs such as driving at night

- Take short stretch breaks or do light exercises in place

- Do not trust your memory; write things down and double check your communications and calculations

- Watch out for your mind playing tricks (like seeing things that are not there) when you are very tired; check strange observations before acting

Learn to Reduce Stress

Stress begins in the mind but causes physical reactions in the body. Although stress can be beneficial in small doses by supplying you with bursts of energy to complete a project on time or compete in an important game, stress that continues over long periods of time can weaken your immune system and lead to exhaustion and illness. People under too much stress may not care for themselves properly or be able to complete tasks effectively.

To keep yourself healthy and efficient, you must learn to relax and reduce stress. The following hints may help:

- Maintain a positive attitude

- Do not try to do more than is possible or take on tasks for which you are not prepared

- Talk with friends or family when you encounter difficulties

- Take time each day to do something that you enjoy, even if it is only for 15 minutes

- Do not worry about things that are out of your control but concentrate on what you *can* do

- Exercise regularly

- Recognize that stress is a normal reaction to many situations, like taking a test, giving a speech, or participating in field training

- Take a deep breath, relax, and do not let stress interfere with accomplishing the task at hand

To help reduce stress in a group or among friends or fellow cadets, give each other moral support if things are tough at home, school, or in the unit. Welcome new replacements into your group and be active in establishing friendships. By building a feeling of esprit de corps, you can minimize stressful feelings of loneliness and isolation. When in the field, attempt to care for other cadets and work together to provide everyone food, water, sleep, shelter, protection from heat, cold, and poor sanitation.

Basic Principles of Sanitation

Poor sanitation can contribute to conditions that may result in diarrhea and **dysentery**. Intestinal diseases are usually spread through contact with bacteria and germs in human waste, by flies and other insects, or in improperly prepared food and water supplies.

Use Purified Water

When you are staying outdoors, in the field, or traveling in foreign countries with questionable water supplies, use only water that is **purified** (see Figure 1.7.3). Fill your canteen with treated water at every chance. To treat or **disinfect** water, bring it to a boil for 5 to 10 minutes. When heated water is not available, disinfect water using one of the following methods:

Key Note Terms

dysentery – any of several intestinal disorders usually caused by infection and characterized by stomach pain and diarrhea with passage of mucous and blood

purified – free from undesirable elements or impurities; cleaned

disinfect – to destroy harmful germs; to purify

Figure 1.7.3: Always use purified water in the field.
Courtesy of Burke/Triolo Productions/Botanica/Getty Images.

The Preferred Method: Iodine Tablets

1. Fill a one-quart canteen with the cleanest water available.

2. Put one **iodine** tablet in the water; two in cold or cloudy water. Double these amounts in a two-quart canteen.

3. Place the cap on the canteen, wait 5 minutes, then shake. Loosen the cap and tip the canteen over to allow leakage around the canteen threads. Tighten the cap and wait an additional 25 minutes before drinking.

Treating with Chlorine

1. Fill a one-quart canteen with the cleanest water available.

2. Mix one **ampule** of **chlorine** with one-half canteen cup of water. Stir the mixture with a clean device until the contents dissolve. Take care not to cut your hands when breaking open the glass ampule.

3. Pour one canteen capful of the chlorine solution into your quart of water.

4. Replace the cap on your canteen and shake. Slightly loosen the cap and tip the canteen over to allow leakage around the threads. Tighten the cap and wait 30 minutes before drinking.

Another Alternative: Tincture of Iodine

1. Fill a one-quart canteen with the cleanest water available.

2. Add five drops of 2% Tincture of Iodine to the water. If the water is cold or cloudy, add 10 drops.

3. Mix thoroughly by shaking the canteen. Slightly loosen the cap and tip the canteen over to allow leakage around the threads. Tighten the cap and wait 30 minutes before drinking.

4. Very cloudy or cold water may require prolonged contact time. Let it stand several hours or overnight if possible.

Guard Against Food Poisoning

Wash your hands for at least 30 seconds after using the bathroom or before touching food. Inspect all cans and food packages prior to using them and throw away any cans with leaks, bulges, or holes. Do not eat foods or drink beverages that have been prepared in **galvanized** containers, which may result in zinc poisoning. When camping or in the field, wash your mess kit in a mess kit laundry or with treated water or disinfectant solution.

Bury Your Waste

On a march, personal disposal bags should be used if available; if not available personal cat holes can be used. Always dispose of your waste immediately to prevent flies from spreading germs from waste to your food and to keep unwanted animals out of your **bivouac** area. Chemical toilets should be used in bivouac area.

Key Note Term

iodine – a nonmetallic element having important medical uses

Key Note Terms

ampule – a small, sealed glass container that holds one dose of a solution, usually a medicine, to be administered by injection

chlorine – a gaseous greenish-yellow element used as a bleach and disinfectant in water purification

Key Note Term

galvanized – coated with zinc

Key Note Term

bivouac – a temporary camp or shelter

Keep Your Body and Uniform Clean

Bathe every day, if possible, or at least once a week. A daily bath or shower helps maintain cleanliness and prevent body odor, common skin diseases, and infection. When you are in the field, however, bathing daily may not be possible. In this case, make sure you take a full shower at least once a week (or at the earliest opportunity) and use a washcloth daily to wash

- **Your face**
- **Your armpits**
- **Your genital area**
- **Your feet**
- **Other areas where you sweat or that become wet, such as between your thighs or, for females, under the breasts**

Powders, such as talcum powder, help to keep your skin dry when in the field. Apply it to places where you tend to sweat and to your feet and inside your socks each morning, especially if you have had prior foot infections. Change to clean clothing regularly. Protection of your feet is extremely important and requires daily attention (see Figure 1.7.4).

Good personal hygiene practices reduce infestation of insects such as body **lice** and mites. Make sure the clothing you wear in the field is loose and does not restrict circulation. Avoid wearing nylon undergarments. Wear cotton, which is more absorbent and allows the skin to dry. Wash your uniform frequently or at least once a week. Use the quartermaster laundry or a stream, lake, or washbasin. Air-dry uniforms, especially underwear and socks.

Key Note Term

lice – small, wingless, parasitic insects that live on warm-blooded animals, especially in hair, and suck the animal's blood

Figure 1.7.4: Cleaning and protecting feet in the field is an important part of personal hygiene.
Courtesy of Michael DeYoung/Corbis Images.

Other Instructions for the Field

There are other precautions that you can take to ensure your health and well-being while in the field and ensure the health of those around you.

Follow Medical Advice: Take medications that help prevent diseases such as antimalaria pills. Use any medication that is prescribed by medical personnel.

Protect Yourself at Night: Use your bed net when sleeping and ensure that it is in good repair. Always follow label directions and precautions with using DoD-approved insect spray.

Wash Your Mess Kit/Eating Utensils: Protect yourself from diarrhea by washing your mess kit/eating utensils. Use a mess kit sanitation center or use treated water or disinfectant solution.

Domestic and Wild Animals or Birds: Do not handle or approach animals in the field. Unless approved by veterinary personnel, do not collect or support with food and shelter any stray or domestic animals in the unit area.

Poisonous Plants: Avoid contact with poisonous plants by properly wearing the uniform and avoid areas where poisonous plants grow. Only eat plants that have been approved by medical personnel.

Conclusion

Practicing good personal hygiene and sanitation are common sense actions that everyone should perform. They are particularly important in the field where cadets have a responsibility to both themselves and others, and leaders must plan and enforce preventative measures.

Remember, correct cleanliness habits, regular exercise, good nutrition, and adequate amounts of rest and relaxation can directly affect a person's well-being. By practicing these preventative measures, you can significantly reduce time lost due to illness and injuries.

The following lesson deals with a common problem in today's world—stress. Knowing how to control stress can help with your emotional and physical health.

Lesson Review

1. **How do you keep clean in the field?**

2. **What is the correlation between physical fitness and hygiene?**

3. **What are some results of poor sanitation?**

4. **Describe one method of disinfecting water.**

Lesson 8

Understanding and Controlling Stress

Key Terms

anxiety
depression
dilated
fight or flight response
generalized
manic-depressive illness
meditation
migraines
visualization

What You Will Learn to Do

- Assess how stress impacts your life

Linked Core Abilities

- Apply critical thinking techniques

Skills and Knowledge You Will Gain Along the Way

- Differentiate between stress and anxiety in overall health
- Identify the physical and psychological effects of stress
- Practice prevention of stress overload including relaxation and anger management techniques
- Identify leadership strategies that promote healthy stress levels within a group
- Explore positive ways to deal with depression and anxiety
- Define the key words contained in this lesson

Introduction

Stress in small doses is a normal, healthy part of life; however, stress that continues over long periods of time can lead to exhaustion and possible mental or physical illness, as illustrated in Figure 1.8.1. This lesson discusses what causes stress, how it can affect you, and ways that you can manage it. Handling stress in your life and recognizing symptoms of stress in others will make your life more enjoyable and your leadership more effective.

The media often portrays the teen years as a carefree time, with few major responsibilities and lots of new and exciting experiences. Many young people know, however, that this is only one side of the coin. You may not have the responsibilities of your parents, but your responsibilities are growing as you grow older. New challenges and experiences, while exciting, can also be a bit scary. Expectations for the future can be exhilarating, but they can also result in anxiety and pressure to succeed. As teenagers make their way to adulthood, they experience a range of emotions and changes that can make their high school years very stressful.

What Is Stress?

Stress is the way your body reacts and adjusts to the psychological and physical demands of life. It can be brought on by situations that cause feelings such as fear, irritation, endangerment, excitement, and expectation. Surprise tests, as illustrated in Figure 1.8.2, can cause stress. Stress in small amounts is beneficial and needed for motivation, improvement, and growth. It can give you a burst of energy to complete a project or run a race, the control and strength to get through a difficult time, or the inspiration to write a poem or paint a picture. Stress can be an important factor in your achievements and progress.

Figure 1.8.1: If a stressor continues for a long time, your body enters the exhaustion stage, and illness can result.
Courtesy of Brent Petersen/ The Stock Market.

Chapter 1 Achieving a Healthy Lifestyle

Figure 1.8.2: A surprise test is just one stressor you may encounter today.
Courtesy of Ken Karp.

Yet times of stress should be followed by times of relaxation to ensure recovery from stress. Experiencing constant stress without a break has a negative effect on people. While stress followed by a period of rest can actually make a person better prepared for the next stressful event, stress followed by more stress without recovery in between can exhaust a person making him or her less prepared to handle the next stressful event. Eventually, constant stress can affect a person psychologically and physically, disrupting normal behavior and resulting in illness.

Physical Effects of Stress

When your mind perceives a situation as stressful, it triggers a series of physical and chemical reactions in your body. These include increased blood flow to the muscles and brain; decreased blood flow to the skin and digestive organs; a shut down of the immune system; and the release of fuel, such as fat, into the bloodstream. While these internal reactions to stress will not be obvious to you, noticeable results of these reactions include increased heart and breathing rates, muscle tension, **dilated** pupils, cold hands, and dry mouth.

These reactions happen as part of a **fight-or-flight response** developed in primitive humans to deal with physical threats by either fighting or fleeing. Either way, primitive man's mind and body placed emphasis on physically responding to stressful situations by providing extra fuel and blood to the muscles while slowing or shutting down other functions.

For modern man, most stressful situations are not life threatening and do not require a physical response, yet being stuck in a traffic jam or pushing hard to finish a report still causes the same physical reactions as those needed for fight or flight. Luckily, once modern man deals with the stress, finishes the stressful activity or the source of stress goes away, the body and all of its functions return to normal.

Key Note Term

dilated – having been widened; expanded

Key Note Term

fight-or-flight response – an involuntary reaction to an immediate danger or thereat, which prepares a person physically to either respond to the danger or run away

Courtesy of US Army JROTC.

On the other hand, if the source of stress continues, the person does not deal with the stress effectively, or the person faces stressful situation after stressful situation, his or her body will not recover its normal state. Eventually, the body's continual reaction to prolonged stress may result in the following physical problems:

- Insomnia
- Grinding or clenching of teeth, especially when sleeping
- Diarrhea
- Indigestion
- Ulcers
- Nausea
- Backaches
- Headaches
- Migraines
- Uncontrollable tics or twitches
- Stuttering
- Allergies
- Asthma
- High blood pressure
- Heart disease

Of particular note is the connection between continual stress and heart disease. Because most of modern man's stressful situations do not require physical action, the fat pumped into the bloodstream to act as fuel for the muscles is left unused, collecting on artery walls and contributing to heart disease.

Psychological Effects of Stress

Generally, the first indications a person may have of stress overload are certain feelings, like irritability or worrying. If the person pays attention to these feelings and takes action to reduce stress, the effects of stress will not continue. If, however, the person ignores these initial warning signs and seeks no relief from stress, he or she will experience more psychological effects and probably begin to experience some of the physical effects discussed previously.

Psychologically, continual stress may cause the following:

- Irritability
- Excessive worrying
- Anxiety
- Inability to relax
- Forgetfulness
- Disorganization
- Inability to concentrate

Key Note Term

migraines – severe recurring headache, usually affecting only one side of the head, characterized by sharp pain and often accompanied by nausea, vomiting, and visual disturbances

Key Note Term

anxiety – eager, often agitated desire; my anxiety to make a good impression

- Inability to complete tasks
- Lack of energy
- Trouble with relationships
- Changed eating habits; over- or undereating with corresponding weight gain or loss
- Use or increased use of alcohol and other drugs
- Lowered self-esteem
- Feelings of discouragement
- Excessive feelings of guilt or self-blame
- Emotional overreaction, like exploding or crying without reason
- Waking from sleep with a sense of doom
- Disinterest in the world and life
- Dissatisfaction with things that were previously satisfying
- Tendency to avoid people and activities, even those that were previously enjoyed
- Unexplained feelings of helplessness or hopelessness
- Depression

When stress continues to go unchecked, negative feelings, like depression and hopelessness, can intensify over time. In severe cases, people can become depressed enough to try to commit suicide. It is important, therefore, to listen to your feelings, relate them to what is happening in your life, and respond to them promptly before the effects of stress get out of hand.

Causes of Stress

Causes of stress and levels of stress experienced under certain circumstances vary from person to person depending on their personalities and tolerance for different situations and experiences. For example, an outgoing person may find public speaking easy and enjoyable, while a shy person may find it difficult and frightening. On the other hand, the shy person may be quite content to study alone, while the outgoing person may find studying alone nerve wracking. Neither of these people is better or worse than the other; they are simply two different people reacting differently to the same situations. Do not compare yourself with others when it comes to stress. What is important is that you understand what causes you stress and learn to manage it before the stress "mismanages" you.

Read through the following items that are common causes of stress for many young people. Think about which ones are stressful for you and whether or not they are things that you can control. Recognizing what causes your stress is a step toward managing it.

Personal Habits

Personal habits can contribute to stress. Listed below are four negative personal habits. Do any apply to you?

Key Note Term

depression – psychiatric disorder characterized by an inability to concentrate; insomnia; loss of appetite; anhedonia; feelings of extreme sadness, guilt, helplessness and hopelessness; and thoughts of death

Courtesy of US Army JROTC.

- Poor time management
- Poor diet
- Irregular sleep habits
- Lack of exercise

Social Activities

Social activities create situations that can be very stressful for young people. Which apply to you?

- Conflicts with family or friends
- Peer pressure to use alcohol, tobacco, or drugs
- Peer pressure to engage in a sexual relationship
- Pressure to be popular
- Lack of money

Major Life Changes

Major life changes affect all people. Have you been effected by any of these major life changes recently?

- Death in the family
- Severe illness in the family
- Parents' divorce
- Parent remarries
- Moving
- Changing schools

Environmental

The environment can affect you mentally as well as physically and can create stress in your life. Are you currently being exposed to any of the following items?

- Air and noise pollution
- Feeling confined
- Overcrowding
- Poor lighting
- Uncomfortable temperature
- Feeling unsafe in your neighborhood, home, or school

Responsibilities

Personal responsibilities are placed on all us at one time or another and can be very stressful. Are you experiencing any of the following items?

- **Participating in too many activities**
- **Having unrealistic expectations of yourself**
- **Constant deadlines**
- **Concern about grades**
- **Concern about college and career decisions**
- **Having to work and go to school**
- **Having to care for younger brothers or sisters**

Stress Strategies

There is no way to eliminate stress completely from life. In fact, as previously explained, a stress-free life would not even be desirable, because stress in reasonable amounts aids performance, creativity, and problem solving. Letting stress get out of hand, however, is a common problem in today's hectic world. Fortunately, once you recognize signs of stress overload in yourself and identify its cause, you can either eliminate the source of stress or, if it is not possible to eliminate it, learn to manage the stress associated with it.

Preventing Stress Overload

The best way to ensure stress does not get the best of you is to follow lifelong habits that promote mental and physical well-being. Getting plenty of sleep, eating well-balanced meals, and exercising regularly will help you cope better with stressful situations; maintaining a positive outlook will help you face difficulties with more confidence. In addition to these common sense approaches, the following can also promote well-being and prevent stress overload.

- **Manage your time with daily, weekly, and/or monthly schedules. In addition to scheduling time for school, study, extracurricular activities, and so on, make sure you allow enough time for sleep, unhurried meals, relaxation, and other things you enjoy.**
- **Take care of your problems as soon as possible; avoiding them will not make them go away. The longer you put off dealing with a problem, the more anxious you will feel about it, and the more stress you will create for yourself.**
- **Keep a journal of the situations you find stressful. For each situation, explain why you find it stressful, how you handled it, and whether or not you believe you could handle it better in the future.**
- **Develop a hobby and/or participate regularly in an activity you enjoy.**
- **Take some time every day to do something you find relaxing—whether it is sitting quietly alone and thinking, talking with a good friend on the phone, or laughing at your favorite sitcom.**
- **Talk over problems with people you trust and who you know are good listeners. Keeping all your thoughts and feelings to yourself can be very stressful. Although you may believe you can handle all your problems on your own, everyone needs at least one person to confide in.**

- Accept that throughout life you will encounter stressful situations that you cannot or should not avoid, but recognize that you also have control over how you approach and respond to those situations. For example, while Shelley dreads going to the dentist, she realizes it is important, and instead of dwelling on how much she hates it, she focuses on the benefits of dental care to her overall health and on how good her teeth will look and feel after the dental appointment. Approaching stressful situations positively and looking to the ultimate outcome of the situation can lower the amount of stress you experience.

- When you do have a choice, do not participate in activities you find stressful and unrewarding. Often, young people will take part in activities because their friends do, they believe their parents want them to, or they just believe they must do it all. Only you know which activities are enjoyable and worthwhile to you, which bring you negative stress, and how many things you can do before getting overloaded. Be honest with yourself and with those who care about you in making decisions about participating in certain activities. If taking aerobics with your friends makes you feel more uptight than healthy and relaxed, and you would really rather get your exercise going for a walk alone, let your friends know how you feel and then do what is best for you.

- Be prepared when you know you will have to face a stressful situation. For example, if you know that you must give a class presentation, plan for it and rehearse it until you feel comfortable with it. By preparing for it, you will be calmer during the time leading up to the presentation and will feel more confident when giving it.

- Do not use tobacco, alcohol, or other drugs. Using drugs does not solve any problems and, more often than not, causes new ones.

- Do not be overly self-critical; remember that making mistakes is part of the growing process and that learning from them will make you more successful in the future.

- If you can, limit the number of changes you make in your life at any one time. For example, if in the same week that you start a new job after school, you also start getting up earlier each morning to jog before school, you are probably putting too much pressure on yourself. To limit your stress level, get used to the new routine of having an after-school job before you add anything else to your schedule.

- Learn a relaxation technique like **meditation**, **visualization**, or deep breathing.

Relaxation Techniques

Try using these relaxation techniques when you notice the warning signs of stress.

Deep Breathing

To relax through deep breathing, follow these steps:

1. While closing your eyes, take a deep breath in through your nose so that your abdomen expands.

2. Slowly exhale through your mouth, letting all the air out of your lungs and allowing your stomach to contract.

3. Repeat for 5 to 10 minutes.

Courtesy of US Army JROTC.

Key Note Terms

meditation – a contemplative discourse, usually on a religious or philosophical subject

visualization – to make visible

The Worry Box

Relaxing through "the worry box" can be done by following these steps:

1. **Start deep breathing.**
2. **Visualize a box that has a lock and key.**
3. **Imagine yourself putting all your worries and fears in the box, then closing the lid, and locking it with the key.**
4. **Imagine yourself putting the key somewhere out of sight—like under a mattress or on the top shelf of a closet—and, therefore, out of mind.**

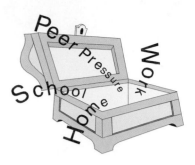

Meditation

Meditation can help you clear your mind and relax. To do so, following these steps:

1. **Find a quiet place where you can be alone for at least 10 minutes.**
2. **Sit on the floor with your legs crossed. Some people put one or both of their feet up onto their inner thighs when meditating. Keep your back and neck straight. Relax your arms with your hands in your lap or on your knees—palms up or down, whichever feels most comfortable to you.**
3. **Close your eyes and try to empty your mind. Many people do this by concentrating on their breathing or on a single word, image, or sound.**

Quick Calming Response

To calm and center yourself quickly, follow these steps:

1. **Turn inward and listen to a sound or word that you find relaxing and choose to use when stress overload hits.**
2. **As you repeat the sound or word inside yourself, slowly take deep breaths in and out, visualizing the release of the "tense air" from your body with each exhaled breath.**

Courtesy of US Army JROTC.

Progressive Relaxation

To try progressive relaxation, do the following:

1. **Sit or lie down in a comfortable position and begin deep breathing.**
2. **As you inhale, tighten the muscles in your head and neck area.**
3. **Relax the tensed muscles as you slowly exhale.**
4. **Continue with all parts of your body, working your way from head to foot.**

Letting Off Steam

Sometimes, stressful situations can make you feel frustrated and angry. To keep the stress from getting the better of you and possibly "losing your cool," try the following:

- **Take several deep breaths, releasing tension with each exhale**
- **Close your eyes and visualize yourself in a calming situation or place**
- **Take a break; if possible, remove yourself from the problem or situation until you feel more relaxed and under control**

- Analyze the importance of the situation. Does it really matter if someone cuts you off in traffic or bumps into you and does not excuse him or herself? Is it worth feeling angry about or wasting your time and energy on? Is it better just to forget it and move on?

- If something is important to you and you can take action, confront the person or situation calmly. If it is not possible to confront the person or problem directly, let off steam, depending upon the situation, by either talking to someone you trust or writing an angry letter, then throwing it away.

- Work off tension with a physical activity, like screaming into a pillow, taking a walk, or lifting weights, as depicted in Figure 1.8.3.

Stress and Leadership

As a leader, learn to manage your own stress effectively, so that you do not create a negative environment for your followers. Recognize that your behavior can directly affect the stress level of your group of cadets. Stress in groups can be increased to counterproductive and unhealthy levels when leaders

- **Act unpredictably**

- **Constantly find fault with their followers, which eats away at their followers' self-esteem and results in increased anxiety**

- **Set up win-lose situations in which either they are right and their followers are wrong or vice versa**

- **Demand too much or too little of their followers**

Figure 1.8.3: Being physically active when under stress helps to release the built-up tension in your muscles.
Courtesy of Ray Morsch/The Stock Market.
Courtesy of Larry Lawfer.

Leaders can keep a group's stress to healthy levels by

- **Allowing some participation in the decision-making process, which creates a feeling of trust and usefulness in followers, and promotes team spirit and cooperation within the group**

- **Giving credit where it is due and praise when warranted**

- **Offering constructive criticism when necessary**

- **Having a good working knowledge of the tasks the group needs to perform**

- **Monitoring and tracking tasks as they are performed and offering guidance when necessary**

As a leader, you must also be aware of any indications that cadets are feeling or acting "stressed out." If you realize someone is showing signs of stress, let them know that you have noticed they have not been themselves lately, or ask if everything is okay with them. Your concern will probably encourage them to talk to you about how they are feeling, and just the fact that they are talking about it and you are listening can help to relieve their stress.

Depression

People often say, "Oh, I'm so depressed," when they are having a bad day or because some unhappy event has recently occurred. Sadness and grief are normal reactions to certain events in life, as seen in Figure 1.8.4. A person who is having a passing blue mood is not truly depressed. For minor low moods, stimulating or enjoyable activities, like running or reading a good book, are often all that is needed to raise a person's spirits.

Figure 1.8.4: Feeling sad is a normal response to a disappointing event in your life.
Courtesy of James Whitmer.

Major depression, on the other hand, is a serious illness that requires treatment. It affects the whole body and involves thoughts, feelings, bodily functions, and behaviors. Most people usually recover from bad events in life after a reasonable amount of time; depressed people do not. And while some cases of depression can be traced to a specific stressful experience, other cases of depression seem to have no apparent reason for occurring.

An episode of depression can occur once in a person's life or many times. A depressed person's symptoms may last for months, years, or a lifetime. Depression can be so severe that the person cannot function at all. Some people who are chronically depressed are able to function but never feel really well, content, or happy. They may be unaware that they are even depressed because they are so used to feeling that way.

Depending on the individual and the severity of the illness, a depressed person will experience a variety of these symptoms to different degrees. Note that many of these symptoms are similar to symptoms of stress.

- **Constantly feeling sad or "empty"**
- **Feeling hopeless, worthless, and helpless**
- **Unable to make decisions, remember things, or concentrate**
- **Loss of interest in normally pleasurable activities**
- **Irritability**
- **Disinterest in school, at home, and in other activities**
- **Not caring about appearance**
- **Avoiding people; staying alone most of the time**
- **Difficulty concentrating, remembering, and making decisions**
- **Problems falling asleep and then problems getting up**
- **Loss of appetite**
- **Feeling tired and "slowed down" all the time**
- **Chronic aches and pains and digestive problems**
- **Frequent thoughts of death and/or suicide**
- **Suicide attempts**

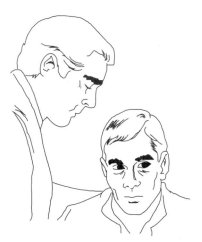

Courtesy of US Army JROTC.

It is important to remember that depression is a real illness and not caused by personal weakness. Potential for developing some kinds of depression may be inherited, and therefore, biologically related. For instance, **manic-depressive illness** seems to occur in people whose genetic makeup is different than those who do not become ill; however, not everyone who has the genetic makeup for the illness gets it. This suggests that other factors, such as stress, also play a role in the development of the disease.

As with stress, physically active people who eat well and get plenty of sleep tend to feel less depressed than people with less healthy lifestyles. Therefore, if you are feeling mildly depressed, take a look at your current eating, sleeping, and exercise habits and try to make some changes there. In addition, do things you enjoy, try

Key Note Term

manic-depressive illness – bipolar disorder

something different that you have always wanted to do, talk to friends, spend time outside because the color green and the sun are known to boost spirits, and try not to pressure or push yourself for awhile.

Likewise, if you know someone who is exhibiting signs of depression, take the time to listen to how they are feeling and offer them your support. Give them the suggestions listed above for lifting their spirits and breaking out of negative habits. Be patient. Often, depressed people are not fun to be around and may even try to push you away, but they really need a friend to understand and encourage them to try to make some changes.

If after giving these suggestions a try, you think his or her depression is worsening or becoming long-term, encourage your friend to seek help. Likewise, if you yourself are depressed and believe it is worsening and continuing, seek help. Doctors, psychologists, counselors, mental health clinics, hospitals, family services, social agencies, and private clinics are among the many people and places that offer help for all types of emotional disorders, including depression.

Anxiety

Anxiety is a feeling that everyone experiences occasionally when dealing with things they fear or worry about. Unlike depression, which makes people feel tired and unenergetic, anxiety makes people feel nervous and energetic, almost as if they cannot sit still. Like stress, anxiety in small amounts and for short duration can be beneficial. It can give you a spurt of energy and sharpen your mind. Too much anxiety, however, can be harmful and lessen your ability to perform. For example, while a little anxiety before giving a speech can heighten your powers of recall, projection, and expression, too much anxiety can make you freeze, forgetting information and stammering through the presentation.

To keep anxiety from getting the best of you, admit to yourself those things you fear and/or worry about. Then, when you know you will have to deal with one of them, make sure you are thoroughly prepared for it: practice for the speech, study for the test, rehearse the dance routine, work out faithfully before the big meet, and so forth. Being unprepared will only fuel your anxiety. When you start to worry or feel afraid, remind yourself that it is a waste of your energy, then visualize yourself doing well instead. Prior to the event or situation, focus on its positive outcomes, use the relaxation techniques discussed previously, and avoid caffeine, which only increases anxiety.

Although it is normal to be mildly anxious about something that frightens or worries us, feeling anxious without a specific reason can indicate an anxiety disorder. When a person experiences anxiety over a long period of time that is related to so many worries and fears the anxiety has become **generalized**, the person is suffering from free-floating anxiety. Often, the effects of free-floating anxiety are the same as stress overload.

When a person experiences anxiety attacks, which are strong, sudden attacks of anxiety for no apparent reason that last only a few minutes, he or she feels panic and extreme stress accompanied by dizziness, faintness, rapid heartbeat, excessive

Courtesy of US Army JROTC.

Key Note Term

generalized   generally prevalent

perspiration, and nausea. A person having an anxiety attack is not able to function until the attack passes. Some people have severe anxiety attacks so frequently that they are constantly fearful and unable to cope with many things in life. People suffering from excessive anxiety, whether free floating or anxiety attacks, should seek help from a counselor who can help them reduce or learn to deal with their anxiety.

Conclusion

Humans experience a wide range of emotions and not all of them are pleasant. Yet, even certain uncomfortable emotions such as stress and anxiety are beneficial in small doses. Sometimes, though, because of hectic, hurried schedules and pressures to do too many things or things we do not necessarily enjoy, stress can get out of hand. When you start feeling and showing warning signs of stress overload, step back and take a look at what is going on in your life. Ask yourself what is causing your symptoms of stress, then take care of it or reduce the stress you associate with it.

Meanwhile, to be prepared for the stressful events that will surely pop up throughout your life; maintain a healthy lifestyle so that you are better able to handle whatever life throws your way. Keep negative stress and anxiety at bay by doing things you enjoy, learning ways to relax, and thinking positively.

Remember, if these uncomfortable emotions ever become extreme, your mental and physical well-being may be threatened. They can even become initial indications of mental illness and physical disease.

This concludes Chapter 1, "Achieving a Healthy Lifestyle." The next chapter covers first aid for emergency and nonemergency situations. This is an important chapter because you will learn to be prepared for anything that might happen.

Lesson Review

1. **Differentiate between stress and anxiety.**
2. **What are the physical and psychological effects of stress?**
3. **List positive ways to deal with depression and anxiety.**
4. **Define the term *depression*.**

First Aid for Emergency and Nonemergency Situations

Lesson 1

The Need for First Aid/ Your Response

Chapter 2

Key Words

cardiopulmonary resuscitation (CPR)
catastrophes
consent
emergency medical service (EMS)
evaluate
first aid
Good Samaritan Law

What You Will Learn to Do

- Assess first aid situations

Linked Core Abilities

- Do your share as a good citizen in your school, community, country, and the world

Skills and Knowledge You Will Gain Along the Way

- Assess the need for knowing how to perform first aid
- Explain the significance of the Good Samaritan Law
- Identify the steps of first aid intervention
- Identify the information needed when calling an emergency number such as 911
- Define the key words contained in this lesson

Introduction

Most people encounter at least one situation requiring the use of first aid at some time in their lives. Whether a friend falls when rollerblading and breaks an arm or your younger brother cuts himself on broken glass and requires stitches, someone should administer first aid until the injured person receives proper medical attention. That someone can be you if you acquire basic first aid knowledge of what to do and what not to do in different accident situations. Remember that first aid may mean the difference between life and death, permanent and temporary disability, or long- and short-term recovery for an accident victim.

In addition to the first aid taught in this chapter, consider taking a first aid class from a qualified instructor. Many schools, hospitals, and fire departments offer first aid classes that provide demonstrations and hands-on experience with medical models of victims. Hands-on training is especially important before actually performing mouth-to-mouth resuscitation and **cardiopulmonary resuscitation (CPR)**, both of which can be hazardous to a victim if performed improperly.

Definition of First Aid

First aid is the immediate care given to an injured or ill individual to keep him or her alive or stop further damage until qualified medical treatment can be administered. It is caring for people involved in accidents, **catastrophes**, and natural disasters such as hurricanes, tornadoes, and earthquakes. First aid includes dealing with the situation, the person, and the injury, as well as encouraging the victim and showing a willingness to help.

Good Samaritan Law

The **Good Samaritan Law** is designed to protect the rescuer and encourage people to assist others in distress by granting them immunity against lawsuits. This law protects people from lawsuits as long as the rescuer is acting in good faith, without compensation and administers first aid correctly and without malicious misconduct or gross negligence (see Figure 2.1.1).

Key Note Terms

cardiopulmonary resuscitation (CPR) – an emergency method to keep blood and oxygen flowing through a person whose heart and breathing have stopped

first aid – the immediate care given to a victim of injury or sudden illness before professional medical help arrives

catastrophes – a great and sudden misfortune

Good Samaritan Law – a law enacted in most states that protects people from lawsuits if medical complications arise after they have administered first aid correctly

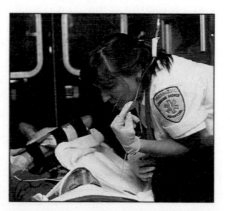

Figure 2.1.1: EMTs are protected from litigation under the Good Smaritan Law.
Courtesy of Dorothy Littell/ Stock Boston.

First Aid Kit

Administering first aid is easier with a first aid kit. It is a good idea to keep one in your house and car and take one along on camping trips and hikes. A well-stocked first aid kit contains an assortment of bandages, Band-Aids, tape, aspirin or aspirin substitutes, antiseptic cream and cleanser, safety pins, scissors, tweezers, cotton, and tissues. To protect against infectious diseases, include rubber gloves and face shields in the kit. Rubber gloves will keep you from contacting blood and body fluids, and face shields will allow you to give mouth-to-mouth resuscitation and CPR without direct contact.

Evaluating the Victim

Key Note Term

evaluate – to determine if an act, process, or method has been attained; to assess; to determine the significance by careful appraisal and study

When you encounter an injured person, you must **evaluate** that person to determine what kind of first aid, if any, is needed. This preliminary check of the person follows a series of steps designed to pinpoint and correct the most serious health risks first and then continue with less life-threatening problems. These steps are explained in more detail later in this lesson. Basically, check for breathing and heartbeat first; severe bleeding second; signs of shock third; and finally for broken bones, burns, and head injuries. Depending on what problems your evaluation of an accident victim reveals, perform the life-saving steps in a sequence that parallels this evaluation sequence:

1. **Open the airway**
2. **Assess breathing**
3. **Assess circulation**
4. **Assess disability**

Key Note Terms

consent – to get approval for what is to be done or proposed by another

emergency medical service (EMS) – medical professional dedicated to the reduction of morbidity and mortality of residents through the provision of Advanced and Basic Life Support care, medically directed rescue, and transportation of the ill and injured

When evaluating a conscious victim, ask the victim if you can help and get **consent** to provide first aid; then get as much information as possible about the situation and how the victim feels. If the victim is unconscious and others witnessed the accident, get as much information from the witnesses as possible. Check the victim for medical alert identification. Many people with heart disease, epilepsy, diabetes, and allergies to medications wear medical alert identification bracelets or necklaces that can give you a clue as to their medical condition.

Have someone at the scene dial 911 for **emergency medical services** (**EMS**). If you are alone and the victim's condition is life-threatening, give first aid first, and then call 911. When calling 911, calmly state your name and exact location, the telephone number from which you are calling, details of what has happened, and the condition of the victim or victims. A dispatcher, as depicted in Figure 2.1.2, will route your call to the appropriate service—either the EMS, police department, fire department, or a combination of these services.

Other important rules to follow at the scene of an accident include the following:

Figure 2.1.2: Dispatchers answer 911 calls and route them to the proper response service.
Courtesy of Frank Siteman/ Rainbow.

- **Remain calm but act quickly.** This will reassure the victim and help him or her to remain calm as well.

- **Do not move an injured person.** If the person has a neck or spine injury or broken bones, moving him or her could worsen the condition. Only move a victim if there is potential danger in remaining at the accident location. If you must move the victim for this reason, pull him or her in a straight line from the shoulders, keeping the head and body in line. Support the head and pull the victim as short a distance as possible.

- **If there is more than one injured person at an accident scene,** evaluate them quickly; then help the most seriously injured first. For example, help the person with severe bleeding before you help the person with a broken arm.

The Life-Saving Steps

The following steps identify evaluation procedures and specify treatment if necessary.

1. **Check to see if the victim is conscious.**

   a. Ask in a loud but calm voice, "Are you okay?"

   b. Gently shake or tap the victim on the shoulder.

   c. Watch for response. If the victim does not respond, go to Step 2.

   d. If the victim is conscious, ask where he or she feels different than usual or where it hurts. Go to Step 3.

   e. If the victim is conscious but is choking and cannot talk, stop the evaluation and begin treatment for clearing the airway of a conscious victim.

2. **Check for breathing and heartbeat.**

   a. Look for rise and fall of the victim's chest.

   b. Listen for breathing by placing your ear about one inch from the victim's mouth and nose.

    c. Feel for breathing by placing your hand or cheek about one inch from the victim's mouth and nose.

    d. At the same time, check for a pulse in the victim's neck.

    e. If there is a pulse but no breathing, stop the evaluation and begin treatment to restore the breathing.

    f. If there is no pulse, stop the evaluation and begin CPR.

3. **Check for bleeding.**

    a. Look for spurts of blood and blood-soaked clothing.

    b. Look for entry and exit wounds.

    c. If bleeding is present, stop the evaluation and begin treatment for stopping the bleeding.

4. **Check for the following signs of shock:**

    a. Sweaty, but cool skin

    b. Paleness

    c. Restlessness or nervousness

    d. Thirst

    e. Loss of blood

    f. Confusion

    g. Faster than normal breathing rate

    h. Blotchy or bluish skin

    i. Vomiting or nausea

If any of these signs are present, discontinue the evaluation and treat for shock.

5. **Check for fractures (broken bones).**

    a. Check for the following signs of neck or back injury:

        • Pain or tenderness of neck or back area

        • Wounds of neck or back area

        • Paralysis

    b. Ask the victim if he or she can move.

    c. Touch the victim's arms and legs and ask whether he or she can feel it.

    d. If you suspect a neck or back injury, immobilize the victim by doing the following:

        • Tell the victim not to move.

        • If you suspect a back injury, place padding under the natural arch of the lower back.

        • If you suspect a neck injury, place padding under the victim's neck and place objects such as rocks or shoes on both sides of the head.

    e. Check the victim's arms or legs for fractures or broken bones. Signs are as follows:

        • Swelling

        • Discoloration

        • Unusual angle or position of arm or leg

        • Bones sticking through the skin

If you suspect a fracture, stop the evaluation and begin treatment for fractures.

6. **Check for burns. If you find burns, cover them with a clean dry cloth.**

7. **Check for head injury. Some possible signs of head injury are as follows:**
   a. **Pupils of eyes unequal size**
   b. **Fluid from ear(s), nose, mouth or wounds to the head or face**
   c. **Slurred speech**
   d. **Confusion**
   e. **Sleepiness**
   f. **Loss of memory or consciousness**
   g. **Staggering when walking**
   h. **Headache**
   i. **Dizziness**
   j. **Vomiting**
   k. **Paralysis**
   l. **Convulsion or twitching**

When first aid is administered correctly and in a timely manner, it could mean the difference between life and death for the victim. Figure 2.1.3 shows emergency medical personnel assisting with an injured person.

If a head injury is suspected, keep the person awake. Watch the victim for signs that would require restoring breathing or treating for shock.

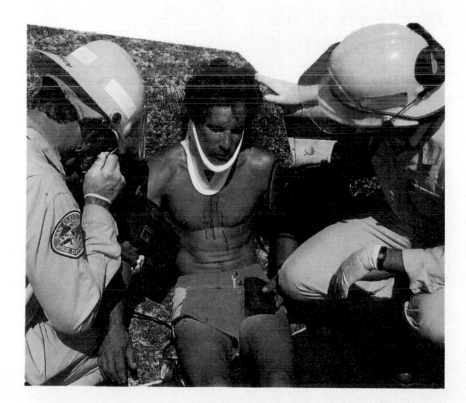

Figure 2.1.3: Emergency personnel are trained to help victims of all types of injuries.
Courtesy of Spencer Grant/ Photo Researchers.

When to Call 911 or Your Local Emergency Number

Call for an ambulance if the victim

- Is or becomes unconscious
- Has trouble breathing
- Has persistent chest pain or pressure
- Is bleeding severely
- Has persistent pain or pressure in the abdomen
- Is vomiting
- Has seizures, slurred speech, or persistent severe headache
- Appears to have been poisoned
- Has injuries to the head, neck, or back
- Has possible broken bones

Also call if there is

- A fire or explosion
- A downed electrical wire
- Swiftly moving or rapidly rising water
- Poisonous gas present
- A vehicle collision

Call the Emergency Number

Call or send someone to call for an ambulance. Calling your emergency number is often the most important thing you can do in an emergency. It is often critical to get professional medical help on the scene as soon as possible. In many communities, you can dial 911 for help in any type of emergency; otherwise, dial your local police or sheriff for medical emergencies, or dial 0, the operator, for assistance. Be prepared to follow these steps:

1. **Speak slowly and clearly.**

2. **Identify yourself and the phone number from which you are calling.**

3. **Give the exact location of the accident. Give the town, street name, and number. If you are calling at night, describe the building.**

4. **Describe what has happened. Give essential details about the victim(s), the situation, and any treatments you have given.**

5. **Ask for advice. Let the person on the other end ask you questions and tell you what to do until help arrives. Take notes, if necessary.**

6. **Hang up last. The person on the other end may have more questions or advice for you. And they might want you to stay on the phone with them until help arrives. Whatever the case, let the other person hang up first.**

Conclusion

First aid is the help that you give an injured person until qualified medical personnel can administer treatment. In other words, think of first aid as aid given first before actual medical treatment. The type of first aid required by an individual depends upon his or her injuries, and you determine what those injuries are by carefully and quickly evaluating the person. This evaluation and the administration of first aid follows a sequence that deals with the most life-threatening problems first—breathing and heartbeat, followed by bleeding; then other health problems—shock, broken bones, burns, and head injuries.

In the following lesson, you will learn life-saving techniques that you can use in a dire emergency.

Lesson Review

1. Do you know how to perform CPR? If so, where did you learn this skill? If not, where can you learn it?
2. What is the Good Samaritan Law?
3. Why is it important to have rubber gloves and a face shield in your first aid kit?
4. What skill can you use to remain calm and aware in a medical emergency?

The First Life-Saving Steps

Key Words

automated external defibrillator (AED)
cardiac arrest
cardiopulmonary resuscitation (CPR)
Heimlich maneuver
rescue breathing
stroke

What You Will Learn to Do

- Demonstrate life-saving skills in an emergency situation

Linked Core Abilities

- Do your share as a good citizen in your school, community, country, and the world

Skills and Knowledge You Will Gain Along the Way

- Describe how to perform rescue breathing
- Identify the steps for performing cardiopulmonary resuscitation (CPR)
- Explain how CPR can keep a victim's heart and brain alive
- Identify the steps for performing the Heimlich maneuver
- Define the key words contained in this lesson

Chapter 2

Introduction

In emergency situations, the people involved may find it difficult to remain calm and think clearly. In the midst of this confusion, one simple trick you can use to remind yourself of the first and most important problems to check for and steps to take are the letters ABC.

- **A stands for airway. Is the victim's airway blocked? If so, clear the airway.**
- **B stands for breathing. Is the victim breathing? If not, restore breathing.**
- **C stands for circulation. Is the victim's heart beating? If not, restore the heartbeat.**

Clearing the Airway of a Conscious Victim

Choking occurs when a person inhales something into the airway leading to the lungs, blocking the airway off and preventing breathing. In many choking cases, people inhale particles of food while eating. In an accident, injured people may choke on dirt, broken teeth, or dentures.

A person whose airway is completely blocked off cannot make any sound because no air is getting to the vocal cords. If a person can speak or cough, some air is getting through to the vocal cords and lungs, and you should let the person try to clear the airway on his or her own. If the person can make no sound and indicates choking by grabbing the throat, the best method to clear the person's airway is the **Heimlich maneuver**, shown in Figure 2.2.1. After performing the Heimlich maneuver, be sure the victim seeks professional medical help.

To perform the Heimlich maneuver on a choking victim, follow these steps:

1. **Stand behind the victim and wrap your arms around the victim's waist.**
2. **Make a fist with one hand and place the thumb side of the fist against the victim's abdomen slightly above the navel and well below the breastbone. Grasp the fist with the other hand.**
3. **Give six to ten quick backward and upward thrusts; repeat this until the airway is clear.**

For an exceptionally overweight person or pregnant woman, use the same procedure, except place the fist in the middle of the breastbone.

If you are the victim of an airway obstruction and no one is around to help, lean forward over a railing, sink, or the back of a chair, as shown in Figure 2.2.2, and thrust yourself down until you dislodge the obstruction.

> **Note**
>
> Don't slap the victim's back. This could make matters worse. For more information about the Heimlich maneuver, check out http://www.heimlichinstitute.org/howtodo.html.

Key Note Term

Heimlich maneuver – an upward push to the abdomen given to clear the airway of a person with a complete airway obstruction; procedure used to expel an object lodged in the airway of a choking victim

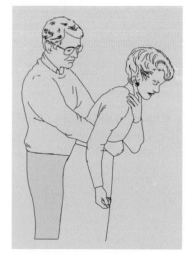

Figure 2.2.1: The Heimlich maneuver can save the life of a choking victim.
Courtesy of US Army JROTC.

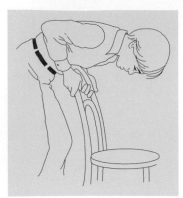

Figure 2.2.2: You can save your life when choking if you know how to dislodge the obstruction.
Courtesy of US Army JROTC.

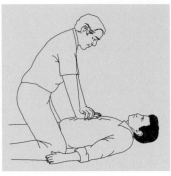

Figure 2.2.3: Kneel over an unconscious victim to clear the airway.
Courtesy of US Army JROTC.

Key Note Term

rescue breathing – the act of forcing air into and out of the lungs of a person by another person

---

Clearing the Airway of an Unconscious Victim

If a person is unconscious and you know that individual has an obstructed airway, perform the following maneuver with the victim lying on his or her back. Figure 2.2.3 shows the position for this action.

1. **Kneel astride the victim's thighs. Place the heel of one hand against the victim's abdomen, slightly above the navel, but well below the victim's breastbone, with your fingers pointing toward the victim's head.**
2. **Place your other hand on top of your first hand and press into the abdomen with a quick forward and upward thrust. Repeat this 6 to 10 times.**
3. **Open the victim's mouth and sweep out any foreign matter using a hooked finger. Be careful not to push anything down the throat.**

For an obese individual or a woman in the advanced stages of pregnancy, use the following procedure:

1. **Kneel to the side of the victim's body. Locate the lower edge of the victim's ribs and run the fingers up along the rib cage to the notch where the ribs meet the breastbone.**
2. **Place the heel of the hand two finger widths above the notch and place the other hand over the first, interlocking the fingers.**
3. **Position your shoulders over your hands and, with the elbows locked, press down 1 1/2 to 2 inches, 6 to 10 times.**
4. **Open the victim's mouth and sweep out any foreign matter using a hooked finger. Be careful not to push anything down the throat.**

Restoring the Breathing

If you discover a victim who is not breathing, it is necessary to start breathing for the victim by forcing oxygen into his or her lungs as soon as possible. This process, called **rescue breathing** or mouth-to-mouth resuscitation, can prevent brain damage and death. By applying this first aid step it will most likely start the victim breathing independently; if not, continue it until you are replaced by a qualified person or medical help arrives. When you are giving mouth-to-mouth resuscitation to a victim, you are a life-support system! Figure 2.2.4 shows the basic position for applying mouth-to-mouth resuscitation.

The following steps describe how to give mouth-to-mouth resuscitation to adults. Procedures that are different for infants and small children are italicized.

1. **Roll the victim gently over if he or she is not already facing up. Open the mouth and check to see if it is clear. Using a hooked finger, sweep out anything you find in the mouth, being careful not to push anything down the throat.**

2. Tilt the victim's head back sharply by pressing down on the forehead and lifting on the jaw. This straightens out the passageway to the victim's lungs. *For infants and small children, do not tilt the head back. Instead, place a finger under the chin and lift it slightly.*

3. Keeping the victim's head tilted sharply back, pinch the nose closed, cover the victim's mouth completely with your mouth, and give the victim two full breaths. *For infants and small children, do not pinch the nose closed. Instead, cover both the mouth and nose with your mouth and give small, slow, gentle breaths.* Each breath should last 1 to 1 1/2 seconds. Pause between breaths to let the air come out of the victim and to breathe in yourself. If the victim's chest does not rise when you breathe into his or her lungs, reposition the head slightly farther back and repeat the breaths. If the victim's chest still does not rise, perform abdominal thrusts to clear the airway as described in the previous section, "Clearing the Airway of an Unconscious Victim"; then repeat the breaths.

4. After the two breaths, listen and feel for breathing by placing your cheek close to the victim's mouth. At the same time, check the victim's pulse by placing two fingers in the groove of the neck next to the Adam's apple, as shown in Figure 2.2.5. This is the location of the carotid artery, which normally produces a strong pulse.

5. If there is no pulse, start CPR immediately as described in the next section.

6. If there is a pulse but no breathing, continue mouth-to-mouth resuscitation at the rate of one breath every five seconds or 12 times a minute. *For infants and small children, give one slow breath every three seconds.*

7. If the victim starts to breathe, stop mouth-to-mouth resuscitation and let the victim breathe on his or her own. Check for other injuries, treat as required, and observe the victim closely until medical help arrives.

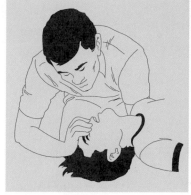

Figure 2.2.4: *Tilt the victim's head and pinch the nose to perform rescue breathing.*
Courtesy of US Army JROTC.

Cardiopulmonary Resuscitation (CPR)

As in mouth-to-mouth resuscitation, when you perform **cardiopulmonary resuscitation (CPR)**, you are a life-support system for the victim. CPR is a first aid procedure performed to restore breathing and heartbeat. It is a combination of mouth-to-mouth resuscitation and a procedure known as closed chest heart massage. Mouth-to-mouth resuscitation supplies oxygen to the lungs, while the closed chest heart massage manually pumps blood through the victim's body, circulating it to the heart and brain. These actions help keep the heart and brain alive until the heartbeat is restored or medical help arrives.

Figure 2.2.5: *After two breaths, check for a pulse as you check for breath sounds.*
Courtesy of US Army JROTC.

CPR can be performed by a single rescuer or by more than one rescuer because CPR can be tiring and is easier if two rescuers are available. The CPR procedures discussed in this lesson are for a single rescuer. Before beginning CPR, you should turn the victim face up, clear the airway, give two full breaths as described in mouth-to-mouth resuscitation, and check for a pulse. Only proceed if there is no pulse, and therefore, no heartbeat present.

Key Note Term

cardiopulmonary resuscitation (CPR) – an emergency method to keep blood and oxygen flowing through a person whose heart and breathing have stopped

Figure 2.2.5: After two breaths, check for a pulse as you check for breath sounds.
Courtesy of US Army JROTC.

Performing CPR on an Adult

To perform CPR on an adult, follow these steps:

1. With the middle and index fingers of the hand nearest the victim's legs, locate the lower edge of the rib cage on the side of the victim's chest closest to you.

2. Slide your fingers up the edge of the rib cage to the notch at the lower end of the breastbone. Place your middle finger in the notch and the index finger next to it on the lower end of the breastbone.

3. Place the heel of the hand nearest the victim's head on the breastbone next to the index finger of the hand used to find the notch.

4. Place the heel of the hand used to find the notch directly on top of the heel of the other hand. Only let the heel of your hand touch the victim's chest; keep your fingers lifted off of the victim's chest. If you place your hands correctly, they will be positioned slightly above the lowest part of the breastbone, known as the xiphoid process. Avoid pressing on the xiphoid process because it breaks easily.

5. Position your shoulders over your hands, with elbows locked and arms straight.

6. Press down on the breastbone 1 1/2 to 2 inches at a very quick, continuous rate. This squeezes the victim's heart against the spine and forces blood through the body.

7. While compressing, count aloud "one and two and three and four . . ." until you get to 15. It should take you about ten seconds to do 15 compressions. Push down as you say the number and release the pressure as you say "and." Compress up and down smoothly without removing your hands from the chest.

8. After the 15th compression, give the victim two full breaths. Be sure to pinch the nose closed and tilt the victim's head back to straighten the airway. Then return to the chest compression.

9. When you complete four cycles of 15 chest compressions and two breaths, check for a pulse again. If there is no pulse, continue CPR.

Performing CPR on an Infant

Performing CPR on an infant is slightly different than performing it on an adult. Follow these steps:

1. Place your hand closest to the infant's head gently on the infant's forehead and leave it there throughout the procedure.

2. Place the middle and ring fingers of the hand nearest the infant's legs on the infant's breastbone about one finger width below the infant's nipples.

3. Give five compressions with those two fingers at a rapid pace, pushing the chest down about 1/2 to 1 inch.

4. Follow the five compressions with one breath as described in the italicized text in Step 3 of mouth-to-mouth resuscitation. Rapidly repeat the five compressions and one breath 20 times a minute until breathing and heartbeat resume.

Performing CPR on a Child

To perform CPR on a child, follow these steps:

1. As with an adult, find the notched center of the child's ribcage with the hand closest to the child's legs. Measure two finger widths above the notch using the other hand, and then place the heel of the hand used to find the notch on the child's breastbone above the two fingers.

2. Place the hand that you used to measure two finger widths gently on the child's forehead and leave it there throughout the rest of the procedure.

3. Using the heel of your hand and keeping your fingers off of the child's chest, give five compressions 1 to 1 1/2 inches deep, followed by one breath as described in the italicized text in Step 3 of mouth-to-mouth resuscitation. Repeat this sequence 12 times a minute until breathing and heartbeat resume.

Heart Attacks

A heart attack occurs when the blood supply to part of the heart muscle is severely reduced or stopped. This happens when one of the coronary arteries (the arteries that supply blood to the heart muscle) is blocked by an obstruction or a spasm. Common signs and symptoms of a heart attack include the following:

- Uncomfortable pressure, fullness, squeezing, or pain in the center of the chest that lasts more than a few minutes or that goes away and comes back

- Pain spreading to the shoulders, neck, or arms

- Chest discomfort with lightheadedness, fainting, sweating, nausea, or shortness of breath

When a person's heart stops beating, the victims is said to be in **cardiac arrest**. CPR can keep the individual alive. If a person has a heart attack, call emergency medical services (EMS). Monitor the ABCs and give CPR as necessary.

Stroke

A **stroke** occurs when blood vessels that deliver oxygen-rich blood to the brain ruptures or when a blood clot forms and blocks the flow of blood in the brain. Common signs and symptoms of a stroke include the following:

- Paralysis on one side of the body

- Blurred or decreased vision; pupils of unequal size

- Problems speaking, slurred speech

- Difficulty breathing

- Mental confusion

> **Key Note Term**
>
> **cardiac arrest** – the sudden stoppage of the heart

> **Key Note Term**
>
> **stroke** – a reduction of blood flow to a part of the brain

- Dizziness or loss of balance
- Sudden, severe, or unexplained headache
- Loss of consciousness

If a person has a stroke, call the EMS. Lay the victim down on one side and cover with blanket. Monitor the ABCs and give CPR as necessary.

> **Note**
>
> To learn more about strokes, check out www.strokeassociation.org to see the American Stroke Association Web site.

Automated External Defibrillators (AED)

Key Note Term

automated external defibrillator (AED) – a device used to treat a patient with cardiac arrest whose heart is beating irregularly

Recently there has been a breakthrough in how emergency medical technicians (EMTs) treat victims of sudden cardiac arrest. The **automated external defibrillator (AED)** is a device that uses a computer chip to analyze the heart rhythm and determines whether a shock is needed. This device allows victims suffering a sudden cardiac arrest a greatly improved chance of survival. Because of the ease of operation, people can be trained in AED use in a few hours, and some say the techniques are easier to learn than CPR. Many AEDs offer voice prompts, which provide operators with clear and concise instructions. Most AEDs have only three buttons: On/Off, Analyze, and Shock. Many airlines have installed AEDs on all their planes, and several cities are locating them in areas where there are large concentrations of people, such as malls, arenas, and stadiums.

Conclusion

This lesson presents the correct techniques for dealing with the most life-threatening conditions of an accident victim—loss of breathing and heartbeat. Use the letters **ABC** to remind yourself of the first problems to check for on an injured person: **A**irway blocked, loss of **B**reathing, and lack of **C**irculation. Perform the Heimlich maneuver to clear a victim's airway, mouth-to-mouth resuscitation to restore breathing, and CPR to restore circulation (heartbeat). For the best and safest results, take a class from a qualified instructor before performing mouth-to-mouth resuscitation and CPR on an injured person.

In the next lesson, you will learn the steps necessary to control bleeding. An accident can happen anywhere at any time. Knowing how to control bleeding is invaluable information.

Lesson Review

1. What are the ABCs of life-saving steps?

2. Demonstrate the Heimlich maneuver, performing it both on another person and on yourself.

3. When performing CPR, what are the differences between performing this on an adult, an infant, and a child?

4. What are the common signs of a stroke?

Controlling Bleeding

Key Words

arteries
dressing
elevated
hemorrhage
pressure bandage
pressure point
veins

What You Will Learn to Do

- Determine first aid procedures for a bleeding victim

Linked Core Abilities

- Do your share as a good citizen in your school, community, country, and the world

Skills and Knowledge You Will Gain Along the Way

- Identify the three types of bleeding
- Identify the best way to control most bleeding cases
- Distinguish among direct pressure, pressure points, and a tourniquet to control bleeding
- Describe how to clean wounds
- Define the key words contained in this lesson

Chapter 2

Introduction

In an accident situation, you may encounter injured persons bleeding from wounds such as scrapes, cuts, or punctures as well as tears or gashes in the skin. The deeper a wound is, the more serious it becomes. Minor wounds to the outer layer of skin do not bleed heavily but still require cleaning to avoid infection. Deeper wounds in which **arteries** and **veins** are cut can be life threatening. These kinds of wounds may involve great loss of blood, and blood may often pulse or spurt out of the wound. Severe bleeding, or **hemorrhage**, can result in shock or death if not treated promptly. It is essential to stop the loss of blood in these cases. If a victim loses too much blood, even CPR will not keep the person alive because there will not be enough blood to deliver oxygen from the lungs to the body.

Key Note Terms

arteries – blood vessels that carry blood away from the heart to all parts of the body

veins – blood vessels that carry blood from all parts of the body to the heart

hemorrhage – Heavy, uncontrollable bleeding

Types of Bleeding

There are three types of bleeding you may encounter in an emergency situation:

- **Arterial bleeding.** Blood loss from an artery. Characterized by bright red blood that spurts with each heartbeat, arterial blood loss is severe and hard to control. Give it first priority for treatment.

- **Venous bleeding.** Blood loss from a vein. Venous bleeding is characterized by a steady flow of dark blood.

- **Capillary bleeding.** Blood loss from the capillaries (the smallest blood vessels); usually characterized by a slow flow of blood.

First aid treatment in all of these cases includes stopping the flow of blood and preventing infection.

Direct Pressure

In most cases, applying continuous, direct pressure to a wound is the best way to control bleeding. To apply direct pressure, place a **dressing** over the wound and apply pressure to the dressing, as shown in Figure 2.3.1. A dressing should be

- **As sterile as possible (If a sterile dressing is not available, use a clean cloth—a washcloth, towel, or handkerchief)**

Key Note Term

dressing – ointment and bandages applied to a wound

Figure 2.3.1: Apply direct pressure to the bandage to stop bleeding.
Courtesy of US Army JROTC.

- **Larger than the wound**
- **Thick, soft, and compressible so pressure is evenly distributed over the wound**
- **Lint free**

If a clean cloth or gauze is not available, use clothing, your bare hands, or your fingers—whatever is the cleanest. Continue applying pressure and the bleeding should begin to slow or stop within 30 minutes.

Stopping Infection

Even the slightest wound requires immediate cleansing. The best way to clean wounds is to wash them with soap and water. At home, use water from the faucet. On a hike, use water from a canteen or the clear running water of a stream. If available, use an antiseptic cleanser instead of soap. Wait until the skin around the wound dries and then put on a bandage. If available, apply an antiseptic cream to the wound before bandaging it.

For a minor wound, cleaning and bandaging it is probably all that is required. Deep wounds, wounds made by animal or human bites, and wounds contaminated by dirt, rust, or other items require medical treatment. Clean and bandage these wounds, and get medical assistance as soon as possible. If a wound contains glass or other objects stuck into the flesh, do not remove them unless they wash out of the wound easily.

Controlling Bleeding to Extremities

Key Note Terms

elevated – raised up

pressure bandage – a snug bandage used to control bleeding

In most cases, direct pressure is the best way to stop bleeding of wounds to the extremities (arms and legs). As you apply direct pressure, keep the injured limb **elevated** above the heart to slow the flow of blood out of the body. After initially applying direct pressure, you may want to apply a **pressure bandage** by wrapping a bandage snugly around the limb, using overlapping turns with a roll of gauze. Do not tie the pressure bandage so tightly that it restricts blood flow to the lower part of the limb. If fingertips or toes appear bluish or if there is no pulse below the dressing, loosen the material used to secure the dressing immediately. After you apply a pressure bandage, only qualified medical personnel should remove it.

Key Note Term

pressure point – a point on the body where a major artery lies near the skin surface and passes over a bone

Pressure Points

In the case of severe bleeding that does not slow or stop using direct pressure, finger pressure may be applied to the **pressure point** on the injured limb between the wound and the heart. Pressure points, shown in Figure 2.3.2, are locations on the body where arteries are close to the surface. By applying pressure at these points, you slow or stop the flow of blood through the artery.

As with mouth-to-mouth resuscitation and CPR, it is better to have first aid training on pressure points before actually using this technique to stop bleeding. If done incorrectly, you may damage healthy tissue fed by the artery you are constricting.

Tourniquet

If heavy blood loss continues, as from amputation, it may be necessary to use a tourniquet.

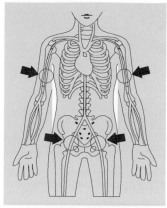

Figure 2.3.2: Use pressure points on the body to help slow or stop bleeding.
Courtesy of US Army JROTC.

> ### Caution
>
> Because a tourniquet is a constricting band that stops the flow of blood below it, it can kill the limb to which it is applied; therefore, only use a tourniquet if no other method works to stop the bleeding and you believe the injured person's life is in danger.

To apply a tourniquet, follow these steps:

1. **Fold a cloth until it is approximately two inches wide and long enough to go around the injured limb (see Figure 2.3.3).**

2. **Tie the material in a loop and position it two to four inches above the wound, but not over a joint.**

3. **Pass a rigid object, such as a stick, under the tourniquet loop and twist it until the bleeding stops (see Figure 2.3.4).**

4. **Tie off the end of the stick with another piece of cloth or string to prevent it from unwinding (see Figure 2.3.5).**

5. **Mark the victim's forehead with a "T" to alert medical personnel that you have applied a tourniquet.**

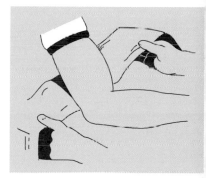

Figure 2.3.3: Fold a cloth so it is long enough to go around the injured limb.
Courtesy of US Army JROTC.

If it is necessary to cover the victim with a blanket, do not cover the tourniquet to make it easier for medical personnel to spot. After you apply a tourniquet, do not loosen or remove it. As with a pressure dressing, only qualified medical personnel should remove a tourniquet.

> ### Note
>
> Remember, use a tourniquet only as a last resort when all other attempts to stop the bleeding fail.

Controlling Bleeding to the Head and Torso

There are different way to control head and torso bleeding. This section details how to use the methods.

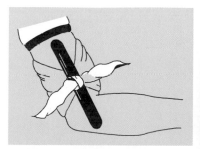

Figure 2.3.4: Use a stick or other rigid object to tie off the tourniquet.
Courtesy of US Army JROTC.

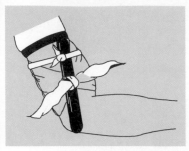

Figure 2.3.5: Secure the end of the stick to keep the tourniquet from unwinding.
Courtesy of US Army JROTC.

Scalp Injuries

For wounds to the scalp, use a pressure dressing. If brain tissue is exposed, tie the dressing loosely over the wound. Do not press the brain tissue back into the open wound.

Facial Injuries

Control bleeding from facial wounds by using a pressure bandage. Position the victim to prevent him or her from breathing blood. Victims who have sustained a severe blow to the head should be kept under close observation as they may have brain damage and could require rescue breathing.

Chest Injuries

A chest injury may result in an open chest wound, which could lead to air leaking from a lung and the collapse of a lung. If conscious, have the victim breathe out and apply some material such as plastic wrap or foil to the wound. Bind a pressure bandage tightly to the wound to prevent leakage of air and slow down blood loss. Have the victim sit up, if possible, or lay that person on the injured side.

Abdominal Injuries

When an open abdominal wound has exposed visceral (internal) organs, cover the abdomen loosely with dressings. Do not force the organs back into the body cavity and do not give victims with abdominal wounds any food or water.

Conclusion

Severe bleeding from wounds in which arteries or veins are cut can be life-threatening to an injured person; therefore, controlling the loss of blood is second in importance only to restoring breathing and circulation. In most cases, applying direct pressure to a wound is the best way to control bleeding. Cleansing a wound to stop infection is also extremely important. If you know these two facts, and the other details on controlling bleeding to the extremities, head, and torso, you can successfully accomplish the second life-saving step in an emergency situation.

In the next lesson, you will learn how to treat shock. You will also learn how to immobilize fractures.

Lesson Review

1. List and explain the three types of bleeding.
2. How does direct pressure help stop bleeding?
3. Why is it important to use bandages that are as clean as possible?
4. Define the term *hemorrhage*.

Chapter 2

Lesson Review

Lesson 4

Treating for Shock and Immobilizing Fractures

Key Words

clammy
closed fracture
dislocation
fainting
ligament
open fracture
splint
sprain
strain
trauma

What You Will Learn to Do

- Determine first aid treatment for shock, fractures, strains and sprains

Linked Core Abilities

- Do your share as a good citizen in your school, community, country, and the world

Skills and Knowledge You Will Gain Along the Way

- Explain causes and effects of shock
- Identify the signs of shock
- Demonstrate how to treat for shock
- Distinguish between closed and open fractures
- Identify procedures for immobilizing fractures using splints and slings
- Distinguish between strains and sprains
- Define the key words contained in this lesson

Chapter 2

Introduction

Whenever you treat someone for a severe injury, you must also treat them for shock. Even if an injured person shows no signs of shock, treat them for shock anyway, since shock can follow all major injuries. By treating for shock, you lessen its severity. If left untreated, shock can become life threatening. There are cases of people who died from shock even though their injuries would not have killed them; therefore, knowing how to deal with shock is a very important part of first aid.

After treating for shock, take care of broken bones or suspected broken bones. If there is a question of whether or not a bone is broken, treat it as if it were broken. Follow the first aid procedures for splinting a fracture carefully because more damage can occur if a fracture is handled improperly.

Shock

Shock from an injury is different from electric shock, although it can be brought on by electric shock, as well as blood loss, burns, psychological **trauma**, heart attack, and other injuries involving pain. Shock disrupts circulation. In an attempt to correct damage from an injury and to protect its blood supply, the body routes blood away from outer tissues to organs inside the body. This may keep adequate blood, and therefore oxygen, from reaching the brain. In severe cases, the injured person can lose consciousness and blood supply to vital organs like the heart, causing death.

Key Note Term

trauma – a behavioral state resulting from mental or emotional stress or physical injury that has a lasting effect on the mind; a physical wound or injury

Shock usually occurs within the first hour after a severe injury. How severe shock becomes depends upon several factors including the type of injury, how much blood is lost, and characteristics of the injured person's nervous system. Increased pain, rough handling, delayed treatment, and emotional reactions such as fear and panic can worsen shock.

Signs of Shock

When a victim is in shock, the skin is pale or bluish and cold to the touch. For a victim with dark skin, check the color of the mucous membranes on the inside of the mouth or under the eyelids, or check under the nail beds. The skin may be **clammy** from perspiration. Other signs that may develop in the early stages of shock include the following:

Key Note Term

clammy – damp, soft, sticky, and unusually cool

- **Restlessness or nervousness**
- **Thirst**
- **Bleeding**
- **Confusion or loss of awareness**
- **Breathing rapidly**
- **Nausea and/or vomiting**
- **Blotchy or bluish skin around the mouth and lips**
- **Fainting**

Key Note Term

fainting – to lose consciousness briefly because of temporary decrease in the amount of blood that flows to the brain

Fainting, or blacking out, is a mild form of shock caused by a lack of blood to the brain. Fright, bad news, breathing polluted air, or standing too long can result in fainting. Before fainting occurs, a shock victim may turn pale, shake, or suddenly fall to the ground.

Treating Shock

Procedures for treating shock include improving circulation of the blood, ensuring an adequate supply of oxygen, and maintaining normal body temperature. To treat a victim for shock, follow these steps:

1. **Position the victim on his or her back, unless a sitting position allows easier breathing. If the victim is vomiting, position that person on the side to let fluid drain from the mouth.**

2. **Elevate the victim's feet higher than the heart, unless the victim has an abdominal or chest wound or an unsplinted leg fracture.**

3. **Loosen clothing that may bind around the neck and waist.**

4. **Keep the victim from becoming cold or overheating.**

5. **Reassure the victim and do not give him or her any food or drink; however, if you know that help is not going to arrive for over an hour, give the victim small amounts of fluids at room temperature every 15 minutes. Add an eighth of a teaspoon of salt, if available, to each half glass of fluid. This will help the victim retain more fluids in his or her system.**

Fractures

Key Note Terms

closed (simple) fracture – a fracture in which the broken bone does not push through the skin's surface

open (compound) fracture – a fracture in which the broken end of a bone pierces the skin

Bone fractures resulting from falls are common injuries. A **closed or simple fracture** is a break in the bone that does not penetrate the skin. An **open or compound fracture** occurs if the sharp edges of a splintered bone have cut through the skin. Both types of fractures are shown in Figure 2.4.1.

In the case of an open fracture, it is obvious that a bone is broken. In the case of a closed fracture, indications of a broken bone include swelling, discoloration, and unusual positioning of the limb in question.

Figure 2.4.1: Closed (simple) and open (compound) fractures.
Courtesy of US Army JROTC.

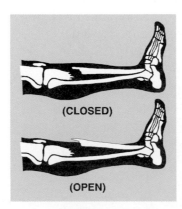

Do's and Don'ts

When treating fractures, what you do is important, and what you don't do is equally as important.

- **Do** call for medical assistance immediately
- **Do** keep the victim from moving
- **Do** treat for shock while waiting for medical assistance
- **Don't** try to set the bone
- **Don't** put the victim in a car to rush him or her to a hospital as that is the easiest way of turning a closed fracture into an open one
- **Don't** give stimulants if there is severe bleeding

Splints

The most important action to take when dealing with a fracture is to immobilize the injured bone to prevent further damage. The best way to immobilize bones is with a **splint**, shown in Figure 2.4.2.

For open fractures, control the bleeding before splinting. Keep the exposed bone moist by covering it with a moist, sterile dressing. The rules of splinting are as follows:

1. Pad all splinting material. Make splints from sticks, boards, cardboard, rolled newspaper, or any other unbendable material.

2. Splint the broken leg or arm in the position in which you found it. Do not try to straighten or reposition the fracture. In most cases, support an arm from above and below and a leg from the sides.

3. Use splinting material that is long enough to immobilize the joint above and below the break. For example, immobilize the ankle and the knee for a fracture in the vicinity of the calf.

4. Tie the splints above and below the suspected fracture. Make two ties above and two below the break. Never make a tie directly over the break.

5. Tie all knots on the outside of the splints.

6. Check that circulation is not restricted by splints tied too tightly.

Key Note Term

splint – to support and immobilize a body part with a stiff material

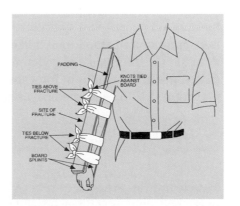

Figure 2.4.2: Splints help immobilize bones to prevent further injury.
Courtesy of US Army JROTC.

Figure 2.4.3: Placing a sling on an injured arm can support the injury.
Courtesy of US Army JROTC.

If no splinting material is available, immobilize a leg fracture by placing padding between the injured leg and the uninjured leg and tying them together. Using the uninjured leg as the splint, draw two ties above and two below the suspected break.

Slings

For arm fractures in which the entire arm is not splinted, use a **sling** (see Figure 2.4.3) to support the weight of the arm. If necessary, pin the victim's shirttail up to serve as a field expedient sling.

Joint Injuries

Joint injuries occur when excess stress or strain is placed on the joint. This can happen during normal activities such as walking or running and is common in sports activities. Dislocations and sprains are the most common joint injuries.

Dislocations

A **dislocation** occurs when a joint comes apart and stays apart with the bone ends no longer in contact. The shoulders, elbows, fingers, hips, kneecaps, and ankles are the joints most frequently affected. Dislocations have signs and symptoms similar to those of a fracture: severe pain, swelling, and the inability of the victim to move the injured joint. The main sign of a dislocation is deformity; its appearance will be different from that of a comparable uninjured joint. The procedures for treating a dislocation include the following:

1. **Do not try to set the joint. Immobilize and support the injured joint as if treating for a fracture.**
2. **Use the RICE procedures (discussed later in this lesson).**
3. **Seek medical attention.**

Sprain

A **sprain** is an injury to a joint in which the **ligaments** and other tissues are damaged by violent stretching or twisting. Attempts to move or use the joint increase the pain. The skin about the joint may be discolored because of bleeding from torn tissues. It is often difficult to distinguish between a severe sprain and a fracture, because their signs and symptoms are similar. If you are not sure whether an injury is a sprain or a fracture, treat it like a fracture. It is better to immobilize a sprain than to take the chance of a victim sustaining further damage from an unsplinted closed fracture. Treatment for a sprain consists of **R**est, **I**ce, **C**ompression, and **E**levation (RICE). Seek medical attention.

Muscle Injuries

Muscle injuries are as common as joint injuries. These can be very painful and need treatment as soon as possible after the injury occurs. The most common muscle injury is a strain.

Key Note Terms

dislocation – the separation of a bone from its joint

sprain – an injury caused by twisting a ligament or tendon around a joint

ligament – a fibrous band of tissue that holds bones together at a joint

Strain

A muscle **strain**, or muscle pull, occurs when a muscle is stretched beyond its normal range of motion, resulting in the muscle tearing. Signs and symptoms include: sharp pain, extreme tenderness when the area is touched, slight swelling, and difficulty moving or using the affected part. When treating for strain use RICE.

RICE: Procedures for Bone, Joint, and Muscle Injuries

As discussed earlier in this lesson, RICE is the acronym for the first aid procedures—rest, ice, compression, and elevation—for bone, joint, and muscle injuries. What is done in the first 48–72 hours following such an injury can greatly affect the recovery.

1. **Rest.** Injuries heal faster if rested. Rest means the victim stays off the injured part.

2. **Ice.** An ice pack should be applied to the injured area for 20–30 minutes every 2–3 hours during the first 24–48 hours. When the skin becomes numb, remove the ice pack.

3. **Compression.** Compression of the injured area may squeeze some fluid and debris out of the injury site. Compression limits the ability of the skin and of other tissues to expand. Applying compression may be the most important step in preventing swelling. The victim should wear an elastic bandage continuously for 18–24 hours.

4. **Elevation.** Gravity has an important effect on swelling. The force of gravity pulls blood and other tissue to the lower parts of the body. After fluids get to your hands or feet, they have nowhere else to go; therefore, those parts of the body tend to swell the most. Elevating the injured areas, in combination with ice and compression, limits circulation to that area, which in turn helps limit internal bleeding and minimize swelling. Whenever possible, elevate the injured part above the level of the heart for the first 24 hours after an injury.

Conclusion

This lesson explained the first aid procedures for treating shock and fractures. Remember that shock can follow severe injuries and can be life threatening if left untreated. Treating a victim for shock involves improving circulation, ensuring an adequate oxygen supply, and maintaining normal body temperature. For fractures, the most important action to take is immobilizing the broken bone using splints. By following these first aid procedures, you can lessen the severity of shock caused by an injury and ensure that no further damage occurs to a victim because of a broken bone, sprain, or strain.

The next lesson covers first aid for burns. Burn injuries can happen anywhere, from the kitchen to the workplace, and knowing how to treat burns is a must.

Lesson Review

1. List one do and one don't when treating fractures.
2. What causes fainting?
3. What are the signs of shock?
4. Describe the differences between a strain and a sprain.

First Aid for Burns

Key Terms

acids
alkalis
bases
caustic
compresses
flush
mottled
neutralized
scalding
smoldering
systemic

What You Will Learn to Do

- Determine first aid treatment for burns

Linked Core Abilities

- Do your share as a good citizen in your school, community, country, and the world

Skills and Knowledge You Will Gain Along the Way

- Characterize degrees of burns

- Describe how to treat first-, second-, and third-degree heat burns

- Describe how to treat electrical burns

- Describe how to treat chemical burns to the eyes and skin

- Define the key words contained in this lesson

Introduction

Burns come from sources such as heat, electricity, and chemicals. In situations where people are injured by these sources, your first aid knowledge should include how to treat them. This lesson covers different types of burns, how to treat them, and ways to prevent them.

Burns

There are several types and degrees of burns that require different treatments. Heat, electricity, and chemicals can produce different burn injuries with their severity depending upon the burn's depth, size, and location. Burns can be painful and may result in shock and infection. They can be very serious if they are spread over a large area of the body, there are other injuries involved, or the victim is very young or very old.

Degrees of Burns

For burns caused by sources of heat, there are different categories of degrees (first, second, or third) based on the burn's depth. The deeper the burn, the more severe and the higher the degree the burn is. All electrical burns are third degree.

Characteristics of First-Degree Burns

There are several characteristics of first-degree burns, as shown in Figure 2.5.1:

- **Least severe**
- **Injury to only the top layer of skin**
- **Reddening of the skin**
- **Produce mild swelling**

Figure 2.5.1 Most sunburns are first-degree burns.
Courtesy of Sinclair Stammers/Photo Researchers.

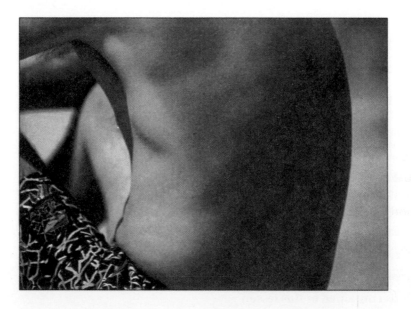

Chapter 2   First Aid for Emergency and Nonemergency Situations

- Cause pain due to irritated nerve endings

- Heal quickly and completely if properly treated

- Caused by brief contact with hot objects, brief exposure to hot water or steam, and overexposure to sun (light sunburn) or wind

Characteristics of Second-Degree Burns

There are several characteristics of second-degree burns:

- Involve deeper layers of skin

- Cause skin to turn red and/or **mottled**

- Appear moist and oozing from the loss of fluid through damaged skin layers

- Produce blisters and swelling

- Usually the most painful type of burn because nerve endings are still intact even though tissue damage is severe.

- Burns covering a large area may cause shock due to extensive loss of fluid from the burned skin.

- Smaller second-degree burns that are properly treated should heal within two weeks with little or no scarring.

- Caused by a deep sunburn, prolonged contact with hot objects, **scalding**, and flash burns from flammable liquids suddenly bursting into flame

Characteristics of Third-Degree Burns

The specific characteristics of third-degree burns are as follows:

- Deepest and most severe type of burn

- May look white or charred (may appear to be a second-degree burn at first)

- Results in deep tissue destruction, reaching all layers of the skin and sometimes even structures below the skin

- Often cause little or no pain because nerve endings are destroyed

- Often cause shock

- Will be covered by scar tissue after healed

- Caused by immersion in extremely hot water, prolonged contact with flames, and electric shock

Treatment of Heat Burns

Treat heat burns based on their degree; therefore, before treating a burn, determine its degree and treat accordingly. When deciding the degree of a burn, in addition to the previous descriptions, it may help to know the source of the burn and/or how hot the source was, as well as how long the victim was exposed to it. If a victim appears to have a combination of burns of different degrees, determine the degree of the most burned part—usually in the middle of the burned area—and treat for that degree. If you are not sure about the degree of a burn, treat it as a third-degree burn.

Keep in mind that the goal of burn treatment is to relieve the victim's pain, prevent him/her from going into shock, and prevent infection of the burned area.

> **Key Note Term**
>
> **mottled** – marked with irregular spots or splotches of different colors or shades of color

> **Key Note Term**
>
> **scalding** – the burning of the skin by a substance that is near boiling in temperature

Treating First-Degree Burns

To treat first-degree burns, follow these steps:

1. Loosen tight clothing and remove jewelry from the burned area before it swells. Have the victim put his/her jewelry in a safe place after removal.

2. Cool the burned part with water by either holding it under cold, running water, pouring cold water over it, immersing it in cold water, or applying cold wet **compresses** to it. Cooling the burn with water helps remove heat from the skin, relieves pain and swelling, and cleans the injury. Continue this cooling treatment for between 5 and 15 minutes until the pain subsides.

3. Gently pat the burned area dry with a clean cloth.

4. Cover the injury with a sterile bandage or clean cloth to keep air off of it, thereby reducing pain, and to provide protection against infection. Keep the bandage loose to keep pressure off of the injury.

5. After a first-degree burn is completely cooled, especially a sunburn, use a lotion or moisturizer to relieve pain and prevent drying of the skin.

Treating Second-Degree Burns

To treat second-degree burns, follow these steps:

1. For second-degree burns, follow steps one through four for treating first-degree burns. If you use running water to cool the injured part, ensure the water is not so forceful that blisters on the burned skin are broken.

2. Elevate the burned part.

3. Ensure the victim drinks plenty of liquids to avoid dehydration.

4. Seek medical treatment for second-degree burns to the face, hands, feet, or genitals or that are more than two to three inches in diameter.

> **Note**
>
> For extensive second-degree burns, monitor the victim for signs of shock and treat accordingly until he/she receives medical treatment. See Lesson 4 for signs and treatment of shock. For second-degree burns to the face, especially if accompanied by smoke inhalation, the victim may have respiratory burns that can lead to swelling and blockage of his/her airway. Monitor the victim's breathing and treat accordingly until he/she receives medical treatment.

Treating Third-Degree Burns

To treat third-degree burns, follow these steps:

1. Remove the victim from the source of heat if he/she is still in contact with it. (See the following section for removing a victim from a source of electricity.)

2. Call for emergency medical services (EMS). All third-degree burns require medical treatment regardless of their size. Until the victim receives treatment, follow steps 3 through 9.

Key Note Term

compresses – folded cloths or pads applied to press on a body part to stop bleeding or cool a burn

---

3. Ensure that the victim is breathing. If not, begin mouth-to-mouth resuscitation.

4. Remove any clothing that is still **smoldering** to stop further burning. If the victim is wearing jewelry that is near or on a burned area, remove it if it comes off easily. Place the jewelry in the victim's pocket, purse, and so on, if available. If not, reassure the victim that you will give his/her jewelry to emergency medical personnel when they arrive.

5. If necessary, expose the burned area by cutting and gently lifting away any clothing. If any cloth sticks to the burn, leave it in place.

> **Note**
>
> If you are in a chemically contaminated area, do not expose the burned area; simply apply a dressing over the victim's clothing.

6. Cover the burned area loosely with cool moist compresses, sterile bandages, or clean cloth.

> **Note**
>
> Unlike treatment for first- and second-degree burns, do not cool a third-degree burn with water because this can increase the risk of shock.

7. Elevate the burned part.

8. Treat the victim for shock. Pay special attention to the victim's body temperature, which can change rapidly due to the skin being burned.

9. Monitor breathing of victims with burns to the face and burns resulting from fire accompanied by smoke inhalation. Treat accordingly.

Don'ts When Treating Burns

It is important to know what to do when treating burns, but it is equally as important to know what not to do. The following list details actions that should never be done when treating burns.

- Do not put butter, oil, or grease on a burn; these ointments can keep heat in the burn and cause more damage, as well as increase the chance of infection.

- Do not use cotton or cottony bandages on burns as they may stick to the injury.

- Do not put ice or ice water on a burn; this can result in frostbite and cause more damage to the skin.

- Do not break any blisters that have formed; blisters help protect against infection.

- Do not put pressure on a burn.

- Do not try to remove stuck clothing, debris, or loosened skin from a burn.

Key Note Term

smoldering – burning slowly without flame but often with much smoke

- Do not try to clean a wound with soap, alcohol, or any other antiseptic product; only water should be used and only on first- and second-degree burns.

- Do not let a victim walk on burned feet even if he/she tells you it does not hurt; third-degree burns can cause little pain because nerve endings are destroyed, but damage is severe and pressure from walking will only increase it.

Prevention of Heat Burns

There are many things you can do to prevent heat burns, including the following:

- Use caution when handling matches and starting a fire, particularly with a flammable liquid.

- If you have young brothers and sisters, store matches out of their reach.

- Use caution around hot liquids, steam, and heating and cooking equipment.

- Ensure hot tap water is not scalding before stepping into a tub or shower or putting your hands under a running faucet.

- Ensure your home has a fire extinguisher and smoke alarms.

- Never use water on an electrical fire; use a chemical fire extinguisher.

- If anyone in your household smokes, remind them not to smoke in bed.

- Keep a box of baking soda in the kitchen to smother grease fires.

- Turn pot handles on the stove so they are not sticking out where someone may bump them in passing.

- For electric cookware, do not let cords hang off the counter, where they can be caught and pull the cookware off as well.

- If a pilot light goes out on a gas appliance, make sure all burners and the stove are turned off and ventilate the area before relighting it or before using electrical switches, which make tiny sparks.

- Do not leave flammable items (such as newspapers or dishcloths) near the fireplace or on or near the stove.

- Turn off space heaters before going to sleep or leaving the house.

- Know what actions to take if a fire starts in your home and practice them with family members.

Treatment of Electrical Burns

Although an electrical shock will often produce only a minor mark on the skin, the injury can be a serious, deep-tissue burn, so treat all electrical burns as third degree. The current from an electrical shock passing through a victim's body can also result in unconsciousness and may slow or stop his or her breathing and/or heartbeat; therefore, treat electrical shock as a potentially life-threatening injury.

If you believe a person has been electrocuted, assess the situation first *before* touching the victim. He or she may still be in contact with the electrical current, and if you touch him or her, you could become a victim of electrical shock as well. Follow these steps to avoid a double accident and provide first aid treatment:

1. **If the victim is still in contact with the source of electricity, stop the current.**

   Shut off the electrical current by unplugging a cord, removing a fuse from the fuse box, or turning off the circuit breaker, as appropriate. Remember that in many cases, just turning off a wall or appliance switch does not stop the electrical flow. Even though you have shut off the electrical current, to be completely safe, move the victim away from the electrical source before continuing. Proceed to step 3.

   If you cannot turn off the electricity or you are outside and the shock is due to a downed power line, either call the power company yourself if you have a phone near you, or if there are other people around, have someone else call the power company. Meanwhile, since it may take you less time to separate the victim from the current than to wait for the power to be cut off, proceed to step 2. Or, if you are alone and/or there is no phone readily available in this situation, proceed to step 2.

2. **Separate the victim from the source of electrical current (see Figure 2.5.2).**

   Push the victim off of or away from the source of electricity—or push the source of electricity off of or away from the victim—using a dry nonconducting material (wood, plastic, cardboard) like a broom, stick, or chair. If available, also stand on something dry and nonconducting, like newspaper or a rubber mat, as you disengage the victim.

   If pushing does not work, use a dry rope or dry clothing to lift or drag the victim off of or away from the source of electricity. This method works better if there are two rescuers: one to lift the victim off and the other to push the electrical source away.

Special Precaution

If the ground is wet, do not attempt to move a victim in contact with an electrical current. Water conducts electricity, and you can be electrocuted as well. In this case, the current must be stopped before you can administer first aid.

---

3. **Check the victim's breathing and pulse. Be prepared to administer mouth-to-mouth resuscitation or cardiopulmonary resuscitation (CPR) if the victim's breathing is shallow or nonexistent or his/her pulse is dangerously slow or nonexistent.**

 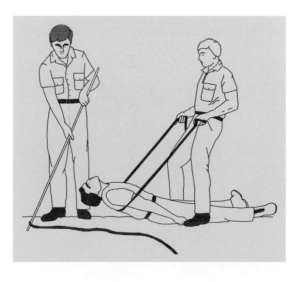

Figure 2.5.2: Removing a victim from the source of an electrical current.
Courtesy of US Army JROTC.

4. After you are sure the victim is breathing, take the time to call EMS if you or someone else has not already done so.

5. Check the victim for two burn sites—one where the electricity entered the body and one where it exited the body. Treat the burns by following steps 4 through 9 for treating third-degree burns, including treating for shock and monitoring breathing.

> **Note**
>
> About 1,000 people die each year in the United States due to electrical shock.

Prevention of Electrical Burns

Electrical burns can be prevented if you know what to do. How to prevent electrical burns:

- Do not use electrical appliances in the tub, while showering, or in or near swimming pools.
- Do not use electrical equipment outdoors if it is raining or the ground is wet.
- Ensure electrical equipment you use outdoors is made for outdoor use, with three-way ground plugs and heavier wiring.
- Ensure outdoor electrical outlets have weatherproof covers.
- If you have very young brothers or sisters, ensure there are child safety plugs in all electrical outlets.
- Do not overload an outlet by plugging in several appliances in a "piggyback" fashion (see Figure 2.5.3).
- Do not use electrical appliances or equipment that have exposed wiring or frayed cords or that overheat or create sparks.
- Do not climb trees that have wires running through or near them.

Figure 2.5.3: Unsafe electrical outlet.
Courtesy of US Army JROTC.

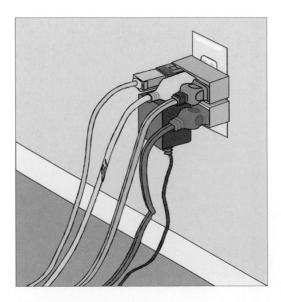

- Look for overhead wires before using long tools like tree trimmers, pool skimmers, or ladders.

- Stay inside during electrical storms; keep away from windows; do not use appliances or the phone, because lightning can travel through wires; and do not take a shower or bath, because lightning can also travel through pipes.

- If you are caught outside during an electrical storm, avoid trees, poles, and metal objects; find low ground and crouch down.

Treatment of Chemical Burns

Chemical burns occur when the skin or eyes come in contact with liquid or dry chemicals that are **caustic** or irritating. You may have products around your house, such as rust and paint removers and drain and cement cleaners, that contain **acids** designed to eat away certain materials and **bases** (also called **alkalis**) used to cut through grease. If used carelessly or improperly, these products may also do the same to your clothes and skin.

The seriousness of a chemical burn depends on the

- Length of time the chemical is in contact with the skin or eyes
- Concentration of the chemical; the more concentrated, the more damaging
- Temperature of the product containing the chemical; the higher the temperature, the quicker the damage.

Treatment of chemical burns involves stopping the chemical action immediately by removing the chemical from the skin or eyes and by removing contaminated clothing that can transmit absorbed chemicals to the skin. Treatment will vary depending on the type of chemical involved, so if there are first aid instructions on the label of the chemical product causing the burn, follow those instructions. If not, use the following basic guidelines for treatment.

Treating Chemical Burns to the Skin

To treat chemical burns to the skin, follow these steps:

1. Depending on the extent of chemical coverage on the victim or in the area, consider wearing gloves and/or safety goggles, if available, to protect yourself from chemical injuries while assisting the victim.

2. Remove any contaminated jewelry or clothing from the victim, including shoes and socks where chemicals can collect.

3. Remove the chemical from the skin.

   For liquid chemicals, **flush** them from the contaminated skin with large amounts of cool running water for at least 15 minutes.

   For dry chemicals, brush them off the skin using a clean, dry cloth. Take care to keep the chemicals from blowing into your eyes or the victim's eyes and avoid brushing the chemicals onto your own skin. Then, if large amounts of water are available, flush the contaminated area for at least 15 minutes. If large amounts of water are not available, do not apply any water to the contaminated area because small amounts of water can react with dry chemicals causing more burning.

Key Note Terms

caustic – capable of destroying or eating away by chemical action; corrosive

acids chemical compounds with a sour taste that have a pH value of less that 7, react with metals to form hydrogen gas, and have the capability to eat away or dissolve metals and other materials

bases – chemical compounds with a slippery or soapy feel that react with acids to form salt, have a pH value above 7, and are used as cleaning materials

alkalis – any base, such as soda or potash, that is soluble in water, combines with fats to form soap, neutralizes acids, and forms salts with them

Key Note Term

flush – to cleanse or wash out with running water or another liquid

Note

If the victim says he/she feels the burning has intensified after you have finished flushing the contaminated area, flush for several more minutes, or longer, as necessary.

4. Cover the burned area loosely with dry, clean bandages or cloths.

5. Minor chemical burns generally heal without further treatment; however, call the EMS for:

- Any chemical burn to the face, hands, feet, genitalia, or joints
- Second-degree chemical burns over two to three inches in diameter
- All third-degree chemical burns
- If there is a **systemic** reaction to the chemical burn and/or chemical exposure

Note

For extensive or severe chemical burns, monitor the victim for signs of shock and treat accordingly until he/she receives medical treatment. For a victim with chemical burns to the face or who may have inhaled chemicals, monitor his/her breathing in case of possible respiratory burns and swelling. Treat accordingly until medical help arrives.

Treating Chemical Burns to the Eyes

To treat chemical burns to the eyes, follow these steps:

1. Position the victim's head so that the injured eye is lower than the uninjured eye. This will prevent the chemical from getting into the uninjured eye (see Figure 2.5.4). If both eyes are injured, proceed to Step 2.

2. If there is only one injured eye, hold the eyelids of the injured eye open and flush with water from the inner corner of the eye (closest to the nose) to the outer corner (closest to the ear). Flush for at least 15 minutes. If both eyes are injured, flush both at the same time.

3. To keep the victim from moving his/her injured eye(s), have the victim close both eyes, then cover them with cloth pads or gauze taped loosely into place. Because eyes move together, both eyes must be closed and covered to keep the injured eye still.

4. Call the EMS or transport the victim to the emergency room.

Don't's When Treating Chemical Burns

Follow the don'ts listed earlier in this lesson in *Don'ts When Treating Burns*. In addition, do not put any other chemicals on a chemical burn in an attempt to **neutralize** the chemical causing the burn—for example, putting an acid on an alkali and vice versa.

Key Note Term

systemic – affecting the body in general; acting throughout the body after absorption or ingestion

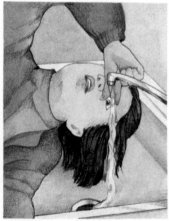

Figure 2.5.4: When flooding the eye, be careful the chemical does not get into the other eye.
Courtesy of Susan Spellman.

Key Note Term

neutralize – to counteract the activity or effect of; to make chemically neutral

Prevention of Chemical Burns

Chemical burns can be prevented, if you know what to do. To help prevent chemical burns:

- Before using any chemical product, read the label—including precautions or warnings—then follow the instructions for use.

- If you have younger brothers or sisters, ensure chemical products are stored out of their reach.

- Use chemical products in a well-ventilated area.

- Do not mix different chemical products; they may react with each other causing hazardous conditions. For example, mixing bleach and ammonia results in dangerous fumes.

- To avoid confusion and accidental misuse of chemical products, leave them in their original containers with their labels intact.

Conclusion

You have just learned important procedures for treating burns as well as when to apply basic first aid and life-saving skills in these situations. Remember that although it is important to administer first aid treatment as quickly as possible in most situations, some rescue situations require careful assessment before you jump in to save someone so that you do not become a victim yourself. Remaining calm, thinking logically and clearly, and knowing what steps to take and when to take them, will help you to successfully perform first aid. In addition, this lesson provided many tips on how to prevent accidents from occurring in the first place.

In the following lesson, you will learn what to do in the event you need to treat poisoning, wounds, or bruises. Knowing what to do when someone ingests a poison can save a life.

Lesson Review

1. What are some of the characteristics of first-, second-, and third-degree burns?
2. How can you prevent electrical burns?
3. What determines the seriousness of a chemical burn?
4. Define the term *systemic*.

First Aid for Poisons, Wounds, and Bruises

Chapter 2

Key Words

abrasions
amputation
avulsion
incisions
lacerations
solvents

What You Will Learn to Do

• Determine first aid treatment for wounds, bruises, and poisoning

Linked Core Abilities

• Do your share as a good citizen in your school, community, country, and the world

Skills and Knowledge You Will Gain Along the Way

• Identify the causes and symptoms of poisoning

• Describe how to treat a poison victim

• Distinguish among the four types of wounds

• Describe how to treat minor wounds and bruises

• Define the key words contained in this lesson

Introduction

Whenever there are small children left alone in the kitchen, accidents can happen, especially when cleaning products are left out in the open. The first part of this lesson introduces the treatment and prevention of injury from poisons. As an addition to your first aid abilities, the lesson ends with a discussion of different types of wounds and their treatment, as well as the treatment of bruises.

Poisons

As consumers, we buy more than a quarter of a million different household products, including materials used in and around the house for medication, cleaning, cosmetic purposes, exterminating insects, and killing weeds. These items are valuable in the house and for yard maintenance, but misuse, especially when products are used in inappropriate applications or quantities, can cause illness, injury, and even death.

Each year more than 6,000 people die and an estimated 300,000 suffer disabling illnesses as a result of unintentional poisoning by solid and liquid substances. Poisonings can happen to anyone, at any time, in any situation. Poisonings at home, however, can be prevented. Although child-resistant packaging has greatly reduced the number of fatalities among children less than five years of age, parents, grandparents, and other caregivers must still be cautious. Following label directions for all products, including medication dosages and the proper storage of potentially toxic products, are important precautions to heed.

- **Poisonings from solids and liquids such as drugs, medicines, poisonous houseplants, and commonly recognized poisons caused 6,300 deaths in the home in 1998 alone.**

- **An additional 500 deaths in the home in 1998 were due to poisonings from gases and vapors such as carbon monoxide.**

- **These deaths are not all among children. Another age group at risk is adults age 25 through 44. Many adults are unintentionally poisoned when they do not follow label directions on medications or household chemicals.**

Poisoning is the effect of one or more harmful substance on the body. Poisons can be inhaled or ingested. Fortunately, most poisonings happen with products of low toxicity or with amounts so small, severe poisoning rarely occurs; however, the potential for severe or fatal poisoning is always present.

Inhaled Poisons

Inhaled poisoning occurs when a person breathes a poisonous substance into his/her lungs. Inhaled poisons include the following:

- **Smoke**
- **Gas used in outdoor cooking equipment and appliances in homes and recreational vehicles**

- Hazardous fumes from household products such as paint and paint thinners, gasoline, **solvents**, and glues, as well as from chemicals used in industrial processes

- Carbon monoxide, which is always produced by wood, coal, and charcoal fires and by gasoline engines, can also be produced by gas, oil, and kerosene appliances such as furnaces, space heaters, water heaters, and stoves.

Carbon monoxide, in particular, is a very dangerous poisonous substance, because it is odorless, colorless, and tasteless, making it difficult to detect. When a person inhales carbon monoxide, it replaces oxygen in the blood, which results in oxygen starvation throughout the body. Exposure to low amounts of carbon monoxide can cause flulike symptoms; continued exposure can cause permanent brain, nerve, and heart damage; exposure to very high concentrations can kill a person in a few minutes.

Running a car engine in a closed garage, using a charcoal grill indoors, and burning a fire in a fireplace with a blocked chimney can all result in carbon monoxide poisoning. In addition, because carbon monoxide forms when there is a lack of oxygen resulting in incomplete fuel combustion, operating fuel-burning equipment without an adequate supply of oxygen (proper ventilation) can result in carbon monoxide poisoning. For example, hundreds of people in the United States each year suffer carbon monoxide injuries from using portable heaters, lanterns, and camping stoves inside tents, campers, and vehicles.

Symptoms of Inhaled Poisoning

Symptoms of inhaled poisoning may not show up immediately. If you suspect inhalation poisoning, keep the victim under observation. If you know the victim has inhaled a poisonous chemical, get medical help whether or not symptoms are present. Symptoms will vary depending on the type and amount of poison inhaled but can include any of the following:

- Dizziness

- Weakness

- Drowsiness

Figure 2.6.1: Car exhaust is a source of carbon monoxide poisoning.
Courtesy of Ted Cordingley.

- Headache
- Mental confusion
- Breathing difficulties
- Heartbeat irregularities
- Unusual breath odor
- Discoloration of the lips and mucous membranes
- Nausea
- Vomiting
- Rashes or burns on the skin
- Unconsciousness

Treatment for Inhaled Poisons

Before rushing in to rescue a victim in a smoke-, gas-, or fume-filled environment, quickly assess the situation so that you do not end up a victim as well. If the poisonous substance is overwhelming and the danger to you is too great, do not attempt to rescue the victim unless you have been trained for rescue in this type of situation. Immediately call the EMS and stay clear of danger.

However, if after assessing the situation you believe you can safely remove the victim from the poisonous environment, do so by following these steps.

1. If you are alone, call for help first before attempting the rescue. This will notify others of the situation; a precaution that will ensure help is on its way in case you are also overcome by the poison.

2. Take several deep breaths of fresh air, then take a final deep breath and hold it as you go in. If available, a damp cloth held over your nose and mouth is a good safety precaution.

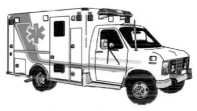

Courtesy of US Army JROTC.

> **Note**
>
> Do not use light switches, light a match, or use any other equipment or appliance that produces flames or sparks while you are in a gas- or fume-filled area.

3. If you can see fumes or smoke, keep your head out of them. For example, fumes from car exhaust are heavy and settle near the floor, so keep your head above them; but in the case of smoke, which rises, keep your head below it.

4. Move the victim out into the fresh air. If for some reason this is not possible, open doors and windows to ventilate the area, returning out into the fresh air as necessary to ensure your safety. Do not administer first aid until you and the victim are out of the hazardous environment or the area is ventilated.

Check the victim's airway, breathing, and circulation (ABCs) and perform mouth-to-mouth resuscitation and CPR as necessary. After you are sure the victim is breathing, call the EMS if you or someone else has not already done so. Even if the victim seems fine after he/she is in fresh air, call for medical help as symptoms may show up later. While you are waiting for medical help, treat the victim for any burns he/she may have suffered and monitor for shock.

Oral Poisoning

Oral poisoning occurs when a harmful substance, such as a common household cleaning product, is swallowed. First aid for oral poisoning depends on the substance swallowed.

Symptoms of Oral Poisoning

Symptoms will vary depending on the type and amount of poison inhaled but can include any of the following:

- **Abdominal pain and cramping**
- **Nausea or vomiting**
- **Diarrhea**
- **Burns, odor, and stains around and in mouth**
- **Drowsiness or unconsciousness**
- **Poison containers nearby**

Treatment for Oral Poisons

Procedures for treating oral poisoning:

1. **Determine critical information:**
   - **Age and size of victim**
   - **What was swallowed**
   - **How much was swallowed**
   - **When it was swallowed**
2. **If a corrosive or caustic substance was swallowed, immediately dilute it by having the victim drink at least one or two eight-ounce glasses of water or milk.**
3. **For a responsive victim, call a poison control center immediately. More than 70 percent of poisonings can be treated through instructions taken over the telephone from a poison control center.**
4. **For an unresponsive victim, or if the poison control center number is unknown, call the EMS and monitor the ABCs.**
5. **Place the victim on his or her left side to position the end of the stomach where it enters the small intestine straight up. Gravity will delay advancement of the poison into the small intestine, where absorption into the victim's circulatory system is faster.**

6. Induce vomiting only if a poison control center or physician advises it. Inducing must be done within 30 minutes of swallowing.

7. Save poison containers, plants, and so on to help medical personnel identify the poison.

Wounds

Wounds are soft tissue injuries that break the skin. Generally, they can be classified as follows:

- *Scrapes* (**abrasions**) are caused by sliding contact between the skin and a rough surface. They are generally shallow injuries with little bleeding.
- *Cuts* (**incisions**) are straight, even wounds made with sharp objects like knives or razor blades.
- *Tears* (**lacerations**) are caused by objects with sharp, irregular edges or by exerted force that leaves jagged, torn tissue.
- *Punctures* are caused by pointed objects such as pins and nails that make small holes in tissue, often with little bleeding.

All wounds can be minor or serious depending upon their size, depth, location, and source. Minor wounds involve only the outer skin layer. They stop bleeding in a few minutes on their own or with gentle pressure and can be treated with just first aid. Serious wounds require first aid followed by medical treatment. Consider a wound serious if the following characteristics are evident:

- The skin is cut or torn all the way through so that it gapes open
- Fat, muscle, or tendons are visible
- Bleeding is heavy and does not slow or stop after applying pressure for 15 to 20 minutes
- Soil or other debris cannot be washed from the wound
- There is loss of function such as the inability to move a cut finger
- It is on the face; even a small wound may leave a scar
- It is on the bottom of the foot
- Its source is a rusty or dirty object, or an animal or human bite

Some extremely serious injuries that generally contain a combination of the four kinds of wounds and always require immediate medical attention are **amputations**, **avulsions**, and crushing injuries. They are generally the result of motor vehicle or industrial machinery accidents or explosions.

- An **amputation** is the complete removal of an extremity, such as a finger or leg.
- An **avulsion** is tissue torn from or pulled away from and hanging off of the body. This type of injury may also result from an animal bite.

> **Key Note Terms**
>
> **abrasion** – a part of the skin that has been lightly torn or scraped
>
> **incision** – a wound that is made by cutting into the body
>
> **laceration** – a wound that is torn and ragged

> **Key Note Terms**
>
> **amputation** – the removal of an external part of the body, most often a limb or part of it, when it has been severely crushed or following the death of an extremity due to impaired blood circulation
>
> **avulsion** – the tearing away of a body part accidentally or surgically

- *Crushing injuries* occur when parts of the body are caught between heavy objects or when the body is thrown against a heavy object or vice versa. In addition to wounds, crushing injuries include bone fractures, as well as possible injuries to internal organs and internal bleeding.

Treatment of Wounds

For a minor wound, clean it by flushing it with cool water and washing it with mild soap. Dry it thoroughly with a clean cloth, apply a thin layer of antibiotic ointment to keep the wound moist and protect against infection, and cover it with a bandage to keep it clean. Change the bandage whenever it gets wet or dirty, and consider leaving the bandage off at night when sleeping because exposure to air also helps the healing process. Contact a doctor if the wound does not appear to be healing after several days or shows signs of infection like redness, draining, or swelling.

For any wound caused by a rusty or dirty object or an animal bite, ask if the victim has had a tetanus shot within the past 10 years. If not, suggest that he/she get one to guard against tetanus infection.

For extremely serious injuries such as amputations, avulsions, or crushing injuries, call the EMS, control the bleeding, monitor breathing, treat for shock, and provide comfort to the victim until medical help arrives. Remember that tourniquets should only be used in extreme, life-threatening situations, and pressure points should only be used if you are trained to do so.

Bruises

Bruises are injuries that discolor but do not break the skin tissue. They can be caused by a fall, a blow, or bumping into something. Though sometimes very ugly and lasting for several weeks, they are usually not very serious. Wrap ice or an ice pack in a clean towel and apply it to the bruise. To reduce swelling, elevate the bruised part for 20 to 30 minutes if the injury is mild or for a few hours if it is severe. Seek medical attention if swelling increases unusually, pain increases, the bruise site appears deformed, or there is an inability to move a body part associated with the bruise.

Conclusion

You have just learned important procedures for treating poisons, wounds, and bruises, as well as when to apply basic first aid and life-saving skills in these situations. Remember that while it is important to administer first aid treatment as quickly as possible in most situations, some rescue situations require careful assessment before you jump in to save someone, so that you do not become a victim yourself. Remaining calm, thinking logically and clearly, and knowing what steps to take and when to take them, will help you to successfully perform first aid. In addition, this lesson provided many tips on how to prevent accidents from occurring in the first place.

In the next lesson, you will learn about heat injuries, from sunburn to heat stroke, and how to treat these problems.

Lesson Review

1. What are common types of inhaled poisons?

2. How can some in-home poisonings be prevented?

3. Compare and contrast scrapes, cuts, tears, and punctures.

4. How would you treat a bruise?

Lesson 7

Heat Injuries

Key Words

dehydration
fatigue
heat cramps
heat exhaustion
heatstroke
perspiring
ventilation

What You Will Learn to Do

- Determine first aid treatment for heat related injuries

Linked Core Abilities

- Do your share as a good citizen in your school, community, country, and the world

Skills and Knowledge You Will Gain Along the Way

- Explain the cause and effect of heat injuries
- Associate the symptoms of the three types of heat injuries
- Explain how to treat heat cramps
- Explain how to treat heat exhaustion
- Explain how to treat heatstroke
- Define the key words contained in this lesson

Introduction

Participating in any vigorous outdoor exercise or activity on an extremely hot day can lead to serious injuries if you are not prepared. Knowing how to recognize the signs and symptoms of heat related injuries can help you prevent a life-threatening accident.

Causes

For your body to work properly, its temperature must be normal, which is around 98° Fahrenheit. You risk health problems, and even death, if your body gets too cold or too hot.

Heat injuries can occur when people are exposed to high temperatures and high humidity. When it is hot, your body cools itself by **perspiring** to sweat evaporates to carry; heat away from your body. However, you risk heat injuries when you lose large amounts of water, salt, or both through perspiring and do not replace the lost fluid, which results in **dehydration**. You also risk injury in high humidity when sweat does not evaporate as rapidly as needed to keep the body cool, causing heat to build up. The body will then perspire even more in an attempt to cool itself, losing dangerous amounts of fluids in the process.

People who may be at risk of heat injuries include those who exercise or work outside in high temperatures and high humidity, those whose bodies do not regulate heat well, such as older people, overweight people, or babies.

Factors to Consider

When perspiring, the body can lose more than a quart of water per hour. Therefore, because the body depends on water to cool itself, you should drink plenty of water when working or playing in hot weather. Salt, which helps the body to retain water, is also lost through perspiring. In most cases, however, you do not need to consume extra salt because you obtain adequate amounts through a balanced diet. In

Key Note Terms

perspiring – giving off moisture through the pores of the skin

dehydration – the condition that results when fluids are lost from the body and are not replaced; symptoms can include thirst, weakness, exhaustion, confusion, and may result in death

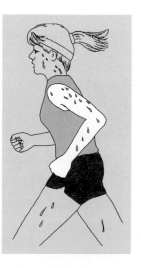

Figure 2.7.1: Heavy perspiring will occur when running or jugging on a hot day.
Courtesy of US Army JROTC.

fact, consuming salt during hot weather activities may pull water away from muscles and other tissues where it is needed and into your digestive tract.

In addition to water intake and diet, consider the type of clothing you wear in hot weather. Wear clothes that fit loosely but also protect the body from sunburn. Wear natural fabrics, like cotton, through which perspiration evaporates better. Some activities require extra clothing or equipment, such as football or hiking with full camping gear. Soldiers may have problems acclimating to hot weather because of the type and amount of clothing and equipment they must wear. In all of these cases, protective gear and equipment may reduce **ventilation** needed to cool the body. So, ensure clothing or uniforms fit well but are not tight, and remove extra pieces of clothing and equipment as soon as they are no longer needed.

Types of Heat Injuries

Overheating of the body progresses through stages. At first, a person may suffer **heat cramps**. If the person ignores the symptoms and continues exercising, working, or playing in the heat, he or she may experience **heat exhaustion**. If heat exhaustion is left untreated, **heatstroke** may follow and can be fatal.

Heat Cramps

Heat cramps are muscular pains and spasms caused by the loss of salt from the body through heavy perspiring. Other symptoms may include stomach cramps, wet skin, and extreme thirst. To treat heat cramps:

1. **Move the victim to a shady area, or improvise shade.**
2. **Loosen the victim's clothing.**
3. **Slowly give the victim large amounts of cool water.**
4. **Monitor the victim and give more water as needed.**
5. **Seek medical aid if cramps continue.**

Heat Exhaustion

When people work or exercise heavily in high temperatures or in a hot, humid place, the body loses fluids through heavy sweating. **Heat exhaustion** occurs when fluids are not adequately replaced or when sweat does not evaporate because of high humidity or too many layers of clothing, causing the body to sweat even more. When the body loses a great amount of fluid, less blood flows to vital organs, resulting in a form of shock. The symptoms of heat exhaustion are as follows:

- **Heavy sweating**
- **Weakness or faintness**
- **Dizziness or drowsiness**
- **Cool, pale, moist skin**
- **Headaches**

Key Note Term

ventilation – circulation of air; a system or means of providing fresh air

---

Key Note Terms

heat cramps – a condition that is marked by the sudden development of cramps in the skeletal muscles and that results from prolonged work in high temperatures accompanied by profuse perspiration with loss of sodium chloride from the body

heat exhaustion – a condition that occurs when a person is exposed to excessive heat over a period of time, caused by the loss of water and salt from the body through excessive perspiration

heatstroke – a life-threatening condition caused by prolonged exposure to high heat

---

Figure 2.7.2: Heat exhaustion may occur after a person participates in vigorous exercise on a hot day.
Courtesy of Bob Daemmrich/ Stock Boston.

- Loss of appetite
- Heat cramps
- Nausea with or without vomiting
- Confusion
- Chills
- Rapid breathing and pulse
- Body temperature above normal but below 102°F

Treat heat exhaustion as follows:

1. Move the victim to a cool, shady area, or improvise shade.
2. Loosen the victim's clothing.
3. Pour water on or apply cold, wet cloth to the skin. Fan the victim if it is a hot day.
4. Have the victim slowly drink at least one quart of water.
5. Elevate the victim's legs.
6. Monitor the victim until symptoms are gone. If symptoms continue, seek medical aid.
7. If possible, keep the victim from participating in heavy activity for the rest of the day.

Heatstroke

Heatstroke, also known as sunstroke, is a medical emergency that can be fatal if not treated as soon as possible. The victim's cooling mechanism stops working when the body perspires so much that no fluids remain to produce sweat. Because the body can no longer sweat and sweating is its defense against overheating, body temperature rises and skin becomes red and flushed. If body temperature rises high enough, brain damage and death can occur; therefore, when you encounter a heatstroke victim, you must cool the victim as fast as possible.

The symptoms of heatstroke are as follows:

- **No sweating**
- **Hot, dry, red skin**
- **Headache, dizziness, nausea, and vomiting**
- **Fast, weak pulse and shallow respiration**
- **Seizures and mental confusion**
- **Unconsciousness or sudden collapse**
- **Very high body temperature**

Treat victims of heatstroke as follows:

1. **Move the victim to a cool, shady area, or improvise shade.**
2. **Loosen the victim's clothing. Remove any outer garments and protective clothing.**
3. **Pour water on the victim or immerse in water, and fan the victim so sweat can evaporate. If you cannot immerse the victim, massage the arms and legs with cool water.**
4. **If the victim is conscious, have him or her slowly drink at least one quart of water.**
5. **Seek medical aid and transport the victim to a medical facility as soon as possible. Perform any necessary life-saving measures.**

Prevention of Heat Injuries

You can prevent heat injuries by taking just a few simple precautions and exercising a little common sense. If possible, limit your exposure to high temperatures and avoid working or exercising outside in hot, humid weather. During work or training periods, or in extremely hot climates, drink at least one quart of water every hour. Also, remember to dress for the hot weather and the activity being performed.

In the military or in the field, prevention of heat injuries is both an individual and leadership responsibility. Leaders should identify people who have a high risk of injury—basic trainees, overweight individuals, and individuals who have symptoms of **fatigue** or a previous history of heat injury. If possible, leaders should schedule heavy or strenuous activities during cooler morning or evening hours.

Key Note Term

fatigue – weakness or exhaustion due to hard work or mental effort

Conclusion

Vigorous exercise in hot weather can lead to heat cramps, heat exhaustion, or heat-stroke. Familiarize yourself with the symptoms of these injuries, which can be serious or even fatal if left untreated. By knowing the signs of heat injuries, and taking precautions, you should be able to enjoy exercising outdoors, even in hot weather.

The following lesson examines cold weather injuries. You will learn about frostbite, snow blindness, and other physical problems connected with exposure to cold temperatures.

Lesson Review

1. What are the causes of heat injuries?

2. What are the types of heat injuries?

3. How would you treat heat exhaustion?

4. What are the symptoms of heatstroke?

Lesson 8

Cold Weather Injuries

Key Words

dehydration
frostbite
hypothermia
insulate
precipitation
subcutaneous
superficial

What You Will Learn to Do

- Determine first aid treatment for heat-related injuries

Linked Core Abilities

- Do your share as a good citizen in your school, community, country, and the world

Skills and Knowledge You Will Gain Along the Way

- Describe factors to consider in cold weather situations

- Explain causes and effects of cold weather injuries

- Identify symptoms of cold weather injuries

- Explain how to treat frostbite, immersion foot/trench foot, hypothermia and snow blindness

- Define the key words contained in this lesson

Introduction

It is common to think that only in areas where snow and frost are present, people are susceptible to cold weather injuries. Prolonged exposure to low temperatures, wind or moisture—whether it be on a ski slope or in a stranded car—can result in cold-related injuries such as **frostbite** and **hypothermia**, no matter where you live if you are not prepared.

Factors to Consider

When thinking about cold weather injuries, there are several factors you need to consider. These factors include weather, stress, clothing, physical makeup, psychological factors, and more. This section discusses these factors.

Weather

Low temperature, high humidity, **precipitation**, and high wind may affect the loss of body heat. Wind chill (the temperature of both the wind speed and air temperature combined) speeds up the loss of body heat and may aggravate cold injuries. By studying the wind chill chart shown in Figure 2.8.1, you can determine the chilling effect that wind speed has on temperature.

Stress

When in a stressful situation, people are more likely to experience fear, fatigue, **dehydration**, and lack of nutrition. These factors increase the possibility of cold injury.

Clothing

When outside during cold weather, you should wear several layers of loose-fitting clothing and dress as lightly as the weather permits. This reduces the danger of excessive perspiration followed by a chill. It is better if the body is slightly cold and producing heat rather than overly warm and sweltering toward dehydration. Wet clothing adds to the possibility of cold injury.

Physical Makeup

Physical fatigue leads to inactivity, personal neglect, carelessness, and less heat production. These, in turn, increase the risk of cold injury. Individuals who have had a cold injury before have a higher risk of being injured again.

Psychological Factors

Mental fatigue and fear lessen the body's ability to rewarm itself and thus increase the possibility of cold injury. Depressed or unresponsive individuals are also at a higher risk of cold injury because they are less active and tend to be careless about protecting themselves.

Key Note Terms

frostbite – an injury caused to body tissue by frost or extreme cold

hypothermia – too little body heat with abnormally low internal body temperature

Key Note Terms

precipitation – any form of water, such as rain, snow, sleet, or hail, that falls to the earth's surface

dehydration – the condition that results when fluids are lost from the body and not replaced; symptoms can include thirst, weakness, exhaustion, confusion, and may result in death

Figure 2.8.1: The wind chill chart.
Courtesy of US Army JROTC.

HOW TO USE THE WIND CHILL CHART

Find the wind speed in the left-hand column, then read across to the column under the actual temperature. This number is the equivalent temperature which would be acting on any exposed skin. For example, if the wind is blowing at 20 mph and the actual temperature is 10° F, the effect on bare skin would be the same as a temperature reading of -25° F under calm conditions. Any movement has the same cooling effect as the wind. Running, skiing, or riding in an open vehicle must be considered in using the wind chill chart.

☆GPO : 1983 0 - 417-503

WIND CHILL CHART FOR FAHRENHEIT TEMPERATURES

ESTIMATED WIND SPEED IN MPH	ACTUAL THERMOMETER READING (° F)											
	50	40	30	20	10	0	-10	-20	-30	-40	-50	-60
	EQUIVALENT TEMPERATURE (° F)											
CALM	50	40	30	20	10	0	-10	-20	-30	-40	-50	-60
5	48	37	27	16	6	-5	-15	-26	-36	-47	-57	-68
10	40	28	16	4	-9	-24	-33	-46	-58	-70	-83	-95
15	36	22	9	-5	-18	-32	-45	-58	-72	-85	-99	-112
20	32	18	4	-10	-25	-39	-53	-67	-82	-96	-110	-124
25	30	16	0	-15	-29	-44	-59	-74	-88	-104	-118	-133
30	28	13	-2	-18	-33	-48	-63	-79	-94	-109	-125	-140
35	27	11	-4	-21	-35	-51	-67	-82	-96	-113	-129	-145
40	26	10	-6	-24	-37	-53	-69	-85	-100	-116	-132	-148

WIND SPEEDS ABOVE 40 MPH HAVE LITTLE ADDITIONAL EFFECT.	LITTLE DANGER FOR THE PROPERLY CLOTHED PERSON; MAXIMUM DANGER OF FALSE SENSE OF SECURITY.	INCREASING DANGER OF FREEZING EXPOSED FLESH.	GREAT DANGER

TRENCH FOOT AND IMMERSION FOOT MAY OCCUR AT ANY POINT ON THIS CHART.

Other Factors

Individuals are also at risk of cold injury if they are

- **In contact with the ground for an extended period**
- **Immobile for long periods of time, such as while riding in a crowded vehicle**
- **Standing in water**
- **Out in the cold for days without being warmed**
- **Deprived of an adequate diet and rest**
- **Careless about personal hygiene**

Types of Cold Injuries

People exposed to severe cold can suffer from the following conditions: **frostbite**, immersion foot/trench foot, **hypothermia**, snow blindness, and **dehydration**.

Frostbite

Frostbite is the most common injury resulting from exposure to the cold. Ice crystals form in body tissues exposed to temperatures below freezing. The crystals restrict blood flow to the injured parts and are like daggers that puncture cell membranes as they grow larger. Body parts most easily frostbitten are the cheeks, nose, ears, chin, forehead, wrists, hands, and feet. People suffering from frostbite may not realize it because the injured part may be numb from the cold.

There are different degrees of frostbite depending on the extent of tissue damage. A **superficial** cold injury can usually be characterized by numbness and tingling or "pins and needles" sensations. It involves the skin and the tissue just beneath the skin. Deep frostbite, on the other hand, involves freezing of the **subcutaneous** tissue and possibly even muscle and bone. With a deep cold injury, victims are often unaware of a problem until the affected part feels like a stump or block of wood. Severe frostbite may result in infection or gangrene and may require surgical removal of the injured part.

Key Note Terms

superficial – not serious; on the surface; shallow

subcutaneous – beneath the top layer of skin

Signs of Frostbite

Signs of superficial frostbite, as shown in Figure 2.8.2, include the following:

- **Redness of the skin on light-skinned individuals; grayish coloring of the skin on dark-skinned individuals**
- **Blisters appearing in 24 to 36 hours**
- **Sloughing of the skin**

Signs of deep frostbite include the following:

- **Signs of superficial frostbite**
- **Painless or numb unthawed skin that is pale-yellowish and waxy looking**
- **Frozen, swollen tissue that is similar to wood to the touch**
- **Blisters in 12 to 36 hours**

Treatment of Frostbite

Treat superficial frostbite as follows:

1. **Move the victim out of the cold and wind.**
2. **Keep the victim warm; rewarm the affected parts gently and slowly. Explain to the victim that he or she will experience pain when warmth restores feeling to the injured part.**
   - **Cover cheeks, ears, and nose with the victim's and/or your hands**
   - **Put the victim's fingertips under his/her armpits**

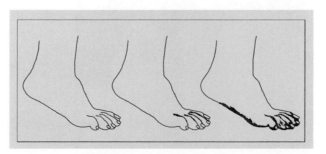

Figure 2.8.2: Signs of frostbite as it appears on your feet.
Courtesy of US Army JROTC.

- Place the victim's feet under the clothing of another person next to that person's belly

3. **Insulate** injured parts by covering them with a blanket or dry clothing.

4. **Loosen tight clothing and remove wet clothing.**

5. **Encourage the victim to exercise carefully, avoiding further injury.**

6. **Seek medical treatment.**

Deep frostbite is very serious and requires extra care to reduce or avoid losing all or parts of the fingers, toes, hands, or feet. It can be prevented as illustrated in Figure 2.8.3. If possible, transport the victim to a hospital or contact emergency medical services immediately; it is preferable that deep frostbite injuries be rewarmed under medical supervision. If this is not possible, rewarm the injured parts, protect them from refreezing, and seek medical help as soon as possible.

The Don'ts of Treating Frostbite

Although there are many things you can do to help a frostbite victim, there are also several things you should not do.

- Do not attempt to thaw the affected part if you believe you cannot keep it warm until the victim receives medical treatment. It is extremely dangerous for an injured part to refreeze after warming. It is less dangerous to leave the part frozen than to warm it and have it refreeze.

- Avoid having the victim walk on frostbitten feet, especially if they thaw. If the victim must walk, it is less dangerous while his or her feet are frozen.

- Do not rub the injured part with snow or apply cold water packs.

- Do not warm the injured part by massage; ice crystals in the tissues will damage more cells when rubbed.

- Do not expose the injured part to open fire; the frozen part may burn because of lack of feeling.

Key Note Term

insulate – to use materials to protect or isolate from the elements of weather

Figure 2.8.3: Avoid frostbite or hypothermia by dressing appropriately for outdoor activites in cold weather.
Courtesy of Paul Mozell/ Stock Boston.

- Do not have the victim move the injured part to increase circulation.
- Do not break any blisters.
- Do not use ointments or other medications.
- Do not let the victim use alcohol or tobacco. Alcohol reduces the body's resistance to cold, and tobacco decreases blood circulation.

Immersion Foot/Trench Foot

Immersion foot and trench foot result from long exposure of the feet to wet conditions at temperatures between approximately 32° and 50°F. Keeping your feet in damp or wet socks and shoes or tightly laced boots for long periods of time may affect circulation and contribute to injury. Inactivity also increases the risk of immersion foot/trench foot. This injury can be very serious, leading to loss of toes or parts of the feet.

Signs of Immersion Foot and Trench Foot

Symptoms of immersion foot/trench foot in the primary stage include affected parts that are cold, numb, and painless. These parts may then begin to feel hot with burning and shooting pains. In the advanced stage of immersion foot/trench foot, the pulse decreases and the skin becomes pale with a bluish cast. Redness, blistering, swelling, heat, hemorrhages, and gangrene may follow.

Treatment of Immersion Foot and Trench Foot

Treat immersion foot/trench foot as follows:

1. **Gradually rewarm the affected foot by exposure to warm air. Explain to the victim that he or she may experience pain and burning when you rewarm the foot.**
   - Do not massage or moisten skin
   - Do not apply ice
   - Do not expose injured parts to open fire or other sources of heat; warm the affected area by covering with loose, dry clothing or other coverings instead.
2. **Protect the affected foot from trauma or infection.**
3. **Elevate the foot to relieve swelling.**
4. **Dry the foot thoroughly; avoid walking.**
5. **Seek medical treatment.**

Hypothermia

Hypothermia is a general cooling of the body to a temperature below 95°F caused by continued exposure to low or rapidly dropping temperatures, cold moisture or wind, snow, or ice. It can also be prevented as shown in Figure 2.8.3. With hypothermia, the body loses heat faster than it can produce it. Inadequate insulation, fatigue, poor physical condition, dehydration, faulty blood circulation, alcohol, trauma, and immersion in cold water can bring on this condition. People at high risk of hypothermia include infants, older people, people with limited mobility due to illness or other medical conditions, very thin people, and people with heart and lung problems.

Remember, cold weather affects the body slowly and almost without notice. Even when well protected by clothing, a person may suffer cold injuries if exposed to low temperatures for long periods of time. As the body cools, it goes through several stages of discomfort and problems.

Signs of Hypothermia

The signs of hypothermia include the following:

- Shivering or trembling, which will eventually stop as body temperature drops (indicates mild hypothermia)
- Cold skin
- Weakness
- Dizziness
- Drowsiness and mental slowness or confusion
- Uncoordinated movements and slurred speech
- Low body temperature; in severe hypothermia, 90°F or below
- Stiff or rigid muscles
- Decreasing pulse and breathing rate
- Unconsciousness
- Shock, coma, and death—all of which may result as body temperature drops and the body freezes

Treatment of Hypothermia

Except in the most severe cases, the treatment for hypothermia is directed toward rewarming the body evenly and without delay. Treat mild hypothermia as follows:

1. Rewarm the victim slowly.
   - If possible, move the victim inside, remove any wet clothing, and cover him or her with blankets. Avoid warming the victim quickly with hot baths, electric blankets, or heat lamps.
   - If you cannot move the victim inside, remove any wet clothing and rewarm him or her beside a campfire or using the body heat from another person.
2. Keep the victim dry and protected with clothing, blankets, towels, a sleeping bag, or even newspapers.
3. Keep the victim awake.
4. Do not raise the victim's feet or legs because blood in the extremities is colder than in the rest of the body and may further chill the body's core.
5. Give the victim warm liquids gradually. Do not give the victim alcohol. Do not force liquids on an unconscious victim.
6. Be prepared to start basic life-support measures.
7. Seek medical treatment immediately.

Treating a person with severe hypothermia is extremely dangerous because of the possibility of shock and disturbances of the heartbeat while rewarming. If possible, as you begin to rewarm the victim, transport him or her to a hospital or contact the EMS immediately. If this is not possible, treat the victim gently because the heart is weak when the body is cold. Stabilize the victim's body temperature by keeping him or her from losing more body heat and continue to keep the victim warm until you can get him or her medical treatment.

Snow Blindness

Snow blindness is the effect the glare from an ice field, or snowfield, has on the eyes. It is more likely to occur in hazy, cloudy weather because people tend to protect their eyes when the sun is shining and believe protection is unnecessary on cloudy days. If a person waits until he or she feels discomfort or pain to use protective eyewear, a deep burn of the eyes may have already occurred.

Signs of Snow Blindness

There are several signs of snow blindness:

- **A sensation of grit in the eyes**
- **Pain in and over the eyes made worse with eye movement**
- **Watery and red eyes**
- **Headache**
- **Increased pain with exposure to light**

Treatment of Snow Blindness

Treat snow blindness as follows:

1. **Cover the eyes with a dark cloth to discourage painful eye movement.**
2. **Try to give the eyes complete rest without exposure to light. If this is not possible, protect the eyes with dark bandages or very dark glasses.**
3. **Seek medical treatment. In most cases, once exposure to sunlight stops, the eyes heal in a few days without permanent damage.**

Dehydration

Dehydration from cold weather occurs when the body loses too much fluid, salt, and minerals. As mentioned in the previous lesson, you can lose large amounts of fluid and salt through sweating. This loss creates an imbalance of fluids, and dehydration occurs when fluids are not replaced.

Dehydration can occur in both hot and cold climates. In cold weather, sweat evaporates quickly and heavy layers of clothing absorb it, making dehydration more difficult to detect because the signs of sweating are less noticeable; therefore, the danger of dehydration during strenuous cold weather activities can become a serious problem. The symptoms of cold weather dehydration are similar to those of heat exhaustion. Treat dehydration as follows:

1. Move the victim out of the wind and cold, and keep him or her warm.

2. Loosen the victim's clothes to promote circulation.

3. Ensure the victim receives proper fluid replacement, rest, and prompt medical treatment.

Prevention of Cold Injuries

You can prevent many cold weather injuries by taking proper care and precautions when participating in cold weather activities. Be sure to receive adequate nutrition, hot meals, and warm fluids. Get enough rest. Practice good hygiene. Wear the right clothing and protective gear. Do not forget to protect your eyes, ears, and face. Wear layers of clothing so you can remove outer layers if you begin to perspire. Avoid tight clothes that interfere with circulation. Replace or remove any clothing that gets wet as soon as possible.

You may not feel cold injuries because of cold's numbing effect, so always try to go out into cold weather with a partner. You can check each other for signs of injury. Exercise and keep active to maintain steady circulation and improve resistance to the cold. Many cold weather injuries can be avoided by planning ahead, staying alert and using common sense.

Conclusion

Whether or not snow and frost are present, cold weather injuries such as frostbite or hypothermia can be a threat to safety. Knowing the proper ways to treat these injuries is very important because although it might seem like a good idea to re-warm the victim, you may in fact be making the injury worse. Read the first aid measures outlined in this lesson, consider how to prevent these injuries in the first place, and you will not be caught off guard when you are exposed to the cold.

The following lesson examines bites, stings, and other poisonous hazards. Insect stings and animal bites are common incidents that you might need to treat, and knowing how to handle a brush with poison ivy and other poisonous plants can save someone a lot of discomfort.

Lesson Review

1. What factors should you consider when preparing for cold weather?
2. What are the signs of frostbite?
3. How would you treat hypothermia?
4. List the symptoms of cold weather dehydration.

Chapter 2

Bites, Stings, and Poisonous Hazards

Key Words

allergic reaction
antivenin
calamine
discoloration
rabies
tetanus
venom

What You Will Learn to Do

- Determine first aid treatment for bites, stings, and poisonous hazards

Linked Core Abilities

- Do your share as a good citizen in your school, community, country, and the world

Skills and Knowledge You Will Gain Along the Way

- Identify types of venoms
- Relate snakes to their bites
- Explain the effects of animal and human bites
- Identify the symptoms of insect bites and stings
- Associate the types of poisonous plants to the reactions they cause
- Determine how to treat for contact with poisonous plants
- Define the key words contained in this lesson

Introduction

With so many outdoor activities to participate in, such as hiking, camping, bicycle riding, skate boarding, and skiing, it is common to come across emergencies involving bites, stings, and poisonous hazards. It is estimated that one of every two Americans will be bitten at some time by an animal. Dogs are responsible for about 80 percent of all animal-bite injuries. Additionally, bee, wasp, and other types of insect stings can be not only painful but also fatal if the person is allergic. Depending on where you live, the type of first aid you need to know for snakebites and plants will vary. Knowing what to do when in the outdoors can mean the difference between life and death.

Snakebites

If you spend much of your time outdoors, it may be common for you to come across snakes; however, your chances of snakebites are remote if you remain alert and careful. There are both poisonous and nonpoisonous snakes, so the severity of a snakebite depends on whether the snake is poisonous or not. Beyond that, the severity of snakebites depends on the type of snake, the location of the bite, and the amount and type of venom injected.

Types of Snakes

There are approximately 130 different varieties of nonpoisonous snakes in the United States. They have oval-shaped heads and round pupils. Unlike pit vipers, nonpoisonous snakes do not have sensory pits with which to sense the body heat of their prey.

Poisonous snakes exist throughout the world, primarily in tropical to moderate climates. In the United States, there are four kinds of native poisonous snakes, as shown in Figure 2.9.1. Three of these four—the rattlesnake, copperhead, and cottonmouth (water moccasin)—are pit vipers.

Pit vipers in other parts of the world include the bushmaster and fer-de-lance in Central and South America, the tropical rattlesnake in Central America, and the Malayan pit viper in eastern Asia. These snakes are shown in Figure 2.9.2.

Courtesy of Z. Leszczynski/ Animals Animals.

Courtesy of Z. Leszczynski/ Animals Animals.

Courtesy of Joe McDonald/ Animals Animals.

Courtesy of Z. Leszczynski/ Animals Animals.

Figure 2.9.1: Left to right: rattlesnake, copperhead, water moccasin, and coral snake.

Figure 2.9.2: Common pit vipers.
Courtesy of US Army JROTC.

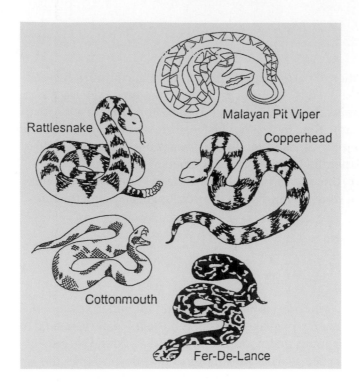

Key Note Terms

venom – a poison produced by animals such as snakes and spiders that is transmitted by a bite or sting

discoloration – altered or changed in color

Pit vipers have slitlike pupils; flat, triangular-shaped heads; small, deep, heat-sensing pits between their nostrils and eyes; and in most cases, hemotoxic **venom**. When a pit viper bites, it injects this venom from sacs through long, hollow fangs. This produces a severe burning pain, along with **discoloration** and swelling around the fang marks. The hemotoxin destroys blood cells, which causes the discoloration of the skin. Blisters and numbness in the affected area follow this reaction. Pit viper bites attack the circulatory system, possibly causing weakness, rapid pulse, and shortness of breath, as well as nausea, vomiting, and shock.

Corals, cobras, kraits, and mambas belong to the cobra family (see Figure 2.9.3). The coral snake is the only one native to the United States. Rings of red, yellow, and black color encircle its body. Although other nonpoisonous snakes have the same colors, only the coral snake has a red ring next to a yellow ring. The cobra, found in Africa and Asia, forms a hood with its neck when on the defensive. The krait, found in India and Southeast Asia, is brightly banded; the mamba in Africa is either almost black or green.

These snakes look very different, but all four inject their venom—a neurotoxin—through short, grooved fangs leaving a characteristic bite pattern, shown in Figure 2.9.4. There is minimal pain and swelling compared to a pit viper bite, but because their powerful venom affects the central nervous system, it can cause blurred vision, drooping eyelids, slurred speech, drowsiness, and increased salivation and sweating. Nausea, vomiting, shock, respiratory difficulty, paralysis, convulsions, and coma develop if the bite is not treated promptly.

Sea snakes are found in warm water areas of the Pacific and Indian Oceans. They have small heads, thick bodies, and tails flattened along the sides. Their fangs are only 1/4 inch long, but their venom is very poisonous.

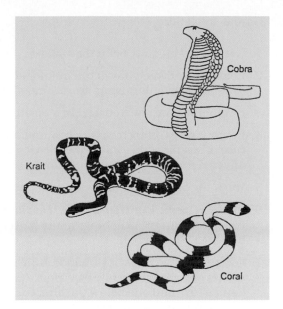

Figure 2.9.3: Members of the cobra family.
Courtesy of US Army JROTC.

Types of Venoms

Basically, venoms are categorized as neurotoxins that affect the nervous system and can cause death by paralysis, hemotoxins that digest tissue including blood cell, or cardiotoxins that affect the heart directly.

Treating Snakebites

Snakebites are rarely fatal if treated within an hour or two of injury, but they can cause pain and illness and may severely damage a bitten hand or foot. Although snakes do not always inject venom, all snakes may carry **tetanus** (lockjaw); therefore, anyone bitten by a snake, whether poisonous or nonpoisonous, should receive immediate medical attention.

One of the most important parts of treating snakebite is identifying the type of snake making the bite. The type of **antivenin** used in medical treatment of snakebites varies depending upon the type of venom injected. If you can identify the type of snake causing the injury, let the EMS know when you call for help or phone the information ahead to the hospital if you plan to transport the victim yourself. If you cannot identify the snake, try to kill it without risk to yourself or delaying first aid; then show it to emergency medical personnel or take it to the hospital along with the victim for identification.

Key Note Terms

tetanus (lockjaw) – an acute infectious disease caused by the poison of a certain bacterium that enters the body through a wound, resulting in muscle contractions, rigidity, and death; it is preventable by immunization

antivenin – an antitoxin used to counteract venom

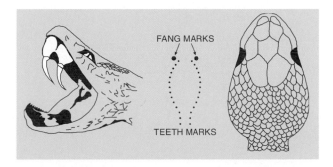

FANG MARKS

TEETH MARKS

Figure 2.9.4: Poisonous snakebites leave characteristic bite patterns.
Courtesy of US Army JROTC.

To treat snakebites, follow these steps:

1. **Get the victim away from the snake.**

2. **Reassure and keep the victim quiet and still. This will keep circulation to a minimum and keep the venom from spreading.**

3. **Immobilize the affected part in a position below the level of the heart.**

4. **Remove rings, bracelets, watches, and other jewelry from any affected limb. In case of swelling, this will make the victim more comfortable and will keep the affected limb from losing blood flow.**

5. **Wash the bite thoroughly with soap and water. Do not apply any ointments.**

6. **Place an icepack or freeze pack, if available, over the area of the bite. Do not place ice directly on the skin or wrap the limb with ice. You are only trying to cool the bite area, not freeze it.**

7. **For bites to the arms, legs, hands, or feet, apply constricting bands two to four inches away from the bite (see Figure 2.9.5). For an arm or leg bite, place one band above and one below the bite. For a hand or foot bite, place one band above the wrist or ankle. To ensure a band is not too tight, you should be able to insert a finger between the band and the skin.**

8. **If swelling from the bite reaches the band, tie another band a few inches farther away from the bite and the old band; then remove the old band.**

9. **Do not give the victim any food, alcohol, tobacco, medication, or drinks with caffeine.**

10. **Seek medical aid immediately.**

Prevention of Snakebites

Most snakes are shy and passive. Unless they are injured or disturbed, they tend to avoid contact with humans. You can prevent snakebites by using caution and common sense. If you are working outside clearing dense undergrowth, wear gloves, long sleeves, long pants, and boots for protection. When hiking in the wilderness, wear boots and long pants. Try to walk in open areas or stay on established paths. Look where you are stepping or placing a hand if climbing or pushing away tree limbs. Check before sitting on a rock or fallen tree. If possible, stay away from brush, rocks, and undergrowth. If you must handle a snake, even a freshly killed one, use a long tool or stick.

Figure 2.9.5: Place constricting bands on either side of the snakebite.
Courtesy of US Army JROTC.

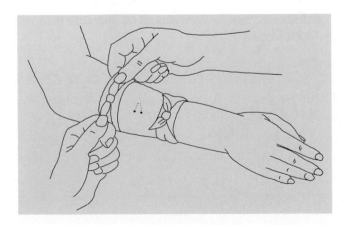

Chapter 2   First Aid for Emergency and Nonemergency Situations

Human and Animal Bites

Mouths of people and animals are full of bacteria, so human and animal bites that break the skin spread germs and may result in serious infection and disease. A person bitten by a diseased animal may come down with tetanus, **rabies**, and various types of fevers. If you think an animal is carrying a disease, notify the proper authorities to have it captured.

To treat a victim of an animal bite, follow these steps:

1. **If bleeding is severe, control it first before continuing with other first aid. Refer to the lesson on** *Controlling Bleeding* **for procedures to control bleeding.**

2. **Cleanse the wound thoroughly with soap or a detergent solution and water. Continue to cleanse and flush the wound with water for five minutes.**

3. **If there is minor bleeding, cover the wound with gauze or a clean cloth, press firmly on the wound, and if possible, raise the injury above the level of the victim's heart.**

4. **When minor bleeding stops, cover the wound with a sterile dressing and secure the dressing in place.**

5. **Immobilize an injured arm or leg.**

6. **Seek medical assistance as soon as possible.**

Insect Bites and Stings

In the outdoors, you may come in contact with various types of biting and stinging insects, including bees, mosquitoes, ticks, fleas, and spiders. Most of these insect bites and stings result in minor reactions, such as itching, redness, swelling, and irritation; however, scorpions and certain spiders can inject powerful poisons when they bite, and some people may have an **allergic reaction** to an insect bite or sting, particularly made by bees or wasps. In these cases, seek medical treatment immediately.

The black widow and brown recluse spider, tarantulas, and scorpions, shown in Figure 2.9.6, are some of the more harmful insects you may encounter. Venom from the black widow is neurotoxic and may cause stomach and muscle cramps, breathing difficulties, nausea, sweating, vomiting, and convulsions. Tarantula venom is basically neurotoxic and may produce symptoms similar to that of a black widow bite, but in some cases can affect the heart and may digest tissue producing a severe local wound. The brown recluse spider can produce severe tissue damage around the bite, possibly leading to gangrene. Although stings from certain types of scorpions are painful but not dangerous, some can cause nausea, fever, stomach cramps, and possible convulsions and shock.

In most cases, bee and wasp stings produce minimal swelling, pain, redness, itching, and burning at the site of the sting. Multiple stings may cause headaches, fever, muscle cramps, and drowsiness. Symptoms from an allergic reaction may include the following:

Key Note Term

rabies – a viral disease affecting the central nervous system of mammals that is transmitted by a bite from an infected animal; it can result in paralysis and death if left untreated

Key Note Term

allergic reaction – a physical reaction, often marked by sneezing, breathing difficulties, itching, rash, or swelling, that some people have when the come in contact with certain substances

Figure 2.9.6: Some biting
and stinging insects can
cause serious health
problems.
Courtesy of US Army JROTC.

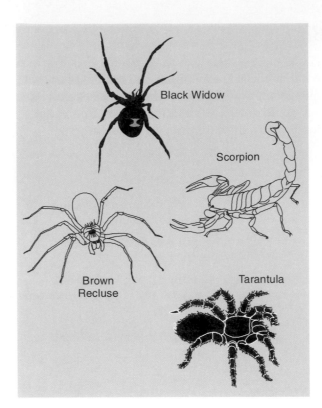

- **Extreme pain at the site of the sting**
- **Itching and hives**
- **Weakness**
- **Anxiety**
- **Headache**
- **Breathing difficulties**
- **Nausea and vomiting**
- **Diarrhea**
- **Collapse, shock, and even death from a serious allergic reaction**

Take the following basic first aid measures regardless of what caused the bite or sting:

1. **Remove any stinger left in the skin by scraping the skin's surface with a fingernail or knife. Do not squeeze the stinger because it may inject more venom.**

2. **For tick bites, remove the tick with your fingers if it will come off the skin easily. Do not pull the tick off if it will not come easily; this may leave the head of the tick in the skin which can cause infection. Instead, cover the tick with Vaseline or thick oil to make it let go and then remove it.**

3. **Wash the area of the bite/sting with soap and water. Apply an antiseptic, if available, to minimize the chances for infection.**

4. **Use an icepack or cold compresses on the site of the bite/sting to help reduce swelling. Do not apply the ice directly to the skin.**

5. Apply **calamine** lotion or a baking soda and water paste to the bite to relieve pain and itching.

6. Treat more serious allergic reactions as you would snakebite.

   - Apply constricting bands above and below the site

   - Be prepared to perform basic life-support measures

   - To positively identify the insect, attempt to capture it without putting yourself at risk

   - Seek medical aid right away

7. If signs of infection such as pus, red streaks leading away from the bite, swollen glands, or fever occur within hours or several days after an insect bite, immediately seek medical attention.

Prevention of Insect Bites and Stings

Wear insect repellent when biting insects are present outside. Reapply repellent every few hours when participating in activities that cause heavy perspiration. Wear appropriate protective clothing when hiking or camping in the wilderness or working in a yard, garden, or other woodsy or overgrown area.

Poisonous Plants

Most plants are harmless, but a few can cause allergic reactions on contact (see Figure 2.9.7). For example, plants of the poison ivy group, including poison oak and poison sumac, produce an oily substance that irritates the skin of many people. Reactions to this substance include a rash characterized by redness, blisters, swelling, and intense burning and itching, as well as headaches and fever. Although the rash usually begins within a few hours after contact, it may appear 24 to 48 hours later.

In general, treat someone who has come in contact with a poisonous plant as follows:

1. Remove contaminated clothing. Set it aside to be washed.

2. Wash all exposed areas of the skin thoroughly with soap and water, then apply rubbing alcohol.

3. Apply calamine or other soothing skin lotion to relieve itching and burning. Avoid covering the rash with a dressing.

4. Seek medical treatment if a severe rash occurs, if the rash is on the face or mouth and may interfere with breathing, or if there is a known history of allergic reactions.

Prevention of Exposure to Poisonous Plants

Become familiar with what poison ivy and other poisonous plants look like so you can recognize a poisonous plant and avoid contacting it. The following are other precautions you should take to limit your exposure to poisonous plants:

Key Note Term

calamine – a pink powder consisting of zinc oxide and some ferric oxide used in lotions and ointments

Courtesy of Gil Fahey/The Picture Cube.

Courtesy of Spencer Grant.

Courtesy of Perry D. Slocum/Earth Scenes.

Figure 2.9.7: Poison ivy, oak, and sumac can cause severe allergic reactions in some people.

- Dress appropriately when participating in outdoor activities
- Avoid areas where you aware that poisonous plants grow
- Do not eat plants or parts of plants that you do not recognize
- Do not put grass, twigs, stems, or leaves in your mouth

Conclusion

Being able to adjust to new environments and protect yourself from harmful conditions is very important when participating in outdoor activities. Factors in nature such as extreme temperatures and humidity; animal, snake, and insect bites; as well as poisonous plants can pose a threat to you if you do not take precautions to guard against the possibility of injury. By being aware of potential hazards, knowing how to treat outdoor-related injuries, and exercising common sense, you can cope successfully with the environment and enjoy your time in the great outdoors.

This concludes the chapter, "First Aid for Emergency and Nonemergency Situations." Through this chapter, you have gain invaluable information about how to keep yourself and those around you safe and healthy. Refer back to the lessons in this chapter if you ever need to know how to administer first aid.

Lesson Review

1. What are the three types of snake venom?
2. Why is it important to try and determine what type of snake caused the bite?
3. What are the symptoms of an allergic reaction to an insect bite or sting?
4. How would you treat someone who has come in contact with a poisonous plant?

Drug Awareness

Lesson 1

Use & Effect of Drugs, Alcohol, and Substances

Key Words

abuse	gateway
addiction	hallucinogens
alcohol	inhalants
controlled substances	intoxicated
dependency	misuse
depressed	narcotics
drugs	nicotine
distilled	stimulants
ethyl alcohol	substance
ferment	tobacco

What You Will Learn to Do

● Assess the impact of drug and substance abuse on life today

Linked Core Abilities

● Communicate using verbal, nonverbal, visual, and written techniques

● Do your share as a good citizen in your school, community, country, and the world

Skills and Knowledge You Will Gain Along the Way

● Identify commonly abused substances

● Recognize the difference between drug use, misuse, and abuse

● Describe reasons why people might use, misuse, or abuse alcohol or drugs

● Identify the risks associated with alcohol and various drugs

● Associate the consequences of alcohol and drug use, misuse, and abuse to life

● Define the key words contained in this lesson

Introduction

Data presented by the *TeenGetGoing* Web site (www.teengetgoing.com) advocated by the JROTC program notes that teen alcohol and drug trends suggest that 90 percent of teens will "use" alcohol and/or other **drugs** during adolescence. Fifty percent of teens will abuse alcohol and/or drugs, and 15 percent will become addicted while still in adolescence. Look around your classroom. What kind of numbers does this represent? This lesson presents the latest information about alcohol and drugs, defines drugs, and explains the difference between drug use, drug **misuse**, and drug **abuse**. You will learn several types of drugs that people abuse, their side effects, and indications of overdose which will allow you to process it in a way that is meaningful both to you and your community.

Drug Use, Misuse, and Abuse

Used under proper conditions, drugs can relieve pain, cure illness, and save lives. When abused, however, drugs can ruin lives and even cause death.

Think about the word *drug* for a moment. It can bring many images to mind from over-the-counter aspirin to stop a headache, a news report about someone who was arrested for cocaine possession, a prescription for antibiotics from your doctor, a drug-related death covered on the front page of the paper, medical research to develop drugs to cure illnesses, the war on drugs, and so on. So exactly what is a drug?

Broadly defined, a drug is any **substance** taken into the body that changes how the body functions, whether mentally or physically. This includes medications used for the prevention and treatment of disease, as well as any **controlled substance** to which a person can become addicted. Whether or not a drug is legal or illegal is no indication of whether or not it is addictive. For example, **alcohol**, and nicotine found in tobacco products are addictive drugs. And just because a drug has a medical purpose does not mean it is not addictive. Many medications, when misused or abused, can cause **addiction**.

Drug use is taking a legal drug as recommended or prescribed for medical reasons. *Drug misuse* is taking a legal drug for medical reasons but not as recommended or prescribed. For example, people who double the recommended dosage of a pain reliever because they think it will make their headache go away quicker are misusing a drug. *Drug abuse* is taking a legal or **illegal drug** for a nonmedical reason in a way that can injure your health or ability to function.

Key Note Terms

drugs – chemicals that cause a change in a person's body or behavior

misuse – the incorrect or improper use of a substance

abuse – improper or excessive use or treatment

Key Note Terms

substance – something, such as a drug or alcohol, deemed harmful and usually subject to legal restrictions

controlled substance – a substance whose manufacture, possession, or sale is controlled by the law

addiction – physically or psychologically dependent on a substance, habit, or behavior that can lead to health, social, or economic problems; dependence on a drug

Why Do People Abuse Drugs?

Some people try drugs out of curiosity or as an act of rebellion. Others cannot resist the peer pressure to try drugs. After people have tried a drug, whether or not they continue to abuse it depends on their individual personalities and situations and on the kind of drug abused.

Most drugs that people abuse produce feelings of pleasure and well-being. When people are unhappy, lonely, stressed, or are missing something in their lives such as friends, love, or satisfying work, they may abuse drugs to avoid their problems or fill a void. But when the effects of the drug wear off, they realize the problems and the voids are still there. So they turn to the drug again.

This cycle is what leads to addiction, a trap that can ruin a person emotionally, socially, economically, legally, and physically. Some drugs are far more addictive than others. For example, a first-time user of crack cocaine has a one in three chance of becoming an addict. This is why it is important to stop before you ever start taking drugs.

What can you do to remain drug-free?

- Fill your life with activities and people you enjoy.

- Believe in yourself.

- Practice saying no before you are actually in a situation where someone offers you drugs, so you will not hesitate to say no when the time comes.

- Think through the consequences of abusing drugs. Where will drugs lead you in life? How long will your body remain healthy if you abuse drugs? How many of your plans can drugs ruin?

- Remember that drugs do not solve problems; they create them.

Many people take drugs without knowing what effect they have on the mind and body. Knowing ahead of time what a drug can do is often enough to convince a person not to try it, especially if one of the potential dangers of abusing a drug is death.

Alcohol

Key Note Term

alcohol – a beverage containing ethanol or ethyl alcohol which causes intoxication

Alcohol, which is legal for those 21 years of age and older, is the most widely consumed and abused drug in the United States. It is socially acceptable in our society for adults to drink in moderation. In excess, however, alcohol is a dangerous drug. Drinking and driving remains the number one cause of death among high school students, as shown in Figure 3.1.1. Heavy alcohol use kills about 50 high school and college students each year because of alcohol poisoning.

Figure 3.1.1: The number one cause of death among high school students is drinking and driving.
Courtesy of George DiSario/The Stock Market.

Alcohol is a natural substance formed when sugar and yeast react and **ferment**. Some alcohols are **distilled**; other are simply fermented. Alcohol is a drug; it is a **depressant** that is absorbed into the bloodstream and transmitted to virtually all parts of the body. Many people don't realize that alcohol is a drug. Some hold the view that experimentation with or use of alcohol is considered normal or acceptable behavior. However, the use of alcohol can cause alcohol addiction and often progresses to further drug abuses. Accordingly, some experts attach the term **gateway** to this substance. The use of drugs such as cocaine and heroin is unusual in those who have not previously used alcohol.

Alcohol abuse can cause serious chemical dependencies, harmful physical and psychological effects, and much suffering by family and friends. As awareness of these ill effects reaches new heights, more and more Americans are joining forces to fight alcohol abuse everyday.

When a person drinks alcohol, it follows the same pathway as food through the digestive system. Unlike food, however, alcohol does not have to be digested by the stomach to be absorbed into the blood. After alcohol reaches the blood, it is circulated throughout the body and affects every part, including the brain and the rest of the nervous system.

Key Note Terms

distilled – heated and condensed to purify, form a new substance, or concentrate

ferment – to produce a chemical change in a carbohydrate material, resulting in alcohol

gateway – a term attached to alcohol and tobacco due to the fact that their use often leads to further drug abuse

Alcohol Statistics

● Ninety percent of teenage automobile accidents involve alcohol

● Drinking and driving accidents are the leading cause of death among 15- to 24-year-olds

● Seventy percent of teenage suicide attempts involve alcohol

Alcohol's Effects on the Body

The effects of **ethyl alcohol** (ethanol) on the human body can range greatly depending on the:

● **Size of the individual**

● **How empty the stomach is at the time of alcohol consumption**

● **State of health and fatigue**

● **Mental attitude**

● **Speed and amount of consumption**

It is also important to note, as illustrated in Figure 3.1.2, that the three most common types of alcoholic drinks—beer, liquor, and wine—contain the same amount of alcohol. Although alcohol may make a person feel "high," alcohol is actually considered a "downer" drug. It slows down or depresses the central nervous system, causing slowed reactions, slurred speech, impaired coordination and judgment, and sometimes unconsciousness. Because alcohol affects reaction time, coordination, and judgment, people under its influence are more accident prone and less likely to make wise decisions. For these reasons, drinking and driving are a very dangerous combination, as well as illegal.

Long-Term Effects

The long-term effects of alcohol abuse include alcoholism; cancers of the liver, stomach, colon, larynx, esophagus, and breast; high blood pressure; heart attacks;

Figure 3.1.2: These different quantities of beer, liquor, and wine contain equal amounts of ethanol.
Courtesy of Ted Cordingley.

Key Note Term

ethyl alcohol – the type of alcohol found in beer, wine, and distilled spirits

strokes; stomach ulcers; birth defects; premature aging; and a diminished immunity to disease due to nonfunction of infection-fighting cells. In men, hormone levels change causing lower sex drives and enlarged breasts; women's menstrual cycles become irregular, possibly resulting in infertility.

The list of effects goes on to include shrinking of the muscles, including the heart; kidney, bladder, and pancreas damage; brain damage affecting vision and memory; depression; and mental illness. Obviously, long-term damage from alcohol abuse can be irreversible and result in death.

Tolerance

When the body becomes accustomed to or builds up a resistance to a drug, the body has developed tolerance to the drug. Tolerance causes a drinker's body to need increasingly larger amounts of alcohol to achieve the effect that was originally produced.

Dependence

When the body develops a resistance to a drug and requires the drug to function normally, dependence occurs. The drinker's body develops a chemical need for alcohol. Dependence occurs as tolerance builds. Dependence is also called addiction.

A dependent person who stops taking a drug will suffer from withdrawal. The signs of alcohol withdrawal include shakiness, sleep problems, irritability, rapid heartbeat, and sweating. The drinker also may see, smell, or feel imaginary objects.

The major psychological symptom of dependence is a strong desire or emotional need to continue using a drug. This need is often associated with specific routines and events. For example, some people drink whenever they face a difficult task or when they feel angry about something.

Brain Damage

Long-term alcohol abuse destroys nerve cells in the brain. Destroyed nerve cells usually cannot grow again. The loss of many nerve cells causes forgetfulness, an inability to concentrate, and poor judgment. These losses interfere with normal everyday functions.

Digestive Problems

Ongoing drinking irritates the tissues lining the mouth, throat, esophagus, and stomach. The irritation can cause the tissues to swell and become inflamed. Repeated irritation increases the risk of cancers of the mouth, tongue, esophagus, and stomach. Alcohol also affects the intestines and can cause recurring diarrhea. Large amounts of alcohol cause the stomach to produce too much stomach acid. The overproduction of acid may lead to indigestion, heartburn, or ulcers.

Liver Damage

Alcohol interferes with the liver's ability to break down fats. As a result of heavy drinking, the liver begins to fill with fat. The excess fat blocks the flow of blood in the liver, and the fat-filled liver cells die. Cirrhosis of the liver is a disease in which useless scar tissue replaces normal liver tissue. Because there is no blood flow in the scarred area, the liver begins to fail. Heavy drinkers suffering from cirrhosis may have high blood pressure, get infections easily, have swelling of the abdomen, and show a yellowing of the skin and eyes. Cirrhosis is the last stage of liver disease and can result in death.

Heavy drinkers often develop alcoholic hepatitis, or inflammation of the liver, caused by the toxic effects of alcohol. Hepatitis causes weakness, fever, yellowing of the skin, and enlargement of the liver. Recovery may take weeks. Sometimes hepatitis can lead to liver failure and even death.

Heart Disease

Excessive drinking contributes to increased blood pressure and heart rate, and irregular heartbeat. These problems can cause disruption in blood flow and possible heart damage. Also, alcohol causes fat to be deposited in heart muscle. Fatty heart muscle, in turn, causes the heart to pump blood through the body less efficiently. Alcohol abuse leads to heart disease, the leading cause of death in the United States.

Fetal Alcohol Syndrome

Pregnant women who drink put the health of their child at risk. A disorder called fetal alcohol syndrome (FAS) refers to the group of birth defects caused by the effects of alcohol on the unborn child. FAS occurs when alcohol in the mother's blood passes into the fetal, or unborn baby's, blood. Babies born with FAS often suffer from heart defects, malformed faces, delayed growth, and poor motor development. Alcohol prevents FAS babies from ever developing the reasoning abilities of healthy babies. Tragically, it is the leading preventable cause of mental retardation in America.

If a woman who is pregnant does not drink, her baby will not be born with FAS. Any woman who is pregnant or planning to become pregnant should not drink alcohol at all.

Short-Term Effects

The short-term effects of alcohol include those that happen within minutes, and sometimes within days, of drinking alcohol. Figure 3.1.3 identifies the short-term effects of alcohol on the body.

Bloodstream

When alcohol enters the blood, it causes the blood vessels to widen. More blood flows to the skin's surface. The drinker feels warm for a short time as the skin flushes; however, the drinker's body temperature drops as the increased blood flow to the surface allows body heat to escape. People who drink alcohol in cold weather to get warm actually accomplish the opposite.

Brain

After reaching the brain, alcohol immediately has a depressant effect and slows the speed of some brain activities. People who drink alcohol may describe the change as relaxing. What they actually experience are physical changes such as a loss of sensation and a decrease in sharpness of vision, hearing, and other senses. Alcohol also affects the parts of the brain that control muscle coordination, which is why drinkers may lose their balance or stumble.

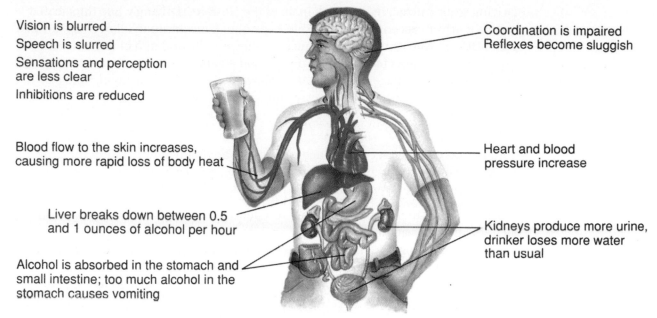

Vision is blurred
Speech is slurred
Sensations and perception
are less clear
Inhibitions are reduced

Coordination is impaired
Reflexes become sluggish

Blood flow to the skin increases,
causing more rapid loss of body heat

Heart and blood
pressure increase

Liver breaks down between 0.5
and 1 ounces of alcohol per hour

Kidneys produce more urine,
drinker loses more water
than usual

Alcohol is absorbed in the stomach and
small intestine; too much alcohol in the
stomach causes vomiting

Figure 3.1.3: How the body reacts to the toxic effects of too much alcohol in the stomach.
Courtesy of Fran Milner.

If drinking continues, alcohol depresses the part of the brain that controls breathing and heartbeat. Breathing rates, pulse rates, and blood pressure, which initially
increased, now decrease. A drinker may lose consciousness, slip into a coma, or die
from alcohol poisoning.

Heavy drinkers and many first-time drinkers may suffer blackouts. Blackouts are
periods of time that the drinker cannot recall. Other people recall seeing the
drinker talking, walking, and in control. The following day, however, the drinker has
no memory of some events from the day before.

Liver

In the bloodstream, alcohol is carried to the liver. The liver chemically breaks down
alcohol into energy and the waste produces carbon dioxide and water. The carbon
dioxide is released from the body in the lungs. The water passes out of the body as
breath vapor, perspiration, or urine. When people drink alcohol faster than the liver
can break it down, they become **intoxicated**.

Kidneys

Alcohol prevents the release of body chemicals that regulate how much urine the
kidneys make. The kidneys produce more urine than usual, and the drinker loses
more water than usual. The drinker becomes very thirsty. In extreme cases, a
drinker may lose water needed for the body to function properly.

Motor-Vehicle Crashes

Almost half of the fatal crashes and about two-thirds of all crashes involving personal injury in the United States are related to alcohol use. In addition, more than
one-third of pedestrians who are struck and killed by motor vehicles are caused by
drunk drivers.

> ### Key Note Term
>
> **Intoxicated** – drunk;
> affected by alcohol to
> the point that physical
> and mental control are
> significantly impaired

Driving while intoxicated is illegal in all of the 50 states. Driving while intoxicated means a driver exceeds the level of blood alcohol concentration allowed by law in a state. Drivers who cause motor-vehicle crashes usually undergo blood, urine, breath, or saliva tests to determine their blood alcohol concentration (BAC, discussed on the next page). If their BAC is above the legal limit, drunk drivers can have their driver's license taken away and can be prosecuted.

Synergism

Some drugs can interact to produce effects that are many times greater than the individual drugs would produce. When drugs increase each other's effects when taken together, the interaction is called synergism.

As previously stated, alcohol is generally a depressant drug. When a person drinks alcohol and takes another depressant, such as sleeping pills, the combination can cause drastic changes in the body. Together the depressants' effects are more than doubled and can cause a dangerous slowing of breathing and heart rates. In extreme cases, synergism of alcohol and other depressants can lead to coma or death.

Overdose

Taking an excessive amount of a drug that leads to coma or death is called an overdose. Severe intoxication causes the heart and breathing to stop, resulting in death from alcohol overdose. Many drinkers assume that they will pass out before drinking a fatal amount. This is not necessarily true. Alcohol continues to be absorbed into the blood for 30 to 90 minutes after the last drink. The drinker's BAC can increase even if the drinker becomes unconscious. First-time drinkers who participate in a drinking contest may die from alcohol poisoning.

Blood Alcohol Concentration

The amount of ethanol in a person's blood is expressed by a percentage called the blood alcohol concentration (BAC). BAC measures the number of milligrams of ethanol per 100 milliliters of blood. A BAC of 0.1 percent means that 1/10 of 1 percent of the fluid in the blood is ethanol. A BAC of 0.1 percent reduces a person's muscle coordination, perception, and judgment.

A variety of factors can affect a person's BAC, including the following:

- **Gender**
- **Age, weight, and height**
- **Amount of food in the stomach**
- **Concentration of alcohol in beverages consumed**
- **Volume of alcohol consumed**
- **Rate of consumption and absorption**

The rate at which a person's liver can break down alcohol is fairly constant. In one hour, the liver can break down the amount of ethanol in a can of beer, a shot of liquor, or a glass of wine. Thus, someone who has three cans of beer in the last

45 minutes of a 3-hour party will become more intoxicated than someone who drinks those three cans of beer over the three-hour period. The effects of BAC on the body are shown in Figure 3.1.4.

Provided the person does not continue to drink, the BAC decreases. The intoxicating effects of alcohol slowly diminish. As reflexes and coordination return to normal, a person gradually becomes steadier. Many people refer to this process as "becoming sober" or "sobering up."

You may have heard that cold showers, exercise, fresh air, or coffee will help a person sober up more quickly. But this is not true. Nothing can speed the liver's ability to break down alcohol. Coffee or fresh air may keep a person awake, but they do not eliminate the intoxicating effects of alcohol.

Behavioral Effects

In addition to the physical effects of alcohol, certain behavioral, or learned, effects are connected to drinking. A person's mood and reason for drinking can alter the effects of alcohol. Sometimes the person's mood and reason for drinking make the effects stronger; sometimes they make the effects weaker. The environment in which alcohol is consumed may influence its effects as well.

At a quiet family dinner, family members may consume wine with no negative effects. The calm nature of the event and the fact that both parents and children expect each other to behave politely creates an environment in which people drink responsibly.

Blood Alcohol Concentration: Effects on the Body

Number of Drinks	Effects	BAC Range*	Approximate Time to Eliminate Alcohol
	Inhibitions, reflexes, and alertness diminished. Judgment and reasoning affected.	.02–.03%	1 1/2 hours
	Drinker gets the mistaken idea that his or her skills and abilities have improved. Self-control declines.	.04–.06%	3 hours
	Unable to think clearly. Judgment, reasoning and muscular coordination is impaired.	.06–.09%	4 to 5 hours
	Most behaviors, including hearing, speech, vision, and balance, are affected.	.08–.12%	5 to 7 hours

*The BAC will vary depending on the alcohol content of the drinks and rate of consumption.

Figure 3.1.4: In some states, a person with a BAC of 0.1 percent is legally drunk. Other states have lowered the legal BAC to 0.08 percent.

Reprinted from *Health Skills for Wellness*, Third Edition, by B. E. (Buzz) Pruitt, Kathy Teer Crumpler, and Deborah Prothrow-Stith, (2001), Prentice Hall, Inc.

At a party in which "getting drunk" is the main theme, alcohol consumption often leads to negative behaviors. The loss of coordination may be exaggerated for comic effect. People who have been drinking may insist that they are still perfectly able to drive. They may not want to admit that they cannot drink as much as others.

As alcohol takes effect, drinkers begin to lose judgment and self-control. At the same time, alcohol decreases drinkers' natural fears. When these two effects are combined, the person's inhibitions are reduced. Inhibitions are the controls that people put on their emotions and behavior in order to behave in socially acceptable ways.

After they lose their inhibitions, drinkers may behave in ways they normally would never consider. For example, a person under the influence of alcohol may express anger in violent or destructive ways. Shy people may behave in outgoing ways, and serious people may act foolishly.

Alcoholism

Some drinkers cannot control their drinking. Their major goal in drinking is to get drunk. People who have an addiction to alcohol suffer from the disease of alcoholism. Psychologically, alcoholics consider drinking a regular, essential part of coping with daily life. Physically, an alcoholic's body requires alcohol to function. An alcoholic's drinking patterns eventually control every aspect of life.

No one is sure why some drinkers become alcoholics, but anyone who drinks, even one drink, is at risk of becoming an alcoholic. Because alcoholism tends to run in

| D E C I D E | DEFINE the problem

EXPLORE alternatives

CONSIDER the consequences

IDENTIFY values

DECIDE and act

EVALUATE results | **Drinking and Driving?**

Janelle attended a party with some of her friends. She planned to get a ride home with Dave, but she had seen him drink four beers since he arrived. Dave was showing some signs of intoxication, and Janelle was not sure if he should drive. Unfortunately, she did not know anyone else at the party who could give her a ride, and Janelle knew that her parents had gone out with friends for the evening. Besides, three of her friends were getting a ride from Dave. "I'm probably getting worried for nothing," thought Janelle. "What could happen in the few miles to my house?"

1. Use the DECIDE process to decide what you would do if you were in Janelle's position. Explain your decision.
2. What role might peer pressure play in influencing Janelle's decision?
3. Suggest a realistic plan that you and your friends could use to avoid situations like the one described above.

Courtesy of Ken Karp |

Reprinted from *Health Skills for Wellness*, Third Edition, by B. E. (Buzz) Pruitt, Kathy Teer Crumpler, and Deborah Prothrow-Stith, (2001), Prentice Hall, Inc.

families, there appears to be some genetic basis. On the other hand, the attitudes in the home in which a person grows up may play a role in whether or not a person develops a drinking problem

Drugs

A drug is any chemical substance that changes the function of the mind or the body. Aspirin is a drug; allergy medication is a drug; marijuana is a drug; beer is a drug; the nicotine in cigarettes is a drug. A drug is neither good nor bad; it is what a person does with a drug that makes the difference.

Use, misuse, and *abuse* are terms thrown around quite a bit when talking about drugs. Use is taking a legal drug as prescribed or recommended for medical reasons. Misuse is taking a legal drug for medical reasons but not as recommended or prescribed. Abuse is taking any drug, legal or illegal, for a nonmedical reason in a way that can injure your health or ability to function. Taking drugs is a serious matter; there is no such thing as recreational drug use. Abusing drugs is not a sport or a hobby and always involves an unnecessary risk to your health.

When people talk about drugs, you often hear that someone is a drug *addict* or that a drug can or cannot cause dependence. Addiction and *drug dependence* mean basically the same thing; however, the term *addict* tends to make people think of a desperate individual living in the back alleys of a big city. But anyone from any background in any place can be addicted or drug dependent. People who are dependent cannot refuse the drug they have been abusing.

A person has a physical dependence on a drug when, after being deprived of the drug for any length of time, he or she experiences symptoms like nausea, vomiting, anxiety, watery eyes and nose, and an overwhelming desire to use the drug. Such symptoms are typical of withdrawal sickness. Withdrawal happens because the body's chemistry has been changed, causing the user to be unable to function comfortably without the drug.

Most people who are physically dependent are also psychologically dependent. Some have psychological dependence without the physical dependence, which can be an equally strong dependence. With this type of dependence, the user feels a powerful motivation to continue abusing a drug for the temporary pleasure or relief of discomfort the drug gives. Because the mind and the body work together very closely, it is often difficult to tell the difference between physical and psychological dependence. The mental craving for a drug may be so powerful that it seems to be a physical need.

Marijuana (Pot, Grass, Weed, Dope, Reefer)

Marijuana (Acapulco Gold, Ganga, Grass, Mary Jane, Pot, Weed, Reefer, Stick, Smoke) comes from the dried flowers, leaves, and small stems of the cannabis plant, as shown in Figure 3.1.5. It is smoked in cigarettes, known as joints, and also in pipes. Marijuana use is illegal in the United States, but in the past it was used medicinally to reduce swelling of the eyes caused by glaucoma and to counteract the intense nausea brought on by certain cancer treatments. Its legalization, especially for these medical purposes, has been a controversial subject in this country for years.

Figure 3.1.5: Marijuana is considered a gateway drug, meaning that people who use marijuana often go on to use other drugs.
Courtesy of Schleikorn/Custom Medical Stock Photo.

The tetrahydrocannabinol (THC) produced by cannabis is the main psychoactive substance that produces marijuana's mind-altering effects. THC is quickly absorbed into the lungs and then travels through the blood to affect the brain. It distorts the senses, including hearing, taste, touch, and smell, alters the sense of time and place, and affects emotions. THC affects sleep patterns and remains in body fat for at least a month after only one joint has been smoked. It causes users to crave food (getting the munchies) and to enjoy eating, which is unusual for a drug. It also tends to dull sexual urges and pleasure.

There are several hundred other chemicals in marijuana that vary between different types of cannabis plants and between plants grown during different seasons. The active chemicals in marijuana affect the brain, altering hearing, taste, touch, smell, and a sense of time and space. The effects of marijuana vary from person to person depending on each person's expectations and how much they smoke and because the chemicals in different marijuana plants vary. People may experience anything from a mild euphoria to uncontrollable laughter to hallucinations. Marijuana can also contain dangerous substances such as pesticides and molds and is sometimes mixed with PCP to make the user believe it is more potent.

Because marijuana is widely abused today and has been around for thousands of years, many people believe that its use poses no harm. However, research studies prove this notion wrong. The effects of marijuana use include the following:

- **Short-term memory loss and shortened attention span, both of which interfere with the ability to learn. Heavy, long-term use is often called "burn out" because the user's thinking is slow and confused.**

- **Increased heart rate and irregular heartbeat.**

- **Weakening of the immune system.**

- **Reduced hormone levels resulting in lower sperm counts in males and irregular menstrual cycles in females.**

- Development of "amotivational syndrome," which results in apathy and loss of ambition and drive.

- Impaired judgment, unsteadiness, lack of coordination, and slowed responses, which make driving a dangerous activity.

- Lung damage and increased risk of lung cancer. This risk is higher than that of smoking tobacco cigarettes because marijuana is inhaled more deeply and then held in the lungs for a longer period of time. Joints also lack filters to cut down on harmful chemical effects.

- Possible depression and moodiness. Some users feel tired and unhappy the morning after smoking marijuana and may respond by smoking a joint to feel better. This cycle may lead to psychological **dependency**.

- Possible intense fear and anxiety, called a "pot panic" and even paranoia and psychosis. This may occur if the marijuana contains higher levels of THC.

- Development of a tolerance to marijuana resulting in the need for greater amounts in order to feel any effects. This may also contribute to psychological dependence.

Key Note Term

dependency – addiction to a substance

The harmful health effects of marijuana use may include rapid and irregular heartbeat, short-term memory loss, shortened attention span, a weakened immune system, fatigue, and a higher risk of lung cancer. In extreme cases, marijuana abuse can result in paranoia and psychosis. Similar to alcohol, marijuana abuse can affect driving ability. As with any illegal drug, marijuana is not tested for safety and purity. It may contain pesticides and molds and may be mixed with other dangerous drugs.

Because of all the effects marijuana has on the mind, body, and the ability to learn, its use may be particularly harmful to young people since they are still maturing physically, sexually, and mentally. Marijuana's effects may prevent you from becoming a healthy, normal adult.

Cocaine, Crack, and Bazuco

Cocaine hydrochloride (Cocaine, Coke, Peruvian marching powder, C, Snow, Flake, Rock, White, Blow, Nose Candy) comes from the leaves of the coca bush, as shown in Figure 3.1.6, and is an illegal drug that looks like white crystalline powder. It is often diluted with other ingredients and then inhaled through the nose, injected, or smoked.

Figure 3.1.6: Cocaine is derived from the leaves of the South American coca shrub.
Courtesy of Dr. Morley Read/Photo Researchers.

Cocaine is a stimulant that affects the nervous system providing short bursts of euphoria, a feeling of excitement, increased blood pressure and pulse rate, and alertness. People often use it to increase mental activity and to offset drowsiness, fatigue, or as an appetite suppressant; however, the intense high of cocaine is followed by an intense low. Repeated abuse of cocaine can result in a strong physical and psychological dependency. The body will ignore all other drives, including hunger, in its drive for cocaine.

Key Note Term

depressed – low spirits; sadness; dejection

Regular use can lead to hallucinations of touch, taste, sound, or smell. Tolerance develops rapidly with repeated use. As the effects of cocaine wear off, the user feels exhausted, **depressed**, and sometimes paranoid, similar to the crashing of amphetamines. Cocaine is considered to be one of the most potentially addictive drugs.

Cocaine stimulates the central nervous system. Immediate effects include dilated pupils and elevated blood pressure, heart rate, respiratory rate, and body temperature. Occasional use results in a stuffy nose, while chronic use decays the mucous membranes of the nose. Injecting cocaine, or any drug, with a shared needle may spread AIDS, hepatitis, and other diseases. Cocaine produces both psychological and physical dependency.

Dealers cut cocaine with other substances, usually table sugar, mannitol, lactose, dextrose, and other drugs (PCP, lidocaine, amphetamines). Strychnine, a poison, has been found in cocaine; talc, which damages the lungs, is also often used.

Occasional use of cocaine can lead to heavy, uncontrollable use, with the dependence becoming so strong that users will not quit even when cocaine severely damages their lives. When users do quit, they may not experience strong physical withdrawal symptoms, but they become depressed and irritable, are tired but unable to sleep, and constantly crave the drug.

Crack (Crack, Freebase Rocks, Rock) looks like brown pellets or crystalline rocks that resemble lumpy soap and is often packaged in small vials. It is smoked. Bazuco is a drug similar to crack. Both of these drugs are illegal.

Crack is street cocaine commonly processed with boiling water and baking soda, which produces a very pure form of cocaine. The effects and the risk of addiction to crack are so great, however, that it is like a completely different drug. It is many, many times more dangerous than cocaine hydrochloride. Its effects are felt within 10 seconds. Cocaine in this form creates a very intense high and a fast, strong addiction. The user also experiences an incredible low after the high has worn off, often throwing him or her into a deep depression. To offset this depression, the user then smokes more crack, which starts the compulsive cycle that leads to a severe dependency. The only person who benefits from this vicious cycle is the drug dealer who now has a desperate customer in constant need of his or her product.

The physical side effects of crack include dilated pupils, increased pulse rate, elevated blood pressure, insomnia, loss of appetite, hallucinations of touch, paranoia, and seizures. A major concern with crack is that dependency is almost immediate. The first experience is often very pleasurable. Then the extreme low afterward is a strong motivator to use the drug again right away, this time to relieve bad feelings. Users of crack are addicted before they know it, turning their lives upside down.

Bazuco, another form of cocaine, is equally if not more dangerous and addictive than crack. Its use originated in Colombia and other South American countries and has now made its way to the United States. It is made from the intermediate step between the coca leaf and the cocaine hydrochloride, called cocaine sulfate. It is mixed with a number of other substances, among them marijuana, methaqualone, and acetone. Its effects are similar to those of crack, as are its dangers and its quick addiction.

The use of any type of cocaine can cause death by disrupting the brain's control of the heart and respiration.

Amphetamines and Methamphetamines (Speed)

Amphetamines (Speed, Bennies, Glass, Uppers, Ups, Black Beauties, Pep Pills, Copilots, Bumblebees, White Crosses, Benzedrine, Dexedrine, Footballs, Biphetamine) look like capsules, pills, or tablets. Methamphetamines (Crank, Crystal, Meth, Crystal Meth, Methedrine, Ice) can be in the form of a white powder, pills, or a rock that resembles blue paraffin. Forms of both drugs are used medically to treat obesity, narcolepsy, and hyperactivity in children.

Amphetamines

Similar to cocaine, amphetamines are **stimulants**. They stimulate the nervous system, increasing physical activity, energy, mental alertness, self-confidence, and producing euphoria. Medically, amphetamines are used to treat obesity, narcolepsy, and hyperactivity in children. For example, the amphetamine Ritalin is used to stimulate the brain center that helps hyperactive children sit still and pay attention.

As a drug of abuse, amphetamines are often referred to as "speed." Many people abuse amphetamines to increase energy and alertness, and in some cases to combat fatigue brought on by use of alcohol, marijuana, or depressants. The body builds up tolerance to amphetamines, however, and greater and greater doses are required to achieve the same effects. Addiction may become severe.

Medically, amphetamines are taken orally, but many abusers inject the drug directly into a vein increasing the risk of overdose and infection. Needles shared to inject the drug can spread hepatitis and HIV. After an injection of amphetamines, the user experiences an intense, short-lived euphoria. An addict may inject the drug several times a day for several days feeling little need for food or sleep. Mental depression and overwhelming fatigue follow abuse, which may cause the abuser to turn to amphetamines again for relief.

In addition to fatigue and depression, the other side effects of amphetamine abuse include extreme anxiety, temporary mental illness, and malnutrition. High doses can cause hallucinations, increased body temperature, high blood pressure, convulsions, kidney failure, lack of oxygen, bleeding of the brain, and death. Withdrawal symptoms include irritability, depression, disorientation, long periods of sleep, and not caring about anything.

Key Note Term

stimulants – drugs, drinks, or other substances that speed up the activity of the mind or body; a drug that speeds up the activities of the central nervous system, the heart, and other organs

Methamphetamines

Methamphetamine is a nervous system stimulant similar to amphetamines that is used medically in much the same way as amphetamines. This drug is abused to produce heightened awareness, alertness, and self-confidence. A smokable form of methamphetamine is "ice." Like crack, it produces an intense high without the use of needles and is extremely addictive. Abuse of methamphetamine may result in bizarre behavior, sleeplessness, depression, high blood pressure, increased body temperature, convulsions, heart problems, seizures, and strokes.

Methcathinone, also called "cat" and "star," is a designer drug similar to methamphetamine that can cause paranoia, slurred speech, tremors, extreme weight loss, and sleeplessness

Barbiturates, Methaqualones, and Tranquilizers

Barbiturates (Downers, Barbs, Blue Devils, Red Devils, Yellow Jacket, Yellows, Nembutal, Seconal, Amytal, Tuinals, Luminal, Amytal, Pentothal, Phenobarbital) look like red, yellow, blue, or red and blue capsules. Methaqualones (Ludes, Quaaludes, Quads, Sopors, Sopes, 714s) look like tablets. Tranquilizers (Valium, Librium, Equanil, Miltown, Serax, Tranxene, Thorazine) look like tablets or capsules.

Barbiturates

Barbiturates are a group of depressant drugs that include phenobarbital (goof-balls), pentobarbital (yellow jackets), amobarbital (blue devils), and secobarbital (red devils). They lower body temperature and blood pressure, slow breathing and heart rate, and as such, have many medical uses. For example, doctors prescribe phenobarbital to reduce the frequency of convulsions in epileptics. Barbiturates are also used medically as an anesthetic and to treat insomnia. The effects of barbiturates vary from person to person and even change within one person from one time to the next.

When abused, the symptoms they produce are similar to those of alcohol. Small amounts can produce calmness and relaxed muscles, but larger doses cause slurred speech and staggering walk. Like alcohol, they distort perception and slow reaction time, which can cause serious accidents like car crashes. Very large doses can cause respiratory depression, coma, and death.

Signs of barbiturate abuse include fatigue, blurred vision, confused or slurred speech, lack of coordination and balance, a reduction of mental and physical activity, and decreased breathing. Abusers will often act like they are drunk, but there will be no smell of alcohol. Long-term abuse may result in double vision, depression, and forgetfulness.

Signs of an overdose of barbiturates include dilated pupils, a rapid pulse, shallow breathing, and clammy skin. An overdose can cause coma and death. Because barbiturates cause confusion and forgetfulness, accidental death occurs when a person has taken barbiturates, becomes confused, forgets, and takes more barbiturates. Accidental poisoning occurs when barbiturates are combined with alcohol. Withdrawal symptoms include anxiety, insomnia, tremors, delirium, and convulsions.

Barbiturate abusers often become extremely depressed, tired, and hopeless. They may reach for the rest of the bottle to "end it all" when in this mental state, or they may become confused, forget how many pills they have taken, and accidentally overdose. For this reason, barbiturates are one of the leading causes of drug-related deaths. The combination of barbiturates and alcohol can multiply the effects of both drugs, thereby multiplying the risks. This multiplication of the effects of two separate drugs when taken together is called the synergistic effect. It can be fatal.

Methaqualone

Methaqualone production has been banned in the United States since 1984 due to its widespread misuse and minimal medical value. Abusers take it to produce a feeling of elation; however, its side effects are headaches, nosebleeds, dizziness, loss of coordination, and leg and arm pain. Tolerance and psychological dependence can develop when used regularly. Using methaqualone with alcohol is known as "luding out" and can cause death.

Tranquilizers

Tranquilizers are used medically to treat anxiety, insomnia, and convulsions. It is very easy to become both physically and psychologically dependent on them. When mixed with alcohol, they can cause death.

Narcotics

Most **narcotics** are opiates, which come from the seed pods of opium poppies. Many are used medically to relieve pain and treat insomnia. Narcotics abuse initially produces a feeling of euphoria that is often followed by drowsiness, nausea, and vomiting. Users also may experience constricted pupils, watery eyes, and itching. An overdose may produce slow and shallow breathing, clammy skin, convulsions, coma, and death. Tolerance develops rapidly and dependence is likely. The use of contaminated syringes to inject certain kinds of narcotics may result in diseases such as AIDS and hepatitis. Narcotics include opium, codeine, morphine, and heroin. Other types of opiates include Percocet, Percodan, Tussionex, Fentanyl, Darvon, Talwin, and Lomotil and come as tablets, capsules, or liquids.

Key Note Term

narcotics – a drug medically used to relieve pain, produce sleep, and dull the senses

Opium

Opium (Paregoric, Dover's Powder, Parepectolin) can look like dark brown chunks or a powder. It comes from a specific type of poppy, generally grown in the Middle East. Opium is one of the weaker narcotics, but it has side effects that make it undesirable as a medication, including slowed heart rate, breathing, and mental abilities, and loss of appetite.

Codeine

Codeine comes in different drugs such as Empirin, Tylenol, and certain cough medicines. It is either a dark liquid varying in thickness or comes in capsules or tablets. Similar to opium, codeine is one of the weakest narcotics. Doctors prescribe it for coughs and pain relief.

Morphine

Morphine (Pectoral Syrup) is an opium derivative, and comes in the form of white crystals, hypodermic tablets, and injectable solutions. Morphine is a very strong painkiller, but because it is also very addictive, it is used in medicine only for severe cases, such as in the later stages of terminal cancer when patients are in extreme pain. Unfortunately, as a drug of abuse, morphine usually results in addiction. Withdrawal from it has painful and severe effects and generally requires the help of a professional to get an addict off the drug.

Heroin and Methadone

Heroin (Smack, Horse, Junk, Harry, H, Brown, Black Tar, Antifreeze) looks like a white to dark brown powder or a tar-like substance. Methadone Hydrochloride (Dolophine, Methadose, Methadone) comes in the form of a solution.

Heroin is a concentrated form of morphine and is so addictive that it is illegal in the United States even for medical use. Unfortunately, it is the most abused narcotic in this country, and its use is on the rise as of the late 1990s. Users of heroin often start by sniffing or smoking the drug in powdered form. Because tolerance develops quickly, they often turn to "mainlining," the practice of injecting a heroin solution into their veins to intensify the drug's effects.

Heroin dulls the senses, easing tensions, fears, and worries. A stupor follows that lasts for several hours in which hunger and thirst are reduced. After 12 to 16 hours without heroin, the user will experience severe withdrawal symptoms, including sweating, shaking, chills, nausea, diarrhea, abdominal pain, leg cramps, and severe mental and emotional pain. To relieve these symptoms, the user must take another dose of the drug. People addicted to heroin often die young, some from overdoses caused by unreliable drugs, others because they cannot distinguish between safe and dangerous doses.

Signs of an overdose include shallow and slow breathing, clammy skin, and convulsions. An overdose can result in a coma and death. When addicted, a person must have more of the drug to keep from experiencing withdrawal symptoms, which are severe and can include panic, shaking, chills, sweating, cramps, and nausea.

Hallucinogens

Hallucinogens alter the physical senses, producing visions, sounds, and smells that are not real, and distorting the concepts of time and space in the user's mind. Because these drugs confuse fact and fantasy, a user may become irrational and resort to violence or suicide to avoid an imagined situation or attacker. Hallucinogens are not physically addictive, but users often become psychologically dependent on these drugs.

Lysergic Acid Diethylamide (Acid)

Lysergic acid diethylamide (LSD, Acid, White Lightning, Blue Heaven, Sugar Cubes, Microdot, Twenty-Five, Sid, Bart Simpsons, Barrels, Tabs, Blotter, L, Liquid, Liquid A, Microdots, Mind Detergent, Orange Cubes, Hits, paper Acid, Sugar, Sunshine, Ticket, Wedding Bells, and Windowpane) can come as brightly colored tablets, imprinted blotter paper, thin squares of gelatin, or as a clear liquid.

Key Note Term

hallucinogen – drugs that cause hallucinations

A "trip" from an average dose of LSD can last as long as 8 to 10 hours. LSD's effects are unpredictable, tolerance to it develops quickly, and its use frequently results in psychological dependence.

LSD is a powerful hallucinogen that scrambles and confuses the senses. A tiny drop taken with sugar or food can cause a person to trip or experience false visions, smells, and sounds for hours. Sensations may be confused and feelings may change rapidly. Music may appear as colors and colors as flavors or odors. Some people say these experiences are exciting; others say they are nightmares. Those having a bad trip may take dangerous or irrational actions to escape from this imaginary situation. In addition to these affects, LSD can cause nausea, vomiting, and misinterpretations of time and distance. Some people experience flashbacks of LSD's effects days, weeks, and years after the original trip. An overdose of LSD can result in psychosis, accidental death, and suicide.

Phencyclidine Hydrochloride

Phencyclidine hydrochloride (PCP, Angel Dust, Hog, Superjoint, Busy Bee, Green Tea Leaves, DOA [dead on arrival]) can be in the form of a liquid, capsules, white crystalline powder, or pills. Of the various types of hallucinogens, only PCP has a medical use as a tranquilizer for animals.

PCP interrupts the functions of the neocortex, which is the section of the brain that controls the intellect and keeps instincts in check. The effects of PCP are unpredictable, but users frequently report a sense of distance and alienation from the world and others. Sometimes a user may feel drunk, but at other times the same dose may cause depression, paranoia, hallucinations, and suicidal thoughts. Time and movement are slowed down; muscular coordination worsens; senses are dulled; and speech is blocked and incoherent.

PCP stays in the system for a long time. Chronic users report persistent memory problems and speech difficulties as well as psychological and behavioral changes. Some of these effects may last six months to a year following prolonged daily use. Mood disorders such as depression and anxiety also occur, and users may exhibit paranoid and violent behavior. In fact, many deaths attributed to PCP do not occur from the drug itself, but from accidents, like falling from high places, drowning, or car wrecks, which are related to the behavior PCP produces. Large doses of PCP can cause convulsions and coma, heart and lung failure, or ruptured blood vessels in the brain. Treatment for an overdose is very difficult and requires hospitalization.

PCP, used as a tranquilizer for animals, can cause frightening hallucinations when used by humans. Abuse can result in seizures, coma, and death or in violent, unpredictable behavior. Some abusers have committed murder and suicide.

Psilocybin (Mushrooms, Shrooms) and Mescaline (Mesc, Buttons, Cactus)

Two other hallucinogens are psilocybin, produced from a type of mushroom, and mescaline, produced from a type of cactus. Similar to other hallucinogens, use of these drugs can cause hallucinations, perception problems, nausea, vomiting, and, in extreme cases, mental illness, suicide, or accidental death. Mescaline effects, while compared to a mild LSD trip, are often accompanied by sweating and severe abdominal cramps. Eating mushrooms poses another danger because many mushrooms look alike and some are poisonous enough to cause death.

Inhalants (Air Blast)

Key Note Term

inhalants – medications or chemicals that are inhaled

Inhalants are toxic chemicals like glue, freon, nail polish, spray paint, and gasoline that are huffed (sprayed into a cloth and held over the mouth and nose) or bagged (sniffed from a bag, bottle, or can) to achieve a brief, mild euphoria. All of these products contain labels warning against inhaling their fumes because of the hazards involved. Some inhalants used medically are also abused, such as amyl nitrate which relieves heart pain and nitrous oxide which relieves anxiety.

Risks involved with inhaling these chemicals include nausea; dizziness; vomiting; headaches; unconsciousness; pneumonia; permanent brain and nerve damage; bleeding of the brain; eventual liver, brain, and kidney cancer; and death due to heart failure and suffocation. Effects of inhalants are unpredictable and depend on what chemical or chemicals are inhaled and how much. Brain damage and death may result after only one use depending on the inhalants involved.

Ecstasy (XTC, Love Drug)

Ecstasy (MBDB, MDE, MDEA, and 2CB) is a "designer drug" that closely resembles cocaine. It produces euphoria that lasts several hours, heightens pleasure, and may even produce hallucinations in high doses. Ecstasy is taken orally and may cause mood swings, overly friendly behavior, insomnia, anxiety, and nausea. In extreme cases, abuse may result in seizure and death.

Rohypnol (Roofies, Forget Pill, Date-Rape Pill)

Rohypnol (GHB include G, Liquid Ecstacy, Somatomax, Scoop, Georgia Home Boy, and Grievous Bodily Harm) is used legally as a medical sedative in Europe and Latin America. As a drug of abuse, it is called roofies, the forget pill, and the date-rape pill. At first, it produces an alcoholic type of high, but then heavy sedation and short-term memory loss that lasts up to eight hours. It earned its reputation as the date-rape pill by being slipped into the drinks of females, who were taken advantage of in a state of sedation brought on by the drug and then unable to remember exactly what happened to them. In addition to the drawback just discussed, dangers of abusing rohypnol include impaired motor skills and slow respiration.

Steroids

Although anabolic steroids are available only by prescription in the United States, many steroid supplements are available over the counter and are marketed under several names. Steroids and steroid supplements are often taken to increase performance in sports. Some people take them to develop muscles. Abusers of steroids take many times the recommended dosages in an effort to bulk up. Steroid abuse has been increasing in recent years, especially among middle-school students. Steroid use has been associated with chemical dependence and withdrawal syndrome. Athletes who turn to steroids risk permanent damage to their bodies and withdrawal syndrome, as shown in Figure 3.1.7.

Adapted from TeenGetGoing Web site, www.teengetgoing.com/Drug/Sdrugs.asp, accessed January 5, 2005.

Figure 3.1.7: This high school athlete is suffering from steroid withdrawal syndrome.
Courtesy of Jeff Jacobson/ Archive.

Key Note Terms

tobacco – the leaves of cultivated tobacco plants, prepared for use in smoking, chewing, or as snuff

nicotine – the drug in tobacco that may act as a stimulant and cause addiction

Tobacco

Many people hold the view that experimentation with or use of **tobacco** is considered normal or acceptable behavior. However, the use of tobacco often progresses to further drug abuses. Accordingly, some experts attach the term *gateway* to this substance. Use of drugs such as cocaine and heroin is unusual in those who have not previously used tobacco.

The hazards of tobacco include cancer and other diseases and can also have ill effects on others. As awareness of these ill effects reaches new heights, more and more Americans are joining forces to fight tobacco abuse every day.

In addition to smoking cigarettes, pipes, or cigars, people who use tobacco products can also do so orally in the forms of chewing tobacco (by placing a wad between the cheek and teeth and sucking on it) and snuff (by placing a pinch between the lower lip and teeth).

Three major components make up tobacco, each having their own ill effects. One such component, tar, causes a variety of cancers and contributes to emphysema and other respiratory problems. For this reason, people often choose to smoke low-tar cigarettes, but even low-tar cigarettes can be unsafe because smokers often smoke more while using these brands. Carbon monoxide, also found in tobacco, restricts the oxygen-carrying capacity of the blood, and can often cause insufficient heart operation. **Nicotine**, the substance in tobacco believed to cause dependency, is absorbed into the bloodstream, reaching the heart and brain within a few seconds of the onset of smoking.

Note

Nicotine in its pure state is a toxic poison and is also used in insecticides.

Some of the diseases associated with long-term tobacco smoking include chronic bronchitis, emphysema, coronary heart disease, and lung cancer. Lung cancer is the leading cause of death among women today. Cigarette smoking is a major independent risk factor for heart attacks (sometimes fatal) in both men and women. Pipe and cigar smokers are more prone to dying from cancer of the mouth and throat than nonsmokers. Smoking also reduces the effectiveness of prescription and over-the-counter medications.

> **Note**
>
> Infections, especially pneumonia and acute bronchitis, are twice as common in young children whose parents smoke than children with nonsmoking parents.

Although chewing tobacco and snuff are not smoked, they increase the risk of disease and damage to the delicate lining of the mouth and throat. As a result, individuals who use these products are more likely than nonusers to develop mouth cancer, throat cancer, and gum disease. Chewing tobacco and snuff can also contribute to heart disease and strokes. The harmful effects of one can of snuff are equal to that of about 60 cigarettes.

Despite the labels required by federal law warning individuals about the hazardous effects of using tobacco products, use continues.

Recent research has indicated that non-smokers who breathe in second-hand smoke (smoke that escapes from the burning end of a cigarette as well as the smoke exhaled by the smoker), can have an increased risk of lung cancer, heart disease, and respiratory disorders. Inhaling second-hand smoke makes the heart beat faster, the blood pressure go up, and the level of carbon monoxide in the blood increase. Smoke from an idling cigarette contains even more tar and nicotine than an inhaled one, in addition to more cadmium, a substance which has been related to hypertension, chronic bronchitis, and emphysema.

As the public becomes more aware of the dangers of inhaling second-hand smoke, the legislation protecting the rights of nonsmokers continues to increase. Smoking is increasingly being banned in both public and private places.

The Chemicals in Tobacco Smoke

With each puff on a cigarette, cigar, or pipe, a smoker inhales over 4,000 different chemicals. Of these 4,000 chemicals, at least 1,000 are known to be dangerous. Table 3.1.1 lists some of the harmful chemicals found in cigarette smoke. Among all the dangerous substances, nicotine, tar, and carbon monoxide can be identified as the most deadly ones found in tobacco smoke.

Nicotine and Addiction

The drug in tobacco that may act as a stimulant and cause addiction is nicotine. A stimulant is a drug that speeds up the activities of the central nervous system, the heart, and other organs. In its pure form, nicotine is one of the strongest poisons

Table 3.1.1: Harmful Chemicals in Tobacco Smoke

acctaldehyde	butylamine	methyl alcohol
acetone	carbon monoxide	methylamine
acetonitrile	dimethylamine	methylfuran
acrolein	dimethyl-nitrosamine	methylnaphthalene
acrylonitrile	ethylamine	nicotine
ammonia	formaldehyde	nitric oxide
aniline	hydrocyanic acid	nitrogen dioxide
benzene	hydrogen cyanide	phenol
benzopyrene	hydrogen sulfide	pyridine
2,3 butadione	methacrolein	toluene

known. Taken in large amounts, nicotine can kill people by paralyzing their breathing muscles. Smokers usually take in small amounts of nicotine. However, over several years the effects on the body of much smaller amounts are numerous and severe.

When tobacco is smoked, nicotine enters the lungs, where it is immediately absorbed into the bloodstream. Seconds later, the nicotine reaches the brain. Chemical changes begin to take place. Nicotine causes the heart to beat faster, the skin temperature to drop, and the blood pressure to rise. Nicotine constricts blood vessels, which cuts down on the blood flow to hands and feet. Beginning smokers usually feel the effects of nicotine poisoning with their first inhalation. These effects include rapid pulse, clammy skin, nausea, dizziness, and tingling in the hands and feet. Nicotine and cigarettes have many adverse effects on the body, as shown in Figure 3.1.8.

The degree of reaction varies from person to person, depending on the person's tolerance to nicotine. The effects of nicotine poisoning stop as soon as tolerance to nicotine develops. Tolerance can develop in new smokers after the second or third cigarette. The smoker begins to experience a "lift," a physical reaction to the chemicals in nicotine. As tolerance builds, however, the user may need more and more tobacco to produce the same feeling. The Surgeon General, the country's highest medical authority, has called nicotine an addicting drug, just like heroin and cocaine.

In a short time, tobacco users develop an addiction to nicotine. A tobacco addict who goes without tobacco for a short time may experience nicotine withdrawal. Nicotine withdrawal is a reaction to the lack of nicotine in the body, which causes

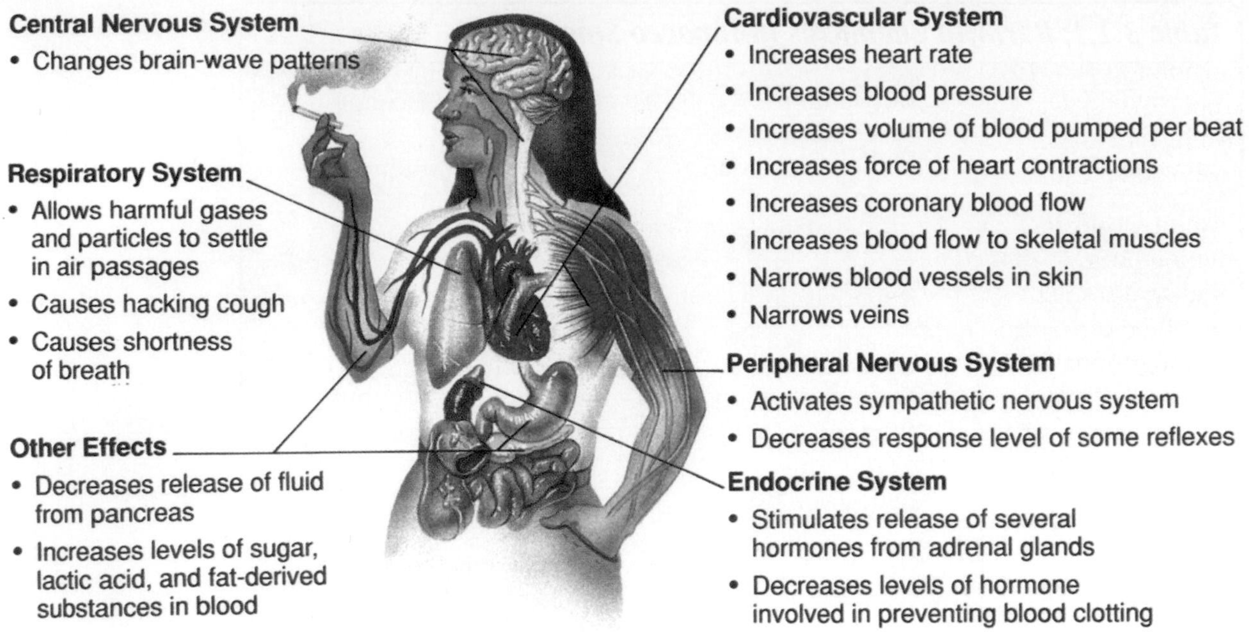

Central Nervous System
- Changes brain-wave patterns

Respiratory System
- Allows harmful gases and particles to settle in air passages
- Causes hacking cough
- Causes shortness of breath

Other Effects
- Decreases release of fluid from pancreas
- Increases levels of sugar, lactic acid, and fat-derived substances in blood

Cardiovascular System
- Increases heart rate
- Increases blood pressure
- Increases volume of blood pumped per beat
- Increases force of heart contractions
- Increases coronary blood flow
- Increases blood flow to skeletal muscles
- Narrows blood vessels in skin
- Narrows veins

Peripheral Nervous System
- Activates sympathetic nervous system
- Decreases response level of some reflexes

Endocrine System
- Stimulates release of several hormones from adrenal glands
- Decreases levels of hormone involved in preventing blood clotting

Figure 3.1.8: Nicotine and cigarettes affect many body systems.
Courtesy of Fran Milner.

symptoms such as headache, irritability, restlessness, increased coughing, nausea, vomiting, a general feeling of illness, and intense cravings for tobacco. Withdrawal effects may begin as soon as two hours after the last cigarette. Physical craving for a cigarette reaches a peak in the first 24 hours.

Tobacco users also suffer psychological withdrawal symptoms when they stop smoking. They feel emotionally and mentally uncomfortable without tobacco. By using tobacco at certain times—when under stress, for example—tobacco users actually condition themselves to rely on tobacco whenever a stressful situation arises. When tobacco users go without tobacco, they may feel unable to handle stress. Many tobacco users begin to depend on tobacco at particular times of the day, such as when they awaken or after they finish a meal. Others begin to depend on tobacco in social or work situations, such as parties or meetings.

Tar

The dark, sticky mixture of chemicals that is formed when tobacco burns is known as tar. Smokers can see evidence of this substance on their fingers and teeth, which turn brown when tar sticks to them. The tar also sticks to the cells of the respiratory system, where it damages the delicate cells that line the respiratory tract. The cells have tiny hair-like structures, or cilia. The cilia beat back and forth and sweep dust and other foreign particles away from the lungs. If the cilia are damaged, foreign particles can enter the lungs, leading to disease.

The tar in tobacco smoke contains hundreds of chemical carcinogens, or cancer-causing agents. Cancer of the lungs, throat, and mouth are caused by the inhalation of tar in tobacco smoke.

Carbon Monoxide

Carbon monoxide is a poisonous, colorless, odorless gas that is found in cigarette smoke. You may be familiar with the dangers of carbon monoxide. Deaths that result from leaving a car engine running in a closed area are caused by carbon monoxide poisoning.

Carbon monoxide has a greater attraction for the oxygen-carrying molecules (hemoglobin) in the red blood cells than oxygen does. When carbon monoxide is inhaled, it takes the place of, or displaces, large amounts of oxygen from hemoglobin. The more carbon monoxide present in the blood, the less oxygen in the blood. Carbon monoxide also makes it hard for the oxygen that is left in the blood to get to the muscles and organs. When a person smokes, the heart works harder but accomplishes less. Because their blood contains too little oxygen to function properly, smokers often experience shortness of breath when they are active.

Chemicals in Smokeless Tobacco

Most tobacco users smoke cigarettes, cigars, or pipes. And yet there has been an increase, especially among teenage boys, in the use of smokeless tobacco. Smokeless tobacco is tobacco that is chewed or sniffed through the nose. Some people who use smokeless tobacco think that the products are safe because no smoke is produced or inhaled. What they may not realize is that smokeless tobacco contains many of the same harmful chemicals found in tobacco smoke, including the highly addictive drug nicotine.

There are two different kinds of smokeless tobacco products. Chewing tobacco is poor-quality tobacco leaves mixed with molasses or honey and placed between the cheek and gums. Snuff is finely ground tobacco that may be held between the lower lip and teeth or sniffed through the nose. One can of snuff delivers as much nicotine as 60 cigarettes. The nicotine in chewing tobacco enters the bloodstream through the membranes of the mouth. The nicotine in snuff gets into the body through the membranes of either the mouth or the nose. After it has entered the body, nicotine from smokeless tobacco has the same effects as nicotine from cigarettes.

Conclusion

When drugs are properly used, they can cure illness and save lives. When abused, however, drugs and alcohol can destroy lives and cause death. It is important to understand that, although people often abuse drugs and alcohol to find happiness and fulfillment, these substances only create more problems and unhappiness. To keep from falling into the trap of drug and alcohol abuse, stay smart, strong, and active. Say no. Recognize the different drugs that are abused in our society and what affect they have on people's health and lives. Understand the dangers of alcohol abuse, not only to the drinker but to family and friends. You can set an example of an informed, drug-free individual.

Chapter 3

Lesson Review

Lesson Review

1. What is the difference between drug use, misuse, and abuse?
2. List three risks associated with the use of alcohol.
3. Is there any "safe" cigarette? Why or why not?
4. Define the term *gateway*.

Critical Decisions about Substances (Interactive Nights Out)

Key Terms

detoxification program
methadone
normal
stress
therapeutic community

What You Will Learn to Do

- Respond to substance use and abuse situations

Linked Core Abilities

- Take responsibility for your actions and choices
- Do your share as a good citizen in your school, community, country, and the world

Skills and Knowledge You Will Gain Along the Way

- Weigh the external and internal factors that influence decisions about substance abuse
- Apply the F-I-N-D-S decision process (See section on F-I-N-D-S in Unit 3, Chapter 10, Lesson 1)
- Employ predeciding techniques as a substance abuse prevention strategy
- Identify two kinds of intervention: interpersonal and enforcement
- Recognize signs of substance abuse
- Describe why people abuse substances and ways to remain drug-, alcohol-, and tobacco-free
- Identity ways to approach/help someone you suspect has a drug problem
- Define the key words contained in this lesson

Introduction

Do you know the difference between substance use, misuse and abuse? Can you recognize the symptoms of each? Substance abuse is a social dilemma that impacts families, employers, friends, and even school systems. In this lesson, you will examine the types of behaviors and characteristics common to substance abusers and apply appropriate responses to substance use and abuse situations.

Obviously, all drug use is not bad. Drugs taken as prescribed by doctors or as indicated on over-the-counter drug packaging can help prevent and cure illnesses and relieve symptoms of illnesses. When taken under these circumstances and for these reasons, drugs are a useful tool in keeping people healthy. However, drugs should only be a small part of an individual's efforts to maintain wellness, since the best way to stay healthy is to maintain a healthy lifestyle. When people are healthy and feeling well both mentally and physically, they do not require drugs. So why do people misuse and abuse drugs when they do not need them?

The reasons for misusing and abusing drugs all have one thing in common: People depend on drugs to change the way they feel, instead of learning to change themselves or their behaviors to solve their problems or face new challenges. You do not need drugs to have a good time; there are many other longer lasting ways to feel good. You do not need drugs to relieve uncomfortable feelings; many other young people struggle with troubles and challenges much like your own. Even adults are often concerned with the same things you are. Many people, young and old, work to change the things that they do not like in their lives and learn to live with those aspects of their lives that they cannot change—all free of drugs. In fact, people who abuse drugs to avoid their problems realize they are not able to solve them.

How Use Develops

Students are usually first tempted to smoke cigarettes and marijuana and drink alcohol at parties and other social occasions because of peer pressure and curiosity. From there, drug abuse may then progress in five stages:

1. **Experimental use.**
2. **Occasional use.**
3. **Regular use.**
4. **Multiple drug use.**
5. **Total dependency.**

This progression of stages is not inevitable; it can be stopped at any stage although stopping becomes more difficult in later stages. The best way to prevent a problem with drugs is to simply not abuse them in the first place.

Experimental Use

Those who experiment with drugs may be more curious about a drug's effects than the drug's dangers. In the case of certain drugs, however, the dangers of addiction, permanent psychological damage, or physical harm takes only one unlucky experiment. Drugs have different effects on different individuals who have no way of knowing what that effect may be. For some, trying a drug once can result in immediate addiction, serious injury to themselves or others, and even death. Remember, those who are now dependent started with experimentation, and they probably never thought that trying a drug once or twice would become an addiction. The many lives ruined by drugs prove that this can indeed happen.

Occasional Use

For occasional drug users, drugs become a way of having a good time with friends in social situations. Using drugs while alone is still relatively uncommon. Drug use may become the major social activity of the group, so it is very easy for occasional use to turn into a regular habit.

Regular Use

Regular users take drugs to maintain a drugged feeling. Though they may deny it, these users are psychologically dependent on drugs. Drug use has become a regular part of their lifestyle, and although they continue to carry out their daily activities at home, school, or work, they are usually barely making it.

Multiple Drug Use

In many cases, once people try one drug and get comfortable taking it, they are more likely to feel comfortable trying other types of drugs. For example, after many young people give in to pressures to try marijuana, and if they continue to use it regularly, it is likely they will try other drugs as well. Unfortunately, as covered in the previous lesson, each drug produces different effects, and while users of one drug may know what to expect when they take it, another drug may be much more dangerous and affect them in a very different way.

Courtesy of US Army JROTC.

> **Note**
>
> The chances that a first-time user of cocaine will become addicted are 1 in 6; the chances that a first-time user of crack will become addicted are 1 in 3; and 1 out of 10 drinkers becomes an alcoholic.

Total Dependency

Dependent users rely on drugs physically as well as psychologically and will go to great lengths to get them. Without drugs, they experience severe physical and mental distress. Dependent users all started with experimental drug use. In many cases, as users grow more dependent on drugs, they crave new sensations and may try more than one drug at a time or different ways of taking a drug. Such habits multiply the risks of drug use. For example, people who start injecting drugs risk contracting diseases like AIDS through shared needles.

Who's at Risk?

Key Note Term

stress – strain or pressure on the body or mind

Anyone has the potential to become dependent on substances, but some people seem to be more susceptible than others. Certain times in life may make someone more likely to try drugs for the first time or to use drugs to escape problems. People who are under a great amount of **stress** are more likely to use drugs; adolescence is a time of great stress and drugs are often readily available to young people. Young people who have family problems are more likely to use drugs, and those with low self-esteem run the risk of continuing to use drugs after just trying them to deal with peer pressure or bad feelings.

The best prevention is simply not to use drugs except as directed for medical reasons and not to drink alcohol until you are of legal age and then only moderately. Children of alcoholics should consider not drinking at all, even when reaching legal age, because their risk of alcoholism is much greater than that of children of non-alcoholics.

Remember, no matter how rough things may get, there are always alternatives to drug abuse, whether it is changing an uncomfortable situation, participating in a healthy activity you enjoy, or seeking counseling for problems you feel you cannot handle alone. Although it may seem that drug abuse is very prevalent in the United States, it does not mean that it is normal.

What Is Normal, Anyway?

Key Note Term

normal – according to a rule or standard pattern; regular, usual

While you may wonder what the term *normal* has to do with drugs, deciding what kind of behavior is **normal** in your life has a lot to do with whether or not you abuse drugs. Many young people are very concerned with being normal, which can mean different things in different situations to different people. Behavior that is normal for one person may not be normal for another. What is normal in one group may be considered strange in another.

When you worry about how your clothes and hair look, if you are saying the right things, or if people will laugh at you for certain things, you are concerned with whether other people think you are normal. In fact, worrying about being normal is very normal. Young people, in particular, worry because they are experiencing so many changes in their lives. This acute awareness of "fitting in" usually decreases as you become an adult and gain a better sense of who you are. Your teenage years are a time for learning what is normal for you. It is not an easy process, so give some thought to the type of behavior you believe is normal.

Do not make the mistake of labeling your emotions as good or bad. You may not enjoy feeling angry, sad, or bored, but these are emotions that everyone has. They teach you about yourself. When you abuse drugs to escape these feelings, you are cheating yourself. Uncomfortable feelings are often messages that you need to change something in your life; look at them as feedback on how you think, act, and view your environment. They are for you to analyze and work with. They are normal.

What you consider normal is generally considered normal by your group of friends. You became friends because you have things in common. But what do you do if your friends want you to try drugs? Is it normal behavior to go along with the group? If what is standard for the group is not for you, then it is better for you not to be what the group considers normal.

If you could run faster than all the others in your group, you would not want to slow down just to be normal. The same goes for drugs. If you know that drugs hurt you, why use them to be considered normal? Why slow down with the crowd when you know you can win the race?

Risk Factors and Drug Abuse

Why do some people abuse drugs? Some people turn to drugs as a way of coping with life's problems and stresses. Other people attempt to improve their mental or physical abilities with drugs. Still others use drugs to try to feel good or get high. Unfortunately, a drug's desired effects are often followed by its unpleasant, harmful side effects.

Risk Factors

Some teenagers who have difficulty coping turn to drugs. Three major types of factors contribute to the risk of drug abuse among teenagers: family factors, social factors, and personal factors.

Family Factors

One of the risk factors for teenage drug abuse is poor family relationships. If teenagers have good relationships with their families (see Figure 3.2.1), they can learn to deal with life's problems and stresses. In a close, supportive relationship, the teen will be able to confide in parents or siblings and find the guidance needed to cope.

Figure 3-2.1: Family attitudes and behaviors influence how teens solve problems or relieve stress.
Courtesy of Choice Photos/ The Image Bank.

However, if family relationships are not close and supportive, the teenager may not get needed guidance. The teen may feel alienated from the family. This alienation may cause the teen to feel closer to peers and therefore more vulnerable to the influence of peers who abuse drugs.

Social Factors

Peer pressure is one of the factors that contributes to drug abuse in teenagers. Most teens who have tried drugs were introduced to them by their friends or peers. They may have initially tried drugs because they were curious. Some continue to abuse drugs because they want to be part of the crowd or be accepted by friends who abuse drugs.

Imagine this situation with Mike. Mike is a 15-year-old high school student who has smoked marijuana almost every day for two years. Mike was introduced to marijuana by some of his friends and continues to use it in order to be accepted by them. Mike says that he can stop using marijuana at any time, although he has yet tried. Mike may not realize that regular use of marijuana often results in a strong emotional need to continue smoking it. One way to avoid drugs is to associate with friends who do not use drugs, as depicted in Figure 3.2.2.

Personal Factors

Stress, low self-esteem, and lack of confidence are personal factors that can place a teen at risk for drug abuse. From time to time, most teenagers experience stress. Stress may occur as a result of a death of a friend or family member, a change in an important relationship, an illness, or an academic or social problem. Some of the symptoms of stress are nervousness, inability to concentrate or sleep, irritability, and depression.

Sometimes teenagers turn to drugs to decrease or avoid the negative feelings and symptoms associated with stress. However, abusing drugs will not decrease the underlying causes of stress. Drug abuse ultimately makes life more stressful. Stress

Figure 3.2.2: One way of avoiding drug use is choosing friends who choose healthy activities instead of drugs.
Courtesy of First Flight.

Chapter 3   Drug Awareness

and negative feelings are a normal part of life. With the proper guidance and advice from positive adult or peer role models, teens can learn techniques for managing stress and negative feelings.

For example, imagine the story of Talia. Talia broke up with Chad after they had dated for two years. Chad kept to himself and pretended the breakup with Talia did not bother him. Chad never really dealt with the sadness over the loss of his girlfriend. Eventually, Chad began to feel depressed; he couldn't sleep very well. Several of his classmates encouraged Chad to get high so that he would get out of his slump.

Perhaps if Chad had been able to talk about his sadness and deal with the breakup of his relationship with Talia, he would not have felt a need to deal with his negative feelings by getting high. Strong social ties and supports can act as powerful buffers, cushioning the negative effects of stress.

Another risk factor for drug abuse is the desire by some teenagers to change their body image or to excel at school athletics. These teens often think that their popularity will increase if they are outstanding athletes. Some athletes abuse anabolic steroids, synthetic drugs that build up protein tissue in the body. Abusers use steroids to boost muscle size and make their bodies stronger.

Other athletes believe that the use of psychoactive drugs such as amphetamines, or speed, will help them concentrate on the game. They may hope that amphetamines will give them extra energy. Still other athletes think that using narcotics, or pain pills, will enable them to continue performing even after they have been injured.

Peggy is a 16-year-old high school athlete who sprained her ankle before the volleyball team tryouts. She wanted to try out, but her ankle hurt a lot. A friend offered Peggy some pain pills and told her that professional athletes take painkillers all the time.

Peggy's friend is wrong. Although most professional and amateur athletes consult their physicians or trainers about aching muscles, sprains, or other complaints, only a few athletes use drugs unwisely. Athletes who use painkillers during competition are likely to sustain more serious injuries that can end their careers. Those who abuse drugs to increase their abilities may face lifelong or life-threatening disorders. For these reasons, organizers of athletic events forbid athletes to use drugs before or during competition.

Legal Risks of Illegal Drug Use

Before deciding to drink alcohol or abuse drugs, remember that abuse of legal drugs, taking illegal drugs, underage drinking, and driving while intoxicated are all against the law. By endangering their lives and the lives of others, users become a societal problem, often requiring legal punishment. Drug laws vary from state to state, but the general trend throughout the United States is toward stiffer penalties for those convicted of drug possession, drug selling, and alcohol-related car accidents. People convicted of these crimes must pay higher fines and must often spend time in jail. If you think trying drugs might be a fun way to spend some time, think about how much fun you would have spending time in a prison.

Turning the Pressure Off

Courtesy of US Army JROTC.

As a teenager, you have many new pressures in your life, as well as many new challenges and experiences. Along with these new opportunities come added responsibilities. While adjusting to these changes that are a part of becoming an adult, you are constantly making decisions. Sometimes you make good decisions and other times you may make mistakes. Making mistakes is normal in a good way because they are part of the learning process. Of course, nobody likes to make mistakes, so try to analyze each situation beforehand to minimize them.

When it comes to drugs, however, it is extremely important to make the right decision before you make a mistake; making just one wrong choice may be too late. Having to juggle pressures from your family, school, activities, job, and friends may overwhelm you at times. The many new situations and emotions you experience can sometimes seem unbearable with no end in sight. Unfortunately, drugs and people who use them and are willing to share them are readily available with what seems like a quick solution to all your problems.

Pressures from society, your family, friends, and yourself may sometimes make it difficult for you to say no to drugs. Our culture often encourages quick solutions to problems; many people would like to believe that taking a pill could cure all types of problems, but there is no magic pill to make it all better. Pills and other drugs only produce chemical reactions in your mind and body, which in turn create artificial feelings and unhealthy side effects.

Advertising, movies, and television shows often glamorize drug and alcohol abuse. It may appear that all the beautiful, fun people are drinking at a bar or taking a refreshing break with the crisp, clean smoke of a cigarette. These types of false messages reinforce the idea of drug abuse as a normal and desirable part of life. You may see your parents drink at parties; you may know students who use drugs; and you may be curious about drugs' effects or tempted to use them to relieve uncomfortable emotions. Though all these situations may make drug abuse attractive to you, the reality of drugs' effects is far from glamorous. The pleasure drugs give is short lived and unreal. They never solve problems; only you can do that, and you cannot function if drugs are a problem in your life.

What you need is a plan of action to cope with all the pressures to abuse drugs. Once you decide that you do not want drugs to be a part of your life, you must develop strategies to resist these pressures as well as healthy alternatives to drugs.

Handling Internal Pressures

The following are tips for being able to handle internal pressures. By being able to cope with what's "inside," you have a better chance of staying drug-free.

Accept and Analyze Your Emotions

If you are feeling something unpleasant, take time to consider the cause of your emotions instead of trying to avoid feeling bad. If you do not address the cause, the uncomfortable feelings will return to bother you. Also, remember that certain amounts of anger, sadness, boredom, and frustration are normal human responses to life that must be accepted.

Seek Out Help When You Feel Overwhelmed

Members of your family, teachers, counselors, and friends can help you. There are also many places that offer help for specific problems, like divorced parents, shyness, alcoholism, or lack of reading skills. You can ask a counselor or instructor at school about them or look for yourself in the phone book. If you are willing to make the effort, there are people willing to help you. Seek them out.

Find Alternatives to Drug Use

If your routine is a big yawn, take a look around and see if there is an activity that looks interesting to you. Photography, auto mechanics, painting, chess, drama, singing, playing an instrument, and part-time employment are among the many activities you could do that would add new challenges to an unexciting routine.

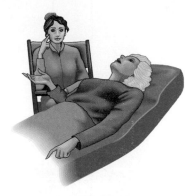

Of even greater importance, these activities pay you back with a real sense of accomplishment and heightened self-esteem as you get better and better at them. Drugs cannot give you these benefits; they can only temporarily produce a false feeling of well-being. In the long run, drugs always take far more than they give and leave the user with nothing but problems.

Release Excess Energy and Learn How to Relax

If you cannot sit still in your seat during class, maybe you are not exercising your body enough. Physical activities such as running, walking, biking, tennis, basketball, weight training, martial arts, skiing, and dance, among others, keep your body in shape while relaxing and focusing your mind during mental activities.

If you have problems relaxing, try the relaxation methods in the chapter on stress, such as meditation, deep breathing, and visualization techniques.

Practice Patience

If there is a situation that makes you feel bad, you cannot think of a way to change it, and nothing you do seems to work, what can you do? *Wait!* You may not like that answer because waiting is difficult, especially for young people. But there will be times in life when the situation is out of your control. This fact is understandably hard for young people to accept. However, change is certain and inevitable. If you wait and stay alert, new solutions and opportunities will become available to you in time. To cope with the stress of a difficult situation until things do change, follow the tips in the chapter on stress. People on drugs never learn this lesson of waiting and miss opportunities to change their lives for the better.

Courtesy of US Army JROTC.

Resisting External Pressures

There are also external pressures that you need to deal with. The following sections give you some hints and tips for refusing drugs when in social situations.

Learn How to Refuse Drugs Effectively

Standing up to peers when they want you to do something that you do not wish to do can be very difficult. When you go against the crowd, you risk rejection, which is scary. However, every time you make a decision to do what is best for you and those you care about, you become a stronger person. You also gain the respect of those people who are your true friends. Your strength and your decisions may even give others the courage to do what is best for them as well. In today's school environment, saying no may not be easy, but it is definitely worth the effort.

Prepare Yourself for Situations Where You May Be Offered Drugs

Visualize different circumstances and different behaviors you can use to refuse offers of drugs. Have answers ready, such as the following:

- **No, thanks, I'd rather do something else**
- **No, I already feel fine**
- **No, thanks, I already have enough problems**
- **No, I'm running in the meet tomorrow (interviewing for a job, taking an important test, acting in a play, etc.)**
- **No, thanks, I'll pass**
- **No, I don't like the way it smells, tastes, and makes me feel**
- **No, I'm not feeling too well, and I don't want to get worse**

Courtesy of US Army JROTC.

If you do not feel comfortable saying no in a situation, find a way to remove yourself from the scene. Suddenly remembering an appointment or some other excuse can get you away from the situation and give you time to think of another way of handling it next time. The important thing is not to do the drugs.

Analyze Media and Advertising

Is the image of drugs projected by advertising accurate? Who gains by making products appear glamorous and sophisticated? People who sell products want you to buy them and will use psychological techniques in advertising to create a demand for their goods. Companies that sell beer, cigarettes, and non-drug-related products, such as cars, have one main goal—they want your money.

Your goal is to do what is best for you. Some products that advertising tries to sell you are opposed to that goal. Your defense against advertisements for products that are useless or harmful is the power to read between the lines of the psychological game. Think about the message an ad is giving and decide for yourself whether it is accurate.

Developing Refusal Skills

In Figure 3.2.3, two of the teenagers are trying to coax their friend into drinking alcohol with them. The friend, however, does not believe in using drugs of any kind. Even so, she worries about what her friends will think if she refuses. Perhaps you have felt this way about saying no to your friends. Maybe you worried that if you refused alcohol, your friends would be disappointed or think you were uncool. You might even have decided to go along with your friends just to avoid the discomfort of saying no.

Refusing your friends is never easy. Nevertheless, being true to yourself and honest with friends are two values that help you develop a sense of your own identity. To

Figure 3.2.3: You can learn to refuse to do something that you're not comfortable with.
Courtesy of Larry Lawfer.

refuse an offer convincingly, you must do more than say no. The following guidelines can help you learn to say no in a way that tells others you mean it.

The answer you give is up to you. Deciding now and practicing what you want to say when the time comes will make your response easier. Avoiding situations where alcohol is served will make it easier still.

Give a Reason for Your Refusal

Don't say no without presenting your personal reason(s) for not going along with the suggestion. Be honest; don't supply phony reasons. Honest answers are more easily accepted by other people. Some answers might be as follows:

- No thanks . . . I don't want to start a bad habit
- I don't need it to have a good time
- I want to keep a clear head
- My parents would be upset if they knew
- I could get suspended from the team
- I don't use alcohol or other drugs

Show Your Concern for Others

Express your concern for those trying to persuade you. You might say things like the following:

- I couldn't stand it if you hurt yourself doing that
- Your parents would ground you for months if they ever found out
- Some people have died from drinking alcohol or taking other drugs
- I'm worried about the amount you drink
- You're only hurting yourself by drinking alcohol

Lesson 2   Critical Decisions about Substances (Interactive Nights Out)

Provide Alternatives

Try to persuade your friends to do something safer or more comfortable. Here are some suggestions:

- **Let's leave this party and go back to my house**
- **This is boring, let's watch a movie at my place (see Figure 3.2.4)**
- **Doesn't anybody feel like going to the gym instead of doing this?**

Use Body Language to Reinforce What You Say

Your body language can either strengthen or weaken your message. To make it clear that you mean no when you say it, you should look your friends in the eyes when presenting your feelings. Try to avoid staring at the ground or glancing away. Also avoid mannerisms that indicate anxiety and nervousness. Do not give power to your persuader by looking away.

Take a Definite Action

If your friends persist in trying to persuade you after you have made your feelings clear to them, it is wise not to continue repeating the point. Instead, try to take a definite action that removes you from the situation and makes it clear that you cannot be persuaded to change your mind.

Here are some examples of specific actions that you can take to remove yourself from potentially harmful situations:

Figure 3.2.4: A movie and popcorn at home is an alternative to drinking.
Courtesy of Larry Lawfer.

- Call for help rather than ride with a drunk driver
- Get up and leave a party
- Widen your circle of friends
- Call other friends and do something else

Apply the Skill

1. Imagine that you are studying for a test with one of your friends when he or she asks you to sit close by during the test and share your answers. Describe how this request would make you feel and some possible ways in which you might respond to the request. If you were to refuse, what honest reason could you give and how would you express it? What do you think would be some of the possible consequences of your saying no? What would be some of the possible consequences of saying yes?

2. Describe two situations from your past in which you said no to others who were trying to convince you to do something you did not want to do. Explain how you felt in each situation. List the things that allowed you to refuse in each of these cases. In which situation was it more difficult to say no? Why? Did you use any of the steps presented in this skill when you refused? If so, describe the steps and how effective they were.

Ways to Say No

Today's young adults experience a great deal of peer pressure to experiment with or use alcohol and tobacco. One way to deal with this peer pressure is to be prepared to offer quick responses when such situations occur. The following are some quick-response ideas that you can use to plan ahead:

- I'm not into body pollution
- I'm kind of depressed, so I don't think I should try it today
- Not today, or, not now
- Nope, I don't want the hassle
- I can't; my mom can smell it on me when I get home
- No, thank you
- When I need it, I'll let you know
- I get grounded if I look sideways at my kid sister; I'd hate to think what would happen if my dad caught me smoking.
- No thanks; I'll wait until it's legal
- No thanks, my grades are bad enough
- I'm into vitamins
- Not for me, thanks, I'm not into chemicals
- No thanks, I'm allergic
- No, I need all the brains I've got
- I don't want to die young

- I'm into health

- I have a big test tomorrow, and I'd like to remember what I study tonight

- Some other time

- If the coach finds out, I'll have to run laps

- No thanks, I just read a new study on its harmful effects

Resisting Peer Pressure

In this activity you will role-play and practice refusal skills.

Materials

- Bag of jelly beans

- Set of five role-playing cards per group

Procedure

1. Work in a group with four other students.

2. Your teacher will distribute a different role-playing card to each group member.

3. Do not discuss your role with other group members.

4. Imagine that you are at a party with friends. Spend five minutes thinking about your assigned role and how you will act during the imagined party.

5. As a group, go to the classroom area designated by your teacher. Each member acts out his or her role.

Discussion

1. Describe your role and explain how you felt playing that role during the imagined party.

2. How do you think player four felt about being pressured to eat the jelly beans when he or she refused?

3. How do you think player three felt when he or she first resisted taking the jelly beans? How do you think player three felt about giving in?

4. How do you think player three felt when player two accepted the jelly beans immediately and then pressured player three to take them?

5. How do you think player one felt about pressuring all the other players?

6. What refusal skills will you use to resist pressure from friends and make your own decisions?

Substance Abuse Intervention

It is important for you to learn about the effects of drug use, the reasons why drugs are harmful, and ways to resist pressures to try drugs. However, imbedded within the principles of good citizenship, JROTC cadets take this one step further. They also learn about the dangers posed by drugs in order to help other students avoid them, thus persuading those using drugs to seek help. Involvement in intervention programs can only help to dissolve the drug problem.

Tell-Tale Signs of Drug Use

As a cadet and leader in the JROTC program, you serve as a role model for other cadets. You send a positive message to your followers about how to successfully function without drugs. You can also help by recognizing signs of problems in other cadets. The following list of symptoms and signs of drug use will help you to determine if someone you know may be using drugs or has a serious drug problem:

- **Changes in attendance, discipline, interests, neatness, and attention**
- **Loss of interest in sports, extracurricular activities, or hobbies**
- **Failing memory**
- **Unusual degree of activity, like excitement, boundless energy, excessive laughter, and excessive talkativeness**
- **Unusual inactivity, such as moodiness, depression, drowsiness**
- **Poor physical coordination**
- **Slurred speech**
- **Deterioration of physical appearance and lack of concern for health habits and dress**
- **Loss of appetite and rapid weight loss**
- **Sudden increase in appetite**
- **Unpredictable outbreaks of temper and arguing**
- **Nervousness and irritability**
- **Reduced motivation, self-discipline, and self-esteem**
- **Wearing sunglasses at inappropriate times to conceal eyes that may be red or have constricted or dilated pupils**
- **Constantly wearing long-sleeved shirts or blouses (to hide needle marks)**
- **Borrowing frequently from others or stealing money (required to purchase drugs)**
- **Chronic dishonesty, such as lying, stealing, or cheating**
- **Appearing frequently in out-of-the way areas, such as closets, storage areas, or restrooms**
- **Guilty behavior and fear of discovery**
- **Association with known or possible drug sellers or abusers**
- **Not giving straight answers when questioned about activities**
- **Appearance of intoxication but no smell of alcohol, indicating possible use of barbiturates or marijuana**
- **Pale and perspiring skin**
- **Runny nose and/or nosebleeds**
- **Use of drug-related vocabulary**
- **Possession of pipes, rolling papers, small decongestant bottles, and lighters**
- **Possession of drugs or evidence of drugs, such as peculiar plants, butts, seeds, or leaves in ashtrays or clothing pockets**
- **Odor of drugs and the smell of incense or other cover-up scents**

All of these signs of drug use may also be caused by other medical, psychological, or personal problems, so if a friend or family member is showing one of the signs, it is in no way an absolute indication that he or she is abusing drugs. Before jumping to conclusions, consider how frequently these signs occur and whether or not the person showing the signs has a logical explanation for them other than drug abuse. Expressing concern and asking questions is the best way to get a person to confide in you.

Remember these are just guidelines of which you should be aware. Many of these behaviors or signs can have causes other than drug use. However, if you notice some of these signs in someone, you can be fairly certain that there is some kind of problem; whether related to drugs or not, the person needs help. You can be a part of that help.

Who You Gonna Call? Where Do You Find Help?

If a friend you know is having problems and is considering abusing drugs to relieve the pain, you can be of help just by being there to listen and by affirming your personal decision that drugs are not a good way to deal with problems. In some cases, this may be all that is needed; a caring and strong presence can go a long way as can an informed discussion about what a particular drug can do to the mind and body. There may be other situations, though, that require specific and professional help that you are not prepared to give.

When you realize that someone you know may have a drug problem, there are some choices of action you need to make. Here are some of your choices:

- *Convince the person to seek help.* **Be prepared with the names of people and agencies that can provide help.**

- *Tell a responsible adult, such as an instructor or counselor, that you are concerned about the person.* **You may be reluctant to do this because it feels like telling on someone. However, especially in cases where you know the person is using life-threatening drugs or participating in dangerous situations, you are really doing this person a favor. Your action may save a life.**

- *If you know of someone selling drugs, report the person to an appropriate authority.* **People who sell drugs have passed the point of having a personal problem. Drug dealers are hurting others.**

Find out what types of help are available at your school and in your community for people with problems. Know the proper procedure for reporting drug-related incidents, and above all, show the cadets whom you lead that you care about their well-being and are willing to help. Your example and your support can have a positive impact on those around you.

CHOOSE TO BE ...
DRUG FREE!

Courtesy of US Army JROTC.

Choosing to Be Drug Free

You may already know about the pressures to experiment with psychoactive drugs. How can you help yourself and others stay away from drug abuse? What can you do to help someone who is abusing drugs?

Treating Drug Abuse and Addiction

Before drug abusers can be helped, they need to recognize their problem. Unfortunately, this may be difficult for them. Many abusers deny their behavior; others deny the problems that led them to drug abuse. Figure 3.2.5 lists some of the signs of drug abuse. This list may help you recognize a drug abuse problem in a friend or classmate and allow you to convince the abuser that he or she has a drug problem.

After drug abusers recognize their problem, many options are available to them. Options for drug abusers include programs in which people withdraw from the drug under medical care and treatment centers in which abusers learn to live drug-free lives. Programs to help abusers and their families are available. Understanding the underlying cause for the drug abuse and involving family members can restore and reinforce the family's stability.

Many organizations counsel people about drug problems. Community hospitals have clinics or programs that provide low-cost or volunteer counseling for teenagers and adults. Local schools and governments also schedule parent meetings, peer group counseling, and drug-free programs. One of the most important aspects of dealing with drug problems, as shown in Figure 3.2.6, is family support.

Exploding Careers: Drug Counselor

A person trying to overcome a drug abuse problem may need assistance from someone outside of his or her circle of family and friends. A drug counselor can help. Drug counselors are trained to help abusers overcome the difficult problem of drug abuse. These counselors also often work with the abuser's family.

Drug counselors work in one-on-one situations, in group situations, in special drug abuse clinics, in hospitals, or for companies with employee drug programs. They also work for telephone hotlines or run private counseling services.

No certification or license is needed for this career. However, a drug counselor must have compassion and an ability to gain a client's trust. A high school diploma and training are sufficient to become a drug counselor. However, college and master's degree programs are available.

Signs of Drug Abuse

- Major changes in behavior
- Lying, cheating
- Sudden changes in mood
- Forgetfulness, withdrawn attitude
- New friends who are suspected of abusing drugs
- Loss of memory
- Poor school performance
- Poor coordination
- Changes in appearance
- Slurred speech
- Irresponsible decision-making
- Attention-getting behavior
- Aggressiveness
- Denial of any problems

Figure 3.2.5: Learning to recognize the signs of drug abuse can make a difference.
Reprinted from *Health Skills for Wellness,* Third Edition, by V.E. (Buzz) Pruitt, Kathy Teer Crumpler, and Deborah Prothrow-Stith, (2001), Prentice Hall, Inc.

Figure 3.2.6: Family support is an important part of recovery from drug abuse.
Courtesy of Mieke Maas/
The Image Bank.

Key Note Term

detoxification program – a type of program where drug users or addicts can get help with drawing from substances

Detoxification Programs

One type of drug abuse treatment is a **detoxification program**. A detoxification program involves gradual but complete withdrawal from the abused drug. People who enter detoxification programs usually receive medical treatment and supervision in a hospital. Drug abusers may stop taking the drug all at once, or physicians may reduce the drug dosage slowly to avoid painful withdrawal symptoms. Detoxification programs always include counseling to help program participants deal with their abuse and to cope constructively with the problems that led to it and were caused by it.

Therapeutic Communities

Key Note Term

therapeutic community – usually a residential treatment center for drug abusers and addicts

Another type of drug abuse treatment is **therapeutic communities**. A **therapeutic community** is a residential treatment center where drug abusers live and learn to adjust to drug-free lives. Members of therapeutic communities lend support and friendship to each other. Often drug abusers are required to undergo detoxification before becoming a part of the community. Therapeutic communities provide medical advice and counseling to help abusers develop a sense of personal and social worth. The staff of therapeutic communities usually consists of health-care professionals and former drug abusers.

Methadone Maintenance Programs

Key Note Term

methadone – controlled substance that is used in heroin withdrawal; produces some effects similar to heroin, but does not produce a "high"

A third type of drug abuse treatment, called methadone maintenance, helps heroin abusers. **Methadone** is a drug that produces many effects similar to heroin but does not produce the same high that causes heroin addicts to crave the drug. This type of treatment involves substituting methadone for heroin. Small, regular doses of methadone prevent withdrawal symptoms. Methadone treatment is intended to eliminate the desire for heroin.

Methadone can cause dependency. Therefore, a trained professional must carefully monitor treatment and slowly lower the dosage. Long-term methadone use causes side effects such as liver damage. Methadone is not a cure for heroin addiction, but it can be a first step.

Making a Public Service Television Commercial

In this activity, you will plan a 30-second commercial to help teens cope with the peer pressure to try drugs.

Materials

Six pieces of poster board

Colored markers

Procedure

1. Work in groups of four to brainstorm ideas, characters, and a theme for a 30-second television commercial. The commercial should give advice to teenagers about coping with peer pressure to take drugs. The theme could be something like "Teen Decisions" or "Wise Choice."

2. Two group members should prepare the visual part of the commercial by illustrating six storyboards. The storyboards will show what will appear on the television screen every five seconds.

3. The other two group members should prepare the audio part of the commercial by writing the script. The script, when read aloud, should be about 30 seconds long.

4. When the visual and audio parts of your commercial are complete, work together to develop music or sound effects to accompany the commercial.

5. Combine the visual, audio, and sound effects and present your commercial to your classmates. Ask for their reactions.

Discussion

1. What was the theme of your commercial? Why did you choose this theme?

2. Who were the characters in your script? What was their message?

3. Did your classmates think your public service commercial was effective for teenagers? Why or why not?

Avoiding Drug Use

You make decisions every day. You decide what to eat, which clothes to wear, and how much to exercise. You may also make decisions about drugs.

Refusing Drugs

Deciding not to take drugs can be a difficult decision when you are faced with pressure to take them. There are ways to avoid drugs in your life. One way is to refuse when someone offers you drugs. To be effective, you can present your personal reasons for not wanting to take drugs. Be honest; do not supply phony reasons. For example, you could say, "No thanks . . . I want to keep a clear head," or "I don't want to become addicted," or simply "I don't use drugs." To make it clear that you mean what you say, look the person in the eyes when presenting your thoughts about drug abuse.

If the person who is offering you drugs continues to try to persuade you, make a definite action that removes you from the situation. This action should make it clear that you cannot be persuaded to change your mind. For example, you can simply get up and leave or enjoy activities with another group of nonabusing friends.

Managing Stress

Another way to avoid drugs is to manage the stress in your life. There are many methods that you can use to help manage stress, including the following:

- **Give in to your emotions. If you are angry, disgusted, or confused, admit your feelings. Suppressing your emotions adds to stress.**

- **Take a brief break form the stressful situation and do something small and constructive like washing your car, emptying a wastebasket, or getting a haircut.**

- **Have a quiet place and have a brief idle period there every day.**

- **Concentrate intensely on something that interest you, reading, surfing the Internet, a sport or a hobby. Contrary to common sense, concentration is at the heart of stress reduction.**

- **Stop to smell the flowers, make friends with a young child or elderly person, or play with a kitten or puppy.**

- **Work with your hands, doing a pleasant task.**

- **Hug somebody you like, and who you think will hug you back.**

- **Find something to laugh at—a cartoon, a movie, a television show, a Web site for jokes, even yourself.**

- **Minimize drinking caffeinated beverages and drink fruit juice or water instead.**

- **Run, swim, ride a bike, or engage in some other form of vigorous exercise.**

- **Learn to manage your time effectively.**

Note

For more information about controlling stress, refer to Unit 4, Chapter 1, Lesson 8, "Understanding and Controlling Stress."

Getting Help

If you decide that the stresses and problems in your life are too much to manage, find someone to help you. Many people are willing to help, but first you must let them know that you need help. Parents, teachers, friends, brothers, sisters, school counselors, school nurses, and members of the clergy are usually available for guidance and support. A second option is to call one of the national hotlines that tell you where to call for drug information and treatment referral in your area. For these numbers, call 1-800-662-HELP.

Alternatives to Drug Use

Turning to drugs to try to feel good or deal with problems is a risky choice. You can get involved in many healthy and constructive activities to lift your mood, feel better about yourself, and deal with the pressures in your life.

Engaging in physical activity is one way to help yourself feel better. Physical activity not only helps improve your mood, but it also relieves the negative effects of stress. Getting enough exercise and getting involved in sports can help you feel energetic, positive, and self-confident.

Helping other people can give you a good feeling about yourself, too. Many social service agencies need volunteers. You could volunteer to read to someone with a visual handicap, make a social visit to an elderly person in a nursing facility, teach a hobby or sport to a youngster, raise funds for a charity, or pick up trash as shown in Figure 3.2.7.

Participating in youth groups can help you feel a sense of belonging and connection to others. The members of these groups support one another as each person strives to find his or her place in the world. Youth groups also volunteer to help others in need.

Working at a part-time job not only provides you with spending money, but can also give you a sense of accomplishment and increased self-esteem. Not only can you learn a new skill, but you can meet new friends. Your family, friends, or school counselor may be able to help you find such a job.

Remember that abusing drugs cannot relieve the pressures and problems in life. It can only postpone decision making and create more problems. Imagine how you would feel if you had to tell lies, hide your physical condition, worry about police, and deal with drug side effects. People who become dependent on drugs spend almost all of their time thinking about drugs, taking drugs, getting the money for drugs, and looking for drugs. Drugs end up controlling their lives. By deciding not to use drugs, you are acting to take control of your life.

Intervening to Help a Friend

Jen had been concerned about her friend Christina's use of marijuana for some time, but last night was the final straw. Jen and Christina were to meet at a friend's party, but Christina showed up two hours late and was high. Christina was feeling drowsy and acting uncoordinated. So Jen drove her home. The next day, Christina told Jen that she was perfectly fine at the party and could have driven herself home. Christina also declared that she could quit smoking marijuana easily at any time.

Figure 3.2.7: Helping others can boost your self-esteem and build friendships with other people.
Courtesy of Bob Daemmrich.

Other friends have started to give up on Christina. But Jen still cares about Christina and fears her friend may be in trouble with drugs. She wants to help, but how can she when Christina is so out of touch with reality?

As seen in Figure 3.2.8, intervening to help a friend who abuses drugs is difficult. You fear you may lose the friend. But your friend's behavior may cause that loss through a fatal accident. Use these guidelines to help save your friendship and your friend.

1. **Stop enabling behaviors.** Enabling behaviors are actions you take that allow, or enable, someone to continue to behave dangerously without facing the consequences. By making it more difficult for people to behave dangerously, you may make them rethink what they are doing. You will help your friend most if you stop

   - **Covering up,** such as saying your friend is at your house when he or she is not.

   - **Giving second chances,** such as repeatedly lending money when your friend has not paid back previous loans.

   - **Making excuses,** such as, "That's OK, everyone's late sometimes."

2. **Talk to your friend.** Talking to your friend about his or her behavior will not be easy, but it is worthwhile if you

   - **Express your concern and** say you are intervening because you are worried about his or her well-being.

   - **Help your friend face the facts about his or her destructive behavior.** Present specific evidence of the problem. Describe behaviors accurately and simply, using dates and times when possible.

   - **Describe your feelings.** Tell how your friend's behavior affects you. For example, Jen might say to Christina, "I was worried something had happened to you when you were late. And when you showed up so high that you were drowsy and uncoordinated, it hurt me."

   - **Don't criticize or argue.** Resist the temptation to be judgmental. You are objecting to the behavior, not the person. Do not get drawn into "no-I-didn't, yes-you-did" arguments. Expect your friend to deny drug dependency or other destructive patterns of behavior. If your friend argues, say "I just want you to know how I feel" and leave.

Figure 3.2.8: A friend may need your help to overcome a drug problem.
Courtesy of Larry Lawfer.

- **Offer specific help and support.** Prepare a list of resources that your friend can go to for help. Include names, addresses, and phone numbers. Offer to go with your friend to the school counselor, a social service center, a member of the clergy, a health professional, or other resource.

3. **Ask another friend to help.** The more people speaking the truth and offering support the better. Be sure to discuss your concerns and guidelines for intervening with the second friend. Work together.

4. **Follow through.** Do what you said you would do, and stop doing what you said you would not do anymore. Be sure your friend knows that your determination to stop enabling is firm and that your offers of support can be counted on.

5. **Seek adult or professional help.** If you think your friend is in a life-threatening or similarly serious situation, find a more experienced person to intervene directly.

Remember, you can only be responsible for yourself. You cannot make another person get help or change behavior. If you have done the above, you have done all you can, and you are a good friend.

Substance Abuse Prevention

Involvement in prevention programs can only help to solve the drug problem. The following is a brief history of substance abuse prevention. Later in this lesson, telephone numbers for self-help groups and prevention organizations are provided.

Prevention History

Historically, various organizations, communities, and governmental agencies founded drug abuse prevention programs based on the theory that people used drugs because they were ignorant of the consequences of such use. According to this theory, failure to recognize any negative effects of drugs resulted in neutral or even positive attitudes toward experimenting with drugs.

During the 1960s, drug education programs focused on providing information. Administrators of those programs often called them *fear arousal messages*, because they dealt with health and social consequences of drug use. However, these programs were somewhat ineffective because youths said that the messages themselves lacked credibility.

By the 1970s, social scientists began to address more personal factors that influenced drug abuse behavior among children and adolescents. Studies showed that a close association exists between drug abuse and a person's attitudes, beliefs, and values, as well as other personality factors such as feelings of self-esteem, self-reliance, and alienation.

One prevention approach that grew from this research was affective education. Rather than focusing on drug abuse behaviors, affective education focused on the factors associated with use. This approach attempted to eliminate the reasons for using drugs by creating a school climate that was supportive of students' social and emotional needs. These programs often focused on training the students in effective decision-making skills. Students in these programs worked to clarify their values, analyze behavior consequences, and identify alternative behaviors.

Some of the other leading prevention approaches in the 1970s focused on alternative activities to drug use. These programs involved youths in community projects to reduce alienation, while others provided alternative opportunities for recreation, socialization, and informal education.

Prevention Today

Today, many schools have drug prevention programs. Sometimes these programs directly involve the students. For example, high school students might perform as "peer" teachers for seventh graders. Some studies have shown that prevention programs led by peers are more effective than programs led by adults. The health programs led by peers were more successful at preventing nonsmokers from smoking. Through role-playing, students acted out situations requiring resistance to peer pressure. Students also made social commitments not to smoke or use drugs.

For most youths, substance abuse appears to be the result, in large part, of social influences. Thus, teaching youths to resist these influences is one approach to the prevention of use. However, not all youths use drugs for the same reason or respond to the same prevention approach. Thus, it may not be effective to focus on any single prevention approach, and it is important to explore multiple strategies.

Changing the Social Environment

Successful drug programs change the social environment to reduce the risks of early drug use. These programs help to provide adolescents with the personal attributes and behavioral skills they need to choose nondrug alternatives, hopefully reducing their tendency to use stronger drugs in the future.

The social environment may provide the necessary conditions for drug use through models and social supports, and through access to drugs. However, not all adolescents in high-risk environments choose to experiment or use drugs regularly. Intrapersonal and behavioral factors may be critical in determining the response to the environment through values and skills available to the adolescent to choose nondrug alternatives that meet their needs. These findings imply concentrating the prevention efforts on both of these factors, rather than on a single factor. They also imply that adolescent drug use is functional; thus, prevention efforts should focus on the functions served by drugs as well as on the more immediate predictors of drug use.

Some models suggest that prevention efforts should focus on this functionality and provide alternative behaviors for drug use rather than simply trying to suppress the underlying need or reason for use. These models often reward adolescents for choosing alternatives to drug use and suggest that such rewards should come from both peers and parents.

Drug Abuse

Drug abuse is using natural and/or synthetic chemical substances for non-medical reasons to affect the body and its processes. For example, people sometimes use amphetamines to stay awake when tired. If abused, drugs can also affect the mind and nervous system. For example, people sometimes use marijuana to change moods and to get high.

Used properly to treat a medical problem, drugs can correct imbalances in body chemistry, protect against disease, and relieve tension, fatigue, and pain. However, when people abuse drugs they can cause

- **Health problems.** Every year, hospitals treat thousands of people for drug-related accidents and mental and physical illness. Drug users can harm their health by losing resistance to disease. Plus, intravenous drug users may be exposed to AIDS and other serious diseases. More than 25,000 die every year from these accidents.

- **Addiction.** When you need more and more of a drug to get the same effect, you risk an overdose, which can kill. The continued use of many drugs can lead to a physical and/or psychological dependence.

- **Legal problems.** Stealing is often the only way to support an expensive habit. Law enforcement officials arrest about two million people each year for alcohol and drug related offenses. Possession of illegal drugs is punishable by heavy fines and prison sentences. A police record can follow you through life and eliminate certain career choices.

- **Financial hardships.** From $10 a week for cigarettes to $100 a day for heroin, drug abuse can be an expensive habit.

- **Social difficulties.** Instead of trying to work out their problems with other people, drug abusers often take more drugs as a solution.

- **Violence.** Certain drugs can trigger violence against others.

- **Loss of friends.** Once hooked, drugs come first—ahead of friendships or anything else.

The facts show that drug abuse is on the rise. Emergency rooms treated 10,000 users of crack cocaine in 1994. In 1985 the cocaine death rate was triple that of 1981. Crack is a $30 billion a year business. Drug-related law enforcement agencies spend $6.5 billion a year fighting crack.

Drug abuse has risen to epidemic proportions in most communities. It touches everyone—regardless of age, race, or economic background. Communities should use information on drugs to help its citizens better understand this serious problem affecting our homes, schools, and neighborhoods.

Drug Abuse Prevention

There are many ways in which you can become involved in drug abuse prevention. You might be able to volunteer at drug treatment and rehabilitation centers. Look in the phone book under drug abuse for information and prevention programs. You may be able to find several local sources for preventive information. There are also toll-free numbers that provide information on drug abuse and prevention.

Many major hospitals have chemical dependency hospitals affiliated with them. These hospitals may offer professional treatment for alcoholism and drug dependency. Some may offer services such as seminars on drug recovery, depression, or anxiety and other individualized programs.

Help and/or information is available from many private and public agencies, facilities, and people. Drug treatment centers and clinics specialize in treating people with drug problems. Hospitals treat on an in- or outpatient basis. Mental health centers can treat people with drug problems by dealing with underlying problems. Public health agencies and social service agencies can give practical advice, make referrals, and so on. Halfway houses provide residential treatment for those with drug problems.

If you need help with a cocaine problem, call 1-800-662-HELP or visit the Web site, findtreatment.samhsa.gov. Volunteer to help others with their drug problems and help to promote prevention programs.

The Office for Substance Abuse Prevention (OSAP) promotes and distributes prevention materials throughout the country. OSAP also supports the National Clearinghouse for Alcohol and Drug Information (NCADI) and the Regional Alcohol and Drug Awareness Resource (RADAR) Network. To learn more information on alcohol and other drugs, write or call the NCADI:

National Clearinghouse for Alcohol and Drug Information
Information Services
P.O. Box 2345
Rockville, MD 20847-2345
1-800 729-6686

Alcohol Abuse

With over 157 million drivers and 105 million drinkers in the United States (in 1990), it is no wonder that people who drink and drive have become the major safety problem on our highways. Approximately 50,000 people die each year on U.S. highways, and alcohol is a factor in at least half of those deaths.

Alcohol can cause a feeling of relaxation and often an unreal sense of cheerfulness. Because of its widespread use, many people do not consider alcohol to be a drug or even dangerous. And, it can be very dangerous. The following list represents just a few of the serious side effects of alcohol:

- **Increase loss of body heat, giving a false feeling of warmth while actually decreasing the body's temperature**
- **Affect a person mentally and physically, even with one drink**
- **Contribute to loss of coordination and slurring of speech**
- **Produce changes in personality and mental functions**
- **Loosen inhibitions, causing intensification of feelings (such as anger and sadness)**
- **Impair clear thinking and judgment**

People who mix alcohol with other drugs multiply the effects of the drugs (known as the synergistic effect). Many drugs interact with each other in harmful ways; consequently, mixing alcohol with other depressants may lead to accidental deaths.

Alcohol Abuse Prevention

Alcoholics Anonymous (AA) is a worldwide group of men and women who help each other maintain sobriety and who offer to share their recovery experiences freely with others who may have a drinking problem. The AA program consists basically of Twelve Steps designed for personal recovery from alcoholism. The organization functions through almost 73,000 local groups in 114 countries. Several hundred thousand alcoholics have achieved sobriety in AA, but members recognize that their program is not always effective and that some may require professional counseling or treatment.

Look for Alcoholics Anonymous in any telephone directory. In most urban areas, a central AA office can answer your questions or put you in touch with AA members. If AA is not in your local directory, write the General Service Office:

P.O. Box 459
Grand Central Station
New York, NY 10163
www.alcoholicsanonymous.org.

Al-Anon is a worldwide organization that offers help to families and friends of alcoholics. Members receive support through a mutual exchange of experiences about how an alcoholic has affected their lives. Alateen is a fellowship of young Al-Anon members, usually teenagers, with someone else's drinking problems affecting their lives. Young people come together to share experiences, strengths, and hopes with each other as they discuss their difficulties. They can also encourage one another to learn effective ways to cope with their problems.

To contact the nearest Al-Anon or Alateen Group, call the local Al-Anon Information Service (Intergroup) in metropolitan areas or write to Al-Anon Family Group Headquarters:

1600 Corporate Landing Pkwy
Virginia Beach, VA 23454-5617
1-888-425-2666
www.al-anon.org.

There are many other places that people can get help for problems caused by alcohol. They can talk with family, friends, a school counselor, or a doctor. Look in the yellow pages under alcohol or alcoholism. Use referral services and get information provided by the local affiliate of the American Council on Alcoholism (1-800-527-5344 or www.aca-usa.org). Remember, it is important to seek help and support for people with drinking problems.

DON'T DRINK & DRIVE

Courtesy of US Army JROTC.

At least 22 states have established formal programs for citizen-reporting of drunk drivers. Oregon has a toll-free hotline and a governor who, at one time, displayed a red star on his car for every drunk driver he reported. During 1982 and 1983—the first two years of Oregon's reporting program—tragic fatalities were the lowest in 20 years. Most will agree that everybody has to work together. The government cannot do it alone. In Nebraska, fatalities dropped 26 percent in the first year of its drunk driver-reporting program.

> **Note**
>
> Drinking is the third leading cause of death in the United States, right behind heart disease and cancer.

Call your police department to see if such a program exists in your area. If not, push for one. There are many other organizations working to get drunks off the roads. For specific information on how you can help, send a stamped, self-addressed envelope to Mothers Against Drunk Drivers (MADD):

National Office
511 E. John Carpenter Frwy., Suite 700
Irving, TX 75062–8187
1-800-438-6233
www.madd.org.

"Know When to Say When," which has been in effect since 1983, is a nationwide consumer education campaign developed by Anheuser-Busch that encourages consumers to be responsible when they drink. It aims at normally responsible, law-abiding citizens who only need reminders of their legal and moral obligations to themselves and others. The purpose of the campaign is to help create a climate that strongly discourages situational abuse. The campaign involves a series of television commercials, a movie, billboards, and newspaper advertisements that remind consumers not to overindulge.

"The Buddy System" is an education campaign aimed at college students and other young adults. It includes a short movie, brochures explaining the program, and posters. The program makes a strong point that friends should be responsible for each other and should help one another avoid drunk driving situations.

Other programs developed to avoid drunk driving situations include free or reduced-price taxi rides home to customers who are unable to drive safely, and designated driver programs. A group designates one person to refrain from drinking so that a safe ride home is available to the other members of the group.

Students Against Driving Drunk (SADD) is a student-run program that works to counteract peer pressure to drink and drive. The founder of SADD, Bob Anastas, suggests that teenagers call their parents if they or their driving friends have been drinking. Anastas has found that such an agreement between parents and teenagers works. Since the founding of SADD in 1981, more than three million students in 6500 high schools in all 50 states have become involved in SADD chapters. The efforts of groups like SADD are beginning to have an impact.

In 1980, traffic accidents accounted for killing 12,214 Americans ages 16 to 21; in 1983, 9054. In 1980, 49% of drivers ages 16 to 21 killed in traffic accidents were legally intoxicated; in 1983, 47%. For information about the parent-teenager agreement, or about starting a SADD chapter at your school, send a stamped, self-addressed envelope to SADD

Students Against Driving Drunk
P.O. Box 800
Marlborough, MS 01752
1-877-723-3462
www.sadd.org.

Each year in the United States, drinking and driving results in costs totaling more than a billion dollars for property damage, insurance, and medical expenses. Drinking and driving accounts for over 500,000 people being injured and more than one million people arrested.

General Information

There are better, safer, more rewarding experiences in life than using drugs. They involve doing something that you find exciting, satisfying, meaningful, and challenging. Some alternatives include sports, dancing, playing music, theater, volunteer work, tutoring, writing, reading, playing games, photography, or crafts. You can find out about other alternatives by asking organizations in your community about programs they offer. Check with schools, community colleges, adult education programs, YMCA, YWCA, Boys' or Girls' Clubs, libraries, and so on.

Drug abuse prevention programs have evolved from the need for action and the need to reach the target school-aged population. The result is a heavy reliance on school systems, use of academic time, and involvement of educators in implementation. Everyone has the opportunity to become involved in community efforts to make citizens aware of the drug problem and how to prevent drug abuse.

Concerning the fight against drunk drivers, there are many things that people can do to help. Your knowledge of the following tips can possibly save a life when you are in a position to influence family members, friends, or other adults who are planning and/or attending a social function that includes alcohol.

As responsible hosts, they should

- **Recognize that every social occasion does not have to include alcoholic beverages.**
- **Place limits on the amount available if alcohol is served. Estimate how much alcohol to have on hand based on the number of guests and the length of the party. As a guideline, plan on one drink per guest per hour; then purchase only that amount.**
- **Provide other activities when serving alcoholic beverages. Drinking should not be the main purpose of any activity.**
- **Create a climate that respects individual choice by providing attractive nonalcoholic drinks.**
- **Be conscious of the drinking age and remember that serving alcohol to a minor is illegal.**
- **Serve snacks so that guests do not drink on an empty stomach and to slow down alcohol absorption.**
- **Create a climate that discourages overindulgence but assume responsibility for guests who overindulge. See that they get home safely by providing or arranging transportation or invite them to stay later or overnight.**
- **Keep a list of telephone numbers of emergency health care, police, and taxi services in case you have a problem.**

As responsible guests, they should

- **Regard alcohol as the highly toxic substance it is; understand its effects on the body, brain, and thought processes**
- **Set a limit on the consumption of alcohol that is well within their personal limits, remembering that this will vary from time to time**

- Eat while they drink, such as low salt snacks or a meal
- If they have exceeded their limit, ask for a ride home with someone who has not been drinking

As friends, they should

- Discourage anyone who appears to be under the influence of alcohol from driving
- Call a cab for anyone who appears to be under the influence of alcohol
- Remember a brief uncomfortable confrontation may save the life of a friend and others

As concerned citizens, they should

- Talk about the dangers of drinking and driving to those who are overindulging. Ensure they understand the dangers of drinking and driving, the effects of alcohol on driving performance, and the consequences of being arrested and convicted of driving under the influence.
- Be a positive role model. Their attitudes and behavior regarding drinking and driving will influence others, especially minors.
- Support education and prevention activities in their local schools.
- Practice other safety measures such as using seat belts and child restraints for protection from drunk drivers.
- Join an organization on the local, state, or national level that is working to educate people about the dangers of drinking and driving.
- Support strong laws and enforcement of those laws. Let government know your feelings.

Help Is a Phone Call Away

The following is a list of numbers to call if you need more information on what you can do to help.

Hazeldon Educational Materials: **1-800-328-9000**

Alcohol Hotline: **1-800-252-6465**

Dare America (CA): **1-800-223-3273**

Center for Substance Abuse Treatment National Hotline: **1-800-662-4357**

Conclusion

Now that you have finished this lesson, you should have a better understanding of drugs, their effects, their dangers, and the correct role they should play in a person's life. You have also learned the importance of remaining drug-free and ways to avoid the pressures to abuse drugs. Use your knowledge to make your life and the lives of those around you better. You do have the power to control much of the way your life turns out. Set an example; your actions do make a difference in the world. Become involved as an individual. Talk to your friends and neighbors about drugs. Ask them to join you in your community's attack on drugs. Reach out a helping hand to your community; join the fight against drugs and become a part of the solution. If you feel you need help to be sober and drug-free, try to be brave enough to call the telephone numbers provided in this chapter. If you know someone who needs help, be a true friend and pass these phone numbers along. Your assistance could save a life.

This lesson concludes Chapter 3, "Drug Awareness." Refer back to this lesson whenever you need to say no or you need contact information to get help for yourself or others.

Lesson Review

1. **What are four clues that might warn you that someone you know is abusing drugs?**

2. **What are two types of drug abuse treatment programs? How do these programs work?**

3. **List two alternatives to drug use. Explain how they work.**

4. **Suppose you were at a party where drugs were being used. What would you do?**

Unit 3: Foundations for Success
Correlated to:
McRel Standards for Life Work, Thinking and Reasoning, and Working with Others, Self Regulation

McRel Standards	Unit 3: Foundations for Success
LIFE WORK STANDARDS (LW)	
LW 2. Uses various information sources, including those of a technical nature, to accomplish specific tasks	Becoming an Active Listener, 22–27; Managing Anger (Emotional Intelligence Program), 201–208; Thinking Maps and Graphic Organizers, 422–431; Using Feedback in the Classroom, 432–436
LW 3. Manages money effectively	NEFE Introduction: Setting Financial Goals, 376–277; Financial Planning: Your Road Map, 278–379; College Preparation, 307–332; Budgeting: Don't Go Broke, 380–381; Savings and Investments: Your Money at Work, 382–383; Credit: Buy Now, Pay Later, 384–385
LW 4. Pursues specific jobs	Career Exploration Strategy, 253–271; Career Development Portfolio, 272–295; Military Career Opportunities, 296–306
LW 5. Makes general preparation for entering the work force	Career Exploration Strategy, 253–271; Career Development Portfolio, 272–295; Military Career Opportunities, 296–306; College Preparation, 307–332
LW 6. Makes effective use of basic life skills	Personal Growth Plan, 16–21; Making the Right Choices, 334–339; Time Management, 346–354
LW 7. Displays reliability and a basic work ethic	Making the Right Choices, 334–339
LW 8. Operates effectively within organizations	Making the Right Choices, 334–339; Goals and Goal Setting, 340–345; Time Management, 346–354; Cadet Etiquette Guide, 355–374
THINKING AND REASONING STANDARDS (TR)	
TR 1. Understands and applies the basic principles of presenting an argument	Left Brain/Right Brain, 42–52
TR 2. Understands and applies basic principles of logic and reasoning	Self-Awareness, 3–9; Making the Right Choices, 334–339; Goals and Goal Setting, 340–345; Time Management, 346–354; Using and Developing Lesson Plans, 398–406

Copyright © 2004 McREL
Mid-continent Research for Education and Learning
2550 S. Parker Road, Suite 500
Aurora, CO 80014
Telephone: 303/337-0990
www.mcrel.org/standards-benchmarks

McRel Standards	Unit 3: Foundations for Success
TR 3. Effectively uses mental processes that are based on identifying similarities and differences	Self-Awareness, 3–9; Appreciating Diversity Though Winning Colors, 10–15; Becoming an Active Listener, 22–27; Brain Structure and Function, 29–41; Left Brain/Right Brain, 42–52; Learning Style and Processing Preferences, 53–70; Multiple Intelligences, 71–76, Thinking Maps, 78–83; Orientation to Service Learning, 230–235; Career Exploration Strategy, 253–271; Military Career Opportunities, 296–306; College Preparation, 307–332; Preparing to Teach, 389–397; Delivering Instruction, 407–414
TR 5. Applies basic trouble-shooting and problem-solving techniques	The Communication Process, 114–119; Becoming a Better Listener, 120–128; Communication in Groups, 129–140; Causes of Conflict, 142–152; Conflict Resolution Techniques, 152–162; Making the Right Choices, 334–339; Using Feedback in the Classroom, 432–436
TR 6. Applies decision-making techniques	Plan and Train for Your Exploratory Project, 236–242; Project Reflection and Integration, 243–251; Making the Right Choices, 334–339; Time Management, 346–354
WORKING WITH OTHERS STANDARDS (WO)	
WO 1. Contributes to the overall effort of a group	Communication in Groups, 129–140; Orientation to Service Learning, 230–235
WO 2. Uses conflict-resolution techniques	Causes of Conflict, 142–152; Conflict Resolution Techniques, 152–162; Managing Anger (Emotional Intelligence Program), 201–208; Conflict Resolution and Diversity (Hate Comes Home), 209–216; Conflict Mediation, 217–222; Violence Prevention (Violence Prevention Profiler), 223–228
WO 3. Works well with diverse individuals and in diverse situations	Becoming an Active Listener, 22–27; Communication in Groups, 129–140; Causes of Conflict, 142–152; Conflict Resolution Techniques, 152–162; Conflict Resolution and Diversity (Hate Comes Home), 209–216; Conflict Mediation, 217–222; Violence Prevention (Violence Prevention Profiler), 223–228; Plan and Train for Your Exploratory Project, 236–242; Cadet Etiquette Guide, 355–374; Using Feedback in the Classroom, 432–436

McRel Standards	Unit 3: Foundations for Success
WO 4. Displays effective interpersonal communication skills	Appreciating Diversity Though Winning Colors, 10–15; Becoming an Active Listener, 22–27; The Communication Process, 114–119; Becoming a Better Listener, 120–128; Communication in Groups, 129–140; Causes of Conflict, 142–152; Conflict Resolution Techniques, 152–162; Becoming a Better Speaker, 191–199; Managing Anger (Emotional Intelligence Program), 201–208; Conflict Resolution and Diversity (Hate Comes Home), 209–216; Conflict Mediation, 217–222; Violence Prevention (Violence Prevention Profiler), 223–228; Career Development Portfolio, 272–295; Cadet Etiquette Guide, 355–374; Preparing to Teach, 389–397; Delivering Instruction, 407–414; Using Feedback in the Classroom, 432–436
WO 5. Demonstrates leadership skills	Communication in Groups, 129–140; Preparing to Teach, 389–397; Delivering Instruction, 407–414; Using Feedback in the Classroom, 432–436
SELF REGULATION STANDARDS	
SR 1. Sets and manages goals	Personal Growth Plan, 16–21; Multiple Intelligences, 71–76; Study Habits That Work for You, 100–112; Plan and Train for Your Exploratory Project, 236–242; Project Reflection and Integration, 243–251; Goals and Goal Setting, 340–345; Time Management, 346–354; NEFE Introduction: Setting Financial Goals, 376–277; Financial Planning: Your Road Map, 278–379; Budgeting: Don't Go Broke, 380–381; Savings and Investments: Your Money at Work, 382–383; Credit: Buy Now, Pay Later, 384–385; Preparing to Teach, 389–397; Using and Developing Lesson Plans, 398–406
SR 2. Performs self-appraisal	Self-Awareness, 3–9; Appreciating Diversity Though Winning Colors, 10–15; Personal Growth Plan, 16–21; Becoming an Active Listener, 22–27; Left Brain/Right Brain, 42–52; Learning Style and Processing Preferences, 53–70; Multiple Intelligences, 71–76; Reading for Meaning, 84–99; Plan and Train for Your Exploratory Project, 236–242; Project Reflection and Integration, 243–251; Career Exploration Strategy, 253–271; Career Development Portfolio, 272–295; Military Career Opportunities, 296–306; College Preparation, 307–332; Goals and Goal Setting, 340–345; Time Management, 346–354; Cadet Etiquette Guide, 355–374
SR 3. Considers risks	Violence Prevention (Violence Prevention Profiler), 223–228; Insurance: Your Protection, 386–387

McRel Standards	Unit 3: Foundations for Success
SR 4. Demonstrates perseverance	Managing Anger (Emotional Intelligence Program), 201–208; Conflict Mediation, 217–222; Plan and Train for Your Exploratory Project, 236–242; Delivering Instruction, 407–414; Using Variety in Your Lesson Plans, 415–421
SR 5. Maintains a healthy self-concept	Self-Awareness, 3–9; Becoming a Better Listener, 120–128; Violence Prevention (Violence Prevention Profiler), 223–228; Cadet Etiquette Guide, 355–374
SR 6. Restrains impulsivity	Becoming a Better Listener, 120–128; Managing Anger (Emotional Intelligence Program), 201–208; Conflict Resolution and Diversity (Hate Comes Home), 209–216; Violence Prevention (Violence Prevention Profiler), 223–228; Making the Right Choices, 334–339; Cadet Etiquette Guide, 355–374; NEFE Introduction: Setting Financial Goals, 376–277; Financial Planning: Your Road Map, 278–379; Budgeting: Don't Go Broke, 380–381; Savings and Investments: Your Money at Work, 382–383; Credit: Buy Now, Pay Later, 384–385; Insurance: Your Protection, 306–387
LANGUAGE ARTS STANDARDS (LA)	
LA 1. Uses the general skills and strategies of the writing process	Self-Awareness, 3–9; Personal Growth Plan, 16–21; Becoming a Better Writer, 164–177; Career Development Portfolio, 272–295; Using Variety in Your Lesson Plans, 415–421; Thinking Maps and Graphic Organizers, 422–431
LA 2. Uses the stylistic and rhetorical aspects of writing	Becoming a Better Writer, 164–177; Creating Better Speeches, 178–190; Career Development Portfolio, 272–295
LA 3. Uses grammatical and mechanical conventions in written compositions	Becoming a Better Writer, 164–177
LA 4. Gathers and uses information for research purposes	Brain Structure and Function, 29–41; Research, 165–166; Project Reflection and Integration, 243–251; Career Exploration Strategy, 253–271; Career Development Portfolio, 272–295; Military Career Opportunities, 296–306; College Preparation, 307–332; Using Variety in Your Lesson Plans, 415–421
LA 5. Uses the general skills and strategies of the reading process	Left Brain/Right Brain, 42–52; Learning Style and Processing Preferences, 53–70; Thinking Maps, 78–83; Reading for Meaning, 84–99; Study Habits That Work for You, 100–112; Using and Developing Lesson Plans, 398–406; Thinking Maps and Graphic Organizers, 422–431

McRel Standards	Unit 3: Foundations for Success
LA 7. Uses reading skills and strategies to understand and interpret a variety of informational texts	Thinking Maps, 78–83; Reading for Meaning, 84–99; Study Habits That Work for You, 100–112
LA 8. Uses listening and speaking strategies for different purposes	Appreciating Diversity Though Winning Colors, 10–15; The Communication Process, 114–119; Becoming a Better Listener, 120–128; Creating Better Speeches, 178–190; Becoming a Better Speaker, 191–199; Conflict Mediation, 217–222; Violence Prevention (Violence Prevention Profiler), 223–228; Cadet Etiquette Guide, 355–374; Using Feedback in the Classroom, 432–436
LA 9. Uses viewing skills and strategies to understand and interpret visual media	College Preparation, 307–332

Unit 4: Wellness, Fitness and First Aid
Correlated to:
McRel Standards for Thinking and Reasoning, Self Regulation, Physical Education, and Health

McRel Standards	Unit 4: Wellness, Fitness and First Aid
THINKING AND REASONING STANDARDS (TR)	
TR 5. Applies basic trouble-shooting and problem-solving techniques	The Need for First Aid/Your Response, 554–561; The First Life-Saving Steps, 562–569; Controlling Bleeding, 570–575; Treating for Shock and Immobilizing Fractures, 576–582; First Aid for Burns, 582–593; First Aid for Poisons, Wounds, and Bruises, 594–601; Heat Injuries, 602–607; Cold Water Injuries, 608–617; Bites, Stings, and Poisonous Hazards, 618–626
TR 6. Applies decision-making techniques	Evaluating Foods, 525–536; The Need for First Aid/Your Response, 554–561; The First Life-Saving Steps, 562–569; Controlling Bleeding, 570–575; Treating for Shock and Immobilizing Fractures, 576–582; First Aid for Burns, 582–593; First Aid for Poisons, Wounds, and Bruises, 594–601; Heat Injuries, 602–607; Cold Water Injuries, 608–617; Bites, Stings, and Poisonous Hazards, 618–626; Critical Decisions about Substances (Interactive Nights Out), 655–685
SELF REGULATION STANDARDS	
SR 1. Sets and manages goals	Choosing the Right Exercise Program for You, 439–462; Checking Your Progress, 453–454; Cadet Challenge, 463–471; Dietary Guidelines, 492–503; Controlling Fat, 504–528
SR 2. Performs self-appraisal	Choosing the Right Exercise Program for You, 439–462; Cadet Challenge, 463–471; You Are What You Eat, 472–478; Dietary Guidelines, 492–503; Controlling Fat, 504–528; Taking Care of Yourself, 529–538; Understanding and Controlling Stress, 439–552
SR 4. Demonstrates perseverance	Checking Your Progress, 453–454; Sticking with an Exercise Program, 458–459; Cadet Challenge, 463–471
SR 6. Restrains impulsivity	Critical Decisions about Substances (Interactive Nights Out), 655–685

Copyright © 2004 McREL
Mid-continent Research for Education and Learning
2550 S. Parker Road, Suite 500
Aurora, CO 80014
Telephone: 303/337-0990
www.mcrel.org/standards-benchmarks

McRel Standards	Unit 4: Wellness, Fitness and First Aid
PHYSICAL EDUCATION STANDARDS (PE)	
PE 1. Uses a variety of basic and advanced movement forms	Cadet Challenge, 463–471
PE 2. Uses movement concepts and principles in the development of motor skills	Cadet Challenge, 463–471
PE 3. Understands the benefits and costs associated with participation in physical activity	Choosing the Right Exercise Program for You, 439–462; Cadet Challenge, 463–471
PE 4. Understands how to monitor and maintain a health-enhancing level of physical fitness	Choosing the Right Exercise Program for You, 439–462; Cadet Challenge, 463–471
HEALTH STANDARDS (H)	
H1. Knows the availability and effective use of health services, products, and information	Taking Care of Yourself, 529–538; The Need for First Aid/Your Response, 554–561; The First Life–Saving Steps, 562–569; Controlling Bleeding, 570–575; Treating for Shock and Immobilizing Fractures, 576–582; First Aid for Burns, 582–593; First Aid for Poisons, Wounds, and Bruises, 594–601; Heat Injuries, 602–607; Cold Water Injuries, 608–617; Bites, Stings, and Poisonous Hazards, 618–626; Use & Effect of Drugs, Alcohol, and Substances, 628–654
H2. Knows environmental and external factors that affect individual and community health	Understanding and Controlling Stress, 439–552; Use & Effect of Drugs, Alcohol, and Substances, 628–654; Critical Decisions about Substances (Interactive Nights Out), 655–685
H3. Understands the relationship of family health to individual health	Critical Decisions about Substances (Interactive Nights Out), 655–685
H4. Knows how to maintain mental and emotional health	Understanding and Controlling Stress, 439–552; Why do People Abuse Drugs? 630; Critical Decisions about Substances (Interactive Nights Out), 655–685
H5. Knows essential concepts and practices concerning injury prevention and safety	A Safe Workout, 454–457
H6. Understand essential concepts about nutrition and diet	You Are What You Eat, 472–478; Nutrition—Nourishing Your Body, 479–491; Dietary Guidelines, 492–503; Controlling Fat, 504–528
H7. Knows how to maintain and promote personal health	Choosing the Right Exercise Program for You, 439–462; Cadet Challenge, 463–471; You Are What You Eat, 472–478; Nutrition—Nourishing Your Body, 479–491; Dietary Guidelines, 493–503; Controlling Fat, 504–528; Taking Care of Yourself, 529–538; Understanding and Controlling Stress, 539–552

McRel Standards	Unit 4: Wellness, Fitness and First Aid
H8. Knows essential concepts about the prevention and control of disease	You Are What You Eat, 472–478; Nutrition—Nourishing Your Body, 479–491; Dietary Guidelines, 492–503; Controlling Fat, 504–528; Taking Care of Yourself, 529–538; Understanding and Controlling Stress, 539–552; The Need for First Aid/Your Response, 554–561; The First Life-Saving Steps, 562–569; Controlling Bleeding, 570–575; Treating for Shock and Immobilizing Fractures, 576–582; First Aid for Burns, 582–593; First Aid for Poisons, Wounds, and Bruises, 594–601; Heat Injuries, 602–607; Cold Water Injuries, 608–617; Bites, Stings, and Poisonous Hazards, 618–626
H9. Understands aspects of substance use and abuse	Use & Effect of Drugs, Alcohol, and Substances, 628–654; Critical Decisions about Substances (Interactive Nights Out), 655–685
H10. Understands the fundamental concepts of growth and development	Nutrition and Pregnancy, 521-523

Glossary

Academic. Belonging or pertaining to higher education.

Acceptable. Capable or worthy of being accepted, adequate, satisfactory.

Active. Characterized by action rather than by contemplation or speculation.

Active duty. A condition of military service where members are on full duty, or subject to call, at all times to respond quickly to the nation's emergencies.

Active listening. To go beyond comprehending literally to an empathetic understanding of the speaker.

Active voice. A term that indicates that the writer has emphasized the doer of the action.

Adaptability. Capability or willingness to adapt.

Admissions. The act or process of admitting.

Advancement. A promotion or elevation to a higher rank or position.

Advocacy service. The act or process of supporting or providing a service toward a cause or proposal that does not require face-to-face contact.

After action review. Reflecting on what was learned after an act.

Agenda. A list or program of activities that need to be done or considered.

Aggression. A tendency to be hostile or quarrelsome.

Allocate. To apportion for a specific purpose or to particular persons or things.

Analogy. Resemblance in some particulars between things otherwise unlike.

Analysis. The separation of a whole into its component parts for individual study; a study of something complex, its elements, and their interrelationships.

Anger management. Learning to control and manage the emotion of anger; managing your anger so it comes out in a healthy and constructive way; employing steps to control feelings of anger or rage.

Annual fee. A yearly fee charged by credit grantors for the privilege of using a credit card.

Annual percentage rate (APR). The cost of credit at a yearly rate.

Anti-Semitism. Feeling or showing hostility toward Jews; persecuting Jews.

Antonym. A word of opposite meaning (the usual antonym of good is bad).

Apologize. To make an apology or express a regret for a wrong.

Apply. The phase in a lesson plan designed to provide opportunities for students to demonstrate their competence and expand their ability to use it in their lives.

Appositive. A grammatical construction in which two usually adjacent nouns having the same referent stand in the same syntactical relation to the rest of a sentence (as the poet and Burns in "a biography of the poet Burns").

Aptitude. The capabilities that you have developed so far that indicate your readiness to become proficient in a certain type of activity.

Aptitude test. A standardized test designed to predict an individual's ability to learn certain skills.

Arbitration. To submit for decision to a third party who is chosen to settle differences in a controversy.

Articulate. To speak clearly and effectively.

Ascendant. Dominant in position or influence; superior.

Assertion. The act of asserting; to state or declare positively and often forcefully or aggressively.

Assessment. The act of evaluation or appraising a person's ability or potential to meet certain criteria or standards.

Associate. To group things together when they have common characteristics.

Attitude. A feeling, emotion, or mental position regarding a fact or state.

Audience analysis. The examination of the characteristics that describe the receivers of communication, to include categories such as age, background, education, political opinions, location, and so on.

Auditory. Of, or pertaining to hearing.

Aural or auditory. Of or relating to the ear or to the sense of hearing: of, relating to, or experienced through hearing.

Authoritarian. Characterized by or favoring absolute obedience to authority, as against individual freedom.

Autobiography. The biography of a person, written by that person.

Axon. Long fibers that send electrical impulses and release neurotransmitters.

Bankruptcy. Financially ruined; impoverished.

Barriers. Obstruction; anything that holds apart or separates.

Bibliography. A list of sources of information on a specific subject; the description and identification of the editions dates of issue, authorship, and typography of books or other written materials.

Bigotry. Bitter, intolerance, and prejudice.

Bi-lateral transfer. The ability of the brain to transmit data processed in one hemisphere and coordinate and integrate it with data processed in other areas.

Biography. The history of a particular person, as told by someone else.

Bodily/Kinesthetic intelligence. The gift of physical prowess, coordination, fitness, and action.

Body. The main part of a paper, lesson plan, or speech.

Bond. An insurance contract in which an agency guarantees payment to an employer in the event of unforeseen financial loss through the actions of an employee.

Brace map. A tool used to analyze a physical object and its parts.

Brain stem. The oldest part of the brain composed of the mesencephalon, pons, and medulla oblongata and connecting the spinal cord with the forebrain and cerebrum. Also referred to as the reptilian brain.

Brainstorming. A teaching method that consists of group problem-solving techniques involving the spontaneous contribution of ideas from all members of the group.

Bridge map. A tool used for seeing analogies; a process of seeing the relating factor or the same relationship to something.

Bubble map. A tool used for describing qualities; describing a process of seeing qualities, characteristics, traits, and/or properties of things.

Budget. An itemized summary of estimated or intended expenditures for a given period along with proposals for financing them.

Capital gain. The amount by which the selling price of an asset exceeds the purchase price; the gain is realized when the asset is sold.

Career. An occupation or profession; the course or progress of a person's life.

Case study. A teaching method that consists of an oral or written account of a real or realistic situation.

Cash flow. A measure of the money you receive and the money you spend.

Cash management. The strategy by which a company administers and invests its cash.

Cause and effect. A process of identifying the interrelationships of what results from an action.

Cerebral hemispheres. When looked at from the top, the brain is composed of two interconnected spheres or lobes, which are the seat of higher-level thinking.

Change orientation. A reflection of satisfaction or dissatisfaction with current emotional skills and abilities; a scale that indicates the degree of motivation and readiness for change in the skills measured by the Personal Skills Map.

Channel. In communications theory, a gesture, action, sound, written or spoken word, or visual image used in transmitting information.

Circle map. A tool used for brainstorming; defining in context; a process where a specific concept is defined and explored.

Clarify. To make understandable.

Classify. To assign to a category.

Classifying. A process of sorting things into categories or groups.

Cluster. A number of similar things growing together, or of things or individuals collected or grouped closely together.

Coach-pupil exercises. A practical exercise format where learners work in pairs or small group, alternately performing as instructor and student.

Cognition. The mental process of knowing.

College. An independent institution of higher learning offering a course of general studies leading to a bachelor's degree; a part of a university offering a specialized group of courses; an institution offering instruction, usually in a professional, vocational, or technical field .

Comfort zone. Behaviors that seem natural; behaviors you exhibit without realizing what you're doing.

Commemorative. Honoring the memory of; speaking in honor of.

Commissary. A supermarket for use by military personnel and their dependents located on a military installation.

Community service. Any form of service provided for the community or common good.

Compare. A test directive that requires that you examine qualities or characteristics to discover resemblances. "Compare" is usually stated as "compare with"; you are to emphasize similarities, although differences may be mentioned.

Comparing and contrasting. A process of identifying similarities and differences of things.

Competency. A major skill or task that describes what a learner will be able to do as a result of a specific lesson.

Complementary. Supplying mutual needs of offsetting mutual lacks.

Compounding. To settle (a debt, for example) by agreeing on an amount less than the claim; adjust.

Comprehension. The act or action of grasping with the intellect.

Comprehensive. Covering completely or broadly.

Compromise. A settlement of differences reached by mutual concessions.

Comradeship. Companionship.

Concept. An abstract or generic idea generalized from particular instances.

Conclusion. The final part of a paper, speech, or lesson plan; also referred to as a summary; a final opinion reached through research and reasoning.

Conference. A teaching method where the instructor involves the entire class in a discussion of the subject being taught by asking leading questions to get the students to think about and discuss the main points.

Conflict. A clash between hostile or opposing elements, ideas, or forces; to show opposition.

Conjunction. Joining words such as and or but.

Constructive. Promoting improvement or development.

Constructive criticism. Feedback that is helpful and productive.

Context. Written or spoken knowledge that can help to illuminate the meaning of a word or passage.

Contrast. A test directive that stresses dissimilarities, differences, or unlikeness of things, qualities, events, or problems.

Conviction. A strong persuasion or belief.

Cooperative learning. A teaching strategy in which teams of students work with and depend on each other to accomplish a common goal.

Coping strategy. Technique used for dealing with a difficult situation.

Corpus callosum. The bundle of fibers (axons) connecting the two sides of the brain; white matter.

Cortex. The highly wrinkled outer layer of the cerebrum and cerebellum (forebrain); gray matter.

Counterpart. Something that is similar or comparable to another, as in function or relation.

Creative. Marked by the ability or power to create: given to creating.

Credit. A trust or a promise to pay later for goods or services purchased today.

Credit history. Record of how a consumer has paid credit accounts in the past, which is used as a guide to determine whether the consumer is likely to pay accounts on time in the future.

Credit report. A record or file to a prospective lender or employer on the credit standing of a prospective borrower, which is used to help determine credit worthiness.

Criteria. A standard on which a judgment or decision is based.

Criteria filter. A standard, rule, or test on which a judgment or decision can be based.

Critical. Of, relating to, or being a turning point or especially important juncture.

Curtly. Rudely brief or abrupt, as in speech or manner.

Debriefer. One who encourages team members and leads discussion after presentation and team reflection.

Debt. A liability or obligation in the form of bonds, loan notes, or mortgages owed to another person required to be paid by a specified date.

Decision making. The process of considering and analyzing information in order to make a decision.

Decision point. The point where a decision to act is made.

Deductible. The amount of a loss that an insurance policy holder has to pay out-of-pocket before reimbursement begins.

Deference. The respect and esteem due a superior or elder; also affected or ingratiating regard for another's wishes; the degree to which a person uses a communication style or pattern that is indirect and effectual for accurate expression of thought and feeling.

Defining in context. A process where a specific concept is defined and explored.

Delayed gratification. To postpone satisfaction until a later time.

Demographics. Dealing with the vital and social conditions of people.

Demonstration. A teaching method that requires hands-on class participation.

Dendrite. Any of the usually branching protoplasmic processes that conduct impulses toward the body of a nerve cell.

Describing. A process of seeing qualities, characteristics, traits and/or properties of things.

Descriptive. Describes how a word derives from the root of its culture.

Differentiate. To make a distinction or state a difference between things so we can tell them apart.

Dining-in. A formal military dinner for military members only.

Dining-out. A formal military dinner to which nonmilitary guests are invited.

Direct service. Involves face-to-face contact with those being served in either project or placement models of service learning.

Discussion. A teaching method where the instructor involves the entire class in a discussion of the subject by asking leading questions to get the students to think about and discuss the main points.

Distance education. Learning that takes place via electronic media linking instructors and students who are not together in a classroom.

Distortion. Twisted out of true meaning; reproduced improperly.

Diversification. To extend (business activities) into disparate fields.

Dominant. Exercising the most influence or control.

Double-bubble map. Comparing and contrasting a process of identifying similarities and differences of things; a tool used to compare and contrast.

Dramatic statement. A phrase or sentence meant to capture the attention of the audience.

Dysfunctional roles. Roles assumed by individuals within a group, that are destructive and block group communication.

Earned interest. A charge for a loan, usually a percentage of the amount earned.

Effective speaking. Expressing your needs feelings and reasons.

Efficient. Productive of desired effects; especially: productive without waste.

Emotional intelligence. A learned ability to identify, experience, understand, and express human emotions in healthy and productive ways.

Empathetic. Of, pertaining to, or characterized by empathy (an understanding so intimate that the feelings, thoughts, and motives of one are readily comprehended by another).

Empathy. The ability to accurately understand and constructively respond to the expressed feelings, thought, behaviors, and needs of others; the capacity to experience the feelings of another as one's own.

Employee. One employed by another, usually for wages or salary.

Employment application. A form used in making a request to be considered for a job position.

Energizer. A learning activity designed to motivate and engage learners.

Enlistment. To engage a person for duty in the armed forces.

Entice. To attract or lure; to encourage someone to participate.

Entrepreneur. One who organizes, manages, and assumes the risks of a business enterprise.

Enumerate. A test directive that specifies a list or outline form of reply; in such questions, recount one by one the points required.

Etiquette. A code of behavior based on rules of a polite society.

Exchange. A store at a military installation that sells merchandise and services to military personnel and authorized civilians.

Expenses. Something spent to attain a goal or accomplish a purpose.

Experiential learning. Gaining practical knowledge, skills, or practice from direct observation of or participation in events or in a particular activity.

Exploratory project. A teacher-planned introductory project to service learning, intended to provide students with a meaningful experience, expose them to how it feels to serve, and to stimulate their thinking about possible service learning activities.

Eye contact. Looking someone directly in the eyes.

Facilitator. One who leads a discussion or guides an activity

Federal income tax. A government levy on the members of a nation to meet its expenses.

Feedback. The return or a response to information, as in the evaluation of a communication; the return of evaluative or corrective information to the sender (point of origin).

Field education. Performing service and training to enhance understanding within a field of study.

Filter. A person who alters information or a method of altering information as it is being passed from one person to another.

Finance charge. The cost of consumer credit expressed as a dollar amount including interest, transaction fees, and service fees.

Financial aid. A grant or subsidy to a school or individual for an educational or artistic project.

Fixed expenses. Expenses that do no vary.

Flexible. Ready to adapt to new, different, or changing requirements.

Flow map. A tool used to determine sequencing; a process of ordering or examining stages of an event.

Focus. A center of activity, attraction or attention; a point of concentration; directed attention.

Fragment. A word group that lacks a subject or a predicate.

Frustration. Feelings of insecurity, discouragement, or dissatisfaction.

Gaming. A teaching method that consists of activities where participants compete to try and achieve or exceed a certain standard in performing a skill relevant to the learning objectives of the lesson.

Gather. The phase in a lesson plan designed to assist learners in gathering new ideas and information.

Global. Involving the entire earth; comprehensive, total.

Goal. An aim or purpose; an end to which effort is directed.

Goal setting. Planning done to reach a desired goal.

Grace period. The period allowed avoiding any finance charges by paying off the balance in full before the due date.

Grants. Monetary awards based on financial need that do not need to be paid back to the grantor.

Grapevine. An informal, often secret means of transmitting information, gossip, or rumor (that is usually incomplete or does not make sense) from one person to another within an organization or institution.

Gross income. For an individual, all income except as specifically exempted by the internal revenue code.

Group performance. A controlled practical exercise where learners work together at a fixed rate.

Groupthink. The situation where a group does not consider all available alternatives due to the desire to reach consensus.

Harassment. The act of annoying continually.

Hate-related words. Derogatory words having to do with race, religion, ethnicity, ability, gender, or sexual orientation.

Hearing. To perceive by the ear; to listen attentively.

Hemisphere. Half of a symmetrical shape.

Hostility. An unfriendly state or action.

Hypothesis. An assumption or concession made for the sake of argument: an interpretation of a practical situation or condition taken as the ground for action.

Idleness. Passing time without working or while avoiding work.

Impromptu. Without planning or rehearsal.

Income. The amount of money or its equivalent received during a period of time in exchange for labor or services, from the sale of goods or property, or as profit from financial investments.

Independent exercises. A practical exercise format where learners work alone at their own pace.

Indirect service. Hands-on involvement in a service activity without any face-to-face contact with those served.

Inference. A test directive, when asked to infer, you are required to make a determination of a given problem based on the proposition, statement, or judgment considered as true within another problem.

Inflation. A persistent increase in the level of consumer prices or a persistent decline in the purchasing power of money, caused by an increase in available currency and credit beyond the proportion of available goods and services.

Information cards. Cards used to collect data for a report or paper.

Inquire. The phase in a lesson plan designed to connect new learning to past experience.

Insurance. Compensation for specific potential future losses in exchange for a periodic payment.

Insurance premium. The periodic payment made on an insurance policy.

Integration. The act or process or an instance of forming, coordinating, or blending into a functioning or unified whole.

Intelligence. The capacity to acquire and apply knowledge; the faculty of thought and reason.

Interest. The cost of borrowing or lending money, usually a percentage of the amount borrowed or loaned.

Internship. An advanced student or graduate, usually in a professional field (such as medicine or teaching) gaining supervised, practical experience (such as a hospital or classroom).

Interpersonal intelligence. The gift of working with people and understanding the complexities of human relationships.

Interpret. A test directive; you are expected to translate, solve, or comment on the subject and usually to give your judgment or reaction to the problem.

Interview. A formal face-to-face meeting, especially one conducted for the assessment of an applicant.

Intrapersonal. Occurring within the individual mind or self.

Intrapersonal intelligence. The gift of inner thought, self-awareness, and self-reflection.

Introduction. The beginning of a paper, speech, or lesson plan.

Introspection. Examination of one's own thoughts and feelings.

Intuition. Instinctive knowledge or perception without conscious reasoning or reference to a rational process; keen insight.

Inventory. An itemized list of current assets: a catalog of the property of an individual or estate; a list of goods on hand; a survey of natural resources; a list of traits, preferences, attitudes, interests, or abilities used to evaluate personal character.

Invest. To commit (money or capital) in order to gain a financial return:

Jargon. Technical terminology or language created for a particular profession, such as computer science, that may seem strange or outlandish to outsiders who do not understand it.

Job.   A position of work or employment that is performed regularly in exchange for payment; a task or undertaking; a specific activity or piece of work.

Job posting.   A published notice of a job vacancy.

Justify.   In a test directive where you are instructed to justify your answer, you must prove or show your grounds for decisions; present evidence in convincing form.

Kinesthetic.   A sensory experience derived from a sense that perceives bodily movement.

Learning objectives.   A supporting skill, knowledge, or attitude leading to mastery of a competency.

Learning outcomes.   Describe what students should know and be able to do as the result of a learning experience.

Learning style.   A particular way in which the mind receives and processes information

Lecture.   A teaching method designed to provide instruction on a task or topic.

Lesson plans.   An organized, well-written plan for how an instructor will facilitate student learning.

Limbic system.   A group of subcortical structures (as the hypothalamus, the hippocampus, and the amygdala) of the brain that are concerned especially with emotion and motivation.

Listening.   Making an effort to hear something; paying attention.

Loan term.   The agreed on length of a loan.

Local.   Not extensive; confined; nearby.

Logical.   Correct or reliable inference.

Logical/Mathematical intelligence.   The gift of reasoning and thinking in symbols and abstractions.

Long-term goal.   A life goal; a goal that requires lots of time and planning to accomplish.

Martial.   Of or relating to an army or military life.

Measurable.   Able to be observed and evaluated for quality.

Mediation.   Working with opposing sides to resolve a dispute or bring about a settlement; the process in which conflicts are resolved with the help of a neutral third party.

Medicare tax.   A program under the U.S. social security administration that reimburses hospitals and physicians for medical care provided to qualified people over 65 years old.

Mentor.   A trusted counselor or guide.

Mid-term goal.   An intermediate goal; sometimes a step to a long-term goal.

Miscommunication.   Failure to communicate clearly.

Mixed messages.   Communication transmitted by words, signals, or other means from one person, station, or group to another with unclear meaning to the receiver.

Mobility.   Moving from one position to another.

Mode.   Method, route, or way.

Modify.   To make basic or fundamental changes to give a new orientation to or to serve a new end.

Modulation.   To change or vary the pitch, intensity, or tone.

Monopolize.   To take exclusive ownership or control.

Mood.   A conscious state of mind or predominant emotion.

Motivation.   Something that causes a person to act.

Multi-flow map.   A tool used for seeing cause and effect; a process of identifying the interrelationship of what results from an action.

Musical/rhythmical intelligence.   The gift of melody, music, rhyme, rhythm, and sound.

Mutual fund.   An investment company that continually offers new shares and stands ready to redeem existing shares from the owners.

Natural.   Based on an inherent sense of right and wrong; occurring in conformity with the ordinary course of nature, not marvelous or supernatural; formulated by human reason alone rather than revelation; having a normal or usual character

Naturalist intelligence.   Environmental awareness.

Needs.   A condition requiring supply or relief; to be in need or want.

Negotiation.   Discussion or conference that is aimed at bringing about a settlement.

Net income.   Income after all expenses and taxes have been deducted.

Networking.   Meeting people and making contacts; the exchange of information or services among individuals, groups, or institutions.

Neural plasticity.   Concerns the property of neural circuitry to potentially acquire (given appropriate training) nearly any function.

Neurons.   A grayish or reddish granular cell with specialized processes that is the fundamental functional unit of nervous tissue in the brain.

Neurotransmitter.   A chemical molecule (as norepinephrine or acetylcholine) that transmits nerve impulses across a synapse, within and between brain cells.

Noise.   That which interferes with the successful completion of communication; a disturbance, especially a random and persistent disturbance that obscures or reduces the clarity of communication.

Nonverbal.   Being other than verbal; not involving words: nonverbal communication.

Objectivity. Expressing or dealing with facts or conditions as perceived without distortion by personal feelings, prejudices, or interpretations.

Observation. An act or instance of examining a custom, rule, or law; an act of recognizing and noting a fact or occurrence often involving measurement with instruments; a record or description so obtained.

Occupation. The principal business of one's life.

Operational. Tells how the object relates to how it works or operates.

Opportunity cost. Choosing one option may mean giving up altogether on another.

Orientation. The act or process of orienting or of being oriented, for example, being oriented on the first day of college.

P.Y.F. Pay Yourself First is the secret to getting what you want and becoming a disciplined saver.

Palate. The sense of taste.

Paraphrase. A restatement of a text, passage, or work giving the meaning in another form.

Part-whole relationships. A process of identifying the relationship between a whole physical object and its parts.

Passive. Acted on by an external agency; receptive to outside impressions or influences.

Passive voice. A term that indicates that the writer has emphasized the receiver of the action.

Payroll deductions. The sum of money to be taken out of an employees paycheck to meet agreed-on obligations.

Perception. Awareness of one's environment through physical sensation. Ability to understand.

Persistence. The action or fact of persisting, to go on resolutely or stubbornly in spite of opposition, importunity, or warning; to remain unchanged or fixed in a specified character, condition, or position; the quality or state of being persistent

Persuasive. Have the power to persuade.

Place cards. A name card for a formal dinner.

Placement. Service learning activities carried out beyond the classroom in a preexisting, structured situation.

Plagiarism. The act of copying the ideas or words of another and claiming them as one's own.

Portfolio. A document that contains a student's achievement over time and provides an in-depth picture of the student's skills and competencies.

Practical exercises. A maneuver, operation, or drill carried out for training a discipline.

Preconceived. To form (as an opinion) prior to actual knowledge or experience.

Predicate. Tells what the subject does.

Predict. To declare or indicate in advance; especially foretell on the basis of observation, experience, or scientific reason.

Prediction. Something that is foretold on the basis of observation, experience, or scientific reason.

Preference. The act of preferring, the state of being preferred; the power or opportunity of choosing.

Prejudice. A judgment or opinion formed without knowing the facts; hatred or fear of other races, nations, creeds, and so on.

Prerequisite. Required before moving to the next step, level, class, and so on.

Prevention. To stop or prevent an event or act from occurring.

Problem-based learning. An instructional strategy that promotes active learning where problems form the focus and learning stimulus and problem-solving skills are utilized.

Process. The phase in a lesson plan designed to provide opportunities for practicing new skills and processing information.

Procrastination. The act of putting off something that needs to be done.

Profession. A principal calling, vocation, or employment.

Project. A task or problem engaged in usually by a group of students to supplement and apply classroom studies. Service learning projects are initiated and planned by cadets with instructor guidance.

Promotion. The act or fact of being raised in position or rank.

Properties. A quality or trait belonging and especially peculiar to an individual or thing.

Protocol. A code of precedence in rank and status and of correct procedure in ceremonies; a form of etiquette observed in ceremonies; a combination of good manners and common sense that allows for effective communication.

Prove. A test directive with questions that require proof or ones that demand confirmation or verification; establish something with certainty by evaluating and citing evidence or by logical reasoning.

Purpose. Something set up as an object or end to be attained.

Quality. Peculiar and essential character; an inherent feature; degree of excellence; superiority in kind.

Quantity. An indefinite amount or number; a determinate or estimated amount; total amount or number; a considerable amount or number, often used in plural; the aspect in which a thing is measurable in terms of greater, less, or equal or of increasing or decreasing magnitude.

Racism. The practice of racial discrimination, persecution, or segregation based on race.

Rapport. A relationship, especially one of mutual trust.

Rate of return. Same as return.

Receiver. One or more individuals for whom a message is intended.

Receiving line. A group of people, including the host and honored guests, who stand in line and individually welcome guests attending a function, as at a formal reception.

Recorder. One who takes notes for the team and organizes information.

Recruiter. A member of the armed services who enlists new members into the armed forces.

Reflection. An activity that requires learners to think about and communicate their learning experiences.

Reflex. Denoting or of an involuntary action in which the motor nerves act in response to a stimulus from an impression made on the sensory nerves.

Registration. The act of registering.

Reinforce. To strengthen by additional assistance, material, or support.

Relating factor. The similar phrase that fits both sides of an analogy.

Relationships. A particular type of connection existing between people related to or having dealings with each other.

Repast. A supply of food and drink served as a meal.

Reporter. One who represents the team voice and reports team findings.

Reserves. A military force withheld from action for later decisive use, forces not in the field but available; the military forces of a country not part of the regular service.

Restraint. The self-control to save your money for a future goal instead of spending it now.

Resolution. The process or capability of making distinguishable the individual parts of an object, closely adjacent optical images, or sources of light such as the sharpness or clarity of a picture.

Resume. A short account of one's career and qualifications prepared typically by an applicant for an employment position.

Risk management. The process of analyzing exposure to risk and determining how to best handle such exposure.

Role-playing. A practical exercise format where learners are given different roles to play in a situation, and apply the concepts being taught while acting out realistic behavior.

Routinization. A process or decision that you have routinely used in the past that helps you in current situations because you have established a decision-making pattern.

Rule of 72. The mathematical rule used in approximating the number of years it will take a given investment to double in value.

Savings. A reduction in expenditure or cost.

Scapegoating. The action of blaming an individual or group for something when, in reality, there is no one person or group responsible for the problem. It targets another person or group as responsible for problems in society because of that person's group identity.

Schema. A pattern imposed on complex reality or experience to assist in explaining it, mediate perception, or guide response.

Scholarships. Grants-in-aid to a student, as by a college or university.

Sensory. Of, or relating to an awareness or a mental process due to a stimulation of a sense organ.

Sensory flooding. Sensory overload, this happens when too much data are getting through to the brain.

Sensory gating. Also called the neuron spike point; regulates the transmission of stimuli to the brain.

Sequencing. A process of ordering or examining stages of an event.

Service learning. An environment where one can learn and develop by actively participating in organized service experiences within one's community.

Setting. The context and environment in which a situation is set; the background; the time, place, and circumstances in which a narrative, drama, or film takes place.

Short-term goal. A goal that can be accomplished in a short period of time; often without much planning or effort.

SMART goals. Specific, measurable, attainable, realistic, and time-bound goals.

Social roles. Roles that individuals assume during the group communication process that help maintain the group.

Social security tax. Federal tax levied equally on employers and employees and used to pay for social security programs.

Sociological. Pertaining to the science of society, social institutions, and social relationships.

Solutions. An action or process of solving a problem.

Sorbet. A fruit flavored ice served for dessert or in between courses as a palate refresher.

Source cards. A card that is used to record the title, author, publisher, copyright date, and place of publication (city and state) of resources being used during research for a project (paper, speech, and so on).

Specialize. To become adapted to a specific function.

Stag. Unaccompanied by someone of the opposite sex; traditionally, a man who attends a social affair without escort of a woman.

State income tax. State tax levied equally on employers and employees, used to pay for state programs.

Statement. The act of stating, declaring, or narrating.

Stereotype. A formulized conception, notion, or attitude.

Stilted. Stiffly or artificially dignified or formal; pompous; lofty.

Stocks. The capital or funds that a corporation raises through the sale of shares entitling the stockholder to dividends and to other rights of ownership, such as voting rights.

Strategy. The art of carefully devising or employing a plan of action or method designed to achieve a goal; the art or science of planning and directing large-scale military operations and campaigns.

Subject. Tells what or whom the sentence is about.

Subjective. Of, relating to, or constituting a subject; relating to or characteristic of one that is a subject, especially in lack of freedom of action or in submissiveness.

Success. The gaining of fame or prosperity.

Synapse. The space between nerve cells; the point at which a nervous impulse passes from one neuron to another.

Synchronize. To happen at the same time; coincide.

Synonym. One of two or more words or expressions of the same language that have the same or nearly the same meaning in some or all senses.

Synthesis. The combining of separate parts to form a coherent whole, as for a concentrated study of it.

Tactile. Of or relating to, or perceptible through the sense of touch.

Task roles. Roles assumed during the group communication process, which help the group, accomplish a specific task.

Taxes. To place a tax on income, property, or goods.

Team practical exercises. A practical exercise format where learners work together as a team to perform the desired tasks.

Team-building exercise. Strategies that can be employed to help foster team dynamics; examples include team color, name, and logo.

Telecommute. To work at home by the use of an electronic linkup with a central office.

Territorial. Of or relating to the geographic area under a given jurisdiction.

Thesis statement. The main point of a paper that you try to support through research.

Thinking process. The organized way in which thinking occurs.

Thought speed. The amount of time it takes for people to hear a thought and process it; typically considerably faster than speaking time.

Time management. The process of effectively using time to gain control of events, conditions, and actions.

Time value of money. The concept that holds that a specific sum of money is more valuable the sooner it is received.

Time wasters. Activities that do not promote the effective use of time.

Timekeeper. One who keeps track of time and plans the schedule.

Tines. Slender pointed parts of a fork; prongs.

Tone. A sound of distinct pitch, loudness, vibration, quality, or duration; the particular or relative pitch of a word or phrase.

Training. To form by (or undergo) instruction, discipline, or drill; to teach so as to make fit, qualified, or proficient.

Training aids. Materials such as computers, handouts, chalkboards, and so on that enhance and support teaching.

Transcript. Complete record of your grades while in school.

Tree map. A tool used for classifying and categorizing; a process of sorting things into categories or groups.

Trigger words. Words that evoke an emotional response that prevents effective listening.

Tuition. The price of or payment for instruction.

Understanding. Knowledge and ability to judge.

University. An institution of higher learning providing facilities for teaching and research and authorized to grant academic degrees; specifically, one made up of an undergraduate division that confers bachelor's degrees and a graduate division that comprises a graduate school and professional schools, each of which may also confer master's degrees and doctorates.

Values. A principle, standard, or quality considered worthwhile or desirable.

Variable expense. A cost that does not remain fixed.

Verbal. Of, relating to, or associated with words.

Verbal/Linguistic intelligence. Strong language and literacy skills.

Violence. Physical force used to do injury; any infringement of rights.

Violence prevention. Discouraging or hindering acts of physical force that cause injury or abuse.

Virtual worker. Employee who telecommutes and performs work tasks virtually, via the internet, phone, and fax.

Visual/spatial intelligence. The gift of visually representing and appreciating concepts, ideas, and information (visual thinking).

Visualize. To see or form a mental image of.

Visualizing. The act of forming a mental image.

Vocal qualities. The characteristic of someone's speaking voice.

Vocational. Of, relating to, or being in training for a skill or trade to be pursued as a career.

Volume. The amplitude or loudness of a sound.

Wants. To desire greatly; wish for.

Unit 4

Glossary

Abrasions. A part of the skin that has been lightly torn or scraped.

Abuse. Improper or excessive use or treatment.

Acids. Chemical compounds with a sour taste that react with base to form salt, have a pH value of less than 7, react with metals to form hydrogen gas, and have the capability to eat away or dissolve metals and other materials.

Addiction. Physically or psychologically dependent on a substance, habit, or behavior that can lead to health, social, or economic problems; dependence on a drug.

Aerobic. Allowing sufficient amounts of oxygen to be delivered to the muscles.

Alcohol. A beverage containing ethanol or ethyl alcohol that causes intoxication.

Alkalis. Any base, as soda, potash, and so on that is soluble in water, combines with fats to form soap, neutralizes acids, and forms salts with them.

Allergic reaction. A physical reaction, often marked by sneezing, breathing difficulties, itching, rash, or swelling, that some people have when the come in contact with certain substances.

Amenorrhea. An abnormal absence or suppression of the menstrual period.

Amino acids. The basic units of proteins produced by living cells or obtained as an essential component of a diet.

Ampule. A small, sealed glass container that holds one dose of a solution, usually a medicine, to be administered by injection.

Amputation. The removal of an external part of the body, most often a limb or part of it, when it has been severely crushed or following the death of an extremity due to impaired blood circulation.

Anaerobic. Working in the absence of adequate amounts of oxygen being delivered to the muscles.

Anorexia nervosa. An aversion to food syndrome; an eating disorder characterized by an extreme (prolonged) loss of appetite.

Antivenin. An antitoxin used to counteract venom.

Anxiety. Eager, often agitated desire: my anxiety is to make a good impression.

Arteries. Blood vessels that carry blood away from the heart all parts of the body.

Automated external defibrillator (AED). A device used to treat a patient with cardiac arrest whose heart is beating irregularly.

Avulsion. The tearing away of a body part accidentally or surgically.

Basal metabolic rate (BMR). The number of calories burned at complete rest; measurement of it indicates an individual's general metabolism or state of health.

Bases. Chemical compounds with a slippery or soapy feel that react with acids to form salt, have a pH value above 7, and are used as cleaning materials.

Bivouac. A temporary camp or shelter.

Bulimia. A disease (or eating disorder) with symptoms of a never-satisfied hunger.

Cadet Challenge. A physical fitness challenge that consists of five exercises taken from the Presidential Physical Fitness Award program.

Calamine. A pink powder consisting of zinc oxide and some ferric oxide used in lotions and ointments.

Calisthenics. Light gymnastic exercise designed to promote good health by developing strength and grace.

Calories. The amount of energy it takes to raise the temperature of one kilogram of water one degree Celsius; a measurement of energy.

Carbohydrates. One of the various neutral organic compounds composed of carbon, hydrogen, and oxygen (including starches and sugars) produced by green plants and used to provide energy necessary for growth and other functions.

Cardiac arrest. The sudden stoppage of the heart.

Cardiopulmonary resuscitation (CPR). An emergency method to keep blood and oxygen flowing through a person whose heart and breathing have stopped.

Cardiorespiratory. Of or relating to the heart and the respiratory system.

Catastrophe. A great and sudden misfortune.

Caustic. Capable of destroying or eating away by chemical action; corrosive.

Chlorine. A gaseous greenish-yellow element used as a bleach and disinfectant in water purification.

Clammy. Damp, soft, sticky, and unusually cool.

Closed fracture. A fracture in which the broken bone does not push through the skin's surface.

Complex carbohydrates. A carbohydrate that is formed by the body after the conversion of extra glucose; it supplies the body with long-term energy.

Compresses. Folded cloths or pads applied so as to press on a body part to stop bleeding or cool a burn.

Consent. To get approval for what is to be done or proposed by another.

Controlled substance. A substance whose manufacture, possession, or sale is controlled by the law.

Curl-ups. One of the five events on the Cadet Challenge and Presidential Physical Fitness test that consists of a sit up movement from a lying position up to the point where your elbows touch your thighs.

Deficient. Having too little of something, such as a nutrient in the body.

Dehydration. The condition that results when fluids are lost from the body and are not replaced; symptoms can include thirst, weakness, exhaustion, and confusion, and it may result in death.

Dependency. Addiction to a substance.

Depressed. Low spirits; sadness; dejection.

Depression. Psychiatric disorder characterized by an inability to concentrate, insomnia, loss of appetite, anhedonia, feelings of extreme sadness, guilt, helplessness and hopelessness, and thoughts of death.

Detoxification program. A type of program where drug users or addicts can get help withdrawing from substances.

Diabetes. A disease that causes too much blood sugar to build up in the body.

Dilated. Having been widened; expanded.

Discoloration. Altered or changed in color.

Disinfect. To destroy harmful germs; to purify.

Dislocation. The separation of a bone from its joint.

Distilled. Heated and condensed to purify, form a new substance, or concentrate.

Diuretics. A food, medicine, etc., that promotes or tends to increase the excretion of urine.

Dressing. Ointment and bandages applied to a wound.

Drugs. Chemicals that cause a change in a person's body or behavior.

Dysentery. Any of several intestinal disorders usually caused by infection and characterized by stomach pain and diarrhea with passage of mucous and blood.

Electrolyte. A substance that, when dissociated into ions in solution or fused, becomes electrically conducting.

Elevated. Raised up.

Emergency Medical Service (EMS). Medical professional dedicated to the reduction of morbidity and mortality of residents through the provision of advanced and basic life support care, medically directed rescue, and transportation of the ill and injured.

Episodic. Occurring, appearing, or changing at irregular intervals; incidental.

Esophageal. Of, or relating, to the esophagus (a muscular tube through which food passes from the mouth to the stomach).

Essential fat. Fat that the body needs in certain amounts to maintain bodily functions.

Ethyl alcohol. The type of alcohol found in beer, wine, and distilled spirits.

Evaluate. To determine if an act, process, or method has been attained; to assess; to determine the significance by careful appraisal and study

Fainting. To lose consciousness briefly because of temporary decrease in the amount of blood that flows to the brain.

Fat soluble vitamins. A vitamin that is absorbed through the intestinal tract with the help of fats and is stored in the body.

Fatigue. Weakness or exhaustion due to hard work or mental effort

Fats. Nutrients made up of fatty acids that are insoluble in water and provide energy to the body.

Ferment. To produce a chemical change in a carbohydrate material resulting in alcohol.

Fiber. Coarse food made mostly of carbohydrates, such as bran or lettuce that serves to stimulate and aid the movement of food through the intestines.

Fight or flight response. An involuntary reaction to an immediate danger or threat, that prepares a person physically to either respond to the danger or run away.

First aid.   The immediate care given to a victim of injury or sudden illness before professional medical help arrives.

Flexed-arm hang.   An alternative event for the pull-up in the Cadet Challenge and Presidential Physical Fitness Test.

Flush.   To cleanse or wash out with running water or another liquid.

Frostbite.   An injury caused to body tissue by frost or extreme cold.

Galvanized.   Coated with zinc.

Gateway.   A term attached to alcohol and tobacco due to the fact that their use often leads to further drug abuse.

Generalized.   Generally prevalent.

Good Samaritan law.   A law enacted in most states that protects people from lawsuits if medical complications arise after they have administered first aid correctly.

Hallucinogens.   Drugs that cause hallucinations.

Heat cramps.   A condition that is marked by the sudden development of cramps in the skeletal muscles and that results from prolonged work in high temperatures accompanied by profuse perspiration with loss of sodium chloride from the body.

Heat exhaustion.   A condition that occurs when a person is exposed to excessive heat over a period of time, caused by the loss of water and salt from the body through excessive perspiration.

Heatstroke.   A life threatening condition caused by prolonged exposure to high heat.

Heimlich maneuver.   An upward push to the abdomen given to clear the airway of a person with a complete airway obstruction; procedure used to expel an object lodged in the airway of a choking victim.

Hemorrhage.   Heavy uncontrollable bleeding.

Hygiene.   Practices or conditions that aid in good health; the science that deals with maintenance of good health and the prevention of infection and disease.

Hypothermia.   Too little body heat with abnormally low internal body temperature.

Incision.   A wound that is made by cutting into the body.

Inhalants.   Medications or chemicals that are inhaled.

Insulate.   To use materials to protect or isolate from the elements of weather.

Intoxicated.   Drunk; affected by alcohol to the point that physical and mental control are significantly impaired.

Iodine.   A nonmetallic element having important medical uses.

Isokinetic.   Exercise in which muscles contract, but very little body movement takes place.

Isometric.   Building muscle strength using resistance without joint movement.

Isotonic.   Building muscle strength using resistance with joint movement.

Laceration.   A wound that is torn and ragged.

Lice.   Small, wingless, parasitic insects that live on warm-blooded animals, especially in hair, and suck the animal's blood.

Ligament.   A fibrous band of tissue that holds bones together at a joint.

Manic-depressive illness.   Bipolar disorder.

Meditation.   A contemplative discourse, usually on a religious or philosophical subject.

Metabolism.   The chemical process by which the body produces energy and maintains vital functions.

Methadone.   Controlled substance that is used in heroin withdrawal; produces some effects similar to heroin but does not produce a "high."

Migraines.   A severe recurring headache, usually affecting only one side of the head, characterized by sharp pain and often accompanied by nausea, vomiting, and visual disturbances.

Minerals.   Natural chemical elements of the earth used by the body to supply necessary nutrition.

Misuse.   The incorrect or improper use of a substance.

Monounsaturated fats.   Oil or fat that is liquid at room temperature, is low in hydrogen, and can lower the level of blood cholesterol.

Mottled.   Marked with irregular spots or splotches of different colors or shades of color.

Narcotics.   A drug medically used to relieve pain, produce sleep, and dull the senses.

Neutralize.   To counteract the activity or effect of; to make chemically neutral.

Nicotine.   The drug in tobacco that may act as a stimulant and cause addiction.

Normal.   According to a rule or standard pattern; regular; usual.

Nutrients.   Substances found in food that nourish the body.

Obesity.   Overweight to the point of injuring health.

Open fracture.   A fracture in which the broken end of a bone pierces the skin.

Osteoporosis.   A condition characterized by a calcium deficiency in the bone mass in which the body pulls calcium from the bones, causing them to lose their density and possibly leading to fractures.

Personal hygiene.   An individual's practice of taking care of him or herself in order to maintain good health.

Perspiring.   Giving off moisture through the pores of the skin.

Polyunsaturated fats.   An oil of fatty acid containing more than one double or triple bond and is therefore cholesterol defensive.

Precipitation.   Any form of water, such as rain, snow, sleet, or hail, that falls to the earth's surface.

Presidential Physical Fitness Award.   An award earned by achieving a standard of 85 percent or higher on the Presidential Physical Fitness Test.

Pressure bandage.   A snug bandage used to control bleeding.

Pressure point.   A point on the body where a major artery lies near the skin surface and passes over a bone.

Protein.   Nutrients that are made of amino acids and that maintain body tissues and supply energy to the body.

Pull-ups.   One of the five events on the Cadet Challenge and Presidential Physical Fitness test that consists of pulling the body up from a dead weight hanging position on a bar to having the chin clear the bar.

Purified.   Free from undesirable elements or impurities; cleaned.

Rabies.   A viral disease affecting the central nervous system of mammals that is transmitted by a bite from an infected animal; it can result in paralysis and death if left untreated.

Referenced Daily Intake (RDI).   Standards developed by the united states government for the regulation of vitamin and mineral requirements.

Rescue breathing.   The act of forcing air into and out of the lungs of a person by another person.

Sanitation.   The promotion of hygiene and prevention of disease by working to keep a clean and healthy environment.

Saturated fats.   A fat that does not melt at room temperature and can raise the blood cholesterol level.

Scalding.   The burning of the skin by a substance that is near boiling in temperature.

Shuttle run.   One of the five events on the Cadet Challenge and Presidential Physical Fitness test that consists of a 30-foot shuttle run.

Simple carbohydrates.   A sugar that is found in the body in its simple state and supplies the body with short-term energy.

Smoldering.   Burning slowly without flame but often with much smoke.

Solvents.   Liquid substances capable of dissolving or eliminating something unwanted.

Splint.   To support and immobilize a body part with a stiff material.

Sprain.   An injury caused by twisting a ligament or tendon around a joint.

Stimulant.   A drink, drug, or other substance that speeds up the activity of the mind or body; a drug that speeds up the activities of the central nervous system, the heart, and other organs.

Storage fat.   Fat that the body keeps in reserve and that can lead to overfat problems or obesity.

Strain.   An injury caused when a muscle or tendon is overstretched.

Stress.   Strain or pressure on the body or mind.

Stroke.   A reduction of blood flow to a part of the brain.

Subcutaneous.   Beneath the top layer of skin.

Substance.   Something, such as a drug or alcohol, deemed harmful and usually subject to legal restrictions.

Superficial.   Not serious; on the surface; shallow.

Systemic.   Affecting the body in general; acting throughout the body after absorption or ingestion.

Tetanus (lockjaw).   An acute infectious disease caused by the poison of a certain bacterium that enters the body through a wound, resulting in muscle contractions, rigidity, and death; it is preventable by immunization.

Therapeutic communities.   Usually a residential treatment center for drug abusers and addicts.

Tobacco.   The leaves of cultivated tobacco plants, prepared for use in smoking, chewing, or as snuff.

Tone.   A degree of tension or firmness, as of muscle.

Trauma.   A behavioral state resulting from mention or emotional stress or physical injury that has a lasting effect on the mind; a physical wound or injury.

Veins.   Blood vessels that carry blood from parts of the body the heart.

Venom.   A poison produced by animals such as snakes and spiders that is transmitted by a bite or sting.

Ventilation.   Circulation of air; a system or means of providing fresh air.

Visualization.   To make visible.

Vitamins.   Nutrients that occur naturally in plant and animal tissue and are required for proper function of the body.

V-sit reach.   One of the five events on the Cadet Challenge and Presidential Physical Fitness test that consists of stretching a number of inches past an established baseline.

Water soluble vitamins.   A vitamin that is dissolved in the water of tissues.

Key Terms Index